THE PERFECT KING

Ian Mortimer has BA and PhD degrees in history from Exeter University and an MA in archive studies from University College London. From 1991 to 2003 he worked in turn for Devon Record Office, Reading University, the Royal Commission on Historical Manuscripts, and Exeter University. He was elected a Fellow of the Royal Historical Society in 1998. In 2003 the first of his medieval biographies, *The Greatest Traitor* was published by Jonathan Cape. He was awarded the Alexander Prize (2004) by the Royal Historical Society for his work on the social history of medicine. He lives with his wife and three children on the edge of Dartmoor.

IAN MORTIMER

The Perfect King

The Life of Edward III, Father of the English Nation

VINTAGE BOOKS
London

Published by Vintage 2008

4 6 8 10 9 7 5 3

Copyright © Ian Mortimer 2006

Ian Mortimer has asserted his right under the Copyright, Designs
and Patents Act 1988 to be identified as the author of this work

This is a work of non-fiction. The author has stated to the publishers
that the contents of this book are true.

First published in Great Britain in 2006 by Jonathan Cape

Vintage
Random House, 20 Vauxhall Bridge Road,
London SW1V 2SA

www.vintage-books.co.uk

Addresses for companies within The Random House Group Limited
can be found at: www.randomhouse.co.uk/offices.htm

The Random House Group Limited Reg. No. 954009

A CIP catalogue record for this book
is available from the British Library

ISBN 9780099527091

The Random House Group Limited supports The Forest Stewardship
Council (FSC), the leading international forest certification
organisation. All our titles that are printed on Greenpeace approved
FSC certified paper carry the FSC logo. Our paper procurement
policy can be found at: www.rbooks.co.uk/environment

Printed and bound in Great Britain by
CPI Cox & Wyman, Reading RG1 8EX

This book is dedicated to my wife, Sophie, who has been so supportive during the months of frustration, stress, worry and euphoria which inevitably occur when trying to encapsulate a life as rich and complicated as Edward III's. She has sat outside the walls of Calais, as it were, and watched Sir Walter Manny take on whole armies armed only with a toothpick. The completion of this book is something in which she too can take pride.

CONTENTS

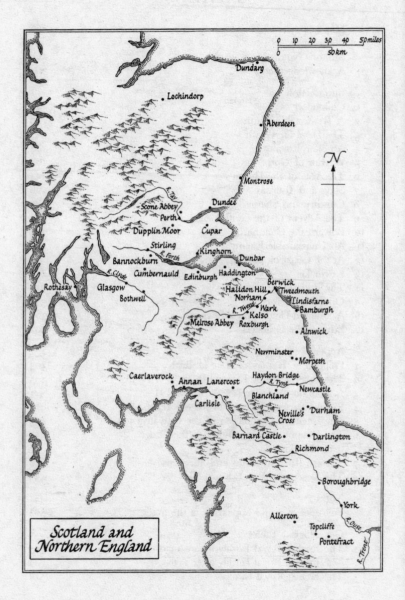

Scotland and
Northern England

Southern and Midlands England

N

York
Allerton
Topcliffe
Pontefract
Burstwick
R. Ouse
Lincoln
Macclesfield
Chester
Nottingham
Walsingham
Norwich
Shrewsbury
Lichfield
Leicester
Great Yarmouth
R. Gt. Ouse
Leintwardine
Kenilworth
Coventry
Bury St Edmunds
Ludlow
Warwick
Northampton
Wigmore
Worcester
Daventry
Towcester
Hadleigh
R. Avon
Bedford
Cambridge
Hereford
Banbury
Harwich
Gloucester
Burford
Dunstable
Ware
Berkeley
Oxford
Berkhamsted
Hatfield
Hertford
Abingdon
King's Langley
Waltham Abbey
London
Malmesbury
Windsor
R. Thames
Queenborough
Bristol
Reading
Chertsey
Merton
Rochester
Sandwich
Ludgershall
Guildford
Otford
Leeds
Canterbury
Wells
Salisbury
Winchester
Dover
Glastonbury
Clarendon
Lewes
Winchelsea
Sherborne
Bishop's Waltham
Southampton
Yarmouth
Melcombe Regis
Corfe Castle
Isle of Wight
English Channel
Dartmouth
Plymouth

0 10 20 30 40 50 miles
0   50   100 km

Havering
atte Bower
Wallingford
Bisham
LONDON
Westminster
Rotherhithe
Isleworth
Reading
Windsor
Kennington
Eltham
Gravesend
Chertsey
Merton
Dartford

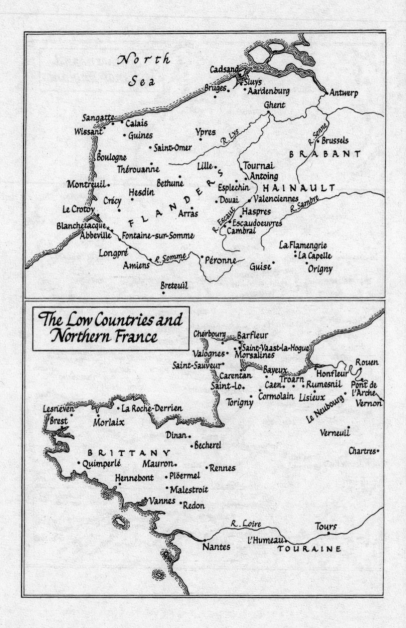

North Sea

Cadsand
Bruges • • Sluys
• Aardenburg • Antwerp
Ghent
Sangatte
Wissant • Calais
• Guines
Ypres R. Lys
Boulogne Saint-Omer R. Senne • Brussels
Thérouanne Lille • BRABANT
Montreuil Tournai
Hesdin Béthune Antoing
Crécy Esplechin • HAINAULT
Le Crotoy Douai • Valenciennes
Blanchetacque F L A N D E R S Arras Haspres R. Sambre
Abbeville Escaudoeuvres
Fontaine-sur-Somme R. Escaut Cambrai
Longpré La Flamengrie
Amiens R. Somme Péronne Guise • • La Capelle
Breteuil Origny

The Low Countries and Northern France

Cherbourg • Barfleur
• Saint-Vaast-la-Hogue
Valognes • Morsalines
Saint-Sauveur Bayeux Honfleur Rouen
Carentan Troarn Rumesnil Pont de
Saint-Lô Caen • • Lisieux l'Arche
Cormolain Le Neubourg Vernon
Torigny
Lesneven • La Roche-Derrien Verneuil
Brest Morlaix
Dinan • Bécherel Chartres •
B R I T T A N Y
Quimperlé Mauron
Hennebont Plöermel • Rennes
Malestroit
Vannes • Redon
R. Loire Tours
Nantes L'Humeau T O U R A I N E

North
Sea

N

Sluys
Antwerp
Bruges
Calais
Ghent
Brussels
Ypres
Herk
Cologne
Boulogne
BRABANT
R. Rhine
Lille
Tournai
PONTHIEU
Bethune
HAINAULT
Koblenz
Crécy
F L A N D E R S
Douai
Arras
Valenciennes
Abbeville
Cambrai
R. Moselle
Péronne
Amiens
R. Somme
Origny
Breteuil
Guise
Noyon
R. Meuse
R. Oise
Cormicy
Pont-Saint-Maxence
Mantes
Rheims
Meulan
Saint-Denis
R. Marne
Poissy
PARIS
Orly
Brétigny
R. Seine
R. Yonne
Orléans
Saint-Florentin
Tonnerre
R. Loire
Rouvray
Bourges

0   50   100 miles
0   50   100   150   200 km

Thouars • · Moncontour

POITOU

Poitiers •

· Chauvigny

Lusignan • Lussac •

· Montmorillon

La Rochelle •

DUCHY

· Saint-Jean-d'Angély

· Taillebourg

· Limoges

· Saintes · Saint-Sevère

Angoulême

Bay of

OF

LIMOUSIN

Biscay

R. Gironde

· Périgueux Auberoche ·

Blaye •

PERIGORD

Saint-Macaire • Libourne •

Bordeaux • Saint-Emilion • Bergerac • · Sarlat

AQUITAINE

· La Réole

Marmande •

R. Lot

Aiguillon • · Montpezat

Cahors

· Agen

Montcuq ·

QUERCY

R. Garonne

ARMAGNAC

· Toulouse

Saint-Sardos ·

Bayonne •

Bigorre •

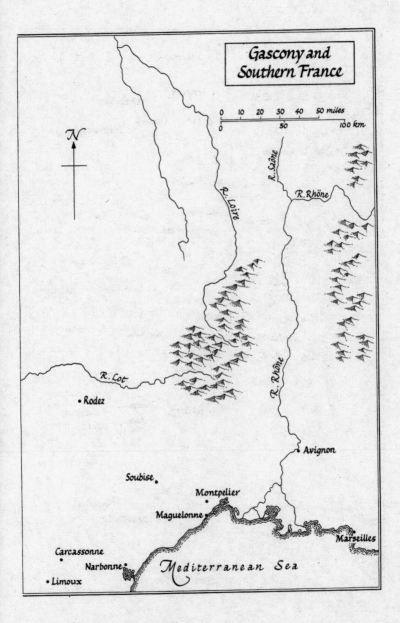

Gascony and
Southern France

0	10	20	30	40	50 miles
0			50		100 km

N

R. Loire

R. Saône

R. Rhône

R. Rhône

R. Lot

• Rodez

• Avignon

Soubise •

Montpelier
•

Maguelonne •

Marseilles

Carcassonne
•

Narbonne •

Mediterranean Sea

• Limoux

ILLUSTRATIONS

Edward II's tomb effigy (*English Heritage*).

John of Eltham's tomb effigy (*Dean and Chapter of Westminster*).

Charles IV welcoming Isabella to Paris (*Bibliothèque nationale de France*).

Edward III washing his hands (*British Library*).

Edward III with hawk (*Master and Fellows of Christ Church, Oxford*).

Young king with hawker's glove, probably representing Edward III (*Dean and Chapter of Westminster*).

Edward III's figure in St Stephen's Chapel, drawn by Robert Smirke (*Society of Antiquaries of London*).

Queen Philippa's figure in St Stephen's Chapel, drawn by Robert Smirke (*Society of Antiquaries of London*).

The Black Prince (*Dean and Chapter of Westminster*).

Edward's son, Lionel (*Dean and Chapter of Westminster*).

Edward's daughter, Joan (*Dean and Chapter of Westminster*).

Edward's daughter, Mary (*Dean and Chapter of Westminster*).

Queen Philippa's tomb effigy (*Dean and Chapter of Westminster*).

Edward III's death mask (*Dean and Chapter of Westminster*).

Edward III's tomb effigy (*Dean and Chapter of Westminster*).

The earliest image of a cannon (*Master and Fellows of Christ Church, Oxford*).

The Loshult gun (© *Antikvarisk-topografiska arkivet, Stockholm*).

Edward ordering a gun attack on Rheims (*Bibliothèque nationale de France*).

Queenborough Castle, by Wenceslas Hollar (*The Trustees of the British Museum*).

Plan of Queenborough Castle (*from a drawing at Hatfield House*).

A gold noble of 1351 (*The Trustees of the British Museum*).

Edward's seventh great seal, 'The Brétigny seal' (*The British Library*).

A fourteenth-century clock (*Ian Mortimer*).

Edward's clock tower at Westminster, by Wenceslas Hollar (*The Trustees of the British Museum*).

Edward's sword and shield (*Dean and Chapter of Westminster*).

Edward's handwriting (*The National Archives*).

Windsor Castle (*Simmons Aerofilms Ltd*).

Edward leading his army across the Somme, by Benjamin West (*The Royal Collection © 2006 Her Majesty Queen Elizabeth II*).

Queen Victoria and Albert dressed as Edward III and Queen Phillipa, by Edwin Landseer (*The Royal Collection © 2006 Her Majesty Queen Elizabeth II*).

AUTHOR'S NOTE

This book deliberately employs the ambiguous use of the term Gascony to describe the English-ruled territory in the south-west of France, in keeping with most books on the fourteenth century. The duchy of Aquitaine – as inherited from Eleanor of Aquitaine – was far more extensive than Gascony but there were times when English authority was squeezed and the two were practically synonymous. It would be convenient to use just the one word to describe the duchy and its extensions, and there is one – Guienne – but it is very rarely used, even by scholars, and would look very odd in a biography. So, in order to avoid the awkward adjective 'Aquitainian' and the even more awkward 'Guiennese', two terms have been used: Aquitaine for the title of the duchy and (later) principality, and 'Gascony' and 'Gascon' when referring to the region generally.

Most English surnames which include 'de' in the original source have been simplified, with the silent loss of the 'de'. Where it remained traditionally incorporated in the surname (e.g. de la Pole, de la Beche, de la Ware) these have been retained. 'De' has generally been retained in French names (e.g. de Harcourt, de Montfort, de Blois). With Italian names, 'de' has normally been retained (e.g. del Caretto, de Controne, de Sarzana) but where it is customary not to keep it (e.g. Fieschi, Forzetti) it has been dropped.

With regard to international currency, the gold florin fluctuated greatly over the period covered by this book. According to the *Handbook of Medieval Exchange*, it was worth as little as 2s 8d in 1346 and as much as 4s in 1332 and 1338. It was also worth different amounts in different places at the same time, and could even be worth different amounts in the same place at the same time. Very roughly speaking, one florin was usually worth slightly more than 3s prior to 1340 and slightly less than 3s thereafter. Many other writers use the rate of 1 florin = 3s 4d, as this allows the easy conversion of 6 florins = £1. In this book this rate is used up to 1340 and the slightly more accurate rate of 1 florin = 3s is used after that year, which implies a conversion of 6.67 florins = £1. The other unit of international accounting used in this book, the mark, was a constant 13s 4d.

ACKNOWLEDGEMENTS

It is impossible to write a book like this without incurring a number of debts of gratitude. I hope that readers will not begrudge me here mentioning the names of my agent, James Gill, and my editors, Will Sulkin and Jörg Hensgen. I am also very grateful to two scholars for their assistance: Dr Paul Dryburgh, who surveyed many of the wardrobe accounts for me in the research stages, and Professor Mark Ormrod of the University of York, who provided me with many valuable hints, photocopies, offprints and references when the book was in a draft form. I would also like to thank staff at the National Archives, the British Library, Exeter University Library, Gloucestershire Record Office, the National Portrait Gallery Archive, Warwickshire County Record Office and Westminster Abbey Library. I am grateful to all those who provided me with accommodation when undertaking research, namely: Zak Reddan and Mary Fawcett, Jay Hammond, Robert and Julie Mortimer, Susannah Davis and Anya Francis. I acknowledge the support of the K Blundell Trust, administered by the Society of Authors, who gave me a grant in the course of writing this book. Finally, I want to say a huge thank you to my family – Sophie, especially, but also Alexander, Elizabeth, and Oliver – for keeping me going.

Ian Mortimer
Moretonhampstead
May 2005

He who loves peace, let him prepare for war.

Flavius Vegetius Renatus, writer on warfare (c. 375)

According to the Theory of War, which teaches that the best way to avoid the inconvenience of war is to pursue it away from your own country, it is more sensible for us to fight our notorious enemy in his own realm, with the joint power of our allies, than it is to wait for him at our own doors.

King Edward III (1339)

When you don't fight, you lose.

Leszek Miller, Prime Minister of Poland (2003)

INTRODUCTION

On 19 October 1330, at dusk, two dozen men gathered in the centre of Nottingham. They were mostly in their twenties, and all on horseback, ready to ride out of the town. But unlike merchants or pilgrims assembling to set out together, these men were silent and unsmiling. Beneath their riding cloaks they were all heavily armed.

The reason for their gathering lay within the fortress which overlooked the town. Somewhere within those walls, high on the massive outcrop, was Roger Mortimer, the earl of March, who kept the young king, Edward III, within his power and ruled in his place. Several of the riders had already been summoned that day to see the brooding dictator. He had questioned each of them in turn; all but one had refused to speak. The only man who had dared to answer back was their leader, Sir William Montagu. He had replied evasively that he would give a short answer to anyone who accused him of being part of a plot inconsistent with his duty. Mortimer had let him go, but not with good humour.

Now Montagu was waiting. He knew it would only be a short time before Mortimer would arrest him and his friends. Mortimer had already given the order that the guards were to ignore the king's commands, and only to obey his own. How suddenly political fortunes changed! It was just four years since Edward II had been swept from power by Mortimer and Queen Isabella, his mistress. It was only seven months since the earl of Kent, the king's uncle, had been beheaded on Mortimer's orders. Shortly after that, the young heir to the earldom of Arundel, Richard Fitzalan, had been arrested before he could carry out his plan to seize Mortimer. Montagu had no wish to suffer the same fate. Nor did he wish to see the young king set aside. He had spent most of the last twelve years at court, and had seen Edward III grow up. But that was how serious matters had become. The future of the English monarchy was at stake. Somewhere in that castle above, young Edward was in fear of his life. Montagu believed Mortimer was plotting his murder and the seizure of the throne.

'It is better to eat the dog than be eaten by the dog', Montagu had remarked quietly to the king, after being dismissed from Mortimer's presence.

But as Montagu knew, it was one thing to suggest 'eating the dog' and quite another to do it. Mortimer had spies everywhere. Although John

Wyard had been the king's trusted friend for several years, it emerged that he was an informer. It had been Wyard who had told Mortimer of Montagu's plot. Mortimer had been thrown into a fury, like 'a devil for wrath'. And now he was on the defensive, perhaps about to order all their deaths. Already he had mustered troops throughout the kingdom, ready to defend his position. He was, after all, a soldier, one of the very few successful war commanders of the last twenty years. He was a clever manipulator and an arch-propagandist. Men like him, when they know their lives are stake, cannot be trusted.

Montagu and his men rode through the town and then south, as if they were in flight. But they were not running away. They were about to embark on a dangerous and adventurous mission. Their courage was swelled through their companionship; they were friends as well as fellow plotters. With them rode William Eland, the castellan or overseer of the castle. It was his idea that had prompted them to ride out into the gloom.

Some way out of the town Montagu gave the signal for them to stop. By now Mortimer would have heard that they had fled, but he would not pursue them until the morning, for there would be no moonlight tonight. They waited until the darkness was nearly complete, and then they turned back and led their horses slowly across to the hunting park by the river. At a thicket which Montagu had chosen as their mustering point, they stopped and waited for those conspirators who had not been interrogated earlier, who had remained in the town, waiting for night to fall.

It grew cold. No one came. Before long they realised that they were on their own. Maybe their companions had been arrested. Or maybe their courage had failed them.

It was Montagu's decision to go on. There were only about twenty men with him, and Mortimer had more than two hundred in the castle. Their plan was a desperate one, to attack through a secret passage which William Eland knew. It led, he said, directly into the building in which the queen was lodged. The king or someone acting on his behalf would unlock the door at the top. Then Montagu and his men had to overpower the guards, arrest Mortimer, and silence those present before anyone could raise the alarm. Most of all they had to stop Mortimer getting a message out of the castle. If he did that, they were all done for.

But the men gathered with Montagu were neither cowards nor weak. They were the very pick of the young English nobility, prepared to die rather than be shamed in honour or arms. Robert Ufford was there, William Clinton, the brothers Humphrey and William Bohun, Ralph Stafford, and John Neville of Hornby. There too were Thomas West, John Molyns, William Latimer, Robert Walkefare, Maurice Berkeley and Thomas

Bradeston. If they succeeded, all their names would be celebrated for centuries. If they failed, they would probably be hanged as traitors the next day, their lands confiscated, their wives and children locked up.

Montagu decided that they could wait no longer, and they would have to go on alone. They tethered their horses at the thicket, and followed Eland carefully along the marshy riverbank. After a while they felt the great rock on which the castle was built. A little further on they came to an opening. They entered the tunnel and began to ascend its long, steep slope.

High above them, within the queen's chamber, Mortimer, Queen Isabella and the bishop of Lincoln were discussing what to do about the intended coup. Mortimer had let the men go in order to organise the case against them carefully. They should be indicted for treason: that was his way of crushing opposition. Parliament would assemble in the hall of the castle on the following day. Those who had fled could be charged in their absence, soldiers pursuing them at the same time. There would be ample opportunity to seize them over the next few days, one by one if necessary. If they fled the country, well, so much the better.

Pancio de Controne, the king's Italian physician, visited Edward in his room elsewhere in the castle. The king had retired earlier, claiming ill-health, to get away from Mortimer. Robert Wyville, Isabella's clerk, was also up and about. Probably either he or de Controne went down to the basement of the queen's lodgings, and checked the bolts on the door to the spiral staircase which led down to the secret passage. This secret door, which few of the important people would have known about, was the keyhole through which the castle could be unlocked. In the silence of the night, while Mortimer and Isabella talked with Bishop Burghersh in Isabella's chamber, the bolts were slid back, leaving the castle open to attack.

About midnight, in the darkness, the door swung open, pushed by the hand of William Eland. If a torchlight was burning there, it would have revealed the determined faces of those following him: John Neville, William Montagu, and the others. One by one they came up the last few steps. They proceeded to climb the stairs, as quietly as possible, up into the tower of the queen's chamber.

At that moment a door opened. Sir Hugh Turpington came out, looked along the corridor, and saw them, their weapons ready. He had no sword with him, but he drew his own dagger, and, without thought for his own safety, yelled the warning 'Traitors! Down with the traitors!' Turpington hurled himself at Sir John Neville. Neville lifted his mace and, side-stepping, smashed it into the head of the royal steward, who fell in a pool of blood. But his final cry had alerted the others. Next came the chamber guards.

Mortimer realised what was happening and grabbed his sword. Two more men were killed defending him. Men rushed at Mortimer; they seized him, and his sword clattered on the floor. Isabella, realising that the attackers could not have got into her apartments without her son's help, screamed into the dark corridor 'Fair son! Have mercy on the gentle Mortimer'.

A few minutes later it was all over. The king went with Montagu from chamber to chamber, ordering the arrests of Mortimer's sons, Geoffrey and Edmund, and Mortimer's henchman, Simon Bereford. The bishop of Lincoln – Mortimer's closest friend – was found trying to escape down a privy chute. He was told he would not be arrested. Mortimer, however, could expect little mercy. He was bound and gagged, and led down to the basement and then pushed through the door into the tunnel. Then he was taken down, out into the park, tied to a horse, and removed from Nottingham and power.

*

It might seem strange to begin an account of the life of Edward III with an event in which he personally played little part, but it is appropriate. For the first four years of his reign Edward had struggled to do anything in his own interest. He had been utterly disempowered by his mother and Mortimer. It is a telling fact that it was his closest and bravest friends who allowed him properly to take the throne. Reliance on his most courageous and capable advisers, who understood bonds of chivalric companionship and the cult of noble achievement, would be a hallmark of his whole reign. When Edward had been crowned, his reign had been greeted as that of a new Arthur, and his young, brave, energetic knights all wished for a place at the round table. They knew that in order to gain such distinction, they would have to earn it. And Edward knew that in order to lead these men, he himself would have to show extraordinary courage. No other medieval English monarch had come so close to being put out of his royal inheritance. Edward was determined to demonstrate that he deserved his crown. It was this determination which inspired his friends to help him.

Within a few years of the Nottingham Castle plot, Edward won his first great battle. By the age of fifty he was famous as the master of European military strategy. Glorious battle had followed glorious battle, orders of chivalry had followed chivalric achievements, so that to be a member of his Order of the Garter was an exceptional honour. He had given England pride, prestige and, through the championing of St George on an unprecedented scale, a new national identity. The nation's wealth had massively increased. The blight of the plague had been weathered. He had taken greater pains than any previous monarch to work with parliament in framing legislation for the benefit of the kingdom. For the next three hundred years he was hailed as simply the greatest king that England had ever had.

Just how great Edward's reputation was, and how long it lasted, can be seen by referring to assessments of his character written between the fourteenth and the seventeenth centuries.[1] A contemporary wrote in a long eulogy that he was 'full gracious among all the worthy men of the world, for he passed and shone by virtue and grace given to him from God, above all his predecessors that were noble men and worthy'.[2] His only failing, according to this writer, was his lechery – 'his moving of his flesh haunted him in his age' – and this was the reason why the author thought his life had been 'cut short'. This was intended as a joke. At sixty-four, Edward had outlived almost everyone of his generation.[3]

Edward's reputation was still shining three hundred years later. In 1688 Joshua Barnes published the first study of Edward and his reign: a huge volume, about 850,000 words long.[4] Its short title is *The History of that Most Victorious Monarch Edward III, King of England and France, and Lord of Ireland, and First Founder of the Most Noble Order of the Garter*. In case his readers had any doubts about the eminence of his subject, Barnes spelled out his own understanding of his theme in the preface: 'the Life and Actions of one of the Greatest Kings, that perhaps the World ever saw'. At the end of the book Barnes gave his judgement on Edward's character. As a collection of superlatives it is unique. Edward was:

Fortunate beyond measure . . . wise and provident in counsel, well-learned in law, history, humanity and divinity. He understood Latin, French, Spanish, Italian, and High and Low-Dutch, besides his native language. He was of quick apprehension, judicious and skillful in nature, elegant in speech, sweet, familiar and affable in behaviour; stern to the obstinate, but calm and meek to the humble. Magnanimous and courageous above all the princes of his days; apt for war but a lover of peace; never puffed up with prosperity nor dismayed at adversity. He was of an exalted, glorious, and truly royal spirit, which never entertained any thing vulgar or trivial, as may appear by the most excellent laws which he made, by those two famous jubilees he kept, and by the most honourable Order of the Garter, which he first devised and founded. His recreations were hawking, hunting and fishing, but chiefly he loved the martial exercise of jousts and tournaments. In his buildings he was curious, splendid and magnificent, in bestowing of graces and donations, free and frequent; and to the ingenious and deserving always kind and liberal; devout to God, bountiful to the clergy, gracious to his people, merciful to the poor, true to his word, loving to his friends, terrible to his enemies . . . In short he had the most virtues and the fewest vices of any prince that ever I read of. He was valiant, just, merciful, temperate, and wise; the best lawgiver, the best friend, the best father, and the best husband in his days.[5]

Maybe some other ruler somewhere has, at some point in history, received praise as great and all-encompassing. But if so, he was not a king of England.

Then something happened, something which none of Edward III's contemporaries could have predicted. Social change allowed a new front of politicised historians to step forward. Less interested in the champions of the past, such men were keen to understand how society had developed. Indeed, within a short while they were only too ready to kick the heroes of yesteryear. Froissart's chronicle – a benchmark of chivalric history – became regarded as a literary masterpiece but worthless as historical writing. Chivalry became the stuff of fiction. Sir Walter Scott led the vanguard of interest in the deeds of knights: a poet and novelist, not a historian. The great historians of the period were exploring how ideas and social movements, coupled with the leadership of political figures, had changed Europe. By comparison, the age of chivalry seemed stagnant, unchanging and distasteful in its glorification of violence and bloodshed.

The development of historical writing along social themes in the early nineteenth century dealt a succession of severe blows to Edward's reputation. History itself became less a matter of narrative than judgement, and this was not just judgement on individuals but power structures and social hierarchies. There is no better example of the High Victorian ethos of historical condemnation which annihilated Edward's glory than Lord Acton's famous phrase: 'power tends to corrupt and absolute power corrupts absolutely. Great men are almost always bad men.'[6] William Stubbs, peering down on the middle ages from the twin heights of an episcopal throne and a professorial chair, condemned Edward as 'ambitious, unscrupulous, selfish, extravagant and ostentatious'.[7] Such attitudes were strongly supported by the popularity of massive, all-encompassing histories which compared individual kings' achievements with the demands of modern society. As a political leader, Edward III was judged to have prejudiced his kingdom's economic and social welfare for a series of expensive and ultimately futile foreign wars, calculated only to add to his own personal grandeur. As a cultural patron he was deemed insignificant because subsequent generations had destroyed most of his great buildings, and as a social reformer he was castigated for attempting to undermine the social changes of the mid-fourteenth century, thereby creating the social tension which led to the Peasants' Revolt. And his love of women generally, and Alice Perrers in particular, was seen as morally reprehensible. In every area in which a great king should be forward-thinking, he was portrayed as conservative or regressive, and in every area in which a king should be circumspect, he was judged reckless.

This change in historians' attitudes towards Edward III was mirrored in the three biographies of him published in the nineteenth century. Although these early biographers should have been able to present the king in relation to the values and needs of his age, and could have resisted the historical trend to condemn him simply on account of the warlike character of the fourteenth century, they failed to do so, beholden to the judgement of academic historians. This is perhaps understandable – they were men of small intellectual stature compared to Bishop Stubbs – but the result was that they developed even more extreme views. They held Edward up as singularly responsible for a horrific international conflict, high taxation and a self-indulgent court. William Longman, the first of Edward's Victorian biographers, writing in 1869, concluded that:

It was the venturesomeness of war, its stirring strife and magnificent pomp that delighted him – as it has delighted barbarians in all times . . . Courage he possessed in an eminent degree, combined, however, with no small amount of chivalrous rashness . . . Of his personal character in other respects but few traces remain, and some of them are not such as to excite much admiration. Conjugal fidelity at that time was not considered a necessary virtue in sovereigns, and certainly was not practised by Edward III. In this matter it is but fair to judge him by the habits of the times, but his disgraceful subjection in his old age to a worthless woman was the natural sequel to a licentious life, and deeply stains the conclusion of his reign. That he was unscrupulously despotic is clear enough from the facts mentioned in the course of this history, and that he was cruel and revengeful is far from doubtful when his conduct to the burgesses of Calais is considered; for he either intended to put them to death in revenge for their courageous defence, or else, with cat-like wantonness, cruelly disregarding their misery, tortured them with the fear of a punishment he never intended to inflict.[8]

This shows a startling disregard for Edward's out-of-date virtues and an exaggerated emphasis on his still-relevant vices. Longman concluded his book with the dictum that we should not be dazzled by the splendour of the victories they [Edward III and his eldest son] gained into a blind forgetfulness of their vanity, or into an unreflecting admiration of two men, who, though possessed of qualities particularly qualified to excite the admiration of unthinking hero-worshippers, have but little claim to commendation of the wise and thoughtful.[9]

That was how he ended a two-volume study of Edward III: an exhortation to disregard the man's achievements and to meditate on the barbarity of his behaviour, completely failing to consider him as a man in his haste to condemn the values of the age.

Longman's portrait was deemed 'remarkable for its justice, its variety of interest, and its completeness as a picture of the times' by Edward's next biographer.[10] The Reverend William Warburton was, in fact, a little more sympathetic to Edward than Longman, and more subtle, pointing out that Edward 'understood better perhaps than any other sovereign of his dynasty the great importance of keeping on good terms with his people', adding that 'almost in every successive parliament he had the credit of making concessions to the nation . . .' However, Warburton's compliments always have a fatal sting in the tail, in this case adding: 'but he was, in all probability, quite as arbitrary as the most arbitrary of his predecessors'.[11] Unlike Longman he does not damn Edward outright for his warrior-gallantry, but belittles him, stating that 'as a soldier and a legislator he looms large between Edward II and Richard II, but seems a man of ordinary stature when measured with the great first Edward or the greater first William'. On and on he goes, diminishing Edward at every opportunity, mainly for his failure to have lived in other centuries. But then Warburton was a man who saw the Black Death as one of the 'real glories' of the fourteenth century, for by it the English serf was freed from servitude.[12] In so doing he shows how little he understands the social priorities of the fourteenth century. He also demonstrates a gross detachment from everyday human existence: the agonising and lonely deaths of one in three of the population of Europe was the antithesis of glory in the fourteenth century, just as it would have been in the nineteenth. For Warburton, another 'real glory' was the *loss* of Gascony, allowing England to 'acquire its insular character'. Probably only Englishmen between the French Revolution and the Great War could have seen the acquisition of an insular character as a positive development. Basically, in Warburton's eyes, Edward was a bland third-rater because he had not contributed to nineteenth-century industrial democracy, as far as Warburton could see. Rarely has a biographer been so unfair in his expectations of his subject.

The third and last of the Victorian biographers was the best writer of the three and the worst historian. Dr James Mackinnon was a biographer of such extreme prejudice and perverse judgement that one quakes under his sentences. Yet, steadying ourselves after reading his outrageous and wrong judgements, we have to reflect that he too was a product of his time. Writing in 1900, in a society whose fear of war was of paramount concern to men such as himself, the fact that Edward was a warmonger was enough to seal his fate.

> Throughout [Edward's French war] we are repelled not only by its heart-less brutality, but by the sordid motives that actuate it. Would-be conquerors of the stamp of an Edward are impervious to considerations of humanity or morality. Let Edward conquer, even if the world perish! But apart from moral and human considerations, it really is marvellous that it did not occur to the aggressor that devastation was a questionable path to a people's love and submission. Without prejudice, I think I may conclude, from a calm view of ends and results, that in this matter of external statesmanship, Edward is without balance, without true insight, without morality, without real grandeur, and his reign is that of a man who exhausted his country in the pursuit of selfish, and therefore essentially unpatriotic objects.[13]

Dr Mackinnon was not entirely negative about Edward. In fact, unlike Warburton, he allowed a few complimentary comments to stand without qualifying them with gratuitous faint-praise. He acknowledged that Edward did not seek to play the despot over the nation, and was 'not devoid of the good qualities of an administrator'. He admitted that he did not rule without reference to the law, that he encouraged free trade (a great virtue in the Great Britain of 1900), that he employed Chaucer and that he was devoted to building 'in keeping with the trend of the age'. But then he socks Edward a huge blow:

> We could wish that there were no reverse side to this picture, yet we greatly fear that the reverse side is *the* picture. It would be going too far to say, as some have done, that he regarded his country solely as a tool of his ambitious schemes of conquest, but he certainly did so in far too large a degree. There must have been something radically wrong in the regal conceptions of a monarch who loaded himself with debt and extorted from an unwilling people . . . enormous sums for the mainten-ance of a war undertaken mainly from motives of ambition . . . Edward made war not only on his enemies but on his people.[14]

Even more extremely, just before going on to blame Edward personally for failing to produce an English poet equivalent in greatness (in Dr Mackinnon's opinion) to Petrarch, he gives the knife he has plunged again and again into Edward's reputation a final twist.

> The strong personality of a virtuous king can make its own moral atmosphere, and exert an incredible influence for good, even if the materials he has to work with are none of the best. The master mind, the noble soul is after all the measure of his age, on the throne at least. For this mastery, this nobility, betokening the truly great man, we look in vain in Edward III.[15]

So why is this book called *The Perfect King*? Surely, if there is such doubt about his achievements, and if we cannot judge past leaders by our own standards, 'perfection' is an inappropriate term for anyone, especially a king. All kings have failings, and Edward III had as many as most men. But I am inspired by the idea that a monarch's vision of kingship is an important factor – perhaps the most important factor – in understanding his life and reign. Kingship is a creative act. To be a good king requires vision, in the same way as to be a good architect or a good military commander requires vision. Obviously vision alone is not enough: a medieval king was required to realise his ambitions under pressure, mindful that thousands of lives, including his own, depended upon his decisons. But we may observe that the least secure medieval kings were those whose concept of kingship did not match their subjects' expectations. 'The perfect king' is not what Edward III was: it is what he *tried* to be. If all statesmen are less than perfect, the best we can hope for is that they have some vision, some principles, and some idealism, at the outset of their careers at least.

The idea that a leader's vision of his role may be the key to understanding his character underpinned the volume which was the precursor to this study: *The Greatest Traitor: the Life of Sir Roger Mortimer*. In that work the centuries of opprobrium and denigration which had encrusted the historical reputation of Mortimer were stripped away to see how he himself would have construed his relationship with the king. He was portrayed alongside other characters who had royal associations to show his role models, his rivalries at court, and the opportunities open to him. In this way his ambitions and vision were contextualised, and his character – or at least his career – could be understood in its varying stages, not as a static finished product but as a human development.

It is harder to do this with a king. Earls can be compared with earls, barons with barons, but the social pyramid permits no comparisons for a monarch. Hence we find kings being compared with each other. This is justifiable in some respects: Edward III was inspired by his grandfather (Edward I) and deeply conscious of his father's failings. But it would be wrong to compare him as a monarch with, say, William I, or even his grandfather, for the challenges he faced were of an altogether different nature. This is why it is intellectually incongruous to find kings compared in the pages of history books, and judged as less or more successful in relation to each other, like so many schoolboys in the curriculum of national progress. Yes, we may play the teacher and call out the names of Edward I, Henry V, Richard I and William I to award them each a gold star for being outstanding war leaders. But in so doing we must consider the opportunities open to them. Why not call out Henry II in the same group? Because he fought no war sufficiently important for that to become the chief characteristic of his reign. This was not because he lacked the qualities of a war leader. His reputation was so great that he did not need to demonstrate his leadership skills on the field of battle. In describing the life of a medieval king, we need to get behind the traditional images of war leaders and legislative reformers to see the individual in relation to his own ambitions and the expectations of his contemporaries, carefully distinguishing between the achievements of the ruler and the reign.

The above problems of royal historical biography – extricating the character of the man from the obscuring effects of historical judgement, distinguishing between the character of the king and the characteristics of his reign, and assessing the king's achievements in terms of his own vision and challenges – are general, and apply to most political leaders. The biographer of Edward III must deal additionally with problems which are peculiar to his reign. The most obvious is the extraordinary romanticism of the sources and the chivalric fervour of the period. To read about the events of Edward's reign is to experience the opposite of the 'willing suspension of disbelief'; one constantly has to question whether events could really have happened as recorded by contemporaries. The opposite effect is at work: the constant nagging of disbelief. Edward III's experiences are so extraordinary that the period 1326–50 reads at times like a fairy tale with footnotes. This raises some serious issues. How can we account for the unattainable ambitions of men who dreamed of chivalrously fighting to the death: an élite whose very *raison d'être* was to don armour and charge into battle, hoping for a glory which was not only personal but spiritual? Will we ever be able to understand them? The age is too much the stuff of *Boys' Own* stories: the valiant warrior, the noble king, the lady and her lover. The modern world simply does not believe in heroics and passions on this scale. Scholarship especially runs scared of fervent quests for glory. If we acknowledge the existence of such feelings, we tend to diminish them: the fearless knight becomes illiterate and ignorant, the passionate lady becomes a woman frustrated by a male-dominated society. We cynically explain the motives of the man who goes on campaign, or fights to the death for his lord. Perhaps only the anonymous men at the bottom of the social spectrum – the landless labourers, who lifted their spades in the years following the Black Death and started to conform to the modern stereotype of the downtrodden peasant, resentful of his servitude – gain widespread and genuine modern sympathy.

There is another side to this romanticism/cynicism coin. At some points in Edward's life the evidence does not read as fable, but should. Edward III and his contemporaries were some of the greatest propagandists who ever lived, and inclined not only to spin a skirmish as a chivalric victory but also to downplay an embarrassment, or to destroy evidence relating to secret or compromising events. This is best represented in the fake death of Edward II in Berkeley Castle in 1327. Edward purposefully suppressed discussion of his father's survival. He personally destroyed evidence (his chamberlain's accounts) relating to the period when we might reasonably have expected him to have been arranging the return of his father's corpse to England.[16] This creates the most extraordinary problems for the biographer, who cannot simply ignore Edward III's relationship with his father's keepers, or the circumstances of his survival, after 1327. With so little definite evidence extant, and so much evidence relating only to nondescript 'secret business', it is hardly surprising that many historians prefer to avoid the debate, and hide behind a cloak of ill-defined scepticism. It does appear – superficially at least – to be the safest intellectual position. But in historical biography, to err on the side of caution is still to err. An understanding of a subject's character will not be illuminated by his biographer's own timidity or ignorance. The bottom line is that the difficulty of treating a hidden or secret aspect of a man's life is not a good reason for his biographer to ignore it, quite the reverse.

The questions arising from Edward II's false death in Berkeley Castle are complicated, as one would expect, and a biography of Edward III is not the place to go into the matter in great depth. But the implications for Edward III of his father's secret survival were far more important than any other writer to date has been prepared to admit. Suffice to say that, as a preliminary to this study, these questions have been revisited, discussed with leading scholars of the period, argued out, checked and revised. The result is the most thorough analysis of the information structures underpinning the narrative of the demise of a medieval English king. In particular, the fake death in Berkeley Castle and its repercussions are discussed at length in an article in *The English Historical Review* (the foremost peer-reviewed historical journal). This concludes that we may be 'almost certain' that Edward II was still alive in March 1330. An analysis of the post-1330 evidence for Edward II's custody in Northern Italy is also being prepared for scholarly publication. Abstracts of these papers appear in Appendices Two and Three of this book respectively.

The last problem facing a biographer of Edward III which needs to be mentioned is perhaps the most obvious. The sheer scope of the man's life is awesome and hugely challenging. Writing this book has, at times, felt like experiencing the most beautiful, escapeless nightmare: the subject is so vivid, fascinating and inspiring; but the man ruled for fifty years! It would take considerably more than fifty years to become fully acquainted with all the documentary and physical evidence remaining from the reign, and to sift it for what is pertinent to Edward himself. True, five other British monarchs have reigned even longer (Henry III, James VI of Scotland, George III, Victoria and Elizabeth II), but their lives would not be easy to encapsulate either. Furthermore, the sheer dynamism of Edward III gives his reign several dimensions not present in any of these others. Edward III was not just head of state, he was his own prime minister, his own foreign minister and his own field marshal. He was his own lawmaker and justice. He was a patron, a consumer, an innovator and an arbiter of taste. He was also a husband, a father and a friend to many. To write a biography of a man who actively associated himself with so many roles is like trying to write a study of a dozen politicians, military chiefs, economists, law lords and multibillionaire art collectors and philanthropists rolled into one.

Perhaps because of these problems, and perhaps because of the derision of his achievements in the nineteenth century, few modern biographers have been tempted to write about Edward III. Just three books purporting to describe his life were published in the last century, and none of these is a detailed study.[17] This might suggest that there is a shortage of writing, especially good writing, on Edward III. But if we look for books on aspects of his kingship we find an abundance in the form of studies of the Hundred Years War, chivalry, his sons (especially the Black Prince and John of Gaunt), his eminent ecclesiastical contemporaries, coinage, literary characters (especially Froissart, Chaucer and Langland), the development of parliament, the development of the English language, the Black Death, local government, the wool trade, social regulation, and the laws of treason. There is a willingness to write about his reign which is strangely contrasted by a reluctance to write about his character. Some scholarly articles, particularly Mark Ormrod's consideration of Edward's personal religion, *are* biographical, and repay repeated reading in an attempt to understand the man. But the vast bulk is like the flotsam which scatters the sea after the sinking of a great ship: it is obvious that something huge and magnificent was here, and has disappeared from view, but one struggles to see exactly what.

This book is by no means the first work to restore Edward III to a more appropriate place in the pantheon of English kings. That distinction probably should go to two very different pieces of mid-twentieth-century scholarship. Edouard Perroy, a Professor of Medieval History at the Sorbonne, wrote his extraordinary book *The Hundred Years War* in 1943–44, while fighting for the French Resistance, or, as he put it, playing 'an exciting game of hide and seek with the Gestapo'.[18] He had no access to his research materials at the time but, in his words, 'suddenly flung into outlawry, abruptly parted from my familiar environment of students and books, I seemed, in contact with this present so harshly real, to gain a better understanding of the past'. And he added that as a result of his circumstances, certain actions had 'become more comprehensible; one is better placed to explain a surrender, or to excuse a revolt'. His Edward was a successful diplomat as well as a military leader, able to outmanoeuvre Philip of France at almost every opportunity: 'a political genius fertile in fresh ideas, but at the same time a cold calculator who drew up long-term plans, knew where he was going and what he wanted, and surpassed his adversary in the diplomatic sphere just as he crushed him on the field of battle'.[19] Perroy also destroyed the idea that the cause of the Hundred Years War was Edward's dynastic ambitions: 'nothing is further from the truth', was his view on the subject.[20] Everyone seriously interested in the fourteenth century has been in his debt ever since.

The other pioneering rehabilitation was May McKisack's landmark lecture, 'Edward III and the historians', delivered in May 1959.[21] In a straightforward and brilliant piece of historical observation, in which practically every sentence is a revelation or a delight (and many are both), she at once showed how Edward III had been the victim – not the subject – of historians since the early nineteenth century. 'Historians whose whole thinking has been conditioned by notions of development, evolution and progress, sometimes find it hard to recognize fully or to remember consistently that these meant nothing to medieval man . . .' Or 'Edward III in the days of his glory is hidden from us by the cloud of contemporary adulation . . .' Wonderful. Perhaps this short lecture should be handed out to all history students in the hope that thereby a little wisdom can be shown to be a powerful tool in assessing a man's achievements. Its fifteen pages end with a final sentence which is the launchpad for most modern writing on the king's character: 'For all his failings, it remains hard to deny an element of greatness in him, a courage and a magnanimity which go far to sustain the verdict of one of the older writers that he was a prince who knew his work and did it.'

Since 1959 various writers have gradually pushed towards a closer and more realistic understanding of Edward III. In 1965 he was the subject of Ranald Nicholson's excellent *Edward III and the Scots*, in which his importance in turning England from a feudal kingdom into a nation was underlined. The 1970s saw little Edward III-related activity, although four biographies of his eldest son (the Black Prince) appeared in just three years. Probably the major contribution at this time was Michael Prestwich's spirited evocation of the period in his *The Three Edwards: War and State in England 1272–1377*, published in 1980. By this date Edward's leadership skills had set him back on the list of England's successful kings, and Prestwich's book brought home Edward's courage and patronage of chivalry, and the adulation of his contemporaries. The 1980s saw the renaissance of serious attention on Edward III, particularly with a series of original and impressive biographical articles by Mark Ormrod. This attention continued in the 1990s and 2000s in works such as Ormrod's own *The Reign of Edward III*, Juliet Vale's *Edward III and Chivalry*, Clifford Rogers' original and revealing book on Edward's military strategy, *War Cruel and Sharp*, and a volume of essays edited by James Bothwell, *The Age of Edward III*. By 1992, after more than a century of prejudice, it was possible for a scholar once again to hold the view that 'The fifty years from 1327 until 1377, which encompass the reign of King Edward III, can be reckoned one of the longest and most successful periods of late medieval English kingship.'[22] Lastly, although it is not a direct study of Edward III, it would be churlish not to mention the first two volumes of Jonathan Sumption's multi-volume work on the Hundred Years War. Outstanding for the very high quality of writing, narrative accessibility, scope and detail (from both the English and the French perspectives), these books reveal Edward as a harrassed, impetuous, frustrated and egotistical man – but a capable, committed and sometimes brilliant war leader – on the bloody stage of fourteenth-century Europe. They certainly provide the best available account of the great conflict which can only briefly be covered in a single-volume biography of one of its many leaders.

Edward's reputation has thus been exalted to the heavens, forced through the mangle of Victorian cultural conceit, and gradually restored to its proper place of exemplary leadership, at least in the pages of military history and chivalry. But from this point on we can lay aside Edward's historical reputation and search for the man himself. What was he really like? Was he really a leader without equal? Was he a cruel, selfish, war-monger? Or was he a loving husband, conscientious ruler and champion of England in the eyes of his people? What should concern us primarily from here on is not how Edward's successors thought of him, nor what the future will think of him, nor even what the most up-to-date academic judgement makes of his successes and failures in relation to his society, but who he was, what he wanted to be, how his contemporaries saw him, and what he thought of himself. To determine these things might be the hardest historical task there is. It is like trying to describe an ancient bonfire on the strength of its wind-blown ashes. But the fact that this man existed, in truth, and lived a life which is so unlike our own, and yet experienced triumph, glory, disaster, suffering, fear, grief and love in ways which we would all recognise, is a good enough reason to make the attempt.

ONE

Childhood

Of all the stages in the life of a resourceful and imaginative individual, childhood is the most important and the most difficult to understand. We need to think about a boy's physical well-being as he developed, as well as his education, social situation and religious outlook. We have to consider his associations with relatives, companions and mentors. With regard to medieval characters, prophecies, feuds and spiritual cults dominated families for generations, and cannot be passed over simply because of their lack of relevance in the modern world. We must understand the strict definitions of hierarchy, and the fighting and leadership skills which noble heirs were expected to display. With regard to royalty, we must also think of the huge weight of public expectation on a young prince. With a growing boy of any class, we must pay a thought to what he simply liked to do, what he found fun. Thus it is fair to say that it is a major failing of all the previous biographies of Edward III that his childhood has either been completely ignored, or covered by a chapter describing his father's shortcomings as a monarch.

It is easy to see why this has happened: there is very little information available on Edward III's early life *except* his father's rule. However, there is no doubt that Edward's relationship with his father was much more important and complicated than merely seeing at first hand how his father's antagonism of the most important nobles led to civil war. What about his personal feelings towards his father? What about the bonds of trust, rivalry, humour, friendship, mutual support, love and (eventually) gratitude which a son often feels for his father and a father often feels for his son? And what about his relationships with other people, for instance his mother? Existing studies say almost nothing of personal relevance between his birth and baptism in November 1312, and his creation as duke of Aquitaine in September 1325. Practically the only personal facts regularly mentioned about him in this period are his creation as earl of Chester, his first being summoned to parliament at the age of seven, and the supposed appointment of Richard Bury as his tutor. With such a shortage of material, it is not surprising that writers have concentrated on the political turmoil of his father's reign, with the overt or implied understanding that young Edward saw his father make a mess of ruling his realm and vowed to try to do better.

We too can try to do better. For a start we may take a very different view on his relationship with his father, about whom we know much more than Dr Mackinnon, who in 1900 began his biography of Edward III with the line 'A more complete ninny than Edward II has seldom occupied a throne.' Edward II's failings as a king did not arise from stupidity or a desire to be obtuse and overbearing towards his subjects. He was undoubtedly one of the most pious kings of medieval England, deeply conscious of his indebtedness to God for his great status, and a sincere believer in the power of the intervention of the saints. He was a man who loved to be generous, and to be seen to be generous. At the same time he could be cruel, and he did not have much of a capacity for forgiveness, or even toleration. He was capable of huge affection, but preferred genuine closeness to the formal bonds of diplomatic and military friendship. He had a keen sense of humour and a rare ability to express it. In 1305 he wrote to his uncle, Louis d'Evreux, sending him 'a big trotting palfrey which can hardly carry its own weight, and some of our bandy-legged harriers from Wales, who can well catch a hare if they find it asleep, and some of our running dogs, which go at a gentle pace: for well we know that you take delight in lazy dogs'.[1] As a young man Edward II's closest companion – and most would say the true love of his life – was the dashing Piers Gaveston, a Gascon knight's son, three years older, who was outrageously witty, unashamedly rude, clever, physically strong, and brilliant enough with a lance to humiliate the proud heirs of England's most important families in the joust, the sport they rated above all others. In the words of a well-informed contemporary, Edward 'adopted Gaveston as a brother' and 'cherished him as a son'.[2] Gaveston in return gave Edward the confidence to be his unconventional self.[3] Above all else, Edward II wished to establish himself as an individual, not a model prince, and in so doing he embarked on a personal rebellion against authority which lasted for much of the rest of his reign.[4]

Gaveston was murdered in June 1312 by the earls of Lancaster, Warwick and Hereford, and the country was plunged into turmoil. Many feared the king's wrath: it seemed that the bloodiest of civil wars was about to break out. The king summoned the earls responsible to London to account for themselves, and they responded with armed force. Lancaster came with a thousand horsemen and fifteen hundred foot soldiers; Warwick with troops from the forest of Arden, and Hereford with a crowd of Welsh 'woodland wild men'.[5] Their troops encamped between St Albans and Ware, within marching distance of the city. Edward, at Blackfriars, urged the citizens of London to defend their gates and walls. He summoned parliament to Westminster to discuss the crisis, and the earls of Pembroke and Surrey urged him to make war on those who had authorised the killing. A papal envoy, Cardinal Arnaud Nouvel, arrived at the end of August, and negotiated directly with the rebel earls at St Albans. He persuaded them to meet the king. But when the earls finally arrived in the city, they came heavily armed. The earl of Gloucester, the king's nephew, then took up the duty of chief negotiator. He achieved little, for the king refused to accept that his most cherished friend was a traitor, and the earls refused to acknowledge that their killing amounted to murder. When Edward left London for Windsor, the recriminations and threats of violence still rattled between the upper ranks of the English nobility. Civil war seemed the most probable outcome.

In such a political atmosphere, on Monday 13 November 1312, Edward III was born at Windsor. The country's relief was described by the contemporary author of the *Life of Edward the Second*:

> Amid this uproar, with various rumours flying hither and thither, while one man foretold peace, his neighbour war, there was born to the king a handsome and long looked-for son. He was christened Edward, his father's name . . . This long wished-for birth was timely for us, because by God's will it had two fortunate consequences. It much lessened the grief which had afflicted the king on Piers [Gaveston's] death, and it provided a known heir to the throne.[6]

All across England there was celebration. A monk of St Albans recorded that 'by this birth all England was made joyful . . . and his father was made happy again, for it tempered that sadness he had felt since the death of Piers'.[7] The monk went on: 'On that day his love of the boy began and the memory of Piers began to diminish.'[8] Edward, it would seem, had redeemed the situation. By his very birth he had pulled the country back from the abyss.

These references to Gaveston and the baby being held in comparable affection are interesting, for they echo those chronicles which refer to Edward II loving his friend as a brother or a son. This was certainly close endearment: no one ever accused Edward II of being a cruel father, or uncaring towards his sisters and half-brothers. He had a particular fondness for female family members – especially his stepmother, Queen Margaret – and maintained his old nurse, Alice Leygrave, for many years. His efforts to bring his friends into the royal family by marrying them to his female relatives – Piers Gaveston is the prime, though not the sole, example – further underline how important family ties were to Edward. The royal family was clearly at the heart of his view of his kingdom and the rest of God's Creation. This explains why his son's birth was of such political – as well as personal – significance to him. The king and many of his subjects would have strongly associated the birth of an heir with God's will, and thus it was a blessing, a gift to the kingdom ordained by God. Edward had received divine confirmation that his line would continue. Most important of all, the whole country – including the rebel earls – had to acknowledge this blessing. There had to be some fear in the earls' camps that God was favouring the king and, by implication, not his enemies.

Edward, in his joy at hearing this news, granted the man who bore it, John Launge, and his wife, Joan (one of the queen's attendants), the extra-ordinary sum of eighty pounds yearly for life.[9] This was more than many knights received, and it is perhaps not surprising that the sheriffs of London proved very reluctant to pay it.[10] But such a huge gift to the bearer of the news was money well-spent. Although it was probably motivated by paternal pride, it had propaganda value too. It helped draw attention to the fact that the king now had a son. Even better publicity was the timely presence of the papal legate, Cardinal Nouvel. Edward jumped at the opportunity to have his son and heir baptised by an emissary of the pope. Accordingly, on Thursday 16 November 1312, Cardinal Nouvel christened young Edward of Windsor in St Edward's Chapel in Windsor Castle. For good measure, Edward asked the other peace envoys in the country – Count Louis d'Evreux, the queen's uncle, and the bishop of Poitiers – to be the boy's godfathers. To these he added five more godfathers: John Droxford (bishop of Bath and Wells), Walter Reynolds (bishop of Worcester), John of Brittany (earl of Richmond), Aymer de Valence (earl of Pembroke) and one Hugh Despenser. The last-mentioned was the father of the man of the same name who, nine years later, finally plunged the country into civil war.

Edward's birth was symbolic for other, secular reasons. England in the early fourteenth century was a country in which the future and the past were interwoven with the present in a series of potent and developing stories. Great families knew their history – none more so than the royal family – and they believed that, to a certain extent, they knew their futures too, through prophecy. This was not personal fortune-telling but public prophecy, which soon was circulated as rumour and eventually captured in literary works. In the widely-circulated 'Prophecy of the Six Kings', probably first written down in its earliest form at about the time of Edward's birth, the six kings following King John were characterised by beasts.[11] Henry III was portrayed as a lamb, Edward I as a dragon, Edward II as a goat and Edward III as a boar 'who will come out of Windsor'. Although a boar might not strike the modern reader as an animal of great significance, it had huge resonance in the four-teenth century. 'The boar who came out of Cornwall' was none other than

King Arthur himself.[12] Moreover, 'the boar who will come out of Windsor' was prophesied to have the head and heart of a lion. He would wear 'three crowns' – an oblique reference to the three crowns of the Holy Roman Empire, one iron, one silver and one gold – and be buried at Cologne amongst the tombs of the Three Kings, the Magi, who were then understood to be the first Christian kings.[13] To many contemporaries, the future was clear: Edward II would lose his kingdom. He would die overseas.[14] After his death, his successor, Edward of Windsor, would win fame as a warrior-king, become Holy Roman Emperor, and win battles across Europe, regaining the lands which his ancestors had lost. The people of England could have some faith that their newborn prince would grow up not just to be a king but a lion-hearted and victorious one.

The large number of copies of this prophecy allow us to be reasonably confident that Edward knew it. A revision updated in about 1327 was incorporated into the most popular chronicle of the day, the *Brut*, written in the mid-1330s, of which Queen Isabella owned a copy at her death.[15] Later in his life Edward specifically renounced any intention of being buried at the shrine of the Three Kings in Cologne, suggesting he knew this was widely expected of him. When personally visiting the shrine in 1338, he gave a large amount of money to be spent on upkeep of the building, so that part of the prophecy was familiar to him by then. But whether he believed all of it, totally, is another question. While certainty in such matters is not possible, it is probable that he recognised that true prophetic writing could contain kernels of truth. When declaring that he wished to be buried in Westminster rather than Cologne, he did not merely pass an idle remark: he swore a solemn oath, so he seems to have taken the original prophecy seriously. And there is good evidence that royal prophecies were taken seriously by Edward's father, for Edward II had faith in one prophetic story in particular: the oil of St Thomas.

The story of the oil of St Thomas stated that when Thomas Becket had been in exile, the Virgin Mary had appeared to him in a dream. She had announced to him that the fifth king after his time (Edward II) would be a benevolent man who would fight for God's church, and reconquer the Holy Land. To assist this king *and his successors* the Virgin entrusted Becket with an ampulla of sacred oil, and directed him to give it to a monk of St Cyprian's monastery. The monk hid it in the church of St George at Poitiers, with a sheet of metal inscribed with the prophecy itself. After an attempt to steal it had failed, it had come into the possession of the duke of Brabant, Edward II's brother-in-law, who had brought it to the king's coronation in 1308. It was not used, however. Ten years later, Edward II claimed that he believed the reason his reign was so unsuccessful was because he, the fifth king after Becket's time, had failed to be anointed with the oil. And in so doing he had failed not only his kingdom, himself and his successors but also St Thomas and the Virgin Mary. So anxious was he for some respite from his failure that he wrote to the recently elected Pope John XXII asking whether he would send a cardinal to anoint him with the oil. The pope refused the services of a cardinal, but said that if the king truly believed the story it would not be sinful for him to be anointed. That Edward II raised such a matter privately with the pope suggests his interest in this prophecy was not merely political, but spiritual too. He believed it.[16]

We do not know how deeply Edward III shared his father's view of this or any other prophecy. It may just be coincidence but the three most important divine figures in Edward III's life – the Virgin Mary, St Thomas of Canterbury and St George – all appear in this story. But in an age when most people believed in destiny, Edward would have understood that it was widely held that he would become a military conqueror abroad and a champion of the church, a man whose leadership had been awaited for centuries. It was an utterly traditional role for a king, very similar to that of his grandfather, the majestic and fearsome Edward I; but it was also wrapped in romance and religious mysticism, and thus embodied all the virtues of fourteenth-century kingship.

If there was a fly in the prophetic ointment, it was the day of the birth. 13 November was St Brice's Day, and St Brice was not the sort of saint by whom one would choose to be governed. He was a pupil of the fifth-century saint, St Martin of Tours, and used to tease his master with sarcastic comments, not always stopping short of insult: calling him half-witted, for instance. St Martin responded by praying that Brice would succeed him as bishop of Tours, and prophesying that he would be treated very badly during his episcopacy. So it happened: Bishop Brice was charged at the age of thirty-three with fathering his washerwoman's child. On commanding the baby to speak in the name of Christ to reveal whether he was the father or not, the people accused him of witchcraft and threw him out of the city. Only after spending seven years in exile at the papal palace in Rome did Brice achieve sufficient composure and sanctity to return to Tours and rule as a more saintly bishop for the rest of his life.[17] Thus it may have been with some trepidation that each chronicler recorded the feast day of St Brice in connection with their new prince's birth. After all, Edward II had been born on St Mark's Day, and that was hardly any more propitious, being widely regarded as a day of doom.[18] The author of the *Life of Edward the Second* ended his eulogy on the young prince's birth with the hope that he would 'combine in his person the virtues that characterised in turn his forebears. May he follow the industry of King Henry the second, the well-known valour of King Richard, may he reach the age of King Henry [the third], revive the wisdom of King Edward [the first] and remind us of the physical strength and comeliness of his father.'¹⁹

The king's instinct was to shower those whom he loved with presents, and so he immediately ordered that the baby be raised to the front rank of the peerage. This was extraordinary. Edward II himself had been sixteen, almost seventeen years old, before he was created earl of Chester; his father had been nearly fifteen. Now his son would bear that title. At the age of twelve days, Edward of Windsor was created an earl.²⁰ No sooner had this been done than the king set about spending money on preparations for his first family Christmas, ordering almost £1,250 to be spent on cloth for his and the queen's retainers and those of the young heir.²¹ After Christmas the baby was provided with his own household, to maintain him in his position as earl of Chester. By 26 January 1313 – aged just ten weeks – Edward was nominally in charge of dozens of greater and lesser servants.

A large household required maintenance. So the king was able to indulge his demonstration of largesse further by granting his son a number of lucrative incomes. The counties of Flintshire and Cheshire were made over to him along with his title. At the age of eight months he was granted the lordship of the Isle of Wight.²² At the age of four he was granted a substantial income from the Exchequer, amounting to the rent of the manor of Petworth and the lands of the young heir, Henry Percy.²³ At the age of five he was granted an additional one thousand marks per year (£666 13s 8d) out of the tin revenues of Cornwall.²⁴ Edward was very well-provided for, not the richest earl in the kingdom – that was his father's embittered cousin, Thomas, earl of Lancaster – but by no means the poorest.

With all these grants came responsibilities. As the earl of Chester, Edward of Windsor was responsible for the administration of justice in all his lands and across many manors held by others. It is, of course, very unlikely that as a baby he heard any of the king's writs addressed to him, but nevertheless he would have had impressed upon him from the earliest age the fact that he had duties towards others. Rents coming in from his manors in the north were collected by his chamberlain and paid out to his officers and into his own 'wardrobe' or treasury. His officers were responsible for raising men from Cheshire for the king's service. When the king needed to raise men from North Wales for the suppression of the rebel Llywelyn Bren in the spring of 1316, it was the three-year-old earl of Chester to whom the writ was directed. Similarly, arrangements to allow foodstuffs to be purchased and conveyed away from Chester, or to arrest outlaws travelling in the region, had to be made with his justiciar.²⁵ The king's reasons for making his son an earl at such a young age were various, and the propaganda element of the outrageousness of the appointment cannot be ignored; but the end result was an education. In later life Edward III would not have been able to remember a time when he was not responsible for the administration of justice, the accrual of revenue from land, and decisions which changed people's lives.

*

The king might have been the most powerful figure in Edward's life with regard to inheritance and status, but he was not the only important person. Edward's mother, Queen Isabella – Isabella the Fair – was every bit as royal as her husband, the only daughter of King Philip of France, who doted on her. She was sixteen years of age at the time of the birth, twelve years younger than the king, and renowned for her beauty and intelligence. She was also connected to most of the royal houses of Europe, due to the geographical position of France and the status of her ancestors. Through her mother, Jeanne, who enjoyed the mouth-watering title of Countess Palatine of Champagne and Brie (as well as that of Queen of Navarre), she was connected to Iberian royalty. Through her grandmother she was related to the dukes of Brabant. Through her cousin, Jeanne, daughter of Charles, count of Valois, she was related to William, count of Hainault, Holland and Zeeland, the lord of Friesland. And so on. She was enmeshed in a complex series of dynastic relationships even more extensive than those of her husband. Edward II's only living close relative in a European royal house was his nephew, the young duke of Brabant. His mother, Eleanor of Castile had died more than twenty years earlier, when he had been only six, and his Spanish cousins were not close. The difference lay in geographical position, and the difficulties of directly exercising royal links. Despite two centuries of taking continental brides, England remained on the periphery of the continental dynastic network. France, respected as the greatest kingdom in Christendom, was at the very centre. Thus for Edward of Windsor, his mother represented rich dynasties and royal links far beyond the shores of Britain. It was perhaps in recognition of this that Isabella's uncle, Louis d'Evreux, requested that Isabella call her first-born son Louis, not Edward. Not surprisingly, the English nobles at the baptism refused.[26]

Dynastic links are easy to account for, but they are not as important for understanding a child's development as parental character. Although Edward II's personality has been reappraised many times in the last hundred years, Isabella's has generally been neglected.[27] Most people still remember her as the 'She-wolf of France'. This name was originally the duke of York's insult to Margaret of Anjou in Shakespeare's *Henry VI Part Three* (Act One, Scene

Four), but it came to be applied to Isabella in the eighteenth century due to the widespread belief that she had been party to her husband's murder. Even though scholarship has moved on considerably, popular reputations of villainy never die. This is both a pity and a problem. Edward's mother was not a she-wolf but a dutiful and highly religious woman who, in later years, when she had been spurned by her husband and had fallen into the arms of a dominating lover, still felt she ought to return to her rightful spouse.[28] When the king lay in prison, scorned by the nation, and bereft of his throne, she still sent presents to him.[29] Edward II's respect for her intelligence and negotiating skills may be seen in his approval of the treaty which she negotiated on his behalf in order to try to secure peace with France in 1325. Nor was this the only time that Edward placed great faith in her skills. She also took part in domestic peace negotiations in 1313, 1318 and 1321.[30] She was a woman of conscience: when she found that two of her sisters-in-law were guilty of adultery with two French knights, she had no hesitation in reporting them to her father.[31] It is not difficult to find instances of her clemency: although she detested Hugh Despenser the younger with a passion, she pleaded for the life of Hugh's father, the earl of Winchester, when he was facing execution. She was known to be moved by pity: in October 1312, while pregnant with Edward, she gave food and clothes to a young Scottish orphan she met; later she paid for him to be sent to London to be educated.[32] She equalled even her husband's piety in her pilgrimages, her devotion to English shrines, and her enthusiastic collecting of relics. She also collected books, especially chivalric tales, and had more than thirty volumes in her library when she died.[33] Bookish and pious, it is not surprising that she had little aptitude for war. An attempt to lead an attack on Leeds Castle in 1321 ended in disaster and the deaths of nine members of her household. Similarly, she never played a leading role in political confrontation except when at the side of her lover, Sir Roger Mortimer. But during the invasion of 1326 she acted as a brilliant and powerful figurehead. Her greatest failing was her ability to spend money – vast amounts of money – with apparently no qualms about the acquisitiveness demonstrated in obtaining such sums. From relatively restrained beginnings at the time of Edward's birth (although sixty men were employed to keep and repair her clothes),[34] her spending in the years 1326–30 amounted to about a quarter of the royal purse. However, if her most notable characteristics were duty, piety, loyalty to those she loved, passion, clemency, trustworthiness, intelligence and conscience, and if her greatest sin was profligacy, she was about as far from the all-devouring 'she-wolf' myth of the eighteenth century as a woman could possibly be.

Of the other people who were important to the infant Edward, one must first mention his nurse, Margaret. She was from Daventry in

Northamptonshire, and in 1312 was the wife of Stephen Chandler.[35] To her Edward remained devoted for the rest of her life. So attached to her did he become that she was still in his household, maintained on the payroll along with his clerks, after he became king. Later, in his twenties, he made every effort to look after her when she encountered legal difficulties.[36] This is not surprising as she was the one person who had always been with him, from birth to adolescence. It was in her care that he remained when, at the end of January 1313, his mother made preparations to return to London. Margaret, who would have been breast-feeding the two-month-old Edward in place of his mother, took the baby from Windsor to Bray on 26 January. The next day they arrived at Bisham, in Berkshire, which was to be Edward's home for the next year.[37] The building they lived in was almost certainly the manor house which had belonged to the Knights Templar until the dissolution of the Order in 1312. His father visited him on 13 February, and stayed for dinner, and again visited on 4 August, on which occasion he granted him the Isle of Wight.[38] His mother visited for four days in early May, and the kindly Queen Margaret (his father's stepmother and his mother's aunt) visited in June. His nurse Margaret also took him to see his mother and father at court. The account for his household expenses at this time records that he was taken to spend twenty-seven days with the royal family in the spring and early summer of 1313.[39]

Edward spent the first years of his life in his nurse's company, receiving gifts and occasional visits from his parents, surrounded by servants and household officials whose roles he would not have fully understood. In April 1314, he was moved from Bisham to Ludgershall in East Wiltshire, an old castle in need of repair, as shown by the order to mend the shingle roofs of the prince's dwellings.[40] It was expected that Edward would stay there for some time, and this still seems to have been the plan at the end of May, when the king's butler was ordered to provide an extra thirty tuns of wine for the prince's household over and above that already delivered, suggesting a very large contingent of men-at-arms protecting the young boy.[41] But in June the king decided to locate his son and heir at Wallingford Castle, previously the chief residence of Piers Gaveston.[42] Perhaps the king, knowing he would be riding north to face the Scots near Stirling – in the battle which came to be known as Bannockburn – wished to make sure his son was secure in case of a disaster. By July the prince and his nurse had taken up residence.[43] It was fitting that he should have come to live in Gaveston's castle: the prince had become the king's symbol of independence, just as Gaveston had once been. Edward conferred gifts and titles on his son in the same way he had given them to Gaveston. The difference was that his son was royal, whereas Gaveston had been born a commoner, not even of baronial rank, and gifts to the heir to the throne were beyond criticism.

The next group of people who might have influenced Edward in these early years – at least the next group whom we can identify – are the officers who administered his household. The most important of these would have been his steward, Sir Robert Mauley, who served him from before July 1314 until at least June 1320.[44] In his official capacity, Mauley would have controlled the men of the household in all their duties, overseeing his own staff and those in the specialist departments of the buttery, scullery, pantry, saucery, the hall, marshalcy and the prince's private chamber. He would moreover have been particularly conspicuous, standing with his staff of office in the hall at mealtimes while the servants took their places at the tables below the dais where the young Edward sat. Next in importance to the steward was the treasurer, or keeper of the wardrobe, who was responsible for Edward's income and expenses. From the beginning until 1316 at least, and possibly until early 1318, this office was held by Hugh of Leominster, a royal clerk who had served as receiver and chamberlain in North Wales in the time of Edward's grandfather, Edward I, and had been in royal service ever since.[45] He would have been able to tell the young prince about his grandfather's conquest of Wales. Perhaps there were other men in the household who could regale the boy with stories of his ancestors' achievements. We can only wonder what Edward might have heard from men such as Grimbald de la Batude, a foreigner who had served both Edward I and Edward II before entering Edward's household.[46]

On 15 August 1316 Prince John, Edward's brother, was born at Eltham. Once again the St Albans chronicler recorded how happy the king was, but this time it is noticeable that there was nowhere near as much effusion of joy. There was no expensive income awarded to the man who brought him the news. There were no comparisons with Gaveston. There was no need. Although far from peaceful, with a serious rebellion in Wales due to the harsh climate of the previous two summers, a rebellion in Bristol, and the Scots' invasion of Ireland, the king was not personally under pressure. His principal enemy, his cousin the earl of Lancaster, had withdrawn to sulk in his vast estates in the north of the country, and for once King Edward had a relatively free hand. He wrote to the prior of his favourite order of friars, the Dominicans, on 24 August requesting that they pray for the king, the queen, Edward of Windsor and John of Eltham, 'especially on account of John'.[47] No doubt four-year-old Edward was summoned to Eltham to see his baby brother. His justiciar in Chester, Sir Hugh Audley the elder, was ordered to pay the queen the rents from the manor of Macclesfield, to cover John's expenses. When their younger sister,

Eleanor of Woodstock, was born on 8 June 1318 it was proposed that all three royal children should live together.

By then, significant changes had taken place in Edward's household. Shortly before April 1318, the king appointed Sir Richard Damory to be Edward's guardian, or, to be precise, 'keeper of the body of my lord Sir Edward, earl of Chester, and surveyor of his household and his lands and all his business'.[48] Damory requested that, since one of his roles was to enquire into the negligence of Edward's bailiffs at Chester, he needed legal assistance. He requested probably the most notable lawyer of the time, Geoffrey le Scrope, or, if Geoffrey could not attend, then John Stonor, another famous royal legal adviser. Damory was given the services of both men.[49] Damory also asked for – and got – the services of Nicholas Hugate to be Edward's treasurer and keeper of his wardrobe.[50] Suddenly, a man had come along who had reorganised Edward's household and set about identifying and correcting the abuses which, it turned out, were being perpetrated across Edward's estates.

Damory was more than just a bureaucratic reformer. He was the elder brother of Roger Damory, whom the king liked so much that in 1317 he gave him the hand in marriage of his own niece, Elizabeth, one of the three sisters and coheiresses of the late earl of Gloucester. This brought Roger Damory into the royal family, and at the same time enhanced Sir Richard's standing with the king. Sir Richard had begun his career in the household of the earl of Hereford, the king's brother-in-law, in whose service he had worked assiduously.[51] After leaving Hereford's service, he had entered royal employment, acting as sheriff of Oxfordshire and Buckinghamshire from 1308 to 1310, and as constable of Oxford Castle from 1311. He also seems to have been associated with the Despenser family.[52] He may be characterised as a man of wide experience, an 'old soldier', probably in his forties, with a dependable track record of responsible command, and with very good connections with the Marcher lords – such as the earl of Hereford – and the royal family. Under Damory's watchful eye, Edward would have had a wooden sword pressed into his hand with the intention that he should learn how to use it, and take his first steps along the long road to becoming a military leader.

*

Edward's household arrangements never remained static for long. In late 1318 his two-year-old brother, John, and baby sister, Eleanor, came to live with him.[53] The children remained together for nearly two years. But on 5 June 1320 Sir Richard Damory, Robert Mauley and Nicholas Hugate were ordered to return High Peak to Queen Isabella for the sustenance of

John and Eleanor. The implication is that they went to live with her. Edward, however, did not return to his mother but to his father. Extraordinarily, on 5 August 1320, although not yet eight years of age, the king summoned him, 'our dearest son', to attend parliament. His political life had begun.

On the face of it, we might wonder what his father expected of him at such a tender age. The boy could hardly be expected to swing opinions in his father's favour through eloquent debate at the age of eight. Edward II himself had not been summoned until he was eighteen. But the king did not expect his son to employ eloquent arguments, or to say anything at all. He merely wanted him there, to be a symbol.[54] Edward of Windsor was not only his father's heir but a statement of his father's royalty and the family's right to rule. The king's message to parliament was clear. If parliament recognised this boy's right to attend and be heard, despite being very young and – through no fault of his own – unwise, then it must also recognise the king's right to attend and rule, however unwise the peers thought him. Edward of Windsor's presence in parliament that October was his father's very powerful demonstration of royal legitimacy. To challenge either of them was to challenge the very institution of monarchy.

There were probably several reasons for the timing of the summons. The least important was that Edward was now of an age at which – had he been the son of a nobleman – he would have been sent to serve in another lord's household. As the king's son, the royal household was the only one suitable, for only there could he learn the basic procedures of kingship. Living at his father's court, it may have been considered fitting that, as an earl, he should attend parliament. A more important reason for the timing was that the king was heading for another confrontation with the barons, and he anticipated very serious trouble indeed.

Edward could have had no idea of the cataclysm which was about to erupt within his small but rapidly expanding world. At the beginning of 1320 he had been living in the care of Sir Richard Damory, no doubt meeting Damory's brother Roger, who was now married to one of his (Edward's) cousins. He would have regularly met his justiciar's son, Sir Hugh Audley the younger, who had married another of his cousins. He would have been familiar with Lord Mauley, his steward's brother. He would have met and heard a great deal about the earl of Hereford, who was married to his aunt. Hereford had been reconciled to Edward II after the Gaveston debacle, and had remained loyal ever since. The prince would have been aware of his more distant kinsmen too, like Sir Roger Mortimer, Lord Mortimer of Wigmore, who had re-established English rule in Ireland after the Scots' invasion. Edward's treasurer, Hugh of Leominster – coming from a Mortimer region – might well have been one of the several clerks promoted into royal service through connections with that family. Edward's justiciar – Sir Hugh Audley the elder – was Mortimer's brother-in-law. What the eight-year-old Edward would have had difficulty grasping was that now, in the autumn of 1320, these men were all gathering to make war on his father, the king. Edward may or may not have been aware of earlier crises, but he could not have failed to hear about this one. This rebellion was being spearheaded by his father's relations and men who had, until now, been his father's loyal supporters.

The cause of the problem was Hugh Despenser, a man to whom the king had entrusted much of his government: too much, perhaps. Despenser's ability to tempt the king to give him whatever he wanted was infuriating for men like the earl of Hereford, Roger Mortimer and Roger Damory. Damory was Despenser's brother-in-law, but Despenser was not touched by family loyalty. Their wives might be sisters but Despenser saw them only as nieces of the king, and thus ways to land and authority, and in particular a way to achieve the earldom of Gloucester. The same problems arose with the other brother-in-law and coheir of the Gloucester inheritance, Hugh Audley the younger. To Despenser, the lords Damory and Audley were not brothers-in-law but rivals.

The rivalry did not stop at Despenser's kin. In 1265 the grandfather of Roger Mortimer had killed Despenser's grandfather in battle, at Evesham, and it was no secret that Despenser wanted revenge. It was said that he had sworn to destroy Roger Mortimer and his uncle, Lord Mortimer of Chirk.[55] When Roger Mortimer and his uncle sought to buy the lordship of Gower, Despenser took action to secure it for himself. Another Marcher lord, John Mowbray, attempted to buy it and consequently fell out with him. Despenser persuaded the king to confiscate it on the basis that it had been obtained illegally, which it had not, merely being transferred in the way that Marcher lands were usually passed on. This united the Marcher lords behind Mowbray and against Despenser. Lord Clifford was another rival, as his mother held several valuable estates which Despenser coveted. Most of all, Despenser had an implacable enemy in Earl Thomas of Lancaster, Edward II's cousin, and when Lancaster spoke nearly all of the north of England listened. This was no local squabble brewing: this was a full-scale civil war between the northern and the Marcher lords, supported by many south-western knights, against the loyalists in the south and east.

This is the reason why it is important to know who was close to the prince in 1320–21. As the baronial revolt – the 'Despenser War' – developed, he would not have been shielded from the news. Nor would he have seen things only through his father's eyes. His guardian, Richard Damory, was torn between supporting the king on the one side, and his brother

Roger and his former lord, the earl of Hereford, on the other. Lord Mauley initially sided with the rebels too. When war finally broke out, the king imprisoned Sir Richard Damory in Banbury Castle.[56] This explains why the eight-year-old Edward was summoned to parliament in the autumn of 1320, and why he probably remained at court thereafter. There was a real danger he would get caught up in the Despenser War, or at least become subject to the influence of the king's enemies.

If young Edward was confused by the rapid development of the situation in the autumn of 1320, he would have been appalled by the eventual outcome. In 1321, after persuading the king to order the banishment of both of the Despensers, the rebel lords were all pardoned for any action they had taken against the favourites. But no sooner was this done than the king raised an army to seek a bloody revenge on those who had forced his hand. In January 1322 Roger Mortimer and his uncle pragmatically surrendered to the king at Shrewsbury; and shortly afterwards the two lords Audley did likewise. But the rest refused to acknowledge any wrong-doing, and retreated to the north, to stand alongside the earl of Lancaster. On 11 March the king declared that everyone who opposed him was a traitor. Five days later, at Boroughbridge, the long-expected battle took place, and Sir Andrew Harclay, acting for the king, was victorious. But young Edward would not have heard the news with any joy. Roger Damory was dead, mortally injured in the battle. The earl of Hereford was dead, killed with a spear thrust up from underneath the bridge into his anus. Most shocking of all was his father's action against the earl of Lancaster. It was utterly inglorious, horrifying even. Edward II ordered his own cousin – a member of the royal family – to be beheaded. He ordered Lord Clifford and Lord Mowbray to be hanged at York. He ordered Sir Henry Willington and Sir Henry Montfort to be hanged at Bristol, Lord Giffard and Sir Roger Elmbridge to be hanged at Gloucester. And so on. All around the country, at the king's order, lords and knights were hanged singly or in pairs in the towns nearest to their lands. Sir Henry le Tyeys, who had been sheriff of Oxfordshire after Richard Damory, and who had then been Edward's constable in the Isle of Wight was hanged in London.[57] And the king ordered their bodies to remain hanging, never to be cut down, but to remain decaying in chains. It was two years before their dessicated and bird-picked remains were finally removed for Christian burial.

We do not know whether Edward was present to see his cousin the earl of Lancaster beheaded, or whether he saw any of those whom he knew on the gallows, but we may be certain that he knew what had happened, and that his father was responsible. His own vassals had been ordered to assemble to take part in the conflict, and, two days before the battle, he himself was summoned to attend the parliament which took place in the wake of the executions.[58] There his father asserted his new authority. He ordered all legal proceedings against the Despensers to be quashed. He ordered his niece, the wife of Hugh Audley the younger, to remain a prisoner at Sempringham.[59] Wives of rebels were to be arrested, as well as their husbands, all their lands forfeit. The sons of Roger Mortimer and the late earl of Hereford were locked up in Windsor Castle.[60] The king's opponents were all dead or imprisoned. One pro-Lancastrian author now described the king fearfully as 'like a lion'.[61] His new-found confidence suggested that he himself believed a new era had dawned. With Despenser to advise him he felt confident enough to order a new campaign in Scotland to reclaim the kingdom he had lost through years of neglect. Perhaps he had in mind his part of the Prophecy of the Six Kings – that the 'goat' (Edward II) would fight with his relation, the 'bear', and would lose much of his land but then he would 'regain what he had lost, and more'.[62] He might have interpreted Lancaster as being the bear, and Scotland as the lands he had lost. If so, he was deluding himself. Perhaps he also deluded his son, but even if he did it is unlikely that the young prince ever forgot that his father began – and ruthlessly terminated – a controversy over a favourite which resulted in the deaths or imprisonment of many of the men whom he had met and looked up to in his childhood.

*

The battle of Boroughbridge totally changed the political scene in England. The king and his favourite were dramatically in the ascendant. Edward himself would have noted the political change reflected in the personnel around him. His officers were replaced with pro-Despenser clerks. Nicholas Hugate was replaced by a one-time Despenser servant, William Cusance, a Burgundian.[63] It is likely that Edward's new steward, John Claroun, another Burgundian, attained his post through his connections with Cusance and Despenser.[64] Despenser's men officiated on behalf of the prince, and probably oversaw his education. Edward did not dislike these new men – Cusance, for instance, remained in royal service for many years and was later directly appointed to important positions by Edward himself – but nonetheless, Despenser's influence and the widespread resentment it caused cannot have escaped Edward's attention. And this would have been accentuated by one person more than any other: Edward's mother.

Queen Isabella loathed Hugh Despenser. After the Scottish campaign of September 1322, which was an utter disaster and almost cost Isabella her life, she blamed Hugh Despenser personally.[65] When four years later, she got the chance to speak her mind publicly, she accused him of abandoning her, and putting her life in peril. She also accused him of 'often dishonouring her and damaging her noble state, of cruelty towards her' and of 'ousting her from her lands' and hindering her relationship with her husband.[66] Eleanor Despenser – Despenser's wife – had more influence over the king than Isabella herself, even to the point where the queen needed Eleanor's help to get the king's approval for her requests. This suggests that something a little more unusual than mere estrangement was going on, possibly involving an incestuous relationship between Edward II and his niece and an attempt by Despenser to have sex with Isabella.[67] But whatever the nature of Isabella's hatred for Despenser, it was sharp and never lessened in intensity.

Edward, though young, was having to grow up fast. He was certainly at the Tower on 17 February 1323, when he dined with his mother. That day Isabella was probably in communication with the king's prisoner in the Tower, Roger Mortimer.[68] Isabella spent much of 1323 and 1324 in London, and almost certainly saw a great deal of Edward and her other children, including the youngest, Joan (born in 1321). But these were not happy times for her. As Despenser's authority grew, hers waned. After the escape of Roger Mortimer from the Tower and his reception 'with great honour' in France in August 1323, the king barely acknowledged her. In September 1324 he removed her children John and Eleanor from her, and put them in the care of Eleanor Despenser. He confiscated Isabella's income. In November he left her just eight marks per day (£5 6s 8d) for food and drink for herself and all her staff. The French people in her household were arrested – a particularly vindictive move in view of Isabella being French – and she was forbidden to do anything to help them. Even the Launge family, who had been so ostentatiously rewarded by the king for telling him of the birth of his heir, were thrown into prison, their endowment still almost entirely unpaid.[69] If Isabella had any solace in the dark days of late 1324, it was the occasional company of her eldest son, Edward, now twelve years of age.

As the Launge arrests suggest, Edward's value as a symbol of his father's royal legitimacy was no longer important. The king had defeated those lords who demanded that his government be constitutional. Edward nevertheless remained high in his father's estimations. He was ordered to attend a colloquium at Ripon to dicuss the war in Scotland, and was summoned to join the army in the summer campaign of 1323.[70] But the main reason we may be certain that Edward remained very much in his father's mind is not regular orders such as these, which were sent to all the earls, but for the very particular role which the king next envisaged his son performing: that of a royal marriage partner, the surety for an international alliance.

The first attempt to find Edward a partner had been made, secretly, in 1318. Various acts of piracy between the men of William, Count of Hainault, and England had encouraged King Edward to look to his kinsman to establish a marriage bond and, with it, peace. He presumed he could rely on his queen to maintain relations with France, so Hainault and Spain were the obvious directions in which to look to advance English interests. On 7 December 1318 he wrote letters authorising Count William to pay heed to the message borne by an embassy of the bishop of Exeter, the earl of Hereford, and the lawyer, John Walwayn. They returned early the following year with a favourable response; so Edward sent them back in 1319 to enquire further. Despite a propitious start, in which the bishop reported that one particular daughter, Margaret, was of fair features suitable to be married to the prince, the matter did not progress.[71] At the end of March 1321, the king wrote a frustrated letter to Count William, asking what his intentions were. The king went on to say that he wished to have an answer quickly as he had been solicited by the king of Aragon, amongst others, for the marriage of Edward.[72] Although Count William did obtain a dispensation for the marriage, further acts of piracy disinclined the king to continue with the negotiations, and Edward remained unwed.

Edward II had not been bluffing. King James of Aragon had indeed been in contact about the possible match, and there were others interested as well. In 1323 Charles de Valois, uncle to Queen Isabella, proposed that his daughter should marry young Edward.[73] The king preferred the idea of an alliance with Aragon, and in 1324 sent an embassy (including his brother, Edmund, and the archbishop of Dublin) with the power to conclude a marriage treaty and dowry.[74] Nothing had come of it by January 1325, when the king received letters from Castile requesting that he consider a double marriage with that kingdom. Edward would marry Eleanor, daughter of King Alfonso, and Alfonso would marry Edward's sister Eleanor (then aged seven). In February yet another embassy was sent abroad to discuss the marriage.[75] Edward's household, newly established at the Savoy Palace in London, waited to see to which great power would yield him a royal bride.

*

As the rift between the king and queen deepened, Edward tried to remain close to each of his parents. But it was his father who remained able to affect his life most directly, as the gift of the Savoy Palace and the marriage negotiations show. It was also the king who arranged his education. We cannot be certain, but it seems likely that in July 1324 this took the form of the appointment of Richard Bury.

Although Bury has often been said to have been Edward's tutor, no record of his appointment has ever been found. One highly respected writer has even gone so far as to say that it is a 'widespread fiction', on the grounds that he was 'illiterate' and more particularly, between 1316 and 1324, he was in Edward's service at Chester.[76] The former of these two objections is ridiculous as Bury had been educated at Oxford and was a royal clerk, and thus very far from 'illiterate'. But the latter objection is valid. While there is no doubt that someone taught Edward how to read and write in both French and Latin,[77] it was almost certainly not Bury. Edward was surrounded by royal clerks, and there may have been several who taught him to read and write. What is more important is the question of who influenced his thinking, and who expanded his intellectual horizons. With regard to this question, it is noticeable that Bury's appointment as Edward's chamberlain at Chester came to an end just before 18 July 1324, when he was described as 'lately' the chamberlain.[78] After this date, although he remained a royal clerk, he seems to have occupied no identifiable position until February 1326 (after which he was regularly appointed by Edward to important positions). The king gave the Savoy Palace to Edward on 14 July 1324.[79] It seems that this may mark the occasion of Bury leaving his post as chamberlain of Chester and becoming Edward's tutor in London.

This would be a tentative assumption, based only on the legend and a coincidence of dates, if it were not for two other facts. Unusually for a royal clerk, Bury was (and is) famous for his very extensive library, and because of this may well have attracted the attention of Edward's mother, Queen Isabella, who was herself a great lover of books.[80] The second fact is the very great trust Edward placed in Bury in later years, suggesting a relationship stronger than that of a distant chamberlain and his lord. When Edward was empowered to appoint a constable of Bordeaux in 1325, Bury was the man selected. While it seems sensible to presume that Bury met the prince on at least an occasional basis prior to July 1324 – perhaps when delivering sums of money from Chester to Edward's treasurer in the south – it seems equally sensible to presume that he saw him more regularly after that date. Edward clearly had a very high regard for the man, and it seems foolish to ignore the probability that this high regard was due to Bury impressing him with his trustworthiness and apparent learning.

The word 'apparent' is used here advisedly. Bury's contemporary, Adam Murimuth, who knew him, described him as a mediocre man of letters who dressed modestly and died like a pauper but who, 'wishing to be considered a great scholar', acquired a huge number of books, so many 'that five great carts were not sufficient to carry them'.[81] Bury's biographer,

William Chambre, claimed he had so many books in his chamber that one could not stand up without treading on them. As Murimuth suggests, large numbers of books are not in themselves a sign of scholarship. In addition, Bury seems only to have written one original text, the *Philobiblon* ('the Love of Books'), and that is a very personal and unusual book indeed. We must therefore ask the question, how scholarly was Bury?

The answer to this question lies in the *Philobiblon* itself. It is an enthusiastic rant about the virtues of books: 'In books I find the dead as if they were alive; in books I foresee things to come; in books warlike affairs are set forth; from books come forth the laws of peace.' Its subject is not scholarship, or a survey of literature, but a justification of the acquisition and possession of books through the knowledge potentially to be gained from them. This is totally in line with what one would expect of a man of great ambition, to whom knowledge was important but whose service did not permit him to spend time in scholarly contemplation. It is likely that Bury's acquisitiveness with regard to books sprang from a thirst for influence, and possession of knowledge – albeit in book form – was one means of gaining this influence. Indeed, one suspects that Bury relished the *potential* of knowledge more than knowledge itself.

If Bury became Edward's tutor, or one of his tutors, in July 1324, our next question has to be what he might have taught his royal charge. We could answer this in two ways. We could elaborate on the formal education of the time, and we might presume that Bury stuck to the curriculum. Edward would have probably found this tedious, as he was inclined to activity and adventure more than study. The alternative is to look at the *Philobiblon* to see whether Bury might have supplied Edward with an education in line with his royal background. This second approach is interesting, especially when one considers that Bury was later held in very high esteem by his pupil. For instance, we may picture Bury in his late thirties telling the twelve-year-old prince about 'Alexander, the conqueror of the earth, and Julius [Caesar], the invader of Rome and of the world, who, the first in war and arts, assumed universal empire under his single rule'.[82] War *and* arts! Edward could not have failed to be struck by Bury's exuberance, for the man was as passionate about his princely responsibilities as he was about books. As he himself put it: 'The history of the Greeks as well as Romans shows that there were no famous princes among them who were devoid of literature.' In a similar passage which seems to be referring to Bury's own pedagogical position: 'We read that Philip thanked the Gods devoutly for having granted that Alexander should be born in the time of Aristotle, so that educated under his instruction he might be worthy to rule his father's empire.' Bury very probably saw himself as an Aristotle to a young Alexander, especially given the conquests which the young man was prophesied to achieve. No wonder, then, that the authors Bury cited included a host of classical writers, with Aristotle at their head.[83] Of all the authors he mentioned, Bury commented on very few in detail, and criticised none of them in any depth, and we may suspect he impressed the prince by pretending familiarity with great thinkers of the past and knowing a little of each of their achievements. Nevertheless, the impact on young Edward of hearing just the names and a smattering of their backgrounds would have been sufficient to catch his imagination. He would have grown up as familiar with Achilles, Caesar and Alexander as King Arthur and characters in the Bible. Bury might not have been a scholar, but he had enthusiasm, and that is a powerful educational tool. If his conversation was as enthusiastic and wide-ranging as the *Philobiblon* suggests, he would have greatly encouraged the imagination of the young prince.

Bury would not have been the only man trying to affect Edward's thinking. Alongside a 'professional' tutor there would have been a whole host of clerks and knights trying to instill in Edward a particular view of the world, or a certain understanding of his future responsibilities as a king.[84] Walter Milemete and William Pagula are two names which are particularly prominent in this respect. Both men wrote advisory works dedicated to Edward, to school him in the art of good kingship. William Pagula's advice, *The Mirror of Edward III*, which survives in two versions and probably was read to Edward, urged him to pay attention to the well-being of his subjects in a way particularly relevant for the civil-war-torn England of the 1320s. Walter Milemete's *On the Nobility, Wisdom and Prudence of Kings* survives today in a single, lavishly illustrated manuscript which was almost certainly intended as a presentation copy for Edward himself. If Edward had it read to him – or read it himself – he would have had an outline for ideal kingship. Walter exhorted Edward 'to know, understand and read the Scriptures and writings in French and Latin; and above all else to have the knowledge to write documents'.[85] He included chapters on not revealing 'the counsels and secret plans of the king', and advised Edward to remove from his presence 'everyone who is covetous, avaricious or jealous'. Justice was given a prominent place among the virtues of the king, followed by prudence, temperance, courage and magnanimity. Mercy required a whole chapter to itself, as did the conduct of the king in war (which Walter drew almost entirely from the classical writer Vegetius). But above all else, Walter of Milemete and William Pagula were at pains to stress the importance of peace among the magnates. International war could be a good and honourable thing, but civil war was nothing short of disaster. Edward had probably learned that for himself in 1322. He would never be allowed to forget it.

*

Medieval history is peppered with minor, almost unknown wars, whose unknown dead are not even commemorated by a recollection of the cause in which they fought, let alone a monument. Few today are familiar with the Despenser War mentioned above; not many more are familiar with the War of Saint-Sardos, which was the cause of the most important event to occur in the life of the young Edward of Windsor.

The War of Saint-Sardos grew out of a long-standing controversy over the rights of the abbot of Sarlat in the French diocese of Agen, held by the English king as part of the duchy of Aquitaine. The Benedictine monastery of Saint-Sardos, established by the abbot of Sarlat, was locally understood to be subject to the same laws as Sarlat itself: subject to French authority, not English. There was a great deal of friction over this matter, however, so that when the monks of Saint-Sardos sought and received French permission for a fortified town to be established on their land, the local Gascon lords took umbrage. One in particular, Raymond Bernard, burned down the existing buildings on the site and hanged the French royal official from the flagpole which he had just dutifully erected. The French were naturally outraged, and blamed the steward of Gascony for not taking action against Raymond Bernard. After a short while King Charles of France also blamed Edward II for not ordering his steward to inquire into the matter. This raised another problem, for Edward II had still not done homage to Charles for his lands in Gascony. In fact, just before hearing of the outrage, he had offered a series of rather weak excuses as to why he could not do so at the present time. Charles offered a brief postponement, but in the summer of 1324 Edward's negotiators – the earl of Kent and the archbishop of Dublin – refused to surrender Raymond Bernard's castle of Montpezat, as they had previously agreed. Charles understandably felt angry, confiscated the duchy, and sent his uncle Charles de Valois to recapture the region from the earl of Kent, whom Edward had ordered to defend it. The English lost several important towns before falling back on La Réole and suing for peace.[86]

In January 1325 King Charles offered Edward II a way out of his predicament. He suggested that Queen Isabella be sent to negotiate with him on behalf of the English. Edward, seeing little other option, agreed, and let his wife return to her homeland to negotiate on his behalf. Despite the antagonisms she had suffered, she did as well as she could, but the English were in a very weak position. When terms were finalised on 31 May 1325, Charles demanded that the king of England should do homage to him for the duchy of Aquitaine, including Gascony. If the king was not prepared to leave the country, there was no alternative but to invest his eldest son with all the French possessions of the English Crown, and to send him instead.

For the king this was a huge problem. If he sent his son, he risked losing control of the valuable revenues of Gascony. Worse, he risked losing control of the boy himself. If the heir to the throne were to fall into his mother's hands, she might prevent him from returning to England, holding him hostage until her income was restored, or even betrothing him to a foreign ruler of her own choosing. Suddenly, for the king, the royal symbolism of his son and heir, which had once been such an asset, seemed a liability, for there was no undermining his son's royal status. On the other hand, if King Edward went to France in person, he would have to leave behind Hugh Despenser, who was exiled from France. This was too similar to the circumstances in which he had lost Gaveston: through becoming separated from him. If Despenser were to lose the king's protection, he stood no chance of survival. There were too many lords in England who sought revenge for the kin they had seen hanged and left to rot after the battle of Boroughbridge.

Edward resolved that he would go himself. It was politically far too dangerous to allow his son to leave his control. Mortimer was still loose, and a small band of discontents was roaming the Continent with him, waiting for their opportunity. Although he did initially appoint the twelve-year-old Edward 'guardian of the realm and king's lieutenant' during his absence beyond the seas, he changed his mind almost immediately.[87] At the eleventh hour Hugh Despenser and his father persuaded him that it would be better if his son should go. In all probability they managed this by hitting on a solution to his dilemma. The real danger lay in allowing the prince to fall into the hands of his mother. So why not demand her return at the same time? If she could be forced back to England, then the French king could be relied upon to protect his own nephew from falling into Mortimer's hands. And by adopting this strategy, the king did not need to risk Hugh Despenser being captured and murdered in his absence.

On 2 September 1325 Edward – two months short of his thirteenth birthday – was given the counties of Ponthieu and Montreuil. He then made the journey to Dover with his father where, on the 10th, he received the duchy of Aquitaine, and 'all the lands the king holds in the realm of France'. Edward's treasurer, William Cusance, was confirmed in charge of all his English lands. Edward himself was placed in the guardianship of the fearless and uncompomising bishop of Exeter, Walter Stapeldon, and Sir Henry Beaumont. Two days later Edward sailed away from England, away from his father and Hugh Despenser, and towards a stranger destiny than had been prophesied for any English king.

TWO

A Treasonable Youth

As Edward made his way to the royal palace at Vincennes, near Paris, to perform homage to King Charles of France, the countryfolk flocked to see him. Here he was, the son of their Princess Isabella, the grandson of King Philip the Fair, nephew of Charles the Fair and the great-great-grandson of St Louis, the famous crusading king of France. Comeliness, spirituality and royalty all ran hand-in-hand in the French royal family, so each member was a spectacle to be seen, as well as a spiritual marvel. Politically too, he was important. Isabella had maintained her French links, visiting France on several occasions, and had attracted considerable French sympathy when she had been neglected by her husband in favour of Piers Gaveston. This appearance in France of her first-born son and the heir to the English throne was not to be missed.

The splendour of Edward's procession and his pleasure at meeting his beloved mother, and the widespread satisfaction that he had performed homage for Gascony, was marred by one detail. The bishop of Exeter's presence was anathema to the queen.[1] She held him responsible for the confiscation of her estates. All France hated him because he was thought to be the impetus for the recent arrest of Frenchmen in England.[2] When the bishop compounded his unpopularity by indignantly demanding in front of King Charles and the court that Isabella return to England immediately, she was in a strong position to refuse. In a sudden and shocking revocation of her loyalty, she launched a bitter attack on her husband and Hugh Despenser, and the full blast was directed at the bishop:

> I feel that marriage is a joining together of man and woman, maintaining the undivided habit of life, and that someone has come between my husband and myself trying to break this bond. I protest that I will not return until this intruder is removed, but discarding my marriage garment, shall assume the robes of widowhood and mourning until I am avenged of this Pharisee.[3]

The bishop, outraged, looked to King Charles to overrule his sister, and to order her to return to her husband. But in words which must have infuriated the bishop, the king declined. 'The queen has come of her own free will', he declared, 'and may freely return if she so wishes. But if she prefers to remain in these parts, she is my sister, and I refuse to expel her.'

With those words the division between Isabella and her husband was made permanent. This heralded a crisis for all concerned, including Edward. His mother had effectively broken from his father, and had publicly received the support of the king of France. Bishop Stapeldon too was alarmed, and hearing a rumour that certain Englishmen in France – probably Roger Mortimer – were plotting to murder him, he fled from the palace in the guise of a pilgrim, catching up with his retinue later and returning to England. Somewhere, yet to show his face in the whole business, was the real protagonist of the split: Mortimer, the man in whom Isabella had placed all her trust.

Roger Mortimer and Isabella had much in common. They were both literate, sophisticated, intelligent and aristocratic, and had known each other for upwards of seventeen years. They had both alienated themselves irrevocably from Edward II and the Despenser regime, which they both hated. Hugh Despenser had for the last two years been in something of a state of panic about Mortimer's possible return to England at the head of an army, and regularly sent scared letters to naval commanders to investigate this trio of German ships or that Hainaulter merchant fleet. He knew from his spy network that Mortimer had gone towards Germany, and had spent some time at the court of Count William of Hainault, but he never envisaged what would happen next. In December 1325 Mortimer returned to France, and Queen Isabella threw herself into his arms. And, together, their attention fastened on young Edward, whose recently confirmed position as duke of Aquitaine gave them the potential to rebuild their authority. They knew that his hand in marriage would command a large dowry from a suitable bride's father. Regardless of the king's attempts to marry Edward to a continental princess, together they could use Edward to raise an army and wrest England from its untrustworthy king and his despotic favourite.

At the end of November, King Edward and Despenser realised their blunder. In less than ten weeks from saying farewell to his son at Dover, 'The Mortimer' – as Edward II referred to his enemy – had control of his son and was plotting with his queen. And that was not all: Despenser's spies told him that the revolutionaries had widespread support in England. Letters from Mortimer had been smuggled into the country. The king gave orders for all imported goods to be searched, but his precaution did nothing to allay the fear. Everyone knew that Mortimer and Isabella would eventually return.

What did Edward himself think of all this? We do not know for certain but it is worth noting that Edward was devoted to his mother, and so he was well-placed to understand her choice of companion, whether or not he trusted him. There is little evidence at this stage that he disapproved of his mother's lover.[4] There is even a snippet of evidence that he may have agreed with the broad thrust of Mortimer and Isabella's plan, in his promising to reward Mortimer with Despenser's rich lordship of Denbigh if they should be successful.[5] We also need to remember that he had much in common with Mortimer. Both men were intelligent, literate, forceful men of action. Both believed sincerely in the virtues of chivalry and knighthood, as can be seen in the way that Edward, when king, enthusiastically shared Mortimer's love of tournaments and Arthurian display. Both men embraced changing technology in warfare – including gunpowder and cannon – while maintaining and encouraging old-fashioned knightly virtues. In terms of religion, both of them were traditional, not particularly pious, but not sceptical either. Both turned to God at crisis points in their lives yet were sufficiently worldly to see the political uses of religious display. When it came to raising taxes and spending money, Mortimer's period of ascendancy was almost a blueprint for Edward's own treasury-busting profligacy. And above all else, Mortimer was a successful leader in battle. Therefore it is likely that Edward saw Mortimer in 1326 as one of the few English lords from whom he could learn something.

Back in England, Edward II knew he could never forgive Mortimer and Isabella, but officially he resisted acknowledging his wife was beyond his control until January 1326. Even then he did not despair of obtaining his son's return. We can trace the king's growing frustration through his letters. After hearing the news from the bishop of Exeter, the king wrote to Isabella and King Charles on 1 December 1325. To Charles he said that it was a lie that Isabella feared Hugh Despenser. He claimed he could not believe that she had given this excuse for not returning to England, and he begged Charles to compel her. He terminated his letter with a request to Charles also to 'deliver up Edward, our beloved eldest son . . . we greatly wish to see him, and to speak with him, and every day we long for his return'.[6] The letter he sent to Isabella was the last he ever sent to his wife. He accused her of lying about her hatred of Despenser, and outlined how he had often commanded her to return to him, and complained that she had always disobeyed. At the end he ordered her to return and to bring Edward with her.

The following day the king wrote to his son. His tone in this letter, the first of three attempts he made to recall his son from France, was more considerate:

Very dear son, although you are young and of tender age, may we remind you of what we charged and commanded you at your departure from Dover. You answered then, with duly acknowledged goodwill, that you would not trespass or disobey any of our commandments in any point for anyone. And now that your homage has been received by our dearest brother[-in-law], the king of France, your uncle, please take your leave of him, and return to us with all speed, in company with your mother, if she will come quickly; and if she will not come, then you must come without further delay, for we have a great desire to see you and speak with you. Therefore, do not remain for your mother's sake, or for anyone else's, under the king's blessing. Given at Westminster, 2nd December.[7]

Edward's reply was suitably contrite. He admitted that he remembered that he had promised not to agree to a contract of marriage, nor to suffer it to be done for him, and to obey his father. But he could not return, he stated, because his mother would not let him. His protestation would have been backed up in mid-December, when the ladies and knights whom the king had sent with Isabella to France returned home. She had dismissed them, and removed all those loyal to the king from her service, cutting herself and Prince Edward off from the influence of the English court.

In January 1326 the king heard that his son had been betrothed to a daughter of the count of Hainault.[8] He wrote to all the sheriffs of all the English counties stating that they should be ready to take arms against the queen, for 'the queen will not come to the king nor permit his son to return . . . and she is adopting the counsel of the Mortimer, the king's notorious enemy and rebel'.[9] The king's only hope now lay in trying to persuade Edward to return to him against his mother's will.

On 18 March, the king wrote to his son again. His letter, which was longer than his last, acknowledged that Edward had done well, and expressed his pleasure in hearing that Edward remembered his promise not to marry without his father's consent. But there was a note of disbelief in the letter, for the king knew about the marriage contract with Hainault. So he indirectly accused his son of concealing the truth. If Edward had done anything contrary to his promise, then

you cannot avoid the wrath of God, the reproach of men, and our great indignation . . . You should by no means marry, nor suffer yourself to be married, without our previous consent and advice; for nothing that you could do would cause us greater injury and pain of heart. And since you say that you cannot return to us because of your mother, it causes

43

us great uneasiness of heart that you cannot be allowed by her to do your natural duty.

Had Isabella returned to England when ordered to do so, the king added, then she would still be high in the king's affections. But her pretences for not returning, said the king, were against her duty. Then he added a particularly hurt line:

> You and all the world have seen that she openly, notoriously, and knowing it to be contrary to her duty, and against the welfare of our Crown, has attached to herself, and retains in her company, the Mortimer, our traitor and mortal foe, proved attainted and judged, and *she accompanies him in the house and abroad*, despite of us, of our Crown, and the right ordering of the realm – him the malefactor . . . And worse than this she has done, if there can be worse, in allowing you to consort with our said enemy, making him your counsellor, and allowing you to associate with him in the sight of all the world, doing so great a villainy and dishonour both to yourself and us, to the prejudice of our Crown, and the laws and customs of our realm, which you are supremely bound to hold, preserve and maintain.

Edward could not have been anything but distressed at this letter. Here was his father using words which were an accusation of his mother's adultery: 'she accompanies him in the house and abroad'. Worse, it amounted to an accusation of treason on Edward's part, which would incur the wrath of God as well as his father's indignation. How on earth was he to make an impression as a monarch when the time came for him to inherit if he was a traitor even before he inherited? But that was not all. The king continued:

> We are not pleased with you; and you should not so displease us, neither for the sake of your mother nor for anyone else's sake. We charge you, by the faith, love and allegiance which you owe us, and on our blessing, that you come to us without delay, without opposition or any further excuse, for your mother has written to us to say that if you wish to return to us she will not prevent it . . . Fair son, do not disregard our orders, for we hear much that you have done which you ought not to have done.

The letter was designed to strike fear into the prince. Among the things he had done which 'he ought not to have done' were two royal appointments. When the king had allowed him to travel to France, he had authorised him to renew the appointments of his agents in the duchy of Aquitaine, both the seneschal of Gascony and the constable of Bordeaux. Edward had instead appointed Richard Bury to be constable of Bordeaux, and had appointed a friend of Mortimer's, Oliver Ingham, seneschal of Gascony. In the latter appointment especially, Edward was probably leaned on by Mortimer, who seems also to have appointed himself Edward's tutor in Bury's place.[10] But the king was laying guilt on to the young duke with seething indignation, and Edward can have felt no pride in not acquiescing to his father's demands. If his father thought that he was defying him, he would be deemed traitorous. If the king knew he had no choice in the matter, he would be perceived to be weak.

By May 1326 Edward knew he was going to be used in a battle between his parents. He could not return to England – he was practically a prisoner – and his marriage to a daughter of Hainault had been agreed. Mortimer had secured the initial contact and forged the strategy in 1324. In December 1325 the countess of Hainault – Isabella's cousin – had travelled to Paris and met Isabella. The pope, seeing that war was likely, despatched envoys to try to secure peace, but their mission was doomed. At the coronation of the queen of France on 11 May 1326, Mortimer carried Edward's robes, an especially prominent position. The papal envoys travelling to England relayed this news to the king, who was furious. To the bishop of Rochester he shouted: 'was there not a queen of England once who was put down out of her royalty for disobeying her husband's orders?' He was referring to Queen Eadburga, who killed her husband in 802 and was exiled from Wessex.[11] The bishop advised the king not to pursue that line of argument any further. But if he hoped thereby to quell the king's anger, he was to be disappointed. The rebels were gathering in France. Edmund, earl of Kent – the king's own half-brother – had decided to stay with Isabella and Mortimer, and had married Mortimer's cousin, Margaret Wake.[12] Sir Henry Beaumont – one of the guardians of the young prince – had also decided to stay. Isabella was marshalling her finances in the county of Ponthieu to pay for ships to invade England.[13]

On 19 June the king could bear it no longer. He sent a final series of letters to King Charles, to the bishop of Beauvais, and to his son. The one sent to Edward fumed that he had 'not humbly obeyed our commands as a good son ought, since you have not returned to us . . . but have notoriously held companionship with Mortimer, our traitor and mortal enemy, who was publicly carried to Paris in your company'. The king insisted that his son had 'proceeded to make various alterations, injunctions and ordinances without our advice and contrary to our orders'. A key line in the letter was 'you have no governor other than us, nor should you have'. Once again the king exhorted his son not to marry without his advice and consent. And, finally, there was a postscript to the letter. The last sentence was as cold a threat as the king could have written:

> Understand certainly, that if you now act contrary to our counsel, and
> continue in wilful disobedience, you will feel it all the days of your life,
> and you will be made an example to all other sons who are disobedient
> to their lords and fathers.

And with that all communication between the king and his son ceased. Edward probably concluded that, no matter what happened now, he could never be restored to his father.

*

In July 1326 Edward and his mother left France and entered Hainault. Despenser had tried bribing Frenchmen to kidnap Isabella and Mortimer. Several chronicles mention that Isabella was in fear of her life, one even stating that she fled by night, secretly advised of her peril by her cousin, Robert d'Artois.[14] They had little time left to organise and mount their invasion. Mortimer had travelled ahead, to see to the arrangement of the fleet. Beyond his presence, and a few disaffected English lords, including the earl of Kent, Henry Beaumont, Sir Thomas Roscelyn and Sir John Maltravers, they would have to rely on Hainaulter mercenaries. And foreign troops on English soil was yet another problem they had to bear in mind. The English were not used to being overrun by foreign armies.

On 27 August it was settled that Edward would marry Philippa, youngest daughter of Count William of Hainault within two years. This was the lynchpin of the plan, agreed in outline in December the previous year. It was on this marriage that Hainaulters' faith in the whole project rested.

Many stories have been told about the marriage, and how Edward and Philippa first met. Biographers in the past, struggling for something to say about him in his youth, have seized on his relationship with his wife and used it to amplify the romantic element in his character. One tale often told is that Bishop Stapeldon, while engaged on his mission in 1319, looked over Philippa and reported that she was fitting as a bride for the future king. Another appears in the pages of Froissart's chronicle, that when Edward arrived in Hainault with his mother, Edward paid more attention to Philippa than Count William's other daughters, and so Edward chose her for his bride. Modernist historians, finding Froissart a fanciful writer, generally dismissed the latter story and accepted the former, stating that Philippa had already been chosen to be his bride, and even claiming that Philippa was born on 24 June 1311 on the assumption that she was the eight-year-old girl Stapeldon saw in 1319. But as a close examination of the evidence shows, it was not Philippa but her older sister, Margaret, whom Stapeldon examined (see Appendix One). As for Froissart's story, he states that he heard the details from Philippa herself: how Edward met four daughters of the count and liked her the best in the eight days they spent together at Valenciennes. Certainly Froissart could be telling the truth, for he served in the English royal household from 1361, and presented Philippa with his poetic and historical works, and relied on her as a historical source for parts of his chronicle. The specific eight-day stay at Valenciennes is entirely plausible, and he correctly names the four girls, apparently in age order: Margaret, Philippa, Jeanne and Isabella. Perhaps Philippa passed over the fact that her elder sister was already married to Ludwig of Bavaria to make it seem that Edward had preferred her to Margaret, his first intended bride, so that she would not appear a second choice. Either way, there is no reason to doubt Froissart's statement that Edward took a great liking to Philippa on this occasion,[15] especially as they were practically the same age, and got on so well together in later years. We may thus have some confidence that, as Froissart mentions in a later entry, when the eight days were up, and it was time for the English to move on, twelve-year-old Philippa burst into tears at Edward's departure.

*

The fleet set sail from Brill on 22 September, straight into a storm. After two days of rough seas and high winds, they landed at Walton on the coast of Suffolk, in the lands of the earl of Norfolk, Edward's uncle. And that was the beginning of another storm, a proverbial whirlwind, as first Norfolk sent one thousand men to their aid, and then other knights and lords joined them. Mortimer's secret messages, smuggled in barrels and other merchandise, and relayed by word of mouth by men travelling as pilgrims, had worked a political miracle.

England had never seen anything like it. Although the invaders had come with probably only fifteen hundred soldiers, men hastened to support them as soon as they landed.[16] Isabella, dressed in her widow's weeds, played the part of a lady in distress, come to avenge the wrongs of Hugh Despenser. She travelled as if on pilgrimage wherever she went. Mortimer, fearful that his presence would cast doubts on the queen's morality and the justification of their invasion, kept a very low profile. Edward on the other hand was championed, as earl of Chester and duke of Aquitaine. It was under the royal banner that the army marched, and no one dared to draw a sword against the future king. Although Edward II ordered the largest army ever to have been summoned – more than forty-seven thousand men – most of these troops did not respond at all, and those who did simply joined the insurgent army as it swept across East Anglia into Cambridgeshire.

Five days after landing, the invaders moved into Bury St Edmunds. Edward and his mother lodged at the abbey, playing the part of dispossessed royalty, while Mortimer stayed with the army. In London, authority was collapsing around the king. Although the Tower had been provisioned for a siege, the king soon saw that he and Despenser would not be able to hold out against the citizens, let alone Mortimer's army. Panic set in, and the king decided to flee westwards before Mortimer cut him off. Already the invading army was moving to the west of London. The royal household and men-at-arms marched out of the gates of the capital in confusion. Weighed down by the sixty thousand pounds of gold that remained in the royal treasury, Edward II and Hugh Despenser began the long journey towards South Wales.

As the king moved westwards, the invaders turned to pursue him. When the king entered the royal fortress of Wallingford on 6 October, they were approaching Baldock. Three days later, as the king marched into Gloucester, they came to Dunstable. On 10 October, while both armies were still far apart, the decisive blow was struck. Edward heard the devastating news that Henry of Lancaster – the most powerful man in the realm, his cousin – had declared for the invaders. Mortimer had succeeded in bringing about the most powerful alliance possible: between the lords of the Welsh Marches, the royal uncles, and the confederacy of northern barons led by Lancaster. This closed off the last avenues of hope for the king. He and Hugh Despenser abandoned their men-at-arms and tried to flee by boat from Chepstow but failed, with the wind against them. They paid a priest to sing a mass in the hope that God would favour them, but God was not listening to his dejected royal supplicant. The wind blew the king back to shore.

Young Edward could never have expected to be greeted with such relief and joy. He and his mother were fêted in town after town across England. His father's promise to make him an example to all disobedient sons now seemed a complete delusion. But if Edward's life and position had been saved by Mortimer's strategic genius, the spectres which Mortimer had summoned up were equally worrying. In London there was anarchy. The mob had broken into the Tower and dragged out Edward's nine-year-old brother, John, and had set him up as ruler of the city. This was a joke in itself, for there was no rule in the city. Rioters and thieves were on the loose. Anyone suspected of collaborating with the Despenser regime was robbed and killed. Bishop Stapeldon, hearing that his house had been looted and was on fire, rode across the city in armour to confront the robbers. The mob caught him in the churchyard of St Paul's and dragged him from his horse and down Cheapside, cutting his head off with a bread-knife in their mad fury. They sent the head as a present to Isabella.

If ever there was an example of how devastating the loss of widespread support could be, it was the destruction of royal power in late September and early October 1326. To Edward's dismay, the country simply jetti-soned his father. All the long centuries of dignity, glory, authority, respect, chivalry and honour – everything which was sacred and powerful about royalty – was stripped away. The king had been forced to run, ignomin-iously, towards Wales, and then forced out to sea. This was distressing for Edward. Mortimer's political machinations, which had served so well to launch their return to the country, now threatened to destroy the very thing that Edward hoped would be saved for him: the authority of the Crown.

At Wallingford, on 15 October, the invaders issued a proclamation. They declared – in Edward's name – that the king had accepted the advice of evil men, and through them the Church had been despoiled, the dignity of the Crown had been reduced, lords had been imprisoned without trial, and fined, put to death, or exiled; and the people had been burdened by heavy taxes. The invaders proclaimed they had come to put an end to this despotism. Edward, seeing his name now being used as an authority for political documents, could only hope that that was true. But on the same day as the proclamation was issued, Bishop Orleton preached a sermon to many hundreds of men at Oxford in which he accused the king of being a 'tyrant and a sodomite', echoing the charges brought against the disgraced Pope Boniface VIII in 1303.[17] It was abundantly clear to Edward that a new tyranny was lurking. His father had now become the target of political lies and anti-royalist propaganda. With Mortimer in charge, the outlook for the royal family was bleak.

On 26 October, Bristol Castle fell to Mortimer. Despite Isabella's pleas for mercy, Mortimer and the royal earls had the earl of Winchester (Hugh Despenser's father) beheaded. By then they knew that the king had fled the country. They also knew that he still had the great seal with him, and a huge amount of silver, so there was a real danger he could have set up a government in exile. But Mortimer and his fellow-advisers had an answer for that too. They argued that when the king left the realm he should have left the seal in the hands of a regent. Since the king was now off the coast of Wales, and had not appointed a regent, there could be said to be a technical absence of regnal authority in England. Here was their oppor-tunity. Mortimer and Isabella agreed that Edward should be regent, and had Edward's new title proclaimed on the same day as Bristol fell.

In the month since the invasion, Edward had seen his father's authority crumble to nothing. Now he himself was titular head of state. But the greater the position he held in theory, the less his power in practice. He was a pawn, not a king, and he knew it. His mother and Mortimer had taken royal power for themselves. The same day he had been appointed to the regency, Mortimer and Isabella had designated Robert Wyville, Isabella's clerk, to keep and control Edward's privy seal. Later they would appoint the Chancellor and Treasurer too. And the man they chose to be Treasurer was Orleton, the bishop who preached the sermon that Edward's father was a sodomite. Edward was as much on the defensive as his father. The heirs to the throne of Edward I were seeking refuge in the last silent places of their kingdom: in the king's case, Neath Abbey in South Wales; in Edward's case, in the quiet counsel of his conscience.

King Edward II and his companions were captured by the earl of Lancaster on 16 December, in open country near Llantrissant. Three men were arrested with him: Hugh Despenser, Simon Reading and Robert Baldock; his other attendants were released. The king was taken to Kenilworth Castle, Lancaster's great fortress in the Midlands; the other three were taken to receive justice at Hereford, where Isabella and Mortimer awaited them with vindictive delight. Isabella had hoped to make Despenser suffer in London, but already he was refusing food and water: there was a significant risk he would die before he reached London. Besides which, Mortimer wanted him to die publicly on the Welsh borders, and to suffer the atrocious torture which Despenser had carried out on one of his own friends.[18] In the debate about carving up the cake that was Hugh Despenser, Mortimer won. At Hereford, on 24 November, Despenser was dragged through the streets of the city, with crowds shouting at him, and with verses from the bible written on to his body. He was hanged on a gallows fifty feet high, beside his henchman, Simon Reading. But Mortimer's *coup de grâce* was the torture he had waited to inflict on his enemy for so long. Before the man was dead, he was brought from his gallows, and his heart and penis cut out. They were thrown into a large fire. Everyone could see that justice in a manner of speaking – had been done.

*

The royal party spent that Christmas at Wallingford Castle, enthusiastically celebrating their victory. Not only had they effected the first conquest of England since 1066, they had done so without great bloodshed, and without losing the goodwill of the country.

First there were the Hainaulter mercenaries to be thanked. From 5 December they began to depart, their job done, while their leader, John of Hainault remained with the royal party. On 26 December the Hainaulter knights who had come in the company of the earl of Kent received presents.[19] The victors had no qualms about being generous; they understood that failure to reward men who had risked their lives was a short-sighted strategy. Besides, they had not only the collossal treasury amassed by Despenser on behalf of Edward II, they also had the personal wealth of Despenser and his supporters. One of Mortimer's knights, Edmund Hakelut, found £1,568 which had belonged to Mortimer's executed enemy, the earl of Arundel, in Clun Castle.[20] The contents of the earl of Winchester's money chest at Winchester Priory was despatched to Isabella. Hugh Despenser's own jewels and treasure were found in the Tower. Isabella took delight personally in distributing this hoard to her Hainaulter friends: a gilded silver enamelled cup as a leaving present for John Marbays on 7 December; a gilded silver, enamelled and engraved cup with base and lid for the lord Haucourt on the 26th. The fairy-tale image of the queen distributing treasure to her knights in shining armour was reality that Christmas.

And the armour *was* shining too. We know because we have records of payments for it being burnished.[21] As soon as Mortimer and Isabella took power, and the regency was established, the structures they put in place began to record their activities. Hence in the run-up to Edward's coronation we have a detailed record of royal expenditure. It is abundantly clear that, although Edward was merely a puppet regent, he was made to look the part of a real ruler, from the top of his nightcap down to the toes of a pair of boots made of cloth-of-gold and silk.[22] Perhaps some of this show can be attributed to Edward II's court. Certainly some should be attributed to Mortimer's influence, as he was known to be a man for whom lavish appearance was important. But now Edward found himself at the heart of a court which was determined to be seen to be royal, official, rich and powerful. Those first days of royal authority left an indelible impression on Edward. If a king wished to be seen as powerful, he needed to dress the part.

For Mortimer, Isabella and the coterie of earls and bishops around them, there were other matters to attend to, besides celebrations. The big question was what to do with the king? As he had been arrested and taken to Kenilworth, and was now back in England, legally speaking he was king again, and Edward no longer regent. Conscious of the problem, Mortimer and Isabella took the precaution of issuing writs as if they had come from Kenilworth in the king's name. This was not a situation which could be allowed to continue.

It is easy for us now to think in terms of deposition. In 1326 it was not. No king of England had ever been deposed. Adolf of Nassau, Holy Roman

Emperor, had been deposed in 1298, and Edward I had forced his puppet king of Scotland, John Balliol, to abdicate in 1296, but both of these instances were very different from the present situation. The Holy Roman Emperor was an elected post, not an inherited one; thus the real power lay with the electors. As for Scotland, it was at this time a semi-autonomous unit on the periphery of England, so the English king was in a position akin to that of the Empire's electors, except that he was the sole 'elector' of the Scottish king. Unwanted rulers of major kingdoms were invariably killed, not deposed. This was not just because of a vicious streak in the medieval character, it was because removing power from a man ordained by God to wield it was a dangerous business. Edward II himself had on many occasions simply revoked parliamentary decisions which had been forced on him. There was a serious case therefore for killing him, and it is probable that Adam of Orleton, given his public denunciation of him as a 'tyrant and a sodomite', led the calls for the king's execution.[23]

Isabella would not countenance her husband's killing. Of the many bishops and magnates at court that Christmas, all must have cast a guarded eye towards Edward, who also did not wish to see his father torn apart by this pack of self-serving hounds. To advocate killing Edward II would secure the lifelong enmity of his son, the king who would immediately replace him. The consensus was thus one of caution. Edward II would be deposed in parliament, and kept safely, in royal dignity, but in prison for the rest of his days.

*

The deposition of Edward II was a display of political theatre, choreographed by Mortimer and the leading bishops. The royal party arrived in London on 4 January 1327. Three days later Edward attended the parliament at Westminster. For the next few days, the bishops preached sermons about how the country should be ruled by Edward, not his father. The archbishop of York, William Melton – who owed everything to Edward II – preferred to see the king abdicate of his own free will. The bishops of London and Rochester agreed. But Mortimer was working hard on twisting arms. He used his contacts among the London merchants, including the mayor, Richard Bettoyne, to intimidate reluctant members of parliament. Outside he convinced the nobles to side with him in a policy of deposition.

On Tuesday 13 January, he was ready to force the issue. Edward was in the palace, but not in the chamber with the barons, knights and ecclesiastical members. Therefore he did not hear the repeated sermons which rang out from nine o'clock. Nor did he hear the speeches which met with the resounding cries of 'Away with the king!' Repeated demands for the country to say whether it agreed to the deposition received the answer, 'Let it be done!' Finally, when those present had been totally swept up in the fervour of the moment, the aged archbishop of Canterbury was called to speak, and he preached on the theme that the will of the people *was* the will of God. The next time the parliament was asked whether the king should be deposed and his son take his place, there was a resounding response: 'Let it be done! Let it be done!' With the crowd all singing 'Glory, laud and honour', Edward was summoned. The doors to the chamber were flung open, and he was led in to witness the tumultuous calls for him to be crowned king.

Edward's reaction is interesting. He refused the throne. As those present at the parliament came forward and swore homage to him, the archbishop of York, and the bishops of Rochester, Carlisle and London very publicly and loudly declined.[24] Their opposition was not to him personally, they explained, but to the process by which his father was to be dethroned. These four men alone were prepared to stand up for the man who had raised them to their positions of authority, and for the rights of the Crown not to be subject to those of parliament. Edward's refusal was perhaps inspired by these men, especially Melton, a capable man whom he trusted. It was plain to Edward that, if his father could be ousted by parliament, then he too could be removed from power. He preferred Melton's counsel: if his father would abdicate, Edward would accept the throne. If not, he would not sanction his father's deposition.[25]

Edward's refusal to accept the throne is the first sign that, even though only fourteen, he was not prepared to bend to Mortimer's will. But Mortimer was a formidable political opponent and a far-sighted manipulator. While he could not be seen to cross Edward, especially now that Edward's candidacy for the throne had been approved by parliament, he soon came up with a solution. He sent a deputation to see Edward II. They gave him news not only of parliament's decision, but also the prince's reluctance to accept it. It was up to the king: either he could abdicate in favour of his son, or he could leave the throne to Mortimer.

On 21 January, in the hall of Kenilworth Castle, dressed in black and weeping, Edward II abdicated. The delegation returned to Westminster on the 24th. The next day it was proclaimed that the king had 'of his own goodwill and by common counsel and assent of the prelates, earls, barons and other nobles and commonalty of the kingdom, resigned the government of the realm'.[26]

The reign of King Edward III had begun.

*

Edward was crowned on 1 February 1327. Mortimer had, in fact, fixed the date even before parliament had decided to agree to the deposition of the old king.[27] He wanted a quick coronation to confirm the official status of what was effectively his administration. For the same reason, he made sure that all the coronation arrangements were strictly in accordance with the long-standing instructions for the anointing of an English king.[28] Edward was dressed in the traditional red samite. Striped cloth lined his path from the palace to the abbey. As he walked along it, surrounded by cheering crowds, with at least ten bishops and many earls and other lords and ladies in the procession, he was accompanied by four knights who held a gold canopy festooned with bells over his head. In the abbey itself, the floor was covered in coloured cloth. The stage – erected specially for the occasion before the high altar – was covered in quilted gold silk. In fact practically everything at the eastern end of the abbey was covered in gold. On the stage the king sat on a gilded throne with gold cushions beneath his feet and gold cloth beneath the cushions, a gold sceptre in one hand, a gold orb in the other and the gold crown of the saint-king Edward the Confessor upon his head. The hangings of the canopy above him were gold with purple cords; the archbishop of Canterbury – who presided over the ceremony – also sat on a seat covered with gold. To anyone staring along the nave, as the Latin chants echoed around the arches, the king would have appeared as the sole man in red at the centre of a dazzling, celestial apparition, in which golden figures moved around him across a golden space and performed the ritual anointing and coronation with golden vessels and golden regalia.

It was thus in an environment of gold, in the most sacred space of the abbey, near the relics of St Edward the Confessor, and the gold-covered remains of his venerated grandfather, Edward I, that Edward swore his vows of kingship. These too were wholly orthodox, consisting of the four-part oath which his father had sworn at his coronation in 1308. Edward III promised to confirm the laws and customs of the people of England, to observe the rights of the Church, to do justice equally to all his people, and 'to hold and keep the rightful laws and customs that the community of the realm shall choose, and to defend and strengthen them'.[29] This last clause had been designed specially to preserve the power of parliament from the encroachments of Edward II's unpredictable self-mindedness. Now, in its repetition at Edward III's coronation, Mortimer forced the same safeguard on the son. Parliament had as great a reason to support this reign as it had had to end the previous one. The king's responsibility to respect the views of parliament was thus confirmed as a permanent feature of the developing English constitution.

Coronations were times for promotion and celebration too. One important part of this was the creation of new knights. After Edward himself
had been knighted – either by Lancaster or John of Hainault – Edward
set about dubbing knights, as custom dictated.[30] Unfortunately for him,
this was yet another aspect of his coronation controlled by others. Mortimer
decided that his own sons should take precedence, and to emphasise their
importance – and thus his own – he ordered that they should be dressed
in clothes suitable for earls. Edward may have felt a need to retaliate with
a few suggestions of his own, and among the knights created on the day
of the coronation we find several who served him loyally for many
years: Ralph Stafford, John Neville, William Percy, John Meules, Ralph
Willington, Gerard Lisle, Hugh Courtenay, Ralph Daubigny, and Peter
Mauley, nephew of his old steward.[31] All these men were dressed splendidly in scarlet, green and brown cloth, with miniver and squirrel furs.
Mortimer's sons were as splendidly dressed as their father, with even larger
furs and cloth of gold adorning their scarlet, green and brown tunics and
mantles.

In all these events of early 1327, from the deposition of his father to
his own coronation, one senses a certain distance in the young king. It is
not so much what is to be read in the records of the events; it is more
what one does not read. The king was crowned, but it may as well have
been Mortimer's coronation. Mortimer's order to dress his sons as earls
was an ominous sign: only kings' sons automatically were accorded the
status of earls. On the day of Edward's coronation, Mortimer was setting
himself up as a king. Pomp there may have been, knighthood and lavish
feasting too; but there are no references to the king doing anything other
than going through with the ceremony. True, there were many gifts given,
but they were given to Mortimer's friends, not Edward's. On the day of
the coronation, Bishop Orleton was given a number of items from the
royal treasury.[32] Mortimer's cousin, Thomas Vere, was handed two gilt
silver basins engraved with the arms of England and France in lieu of his
being chamberlain at the coronation. Another of his cousins, Thomas
Wake, was given a gilded silver salt cellar in return for playing the part of
pantler. The earl of Lancaster, an older royal cousin whom Edward did
not wholly trust,[33] was handed a number of silver dishes and spoons
stamped with images of leopards in lieu of his being steward on the day.
Mortimer's friend, Richard Bettoyne, mayor of London, who had helped
threaten the members of parliament into supporting the deposition, and
who acted as chief butler at the coronation, was allowed to keep an
engraved gold cup and an enamelled gold ewer.[34] Even Isabella, Edward's
own mother shocked him on the day of the coronation, awarding to herself

the annual sum of twenty thousand marks (£13,333): probably the largest personal income appropriated by an individual in medieval England. Adam Murimuth, a canon of St Paul's, was stunned: 'to her son she left barely the third part of his kingdom,' he wrote.[35] This was not quite accurate, it amounted to only a third of the royal revenue.[36] But the spirit of his exclamation was correct: the remaining two-thirds were controlled by Mortimer and Isabella.

The impression one has is that of a boy – albeit a king – with few close friends, shuttered off from the world, partly through his unique position and partly through the threatening ambitions of his mother and Mortimer. Around him the majesty of the court was swirling and laughing, delighting in its newly found wealth. But at the eye of the whirling storm he sat alone on his throne, not knowing what was going to happen next.

THREE

The Devil for Wrath

Two days after his coronation, Edward presided over his first parliament as king. It was obvious that two of his lords would dominate. One of these was the earl of Lancaster: garrulous, proud, and angry that for so long he had been deprived of his rightful inheritance. He was a royal earl, a grandson of Henry III, and the richest lord in the country, and therefore had a good reason to consider himself pre-eminent. But Isabella did not like him, nor did she trust him. The other lord was Mortimer, who disliked him every bit as much as Isabella, and did not trust him at all.

Lancaster stormed through that first parliament. As Edward watched from his throne the earl put forward a whole gamut of petitions. He proposed that he and the invaders should be pardoned for any wrong-doings, that his dead brother Thomas be pardoned for his part in opposing Edward II, and that accordingly he should receive his brother's full inheritance. Edward listened and assented, refusing only to grant the part of Lancaster's inheritance which Isabella had already taken for herself. Mortimer kept a low profile. Lancaster continued. As the king was under age, there should be a council of regency, composed of twelve or fourteen men, which he (Lancaster) would lead.[1] And so the whole Lancastrian programme was rolled out. Many grievances dating back to the days of Thomas of Lancaster were aired: curbs on the abuses of gaolers, restrictions on the appointments of justices of the peace, rules against the king making contracts with lords to supply troops, restrictions on taxation. Lancaster was given an open field.

The power game which was developing during that parliament was subtle. Lancaster was trying to set the political agenda, as his brother had done before him, and to use parliament to reinforce his influence over a weak monarchy. Edward was in no position to do anything but take advice and play the official role of monarch, acquiescing to the council of regency. Mortimer's strategy was totally different. He would not challenge Lancaster in parliament. He would allow the earl to dominate that forum. He did not mind if royal authority *appeared* weak. But through Queen Isabella, Mortimer had royal influence. He would let Lancaster play the part of a political leader while, behind the scenes, he played the king.

Mortimer's subtlety in wresting control from Lancaster went much further than parliamentary contests. When Edward II had abdicated he had been promised that he would continue to enjoy regal status as he had before.[2] And so he did at Kenilworth, under Lancaster's guard. But certain lords did not see why the ex-king should be kept in prison. In addition, in March the Dunheved brothers, fanatical supporters of Edward II, tried to set him free. Mortimer could see that, whoever had custody of the ex-king wielded an instrument of great power. Since medieval kings were, by their very existence, royal, they could revoke any law which had been forced upon them. If Mortimer and Isabella were to lose favour, and if Edward II were to be freed, they might see the country reinstate the old king. Edward, still under-age, might find his father, as his guardian, commanding him to give up power. Mortimer and Isabella decided that Lancaster could not be trusted with such political leverage. As a result, Mortimer secured a royal writ to remove Edward II from Kenilworth. In March he left court and supervised the removal himself, with an armed retinue, much to Lancaster's fury. The old king was taken to Berkeley Castle and placed under the care of two of Mortimer's most trusted supporters: his son-in-law, Lord Berkeley, and his old comrade-in-arms, Sir John Maltravers.

To Edward, these developments were deeply disturbing. Neither Mortimer nor Lancaster was to be trusted. Lancaster was clearly following his own agenda: insisting, for example, that the young king confirm that he was bound by Magna Carta and the laws of the forest. And Mortimer was clearly a law unto himself, working through people, not institutions or ordinances. Isabella too was another force in the land. Her priority, however, was more straightforward. She sought money, in vast quantities. In addition to her twenty thousand marks a year, she now demanded another twenty thousand pounds to clear her debts.[3] Edward could not stop her any more than he could stop Mortimer.

Although only fourteen, and therefore seven years short of being able to rule without a council of regency (in theory), Edward knew that young men who proved themselves in war could dispense with the need for councils and advisers. Richard Bury, full of historical anecdotes, had probably advised him that Mortimer himself had been advanced to his inheritance because of his soldierly prowess at a time when the then king needed knights. So too had some of the young men at court, such as Robert Ufford. Edward was supposed to be the new King Arthur. Had that legendary leader not also won renown as a youth, and come to the throne in his fifteenth year? Edward could see that in order to prove himself a king, he would have to be more than a well-dressed puppet on the throne.

The royal accounts for 1327 are littered with payments for armour for Edward.[4] He commissioned his armourers to produce hauberks, greaves, lances, bascinets with visors (the latest style of protective helmet), gauntlets, trousers and breeches, and many other items of personal armorial wear. He ordered decorated aketons (protective stuffed leather jerkins), gilded lances and armour for tournaments. Some of his tournament armour was decorated with images of flowers and animals; some with royal emblems, such as leopards and crowns. Most importantly, he put this armour to use, as shown by a payment for enlarging his hauberk.[5] Edward took part in tournaments, and, aware of what was expected of him, he made himself as obvious and as visible as possible. Although only fourteen, he was trying to live up to his destiny.

*

Edward's need for a war to assert himself had an unlikely parallel north of the border. The Scots were no less aware than the English that this new king was prophesied to be the all-conquering King Arthur. In order to retaliate with a little propaganda of their own, they chose the day of the coronation to launch an attack on Norham Castle. Their plan went disastrously wrong after the governor of the castle heard rumours in advance, and the attackers were repulsed with the loss of several men. Nevertheless it was an indication that the Scots were no longer satisfied with the truce which had been signed in 1323. In particular, they were not happy that a promise made by Mortimer and Isabella before the invasion had not been honoured. To ensure Scots neutrality, Mortimer and Isabella had assured the Scottish representatives that if the invasion was successful, they would recognise Scotland as an independent kingdom.[6] Isabella had entered into further negotiations just after Christmas 1326, but talks had already broken down. Robert Bruce was growing ill and old: an independent Scotland was his last great ambition. By the spring, he wanted action.

Mortimer and Isabella did not want war. They had gone so far as to sign an embarrassingly one-sided treaty with France in March in order to make sure they would not have to fight in Gascony.[7] Lancaster, however, had good reasons to want the north armed and ready to fight. Bruce had demanded that the northern English barons give up their rights to their Scottish estates. In reality, the northerners had long since lost control of these lands, but they cherished their nominal rights nonetheless. Isabella could not persuade Lancaster and the other northern lords to surrender them. Thus there could be no lasting peace, and thus there would be repeated attacks on the northern marches of England by the Scottish king's men until the matter was resolved. Negotiations led by Lord Percy in February and March failed. In April, the army was ordered to muster in preparation for an attack. Mortimer and Isabella still hoped for a peaceful settlement but Bruce did not trust them. Moreover, he knew that, if they wanted peace, he could not lose by waging war. He would send an army to harry the northern counties until the English leaders bought the peace they wanted by recognising Scotland's independence.[8]

The consequent campaign was arranged with more ceremony than strategy on the part of the English. Positions of authority went to all three royal earls – Lancaster, Norfolk and Kent – with Lancaster in overall control. But no one doubted that Mortimer was really in charge. He had considerably more battlefield experience than the earls. Hainaulter mercenaries joined them at York, where a riot – which resulted in several hundred deaths – was only quelled by the king and his magnates riding through the streets to restore order. Edward could take a measure of pride in his appearance being the decisive factor in calming the riot, but the omens for the campaign were not good.

Still, this was his great opportunity, and he was determined to make the most of it. On 1 July he set out with the army and began the march to Durham, with trumpets sounding and pennons fluttering. Although the chronicler who recorded these details – Jean le Bel – does not describe the pennons in detail, they bore the arms of St George.[9] This was not the first time St George had been adopted by an English army in the field; both Edward I and Edward II had carried pennons bearing the red cross on white background.[10] But on that occasion the pennons had been mixed with those of St Edmund and St Edward, kings of England. This time, only the arms of St George were specifically made. Eighteen hundred of them were ordered to be taken to Stanhope. During the campaign, more were ordered, including some for the king's own trumpet. It seems Edward was calling the warrior-saint to stand by him, perhaps as an emblem of his prophesied status as a champion of God.

Unfortunately for Edward, the English forces were slow and cumbersome. The Scots by comparison were supremely manoeuvrable. Under the command of Sir Thomas Randolph and Black Douglas, they ran rings around the English force. Seeing they had been outwitted again, and not knowing whether the Scots were planning to attack the queen mother at York, or were in retreat to Scotland, one of the commanders ordered a sudden dash to the north to cut them off.[11] It was an unwise decision, for it split the footsoldiers from the mounted men-at-arms. And the supply wagons were left far behind. By the time the English had regrouped at Haydon Bridge, on the River Tyne, many of the men were hungry, soaked with the heavy rains, tired, and starving. Worse, they had no idea where their enemy was.

At this point Edward tried to take control of the situation. He sent word among his bedraggled and downhearted men that whoever would tell him where the Scots were would receive a knighthood and an income of one hundred pounds a year for life. Esquires set out immediately in all directions. One, Thomas Rokeby, not only found the Scots, he was captured by them. When he told them of his mission they laughed and let him go. Rokeby returned to Edward and admitted he had been captured. Edward acknowledged his honesty and, true to his word, knighted him. Rokeby might have been successful in a most inglorious fashion, but he had given Edward the initiative he wanted. He also gave Edward the opportunity to demonstrate that the king intended to honour his promises. The king ordered the army to be prepared, and masses to be sung, and called for his confessor.

The army set out that morning. They passed the burnt-out ruins of Blanchland Priory and continued on towards the Scots' position. Edward was determined to do battle: his mind was fastened on what was required of a king. And the men around him, his bodyguard, would have been aware that this young man truly meant to fight, and that they were bound to fight to the death to protect him. At about midday, as they came towards a steep hill on the far side of the River Wear, the Scots army appeared, gathering themselves into battalions on the slope.

The tension mounted, on both sides. The Scots were in an unassailable position, but Edward was not going to hold back. More than just Scottish independence was at stake: Edward's self-esteem and personal authority hung in the balance. The English army drew up below the Scots' position, on the near side of the river, in readiness. Edward, on horseback, rode among them, calling out encouragement. This was unusual for an English king; his father certainly had not done likewise. But Edward wanted everyone there to see he was different from his father. He wanted men to see that he would willingly share their danger. Occasionally he stopped, and dubbed a man a knight there and then. Then he rode on, telling the men that, under pain of death, no one was to attack until the order for the whole battalion to move was given.

Then the advance began. The army moved forward in slow time, to see whether the Scots would withdraw. They did not. Closer and closer the English approached, the crosses of St George flapping in the wind before them, until the two sides were in arrow range, and they could recognise the nobles on the opposing side by their coats of arms. The Scots stared back. The English came to the river. Then Mortimer called a halt.

After the failure of a contingent of archers to break the Scots' position, Mortimer called off the attack.

Edward was furious. Who was Mortimer to give orders? And who was he to take away Edward's chance of glory? But the truth was that Mortimer was in control, and even he was nervous. His priorities were to keep the young king from danger, to drive the Scots out of England and allow them to pass back into their own country without great loss, so that they would sign a treaty. He could not see how he could attack the Scots in their present position without risking all these things; they had chosen a spot which was too well-defended. The young king had to be held back. To break the deadlock, Mortimer agreed to allow heralds to cross the river to ask the Scots to fight a fair pitched battle, as the king wanted.

This move bought Mortimer time, but that was all. The Scots' reply was calculated to enrage Edward even further. 'The king of England can see we are in his land, and he can see what we have burnt and pillaged wherever we have been. If the king is displeased, let him come and seek redress.'[12] Edward's response was to camp exactly where they were. Although he could not go forward because of Mortimer, he would not retreat on account of the Scots. The English nobles spent an uncomfortable night in the open, in their armour, while the Scots banged drums and kept them awake, to demoralise them.

So began a long stalemate. Edward wanted to attack. Mortimer would not let him. The English lords were set to besiege the Scots in their well-defended position. This stalemate was only broken to be replaced by another, when the Scots suddenly left their camp to take up position in an even better-defended spot. The siege began again: the English weary with the wait, and Edward frustrated that he was being denied a battle in which to prove himself a man.

It was at this second site, still on the banks of the River Wear, that the Scots made their move. On or about 3 August, the English had placed their guard for the night as usual. But unknown to them, Black Douglas – the famous Sir James Douglas who was to die in Spain, flinging the heart of Robert Bruce into the midst of the enemy that was pressing his men on all sides – took two hundred men along the river bank and crossed quietly in the moonlight.[13] The English camp was quiet and unsuspecting. Most Englishmen were asleep. Suddenly the Scots rushed in, slashing the ropes of the tents and thrusting down with spears on the sleeping men caught beneath the tangled canvas, ropes and poles. The leaders were sleeping in their armour, and were quickly awake, but they could do little to organise resistance, and many men were slain. Edward himself was badly shaken, for as he slept, Black Douglas cut the ropes supporting his pavilion. The plan had been to capture the young king, but one of his chaplains within his tent managed to conceal him, saving him from a terrible humiliation.[14] All through the camp the cries of 'A Douglas! A Douglas! You shall all die, English thieves!' rang out and caused terror. Then, as quickly as they had arrived, Douglas and his Scotsmen left the English to tend to their wounded men as they lay screaming, dying of their wounds, in the night.

The next few days were unremarkable in terms of military encounters. Black Douglas had made his point well: the Scots were in the ascendant because the English had too much to lose. Even the English and Hainaulters marvelled at the Scots' audacity. But for Edward it was a startling introduction to war. He had come close to being killed. He had seen and heard men butchered around him. He had seen the dead, their lifeless flesh, the grass soaked with blood. The sight was hideous, but in his comprehension of war and his duty, what he perceived to be required was not a man who would shrink from the sight of death but a man who would lead his men despite such horrors. So completely did Edward believe in his duty to lead a fighting nation, that he saw himself as the failure of Stanhope Park, and Douglas as the victor, even though the English generally saw themselves as the army which forced Douglas to retreat. When a few days later the Scots once more tricked the English, and escaped by night, leaving their leather cauldrons bubbling with stewed meat in a final insult to the army of King Edward, the young king broke down and wept. The tension had been great; the stakes had been high, and in all the suddenness of the Scots' departure it became clear to Edward that he had lost in every way. The Scots had succeeded in harassing the English and getting away without a battle. Mortimer had succeeded in stopping them invade England further, and in protecting the king. And Edward was as powerless as ever.

*

There was one small consolation in the failure of the attack on the Scots: Edward had at last been able to speak out against Mortimer openly and in full view of the leading nobles of England. They had all cowered under Mortimer's reply – Lancaster included – but just by speaking his mind Edward had distanced himself from the growing authority of this dictatorial Mortimer. When the court was informed in September 1327 that there was a rebellion growing in South Wales and Mortimer declared that he would leave court to attend to it in person, Edward can only have been relieved. He could not possibly have foreseen the depths to which he would shortly be plunged.

The court travelled from York to Nottingham, and from Nottingham to Lincoln. There, on 15 September, parliament assembled. Mortimer still had not returned, and Edward was able for several days to imagine that he was king in practice as well as in name. Many issues were raised – charters were confirmed, pardons were issued, terms of military service were established, taxation was discussed, the debts of the Crown were negotiated, and the franchises of cities reaffirmed – and no fewer than seventeen Acts were passed. Mortimer only returned on the fifth or sixth day. At the end of the parliament on Wednesday 23 September Edward could reflect that at last his authority was growing, and that perhaps soon he would be king *de facto* as well as *de jure*. But late that night a messenger, Thomas Gurney, arrived from Berkeley Castle. He was carrying two letters: one for the queen and one for Edward. His father, the late king, was dead.

Although Edward's relationship with his father had been difficult, it was not the man but his unsuitability as a king which had come between them. Had his father not been a monarch – if he had been a minor lord – he would have been able to enjoy a much simpler life, and he would have been far happier. But as a king, unloved as a child, expected to be a warrior and a leader against his temperament, and placed in a position of responsibility which he simply could not understand, his unhappiness and the unhappiness of his family had been guaranteed. Edward had witnessed the arguments at court and fully comprehended the depth of his father's failures of responsibility. But did these failures deserve to be punished with loss of royal status, liberty, and life? Edward did not think so. He wrote to his cousin, the young earl of Hereford, the next day, with the principal purpose of giving orders for the reinforcement of the northern border against a possible further Scottish attack, but he was unable to refrain from passing on the news that 'my father has been commanded to God'.[15]

Edward could not have helped but dwell on his father's death. Natural causes? It must have been an illness brought on by grief, some said.[16] But the man was strong, forty-three years of age. Edward dared not repeat a suspicion that his father had been killed, but it probably occurred to him. On the other hand, his mother did not appear particularly grief-stricken even though she had been fond of her husband, and had sent him presents in his captivity at Berkeley. But since her liaison with Mortimer, Edward was not sure how to interpret her reaction. Mortimer himself gave nothing away. He gave permission for the abbot of Crokesden to commemorate the old king's death annually on 21 September, and allowed the prior of Canterbury to do likewise. But he refused permission to the monk Robert

Beby to receive Edward's body in order to bury him with his father, mother and grandfather in the church of Westminster Abbey.

From the 24th or 25th messengers carried the news that Edward II was dead across the country. Lords and knights leaving Lincoln after the parliament took the news with them on their return journeys. A huge canopied hearse was ordered for the late king, to be sent to Gloucester Abbey. Various knights and priests were detailed to join the bishop of Llandaff in the continual watching of the shrouded body from the time of its delivery to Gloucester until its burial. Eight hundred gold leaves were purchased for gilding a leopard onto the cover placed over the body.[17] Knightly robes and tunics were commissioned for the attendants.[18] Four great lions were made by John Estwyk, the king's painter, who gilded them and covered them with draped garments adorned with the royal arms, to be placed at the four corners of the late king's hearse. Four images of the Evangelists were also built by Estwyk to sit on top of the hearse. Eight incense-burners in the form of angels with towers of gold, and two rampant leopards, were made for the exterior of the hearse.[19] A wooden effigy of the dead king was carved, dressed in his robes and given a gilded copper crown.[20] Oak beams were supplied to keep the crowds away from the hundreds of candles which were to be placed on and around the hearse. Armour, including two helmets, was purchased for the deceased king.[21] Everything was packaged and transported by road to Gloucester, ready for the funeral, which was scheduled for 20 December.

In the meantime, Edward was jousting.[22] At first, this seems incongruous, and somewhat disrespectful. The young king, having just lost his father, continued to follow his favourite pastime. But we must remember that Edward was no ordinary young man, and martial prowess was a duty which consumed him completely. Jousting was part of his education as well as a pastime. One can read just as readily that Mortimer ordered the tournaments to take place, to divert Edward's attention. It was a full three months between receipt of the letters announcing Edward II's death and the funeral. Life, with all its demands on the young king, had to continue.

On the day of the funeral, Edward, his mother, his uncles, and Mortimer were among the several hundred mourners who gathered for the late king's obsequies. Hundreds of candles burned on and around the magnificent hearse. High within its structure the crowned wooden effigy of the king was clearly visible, lying on top of the sealed wooden coffin, which encased the lead coffin in which the embalmed body lay. Isabella was given a silver vase with the man's heart inside, in accordance with her long-stated wish to bury his heart with her.[23] As the monks of the abbey sang a mass, the royal family watched the coffin taken from the hearse and lowered into the tomb on the north side of the nave. The monks carried on singing for the soul of the departed man and the royal party withdrew. They stayed only for one night in Gloucester, and then left, travelling to Worcester, which they reached the following day.

Over the last three months Edward had come to terms with his father's death. He still must have felt a sense of loss, and not just on personal grounds, for his father was the only other man in England to have borne the burden of kingship. In those three months too he had grown more wary of Mortimer, who, if he had murdered his father, might equally turn against him. Mortimer had, after all, demonstrated how he could use parliament to remove a king, and then how he could have that ex-king buried without anyone publicly asking questions as to the manner of death, or even seeing the corpse. In this mixture of personal loss, fear, and growing responsibility, the next development in Edward's reign must have been utterly devastating. He must have felt his whole world shaken. Shortly after the funeral, probably while journeying to Worcester, he was told that his father was not dead.[24] The whole episode had been a fabrication. The letters sent by Lord Berkeley announcing the death had been false. Edward had been tricked.

Although we may now piece together the process whereby Edward, parliament and the rest of the country had been misled (see Appendix Two), we cannot know what the young king thought in the days and weeks after receiving this shocking news. However, it is reasonable to suggest that, along with the resentment towards Mortimer, he felt an element of self-recrimination. Mortimer had set the trap, but he (Edward) had walked blindly into it. As soon as he had been informed of his father's death, he had started circulating the news. On the very next day, in fact. Why did it never occur to him to check the identity of the corpse, to insist on seeing his father's face? But Edward was intelligent enough to realise that his mother and Mortimer between them would have prevented him from making sure. And his mother may well have suggested that it was in all their best interests that his father lived out the rest of his days in obscurity. It had been already agreed that the man should be kept perpetually in prison. But any relief Edward felt in knowing that his father was alive would gradually have been eroded by the disturbing implications of this news. Mortimer had power over his father. His father had been forced to abdicate. What if Mortimer were to turn against him? Edward would be exposed as having officially announced his own father's death and having subsequently attended the funeral, when a false body was lowered into a royal grave. How on earth could he, Edward, do anything but support this upstart monster, Mortimer? He had not only been tricked, he had been trapped. And his mother was part of the plot. There was no one to whom he could turn.

*

On Sunday 24 January 1328 Edward met Philippa of Hainault, his bride, at the gates of York. It had been more than a year since he had last seen her, at Valenciennes, but the kind and pretty Philippa was a most welcome sight. She was practically the same age as Edward, probably eighteen months his junior.[25] She was of the same blood, being his second cousin on his mother's side. Most important of all, she was temperamentally his ideal companion. She had a sense of humour, loved romances, and displayed a sympathetic understanding of people. Her wedding present for her husband was an illuminated collection of texts for aspiring rulers, including the 'Book of Julius Caesar' and the 'Government of Kings', and a book of statutes and music, with an illuminated picture of Edward in his favourite pose, holding a falcon: altogether a well-considered gift.[26] Side by side they rode into the city, with the crowd celebrating in widespread and heartfelt joy at their union. Either the next day or on Tuesday 26th they were married in the cathedral by the archbishop, William Melton, with Bishop Hotham of Ely in attendance, watched by Mortimer and Isabella and thousands of lords, knights, esquires, priests and citizens of York.[27] The Hainaulters were as fervent in their celebrations as the English. Count William of Hainault, struggling with gout, had accompanied his daughter and his brother, Sir John, bringing a large contingent. Of course there were tournaments. Philippa watched as Edward fought, with the pennons of his chosen protector, St George, flying above him.[28]

For Edward the wonderful thing about Philippa was that, for the first time, he had someone totally loyal in whom he could confide. Isabella could read his letters and Mortimer could spy on his conversations, but neither of them could come between him and his wife. She very quickly became his support in his struggles with the leaders of the regime. Although Edward could not reduce Mortimer's authority, he could obstruct his plans. Also with Philippa came a number of young pages and Hainaulter servants who owed no allegiance to anyone but her. One, Walter Manny, would prove a lifelong friend to Edward. When Edward's household officers were appointed by Mortimer, and when he had to entrust his secret business to men like John Wyard – a man who would one day betray him – he needed all the friends he could get.[29]

Before the end of the wedding festivities, dark news was received in York. King Charles of France, Isabella's last brother, had died, leaving no heir. Since females were barred from inheriting the French throne, Isabella had no claim herself; but she could pass on her claim to her son. Indeed, with all her brothers dead, if Isabella wanted her dear father's dynasty to continue to occupy the French throne, she had no alternative but to make a claim on behalf of Edward.

As far as Edward was concerned, the French claim only added to his problems. In the parliament which met at York directly after the wedding, it became clear that Mortimer and Isabella were preparing to give up his sovereignty of Scotland. This would alienate his northern barons, and lose Edward part of his inheritance. More personally, his grandfather, Edward I, had fought long and hard for control of Scotland; it should not be given up without a fight. To Edward, Scotland symbolised everything that was ignoble about the government exercised in his name. He also knew that unless he made it clear that he personally did not agree to giving up Scotland, a large contingent of English lords would blame him, for not standing up to Mortimer.

Mortimer and Isabella were unassailable. On 1 March letters were issued in Edward's name which outlined the terms of the permanent peace. Edward had to renounce all his claims and those made by his ancestors. The borders of the time of Alexander III (d.1286) were to be recognised. All English lordships in Scotland were to become Scottish lordships. All English actions against the Scots at the papal curia were to be dropped. Most personal of all these insults to Edward's status was the clause about a royal marriage. One of his sisters would be forced to marry the heir to the kingdom of Scotland, David, the eldest son of Robert Bruce, a man whom most Englishmen held to be a traitor.[30] To agree publicly with any of these terms would be humiliating. Edward began thinking about how he could make his disagreement publicly known.

Edward's quiet planning was given an unexpected boost a few days later. For the first time since the invasion, his mother, Mortimer and Lancaster all left him. On 2 March he issued a writ urging the sheriffs throughout the kingdom to assist his mother wherever she went on her pilgrimage.[31] On 5 March the next parliament was summoned to meet at Northampton at the end of April.[32] And then they began to depart. Mortimer disappeared off to Wales, probably with Isabella.[33] Lancaster and his kinsman, Thomas Wake, remained with Edward until 8 March and left shortly afterwards. Edward was left in the keeping of the bishops of Lincoln and Norwich, Gilbert Talbot, John Maltravers (then steward of the household), William Zouche, and John Darcy.[34]

This unprecedented departure prompts us to wonder what was going on in March 1328. And we might well wonder, for one of the reasons why Mortimer left court was to attend to his business in secret. We might say that, if contemporaries did not know what he was up to, what hope have we seven hundred years later? It is like trying to find where a needle was in a long-since vanished haystack. But the problem is potentially very important. For another of the characters who disappeared from court at this time was the earl of Kent, Edward's uncle. He was away for the same period as Mortimer, and returned to court at the same time as him.[35] This is interesting because these two men seem to have fallen out at this point. They had been close in France in 1325–26, and Kent had married Mortimer's cousin, Margaret Wake. Kent had urged a gift of a manor to be given to Mortimer after the invasion; Mortimer had responded on 3 March 1328, offering Kent some of Hugh Despenser's old lands. But thereafter there is no evidence of closeness between them, and later there was great hostility. The reason this is relevant to Edward III is that, at some point in 1328, almost certainly before March, Kent discovered that Edward II was still alive.

This was the third great worry (along with France and Scotland) that weighed on Edward III's mind in the summer of 1328. In 1327 there had been three attempts to rescue his father from prison: what if it were to happen again? Edward would then be entirely dependent on Mortimer to protect him. But how did Kent know? In 1330 he confessed that a friar had conjured up a devil, who had told him; but this was merely a ruse to cover up his true source. This was almost certainly Sir John Pecche, a man of fluctuating loyalty, who returned unexpectedly from abroad in about January 1328. He was the keeper of Corfe Castle, where the old king was being held.[36]

Edward, still only fifteen-and-a-half, was under huge pressure when parliament gathered at Northampton. War with France was being discussed. The independence of Scotland threatened England. And the earl of Kent's knowledge was potentially the greatest danger of them all. Disempowered by his mother and Mortimer, and separately undermined by his uncle, what could he do but try to manoeuvre himself between their contests, and look to his own safety, while trusting that others would speak out on his behalf? Lancaster, as head of the council of regency, did speak up. But he and Mortimer were so hostile to one another by this stage that Mortimer had no qualms about using Edward's name and authority to threaten his rival. When Mortimer declared outrageously that he spoke for the king, and the king's will was that Scotland should be independent, Lancaster declared that this 'shameful peace' was none of *his* will. Mortimer stood firm, knowing Edward could not oppose him. As everyone was in some way compromised by, or afraid of, Mortimer, no one else followed Lancaster's lead. Edward was forced to ratify the treaty.

Parliament broke up, and Edward had to acknowledge he had lost a part of his kingdom. Once more he had failed to live up to his responsibilities. Once more he had been publicly humiliated.[37]

*

It is easy to dismiss Mortimer's role in 1328 as that of a self-interested dictator. But even Edward would have acknowledged that his adversary was more than that. Mortimer believed he had relieved the country of a tyrant, and was now acting in the manner of a benign governor. He had done so before – quite legitimately and successfully – in Ireland in 1317–20. However, now his position was complicated by his illegal appropriation of royal authority. Even if his actions had been enlightened they would never have been agreeable to Edward. Mortimer's mere existence was a blow to royal authority, for it prevented him from ruling in the proper capacity of a monarch.

As a result, the strains on the relationship with his mother and Mortimer were felt most acutely by Edward. After Northampton, Mortimer and Isabella dragged Edward and Philippa to Hereford, there to attend the double wedding of two of Mortimer's many daughters and the post-nuptial tournament. This was another opportunity for Mortimer to spread his largesse, and to be seen as rich and powerful. But simply by being there, at Mortimer's beck and call, was a humiliation for Edward. And so it went on, day after day. From Hereford the royal party slowly made their way to Mortimer's castle at Ludlow. After two days hawking and jousting, they made their way back south to Worcester. There they waited for Henry of Lancaster, so Mortimer and Isabella could discuss the war with France. It might have been Edward's inheritance they were discussing, but it was Mortimer, Isabella and Lancaster who were doing the talking.

Faced with such humiliations, we might wonder why Edward did not speak out more often against Mortimer and Isabella. He probably did, but his opinions rarely reached the distant chroniclers. Also he was still young, only fifteen, and relatively insecure. He did not yet have the circle of determined supporters of later years; his contemporaries were relatively young. We must also remember that he was fond of his mother. And as for Mortimer, he did have his uses. At least he acted as a protection against Lancaster. At Worcester it became clear to Edward that, while Lancaster might argue with Mortimer about France and Scotland, what Lancaster most wanted was to control the king. Lancaster realised that Mortimer had outwitted him; he had to diminish or destroy Mortimer if he wished to take his place.

Mortimer's and Lancaster's arguments at Worcester were met with an outburst by Edward himself. In defiance of his two over-mighty magnates, Edward tried to impose his own will, to resist the demands on him to attend the marriage of his sister Joan with the son of Robert Bruce.[38] Mortimer and Isabella in turn countered that these matters had already been agreed at Northampton. But this time Edward did not back down. People had already cruelly renamed her 'Joan Makepeace', as if she were just a diplomatic tool. He refused to attend the wedding. He would stay in England while they went north. It was argued that this would damage the value of the alliance; but in Edward's eyes there was no alliance, for there was no peace. Seeing that there was nothing they could do to force him to come with them, his mother and Mortimer had no choice but to leave him behind.

*

In August 1328 Edward's brother, John, turned twelve years of age. Like Philippa, he was a natural ally against the growing oppression of Mortimer. Having been raised as a prince under the guardianship of a king, John could see the situation entirely from Edward's point of view. He was now being ruled by a baron. This led to what was probably Edward's next stand. When Mortimer demanded that, at the forthcoming Salisbury parliament, he be given the hugely significant title of Earl of March, Edward countered by pushing his brother forward to receive the rich earldom of Cornwall.

By this stage relations between Mortimer and Lancaster, and between both men and Edward, had reached a new low. On 7 September, Lancaster had threatened Mortimer and the king with an army at Barlings Abbey, near Lincoln. Edward was clearly shocked. A London rebellion was being planned also, and Edward was again dependent on Mortimer to send men to eliminate opposition from that quarter. Lancaster issued a whole string of accusations against Mortimer. As the date for the Salisbury parliament approached, it looked as if only pro-Mortimer supporters would attend. Lancaster's faction were preparing not for discussion but for war. That Edward was personally in danger was not in doubt. At the end of September Lancaster sent an armed force to capture him in East Anglia. It was only Edward's speedy reaction – forcing the court to travel 180 miles westwards in six days, towards the relative safety of Mortimer and Isabella at Gloucester – which saved him from falling into Lancaster's hands. If that had happened, Mortimer and Isabella would have lost their royal power, and Lancaster would have gained it. Civil war would have ensued.

Lancaster failed to arrive at the Salisbury parliament. The agenda was thus Mortimer's. No statutes were enrolled. The main items of business were the civil disturbances, the likelihood of war, and Mortimer's title. On the last day of October Edward ceremonially strapped the sword on to his mother's lover, and exchanged the kiss of peace with him, and in so doing created him earl of March. It must have been a far greater pleasure for him to do the same for his young brother, John, and the twenty-three-year-old James Butler, whom he created earl of Ormond.

Mortimer's title only infuriated Lancaster more. Throughout the latter part of 1328 it looked as though a great battle would be fought to establish who had the right to rule in Edward's name. At Winchester, Lancaster was persuaded to retreat at the very hour that Mortimer's vanguard arrived in the city. Skirmishes took place, but the two armies narrowly avoided one another. In London, Mortimer harangued the citizens who had dared to take Lancaster's side. Finally, at the end of December, Mortimer declared war on Lancaster in Edward's name. The young king could not have known what to think as his mother also donned armour and took part in a sudden overnight charge which resulted in Lancaster's capitulation near Bedford.

*

The year 1328 had seen Edward being fought over by Mortimer and Lancaster, like a wounded gazelle being trapped between two lions. Victory for Mortimer hardly made Edward's sleep any easier. The real danger for the gazelle begins when one lion has defeated the other and may safely consume its prey.

Edward's uncles, the earls of Norfolk and Kent, had initially sided with Lancaster. They had deserted him at the last, rather than take arms against the king. Like Edward himself, they saw no victory in Lancaster's defeat. Kent in particular wanted to see Mortimer removed from power: that was why he had sided with Lancaster in the first place. And in his opinion Edward was too young and inexperienced to throw off the irons of Mortimer's authority. In spring 1329 Kent took matters into his own hands. He planned a mission overseas to see Pope John XXII and began his arrangements for the rescue of Edward II.

Edward was also planning an overseas trip; or, rather, Mortimer and Isabella were planning one for him. Isabella had been persuaded to relinquish her claim to the French throne on Edward's behalf, largely because the risk of civil war made an overseas expedition impossible. Instead she had been persuaded reluctantly to recognise Edward's cousin, Philip de Valois, as king. But this rankled with her, as indeed it did with Edward himself. When Philip had demanded that Edward come to France to do homage for his French possessions, Isabella retorted that 'the son of a king would never do homage to the son of a mere count'. This infuriated Philip. He confiscated the revenues of Gascony and sent envoys to demand that Edward do homage as initially stated. Edward could see his French possessions slipping from his grasp as quickly as his Scottish ones. Mortimer agreed that he should do what was required of him, and perform homage. After a flurry of diplomatic missions, Edward appointed his younger brother, John, custodian of the realm during his absence. He said farewell to him, his mother, and Mortimer at Dover at the end of May.

Edward had many men with him, including Hugh Turpington and John Maltravers, Mortimer's most loyal knights. He also had close friends in William Montagu, Thomas West, Geoffrey le Scrope, Pancio de Controne and Robert Ufford. Montagu, now aged about twenty-seven, had been at court since his father's death in 1319, when he had become a royal ward. Thus he had known Edward since the age of six. Thomas West was one of Montagu's retainers.[39] Ufford was thirty years old, and had known Edward as long as Montagu. The Italian de Controne was Edward's personal physician. Le Scrope was the prominent lawyer who had assisted in Edward's household many years earlier. With the possible exception of le Scrope, all these friends of Edward's had seen their hopes for the future threatened by Mortimer. To them Mortimer represented the traumas of the old reign. And they knew Edward needed their help. He had already lost his rights to Scotland, and was on the verge of surrendering his rights to France. His royal power had been held from him, his father held prisoner, his uncle Kent alienated from court. We do not know when Edward began to confide in Montagu and Ufford, but we might assume from their presence on this trip that they were there at Edward's insistence, and that Edward was already closer to them than he was to Mortimer's henchmen.

Edward and his men landed at Wissant on 26 May, after a two-day crossing. They made their way via Crécy and Montreuil to Amiens, where on 6 June, in the choir of the cathedral, Edward swore homage to Philip. Something about the ceremony, however, was not right. Various writers later postulated that Edward had not put his hands between Philip's when swearing the oath; others thought that he had not sworn fealty, and thus refused to serve Philip in war.[40] One thought Philip was planning to arrest Edward after the ceremony.[41] Another story was that Isabella summoned him to return immediately.[42] Whatever the truth of what happened, Edward left France in a hurry. He did not beg leave of the French king; he simply left. Within six days he was back on English soil. Two days later he was at Canterbury.

Why did Edward depart so suddenly? So many problems were billowing like smoke out of England that it is difficult to know which was the most important. One is the possibility that Isabella was pregnant, with Mortimer's child.[43] This would have threatened Isabella especially, and it may be that she and Mortimer immediately sought Edward's acquiescence, if not his approval. However, it is unlikely that Isabella would have upset a diplomatic agreement for the sake of not telling Edward such news for a few more days. It is more probable that something directly threatened Edward as well as Isabella and Mortimer. This is very unlikely to have been a French plot to arrest him. The message would have been poorly directed if it had reached him having travelled via England. Also, on his return to England, Edward authorised the negotiations for a marriage between his brother John and a daughter of the king of France. The most likely explanation is that this was the point at which Mortimer and Isabella discovered the nature of Kent's plot to rescue Edward II.

Historians have traditionally assumed Edward II had been dead for the last two years. If any acknowledged that this was not certain, they still assumed that Edward II had disappeared from English politics altogether, and that he may as well have been dead.[44] But it has become clear that this was not the case: Edward II's shadow haunted Edward III far more than has hitherto been realised. Edward was a nervous young man, beset by troubles. And the knowledge that his father was alive, and that he himself, through his royal position, had helped create the lie of his father's death, troubled him mightily. In later years it became usual for members of the royal family to be buried with their faces exposed, precisely to avoid the confusion which now beset Edward and his contemporaries.[45] The news that Kent had gone to the pope to inform him that Edward II was still alive must have alarmed Edward as much as it did Mortimer and Isabella.

Kent had been planning his trip for several months, since at least April if not earlier.[46] But he was still in England in May, and seems not to have left until early June.[47] It seems that Isabella may have ordered Edward to hurry home in the fear that Kent, after his support for Lancaster, might himself have sought to kidnap Edward while in France, possibly to stage his own *coup d'état*. Kent was no fool, despite often being referred to as one, and he too could have used custody of the young king to steal power in England, just like Mortimer or Lancaster.[48] All we know for certain is that, as Edward was swearing homage to King Philip on 6 June, his uncle was crossing or about to cross the Channel with a view to taking action against Mortimer and Isabella's regime by replacing Edward on the throne with his secretly imprisoned father.

The situation would have been made clear to Edward on his arrival back in England. If we are right in thinking that Isabella was pregnant at this time, Edward would have been forced to grapple with that fact also. Problem after problem seemed to loom before him. And Mortimer, the architect of so many of these problems, seemed more confident than ever. That autumn he held a great feast at his newly rebuilt castle of Wigmore, at which he (Mortimer) played the part of King Arthur in the king's presence. The symbolism was unambiguous. Mortimer was playing the king himself in front of Edward, the real king. This was more than mere play-acting.

Although not yet seventeen, Edward realised he had to take steps to reclaim power. He decided that his first move must be to convince the pope of his integrity. A week after the tournament at Wigmore, he sent William Montagu to Avignon. The mission was secret: ostensibly Montagu was to see Otto, lord of Cuyk, whom Edward said he wished to employ.[49] But Mortimer was quick. On learning of Montagu's trip, he instructed his own man, Sir Bartholomew Burghersh, to accompany Montagu. Undaunted, Montagu did what Edward had bade him, and saw Pope John XXII. On the journey he may have been able to persuade Burghersh to change allegiance, at least tacitly, for he was able to see the pope and tell him of the plight in which Edward found himself, and how the country was being run against his wishes by Mortimer and Isabella. Pope John told Montagu to return to England and let Edward send him a secret letter bearing a sign or cipher by which he could discern which letters to him came with Edward's blessing and which did not.

Sending Montagu to Avignon meant Edward was temporarily without his most trusted friend. But others were beginning to rally to his cause. Most important of these was Richard Bury, Edward's old tutor, whom he had managed to keep with him. Bury had been a cofferer in 1327, and keeper of Edward's wardrobe from August 1328. On 24 September he was raised to the position of keeper of the privy seal. This was crucial: it meant that one of Edward's trusted servants had custody of the means by which his personal instructions could be authenticated. It marked a distinct setback for Mortimer and Isabella, and the best-informed chronicles begin to note that at this time Mortimer was beginning to perceive Edward as a threat.[50] In particular, when the pope asked Montagu to arrange the means by which he could distinguish between Edward's and Mortimer's written intentions, Bury wrote a letter which Edward himself signed with the words 'Pater Sancte' (Holy Father).[51] This is today the earliest surviving writing in the hand of an English monarch.

Everyone was playing a deadly game. Mortimer could see his influence waning. But as the basis for his confidence diminished, Edward saw him growing more arrogant and more dangerous. The child which may have been born to Mortimer and Isabella at Kenilworth in December 1329 would have made nothing easier for any of them. Isabella too was vulnerable. Lancaster, only superficially forgiven for his rebellion, was out of the country, on a diplomatic mission, possibly coordinating activity from France. To make matters more dangerous still, rumours about Lancaster's return, or Kent's return, with an army of mercenaries were circulating. On 7 December 1329 Mortimer and Isabella issued a warrant to arrest anyone spreading such rumours.[52] Feelings were running high, and, at the height of these feelings, Kent returned. The man with the knowledge and power to blow the whole situation sky high was back in England.[53]

No one knew quite what to expect at the beginning of 1330. Edward now learnt that Philippa was pregnant, and expecting their first child. Mortimer, fully aware of the danger to them all, was plotting. So too was Kent. They all came together for the coronation of Queen Philippa at Westminster Abbey on 18 February.[54]

The records do not show how tense the situation was. The only documents which shed any light on that day are those which show what the queen was wearing. The fantastic ostentation is worth quoting, for it contrasts so completely with the antagonisms at court. It was almost as if Edward was ordering Philippa to spend as much as she possibly could in order to emphasise his right to empty the royal purse. For her journey from the Tower of London to Westminster on the eve of her coronation, Philippa wore a tunic comprising nine-and-a-half ells of green velvet cloth; for the cape she wore on the same occasion 'three of the very best red cloths of gold spinet', along with a selection of miniver furs.[55] The next day – the day of her coronation – she wore, in the morning, a robe of seven cloths 'of green gold spinet of the very best quality'; a fur hood and fur cap. Then she changed, and wore a lined tunic and a lined mantel of red and grey samite for her anointing and coronation. This took place before the high altar of Westminster Abbey, Philippa being crowned by the new archbishop of Canterbury, Simon Meopham. She changed again for lunch, and wore a tunic and a mantel 'of the very best purple cloth of gold spinet and a hood of miniver fur'. For supper she changed again, and wore a robe of the very best gold spinet, a miniver fur and a miniver hood and fur cape. Finally, after her coronation, she dressed in a robe of the very best cloth of gold, and yet more furs, this time of ermine. According to the annalist of St Paul's, there was a great procession, and the queen rode between Edward's two uncles – Kent and Norfolk – who dressed as pages and rode on palfreys with her to the abbey. One wonders at the pleasantries which passed, the conversations which bubbled over the deep anxiety felt by Kent, Edward, Philippa, Mortimer and Isabella.

In fact the situation was worse than any member of the royal family could have guessed, including Kent. Mortimer now had the means to bring the crisis to a head. He had managed to obtain from his agent, John Deveril, at Corfe Castle, written proof of the earl of Kent's plot to release Edward II and dethrone Edward III. The incriminating letter had been written by Mortimer's own cousin, Margaret Wake, Kent's wife. Mortimer had to respond. His response would be cold and severe. He would have to betray the continued existence of the old king, but that perhaps was not such a bad thing for him, as he would thereby undermine Edward's authority. Either way he could not delay. Kent's plot was about to spring Edward II from Corfe. The archbishop of York had even written to the mayor of London to arrange for the delivery of clothes for the old king after his release.[56] The rumours were rife, incriminating letters were being passed from hand to hand. Mortimer must have considered this might be his only chance to save himself and Isabella, and perhaps to stave off a civil war between his own faction, fighting in the name of Edward III, and those who, like Kent, wished to see Edward II restored.

*

At Winchester, on 13 March, Mortimer made his move. In the hall of the castle, in the king's presence and with the lords all assembled, he announced that he had arrested the king's uncle, the earl of Kent, on a charge of treason.

The stakes could not have been higher. Calculations had been piled on calculations; risks on risks. Edward probably trusted Mortimer to keep his father's survival secret, even at this stage, even though many of those attending parliament knew the truth. If the ex-king's survival became an open matter for debate, then he, Edward, could be accused of breaking the terms of Magna Carta, and keeping a man wrongly imprisoned. His uncles had, in fact, already accused him of exactly that crime.[57] If his father were to be released and restored – and such was the opposition to Mortimer now that many thought this an appropriate course of action – Edward would find himself dethroned. Mortimer would be hanged and quartered, Isabella divorced and sent to a nunnery. Edward himself might even be arrested for treason. He might very easily find himself in Kent's place. All the key personalities had much to lose, and for once Mortimer was not an exception.

What Edward was probably only just beginning to understand was how far the information about his father had gone. Kent had been very successful in attracting support. The pope had promised unlimited funds. The archbishop of York had offered £5,000. Sir Ingelram Berengar had discussed the plan with Kent several times, the last in Kent's room above the chapel at Arundel Castle. Sir Fulk Fitzwarin said it would be the 'noblest deed ever accomplished'. Lord Beaumont was deeply implicated, so too was Sir Thomas Roscelyn. Kent's brother-in-law, Lord Thomas Wake, another of Mortimer's cousins, was an accomplice. So were Lady Vesci, the Scottish earl of Mar, and Sir John Pecche. Add to these Lord Zouche, the bishop of London and the earl of Lancaster, and things began to look very grave for Edward indeed.

Mortimer proceeded undaunted. He himself acted as the prosecutor, in a court specially arranged for the purpose of trying Kent. He made no attempt to cover up the secret of the ex-king's survival and custody.

> Sir Edmund, earl of Kent, you should understand that it behoves us to say, and principally unto our liege lord, Sir Edward, king of England – whom Almighty God save and keep – that you are his deadly enemy and a traitor and also a common enemy unto the realm; and that you have been about many a day to make privily deliverance of Sir Edward, sometime king of England, your brother, who was put down out of his royalty by common assent of all the lords of England, and in impairing of our lord the king's estate, and also of his realm.[58]

If Kent had harboured an illusion that rescuing a wrongly imprisoned kinsman was in some way not a crime, then it was shattered instantly. He falteringly replied: 'In truth, Sir, understand well that I never assented to the impairment of the state of our lord the king, nor of his crown, and that I put myself to be tried before my peers.' But he must have known that no plea could save him from Mortimer's judgement. And Edward too must have realised that Mortimer was going to push all the way: there would be no pretending that Edward's father was dead. If Edward himself openly denied it, then Mortimer could denounce him there and then, and reveal all. The whole royal family was on trial.

Edward kept silent. Mortimer continued. He held up a letter which, he explained, had been handed to his agent at Corfe Castle. It bore a seal. To Kent he showed the letter and said: 'Sir Edmund, do you not know this letter that you sent to Sir John Deveril?' The earl's seal was clearly visible, and he agreed it was his, but it was of no value, he protested, as he had sent many letters. Perhaps Kent genuinely did not know what this particular letter said. But Mortimer knew. He began to read the letter aloud:

> Worshipful and dear brother, I pray heartily that you are of good comfort, for I shall ordain for you, that you shall soon come out of prison, and be delivered of that disease in which you find yourself. Your lordship should know that I have the assent of almost all the great lords of

England, with all their apparel, that is to say with armour, and with treasure without limit, in order to maintain and help you in your quarrel so you shall be king again as you were before.

There was no denying this evidence. Edward could see that his uncle was damned. Worse, he himself was demonstrably guilty of keeping his father hidden, and of having given orders for, and attended, a fake royal funeral. Could he plead ignorance? Would anyone listen if he did? His confidence had been broken, and broken again, so that many of the men now present suspected that he himself may have led Kent into this trap, and here, almost crowing, was Mortimer, who was setting his father and uncle against him.

Still Edward kept silent. The sentence was read out. Kent was told that:

the tenor of this your letter is that you were on the point of rescuing that worshipful knight Sir Edward, sometime king of England, your brother, and to help him become king again, and to govern his people as he was wont to do beforehand, thus impairing the state of our liege lord the present king . . . The will of this court is that you shall lose both life and limb, and that your heirs shall be disinherited for evermore, save the grace of our lord the king.

The sentence resounded around the hall. Edward heard the words 'save the grace of our lord the king' and knew he could no longer keep silent. The moment had come to decide. Kent, having heard that he was to die, in tears began to plead for his life. He admitted he had not considered the king in all his plotting, and he wholly submitted to him. He promised, if the king so desired, that he would walk through the streets of Winchester, or even all the way to London, barefoot, with a rope around his neck, in atonement. The man was terrified and humiliated, and begged Edward, his nephew, for his life.

'Save the grace of our lord the king.' Edward's kingship had crumbled into disaster. Everything – loyalty, affection, kinship, pity – suggested that he should save his terrified uncle, who had acted only out of love for his brother. But in Mortimer's open assertion that Edward II was still alive, Edward could see that he himself was under threat. Mortimer claimed descent from Arthur: the line which, it had been prophesied, would one day rule all England and Wales. Mortimer had presented his sons as earls; he had claimed the premier earldom in the kingdom; he had defeated his only rival, Lancaster, and was speaking and acting as if he, not Edward, was king. He had already once put himself forward as a possible monarch.

This trial was not about the earl of Kent, it was about Mortimer's power. Mortimer was the enemy here, not Kent. The prosecutor was the guilty party. But there was nothing Edward could do to stop him. Nor would he ever be able to stop him if men like his uncle saw his father's restoration as the best way to prevent Mortimer from achieving the throne. Edward realised he had to demonstrate to all those who knew that his father was still alive that he would never give up his right to be king. With a pitiful heart, he understood what he had to do.

He sentenced his uncle to death.

*

On 19 March 1330 the earl of Kent was led out of prison, his hands bound. He was to be beheaded. Bravely, the captain of the guard declared that his men had refused to carry out the sentence. This embarrassed Mortimer, but the captain was steadfast, and so were his men. Mortimer and those who had gathered for the execution waited. Eventually Mortimer ordered the gaols to be searched for a man prepared to do his bidding, and a latrine cleaner, himself sentenced to death for murder, agreed to kill the earl in return for his life. He was brought out to confront his royal victim. So the blow was wielded by a criminal. And thus Edward sacrificed his uncle.

The fall of the axe meant one thing was certain: Edward would avenge his uncle's death. From that moment on there could be no drawing back from his determination to put an end to Mortimer's rule.

Mortimer was not unaware of the changed situation, but he was too involved to be able to extricate himself. How could he? He had kept Edward II alive – perhaps out of consideration for Isabella's wishes, perhaps out of his own desire to control the young king, perhaps both – and now he was guilty of having kept an anointed king hidden, illegally, for more than two years. If he withdrew from court now, Edward III would surely come after him and seek revenge. Besides, he would lose Isabella if he withdrew, or went into exile; and he may well have been devoted to her emotionally, even beyond the limits of his excessive ambition. From Mortimer's point of view, all he could do was to keep his nerve, to use his wits to keep in control, for as long as possible.

From the day of Kent's execution, Mortimer had exactly seven months of freedom left. In that time he certainly used his wits. He rallied troops, he appropriated lands and wealth, and he did all he could to keep Edward in his place. A plot arranged by Richard Fitzalan, heir to the earldom of Arundel, was discovered by Mortimer and foiled.[59] But Mortimer's authority was diminishing by the day. Magnificent he may have been, feared he certainly was; but the young generation of knights at court were of a mind to fight for their king. Long before 19 October Edward knew whom he could trust. William Montagu had returned from Avignon, and he was willing to take action. It did not matter how many troops Mortimer inspected in his show of strength. The revolution would not be an invasion, it would come from within. The only question for these young knights of St George was how to strike the dragon, and avoid being scorched in its dying fire.

The politeness continued. Edward had learnt how to play the games of diplomacy. As late as 28 July Edward included Mortimer amongst those to whom he gave elaborate Turkish clothes for the summer season, along with his mother, his wife and his sister, Eleanor.[60] They were still at Woodstock then, where Edward learned he had become a father. Philippa had given birth to a son, Edward – the future Black Prince – on 15 June. Edward was ecstatic, and gave the valet who brought him the news forty marks yearly for life.[61] Maybe this was why his mood was light enough for him to give Mortimer presents of Turkish cloth that summer. Maybe these were the last attempts to cover up the plots being hatched. Either way, it is much easier to give gifts to a mortal enemy knowing you have marked him down to die.

The third day of the parliament held at Nottingham Castle was 19 October. Tempers had flared in the days before, the hatred and fear on all sides had become obvious. Mortimer had arrived to find that Lancaster had been given rooms in the castle. He flew into a rage and demanded to know who had dared house so great an enemy of the queen so close to her. On his orders the earl was directed to be removed and lodged at a merchant's house in the town. Mortimer also gave orders that the men of the garrison were to obey his orders, and not the king's. This was utterly outrageous. Just as shocking was his confiscation of the keys to the castle, which he handed to Isabella.

The king's friends were near to taking action. They hesitated at this last violent outburst from Mortimer, not quite knowing what he was planning. Some urged Edward to accuse Mortimer openly of murdering Edward II, and to arrest him.[62] That way, even if the king's father were to appear in public, he could be declared an impostor and set aside. But Edward was reluctant to follow this path: it held too many pitfalls. Besides, he now knew that his secret information was being passed directly to Mortimer by John Wyard. As first Montagu, and then Humphrey and William Bohun, Ralph Stafford, Robert Ufford and John Neville of Hornby, were each led before Mortimer and interrogated, Edward realised that a more immediate and complete strategy was required.

At this point William Eland changed the course of history. Eland was the man who told the plotters about the secret passage which led from the riverbank up into the queen's apartments. It seems that he told Edward first, and the king sent him to Montagu with orders to give him the same information. This is the most likely sequence of events given the wording of Montagu's charter of reward. Edward states clearly that he revealed his own secret design for the arrest of Mortimer and his accomplices to Montagu, and that Montagu was 'strenuous' in carrying out the plan.[63] Sir Thomas Gray, writing twenty years later, tells us that the king instructed Montagu to order Eland on pain of death to leave a postern gate to the park open, which suggests that, until that moment, there was some doubt over Eland's loyalty. This postern may have been at the bottom or the top of the secret passage, or possibly both. The chronicle known as *The Brut* relates a conversation between Montagu and Eland in which Montagu asked Eland for the keys of the castle that night, and Eland pointed out that Isabella kept them under her pillow, but told him about the secret passage. Edward saw his opportunity to seize Mortimer without alerting his troops.

We cannot know the precise movements of each person that night, but some things are clear. The lower entrance to the passage was left unlocked by Eland or on his instructions, and perhaps an upper door was unlocked by one of Edward's accomplices within the castle. Eland himself was with Montagu. From the inclusion of certain non-combatants among those rewarded for assisting in the coup, especially Pancio de Controne and Robert Wyville, it would appear that these men also helped in the operation, very probably assisting in the entry of the armed men.[64] As de Controne was a physician, it is possible that his role was to support Edward's alibi of ill-health, as Edward would not have wanted to be with Mortimer and Isabella when the fight to arrest them broke out.

According to Sir Thomas Gray, after ascending the stairs from the tunnel, Montagu and his accomplices were undetected as it was 'mirk night'.[65] The followers of the nobles had left the castle and returned to their lodgings in the town. Isabella, Mortimer, his sons Geoffrey and Edmund Mortimer, Simon Bereford, Sir Hugh Turpington, and Bishop Burghersh were in the hall of the queen's lodgings discussing what action was to be taken against the plotters. Various other esquires and men-at-arms stood guard, but they were few. Most of Mortimer's men were billeted in an outer ward of the castle, at a considerable distance, or on watch on the outer walls. As steward of the household, it was Turpington's responsibility to make sure that the servants and guards were attending to their business. He was probably in the course of a routine check about the castle when he saw the armed group advancing up the stairs to the queen's apartments. Had he withdrawn at that moment he might have saved himself, but Turpington had fought alongside Mortimer since at least 1310, and his response was unquestioning and immediate. Turpington's dying shout alerted everyone within the hall, and, in the next few moments, as Montagu, Neville and the other assailants rushed to the door of the hall, the household esquires ran to defend the entry. In the struggle which followed, several esquires were injured and two were killed: Richard Crombek and Richard Monmouth. As they fought, Mortimer left the hall and went into the queen's chamber to seize his sword. Bishop Burghersh followed him, not to fight but to try and escape. But Montagu had enough men to capitalise on the surprise of his attack. Within a short while Mortimer had been disarmed, and his sons Geoffrey and Edmund had been arrested, along with Simon Bereford. Isabella, inviolable as the king's mother, simply screamed despairingly at the door of the chamber into the dark corridor beyond, suspecting Edward to be present.

All the prisoners were marched down to the basement of the queen's apartment, and down the spiral staircase into the secret passage, down to the riverbank and through the park. They were taken to Leicester. Such was Edward's fear of Mortimer that he rode with the men who removed him, and ordered them to hang him as soon as they reached Leicester. But Lancaster, who had also ridden with Edward and his knights, urged him to use parliamentary approval for Mortimer's execution. A show trial was needed, if only to reinforce the idea that Edward II was dead, and that Mortimer had killed him. Lancaster – who had now become reconciled to Edward, and clearly must have apologised for his earlier behaviour – persuaded the king. Mortimer was taken to the Tower of London.

Just as the execution of his uncle had been a pivotal moment in Edward's development as a man, so now the destruction of Mortimer's authority was a pivotal moment in his development as a king. Having accompanied Mortimer all the way to London, Edward ordered him, his son Geoffrey Mortimer and Simon Bereford to be walled up in one of the rooms.[66] The doors and windows were accordingly filled in by a mason. Six royal sergeants-at-arms under the command of two knights of the royal household, Robert Walkefare and Arnold Duroforti, were stationed around the room to make sure Mortimer did not repeat his 1323 escape.[67] There, in the darkness, Mortimer waited for a month before he was sentenced. Perhaps Edward ordered this in reflection of the conditions in which his father had been held.[68] On this we can only speculate. But one aspect of the incarceration is very interesting: it was not just any room into which Mortimer was sealed. It was the one next to Edward's own.[69]

FOUR

Absolute Royalty

On 26 November 1330 Edward had Mortimer dragged before parliament, bound and gagged. He sentenced him to death for fourteen specific crimes, most of which were prefaced by the accusation that Mortimer had 'accroached the royal power'. It has generally been assumed that this marks the moment when Edward took absolute control of his kingdom, and it is true that with Mortimer's downfall the major obstacle to Edward's direct rule was removed. But many challenges remained. Before he could recognise his ambitions, Edward would have to wait until he was older, more trusted as a leader, and more confident.

First there was the problem of what to do with the old regime, its victims as well as its supporters. There was the issue of the lands and treasure which Mortimer and his friends had amassed, including the fortune gathered by Isabella. What should Edward do with the people they had obstructed or disempowered, and the estates of those they had executed, such as Hugh Despenser and the earl of Kent? Disinherited lords could be reinstated, as with the earl of Kent's son; but what about those whom Mortimer had locked up for good reason? What about Mortimer's family and the families of his supporters? And what about their actions before 1326? One of Mortimer's Irish tenants, Hugh Lacy, came to court seeking redress for accusations of treason brought against him in 1317, when Mortimer had been a highly respected King's Lieutenant of Ireland.[1] Such grievances had to be treated on their individual circumstances. It would have been unwise simply to revoke all of Mortimer's actions.

Edward proceeded cautiously. On the way south from Nottingham, just four days after the arrests, he ordered Mortimer's treasure to be handed over to Richard Bury, along with that of Queen Isabella.[2] Mortimer's lands were confiscated. Isabella voluntarily surrendered her vast estates at the end of November.[3] The pope was very quick to get involved, writing to Edward immediately requesting that he deal leniently with Isabella and Mortimer.[4] In fact, so seriously did the pope take the matter that he sent two copies of his letter on behalf of Isabella to Edward, in case one should be lost. The pope wrote at the same time to Queen Philippa, the earl of Lancaster, William Montagu and the bishop of Winchester exhorting them all to use their influence to help Isabella, Mortimer and the bishop of Lincoln. Such intentions were not lost on Edward, who knew he would need the pope's support in the years to come. Isabella was placed temporarily under house arrest. The bishop of Lincoln was left unmolested.

The real problem facing Edward was how to proceed against those who were the closest intimates of Mortimer, the handful of men who knew what had happened to Edward II. This was a matter of the greatest delicacy. The strategy he adopted was brilliant: Mortimer had concocted the 'death' of Edward II; so Edward III would maintain that his father really *was* dead, and that he had been murdered on Mortimer's orders. In this way, although he had no idea where his father was, he could set aside any attempts to restore him during his own minority, just as Mortimer had done. He also could restore the son of the earl of Kent to his rightful inheritance and pardon his poor dead uncle, which he did. But this strategy did carry one great difficulty. It raised the question of how Edward should treat the men who thus were implicated in a fictitious royal murder. Obviously he would have to take action against them. Fortunately, all the ringleaders fled except one. Lord Berkeley remained. Defiantly he maintained in parliament that the ex-king was not dead.[5] Edward showed great awareness and intelligence in his response. He quickly took the initiative and came to an understanding with Berkeley. The official announcement of the death would be maintained, but Berkeley himself would not be held guilty of the fictitious death.[6]

In this context, Mortimer was the least of Edward's worries. He was sentenced to be dragged to the gallows at Tyburn, then hanged. On the day of his execution he was made to wear the black tunic he had worn at Edward II's funeral.[7] Isabella's movements were restricted for several months. Then she received her liberty and the income she had held before the ascendancy of the Despensers: the substantial sum of £3,000 per year. Edward waited a week after the parliamentary trials before ordering the arrest of Maltravers for arranging Kent's death and the arrests of the other men involved in the supposed 'murder' of Edward II. They had already fled, of course, but Edward had to be seen to be taking action against the supposed killers of his father. Moreover, he wanted one of Mortimer's supporters in particular brought to him. This was Thomas Gurney, the man who had originally brought him the news of his father's 'death', knowing it was false. Gurney was arrested in Spain, and died three years later of a sudden illness on the way back to England. As for other members of the Mortimer faction, the dictator's widow, Joan, eventually received her lands back, with a full recompense for her lost income.[8] Lord Berkeley was notionally held over on the charge of appointing the men who were supposed to have killed Edward II, but he was neither incarcerated nor deprived of his lands or revenues.

In this way Edward coped with a serious dilemma. On the one hand he had to be seen to take firm action against Mortimer's adherents. On the other, he had to be careful lest he be accused of creating false 'crimes' in order to discredit men for the sake of his own reputation, especially in the case of Lord Berkeley. Only two men – Mortimer himself and his henchman, Simon Bereford – were executed as a result of the coup. Even Geoffrey, Mortimer's son, who was walled up with his father in the Tower, was released without charge. Mortimer's eldest son, Edmund, was allowed to inherit some of his family estates within a few months of his father's execution. Edward never even pursued Sir John Maltravers, the other man responsible for the ex-king's security, along with Lord Berkeley.

Not only would it have been unwise for Edward to persecute those who had supported Mortimer, it would have served no purpose. Mortimer had surrounded himself with the cleverest and most able men of his generation. Indeed, virtually all the prominent men at court in the last year of Mortimer's ascendancy were retained by Edward III in the first year of his. We know this by assessing who witnessed royal charters in the period before and after the coup of 19 October 1330 (See Appendix Four). Bishop Burghersh of Lincoln, who spent more time at court in 1330 than any other bishop, was retained by Edward III even though he was no longer Chancellor. The pope wrote commending his skills to Edward, who acknowledged in his reply that Burghersh had 'more good in him than all the other bishops'.[9] This is remarkable in view of Burghersh being Mortimer's closest friend and adviser.[10] Nor was he the only Mortimer ally to win Edward's approval; even Oliver Ingham attested a charter in 1331, despite being a Mortimer agent; and two years later he was appointed seneschal of Aquitaine. Leaving aside the steward of the household (who attested charters by virtue of his office), all but one of the fifteen men who had witnessed more than three charters in 1330 under Mortimer's period of influence performed the same courtly function in 1331, the exception being Geoffrey Mortimer. Edward restricted his reforms to replacing the Treasurer and Chancellor with men of his own choosing. The men he selected for these posts were William Melton (archbishop of York) and John Stratford (bishop of Winchester) respectively.

All this points to another significant feature of Edward's character: forgiveness. Edward was not averse to executing his enemies, as later events would show, but if a man could prove useful to him, he did not let past enmity stand in the way of reconciliation. Already by 19 October 1330 Lancaster – the rebel of 1328 – had been restored to favour. More surprisingly, Geoffrey Mortimer was permitted to live quietly on his estates in France. Although Maltravers was sentenced to death for his part in procuring the death of the earl of Kent, he too was allowed to live untroubled in

Flanders. He was allowed to return to England secretly for a conference with Edward's advisers in 1335, was employed by Edward in Flanders and Ireland not long after that, and eventually restored to his estates and lordship.[11] Bartholomew Burghersh, who had shadowed Montagu's mission to the pope, was appointed seneschal of Ponthieu.[12] Such an ability to forgive meant Edward did not permanently alienate key magnates and prelates from court. He did not disable his government by vindictiveness upon the disempowered ministers. Nor did he create new enemies. In fact, so much did he sympathise with the judgement of those who had supported Mortimer that a year later, in January 1332, he announced that a grant made before October 1330 was not questionable merely on the grounds that it was made in the time of 'evil counsellors'.[13] Mortimer had not been a bad administrator. He had committed only one unforgivable sin in Edward's eyes. He had appropriated Edward's royal power.

*

It is particularly unfortunate for the biographer that the sorts of documents which survive from the fourteenth century – financial accounts, administrative and legal records, royal writs and chronicles written by clerks with one eye on posterity and the other on morality – rarely give an impression of how much fun was had at court. The weight of evidence is always on the side of business, whether the king's or God's. Nevertheless, we can be confident that Edward was ecstatic at his success in capturing Mortimer, and, as soon as the man was dead, he revelled in his position. As Sir Thomas Gray put it, 'so this king led a gay life in jousts and tournaments and entertaining ladies'.[14]

Edward certainly enjoyed the jousts and tournaments which Gray mentioned. We can point to a whole gamut of tournaments, games, staged battles, promenades and masked events provided by Edward, rather like a Roman Emperor providing games for the entertainment of his citizens. These events, whether private (for a few dozen nobles and knights) or public (for the citizens of London) all helped Edward recreate the cult of kingship. They were dramatic events too, with the emphasis on spectacle. For the games at Guildford, on 1 and 6 January 1331, Edward ordered canvas and Spanish wool to be purchased to make 'the hair and hides of men and deer', perhaps to be used in mock hunts.[15] For the same games he also ordered two banners and four pennons to be made, presumably for the two 'armies' which would compete in the tournament, and 'ten dozen false faces complete with beards, both for knights and squires'. Masks became a common element of Edward's games. So too were mock animals and mythical beasts. The costumes of merchants, friars, devils, dragons, angels and women never ceased to be popular, and were still being invented for Edward's entertainments twenty years later.[16]

What is often overlooked about all this display is that it was not just an occasional happening, it was a regular occurrence. To get an idea of just how regular, we have to examine Edward's accounts for references to payments for armour and costumes. Of course, many festivities have left little or no trace, when only a small amount of armour was purchased specially. Nevertheless, it is reasonable to estimate that Edward attended some sort of 'games' on a monthly basis in the summer and on the major feast days in winter: so a total of about ten or eleven tournaments per year, each lasting between two and four days.[17] In between these were the preparations for the events. And of course the events themselves were in many respects training exercises for real battles and duels. Edward was encouraging his subjects to live the romantic chivalric life. For Philippa and her ladies at court this took the form of a massive display of wealth through their rich and varied appearance, and extravagance in practically everything they did. For Edward's knights, it took the form of regular displays of prowess in the joust, and dressing up and acting archetypal roles from popular culture and imagination. Edward was leading the royal family in a recreation of a semi-legendary realm. His purpose was a demonstration of absolute royalty. It was the biggest pro-royal propaganda statement since his grandfather Edward I had constructed a whole series of castles in the newly conquered north of Wales, including one (Carnarvon) modelled on Constantinople, capital of the Eastern Roman empire. If Froissart's chronicle with its tournaments and feasts, romantic deeds and chivalric honour seems far-fetched, it is not because it was trying to misrepresent Edward's court, it is because it was trying to represent it faithfully.

Absolute royalty in 1331 harked back to one figure above all others, King Arthur. The Arthurian legends had, for a number of years, offered various kings the model for a band of knights who were indomitable and who would win fame, love and virtue. In his old age Edward I had tried to create just such a band to wage war against the Scots; it had failed, partly due to its size (more than two hundred knights) and partly due to Edward II's lack of determination to continue his father's war. Edward III imagined his band of knights in a new way. If he was to be the new Arthur, then he too needed a band of close-knit, peerless Knights of the Round Table. The late thirteenth-century Round Table, which now hangs at Winchester, has places for twenty-four knights as well as the king.[18] Later Edward formed a chivalric band with a similar number of knights (twenty-six as opposed to twenty-five). Over and over again in Edward's accounts of the 1330s we read of aketons (embroidered, padded tournament jackets), tunics and mantles being made for small groups of men. Edward's vision of his companionship was simple: a group of about two dozen friends, brothers-in-arms. From the beginning of his reign there was an attempt to make the Arthurian legends come true. If the Round Table could be made a reality, there was no reason why Edward's knights could not actually sit around it, nor any reason why they should not be as brave as the legendary knights of King Arthur. They had already begun to show their courage. It is no coincidence that the first set of aketons for a band of courtiers was made for the men who had assisted in the capture of Mortimer.[19]

Edward III's vision of kingship cannot be separated from the legends of King Arthur. So strong was their pull that Edward visited Glastonbury – Arthur's legendary burial place – soon after he took power, in December 1331.[20] There were other examples of bonded knighthood for him to draw upon too. In Castile, Alfonso XI had recently established his Order of the Band, a group of knights distinguished by their extravagant dress.[21] Before that even, in the 1290s, the Count of Holland had established a tourneying society.[22] And then there were the religious knights. Edward's first home as baby, Bisham Priory, had been a house of the Knights Templar. He would have remembered nothing of this place from his living there, but he would have passed it many times in later years, and he cannot have been unaware that once there had existed in England an order of knights who dedicated themselves to fight for the patrimony of Jesus Christ, the Holy Land. The very oaths sworn by knights when they received knighthood exhorted them to noble deeds and Christian virtues: to higher purposes than self-aggrandizement. It was these higher purposes which Edward hoped would appeal to his own company of knights.

We might have expected this burst of knightly expectation, tourneying and chivalric virtue to have been accompanied by a range of rewards liberally scattered amongst the men who had freed Edward from Mortimer. This was not the case. The rewards were few. Montagu was rewarded with the lordship of Denbigh for leading the plot to arrest Mortimer, which was fitting, as that lordship had been Mortimer's reward for freeing the country from the previous royal manipulator, Hugh Despenser. Men such as the earl of Lancaster and the lawyer Geoffrey le Scrope were also rewarded, and certain knights who had taken part in the arrest received charters in their favour. But there were no huge grants of land and titles. For several years no knight who had assisted in the attack of 1330 was advanced in rank. Edward was fastidiously careful not to be seen to appoint another favourite who would grow rich, ambitious and assume Mortimer's place. Men under Edward III would have to earn their titles and glory. Relieving the king of Mortimer's influence was merely a first step.

There were other reasons not to distribute rewards liberally so early in his career. Edward was still under age – he only turned nineteen in November 1331 – and although he had taken control of the realm he had yet to prove himself as a leader. His letters at this time are marked by his eagerness to ask for advice, whether from parliament or the pope. His approach to his royal status was hands-on and immediate, but his approach to overseas and military affairs was tentative. Would his lords and knights trust his judgement on the field of battle? Would men follow his orders in the face of danger? Although it had been prophesied that he would be an all-conquering king, that was not prophesied to happen during his father's lifetime, and Edward did not yet know whether his father was alive or dead. All he knew in 1331 was that it had been foretold that his father would lose all his lands and then regain them and more, and that he would die overseas.[23] His father had now lost all his lands. If Edward were to leave the realm and if some lord seized the opportunity to reinstate his father, if he was still in Britain, the prophecy might yet come true.

Thus we can see that the consolidation of his reign was Edward's priority in 1331. Every statement was carefully designed to reflect his royalty, from the organising of a tournament to the creation of his crest: a crown surmounted by a gem-encrusted gold eagle.[24] But although we may see the process of 'absolute royalty' as layer on layer of propaganda, we should not presume it was cynically done. This was part of his real identity: he was reinforcing his legitimacy, unlike Mortimer whose propaganda had been concealing his illicit use of authority. We cannot separate the image that Edward wanted to project – his vision of kingship – from the nineteen-year-old man himself. In Edward's own eyes, he really *was* the new Arthur. It had been prophesied thus; now it was up to him to make the prophesies come true.

*

In 1331 Edward wrote to the pope asking whether he should go to Ireland 'which needed much reformation'.[25] At the same time he asked about 'crossing the sea', by which he seems to have been asking a question about whether he should go on crusade.[26] The pope's answer to the latter question was that all Christian princes should go on a crusade. His answer to the former was that, if England was safe, then Edward could travel, if his presence in Ireland would do some good, although he ought to delegate the 'reformation' of the country to someone else. Edward summoned the young earl of Ulster and the archbishop of Dublin to come secretly to him in England to advise him on his planned trip to Ireland, and even set a date for his journey there in 1332.[27] But one has to wonder why Edward was asking the pope about visiting a part of his own kingdom, and why he needed the earl to come to him to advise him on his going there, especially since he never actually went.

Traditional explanations of Edward's Irish interest have been based on the lawlessness of Ireland in 1331. One might reasonably speculate that Edward was trying to impress the pope with his concern for the more lawless reaches of his kingdom and the Holy Land. Every Christian ruler in the middle ages was engaged in a constant public relations battle with the pope, who organised much international diplomacy, acted as a mediator in conflicts, appointed the archbishops, bishops and archdeacons throughout Christendom, and thus had much influence in the internal and external affairs of any country. But with a man so given to secret business and propaganda as Edward, it is worth asking a much more radical question. Was Edward seeking information from the pope regarding his father's possible whereabouts in Ireland?

This is an exceedingly difficult question to answer. But it is worth considering in regard to these requests of 1331. Edward may have been eager to go to Ireland not just for the reformation of the country but perhaps also to ransack Mortimer's castles there for information regarding his father's whereabouts. In this respect there is some evidence that Edward II was taken to Ireland after Kent's execution. This is a document known as the Fieschi letter: an account of Edward II's later life up to and including the year 1335 written at Avignon by a papal notary, Manuel Fieschi. This has hitherto been considered by scholars to be a contemporary forgery. However, the main reason for supposing this was the long-held assumption that Edward II had died in Berkeley Castle in 1327. That we now know that Edward II was alive in 1330 does not automatically make the Fieschi letter genuine, but it allows us to consider its contents seriously, and there are a number of reasons to consider that it was written in good faith (see Appendix Three). In particular it states that Edward II was taken to Ireland after Kent's death. If this was the case, Edward might have heard from one of Maltravers' men that his father had been taken to Ireland in 1330, and might have presumed he was still there, or Mortimer's agents there knew what had happened to him.

Alternatively, we might consider another possible attempt to locate his father. The Fieschi letter suggests that, after Mortimer's execution, Edward II was released from captivity in Ireland and crossed to Normandy in the guise of a pilgrim. This would have been in early 1331. On 3 April 1331 Edward III suddenly departed from court with about twenty men, all dressed as if going on pilgrimage, to Northern France. Adam Murimuth noted the king's journey in his chronicle. He stated that Edward, Montagu and the bishop of Winchester, with about fifteen other knights crossed the sea dressed as merchants. They had it proclaimed in their absence that they had gone abroad 'on pilgrimage and for no other reason', and that John of Eltham was appointed custodian of the realm until the king returned.[28] Murimuth supposed that Edward had gone in disguise to cover up the fact that he was going to swear homage to King Philip for Aquitaine. Modern scholars have tended to agree, on the basis that Edward had failed to do homage properly before, and therefore needed to repeat his aborted performance of homage to Philip's satisfaction.[29] But this is far from certain, not least because Philip had just agreed – on 9 March 1331 – that no fresh performance of homage was necessary; all Philip required was a letter assuring him that Edward had meant to swear to be Philip's liege man.[30] Even though Edward did indeed meet Philip at Pont-Sainte-Maxence, his journey may have had a double purpose, especially as it was clearly arranged in great haste and he was hot on the heels of his father, according to the Fieschi letter. It is also significant that in setting off, Edward rode at very high speed, travelling from Eltham to Dover in a day. We cannot rule out the possibility that a merchant with royal connections had informed Edward that his father was travelling with pilgrims in Normandy, causing Edward to set off immediately with a number of trusted men to look for him.

Both of these possible attempts to find Edward II are tentative, and from a historical perspective it is safest to presume that Edward had no second agenda in going to Normandy or Ireland in 1331. However, from a biographical perspective it is important to be aware that Edward may have been conscientiously undertaking a search for the man, in the most extreme secrecy. In addition, there are other circumstantial indications that he was trying to discover his father's whereabouts. On 31 May he despatched Giles of Spain to seek out Thomas Gurney on the Continent and to bring him back to England.[31] It is very interesting that the man he chose for the task of rounding up the 'murderers' was one of the earl of Kent's supporters, and thus a man who knew Edward II was probably still alive. Later in the year Edward became aware of a dispute between his clerk, John Melburn, and William Fieschi (a kinsman of Manuel Fieschi). William had been removed from his prebend at Strensall in May 1330 and Edward had caused it to be given to John. Before October 1331 Edward discovered that William was attempting 'to draw John into a plea outside the realm concerning certain matters which ought to be brought to the king's attention'.[32] Edward prohibited his preferred candidate, John, from leaving the country until October, and then, when he did let him go to Avignon, he had strict instructions not to engage in other matters apart from his right to the prebend. The evidence – as so often with Edward's secret business – permits nothing more than a question to be raised, but when the question is so important it cannot be ignored. It might well be that Edward heard hints as early as 1331 of as to where his father might be, or where he might be going, and how safe he was, or how compromised.

*

After his incognito dash to France, Edward threw himself back into promoting his chivalric regality in England. At the beginning of May he and his men took part in a tournament at Dartford. It was hosted by William Clinton, and Edward fought as a knight on Clinton's side. This is the first recorded instance of him taking part in a tournament as a common knight, not as the commander. In putting himself at risk, he was encouraging his knights to respect him for his valour and for his own qualities, not just his rank. And he did put himself at risk. At the end of this tournament, as he was leaving the field, his horse – a magnificent destrier (warhorse) – threw him to the ground. So displesed was Edward, and so angry, that he changed it for a humble palfrey. Although several of his knights were surprised, and declared it was not becoming for him to ride such a modest steed, Edward was later proved to have been fortunate, for his hot-tempered and sweating destrier threw its rider into a deep part of the river. Had Edward still been riding it, dressed in his armour, he would have drowned.[33]

One month later Edward took part in another tournament at Stepney, a four-day event held to celebrate the first birthday of his son, Edward of Woodstock.[34] This event was proclaimed by Robert Morley, who fought against all comers with fifteen men, all dressed in green cloaks decorated with golden arrows.[35] In late September yet another tournament was held, this time at the invitation of William Montagu. Unusually, it was held in the very centre of the city of London, in Cheapside. After a mass sung in memory of his father, and the usual pittances had been doled out to paupers in order to keep up the appearance of his father's decease, Edward joined Montagu and his other chosen knights in dressing as Tartars and leading in procession the 'most noble and most beautiful women of the realm', all dressed in red velvet tunics with white hoods (the colours of St George). Each woman was led by a silver chain attached to a knight's right hand.[36] Edward himself led his sister, Eleanor, in the procession, but no doubt paid attention to the damsels around him. Extending invitations to ladies of merchant class was novel. Although the reference to their beauty might explain Montagu's readiness to invite them, in Hainault it was customary for the nobility to fraternise with the richest merchants, and thus the inspiration may have been Queen Philippa's, not Montagu's. Either way, the extension of royal favour to the merchant class was a marked development of Edward's reign, and led to many leading merchants and mayors being knighted.[37]

Unfortunately on this particular occasion, there was a less than glorious start to proceedings as the high wooden stand in which Queen Philippa was sitting collapsed, and many ladies and knights were injured. Edward furiously declared he would take revenge on the workmen, but before he found the men responsible – whom he would probably have hanged on the spot – Queen Philippa herself begged for him to spare their lives.[38] It was typical of Queen Philippa that she should seek mercy for the men. And it was equally typical of Edward that he should immediately respond to the challenge of disaster with threatened force. Edward did spare the workmen; it did not matter to him whether they lived or died, only that he was the one who made the decision. But perhaps the most telling point with regard to this anecdote is that despite the near death of his wife, he ordered the tournament to continue. Edward was a young man who needed to control events, and, though he might have been persuaded not to hang his negligent workmen, nothing was going to turn him from his intended path.

*

Edward's strong mental grasp of a situation, and instinct to control it, was very similar to that exhibited by his grandfather, Edward I. Edward felt a strong affinity towards 'the Hammer of the Scots', as his grandfather was called, who had died six years before he was born. He regularly made spiritual gifts at his grandfather's tomb in Westminster Abbey and treasured the knife that an assassin had used in an attempt to murder Edward I in the Holy Land (on which occasion Edward I had overpowered and killed his assailant).[39] We might also fairly assume that the genes of the elder Edward conditioned the temperament of the younger. But just as important was the legacy of the man's reputation. For the Hammer of the Scots had not just been a warrior, he had been a great lawgiver and a great leader.

Edward had made much progress in the year since Mortimer's fall, but in terms of leadership he had hardly proved himself. His entertainments were glorious spectacles, but so had been his father's musical interludes and carnivalesque capers. Tournaments were entertaining, and they showed personal mettle, and his companions' collective spirit, but they were not an indication of responsibility, and hardly a measure of political judgement. For that, Edward needed another proving ground, and one in which his grandfather had excelled. Parliament.

A week after the Cheapside tournament, parliament met at Westminster. Edward had agreed the previous year that parliament should meet annually, and although later in his reign he did not always abide by this resolution, for the moment it suited his purposes to do so. It gave him the perfect opportunity to assert himself – and more importantly, to be seen to assert himself – over his nobles. He also came with a specific agenda. He asked the lords to give up the unpopular practice of 'maintenance': shielding their tenants from the law when they had committed a crime.[40] This had been going on for some years, and Edward was directly confronting his nobles by issuing what was in effect a manifesto of fair rule for all, in line with the coronation oaths he had sworn.[41] His request that they give up such practices – rather than forbidding them outright – indicates vestiges of nervousness, or uncertainty, but he clearly hoped to mark out a policy. Unfairness and extrajudicial processes were aspects of lordly domination which he had known only too well.

One particular question raised at the parliament of 1331 was whether England should go to war with France. Edward wanted to know specifically whether he should seek to recover the lands lost to the English Crown in the war of Saint-Sardos by force or by diplomacy. Parliament responded that diplomacy was the preferred course. Edward consequently embarked on a tortuous series of diplomatic negotiations to try to recover the Agenais. Edward himself probably felt that the time was not right for a continental campaign. But the real question here is why he asked parliament at all. Surely, now that Mortimer was dead, and the consolidation of the reign was Edward's priority, he did not need a war? Was the question just put to demonstrate to parliament that he was prepared to listen to their advice?

The diplomatic situation in France was stable but not to Edward's advantage. To paraphrase his mother's words, he had been forced to do homage to the son of a count. France was a sore in his mind. After his claim to the throne of France had been withdrawn, his rival, King Philip, had very soon led the French to a remarkable victory at Cassel against the Flemish. Philip had exhorted his men to feats of daring and chivalry, and they had responded to his leadership. Philip was determined to win glory for France by leading a crusade. Philip's name was becoming synonymous with all the virtues which Edward wanted associated with his own. After Edward's renewal of homage in 1331, Philip had even greater superiority in the chivalric pecking order. Although Philip was much older – he was thirty-eight in 1331 – Edward saw the new French king as a definite rival in fame as well as power and royalty. When Philip first expressed his desire to go on crusade, Edward, not to be outdone, supported him. Thus there was a personal dimension to the struggle. Lastly, Scotland rankled with Edward no less than France, and both kingdoms were bound by an alliance to defend the other against England. When Edward suggested using force to reclaim the Agenais, he was not just suggesting war with France, he was suggesting an armed struggle which would force the Scots to join France and attack England, and thus break their truce.[42]

Edward's relations with Scotland were complicated. He had been forced to ratify the Treaty of Northampton by which he recognised the independence of Robert Bruce's kingdom of Scotland. Bruce had died in 1329, leaving the country in a weak state, with no obvious leader, but Bruce had done his best to ensure the succession. Edward's ten-year-old sister Joan had been married to the seven-year-old king, David II, and her coronation was planned for November 1331. On the other hand, there had been many lords who had never accepted the 'shameful' treaty, due to the loss of their lands north of the border. Edward himself had never forgotten the ignominy of being forced to relinquish part of his kingdom. Nor had he forgotten that the Scots nicknamed his little sister 'Joan Makepeace' on the day she was taken north. He had not forgotten their insults at Stanhope Park, nor their dealings with Isabella and Mortimer rather than him, when he had been the rightful king. As for his sister's marriage, although she was married to his enemy, she was still under age, and so the marriage could not yet have been consummated. That of course was a technicality. The important fact was that Edward was not going to let her status be the cause of his own disinheritance.

As it happened, parliament's decision not to pursue a war in the Agenais was overtaken by events. Edward Balliol emerged as a leader of the claimants of Scottish lands, 'the Disinherited' as they came to be known. Balliol was the son of the ousted king of Scots, John Balliol, who had ruled the country under Edward I. It made perfect sense for Edward to allow this adventurer to try his luck. If he was successful, he would rule Scotland as Edward's client king, and, by keeping the northern border secure, he would permit Edward to concentrate on France. If he was unsuccessful, he would tempt the Scots to break the terms of the truce, so that they would probably appear the aggressors in any subsequent war. Balliol swore homage to Edward, and Edward tacitly gave his approval for Balliol to use English ports to gather and launch his invasion.[43] Several of Edward's friends decided to go with Balliol, including Sir Walter Manny and Sir Thomas Ughtred, and they went with his blessing. Although Edward issued written orders for the sheriffs to stop the invasion, this was almost certainly a smokescreen; it is likely that he also issued verbal orders for the written orders to be disregarded.

For Edward, this new Scottish strategy meant a period of waiting. He spent Christmas 1331 at Wells with Philippa, who was three months pregnant with their second child. They stayed there until the completion of the games on the night of Epiphany (6 January). Presents were exchanged;

Philippa gave Edward a silver goblet and ewer, the goblet being 'enamelled on the outside with images of beautiful castles, ships and beasts, and on the inside with a great castle at the base with its banners unfurled and the king seated in the middle, and enamelled on all sides with the arms of England among leopards bearing the same arms'; the ewer was enamelled with legendary figures: Julius Caesar, Judas Maccabeus, Charlemagne, Roland, Oliver, Arthur, Gawain and Lancelot of the Lake.[44] Philippa must have commissioned this herself, and it is striking that several of the heroes from books in Richard Bury's library are represented. The conqueror of Jerusalem (Judas Maccabeus) sat alongside the conqueror of Europe (Caesar). Philippa knew her husband's tastes well.

While Edward waited for the resolution of Balliol's gamble, he had many other claims on his attention. He was still considering going to Ireland in August 1332.[45] He was concerned about the state of the University of Cambridge. He ordered the arrest of renegade friars wandering around the country. He ordered the bishop of Winchester to arrange the marriage between his sister Eleanor and Reginald, count of Guelderland. He ordered the repair of his castles in Gascony. He responded to the news that Thomas Gurney had been caught in Bayonne. He received ambassadors from Armenia (in relation to a crusade there), Savoy, and the pope: the last exhorting him not to fight the French. He sent ambassadors to Flanders, Rome, France, Portugal and Spain. In March, he urged parliament to encourage Flemish weavers to come to England to teach the English how to improve the making of domestic cloth, his first foray into economic policy. In April, despite parliament's expressed desire that he should put off going on a crusade with Philip of France for three years, he sent the bishop of Winchester to negotiate this, and wrote to the pope about the plan.

As this list shows, economics, family relations, foreign policy, defensive strategy and crusading were all bubbling together in one great royal melting pot. This was merely what a king did. Throughout 1332 we see Edward moving around the country – rarely spending a week in the same place – feasting on the major saints days, attending mass, holding parliament, receiving ambassadors, jousting and granting charters. For relaxation he indulged in hunting, gambling with his friends, and being told chivalric stories of military and romantic prowess. At the end of April the court came to rest at the royal manor of Woodstock, at which it had been decided Philippa would have her next child. There, on 16 June, his first daughter, Isabella, was born.[46] Two weeks after the birth, the king was off again, travelling through Burford to Devizes, to his manor at Clarendon; then, via Abingdon, back to Woodstock to attend the churching of Queen Philippa. Of course, there was a lavish tournament in celebration. No expense was spared in the decoration. The altars of the church itself were decorated in purple silk embroidered with birds, beasts, baboons and snakes, and Philippa's state bed hangings were similarly decorated with these animals and the arms of England and Hainault.[47] The feast that day (19 July) cost more than £292: about ten times the usual daily expenditure on feeding the royal household.[48]

On 12 July, at Woodstock, Edward decided to delay his Irish campaign until Michaelmas, in order to learn the results of Balliol's adventure. Balliol and the disinherited lords landed with eighty-eight ships and fifteen hundred men at Kinghorn on 6 August.[49] They soon met with considerable opposition. Although the southern Scottish forces, under Patrick of Dunbar, were too far away to prevent the landing, the huge army of Donald, earl of Mar, confronted them four days later. Balliol had been led to believe that Donald of Mar would come over to his side, but, now he was actually there, he found Mar planned to slaughter him and all the Disinherited. On the night of 10 August, knowing that thousands of men were ranged against them, and knowing even more men were on their way to assist in the massacre, Balliol and his experienced military adviser, Henry Beaumont, made a desperate decision. They decided to seize the initiative and fight. The longer they delayed, the greater the risk of having to resist an even larger army. The other lords with them were aghast, and accused Beaumont of leading them into a trap. 'By no means', he replied, 'but since the affair has gone so far, for God's sake, let us help ourselves. For no man knows what God has in store for us. Let us think of our great right so as to show we are descended from good knights.' Most inspiring of all, he found a Scotsman who was prepared to show them the ford across the River Earn. That night, while the men-at-arms loyal to the earl of Mar drank the night away on the moor, and their footsoldiers slept, Balliol and Beaumont led their men across the Earn and slaughtered the Scottish footsoldiers in their tents. But as light came up, to their amazement they realised they had only engaged half the enemy, and now the great mass of Mar's men was ranged against them. Desperate measures were called for. Facing death, the English men-at-arms dismounted, and set themselves to form a defensive line of pikes, with archers on the flanks. Beaumont ordered the pikes set into the ground, and the archers to aim at the faces of the oncoming Scottish riders.

Desperate measures they may have been, but what happened that day was truly remarkable. The English archers, well-organised and well-trained, stood their ground and drove the flanks of the Scottish army into the centre of the charge, where they disabled their own compatriots. For centuries the great charge of a body of knights – the utterly destructive fast-moving mass of armoured power – had held sway on the battlefields of Europe. Here, on the slopes of a Scottish moor, Dupplin Moor, everything changed. The archers destroyed the force of the charge. When the Scots front line had finally staggered on to the English pikes, they drove the English back twenty or thirty feet. At that point Lord Stafford cried out: 'Englishmen! Turn your shoulders instead of your chests to the pikes!' A little later another Englishman cried out 'Cheer up, Englishmen, and fight like men, for the Scots in the rear have now begun to fly!' As the chronicler who noted these exclamations recorded, the English took heart, and the Scots were dismayed. The battlefield became a slaughter ground. The same chronicler adds 'a most marvellous thing happened that day, such as was never seen or heard of in any previous battle: the pile of dead rising up from the ground was more than a spear's length in height'.[50]

Back in England, Edward was still thinking about his expedition to Ireland.[51] On 4 August, alarmed at the discontent he was hearing from the Scottish Marches, he gave orders that Lord Percy was to hold the Scottish border, in case the Scots under Patrick of Dunbar invaded. He empowered Percy to raise the men of five counties. Then, at Wigmore on 10 August, he heard that Balliol had landed. A few days later he was told the news of Dupplin Moor. Three Scottish earls had been killed in the battle, along with many thousands of footmen and men-at-arms. English losses were put at two knights, thirty-three esquires and no archers or footsoldiers. It was extraordinary, and Edward could not have anticipated such an outcome. It presented something of a problem too, as Balliol was now in a position to make himself King of Scots or even King of Scotland.[52] Parliament was ordered hastily to assemble on 9 September. Taxes were granted for Edward to place the kingdom on a war footing, if necessary. It was agreed immediately to remove the administration to York, and to hold another, fuller discussion there. The Irish campaign was cancelled.

The strangeness of Balliol's campaign was not yet complete, however. The Scots had regrouped under Sir Andrew Murray and Sir Archibald Douglas. They had also employed the services of the pirate, John Crabb, a man whose viciousness on the seas struck fear into land-loving knights. Crabb set out from Berwick to attack the English vessels, and, though he managed to capture one, the rest of the fleet managed to drive him off. Crabb himself was later captured by Sir Walter Manny.[53] Even more extraordinarily, Murray managed to fall into the hands of his enemy. According to the Lanercost chronicler, he tried to separate Balliol from his army by breaking down the bridge at Roxburgh. Balliol's army 'repaired the bridge with utmost speed, and some of them, not waiting till this was done, plunged into the great river, armed and mounted, and swam across and pursued the flying Scots for eight miles' in which pursuit Murray was seized.[54] Both Crabb and Murray were sent to Edward.

If a man like Crabb had fallen into the hands of Edward I or Edward II, he would have been summarily executed in the most public place possible. Edward did not kill Crabb. Herein we may catch another glimpse of his strategic forgiveness. Crabb was a destructive weapon, and a rare one at that, being used to maritime warfare. He was also a man without loyalty, and so as a weapon he could be turned to anyone's advantage. Having received the man in chains from Sir Walter Manny, Edward could offer Crabb a reason to be loyal: to serve the man who would permit him to live. This was not just opportunism, it was forethought too. Through it Edward gained a man who would one day prove very useful.

Balliol was crowned King of Scots at Scone Abbey on 24 September. Two months later he wrote to Edward laying out how he saw his relationship with the English king. Sensitive to the fact that he had, by his coronation, disinherited Edward's sister, he kindly offered to marry her (if she was willing) and to make her queen of the Scots. Parliament discussed the coronation in early December. Edward's lawyer, Geoffrey le Scrope, laid out the three alternatives: to support David II in line with the 1328 agreement, to support the new king, Balliol, or to dispense with them both and allow Edward to assert his rights in Scotland by force as overlord of the kingdom. Edward himself made clear he wanted the 1328 treaty to be considered null and void on account of it having been made while he was still a child. But as to what he should do otherwise, parliament could not decide.

This would have left Edward with a problem but for the next event in Edward Balliol's strange saga. Sir Archibald Douglas and Patrick of Dunbar managed to surprise Balliol at Annan in a night attack during the Christmas festivities. Most of the men with Balliol were killed in their nightshirts; Balliol himself only escaped by smashing through a partition wall, and jumping on to a horse and riding away bareback, without a harness, towards Carlisle. In losing his kingdom as suddenly as he had won it, Balliol had avoided being betrayed by Edward, whose definite preference was to reclaim all of Scotland as his own.

Parliament was still cautious. Edward was now twenty, eager to prove himself and desperate to avenge the treaty of 1328. Those who arrived at York in January could see that the young man was determined to lead his band of knights to war. A cautious parliament was no match for him. Although he would have preferred all the lords, prelates and commons to support him in his military endeavour, he also wanted parliament to remember that they were merely there to advise him. They might have agreed to his father's deposition but they were still ruled by him, not vice versa. He had made a statement to that effect, in the parliament of September 1331, when he had refused a petition to restore Edmund Mortimer to all his ancestral lands.[55] He had replied that such a matter was his own prerogative, and he would do as he saw fit. Now he did as he saw fit again. When the Chancellor declared that parliament had failed to come to a conclusion on the Scottish situation, Edward took matters out of their hands. He appointed a council of six wise men to advise him. These were the archbishop of York, the bishop of Norwich, Henry Percy, William Clinton, William Denholme and William Shareshull.[56]

As the knights and representatives of the counties made their way home-ward from York, they may have reflected on the events and presumed that the situation was a difficult one. If so, they were deluding themselves. The situation was simple. Edward wanted war, and Edward was now old enough, trusted enough and most of all confident enough to have his chance of glory. Parliament had disempowered itself with regard to foreign policy. Had it been united, and if the lords and commons had spoken together against any war in Scotland, then Edward would have been restrained. But they had not been united, and Edward had encouraged their disunity by having Geoffrey le Scrope offer a variety of strategies: to support David II, Balliol, or Edward himself. What le Scrope had not suggested was that nothing should be done. The only way parliament, if divided, could restrain the king was by witholding necessary taxation. But parliament had already voted sufficient funds to be allocated to the defence of the north. The six wise men were not chosen to advise on whether to go to war but, as 'wardens of the Marches' to help Edward make the attack seem like a defensive manoeuvre. That was at least how Edward justified his actions to the pope. He was defending the north of his kingdom.

*

Edward spent March 1333 at Pontefract Castle in Yorkshire, making arrange-ments for the attack. He already had a strategy. He would besiege Berwick, the prosperous town on the north of the River Tweed. This was shadowed by the strong castle which had fallen to the Scots in 1318 but which had resisted the English the following year. It was the sole southern Scottish castle of sufficient importance to the Scots that they had reinforced its defences rather than destroy them. Before Edward left Pontefract he sent orders for two great siege engines to be built and shipped to Berwick, and for teams of quarrymen to make hundreds of large stone missiles.[57] He also gave orders for gunpowder to be obtained from a York apothecary.[58]

Gunpowder – or, more precisely, the use of firearms – was a recent inno-vation. Although gunpowder had been known in Britain for at least eighty years, the first unequivocal documentation attesting to the use of cannon in Europe dates to 1326. In that year, Walter Milemete included an illustration of a cannon in his *On the Nobility, Wisdom and Prudence of Kings* (presented to Edward). That same year, orders were given by the Council of Florence for metal cannons and cannonballs to be made: the earliest certain appearance of cannon in Italy. Milemete's gun was shaped like a tall bronze vase lying on its side, and an example of just such a bronze gun was discovered at Loshult in Sweden in the nineteenth century.[59] Modern tests have shown that it probably had a range in excess of three-quarters of a mile.[60] Edward probably saw examples used in 1327 on the Stanhope campaign, when Mortimer had employed 'crakkis of wer' (as the Scottish chronicler called them).[61] So, in 1333, Edward was employing the most recent military technology, tried perhaps only once previously in British military history.

The really startling thing about this is not that Edward was prepared to try new methods; it is the irony that he – the great king of chivalry, the champion of the joust – was the man who more than any other medieval leader was responsible for the development of the gun, the instrument which ultimately led to the destruction of both chivalry and jousting. It seems paradoxical, until we recall that knighthood was a means of channelling military strength and encouraging men to fight. Newly made knights often died in their first battle, attempting to prove themselves worthy. Knighthood was basically a ritualised form of motivating and mobilising society for war, and the men around Edward – his new Arthurian knights – were highly motivated and well-equipped. This is why in March, knowing the country was on the verge of conflict, Edward had ordered every man of sufficient income – forty pounds per year – to become a knight. Edward's chivalric ethos was not just a romantic, wistful throwback to the days of yore, but a military operation. In later years he organised the casting of guns and the manufacture on a large scale at the Tower of London: more than two tons of gunpowder being made there in the year 1346–47.[62]

In his adoption of new techniques and strategies, it is evident that Edward had the ability to grasp new ideas quickly and exploit their potential. He seized on the principle underlying the victory at Dupplin Moor and summoned Henry Beaumont to advise him at Berwick. New types of siege engines were probably another innovation.[63] And the presence and use of ships under the captured Flemish pirate, John Crabb, again shows an instinctive grasp of how best to direct his resources. Crabb knew the walls of Berwick inside out, including their weaknesses. He had defended them successfully against the English in 1319.

In April the country mobilised. Men marched towards Berwick from across England and Wales. Corn was transported by road from sixteen counties in preparation for the siege. The abbot of St Mary's, York, was directed to act as an unofficial war treasurer.[64] The men of Tadcaster were ordered to assist in buying more stones for the siege engines. The archbishops of York and Canterbury were both requested to 'exhort' their clergy to pray for the success of the siege. On 10 April Edward made an offering of a red and silk cloth embroidered with gold at Durham Cathedral.[65] On the 23rd the siege began, in advance of his arrival, and by the 30th Edward arrived at Alnwick. After responding to the pro-Scottish entreaties of King Philip of France with the statement that the Scots had invaded his land several times, he proceeded to Tweedmouth, just across the river from the fortified town and castle. With the king's arrival there on 9 May, the siege proper began.

Edward ordered the water supply to the town to be cut off. The four aqueducts were broken.[66] Then, day after day, the siege engines projected boulders into the town, and the guns blasted away at the walls. Edward had made a 'fair town of pavilions outside the walls' and built ditches around them, so that the attackers themselves were well-defended.[67] Within Berwick houses were destroyed and churches razed to the earth. Food began to grow short in the town, but still the people held out, hoping that the main Scots army would arrive and relieve the siege, despite Crabb's purposeful directing of the guns.

The siege dragged on. While Edward waited he gave some time to family concerns. He organised the raising of money towards his sister's marriage to the Count of Guelderland from the prelates (which had taken place the previous year), and he gave to his three-year-old son, Edward, the title of earl of Chester, which he himself had received as a baby. He took his wife Philippa to visit the Holy Isle of Lindisfarne and its monastery. Then, having returned her to the safety of Bamburgh Castle, he returned to the pavilions, and the waiting. He played chess and dice, losing seventy-six shillings on 8 June. Two days later he lost another five shillings. Tedium set in, between the ear-splitting blasts of the guns and the distant crash of stone shot smashing into the wooden houses of the town. The ennui was slightly relieved the following week, when he heard that his sister had given birth to his first nephew. But soon it was back to gambling. Having lost twelve pounds in his pavilion on 25 June, Edward ordered a direct attack on the castle.[68]

On 27 June, in an assault carefully planned by someone with knowledge of tides as well as Berwick's mural weaknesses – one thinks immediately of John Crabb – the English ships and landward soldiers went into action. Seeing the ships approaching the town, at high tide, the Scots set alight a quantity of pre-prepared tar-soaked faggots, and launched them at the assailants. But their strategy met with disaster, for some of the faggots went awry and were blown back over the walls. These set some houses alight. The fire then spread to other buildings, until their desperate defence against the English had become a defence against the ravages of the fire. Edward watched, contented, and when they sent to him begging for a truce, he assented, on condition that Sir Alexander Seton, commander of the castle and town, surrender twelve hostages. The hostages were all to be children of the prominent men of the town.[69] The truce was to last fifteen days; if the Scots army had not come to relieve the town by then (thus allowing Edward a pitched battle), then its occupants would surrender.

Seton had already lost two sons in the war against England. The eldest, Alexander, had been killed resisting Balliol the previous year. The next, William, had drowned the previous day while fighting off the English attack from the Tweed. He had tried to jump from one Scottish boat on to an English one, but a sudden surge in the river, which was tidal, swept his vessel away, and he had fallen between the two boats and drowned. Now Seton's last remaining son, Thomas, was sent with eleven other sons of prominent men to Edward as hostages. Sir Alexander probably thought that this would be taken as a gesture of sincerity. Ironically, his own compatriots would destroy all hope of that.

On the last day of the truce, Sir Archibald Douglas reached Berwick. Behind him marched the whole Scottish army, drawn from all over the kingdom.[70] His men forded the Tweed and razed the English settlement of Tweedmouth on the other side of the river, killing the inhabitants and burning the buildings. Edward could only look across the river as the smoke rose, and as the Scots crossed back over by low tide to hurl meat and bread over the walls of Berwick to the besieged. Some of the Scots under Sir William Keith even tried to cross the bridge, which had been in ruins for the last thirty years; and after a sharp engagement with Sir William Montagu, they managed to enter the town. Keith claimed that he had relieved the siege, and, in view of this, he replaced Seton as commander of the town and the castle. Counter to Seton's orders, he declared there would be no surrender.

Edward was utterly furious, not just because of the relief of the town on the last day of the truce but by the continued defiance of his will. The relief had come from the English side of the river, he claimed, and therefore was not valid. He *wanted* a battle. But most of all he was angry because the Scots were not yet afraid of him. He wanted them to bend to his will. He was determined to rid them of the notion that he was as weak as his father. When Douglas brashly sent messengers announcing that the Scots would now attack England, and in particular Bamburgh Castle, where

Queen Philippa was lodged, Edward decided only a vindictive and personal attack on the Scots' leadership would make an impression. He ordered a particularly high gallows to be erected outside the gates of the town. And then, when it stood there, defying the Scots, he dragged out young Thomas Seton, the last and youngest of the Seton sons, and hanged him there and then, in front of his father's eyes.[71] He sent a message to Seton and Keith that each day he would hang two more of the boys, until they were all dead. And that would teach the Scots to break their covenants.

It was a hideously cruel act. But the hanging of Thomas Seton more than anything else impressed Edward's seriousness upon his adversaries. They now saw that this was no self-indulgent Edward II-figure; this was a new Hammer of the Scots, with the capacity for utter ruthlessness. Rather than see the high gallows used again, Keith sent messengers to seek another truce. On 15 July it was agreed that if the castle and town had not been relieved by vespers on 19 July, the following day everything would be handed over to Edward. Keith was confident that the huge number of men with Douglas and their long years' experience of fighting the English would prove more than a match for Edward's army. Under the terms of the new agreement, Keith left Berwick and crossed the Tweed to find Douglas, who was destroying the neighbourhood of Morpeth in an attempt to draw Edward's attention away from Berwick.[72] The two men decided they would meet the English in a full-scale battle.

On the morning of Monday 19 July the Scots began to move over the hills towards the English position. Even though they tried to approach from the north, hidden by the higher ground, Edward's scouts soon established where they were. The Scots intended to appear on the higher hill in the full force of their numbers, which chroniclers on both sides state far outnumbered the English, hoping to terrify their enemy. Edward arranged his army on Halidon Hill, a carefully chosen position. To reach it the Scots would have to descend and cross a marsh, and then climb the steep slope. In case they tried to relieve the town from another angle, by skirting the English, Edward despatched five hundred men to guard the approach to the town.

The Scots drew up their forces, and waited. Edward had set his army into three battalions, facing them. The battalion on his right was commanded by his uncle, the earl of Norfolk, and Sir Edward Bohun. That on his left was placed under the command of Edward Balliol. Edward himself assumed command of the central battalion. Then, with Dupplin Moor in mind, Edward ordered all his knights to do a very unknightly thing: they were all to dismount and fight on foot. Edward alone remained mounted, but only so he could ride up and down the lines of his men, urging them to win honour for their country, and to avenge the murders which the Scots had perpetrated in the north of England. Then he too dismounted, and sent his warhorse away. This was the moment he had been trained for, and for which he had waited all his life. Above him, and all around him, the cross of St George flapped on a thousand pennons. Beside him, was displayed the banner of St Cuthbert, whose shrine he had visited at Durham.[73] This was the ultimate test of royalty. He took his place on foot in the front line of his battalion.

The Scots delayed, waiting for the tide to shift. With superior numbers they believed they could force the English back into the swollen river.[74] Their champion, a giant called Turnbull, stepped forward and challenged any Englishman to single combat. A Norfolk knight, Sir Robert Benhale, begged Edward to allow him to answer this challenge. Edward assented. Benhale proved the better man, his sword play being quicker than that of the giant, whose limbs he sliced off.[75] It was a good sign for Edward. But then, among men nervous with the approach of battle, he watched as the Scots advanced. There were thousands of them. And as they advanced he heard Sir Archibald Douglas call out the chilling declaration: 'No prisoners'. No one was to be taken for ransom.[76] Edward had no choice but to respond with a similar call. The English too would fight to the death.

Edward and his commanders had chosen the site well, knowing the Scots would have to come at them in order to relieve the town. The Scots' only alternative was an indirect approach between the hill and the river, and that was too dangerous by far. But the Scots had the advantage of numbers, and now they chose to charge directly at the English ranks. As they lumbered forward, they were slowed by the marsh and the slope. The English watched, and waited, and when the Scots were committed, the trumpets sounded for the English archers to attack. Immediately wave after wave of arrows flew down the slope into their enemies' faces. Then Balliol's own trumpets blasted the infantry advance, and his men rushed forward to engage the front line. The Scots, turning their heads away from the arrows, could not muster their courage to charge and found themselves trapped between their fellow men still advancing behind them and the deadly arrows ahead. So it was with those facing the central English battalion. Edward himself was the first man to throw himself into the difficult, hand-to-hand combat.[77] Soon the whole hill was a mass of bitter, fighting, dying men, terrified by the arrows, furiously battling for every inch of hillside. Ranks of brave Scotsmen came forward, but none could break through the English lines, not even those who had been detailed specially to cut their way through to the town under Archibald Douglas. These men especially won the respect of the English, their fighting spirit pushing them on far beyond the point when their adversaries believed they would retreat.

Towards evening, the men fighting uphill, wearied by the effort and dispirited by the constant raining down of arrows, began to slip back. Balliol's battalion broke through the Scots' lines, forcing them to retreat and then flee. As soon as this first section was in flight, Edward knew it was only a matter of time before the others too would break. He pressed his advantage, yelling encouragement to his hard-pressed men. And they responded. Although the earl of Ross shouted a challenge for all the Scots to fight to the death, and made a stand, the rearmost had already begun to make their escape. The second and third lines of the Scots retreated, then turned and ran for their lives. The earl of Ross stood his ground, and fought on, as the men beside him were hacked down one by one, until eventually he too was killed.

Now Edward sent for the horses. He wanted revenge for the insults, peace treaties, disrespect, and the hostility shown lately to his queen. He had much to prove. The Scots were now set to pay for the years of humility which had been forced upon him by Bruce, Philip of France and Mortimer. And having offered no quarter, despite facing the king of England – their overlord, in Edward's opinion – they could expect no mercy. He rode with his knights here and there in pursuit of the Scots, striking down everyone whom he could reach. As one contemporary put it:

> there men might have seen the doughtiness of the noble King Edward and of his men, how manly they were in pursuit of the Scots, who ran in dread. And there might men have seen many a Scottish man cast down on to the earth, dead, and their banners displayed and hacked to pieces, and many a good hauberk of steel bathed in their blood, and many times the Scots regrouped in companies, and every time they were defeated.[78]

The devastation was utter. No quarter had been ordered and no quarter was given. Most of the earls of Scotland who had not been killed at Dupplin Moor lay dead: Carrick, Ross, Lennox and Menteith. Sir Archibald Douglas himself was killed. Chroniclers reckoned the Scottish dead in tens of thousands. Berwick had fallen. The Scots had been defeated. But far more than this, Edward had proved himself in battle, and against superior numbers. His enemy had flaunted its strength at him, and had issued the challenge of a fight to the death, and he had responded. He emphasised his point on the day after the battle, when he ordered one hundred captured Scotsmen to be beheaded.[79] No prisoners. The town and castle of Berwick was a smoking, dilapidated wreck, largely destroyed by his guns and siege engines. Amid the gore and terrible destruction, Edward had proved himself a terrifying king.

FIVE

Warrior of God

Halidon Hill answered the two most important questions in Edward's mind in 1333. He had proved he could lead his men into battle – a test of his confidence in himself as much as theirs in him – and success had shown that God favoured him. In England there was general delight at 'this gracious victory', as one chronicler described it.[1] After the battle, the Scots surrendered Berwick, and Edward returned to England 'with much joy and worship'. In London, the citizens followed their clergy in procession from St Pauls to Trinity Church, solemnly singing thanks to God. The English poet Laurence Minot was moved to write his first extant poem, and exemplified the shifting of opinion, from his initial fears – 'of England had my heart great care / when Edward first went to war' – to his pride in England's victory, which he specifically associated with the king: 'the Lord of Heaven might Edward lead / and maintain him as he well may'.[2] All the 'great care' and caution of parliament in January 1333 was forgotten.

Thanks were due to God as well as to his fellow fighters. Three days after the battle Edward sent letters to all the archbishops and bishops in England, Wales and Gascony requesting that they give thanks for his victory. A week later he set out south, first making for Bamburgh Castle, where Queen Philippa was waiting for him.[3] He stopped at most of the shrines on the way south and gave alms at each of them.[4] He returned to Durham, and gave thanks at the tomb of Saint Cuthbert, beneath whose banner he had fought. As he approached East Anglia he made a brief visit to the great shrine at Walsingham. Some chroniclers described this victorious journey southwards as a pilgrimage.[5] He gave alms to those who had been injured in the battle, and paid a hermit who lived near Norham to assist in the burial of the dead.[6] In order to commemorate his victory he ordered a nunnery in the locality to be repaired at his cost. It was a symbol of victory in more ways than one. The money was to be paid by the people of the wrecked town of Berwick.

Edward clearly wanted to project a religious dimension to his victory, to emphasise that he – and thus the English – had been favoured by God. But how religious was he? Edward's reputation as a paragon of religious kingship was firmly established by the end of the 1340s, and that reputation never diminished in his lifetime. But was it real or just another part of his chivalric propaganda programme?

In considering this we need to be aware of a whole string of problems affecting past judgements on his religious life. First it has to be said that most nineteenth- and early twentieth-century historians labelled Edward unreligious because they wished to castigate him as a warmonger. Since their own interpretation of Christian doctrine excluded the promotion of war, they decided Edward could not possibly have been a religious man, thereby completely disregarding the differences between their own steady, supposedly enlightened age and the fourteenth century. In Edward's day, war could be seen as an instrument by which leaders carried out God's will. We also need to remember that even though Edward consciously used religion to bolster his reputation, it does not necessarily follow that he did it cynically, or *only* for this reason.[7] His coronation had been laden with religious symbolism, and was basically a ritual designed to establish the changed earthly and spiritual status of the king; but there is no reason to believe such a demonstration did not have as profound an effect on the king as on his subjects. It is the same with his other religious demonstrations, including those during and after a battle. They had a political purpose, but that does not mean that Edward did not believe in them.

Edward was still not yet twenty-one, and this alerts us to another misjudgement frequently made in historical assessments of medieval spirituality. We cannot presume that a man's faith remained consistent throughout his life, and that his spiritual outlook was the same at twenty as it was at fifty. This is not to say that Edward experienced a 'road to Damascus' conversion at any point in his life, but it does mean we should be cautious about reaching for evidence from his fifties or sixties (when the reformer John Wycliffe was influential at court) to explain his religious outlook at the age of twenty. Indeed, in 1333 the great religious debates of the fourteenth century were still in their infancy, and William Ockham (who was in the vanguard of the reformers) was a refugee from papal censure, in exile, having been imprisoned by Pope John XXII for heresy. It is not surprising therefore that Edward's life was largely unaffected by popular religious dissent.[8]

Edward himself *was* a religious man. He was chosen by God to be king, that was a fundamental and widespread understanding. As an anointed king, he was the instrument through which God might cure men and women of certain diseases, notably the King's Evil (scrofula) and epilepsy. Edward undertook 'touching' for the King's Evil in thousands of cases in the 1330s and 1340s.[9] When processing into a city, he often distributed alms to all the main orders of friars, not just the Dominicans (his father's choice) or the Franciscans (his mother's) but Carmelites and Austins as well.[10] But if we try to differentiate between his religious acts and his actual faith, we may observe that many of his religious acts were routine. Religion formed his outlook on a world which was largely Christian or Moslem, as far as he knew. Every feast day and every Sunday he would hear a mass. Family events required religious observance, such as the birth of a child or the mother's churching a few weeks later. Visits of certain dignitaries – especially emissaries from the pope – required ecclesiastical audience. Religion was thus a function of his everyday life, and a part of his royal status. Piety and power went hand-in-hand, and it would have been difficult for him to further his political and diplomatic ambitions without seeming a perfectly religious king. Edward needed religion to reassure his people (bishops and archbishops included), so they would have faith in him as worthy of God's favour and their respect.

In keeping with his royal status, Edward possessed many religious objects. The keeper of his wardrobe in late 1332 reported that he had a gilded silver crystal reliquary vase bearing divers precious stones topped by an engraved silver image of the Crucifixion.[11] The same source mentions two gilded silver basins engraved with images of Christ, and numerous ecclesiastical bowls, chalices, vestments and candelabra. There were also many religious books – chorals, missals, graduals, antiphons, martyrologies and gospels – including a text of the gospels illustrated throughout with silver and gilded images. Interestingly, one of the ceremonial copes worn by Edward's priests included images of the martyrs and their sufferings – Saints Thomas, Laurence, Denis, Blasius, Edmund and Stephen, and the beheading of Saint John the Baptist – all ornamented with gold and silver. Physical suffering as worship, and ultimately a means of obtaining redemption – the cult of the crusader – was here apparent for him to dwell on, if he felt so inclined.

And then there was the relic collection. Both of Edward's parents had gathered relics with a pious fascination, and Edward had inherited his father's collection, and probably his fascination too. In 1332 he had 'eight silver gilded images of saints, each standing and carrying their own relics', the saints being St George, St Leonard, St John the Baptist, St James the Less, St Agnes, St Margaret, St Mary Magdalene, and St Agatha. He also possessed relics of the saint-king Edward the Confessor, St Stephen, St Adrian and St Jerome. And most important of all he possessed a thorn from the Crown of Thorns and the Neith Cross, a fragment of the True Cross, which he kept safely with his other relics at the Tower of London.

To go beyond the religious routine of royalty, and to investigate Edward's actual faith, is much more difficult. The problem lies in that virtually all the evidence relates to his *showing* his religion, and thus potentially relates to a religious or a political statement rather than his spirituality. The temptation therefore is to do the opposite, and to look for signs of his apparent *lack* of spirituality, such as his merciless hanging of Thomas Seton at Berwick, his massacre of one hundred after the battle of Halidon Hill, and his order to execute those who had imperilled his queen's life at Cheapside. But it would be rash to presume that what we assume to be 'mercilessness' automatically implies a lack of faith. If the punishments were ruthless rather than merciless, it would be possible to see how they could have been compatible with spiritual conviction. No one would doubt that Edward II was deeply spiritual and yet he too was capable of atrocious acts of barbarity, such as the massacre following Boroughbridge. We must remember that Edward was able to forgive men, and to a far greater extent than his father. He forgave Mortimer's supporters, and he forgave the Cheapside workmen after Philippa pleaded for their lives. Also, to kill men in or after a battle was not an ungodly thing to do. Subjects who took up arms against the king were flouting God's law, and, if exacting retribution in the name of the saints, to punish them with death was not necessarily an irreligious act.

There are some signs that, even at the age of twenty, Edward had strong spiritual beliefs and was convinced – if not fervent – in his faith. Three points particularly stand out in relation to this early stage of his life. The first is that he often gave away his possessions – even presents which had been made specially for him – but he did not give away relics. The lavishly illustrated books which Philippa gave him at their wedding were broken up and given away, as was the wonderful basin decorated with Caesar, Judas Maccabeus, Arthur and other figures which she gave him in 1333.[12] Religious artefacts were treated more carefully, suggesting either genuine religious passion or a streak of superstition, or both. Next we may note that some of Edward's religious choices were passionate and lifelong. For instance, there is a marked contrast between his patronage of the local, Northern English saints in the 1330s (when fighting in Scotland with armies of Northern Englishmen) and his lifelong adoptions of St George, St Thomas the Martyr and the Virgin. He made almost yearly pilgrimages to the shrine of St Thomas at Canterbury, the saint who best represented the guilt of English kings. He paid even more attention to the cult of the Virgin. Most chroniclers record him swearing an oath in her name. From the 1330s to the 1350s he made special efforts to visit her statues. In 1338, when making an exceptionally rapid journey north, he took the time to stop at the image of the Virgin Mary in Darlington and donated two cloths of gold to the church there.[13] As this was a 'secret' journey, one could well have forgiven him for not making such a detour, or such a gift, and thus it points to a real engagement with the cult.[14] Likewise he went miles out of his way secretly to visit a statue of the Virgin in Herefordshire in the 1350s. In later years he even included her image on his seal. Such sustained support went beyond religion as a matter of routine, and beyond a mere propaganda statement. We have to consider it as an indicator of genuine, lifelong devotion.

The third sign of his youthful spirituality is his combination of war and spirituality. The crusade, promoted by his rival Philip, remained on the agenda even while relations with France were deteriorating. It was still being discussed in July 1334, and even in September of that year Edward sent negotiators to set up a meeting between himself and Philip so they could discuss it.[15] This should not be taken too seriously as an indicator of faith, for there were political overtones to the crusade of the 1330s. Nevertheless there is no doubt that, beyond crusading, war and spirituality were interwoven in his imagination. Edward's personal appropriation of St George as his personal saint as well as the national one is particularly revealing. Although his choice of saint was military, and thus perhaps political, he was under no obligation to justify his militarism with religious patronage, it was a matter of choice. It was, moreover, a choice made at a very young age.[16] He could simply have established a jousting society, like the count of Holland, but instead he subjected his militarism to saintly protection. And then he worked tirelessly at promoting the saint. Even some of Edward's tournament armour at this time was white with a red cross, putting him in the position of being St George's champion, wearing the saint's arms.[17] This put a heavy responsibility on the wearer, to live up to the expectations of a saint, especially if he went into battle invoking the saint's protection. Edward may have been deliberately publicising his relationship with St George, the Virgin, St Cuthbert and a number of other English saints, and he may have been making 'a show of his religion', but it was very probably based on a sincere spiritual footing. Had he or his followers perceived that St George had reason to doubt his sincerity, he and they could have expected retribution of a kind which would have put an end to him, and them, and all their ambitions. His confidence never seems to have suffered in this way – not in battle at least – and so we may be sure that his faith remained firm, ardent, and grateful to the victory-delivering saints.

As a result of all this, we may look at Edward as a young man who genuinely believed that he was a soldier of God, a champion of St George. His spirituality may have extended no further than the point of his sword, but his approach to God was that of a genuine supplicant, not a cynic. He had no pretensions to be spiritually humble, nor did he have any leanings towards theology, nor was he yet a great patron of ecclesiastical architecture. But he did believe in his calling as a warrior, and he believed his cause – to fight for England – had been divinely sanctioned. As he came south from his victory at Halidon Hill in 1333, he repeatedly gave thanks to God, both for his own sake and for the sake of all those who were with him. His leadership, his warring, his diplomacy and even the well-being of his kingdom were all founded on the fact of his divine appointment, and the success of his reign depended on his retaining God's favour. Much more than just English military skill had been put to the test at Halidon Hill, and confirmed.

*

Edward spent Christmas 1333 at Wallingford Castle. The feasting was sumptuous, the joy of the court was unbridled and royal extravagance was let loose. All the objectives Edward could reasonably have set himself to achieve by the age of twenty-one had been met and surpassed. Any doubts he had had in 1330 about his taking power from Mortimer were long-since forgotten. Any doubts he had had in his own abilities had proved to be merely a youthful lack of confidence. Although he had been very cautious about handing large rewards to his nobles, now in return for their part in his victory he richly rewarded men like William Montagu, to whom he gave Wark Castle and the Isle of Man. There was no longer any threat to his kingship. Indeed, it is likely that in February 1333, even before the siege of Berwick, he received further information about his father's whereabouts, reassuring him that the man was not in England, but under papal protection.[18]

Edward's family life was broadening out too. He had forgiven his mother for supporting Mortimer, and left her free to indulge herself in collecting jewellery and relics, and even augmented her income.[19] Rumours of her affair and the possible birth of a bastard son of Mortimer's had lingered on, and had reached the papal curia, but the pope now wrote to express his relief that such rumours had been 'discredited'.[20] Interestingly, although close relationships between sons and their mothers often impact negatively on their wives, there is some evidence that Philippa was supportive of Isabella. When Isabella's name had first fallen into disrepute, Philippa had helped her, and the pope had written to acknowledge and thank her for her support.[21] So it seems that Edward's family life was as happy as could be. In March 1334 he granted Philippa the revenues of the earldom of Chester to support the infant earl, Edward, and their other children. Philippa was now expecting their second daughter, Joan.[22] More children meant more possible marriage alliances, and Edward soon began considering how best to marry off his family. His daughter Isabella he planned to marry to the heir to the Castillian throne.[23] His brother John he decided should marry Mary, daughter of the lord of Coucy.[24] Two years earlier he had tried to negotiate a marriage between his three-year-old son, Edward, and a daughter of Philip of France, but the worsening relations between the two countries had ended that. Little Edward remained 'on the shelf'. Newly born Joan also escaped her father's enthusiastic international match-making, for the moment at least.

In the wake of Halidon Hill the exuberance of the court hit a new high in its tournaments and games. It is difficult even to begin to represent the vast expenditure and huge range of elaborate costume and gilded and decorative armour which Edward now ordered for himself and his courtiers. One writ of March 1334 may be considered representative. It included:

Eighteen green surcoats made for the king's knights embroidered on the chest with two images, one of a knight, the other of a damsel, and covered with leaves and branches of gold. Thirty-one striped blue surcoats with hoods for the king's squires embroidered on the chest with the heads of a knight and a damsel encircled by silver foliage. Seven surcoats made of cloth of gold with blue sleeves for the king's minstrels, on each sleeve an image in gold and silver of a minstrel performing his art. Three hoods of scarlet with peacocks, snails and other beasts worked in gold, silver and other colours, all encircled in gold. Two suits for the king to be worn in the joust, one of which is of Tartar cloth fringed with gold and bearing escutcheons (shields) containing images of a lioness and leaves in gold and vermilion velvet; the other likewise with a lioness in a field of silver, studded with silver rosettes and quartered with red velvet, along with a banner of the same livery. Seven blue surcoats trimmed with miniver and embroidered with velvet leaves. Seven brown scarlet hoods studded with one thousand white pearls around the edge, the pearls being provided by the king for two of the hoods and by John (of Eltham) for the remaining five. Five more brown and scarlet surcoats made for the king and trimmed with miniver and embroidered with a letter 'M' above the arms, within which are two silken figures holding a roll bearing further silken letters.[25] A bed for the king made of silk, sparkling with powdered gold and studs of jasper and decorated with foliage and baboons . . . ten cotehardies (tunics) for the joust made of Norwich worsted and russet. Three russet coats for the king, William Montagu and John Meules, each coat bearing two figures on the chest each carrying a roll in their hand. A russet coat for the king with a roll above the arms bearing silken letters. Four surcoats of brown scarlet trimmed with miniver for the king, William Montagu, Robert Ufford and Ralph Neville, each bearing little spaces above the arms containing a figure holding a roll of silken letters . . . Twelve black surcoats for the king; twelve hoods lined in red scarlet and adorned with red roses. Thirty-five coats for the king's esquires lined with white woollen cloth; thirty-five lined hoods for the same esquires. Two suits of armour for William Trussell and two for William Lengleis. A harness for the king for three horses bearing the arms of William Montagu. Four aketons for the king of red cloth adorned with divers heads and leaves. A suit for Thomas Purchaz and two aketons for the king. Six white surcoats of embroidered cloth. A suit of armour for the king embroidered with baboons and other animals; a hood studded with pearls; a pair of pearl garters for the king encrusted with gold. A surcoat and hood of red velvet for the earl of Chester, the king's son, the hood being embroidered with pearls and the surcoat with gold and silver; fifty-six pearls delivered to the prince's tailor to make buttons for the prince's surcoat, each pearl being priced at 12d. A surcoat of russet adorned with golden branches and foliage made for the king and lined with fur . . .[26]

Imagine a total of commissioned items amounting to twenty times this list for a single year. The quantity of costume, its richness and the imagination which went into designing and making it, are extraordinary, even for a medieval king. This particular writ includes a series of hangings 'all of which have been ornamented at the king's request' showing that Edward was personally behind at least some of the court's brilliant decoration. The unbounded extravagance of this display is something to which historians have rarely done justice, and biographers have never even mentioned. Edward's mounting debts have usually been blamed exclusively on his wars, but making new and dazzling costumes for dozens and sometimes hundreds of men on a monthly or even more frequent basis cannot have helped the royal finances, especially when they were made of expensive cloths and – for the élite – decorated with furs and pearls.

Picking out choice items from an adjacent writ enrolled on the same parchment roll, we see that Edward's St George tournament armour was accompanied by 'three horse harnesses of the same livery with pennons, flags and standards'. He also ordered 'two great suits of armour for tournaments, one for the joust embroidered with the arms of Lionel'. This was for just one tournament, that at Dunstable in January 1334. The reason for Edward's choice of Sir Lionel – a knight of the Arthurian Round Table – was not that he was a hero, for he tried to kill his beloved brother. It was a reference to growing up under Mortimer. Lionel and his brother, Sir Bors, had grown up under the domination of an interloper lord who had made himself king at their father's expense. No fewer than 135 knights and esquires took part in the Dunstable tournament, and Edward seems to have clothed many of them elaborately. And for the next tournament, he clothed them all in something different. The whole court and all its chivalric onlookers were dressing up, role-playing and changing identities in line with the king's whims and passions.

So many clothes are mentioned in the accounts that it is difficult to believe that Edward wore any single item regularly, perhaps with the exception of his golden and gem-encrusted eagle crest. This goes for armour as well as daily wear. In 1330 he employed seven armourers, including several foreigners, showing that he used not just the best local manufacturers (such as Thomas Copham, and William Standerwyk) but foreign-born experts, such as John of Cologne, Gerard of Tournai and Peter of Bruges. He also imported pieces of German and Italian armour.[27] In 1338 his list of armourers included several more foreigners, James of Liège, Gottschalk and Arnold of Cologne and Herman Keplyn.[28] And all these men were turning out quantities of equipment. At Barnard Castle in July 1334 he ordered the controller of his wardrobe, William Zouche, to account with Gerard of Tournai for a total of one hundred and seven pieces of armour then brought to his chamber, including a number of 'black helmets for war', burnished helmets, tournament helmets 'with gilded eye-holes', a complete suit of jousting armour and, most interestingly, 'a plate corset lined in white silk for the king's person [and] an identical corset for the person of William Montagu', early appearances of the breastplate.[29] Armour developed very rapidly over the course of Edward's reign, so that the general coif or hauberk of chainmail – ubiquitous in 1330 – had become a thing of the past for the leading knights in his army by 1345.

Those who benefited most from all this elaborate costume-making were, of course, those closest to Edward: his wife and his selected band of knights. Even after Halidon Hill, Edward continued his bonding exercise with his leading men by giving them costly tournament gear and linking them into a fraternity of warriors. He himself would fight in their mock-armies during a tournament, or joust in their coats of arms. On many occasions he ordered a pair of suits so that a particularly favoured knight should be seen to be dressed like the king. In late 1334 or early 1335 he ordered 'two surcoats of tawny-red decorated with various birds, from the mouth of which springs forth a roll bearing song lyrics and another bearing a different legend', one of these surcoats being for the king, the other for Sir William Montagu.[30] Over and over again we read of clothes being given away. Some of these were for the king and later distributed after being made or worn once.[31] Others were made expressly for the band of his intimate knights.[32] Yet other items were made so that Edward and his son were seen in the same livery, accentuating their royalty. On one occasion, although his son was still only a toddler, Edward ordered for himself, his son Edward and Sir William Montagu a brown coat and mantle each. These were:

> embroidered with gold trees and garnished with silk fowl, trimmed with gold throughout, and decorated with birds on branches; on the breasts of these birds were two embroidered angels studded with pearls holding a golden crossbow crafted with gilt silver and a string of pearls.[33]

In this way the little prince was tied into the band of close knights at court. By the age of four he had a little palfrey of his own, and was receiving decorative apparel for it. By the age of seven he had his own suit of armour.[34] He would have never have known a time when he was not associated with the military élite of England. The only significant difference from Edward's own upbringing was that his son was surrounded by this new confraternity of knights, led by his warrior father, which was most unlike growing up at the court of Edward II.

*

Edward in 1334 was fully adult, a proven leader, favoured by God, and a dazzling king of a magnificent court. His family was fine, and growing; his marriage was a good one. And to cap it all, he had the two things which most men who have reached a pinnacle of achievement lack: health and youth. But he also had problems. In his very victory, in his chivalry and public religiosity, in his encouragement of overseas diplomatic links through marriage, and in his refusal to compromise over the Agenais, Edward had established a culture of triumphant belligerence which neither Scotland nor France could ignore. In particular, he had failed completely to reverse the tide of Scottish patriotism, and had failed to press home his advantage after Halidon Hill.

In terms of *conquering* Scotland, Edward had been rather short-sighted. In his determination to confront the Scottish army he had concentrated wholly and exclusively on one big battle. Although he had proved his leadership qualities during that battle, he had ignored the wider aspects of subduing a country, expecting that it would capitulate. He was not far wrong – only five castles continued to hold out against his rule – yet he did not attempt to subdue these last few rebels. Instead he let Balliol take responsibility for putting down all opposition. Edward concentrated instead on exerting his maximum gains from Balliol, in terms of grants of land. The ease with which he could control his client king fooled him into thinking that he had power over Scotland. In reality, Edward provided insufficient men to keep the northern kingdom subdued, and this, coupled with Balliol's own shortage of men, allowed the Scottish rebels to regroup. Most of all, Edward let slip through his fingers the one man he should have secured above all others, his brother-in-law, King David II.

The landing of David II and Queen Joan in France in May 1334 merely confirmed what Edward had hitherto only suspected: France would continue to support his enemy. While Edward took part in yet more extravagant jousts at Burstwick, including gunpowder demonstrations,[35] the Scottish rebels were covertly winning over many of the leaders who had ostensibly acknowledged Edward's overlordship. France too was shifting towards a position of war. The newly installed archbishop of Canterbury, John Stratford, was deep in negotiations with the French king. At the beginning of July Stratford returned with the news that Philip was prepared to bargain over the Agenais but he demanded to know why Edward continued openly to support Balliol against his own brother-in-law, whom Philip regarded as the rightful king. Why had Edward again received Balliol's homage as King of Scots? This greatly complicated the discussions over the Agenais and put negotiations about the French throne beyond the reaches of diplomacy. Significantly it ensured that any refugees from English administration north of the border had a safe refuge south of the Channel, where they could regroup and plan.

Edward did not doubt the seriousness of this resumption of the alliance against him. After Stratford's return to England, Edward attended one more tournament at Nottingham, but this was probably the last for some years.[36] He sent messengers back to Philip to discuss a possible meeting between the two men about the crusade, as if this was a carrot with which to tempt Philip into sacrificing David II. But although Philip might have been prepared to do almost anything to be able to lead his expedition to the Holy Land, he could not acquiesce to Edward's demands. He had to maintain his opposition to this young English lion, and hope that by encouraging others to oppose him, Edward would receive such a setback that he would learn some humility. If Edward were to receive a bloody nose in Scotland, for example, the way would be left free for Philip to lead his crusade without Edward, and without having to share the glory.

What Philip probably could not have appreciated was how much the tentative eighteen-year-old he had met in 1331 had grown in confidence. Edward had already decided on his course of action, and it was straightforward. He was not going to compromise with Philip de Valois, David II or anyone, under any circumstances. As early as August 1334 he was thinking of a new expedition to Scotland. He summoned parliament to meet in September, and made preparations for the defence of the north.

Balliol's allies were deserting the English cause, Berwick was threatened with attack and, amid all this distant confusion, the idea that only he, Edward, could quell the Scottish revolt greatly appealed to him. At the September parliament he personally paid for a settlement between two of his warring lords – Edward Bohun and Henry Percy – in order to secure their support.[37] He asked parliament to grant him a tax for the forthcoming war. As parliament deliberated, news came that one of Edward's principal agents in Scotland, Richard Talbot, had been captured. Another, Henry Beaumont was besieged in Dundarg Castle, and yet another, David of Strathbogie, had been pursued and forced to swear allegiance to David II. It only remained for Edward Balliol to take the fast road back to safety in Carlisle for the north of England to be threatened once more. Parliament gave him everything he wanted.

No one can doubt Edward's resolution in organising his new Scottish campaign. Troops were to assemble at very short notice, on 6 October, at Newcastle. Monthly loans were secured from the Italian bankers, the Bardi. Clerics and laymen were induced to give personal loans to the king. New means of taxation were devised to maximise Edward's ability to raise and sustain an army.[38] Old forms of taxation were revamped to guarantee delivery of specific amounts of silver.[39] Once again, all those of sufficient income were ordered to become knights. Edward was not just mobilising English society, he was forcing it through a socio-economic funnel so that it might more efficiently respond to his demands. By the end of December 1334, negotiations with Philip had been terminated, the army had gathered, banners bearing the royal arms and the arms of St George and St Edmund had been ordered, hundreds of pennons bearing St George's arms were in the making, and Edward was dressed in new armour and surrounded by a bodyguard of two hundred mounted archers picked from the men of Cheshire.[40]

Archers were an essential part of Edward's new army, and his willingness to employ them was one of the real achievements of his war policy at this time. It was experimental, cutting-edge strategic thinking, combining the manoeuvrability of the Scots army in 1327 with the firepower of the English archers at Dupplin Moor and Halidon Hill. On this expedition there were 481 mounted archers in his own household.[41] He also provided 371 knights and men-at-arms. Other lords provided at least 838 knights and men-at-arms and 771 mounted archers.[42] The sheriffs of the English counties also were required to raise and send large numbers of infantry archers. Lancashire alone was expected to provide four thousand, Yorkshire more than five thousand. Only a fraction of these turned up, but the message was emphatic. The sheriff of Lancashire may well have scratched his head on receiving the royal writ, and wondered where he was going to find four thousand men who could shoot longbows rapidly and accurately, but he would have known that this was what could be expected in future campaigns.

Edward had two significant challenges to overcome. The first was that he had chosen to fight the Scots in winter, in Scotland. Moreover, of all Scottish winters he had chosen one of the very worst. In the words of one Yorkshire contemporary:

> that year, about the feast of Saint Martin (11 November), frost, snow and hail began to fall, and they lasted continually for four months. And on the eve of St Andrew the Apostle (29 November), about midnight, flashes and bolts of lightning were seen, and terrible thunder crashes were heard. And in the same night, about the hour of dawn, the west wind blew up a tempest and blew snow everywhere, such that no one could remember ever having seen such bad weather. The new nave of Whitby Church was blown down . . . the columns within the outer walls collapsed . . . and similarly many houses and churches throughout England and other places were destroyed.[43]

With weather so appalling it is a wonder that Edward managed to sustain a campaign at all. Having marched north from Newcastle on 14 November, many of his men would have been billeted in tents at the time of the storm; and after such a blowing and a soaking, four months foraging in frost and snow on reduced wages cannot have been a happy experience for anyone.[44] Those sleeping on the decks of the many ships Edward had requisitioned to attend off the northern coast must have had a particularly grim experience.

Edward's second challenge was how he was going to engage the Scots in battle. As his father had learned, there was little point amassing an army if the enemy did not appear. After a period of service – three months in this case – the English troops could begin to return home, as the Scots knew. Edward's choice of strategies to try to bring them to battle was limited. One was to try and relieve Dundarg Castle, where Henry Beaumont was besieged by the Scottish leaders Sir Andrew Murray and Sir Alexander Mowbray; but that was a remote place, and offered little strategic advantage other than freeing Beaumont. Besides, not all the Scots were at Dundarg, and to try to relieve that siege would have been to follow their agenda, to respond to their initiative. Instead he began to establish a new centre of operations at Roxburgh Castle. There he ordered his masons to restore the walls of his grandfather's fortress, and spent the harsh Scottish winter, surveying the snowy emptiness around him.

No Scotsman in his right mind was going to attack Edward at Roxburgh, surrounded by his archers. The view from the castle walls remained empty, barren, and frozen. Troops, coming to the end of their periods of service, began to depart. Beaumont capitulated and surrendered Dundarg on 23 December 1334. Edward saw he was going to be left stranded. His reaction was to demand more men; those who had failed to respond to the summons before were now summoned again, and threatened with the forfeiture of their estates if they failed to come. But everyone could see that Edward was slowly being defeated by the Scots' strategy of avoidance, the cruel weather, and the need for the English infantry to return home to their farms and their spring sowing.

By the end of January 1335 Edward realised he had no option but to retreat. Until the last he continued to demand reinforcements to replace his dwindling army, but on 2 February he left Roxburgh and headed south. To keep pressure on the Scots, he ordered as many ships as possible to begin a naval blockade. This included merchant ships as well as the handful of royal ships regularly maintained by the king. Mariners who would not volunteer were press-ganged into serving, and ordered to seize any ship taking cargo to or from the Scottish rebels. If Edward could not defeat them in battle, he would try other methods of attack.

Edward was having to learn some hard truths about war. The battles he had yearned to fight as a teenager were turning out to be long, drawn-out campaigns. Strategies of supply mattered just as much as battlefield heroics. Leadership involved far more careful diplomacy than military glory. The French now demanded that Edward negotiate a solution to the Scottish question with them, and without the means to pursue a new offensive he had no option but to receive ambassadors. They arrived in March, quickly followed by envoys from the new (French) pope, Benedict XII. In early April Edward agreed to a truce until the summer, and even acknowledged the right of four Scots partisans to attend parliament, to present their case, as requested by the French envoys.[45]

It was not just warfare which was teaching Edward a few hard lessons. When parliament met at York on 26 May, it discussed money too. Money was becoming a subject of interest to Edward, who knew that continual failure to pay his men's wages would defeat his army as completely as any enemy. Moreover it would damage his ability to raise subsequent armies. If he wished to continue to fight his wars, he needed higher income from taxation. As taxation was granted or withheld by parliament, it seemed advisable for him to work with parliament to increase their willingness to grant him money. And parliament too wanted to use its influence to increase its wealth. At York in 1335 Edward began to pay his first serious attention to economic reforms. He passed the Statute of York, whereby free trade was permitted: 'merchant strangers may buy and sell within this realm without disturbance'. The Londoners were astonished by this, and complained bitterly that it went against charters to run their own affairs which Edward had previously granted them. But for the moment Edward was resolute. He only acted to reverse his free trade policy with regard to Londoners a few years later, when he found it in his interest to do so.

Whoever had convinced him of the merits of allowing foreigners to trade freely had also set his mind thinking with regard to other financial matters. The Statute of Money was also passed, in an attempt to make sure that no gold or silver left the realm. Money was flowing from the kingdom to the Continent as a result of an unfavourable balance of trade.[46] The cause, however, was not properly understood. It was thought that the shortage of silver was due to hoarding and people taking silver abroad. To prevent this, pilgrims were restricted to using Dover as their sole port, searches were to be made for money, it was forbidden to melt down money to make silver vessels, and no counterfeit sterling was permitted to be brought into the realm. Although it was not the solution, it was at least an honest attempt to tackle the problem.

None of this distracted Edward from his war in Scotland. Everything came second to his military plans. He spelled the matter out clearly to the French and Scottish envoys that, as soon as the truce expired, he would attack again. As far as he was concerned, the truce served only one purpose. It was to give him time to gather his resources and to prepare for the next stage of the war. And he was serious. He had issued the summons for the next campaign, on 27 March, only a few days after he had left Roxburgh. When a gang of Frenchmen led by a Scotsman seized an English ship at the mouth of the Seine, stole its cargo and killed its crew, Edward had yet another excuse to renew his Scottish onslaught. Orders went to Ireland to prepare a great siege engine there and for the Irish justiciar, John Darcy, to raise more troops. Writs were sent out to the counties to demand specific numbers of men for the summer campaign.[47] By June Edward was ready to fight again.

The army was set to muster at Newcastle on 23 June 1335.[48] This time Edward was joined by a foreign ally, Count William of Juliers (now a part of Germany), who had married Queen Philippa's sister. From the shires another large contingent of archers was ordered: more than 5,500 of his total army of more than thirteen thousand.[49] Balliol came south to join him and take part in the war council. Two armies would proceed, one led by Edward, the other by Balliol. With Edward rode his brother John, earl of Cornwall, the count of Juliers and the earls of Warwick, Lancaster and

Hereford. Balliol rode to Berwick with the earls of Arundel, Oxford and Angus. The contrast with the reign of his father, who rarely managed to persuade more than two or three earls to join in a Scottish expedition, was striking. Any Scotsmen unfortunate enough to witness the approach of either of the two armies would have had no doubt that this was a serious display of English military strength.

Edward was in his element. Leading his men, he could forget his ecclesiastical advisers and his money troubles, and he could fully exercise his favourite faculty, to command. This was the exertion of real power, combined with the unquestioning loyalty of his men, and the comradeship of his friends. In south-west Scotland, in the forest of Dalswinton, he brought forward a destrier clothed in Sir William Montagu's arms, and gave it to him as a present. He also gave Montagu one of his two precious eagle crests.[50] This was honour indeed, and it pleased Edward to favour Montagu in this way. As he had recently been reminded, his friends would not necessarily always be with him. Sir Edward Bohun, one of the men who had risked Mortimer's wrath in 1330 and who had commanded one of the battalions at Halidon Hill, had drowned crossing a river in the appalling weather of the winter of 1334. On the way into battle, there was no saying who would be the next of the companionship to be struck down.

The summer campaign of 1335 was war without compromise. Knights were dubbed, prayers were said, and then the looting, raping, killing and burning began. Few who found themselves in the path of the English armies escaped. Even monastic property was destroyed: Welsh troops under Balliol's command attacked a nunnery and a monastery.[51] Gradually the two armies closed in on Glasgow. At Cumbernauld, Balliol found the tower held against him. After burning it, he captured more than two hundred men and women found sheltering inside. The men he killed; the women he spared. Chivalry – an intense contrast of light and dark even in peacetime – became horrific in times of war.

Edward pushed on to Perth. Wherever they went, the English wrought destruction. The sailors of Newcastle attacked Dundee and burnt much of the town, including part of a friary; they also burnt a friar and looted monastic property.[52] The conduct of such individual raids was largely beyond Edward's control, but he did nothing to stop the destruction. His thirteen thousand troops were taken on swift marches up and down the kingdom as much to strike fear into the hearts of the Scottish civilians as to engage with their troops. It had become part of his policy to demonstrate his power in person by showing he could, at will, destroy any semblance of nationalist power in Scotland. It was a logical strategy. After repeated campaigns of this nature, who could reasonably be expected to serve a rebel leader, and entertain further death and destruction? That Edward would never earn the love of the Scottish people in this manner was relatively unimportant, in his opinion.

Then came August 1335. Although Edward did not yet know it, the French parliament had declared that France would support the Scots with six thousand troops, including one thousand men-at-arms.[53] There was a message to this effect on its way to him. Philip also invited Edward to submit his quarrel with David II to the arbitration of himself (Philip) and the pope, for Edward's quarrel was endangering the crusade. At the same time, Robert of Namur was making his way to Edward, to help him in his campaign. With only one hundred supporters, however, Namur was chased by the Scots to Edinburgh, where he was captured. More humiliatingly, after his English guides had been killed, he was set free upon swearing an oath that he would not fight in Scotland. Namur then went to Berwick, and caught ship with Philippa, joining Edward at Perth. Namur was a nephew of Robert d'Artois, a cousin of Edward and a bitter enemy of Philip. There was also a message on its way to Edward placing the disagreement between Philip and d'Artois beyond negotiation. All these messages and men were closing in on Edward over the course of August. The battle lines of the first stage of the first great war of European nations – the Hundred Years War as it came to be known in the nineteenth century – were being drawn up.

On 7 August Edward was at Perth. The French message had still not reached him, but his messengers had brought news that the French were gathering ships in the Channel. Rumours of Philip's plans to aid the Scots had also reached him. And the vulnerability of his kingdom, stripped of its fighting men, was very much on his mind. On 12 August he designated men to represent him at a council in London, and appointed others to array and lead the Londoners if the realm should be invaded. On 18 August the seriousness with which Edward regarded the threat of invasion was shown by his order to remove his infant son, Edward, to the safety of Nottingham Castle. The rumour in the north was that Philip had requisitioned seven hundred and fifteen vessels, in alliance with the king of Bohemia.[54] Edward divided his kingdom into three and ordered local magnates to oversee the defence of each part. Ships were requisitioned to defend the coasts. Beacon fires were to be assembled. Edward ordered Montagu to defend the Channel Islands. England and Wales were poised to expect a French armada, to be launched by Philip of France in the name of David II.

The situation had developed to a point of war between England and France on account of the intransigence of their two leaders. On a personal level, this was merely the natural arrogance of medieval warrior-kings. But at a diplomatic level, royal pride could have serious consequences. It was only to be expected that not backing down should become a point of honour between the two kingdoms as well as the two kings. And both men dominated their courts so completely that royal advisers were urging both kings on to greater declarations of bellicosity. Neither side was proceeding with caution. Having said that, there was a fundamental difference between their two positions at this time. Edward was on the offensive, and he did have a legal claim to back up his actions. Thus he had something to gain, and the initiative accordingly lay with him. In any compromise, it was Edward who stood to benefit most. And in the matter of Scotland, Philip had nothing to gain at all. Even if he had been successful, and had forced Edward to acknowledge the right of David II to rule, Edward would merely have turned his attention elsewhere, perhaps to an attack on France. This is why, although Philip did not let on as much, the pope had secretly urged him to back down and to give up the Scots cause.[55] Philip's sole achievement in sending a few dozen ships to raid the English coast was to shock the richest and hitherto most secure towns of the kingdom into the realisation that they too were vulnerable to attack from France, even though France had no claim on England. Until then only northern England had recently experienced foreign aggression at first hand. When the good burghers of Southampton and Portsmouth found themselves set upon and their houses burnt, Edward's ability to raise money for a foreign war was suddenly increased.

August 1335 was the point of no return in the developing struggle between Edward and Philip. When Philip's letter of support for the Scots finally arrived, Edward replied that his pacification of Scotland would be over quickly and would not impede arrangements for the crusade. He added that Philip had no right to get involved, as this was a purely domestic matter between him and his subjects. Quietly, the pope was saying much the same thing to Philip. Even more telling was the capture by the garrison of Roxburgh of the Scots patriot, the earl of Moray. With his capture, pressurised by Edward's army, the other Scots leaders saw they now had little to gain and much to lose, and gave themselves up. David of Strathbogie surrendered and received his English estates back. The earl of Fife surrendered Cupar Castle. Alexander and Geoffrey Mowbray gave themselves up, and promised to renew their allegiance. Robert Stewart – next in line to the throne after David II – also surrendered. To cap it all, Edward's Irish invasion force finally arrived and proceeded with an onslaught on Rothesay Castle. Although they were unsuccessful, Edward had emphatically made his point. He could bring three armies against

Scotland simultaneously from three different directions, as well as a naval attack on the Perth and Dundee region. If Scotland wanted a king, it would have to be one appointed by him. And if Philip wanted to mediate in Scottish affairs, he would have to use force.

As Edward returned to the lowlands of Scotland in September, he was minded to make another permanent reminder of his Scottish foray. Edinburgh was the weak link, where Robert of Namur had been captured. To secure the Scottish city would be further to strengthen his grip on the lowlands, and a safeguard on the English border. Bruce had originally conquered Scotland through subduing and reducing the English fortifications; now Edward set himself the task of rebuilding them, and reinforcing them. He maintained Roxburgh and Berwick on the border. With Edinburgh now a third castle under his control, and Caerlaverock a fourth, it seemed that Edward had reinforced the border for the foreseeable future. There was just one flaw in his plan. It was obvious to the man whom he appointed to command Edinburgh, John Stirling. Edward was bent on saving money, coming away from Scotland with more than £25,000 of wages still unpaid.[56] Therefore he ordered the smallest garrison which conceivably could maintain each fortress. How would they withstand the next wave of attacks? John Stirling realised that such small numbers were insufficient to guard them against all eventualities. Only in 1337 did Edward begrudgingly acknowledge that Stirling was right.[57]

*

Edward's policy towards Scotland – a state of continual war, punctuated by occasional large-scale expeditions – had worked satisfactorily. The long respites in the fighting meant his men could return home to their communities while he himself could set about arranging further instalments of much-needed cash to pay for the next expedition. Keeping the war going – never agreeing to peace but only a series of truces – allowed him to keep the pressure on the Scots, and eventually to wear them down. Hence he remained on the border through the winter, to emphasise his readiness to resume the fighting. Christmas was spent not in comfort with Philippa but at Roxburgh Castle, looking out at the frozen flood waters which covered the land.[58] The war, he was reminding the Scots, the French and the pope, was not over. Unless a permanent peace could be arranged, and one which was on his terms, he would raise another army the following year, and yet another the next.

Edward was not going to initiate such a peace agreement. This was not just because of his pride; each time the Scots or French asked him to renew the truce he could demand more concessions. But in late 1335 Philip of

France and the pope were particularly eager to see a permanent settlement come about. Philip had been told in no uncertain terms by the pope that his cherished crusade was dependent on peace in Europe, and especially between England and France. Accordingly both Philip and the pope sent negotiators to see Edward. Edward was in no rush to come to any agreement, and it was January 1336 before any measure of acceptable compromise was tabled. Edward renewed his truce with Scotland for a further three months – to 12 May – and demanded that the Scots who had not surrendered to him (now led by Sir Andrew Murray) should give up their sieges of two Scottish castles. It was agreed that Edward Balliol would rule Scotland for his lifetime and that David II would be his heir. Andrew Murray himself seems to have agreed to this. The only other party whose agreement was required was David II himself, still in exile in France. This was merely a formality: David was still only twelve years old and had no real personal authority. But messengers, not ambassadors, arrived from the king of Scotland at the Westminster parliament in March 1336. David II had refused, and he had refused to countenance any further compromises or truces. The papal nuncios and the French envoys – who were present at the parliament – were probably no less aghast than Edward.[59]

Edward's reaction was utter disbelief, followed swiftly by anger. It certainly seems strange to the modern reader that David II did not agree to the peace. But we are too detached from the hatreds, pride, jealousies, animosities and envies of the period, and the sources barely convey how much hatred there must have been on somebody's part to come to this decision on David II's behalf. For it was not David's own decision – the boy was too young – and therefore someone in his faction ordained this course of action. It could have been Andrew Murray and his associates, adopting a strategy of parleying with Edward but continuing resistance through their safely-protected boy-king. Or it might have been King Philip, secretly persuading David's guardians that they could only lose by this deal. Whoever was behind it, the rebuke set Edward on a path of angry war, and crucially it caused the pope to call off the crusade. Edward now knew that, when Philip's disappointment had worn off, it would leave him with all his men and ships unused, his weapons sharpened for war, and no obvious enemy except the man who had come between him and his dream of reconquering the Holy Land.

*

On 3 April 1336, Edward had dinner on his ship called the *Christopher*, which was then moored in the Thames near the Tower of London.[60] We do not know who was with him, but we may suppose he did not dine alone; eating on board a boat was a way to achieve a high degree of privacy with regard to one's companions as well as what was said. He had been staying at Eltham, and seems to have come briefly to the Tower for this meal. The next day he began a journey to Waltham Abbey, the pilgrimage site in Essex which he often visited. He stayed at Waltham for a week, during which he granted at least three requests to found chantries to pray for his father's soul,[61] then returned to the Tower on 13 April. All this seems curious when we consider that the truce with Scotland was about to run out on 12 May, and that Edward was supposed to be heading north again with his troops, as he had previously arranged. He even took the unusual step (for him) of appointing someone else to lead the army. It so happens that this delay coincides with the appearance of Niccolinus Fieschi. On 15 April, Edward issued letters confirming the engagement of Niccolinus, otherwise known as 'Cardinal', as a member of the king's council, with an annuity of £20 and robes befitting a knight.[62]

Niccolinus was a relative – perhaps first cousin once-removed – of the author of the Fieschi letter, Manuel. Edward had previously received him at Westminster in February 1333, and his visit then had coincided with Edward sending his trusted friend Richard Bury to the papal court on 'secret business'.[63] Now his reappearance coincided with another important date, for the Fieschi letter was very probably written in early 1336.[64] Niccolinus's arrival marked the start of a long and important relationship with Edward, in which Niccolinus undertook much secret business for the king at Avignon and other places, and was paid the very significant sum of between two and three hundred pounds each year in lieu of this work, his status rising eventually to the point of helping to negotiate several international treaties on Edward's behalf.[65] This points to an extraordinary level of trust placed in a man who was not only a foreigner, but a foreigner who was related to the author of that letter and who had prior obligations to two potentially hostile foreign powers: the Genoese (who fought on the French side in the forthcoming war) and the pope.

If Edward received the Fieschi letter at this time, as seems likely, then this marks the point when he finally learnt where his father was: Northern Italy. But however relieved he may have felt, this news raised as many problems for him as it solved. Firstly, if we are right in thinking that Edward II had been held all this while by his kinsman Cardinal Luca Fieschi, with the acquiescence of the pope, then the peace negotiations were delicate, as the pope was French and Cardinal Fieschi had just died.[66] For this reason, as well as his own standing in England, it was of paramount importance to Edward that the information itself remained secret. Prayers and masses were said for Edward II just as before. Chantries were founded to help his soul even more frequently than before. But Edward did start at this point to resolve the conflicts which had arisen from the problem involving his father. One example is his smoothing out of the anomaly of the accusation still hanging over Lord Berkeley – of appointing the men who supposedly murdered Edward II – which he did through wholly acquitting him at the next sitting of parliament. Another was that he purchased the land for his father's intended foundation of King's Hall at Cambridge University (now part of Trinity College), which he properly recognised and endowed by charter the following year.[67] A third is that he turned his attention to his father's tomb, with the fake body in it, at Gloucester. On 15 September 1337 Edward paid a visit to Gloucester (his first since taking power in 1330).[68] There he saw the newly elected abbot, Adam Staunton, and may have indicated his intentions eventually to bury his father in the tomb.[69] His idea as to how to get the bodies changed over was beautifully simple: he lent his own great mason and architect, William Ramsey, to supervise the rebuilding of the choir there.[70] Lastly, it is possible that we may discern a fourth resolution, that of his own relationship with his long-lost father. It would appear that he asked Niccolinus Fieschi to arrange for him to meet his father in person.

*

By mid-May 1336 Edward was ready for another attack on Scotland. He set off at an extraordinary pace. He was in or near Reading on 16 May.[71] Thereafter his progress north was very quick indeed. On 4 June his wardrobe was at Towcester, the next day Northampton, the next day Leicester, the next Allerton, the next Pontefract, the next Topcliffe, and on 10 June Edward arrived in Durham. After a quick supper with the bishop of Durham, Richard Bury, he went on northwards, his tired servants reaching Kelso on 15 June and Perth on the 19th. So sudden was his arrival in Scotland that not only was the enemy surprised to see him arrive; his own army was too.

Edward's haste was not just due to a desire to catch up with his army, led in his absence by the earl of Lancaster. He was also acutely aware of the growing ambitions of France. Philip had realised the weakness of a policy which committed him to a war in Scotland and which he was never prepared to support with force. He had accordingly persuaded the French parliament to act on its resolutions of the previous year to land a French army in Scotland. Invading armies needed landing places where they could enjoy safety and find supplies. Edward thus had plans to destroy any possible form of nourishment within reach of suitable landing places on the east coast of Scotland. Abbeys were emptied of their food supplies, cattle slaughtered, corn fields burned. Whole towns were destroyed.

Edward personally saw to the destruction of Aberdeen. Against the vigour of the English army in full destructive flow, the Scots could do nothing. William Keith, Andrew Murray and William Douglas may have felt bitterly angry that Edward was wrecking their countrymen's homes, food supplies and livelihoods but they too would have seen that this was a strategic necessity. The ambition to be a 'perfect' king was not incompatible with the ruthless destruction of food supplies and defensive structures, or any other aspect of the efficient prosecution of a bloody conflict.

While Edward was savaging the north, and chivalrously rescuing the widow of the earl of Atholl from a siege at Lochindorp, a great council was held at Northampton. Edward had appointed the archbishop of Canterbury (Chancellor), Henry Burghersh (Treasurer) and his brother, John, to preside at this council, but on one day at least it seems Philippa took charge.[72] Beside the archbishop of Canterbury, seven bishops, and forty-six barons, knights and other magnates were present. They decided another embassy should be sent to France, to seek a compromise to the conflict which was developing. Edward agreed, and sent word accordingly to the bishops of Durham and Winchester. He also summoned his brother to help him in Scotland. As a precaution, he placed all the royal castles of southern England on a state of alert, and instructed the earls of Arundel and Surrey to defend their fortifications at Arundel and Lewes.

At the end of the summer, the crisis suddenly worsened. Edward summoned another council to meet at the end of September, this time at Nottingham. The envoys proposed by the previous council had been utterly unsuccessful in trying to get a compromise from Philip, who was determined to go to war. In fact, Philip declared openly to Edward's envoys that he would send an army to help the Scots, and would do all he could to assist them. The French fleet – amassed by Philip to fight the infidel – was now sailing around the southern English ports attacking any English ships they found. Edward wrote to his admirals on 18 August urging them to intercept the enemy and declaring that 'our progenitors, the kings of England, have before these times been lords of the English sea on every side . . . and it would very much grieve us if in this kind of defence our royal honour should be lost'.[73] But Edward's claim to sovereignty of the seas was of little help to the crews of those merchant vessels which the French caught. Those who were trapped at sea had the choice of the sword or the waves. No merchant was safe. Englishmen in Ghent and Bruges began to be rounded up on the orders of the count of Flanders, Philip's ally. At the height of this extreme panic, which Edward was powerless to control from Scotland, he received utterly dreadful news. John of Eltham, his only brother, had died suddenly.

John was just twenty years old. Edward had been fond of him, had raised him to the earldom of Cornwall, and had shared with him the terror of Mortimer's dictatorship. John alone had benefited from a flood of estates and rewards after Mortimer's fall, when Edward was too cautious to distribute largesse to his non-royal friends.[74] He had been the Sir Bors to Edward's Sir Lionel: the two brothers growing up under the rule of the usurper 'King Claudas'. John's marriage was a subject to which Edward had given very considerable thought, first favouring Jeanne, a daughter of the count of Eu, then Mary of Blois, then Mary of Coucy, and lastly a daughter of King Ferdinand of Castile.[75] John's death also marked the loss of the only one of Edward's brethren still in England. His sister Joan was in France, married to his enemy David II, and Eleanor was married to the count of Guelderland, in the Low Countries. Of his family he had only his wife and three children, his forty-year-old mother, and one uncle left. In this light it is all the more shocking to read of a rumour that the cause of John's death was murder. And a most extra-ordinary murder too. He was supposed to have been stabbed in a rage by Edward himself.

The shock of this story tends to deflect attention from the impact of John's death on Edward. Edward was exceedingly upset. He ordered nine hundred masses to be said for John's soul.[76] A year later, John's death was still giving him bad dreams, as his household accountant noted, after extra alms-giving by the king; but the cause of those bad dreams was almost certainly not regret for a knife wielded in rage.[77] John had died on 13 September at Perth, and although it is probable that Edward was at Perth at the time, the source of this story, *The Scotichronicon*, is very doubtful.[78] It was written about twenty-five years later by John Fordun, a clerk from Aberdeen, which Edward had just burnt to the ground. We therefore have to accept that the truth remained hidden from all Edward's English companions for twenty-five years before being leaked to an embittered and relatively unimportant Scottish clerk. Sir Thomas Gray – writing while a prisoner in Scotland in 1355 – stresses that John died a 'good death', which probably implies fortitude in the face of an illness sent by God.[79] Most fourteenth-century English chroniclers record the death; not one of them states he was murdered.[80] Barnes believed that he died of a fever brought on by his military exertions.[81] There is little room for doubt that Fordun's story of Edward stabbing John to death was not a rare fragment of a hideous truth but a choice piece of Scottish propaganda. An inspiration for the theme of the story may be found in Edward's adopted role of Sir Lionel, for this Arthurian knight attempted to kill his brother Sir Bors. In the wake of the destruction of Aberdeen, men from the town may have believed that Edward was so ruthless in destroying the land of which his sister was queen that he *could* have killed his own brother.

Edward probably remained at Perth until the third day after his brother's death. He had sent his wardrobe ahead to Nottingham in readiness for the council to be held there, but still he lingered by the body of his brother. He seems still to have been at Perth on 16 September.[82] This left him a mere eight days to reach Nottingham, more than three hundred miles away. When he finally moved off he hastened south at a breakneck speed.[83] He entered his council chamber at Nottingham Castle on 22 September, tired from a very long journey, distraught, and facing the gaunt faces of men who knew that the kingdom was facing imminent invasion.[84] Worse, the Scots had been pricked into action by the French support. Andrew Murray was burning and levelling his own lands – in emulation of Edward at Aberdeen – to stop the English being able to station an army there. The isolated English castles were already under attack. In this climate, it is no wonder that the council granted Edward his taxes without question. Men were raised from the shires. An immense defensive army was conceived, and large sums of money were secured from the Bardi and Peruzzi banking houses as a means of paying troops. Edward summoned naval help from Bayonne. He even wrote to the king of Norway to request that that monarch refuse to supply ships to Philip. In doing so he admitted that he was likely also to face the opposition of the counts of Hainault and Guelderland, his relatives. Far from setting an example of perfect kingship, he now looked very beleaguered indeed.

As it turned out, the invasion threat was more imagined than real. By the end of October the large army ordered for the defence of the country could be sent home, and the naval contingents of the south coast could be safely directed to protect the merchant fleet heading to Gascony. They were to be replaced by ships raised from Great Yarmouth and twenty-four other ports. Further protection measures were made – including a repeated order to Bayonne to send ships, and an order to protect the port of Dartmouth in Devon – and gradually the sense of fear calmed. But as it calmed in England, it grew in Gascony. In the Agenais, fear of attack became reality as a French army was sent to assault Gascon outposts, and plans for the seizure of the whole duchy of Aquitaine were contemplated.[85] Philip was now writing to Edward saying that he should expel Robert d'Artois from England, or, rather, send him to France in chains for judgement as an enemy of the French king. In Scotland, to which Edward had returned after the council at Nottingham, his rebuilding of Bothwell Castle was hampered by constant attacks from William Douglas. For Edward, the glories of war had turned into the long, bitter reproaches of diplomacy.

It was a discomfiting contrast to the glorious tournaments of the years after Mortimer's fall.

Edward left Bothwell in mid-December and came south with his brother's embalmed body.[86] Philippa travelled with him as far as Hatfield, where they spent Christmas together. Heavily pregnant, she remained at Hatfield while Edward went on with John's corpse to the Tower, arriving on Friday, 10 January. The next morning, he walked with it in a great solemn procession to St Paul's Cathedral, surrounded by clerics and citizens, where it lay the night. The following day, Sunday, he attended mass in its presence. After mass it was taken to Westminster Abbey. The next day solemn exequies were celebrated by the archbishop of Canterbury in the presence of the king and many earls, prelates and barons. Funeral feasts were arranged at Westminster and St Paul's. Finally, on Wednesday 15 January, John of Eltham was laid to rest in St Edmund's Chapel, Westminster. As a mark of respect, Edward commissioned one of two exceptionally fine alabaster effigies for his tomb. The other was for their father, to be incorporated in the tomb at Gloucester.[87]

The day after John was lowered into the stone floor of Westminster Abbey, Philippa gave birth to a second son, William of Hatfield. Edward responded to the good news by making a journey to Canterbury to give thanks at the shrine of Becket.[88] But beyond this, the birth of a second son was greeted with muted enthusiasm. The reason is not hard to find. The child was sickly, and dead within weeks. Edward seems to have been disturbed by this, as he decided that his dead baby should not be buried in the family mausoleum at Westminster. Instead he sent its corpse all the way to York Minster. Although grief for a lost new-born was, in medieval times, often less profound than today, it was another blow. God was not favouring Edward. He had lost his brother and now a son. And that was not the end of his worries. The French had attacked Portsmouth and Jersey. In Scotland the rebels had won a series of victories against the under-resourced English garrisons. Bothwell Castle, only just repaired, was under attack and soon to be destroyed. It was as if Edward had never fought and won at Halidon Hill. His achievements were being undone, the winter had set in very cold, and bad rumours were spreading. It was said that a calf was born with two heads and eight feet. A very bright comet was seen which 'darted forth its rays with terrible streams', as if a precursor of devastation.[89] If Edward was a warrior of God, then God required something more from him than this. It is a telling sign that most chroniclers do not mention the birth, let alone the death, of his doomed baby.

SIX

The Vow of the Heron

'The Vow of the Heron' is a political poem about Edward, written in the Low Countries in the mid-1340s. It relates how, in September 1338, Edward was sitting in his 'marble palace' in London with his courtiers and 'ladies, girls and many other women' around him. He was thinking about love and had no plans to make war, when Count Robert d'Artois returned from a hunting expedition with a heron he had caught. Having had the heron plucked, stuffed and roasted, d'Artois had two girls carry the bird on a silver plate to Edward, accompanied by minstrels playing the viol and the gitterne. D'Artois declared before all the court: 'I have caught a heron, the most cowardly bird there is, and therefore I will give it to the greatest coward alive, King Edward, the rightful heir of France, whose heart has clearly failed him, for he fears to maintain his claim to the throne.' In the story, Edward was embarrassed, and, red-faced, replied: 'Since I am so accused, I swear on this heron that I am no coward but that I will cross the sea within a year to claim what is mine.' Having heard the king's promise, d'Artois smiled wickedly, and let the girls go forward to sing of sweet love-making to the king as the courtiers embraced their mistresses around the palace.[1]

This poem gives us a vivid glimpse of how Edward was imagined by his enemies at this time, and in particular how he was seen in relation to the war. He was the sole protagonist. His warmongering could not even be excused by his leadership of a parliament which had resolved to take up arms. He *personally* decided to begin the conflict, and his cause was a selfish one: a frustrated claim to the throne of France, and the shame of accusations of cowardice. In the story of the Vow of the Heron the catalyst who turned this frustration into violence – Robert d'Artois – was a sinner, a heretic and a traitor. Furthermore, Edward's decision was portrayed as being taken in the midst of a lascivious court in which nobles paraded their mistresses openly, flaunting their immoral behaviour before God. It all added up to a *mélange* of vice, dishonour and unworthiness.

Considering the need for pro-French propaganda, especially in the small countries whose rulers wanted to persuade their people to support them in their alliances with King Philip, there is nothing particularly surprising in the story itself. What is surprising is that modern popular understandings of the causes of the war are largely based on it. In Queen Philippa's entry in the old *Dictionary of National Biography*, this vow was regarded as a real event, a chivalric ceremony in which Edward swore to make war. In twentieth-century classrooms, Edward was almost always portrayed as the guilty party on account of his dynastic ambitions and his claim to the kingdom of France (his 'absurd' claim, as the *Encyclopaedia Britannica* called it).[2] However, as we have already seen, Edward was very cautious about the developing diplomatic situation, and had proved scrupulous in his consultation with parliament and his council. As scholars have universally acknowledged for the last fifty years, his war-related claim that Philip had illegally seized the throne of France cannot be treated separately from his claim to Aquitaine, which Philip now openly and directly threatened.[3] When he finally did claim the French throne, it was principally a technical shift to permit the Flemish legally to renounce allegiance to Philip. In this way we may see that Edward was not proceeding without parliamentary support. His decision to fight, while not encouraged by parliament, was nevertheless ratified by it. And hostilities broke out long before Edward finally and irrevocably claimed the title King of France. The dynastic claim was a symptom of the conflict, not a root cause.

In considering the events of 1337–40, Edward's dynastic ambitions are less important than Philip's dynastic vulnerability. When Edward's claim to the French throne had first been put forward, during his minority, it had proved impossible to sustain it with any force. In addition, regardless of any legal claim or dynastic right, the French nobles preferred an exclusively French king to a part English, part French one, for the simple reason it was better to have a head of state who would have to consider their interests before those of the English. Thus Philip had become firmly established as the French king soon after his accession. Edward was in no position to risk a continental war in the early 1330s, and was well-advised by his parliament in 1331 to seek a peaceful solution to his disputes with Philip. This he did. But the fundamental problem had never gone away. In reality, it was in neither England's nor France's interests for Edward to be king of both nations; and Edward would have acknowledged that his dynastic claim to the throne of France would have been difficult (if not impossible) to assert and maintain without conflict. In later years he was happy to agree to peace treaties in which his claim was laid aside. But the very fact he had a claim could be used to his advantage if Philip tried to push his overlordship of the duchy of Aquitaine – and thus his overlordship of Edward himself – too far.

In order to counter this dynastic vulnerability, Philip had adopted a strategy of sustained diplomatic antagonism towards Edward. First he had claimed in 1331 that the form of homage which Edward had paid him was insufficient. Next he had refused to restore the parts of the Agenais seized from the English by his father. Then he had insisted on supporting the Scottish claim of David II, and had used Edward's championing of Balliol to accuse him of threatening the crusade. After that he had threatened to invade Scotland, and had embarked on a policy of naval piracy, killing English sailors, looting English ships and burning English ports. Now he claimed Edward should not shelter d'Artois. As each dispute had been smoothed over by the patient negotiators, Philip had found another. While Philip may have benefited domestically in the short-term from such a policy, he was like a boy showing off to his peers by prodding the English lion's rump with a sharp stick. That the lion did not immediately turn and bite – as Edward would have preferred – is probably due to three factors. These were the repeated advice of the English parliament and councils of magnates that the French question should be settled by negotiation, not war; Edward's higher priority on asserting his Scottish rights; and a series of papal initiatives, including the crusade.

Philip's demand that Edward should surrender d'Artois was thus just one more in a long string of grievances. If there had been no d'Artois, war would have been no less likely, as some other problem would have been put forward by Philip as a justification for taking action against the English king in Gascony. As it was, d'Artois was the best excuse Philip could find. On 30 November 1336, the pope wrote to Edward stating that Philip would not receive his peace envoys as Edward was protecting d'Artois.[4] At the same time the pope asked Edward to send him (the pope) envoys equipped to agree a peace treaty. In the pope's view, all was not lost. Even if Philip would not negotiate, the pope would.

Edward would have heard the pope's view of the d'Artois dispute in December 1336. Such a contrived reason to break off diplomatic relations would certainly have infuriated him, and may well have convinced him that Philip was bent on war.[5] This in turn may have triggered Edward's next series of innovations. Out of the despondency of his brother's death, his infant son's death, and losses in Scotland, he saw a chance to recapture that enthusiasm and chivalric brilliance of the early 1330s. Philip's antagonism had the result of challenging Edward to concentrate his attention and the bulk of his resources on France. It was exactly what Edward needed to enthuse himself, his court and parliament – and thus the country as a whole – into purposeful optimism for the future.

The seeds of the new initiative probably were sown in the days around his brother's funeral. On 23 January 1337, almost immediately after his return from Canterbury, Edward held a council in the Tower of London.[6]

Gascony and Edward's claim to the French throne were again discussed, but, as before, his counsellors urged him to seek peace, not war. English interests, it was said, would be best served by reinforcing the English fleet and building a league of allies against Philip, as Edward's grandfather, Edward I, had done in 1297. Edward listened, and took these debates into parliament with him in early March 1337.

The first day of the parliament, 3 March, was momentous. Edward raised his six-year-old son, Edward, to be the duke of Cornwall. Never before in England had there been a duke; the title was connected solely with continental possessions. But in the wake of his brother's death Edward had the idea of endowing his eldest son with the richest available earldom (Cornwall) and giving him the pre-eminent title among the nobles. In this he was emulating his grandfather's creation of his son and heir (Edward II) as prince of Wales. Edward could not pass on that title in good faith, knowing his father – who had retained the title Prince of Wales – was still alive. So he did the next best thing: a royal dukedom. All the chroniclers were impressed, and almost all recorded the creation.

The parliament of March 1337 was radical. Innovation loomed large. The ban on all exports of unworked wool – proposed in late 1336 – was reinforced with parliamentary support. From now on weavers would be regularly invited to ply their craft in England and to teach the English how to make cloth. Grants would be offered to entice them over from the Low Countries. In this way the cloth trade could be developed and enhanced. And to maximise the potential and increasing demand, the wearing of imported cloth was banned, except of course for the king and his nobles. No one should wear imported furs unless they had an income of one hundred pounds per year. This 'sumptuary law', together with a similar statute of the previous year, was the first of its kind in England. Although the high income required for the wearing of furs might be seen as exclusive, the criterion is a money-related one, not restricted to the nobility. This permitted rich merchants and their families to continue to wear furs, and thus set men like the London merchants William de la Pole and John Pulteney – whose friendship and finances were beginning to make a real impression on the king – up alongside the barons. In so doing Edward was extending his principle of inviting leading townsmen to tour-naments, and enforcing the requirement for all men with an income from land over forty pounds per year to be knights. A sensibility to the advan-tages of broadening the upper and middle tiers of the class structure was clearly at work.[7]

The major event of the parliament of March 1337 was not a law, nor anything to do with the wool trade, nor the creation of a duke, but the creation of six earls. This delighted chroniclers: so many in one triumphal creation! It was a clever move. In the past kings had been dogged by accusations of favouritism, but in raising six deserving men to such high status, no one could look at Edward favouring this or that one over the others. Each chronicler dutifully wrote down who received which earldom, documenting their names reverently, as if a new tier of chivalry had just been invented, which is, of course, what Edward had in mind. First and foremost was his closest friend, the thirty-four-year-old Sir William Montagu, captain of the plot to capture Mortimer and a war leader at Edward's right hand ever since. He became earl of Salisbury. Lancaster's eldest son, the twenty-six-year-old Henry of Grosmont, was created earl of Derby. The twenty-five-year-old William Bohun – another of those who had assisted at Mortimer's arrest, a frequent participant in the Scottish wars, and recently married to the widow of Mortimer's heir – was created earl of Northampton. Hugh Audley, son of Edward's childhood justiciar, was created earl of Gloucester. Despite being Mortimer's nephew, Hugh had joined Lancaster's attempt to overthrow Mortimer in 1328, and had been unswervingly loyal to Edward ever since, providing him with troops for his Scottish wars and serving in person on the last two campaigns. William Clinton, another of the knights who had seized Mortimer in Nottingham Castle, was made earl of Huntingdon. Now thirty-two years old, he also had continued an active military life, being warden of the Cinque Ports and admiral of the western fleet during the French raids. Finally, Robert Ufford, who at the age of thirty-eight was the oldest of the new earls, was created earl of Suffolk. He too had assisted in arresting Mortimer. In surveying the credentials of those now raised to earldoms, it is striking how the removal of the dictator Mortimer was a common factor. It shows Edward continued to acknowledge and value the help he had received in throwing off the dictator's oppression.

The end of the parliament was one huge feast. More than £439 – the equivalent of yearly wages for about one hundred and forty skilled labourers – was spent on this one meal.[8] Edward held a great court for the men, while Philippa held a lesser court for the ladies.[9] Twenty men were specially knighted to mark the occasion. Lord Berkeley received his official acquittal of any wrongdoing against Edward II. Two days later, on 18 March, grants were dispensed to the new earls and some of the knights, to keep them in the style befitting new men of rank. With Edward dining in state we might fairly see him presiding over a court full of confidence, looking to the future. Yet in reality it was a court beset by problems. As Edward feasted and his musicians played, and the new earls shared his dais, the Scots were planning an attack on the great stronghold of Stirling, and the French king was making plans to confiscate not just a few more English castles but the entire duchy of Aquitaine. If anything kept the smiles on the faces of the courtly retinue as they feasted that day in March 1337, it was that in Edward they had a man who, when faced with personal disaster, did not disappear in his own hunched conscience, or disdainfully shun his responsibilities as his father had done. This king faced up to his problems: he even found strength in them. He might have been aggressive, ruthless and dominating but he could turn his own mood and the mood of the court – and eventually that of the whole kingdom – simply through the force of his will.

*

The parliament was followed by a flurry of diplomatic initiatives. Even while parliament was still sitting the new papal nuncio in England, Bernard Sistre, was despatched back to Avignon with letters of credence from the king and a spoken message: 'secret business' as it is habitually described in the records. Diplomatic exchanges were made with Alfonso of Castile, the elderly and dying count of Hainault (and his son – just in case), and the counts of Flanders, Guelderland and Juliers. Edward sent his negotiators to the Flemish cloth-working towns of Bruges, Ghent and Ypres, to discuss allowing the purchase of English wool. He sent several letters to the Gascon port of Bayonne, requesting warships, and prepared a defensive strategy for Gascony. He even sent messengers to Philip of France, still trying to find a way to negotiate rather than fight. This was certainly not appeasement – Edward's attempts to build a federation of forces against Philip were not likely to end in a climb-down, and Edward's only compromise was an offer to give up d'Artois if the man was given safe passage to his trial and Philip gave up his support of the Scots – but neither was it hankering after a European conflict.[10] Considering that the French had burnt Portsmouth again and attacked Jersey during the parliament of March 1337, Edward's final attempts at a negotiated settlement appear very restrained.

Edward's busy diplomatic embassy – led by Henry Burghersh (bishop of Lincoln), William Montagu and William Clinton (earls of Salisbury and Huntingdon respectively) – were given the task of presenting Philip with a series of demands, to permit diplomacy to continue. They were not welcome to proceed into France. Instead they remained at Valenciennes, dishing out royal grants and pensions to all those who might prove useful, until a grand meeting of diplomatic representatives took place there in early May. Straightaway the battle lines became clear: Louis, Count of Flanders, stood resolutely in support of Philip of France, and, like Philip himself, failed to attend the diplomatic party (although both men had been invited). John of Luxembourg, king of Bohemia, also refused to desert Philip. On Edward's side were the count of Hainault and his heir (Edward's brother-in-law, the count dying just after the meeting), the count of Guelderland (Edward's brother-in-law), the duke of Brabant (Edward's first cousin) and a host of minor counts and margraves: Berg, Juliers, Limburg, Cleves, Marck and Namur. Peace was discussed, and the intransigence of the French king examined. Then, seeing as Philip's allies had not sent representatives, the discussions turned to war. Edward's representatives took the lead. Edward would pay handsomely for the support of the other nations if war broke out. Even Edward's close relations were promised large amounts of money. William Montagu himself had some doubts about the strength of the coalition, and he was not alone in thinking that the German princes were only after Edward's gold, or England's wool (which for the cloth-working towns was just as valuable).[11] The pope was also inclined to think the worst of the German princes' love of money. But nevertheless the negotiations continued, and towards the end of May it was clear that a military alliance had formed against France, led and financed by England.

Edward remained at Westminster until 3 May. That day he began to head north with his army at a huge speed, reaching York in time for him to dine with Richard Bury and the earls of Northampton and Gloucester on the 11th. The infantrymen with him were forced to march 'night and day' as he raced towards Stirling Castle, the strategically important fortress now besieged by the Scots.[12] Edward saw an opportunity to engage them in battle and, if not to defeat them permanently, at least to do them such lasting damage that his policy of constant attrition would be sustained. But in reality his efforts and attention were now being directed towards the Continent, and the Scots understood that they merely had to return to their old tactics of waiting until the English king had departed before they attacked again. Thus, as Edward approached Stirling Castle, the Scots disappeared. They remained in hiding as long as Edward was in the vicinity. With the French supplying them through Dunbar, and Edward having to return south to deal with his alliance, they were safe, and free to fight another day.

It was while Edward was at Stirling, reinforcing his garrisons and repairing the walls, that Philip finally plunged Europe into war. On 24 May he confiscated the duchy of Aquitaine. So much attention had been paid to the English province over the last thirteen years – since the War of Saint-Sardos – that Philip cannot have had any doubt as to what would be the results of his action. He had asked the question which could only be answered by force of arms. The question was whether he ruled as an absolute king of a nation which included the duchy of Aquitaine (as if Edward was just another French vassal), or was Aquitaine beyond his control, absolute rule there being the prerogative of the king of England. Having confiscated the duchy, and done away with diplomacy, Philip VI had given Edward the choice of responding with force or forever losing a major part of his birthright. For Edward, who had championed the virtues of chivalry all his young life, and who had repeatedly proved himself prepared to use war to attain his ambitions in his other threatened territory, Scotland, this was no choice. It was a declaration of war.

Edward immediately returned to the south. He gave orders for his already extensive coalition to be augmented still further. Alfonso of Castile was already at war. Promises were made and pensions offered to the palatine count of the Rhine, the counts of Geneva and Savoy, and more than a dozen others. Most important of all, negotiations for an alliance were made with the Holy Roman Emperor, Ludvig of Bavaria. For Pope Benedict XII, the news that Edward was in discussions with Ludvig – a heretic and an excommunicate – can only have caused him to pull out his hair. When it emerged that Philip too was in negotiations with the heretic emperor, he must have despaired. He wrote in mid-June to the archbishop of Sens and the bishop of Rouen, to see what they had done to prevent the war. At the end of June he wrote again. He wrote to both kings urging them to follow the path of peace, and sent a diplomat to each of them in turn, and castigated them for being so cordial to an excommunicate ruler. But despite his best efforts, it was apparent to all that Ludvig would side with either Edward or Philip, and there would be a great European war. All the pope could do was to try to use his influence to stave off the onslaught as long as possible.

In theory Edward could have taken action with no further reference to parliament, but he was dependent on his people for finance, not to mention their goodwill. He had carefully brought every single decision regarding war with France to a council or parliament, and always he had abided by the decision not to take military action. Hence in May he had held a great council of magnates and prelates at Stamford to consider the repercussions of Philip's actions in Gascony. In July he held another.[13] Diplomacy had failed. War was now unavoidable. Philip's catalogue of errors was growing longer by the season. He had failed to address the question of the Agenais, had attacked English shipping, had attacked English ports and the Channel Islands, had threatened to invade Scotland, had supported Edward's Scottish enemies, and had confiscated Aquitaine. In July 1337 he finally sent an army to invade the duchy and to prise the castles there from English control. His actions had caused several Gascon families to withdraw from openly supporting Edward. Far too much was at stake now to let these matters pass without recourse to military action.

Edward was not set on sending an army directly to Aquitaine. Troops to help defend the duchy had been summoned in preparation, but a full-scale attack on the French there would have left England unprotected, and if Philip held back sufficient men from the duchy and used them to attack the coast of England, it would be very difficult to defend it. Besides, Edward could see other options. He chose in the end to send a limited force to the duchy, under the command of John of Norwich, and to retain men in England to constitute a second army, to assemble on the borders of Northern France, and to join with the forces of his many allies, thus directly threatening Philip's kingdom. He also played his trump card: English wool. Tens of thousands of sacks of it. For a year he had withdrawn wool from export; now, directing this precious resource carefully towards the looms of his allies in Brabant and away from those of his enemy, the count of Flanders, he could enrich his friends and impoverish his opponents. Moreover, he could do this at a profit. Through setting up an English wool company, under the oversight of the London merchants William de la Pole and Reginald Conduit, Edward could borrow large amounts of money advanced on an income to be derived from exported English wool. Using his political authority, Edward could ensure that the wool was bought at a minimum price through compulsory purchase and sold at a premium to the merchants in Brabant.[14]

The opening hostilities in the war were half-hearted. Philip's large army under the command of the count of Eu had marched into the Agenais at the beginning of July. At this time, Edward's small army under John of Norwich was still in Portsmouth, about to set sail. This left the French free for a short while to attack fortified towns and seigneurial castles in the region; but they did not do so with any great conviction. At the end of June Edward had sent letters to sixty-seven Gascon magnates thanking them for their loyalty to him, and similar letters to the leading citizens of more than twenty towns.[15] His hopes that they would prove loyal when the French invaded proved well-founded. The fortified towns of Saint-Macaire, Saint-Emilion and Libourne each withstood a brief siege.[16] Other, smaller fortresses did not, but they were cheap gains for the French. If they fell so easily, they would be difficult to defend when the time came for a counter-attack. And Philip was more anxious about the counter-attack than he was about the initial progress of his army in the south. The growing awareness that Edward had not sent a large force to Aquitaine but was holding back, probably to attack the north of France together with his allies in the Low Countries, severely worried him.

In late August Edward won the auction for the Holy Roman Emperor's support. He undertook to pay Ludvig an advance of 300,000 florins (£50,000) in return for two thousand men. It was a very large sum. And he was distributing grants of this magnitude all across Germany: at 15 florins for each man-at-arms per month (£27 per year), he was engaging imperial, royal and ducal support by advancing sums equivalent to ten months in the field. He was betting heavily on victory. And well he might: he seemed to be emerging as the surer diplomatic hand and the more capable strategist. Philip had invaded Aquitaine but it was Edward who had taken the military initiative in threatening the north of France. And he had not even left England.

Edward summoned parliament to Westminster to discuss the wars with Scotland and France in September 1337.[17] Parliament took the remarkable step of granting taxation for the next three years: an unprecedented grant, which demonstrates how much the kingdom supported his leadership. One of the reasons for this probably lies in Edward's policy of making proclamations throughout the country, so that the people were aware of the dangers posed by French aggression. More than any other previous king, Edward consulted his subjects on his foreign policy, sending out important representatives such as the archbishop of Canterbury and William Bohun, earl of Northampton, to explain his decisions to the leading men of the counties.[18] The result was that parliament agreed that Edward should go to take charge of the military alliance formed in the Low Countries, and to meet the Holy Roman Emperor, Ludvig of Bavaria.

*

It might appear that all was going well for Edward in late 1337, and that the root of his problem – King Philip and Aquitaine – was soon to be confronted. He was about to set out to join with his magnificent array of allies, to attack a strategically indecisive French king who was not prepared to take risks or to stretch himself financially as far as Edward. But not only had his problems of Scotland and France not gone away, he had manoeuvred himself into a position of extreme debt. The three years' taxation would not even repay his borrowing to date, let alone his planned future expenditure.[19] Worse, he had put himself at the mercy of his allies, and was now dependent on them doing what they had promised to do. Worse still, he had committed himself to providing men he simply he did not have at his immediate disposal. Leaving troops in the north to hold the border against the Scots, leaving an army – albeit a small one – in Aquitaine, and securing the southern coast meant that there were fewer troops to take abroad. And whereas he could borrow money from the

Italian merchants and Conduit's and de la Pole's wool company, and promise to pay sums he did not actually have, he could not borrow men. His advisers cautioned him that the grand expedition might have to be cancelled.

Edward did not cancel, he postponed. At which point Philip agreed to peace negotiations. Edward, too good a diplomat to refuse to deal with Philip, but eager not to lose momentum, upped the stakes by agreeing to negotiate but at the same time threatening to claim the throne of France. On 6 October 1337, three days after he had despatched a high-level diplomatic mission to France, he issued writs to the count of Hainault, the count of Juliers, the duke of Brabant and the earl of Northampton, appointing them his lieutenants in France, using the title 'King of France and England' in one set of documents and 'King of England and France' in another.[20] Such a declaration was not just a fist in the face of the French king, it was an insult to the pope, who regarded Edward's potential claim to the throne of France as possibly the most destabilising aspect of the whole controversy. Benedict XII had just written to the two cardinals he had deputed to deal with Edward and Philip, ordering them to proceed to England straightaway, without waiting for Edward to cross to France. As Benedict put it: 'for once there [in France] he cannot easily return, and the Teutons who want to get his pay would incite him to war. That the spark may not become a flame, the nuncios should dissuade the king from crossing the sea.'[21] Now this new claim to the throne was guaranteed to undermine any possible peace negotiations. It threatened to undermine the basis of French sovereign power, and thus Philip's right to act in Aquitaine. Although Edward did not follow up this claim with further writs issued in his name as king of France, that he had done so once, and on an international stage, was enough.

In early November the pressure on Philip increased further. On the 6th the pope wrote to him outlining in full the implications of Edward's alliance with the rulers of the territories of Germany and the Low Countries. Benedict informed Philip that Edward was planning to bribe Ludvig of Bavaria to resign his position as Holy Roman Emperor. If this were to happen, Edward would be elected in his place, with command over the German princes. Even if Ludvig were not to resign, Edward was going to be appointed Vicar of Lower Germany (the Low Countries) for life 'so as to be nearer to France, and so better able to attack it'.[22] The pope further informed Philip that his enemies had gathered men, money and supplies, so that he (Philip) was almost entirely isolated. This confederation, the pope claimed, was to last for the lifetime of Edward and Ludvig and their sons. Further marriage alliances would bind the allies closer together. In short, the pope was outlining how Philip had been totally outmanoeuvred by Edward, who now had most of Europe behind him. The only chance Philip had was to make peace with England.

As it happened, Edward still faced many problems gathering men and money before he could set out. Without him – the undisputed leader – the rest of the confederation was worse than useless, a drain on English resources. It looked as if William Montagu and the doubters would soon be proved right: the heavy expenses of the coalition would hamper Edward's ability to raise an army, not help it. Frustrated by the slowness of gathering troops, Edward ordered the one fleet he had in readiness, under Sir Walter Manny, to set out and harass the French ships and ports. At the same time he urged the army in Aquitaine to seize back all the castles and fortified houses which the French had taken in July. On both fronts Edward's men did his bidding. In Flanders, the tables were almost entirely turned. Eager for battle, Manny's fleet failed to capture Sluys but lured the garrison into combat at Cadsand, where he won a bloody victory, directing his archers to massacre the Flemings assembled on the shore.[23]

Manny's victory did not make anything easier for Edward. He was still short of men. His lack of money was greatly exacerbated shortly afterwards when Bishop Burghersh, in a rash attempt to shore up the alliance, promised unrealistic amounts of cash to the duke of Brabant and other waverers. They had begun to question Edward's resolve, especially when the cardinals sent by the pope urged him to agree to a truce, and threatened him with everything from excommunication to an alliance between the apostolic see and Philip. The duke of Brabant – whose support for Edward had been kept secret – was just one of those tempted to open an alternative secret diplomatic channel with France. Burghersh panicked, and seized the wool which Conduit and de la Pole were about to sell. Needless to say, having no mercantile skill or experience of his own, and no appreciation of theirs, his efforts to obtain more money than the merchants proved an utter failure.[24]

Edward was faced with financial disaster. He had already borrowed more than a hundred thousand pounds.[25] But when a king like Edward finds himself in such a predicament, his lifestyle does not alter, nor does his largesse. Edward now rose above his financial problems in style. He paid Sir Walter Manny eight thousand pounds for one single prisoner captured at Cadsand: the half-brother of the count of Flanders. For his games at Christmas 1337 he ordered an artificial forest foliated with gold and silver leaves, as well as more than a hundred masks, some with long beards and others in the forms of baboons' heads, to entertain the court.[26]

For his games on 13 April 1338 at Havering he built mock siege engines and lavished new clothes on all the participants as usual.[27] But the clothes he ordered for himself raised the art of dressing like a king to such heights that previous superlatives are hardly adequate. His hood, for example, was made of black cloth and

> decorated on one edge with images of tigers holding court made from pearls and embossed with silver and gold, and decorated on another edge with the image of a castle made of pearls with a mounted man riding towards the castle on a horse made of pearls, with trees of pearls and gold between each tiger, and a field and a trefoil of large pearls embroidered well in from the edge[28]

No fewer than 389 large pearls, three enormous pearls and five ounces of small pearls were used in making it. The other clothes he and the earls of Salisbury and Derby wore were equally stunning.[29] His only concession to impending financial ruin and his inability to raise enough men to invade France was to answer the cardinals who had so threatened him with an offer not to invade France for two months. Faced with no prospect of obtaining better terms, they accepted.

*

In dealing with the cardinals, Edward told them an extraordinary thing. He claimed that any truce he made with France would have to be ratified by parliament, because in England parliament ratified all matters regarding war and peace.[30] The cardinals did not believe him, and presumed this was merely a diplomatic ploy. But, as we have seen, although Edward was grossly exaggerating the legal basis for parliamentary ratification, it was not entirely untrue. Moreover, it was a development of Edward's reign, and very much his own initiative. Mortimer had used parliament to sanction the forced abdication of Edward II in 1327, but war remained outside its remit until Edward had put the question in 1331. From then on, discussions about whether to go to war or not had never excluded parliament's voice. Although any real decision-making still lay with the king, parliament was consulted, if only to determine the strength of support for the king's policy.

The other point to note about parliament in 1338 is that it was no longer just the lords temporal and spiritual. Commoners played an increasingly important part. When Mortimer had summoned representatives of the shires and towns to the 1327 parliament, they had been drawn together merely to add weight to the voices of the leaders and to depose the king with the assent of all the people. Edward jumped on this idea of popular assent, and encouraged popular representation. By 1338, commoners were summoned to parliament as a matter of course. They met separately to the lords, and they were not consulted on every matter, but they had a presence and a voice. They presented their own petitions, and could expect some answer from the king. In effect, a great bargaining was going on between king and people. The commoners or representatives of the shires and towns – forerunners of modern Members of the House of Commons – wanted grievances addressed, but more importantly they wanted to know that they had a forum for raising complaints. The king wanted popular support for his main policies, and to ensure that taxation would be forthcoming when those policies entailed keeping an army in the field, or bribing continental princes. Edward was offering parliamentary power in return for money and support, and enlarging the representation of parliament to include the wealthy and important provincial townsmen and landowners, as well as the lords and bishops.[31]

In February 1338 parliament was put to the test. Edward wanted to know whether the representatives of the shires would continue to support his policies in war as well as peacetime. In particular, did parliament support his continental alliances, and his plans to go overseas, and could he rely on parliament to promise further financial support?[32] With regard to Scotland he wanted to know whether he had continued support for his new attack on Dunbar Castle, through which the French were supplying the Scots nationalists. This was held by the fearsome Black Agnes, daughter of Sir Thomas Randolph and widow of Patrick of Dunbar. As the name implies, she was no wan Scots lass. As Montagu and four thousand men hammered at the gate with a battering ram and blasted away at the walls, this woman yelled defiance from the battlements at the English and berated her garrison, probably terrifying them more than the enemy. A good handful of women in the mid-fourteenth century were truly militaristic, able to inspire and lead their men in battle as well as most men. Black Agnes was certainly one of them. When a boulder from a siege engine smashed into the battlements near where she was standing, she took a cloth and ostentatiously began to dust the walls.

Parliament in February 1338 supported Edward wholeheartedly. The Scots were more dangerous than ever. The French were making plans to invade England, and in March the first incursions of their long-awaited onslaught took place.[33] Portsmouth suffered yet again, as did Jersey. Parliament urged Edward to go to the Low Countries to take command of the allied army and once and for all to bring King Philip of France to his knees. On 24 February the truce was extended until midsummer. The cardinals, the pope and King Philip were informed. But on the very same

day orders were given for the northern and southern fleets to assemble at
Orwell and Great Yarmouth a fortnight after Easter (12 April), ready to
set out the following month. And when Bishop Burghersh was given his
instructions to take new proposals for peace to the French king in May,
the letters he carried were not of a conciliatory nature. In them Edward
addressed Philip as 'Philip de Valois, he who calls himself king of France',
and stated that he, Edward, had a stronger right to the French throne than
Philip.[34] He added his intention to conquer his inheritance by force of
arms. In confiscating and trying to seize control of Gascony, Philip had
thrown down the gauntlet. Now Edward picked it up.

*

There were many delays before he could set out. The fleet proved very
difficult to gather, with much corruption on the part of the royal officials
who were charged with gathering men, money and materials. Edward's
haste may have added to the problem, as men stole what they had been
ordered to requisition from others for the king's use, and then took advantage of the need for materials and foodstuffs to sell on what they had
already obtained. The problem of 'purveyance' – the requisitioning of
food and other necessities for the royal household – became far more widespread as supplies for the forthcoming war were also seized. Edward himself
was probably aware of the tension this caused; William Pagula had
written in *The Mirror of Edward III* about the injustice of royal purveyors
who would seize a hen from an old woman from which she got four or
five eggs a week, or take a sheep from a man who had only taken it to
market to pay his rent.[35] But Edward was unable or unwilling at present
to curb such injustices. He was preoccupied with his political agenda, not
the process of carrying it out. In April 1338 he wrote to his friend, Sir
Walter Manny, expressing surprise that he had failed to assemble sufficient
ships to cross the sea.[36] The Exchequer was still based in York, to which
city it had been moved in 1333 during the Scottish wars. And Edward
personally contributed to the inefficiencies by removing himself from
business. In late March he made another very fast journey to Scotland,
travelling from London to Newcastle in less than seven days, and
completing the whole journey from London to Berwick and back (more
than seven hundred miles) in less than nineteen.[37] If we are right in
assuming that this is the 'secret' journey described in the record of his
daily alms-giving as taking place in May or June, during which he took
the time to go to Darlington to give two cloths of gold spinet to the image
of the Virgin in the church there, then we have an explanation for his
sudden journey, for it records that the king went 'secretly to Scotland to

visit and comfort the garrisons and commanders of certain castles there'.[38] It seems that this was the point at which Edward decided he could spare his Scottish troops no longer, and instructed Montagu to call off the siege if the castle had not capitulated by a certain date. In the hope of speeding up the siege, Montagu told Black Agnes that her brother (who was then a prisoner in England) would be executed beneath the walls of her castle if she did not submit. She laughed and replied that, if they did that, she would not be disappointed, for she would inherit his earldom of Moray.[39] There was no persuading this woman. Montagu realised that if Edward wanted to campaign in France, he would have to give up Dunbar Castle. Black Agnes on her own constituted a whole second front.

Edward, Philippa, their daughters and most of the royal household – their clerks, their musicians, their cooks, their pantlers and butlers (including John Chaucer, father of the great poet Geoffrey Chaucer) – and several thousand soldiers assembled at Orwell on 12 July 1338, seven weeks after their original intended date to set sail.[40] Edward gave presents of a pair of decorated silver basins to each of his daughters, Isabella (now aged six) and Joan (now aged four) in the days before travelling.[41] A new seal of absence was struck and delivered to the Treasurer, the previous great seal being delivered to the king on his great ship the *Christopher* on the 14th.[42] The elaborate arrangements for governing England in his absence (the Walton Ordinances) were drawn up. John Stratford, archbishop of Canterbury, was appointed chief officer during the regency of the eight-year-old duke of Cornwall. Finally, on 16 July 1338, Edward and his fleet finally cast off and sailed from Orwell, picking up the rest of the fleet from Great Yarmouth a couple of days later. The fleet was numerous, and decked out to create the most striking impression, Edward's great ships carried specially made huge streamers, thirty or forty feet in length, showing the royal arms as well as those of St Edward (on Edward's own ship, the *Edward*), St Edmund, and St George.[43] The largest of all was decorated with the life of St Thomas and was seventy-five feet in length; this probably adorned the mainmast of his great ship, the *Thomas*. On the 21st the royal entourage landed at Antwerp, and was received by Edward's allies, all assembled for the occasion. His first night in Brabant was far from a comfortable one: the entire household had to flee the building they were staying in as it burnt down. The new leader of the great confederation of allies against France found himself and his pregnant queen fleeing from their beds in their nightshirts, and being accommodated at the abbey of St Bernard nearby.

The fire was not an auspicious start to the campaign. Still less auspicious, after the formal greetings, was the allies' support, or, rather their lack of it, which may be accurately characterised as a hesitancy to go to war. Edward was of the opinion that he had paid them well; he wanted to know when they would be ready for action. In particular he planned to lead a preliminary attack on the Cambresis region – which bordered on the south-west of Hainault – in the next few weeks. His allies dithered. They pointed out that much money had been promised, and little had been delivered. They wanted to see his gold before they committed themselves to fight for him. Edward, regarding it as a royal prerogative to distribute largesse without checking his balance of accounts, had to face the fact that they would not be persuaded. They would not fight Philip for prestige alone. The problem was, as Edward knew, that he had very little actual gold.

Edward could still raise money but it was soon apparent that it would be years, not months, before he could meet his debts in full. Furthermore he had not just to meet his debts, he had to show his allies that he would go on being able to meet them. The Bardi and the Peruzzi banking houses were called upon and advanced a further eight thousand pounds. Paul de Montefiore (an Italian administrator and trusted confidant of Edward) raised another eight thousand. William de la Pole advanced eight times this amount against promised wool customs. Sir Bartholomew Burghersh (brother of the bishop of Lincoln) set about raising money through loans from continental and English magnates with the king. He and Paul de Montefiore mortgaged quantities of royal treasure, including Edward's great crown of gold. Nor was this the most desperate money-raising measure undertaken: back in England his government licensed the clergy in Devon to start digging for buried treasure.[44] No reports of treasure survive, but somehow enough money was raised to fill the royal coffers, and to sustain obligations and payments of more than four hundred thousand pounds over the next year and a half.[45]

While all this was going on, the Holy Roman Emperor also had begun to have doubts. It was suspected that Edward had promised more than he could afford to the lesser lords of the Low Countries and Germany; it went without saying that he would be even more at a disadvantage when it came to paying for the services of the Holy Roman Emperor. As a result of this information, no doubt passed back to him from his first-class intelligence network, Edward seized the initiative. Rather than wait for his money-gatherers to make careful apologies for him, he had a brief meeting with several of his diffident allies, paid them some small sums, and then took his essential entourage quickly down the Rhine to Cologne, instructing the rest of his household to follow by barge.[46] Entering Cologne, he ostentatiously gave money away, making small but careful donations at the houses of all the orders of friars in the city, offering oblations at the shrines of the cathedral, including the shrine of the Three Kings, where it had been prophesied that he would be buried. To the cathedral itself he made the very generous donation of £67 10s.[47] He spent the night in Cologne, and then next day was off again, on his way down to Koblenz. On 30 August he arrived just outside the city, and stayed on the island of Niederwerde, awaiting a response from the emperor. In the meantime he sent gifts to the emperor and the emperor's wife (Philippa's elder sister, Margaret).[48]

Edward's judgement had been good. His instinct to take immediate action to secure support proved decisive. Through lavishing money publicly on people, living as sumptuously and ostentatiously as he could, and through paying the emperor the next instalment of his treasure, he forced Ludvig's hand. With all his subservient princes and petty kings present, Ludvig could not possibly go back on his earlier agreement. Any thought he had of reopening the auction for his army was ruled out, as Edward's presence and very high profile demanded an immediate and public response. The affirmation which Edward sought – an official position to confirm his leadership of the allies in the Low Countries – came on 5 September, when he met Ludvig in a great ceremonial meeting in the marketplace at Koblenz. The two leaders processed into the cathedral and Edward, dressed in a robe of scarlet, sat at the foot of the imperial throne. The emperor himself sat in splendour, wearing his crown and holding a sceptre, with a naked sword held aloft behind him by Otto de Cuyk.[49] Edward could not resist one show of independent pride, refusing to kiss the emperor's feet. But this irregularity was quickly smoothed over, and, with most of the great men of Germany watching, Edward was crowned Vicar of the Holy Roman Empire.

This new title was worth more than gold to Edward. It was pure and powerful propaganda. That he understood this is evidenced by the fact that he had had fifteen rich robes made in advance to be worn by the emperor, himself, the duke of Brabant and twelve other noble leaders of England and Germany.[50] Two days after his coronation the resplendent king of England rode back across to Antwerp, arriving there on 13 September. Five days later he summoned all his allies, or, rather, his new subjects, to attend him at Herk, in Loos, to hear the Imperial letters. On 12 October they gathered in the town hall. The walls were hung with 'rich and fine cloths, like the king's presence chamber'.[51] The king himself was seated five feet higher than everyone else, and wore his new golden crown. He had the official letters of office read out, appointing him Vicar Imperial for life, lieutenant of the Holy Roman Emperor. His wars were to be treated as wars of the empire. All those subject to the authority of the emperor were to swear fealty to him. The war against the French in the Cambresis would begin the following summer. After all the solemn celebrations, Edward returned to Philippa, now eight months pregnant, at Antwerp at the beginning of November.

*

On 6 September, the day after his coronation, while still at Koblenz, Edward commended the services of one Nicholas Blank de Fieschi, master of a certain galley lately sent to him in England, and at the same time released the man from his covenants agreed in Marseilles with Niccolinus Fieschi on Edward's behalf.[52] Whatever the task for which Niccolinus had engaged Nicholas Blank (who was probably his nephew), it was now finished. It so happens that this coincides with the arrival at Niederwerde of one Francesco Forcetti or Forzetti, probably a member of the Forzetti family of Florence.[53] The reason this deserves notice in a biography of Edward III is that with Forzetti was a man called William le Galeys – William the Welshman – 'who calls himself the father of the king of England'.[54] It appears likely that on 6 September 1338, on the island just north of Koblenz, Edward finally came face to face with his father, Edward II.

The meeting had been planned well in advance. Edward II as 'William the Welshman' (a name reflecting his one remaining royal title: Prince of Wales) had originally been taken to Cologne, where Edward had visions of meeting Ludvig, but due to his need to meet the emperor sooner rather than later, he had gone straight on to Koblenz. Hence William the Welshman had to be brought to him by his minder, Forzetti. That Edward had either directly or indirectly deputed Forzetti to bring his father to him is suggested by his description as a royal sergeant-at-arms on this, his first appearance in the royal accounts. (Sergeants-at-arms were middling status, well-respected men, superior to esquires of the royal household but less important than knights, expressly sent on missions to do the king's personal bidding.) So it seems likely that it was on an island in the middle of the Rhine, near Koblenz, that Edward met his father again. And the meeting went well. Forzetti was paid in advance for the expenses of looking after Edward II for three weeks in December.

Of all meetings between members of the royal family, this and its follow-up in December must have been the strangest that ever took place. Indeed, the whole story of Edward's survival is so amazing that historians have normally refused to believe the evidence, and preferred to present the whole episode as a series of hoaxes and deceptions. It goes against the grain of professional sobriety to present such an extraordinary story as fact, or anything other than the plot of a nineteenth-century Italian opera. But this was neither a hoax nor a deception. Edward had last seen his father in 1325, thirteen years earlier, when he had still been king, and when Edward himself had been twelve. In the months afterwards his father had written letters to him which, although they did contain shards of fatherly affection, remonstrated with him in the severest terms. Perhaps Edward had forgotten the dire pronouncement that his father would make him an example to sons everywhere to obey their fathers. Perhaps Edward II himself had forgotten that he had said it. What is undoubtedly true is that now the tables were reversed. Edward was king, and his father diminished. Indeed, Edward II had officially been dead for the last eleven years, and Edward himself had advocated that his father should continue to be treated as such. Both men probably experienced some feelings of guilt, and we may especially suspect Edward III did, as he had sanctioned the execution of his father's beloved half-brother and refused to acknowledge his father's continued existence. But he could explain now. He had kept his father alive by sacrificing his uncle. He had punished Mortimer. Moreover, he had won at Halidon Hill whereas his father had lost at Bannockburn. That was why he was a king and his father now a penniless hermit.

The reasons for picking December as the time when he would meet his father again was due in part to Edward's great demonstration of imperial authority at Herk in October, but more importantly because it would be a time for the old king finally to meet his grandchildren. Not only were little Isabella and Joan at Antwerp. On 29 November 1338 Philippa gave birth to a son. Edward was overjoyed, and promised the man who brought him the news a reward of one hundred pounds.[55] He gave the child the Arthurian name Lionel, which he had himself adopted as a nickname in his youth. It may have been conceived as a tribute to his dead brother John, or with the idea that Lionel would be a lifelong companion to his elder brother, or maybe it was a reminder of how he himself had come through the test of living under the shadow of Mortimer's authority. We do not know, but, given the stories of brotherhood and suffering with which this name was associated in the Arthurian cycle, and given Edward's own earlier adoption of the name, it was probably not selected just because he liked the sound, especially not in his father's presence.

We have only one vague possibility as to what was actually said at this meeting. Father and son seem to have discussed Edward I. It is noticeable that every year for the rest of his life after this meeting, Edward III ordered the wax torches to be renewed around the tomb of the old king at Westminster, this being done on or about the anniversary of his death. It is not possible to be certain, but it seems likely that Edward II had reflected over the years on his confrontational relationship with his own father, and hoped that his son would make amends with the old man on his behalf, if only in the way he was treated in death.

We have no further definite location for Edward II after December 1338. It is likely he stayed for the Christmas feast – always a lavish event in Edward's court, costing that year £172, including £56 on cooking – and probably for the churching of Philippa at the end of December. Niccolinus Fieschi probably left Antwerp the following February. There is no further reference to Francesco Forzetti until October 1340, when he was back in England, dealing with the Italian wool business.[56] We do not know whether Edward himself took charge of his father from this point, or whether he remained in the custody of the Peruzzi as security for some of the loans they still hoped to reclaim from Edward. All we may say is that, wherever he was taken, he lived out the rest of his days in peace.

*

Edward's journey to the Low Countries alarmed Philip. In August he responded by gathering an army and going to Saint-Denis to take the semi-mystical, ceremonial war banner of the Oriflamme. He expected Edward to invade immediately.[57] At that moment Edward was in no position to attack; but this did not make Philip any more comfortable. He tried to shift the confrontation to England, sending fifty ships to Southampton. Several thousand men landed there on a Sunday, while all the inhabitants were at church. They sacked the town, and as the inhabitants left the chuches they ran away. The French took what they wanted at their leisure. It is recorded that where they found poor people, they killed them, and where they caught any women, they raped them. And where they caught a man of wealth or status, they hanged him in his own house. Then they set the whole town on fire.[58] Guernsey too was taken and its garrisons killed. For Edward, worst of all was the capture of an English wool fleet, five ships, including one of the most prestigious, the *St George*, and two of his largest and most important: the *Christopher* and his flagship, the *Edward*. The sailors manning the royal vessels surrendered after being outnumbered. Even though Edward's personal clerks were among them, they were all thrown overboard and drowned.

Philip was not the only leader threatened by Edward's move to the Low Countries. The pope too was disappointed to see Edward cross to Brabant. As he shrewdly observed, such a move would force him to start paying his allies, and he would soon want to see some military gain in return for his investment. But what really infuriated the pope was Edward's alliance with Ludvig, the heretic. Regardless of the fact that Philip also would have enlisted Ludvig's support if he had been able to, the furious pope took sides. He wrote to Philip informing him that he had heard, from someone who had been at Koblenz, that Edward was planning to attack France the following May.[59] The pope added that he suspected also that this information might be deliberate misinformation, and so he urged Philip to be cautious. To Edward, he was less cordial, barely concealing his indignation despite his considerable diplomatic skills. He pointed out to Edward again that John XXII had excommunicated Ludvig for good reason. He added that he had offered to take Ludvig back into the Church if only he would give up his support for the anti-pope and be reconciled to the Avignon papacy, but Ludvig was adamant. In this light the pope was amazed that Edward was prepared to go to Germany, risking excommunication. He stressed how hard he had worked to maintain peace between Philip and Edward, sending cardinals to negotiate with them. He called on Edward 'to free himself from the bonds and snares in which he is involved by his relations with Ludvig'.[60] At the same time (1 November) he wrote to the archbishop of Canterbury asking him to intercede and show the king how wrong he was to accept an office from an excommunicated ruler. He also wrote to the archbishops and bishops in the Low Countries and Germany forbidding them to swear to serve Edward. He also copied all these letters to the cardinals supposed to be negotiating between the two kings. As demonstrations of Benedict's anger went, this was severe.

Edward's principal worry lay in England. As soon as he had set sail, three years of good harvests, combined with a lack of silver in the money supply, had disastrous results. Deflation – crashing prices – set in. With money being sucked out of the kingdom, and Edward's officers impounding wool supplies for shipment to the Low Countries and Italian markets, and the royal purveyors seizing whatever they wanted under cover of it being for the king's campaigns, the country was fast approaching an economic crisis. Coming on top of the three-year taxation granted in 1337, this meant social catastrophe. And then the winter came, and with it came rain and cold. Where there had been plenty of supplies but no money, now there was neither money nor food.

Edward's reaction to his logistic and economic problems was to blame his advisers. As he saw it, it was not his role to understand why supplies were late, or why money could not be raised; it was his role to enforce discipline on his enforcers, so that his instructions were carried out. In a fit of anger he sacked his treasurer, Robert Wodehouse. This was most unfortunate, as Wodehouse was probably the man responsible for managing what would yet prove to be a turn-around in Edward's ability to raise money from wool in England.[61] Wodehouse wrote to John Molyns lamenting the way he had been treated, and expressly mentioning the king's lack of gratitude for his efforts. It was in a similarly angry mood that Edward responded to the pope's letter, appointing the highest status embassy possible to treat with Philip – Montagu, Richard Bury, the archbishop of Canterbury, Sir Geoffrey le Scrope and Bishop Burghersh – but expressly forbidding them to address Philip as king of France.[62] This was not the same as claiming the throne (as he had done briefly in October 1337), but it was close.

Under severe pressure on all fronts, including his own companions who doubted his strategy, Edward was beginning to show some of the character traits of his father. He was acting in a high-handed fashion, yet not more so than most kings of the middle ages, but like his father he rounded on men who were genuinely trying to help him. His utter faith in his own royal irreproachability, coupled with his frustration with the faults of his advisers, threatened to cloud his judgement. When frustrated, Edward tended to try to force his will on those around him. Wodehouse was just one example. Another example is his order in May that all debts to him were not to be paid in instalments, in the traditional manner, but all were to be paid instantly and in full, an impossible demand.[63] It is possible to argue that other examples are to be found in his high-handed appropriation of various rights in England, largely in order to raise money. If an heiress was unmarried – whether a spinster or a widow – Edward assumed the right of appointing her husband, partly to raise money, and partly to use the revenue from women's lands to provide an income for his most trusted war commanders.[64] Lands of felons which had formerly reverted to their feudal lord were confiscated outright by the king and used to endow the new and rising members of the nobility. Priories dependent on foreign monasteries had their revenues temporarily confiscated and handed over to provide incomes for Edward's associates. To those who gathered for the parliament at Westminster in February 1339, it was worrying that Edward was demanding more from them in taxes, and yet not even prepared to return to England to meet them and hear their grievances. Having empowered the commons and given them a voice, he was now running a very great risk by failing to listen to them.

It was at this point that Philip invaded Aquitaine for the second time. Believing the pope's advice – that Edward's campaign in the Cambresis would not begin until May – and probably trusting his own spies' validation of this information, he judged it safe to withdraw his forces from the north. Having done so, he threw them into a sustained onslaught on the English forces in the south-west. It was an inspired strategy; Edward was unable to take his army across France and unable to mobilise a sea-borne force to defend the duchy. He had also failed strongly to support those who had previously resolutely held out for him, so that their resolve was weaker on this second occasion. He had only one option left open to him: to invade France without delay, diverting Philip's attention from the south-west. He summoned all his allies to gather for an invasion on 18 December, but, to his great anger, the response was not even lukewarm. They had settled their minds on a war in May 1339, and nothing would move them to risk everything now, in winter.

The strategic drawbacks of the alliance were now apparent. It was holding Edward back from attacking Philip, it was preventing him from taking action against the French fleet, and it was quickly bankrupting him. And it was sapping his moral authority too. It would not be long before he was reduced to little more than a paymaster for the German confederacy. He had lost papal support, and had infuriated Philip into attacking England itself as well as English trade. His own kingdom was on the brink of economic turmoil, and he was in grave danger of parliamentary opposition. But even if Edward could now see that he had been wrong, and that he had made mistakes, he was aware that to give up on the alliance now would be a waste of all he had invested. In order to maintain a degree of pressure on Philip through the alliance, it was important for him not to lose his nerve.

Edward's saving grace was that, unlike his father, he had a sense of purpose, and it was a noble purpose by the definitions of the time. He also had a self-belief which allowed him to cope with the problems which he had brought upon himself. He could rant at his ministers, he could sack them and he could even order the council back in England to stop paying the civil servants (which he did, to their shock and indignation), but while he kept focused on England's war with France, and while he continued to inspire those around him, no one was in a position to question him or take action against him. It was this focus, confidence and leadership which now he used to draw himself out of his predicament. He marched to Brussels with his army and threw himself into negotiations for the campaign. When these had proved futile, he declared to his allies that, if they would not fight, then he would. He would lead his army into France, and do battle, with or without them. He set down his terms for renewing negotiations in a final ultimatum. He demanded five things: that the losses on either side should be made good, that friends of either king could freely pass over the lands of both kings, that merchandise should be freely transported, that the king of France should offer no further help to the Scots and that Philip should restore those parts of Gascony which he had recently occupied.[65] It was not an excessive list; the first three were merely normal affairs. The pope, still in a hostile mood towards Edward, declined to accept the fourth point, advising merely a truce between England and Scotland, and preferred not to comment on the fifth point. King Philip refused to accept the ultimatum outright.

Edward, having made up his own mind, and seeing the pope and Philip practically united in their opposition to English interests, now put his own grievances to the pope and the college of cardinals in a long letter dated 16 July.[66] He stressed the dangers of war, asserted that he loved the ways of peace ('as God knows'), but claimed that Philip (whom he described as his 'persecutor') had illicitly occupied the throne of France, and therefore threatened war. His basis for this was that although a woman was barred by Roman Law from occupying the throne, this bar only applied to the woman herself, and not her male offspring. If the bar attended to her male offspring, then Jesus had no right to be described as of the line of David, as his mother Mary, bearer of God's child, was the parent through which this claim descended. As Edward was the nephew of the last king, and Philip was a cousin, he had a prior claim, as Philip's was collateral. (Contrary to popular belief his claim had absolutely nothing to do with Salic Law, a local land inheritance law whose relevance was pretended by French writers in the next century.)[67] Edward went on to state that he had done nothing to provoke Philip, and that he deplored the invasion of Aquitaine and France's support for the Scottish nationalists. He stressed how wronged he felt. The letter is very revealing, especially the sentences immediately following this claim of self-defence. Edward claimed that:

We only make a shield against him who levelled a deadly blow at our head . . . At this he storms, Holy Father, he storms, is uneasy and complains: he, who sought by his subtle devices to find us unadvised and unprepared. But according to the Theory of War, which teaches that the best way to avoid the inconvenience of war is to pursue it away from one's own country, it is more sensible for us to fight our notorious enemy in his own realm, with the joint power of our allies, than it is to wait for him at our own doors.[68]

Here we see the fundamental principle of Edward's strategy clearly spelled out: taking the fight into France protected England. When twentieth-century historians came to assess the 'profit and loss' account of the English during the Hundred Years War, they completely ignored this element of his strategy, only counting Edward's territorial conquests and losses.[69] But Edward could win and lose in France, and have nothing material to show for his troubles at the end of the day, and still would have achieved something because he had protected England from French attack. In this same letter Edward stressed that the more he thought about Philip paying for an army out of money originally gathered to fight the crusade, the more it pained him. Benedict had granted a clerical subsidy for the crusade, and another for the defence against Ludvig, and permitted Philip to use both to fight the English, which rankled with Edward. But no matter how interesting and revealing the letter was, Benedict was having none of it. In keeping with his new policy of favouring the French, he did not even reply.[70]

Edward marched into France on 20 September 1339. Some of his allies followed him; Ludvig did not. The duke of Brabant was still in negotiations with Philip. Promises for payments were made, promises to leave hostages to ensure final payment were added, and Edward himself was forced to promise that he would remain in the Low Countries as security for the debts he had incurred. The cardinals who had tried hard to bring Edward to accept Philip's absolute rule in France and his right to intervene in Scotland remained with him. On the first night Sir Geoffrey le Scrope led one of them, Bertrand de Montfavez, cardinal deacon of St Mary in Aquiro, up a tall tower, showing him the result of the first day's work. It was a dark, moonless night, and as he looked out it was clear that every village for fifteen miles in every direction was on fire. The cardinal was reminded of something he had once declared to Edward in his negotiations: 'the kingdom of France is surrounded by a silken thread which all the power of England will not suffice to break'. Scrope said calmly to the cardinal: 'does it not seem to you that the silken thread encompassing France has broken?' Seeing the terrible outcome of the invasion, the cardinal grew faint, staggered and collapsed.[71]

Edward's strategy was simple. If he could bring Philip to battle and defeat him, then he would gain glory, win his arguments over Scotland and Aquitaine and limit his liabilities to his German allies. Hence the utmost destruction of France was undertaken. He besieged the town of Cambrai and destroyed as much land and as many villages as he could. But Philip did not give battle. Reactions were mixed. The duke of Brabant joined Edward at the end of September, but the young count of Hainault deserted him, and joined Philip. Further delays would mean further expense, further doubt in his resolution and inevitably more defections. Edward had no option but to go forward, and to take the fight to the French army, which was more than double the size of his own, even including his allies' troops. With caution he advanced directly towards Péronne, where the massive French army had gathered.

On 14 October Edward brought his army within a mile of the French. Everything he stood for and believed in – chivalry, glory and royalty, divine support and the prophesies that he would be a great conqueror – was about to be put to the test. But in order to implement the military strategies he had learnt in Scotland, he needed to force the French to attack him. And in order to withstand an attack by superior numbers, he needed to draw his men up in a particularly well-defended situation, so he could catch the French in the cross-fire. Although he had found the French, and they were ready to do battle, Edward was not in a well-defended position. His smaller army was in fact exposed. He had no option but to withdraw. In the ensuing discussions about future strategy, the German allies declared they were running short of supplies. They wanted to go home.

Edward had not waited a whole year on the Continent simply to withdraw at the first onset of his allies' fear and hunger. He had held back from encountering the French in a weakly defended position, but his resolution to do battle went far beyond this one encounter. He reinforced his original strategy, sending out the earls of Salisbury, Derby and Northampton to destroy whatever they could. He also sent Sir John of Hainault, whose men stormed into the town of Origny, looting, burning and destroying. A Benedictine nunnery was looted, and the nuns themselves raped. Sir John then proceeded to Guise, which he burnt. In the castle at Guise was his daughter, Jeanne, married to the heir of the count of Blois, a Frenchman. Jeanne pleaded with her father to save the lands and heritage of the Blois family; but Sir John had his orders, and he carried them out mercilessly. Those who fled were hunted down in the woods by the lord of Fauquemont.[72] More than a dozen villages and towns were utterly wasted by the English troops in the next two or three days. The destruction would have made Cardinal Bertrand faint again, but the result was precisely what Edward wanted. A messenger from Philip came to him at La Flamengrie, offering to do battle on a certain day, either 21 or 22 October, in a place unencumbered by rivers, walls or earthworks. It was now down to Edward to choose the site of the battle.

He chose carefully, a place between La Flamengrie and La Capelle, on the evening of 22 October. The huge French army was just four miles away. He and his advisers had one major strategy in their minds: the tactics which had proved so effective at Dupplin Moor and Halidon Hill. They would invite the traditional charge of mounted men at them, and they would situate their archers on either side to destroy the charge. Edward's position had a dense wood on one flank, and a slope in front of him, which would naturally reduce the speed of the French attack. On the morning of the 23rd, the king and his men attended mass, and then set about the final preparations for the battle. All knights were ordered to dismount, regardless of the fighting practices of their respective leaders. Their horses and baggage were placed in a small wood behind the three battalions of men. Trenches were dug to protect the archers from a direct charge. Then the English and their allies formed up in three battalions. The first and largest, including the English household knights, was commanded by Edward himself. The second, composed mainly of men from the Low Countries, was commanded by the duke of Guelderland and Sir John of Hainault. The third was commanded by the duke of Brabant. On the wing was another force, commanded by Sir Lawrence Hastings (whom Edward now created earl of Pembroke), the earl of Warwick, Lord Berkeley and Sir John Molyns. The express purpose of this small battalion was to hold the rear, and to rally the Germans if they tried to desert. When all was ready, Edward mounted a humble palfrey and rode along the lines, with Robert d'Artois, Sir Reginald Cobham and Sir Walter Manny, making knights of valiant men and shouting out exhortations to all the troops not to dishonour themselves or him in the forthcoming battle. Then Edward and his companions took their position at the front of the English household knights, with banners held aloft, and pennons flying above each battalion.

Nothing happened. Morning passed, noon came. The French army, restless, sent up such a great shout at the sight of a hare running across the ground in front of them that the count of Hainault at the rear of the army, thinking the attack was about to begin, knighted fourteen men in preparation for the battle. Froissart took great delight in noting that they were thereafter called 'Knights of the Hare'. Such was his embarrassment at this *faux pas* that the count withdrew his forces. A little later, a letter arrived from the king of Jerusalem and Sicily, supposedly telling Philip that he had consulted the stars to tell Philip's fortune and the prognostication was that Philip should never risk doing battle with Edward directly, for he would always lose. More serious were the discussions raging among the advisers gathered around Philip. The trenches dug in front of the English ranks were so deep, said some, that they would not be able to sustain their charge. Others argued that Philip was obliged to give battle, for it would be dishonourable to withdraw now. Dishonour or not, it was those who advocated withdrawal who prevailed. The danger to France was too great. Philip agreed, and ordered the building of his own defences to protect his army in their current position. There would be no battle.

Edward was let down by both his enemy and by his allies. The latter assured him that they thought that he had won the moral victory, as Philip had gone back on his promise to fight. But Edward knew that that was not true. The victory was as much Philip's, for, seeing that no battle was to take place, the allies now began to withdraw. Edward had no option but to follow them. The only loser of the battle – the battle that never was – was Edward.

*

Edward's lack of success was not obvious to those who were with him on the campaign, but his failure to make significant inroads into France was soon magnified by a string of other calamities. The Scots had recovered practically all of Edward's hard-won Scottish lands, including Cupar Castle, the county of Fife, and the strategically important castle at Perth, which Sir Thomas Ughtred was forced to surrender on 16 August after a hard siege. Worse, while Edward had been facing the French army in October 1339, his regency council in England had been facing the anger of parliament. High prices, high taxation and widespread suffering at the hands of Edward's purveyors had bubbled over into angry parliamentary representations. Warned of this, Edward had directed the head of the regency council, Archbishop Stratford, to grant concessions if necessary. The order that all debts were to be paid in full was to be relaxed, as was the confiscation of the property of felons.[73] But such concessions did not go far enough. Although Stratford made no secret of the king's indebtedness, and at three hundred thousand pounds may even have exaggerated it, both houses of parliament refused to rush to Edward's financial rescue.[74] The lords called for the abolition of higher wool duties. The commons supported them, and added a trenchant demand that, unless purveyors paid for what they took, they should be arrested as thieves. The king's purveyor-in-chief, William Wallingford, was arrested. Commissions of enquiry were set up into purveyance in various counties. Although the lords were still prepared to see further taxation imposed, the commons refused, preferring further consultation in the counties before any decision was made. Edward now had to face the opposition of his own parliament in addition to that of his enemies and the half-heartedness of his allies.

Edward returned to the Low Countries, still bound by the agreements of the previous autumn not to leave until all his debts were paid. That now looked a very far-off time indeed, especially since the commons' refusal to pay a new subsidy towards the war. But Edward now proved adaptable to his changed and challenging circumstances, and entered into new negotiations with the new leaders of Flanders, in particular a wealthy merchant called Jacob van Artevelde.

Van Artevelde's name remains famous to this day principally on account of his revolution. When Count Louis of Flanders professed his loyalty to his overlord, Philip of France, his people were starving, penniless and riotous. The reason was Edward's strategy of disposing of his wool at staples (designated places of trade). Flanders depended on English wool to make cloth. Starved of their raw material, and seeing more and more of their fellow cloth-workers drawn to England to ply their craft there, the great trading cities of Bruges, Ypres and Ghent had rapidly become places of violent dissent. First to tumble into revolution was Ghent, which saw an emergency committee of governors appointed in early January 1338. Five captains of the people, led by Jacob van Artevelde, took control of the city. Utterly ruthless, and unscrupulous in his use of violence to attain his ambitions, he soon destroyed any authority Count Louis had left. Bishop Burghersh immediately saw the opportunity to gain a diplomatic advantage, and quickly negotiated an agreement whereby Flanders would remain neutral during the forthcoming hostilities. Pleased with Burghersh's coup, Edward maintained good relations with the Flemings thereafter, hoping in due course to draw them also into his grand alliance, and closer than some of the more reluctant princes who had already contracted to serve him.

Edward's favour persuaded the Flemings that their interests were best served by supporting England. Van Artevelde had the idea of going further than this, using English military support to gain control of parts of Flanders lost to the French after the battle of Cassel. He hatched a plot with Edward that he would attack Lille, Douai and Bethune while Edward's invasion was in progress. However, by the time van Artevelde made his move, Edward's army was already returning from La Flamengrie. The withdrawal of the allies from the battlefield relieved the pressure on Philip, and the Flemish, having declared war on the French, realised that they had jeopardised their position. Had van Artevelde at this stage sought reconciliation with France, he would have seen his own position swept away and his life forfeit for treason against his lord, the count of Flanders. His only option was to join the alliance completely, and become an ally of England.

For Edward, this had one huge implication. If the Flemings broke their allegiance to the king of France, then automatically the whole country would fall under an interdict. They would also be obliged to pay to the pope a huge sum – two million florins (£333,333) – if they were to renounce allegiance. Such sums and such risks were beyond the townsmen who had seized power from the count. But there was a solution. If Edward were publicly to claim the title King of France, then, in maintaining loyalty to him, they would not be breaking their oaths, nor would they be obliged to pay the fine.

At Brussels in the first week of November a great tournament was proclaimed to celebrate the end of the campaign. Once more Edward indulged in costly gift-giving, as keen as ever to play the propaganda card of international largesse. But behind the scenes, serious negotiations were taking place about the Flemish situation and the claim to the throne of France. On 3 November Brabant and Flanders signed a treaty of mutual protection and trade. Edward was still hampered by debt, facing the opprobrium of the English commons in parliament, and worried about the situation in Scotland. He was probably compromised by the pope, though not in the same way as the Flemings.[75] He also had to face the fact that a public claim to the throne of France would be practically impossible to put into effect, and this carried with it the danger of ridicule for claiming something which was inappropriate and embarrassing. Nevertheless, he wanted the Flemings on his side, and he agreed a treaty. It would leave him no option but to claim France as his own inheritance.

The decision was not an easy one. Just how difficult it was can be seen by reflecting on Edward's previous claims. His mother had first claimed the throne on his behalf in 1328. Edward had never renounced this, but had been forced to do homage to Philip in 1329. As he is supposed to have said in the Vow of the Heron, he was a young man then, and the homage was not of his own will. But he had done homage again in 1331. Not until 1337 had the question been raised again, and though debated by the king's council and parliament from January that year it was only in the documents of 6 and 7 October that he actually styled himself 'King of France'. By the 19th, after an intervention by the papal emissaries, he had stepped back from claiming the throne and changed his strategy to objecting to Philip claiming it. This remained the position for more than twenty months, until his letter of 16 July 1339, in which he demonstrated to the cardinals why his claim was superior to Philip's. But still he did not actually claim the title. There was a real reluctance, much more than a mere hesitancy. Contemporary writers stressed how much discussion and thought had gone into it. It was only when the Flemish councils insisted that they would not support Edward unless he claimed the throne that the decison was made.

On 26 January 1340, Edward finally claimed the title King of France. Although he had probably weighed up every consideration which had occurred to him, his advisers, his allies and his councils, he could have had no idea how significant this decision would be in English history. He radically altered the focus of the war from being a mere dispute about feudal rights in Aquitaine to an argument about the sovereignty of the whole of France and its dependencies. That argument – to which French historians gave the name 'the Hundred Years War' in the early nineteenth century – did indeed continue for more than a hundred years. In fact it may be argued it lasted for a hundred and fifty years, for although the final battle was fought in 1453, peace was not agreed until 1492. It has been described as 'perhaps the most important war in European history'.[76] It was not until 1802 that George III finally dropped the formal title 'King of France', after the French Revolution had destroyed the Bourbon monarchy. It is difficult to think of any other single initiative of an English king before Henry VIII's break with Rome which had such long-lasting, widespread and dramatic consequences.[77]

SEVEN

Sluys and Tournai

Before his birth it had been predicted that Edward would wear 'three crowns'. The prophecy probably meant the iron, silver and gold crowns of the Holy Roman Emperor, the title currently borne by Ludvig of Bavaria.[1] Ludvig declined to give up his title, but Edward was not to be outdone. He already had a good claim to wear the sovereign crown of England, and a claim on the overlordship of Scotland. To these he had added the vicarial crown. But even these three were not enough. Now, in the market square of Ghent, in Flanders, he went one better, exceeding the prophecy with a claim on a fourth crown: that of France.

In reality only his English title imparted genuine sovereignty. Scotland was almost lost. The Holy Roman Empire had proved an expensive and weak ally, and its counts, margraves and dukes had shown themselves to be undutiful subjects. And Edward had not conquered so much as an inch of French soil. Those who witnessed his proclamation as king of France on 26 January, sitting on a makeshift throne in a marketplace, might have wondered if this was another gesture, as devoid of power as the last. But Edward's French claim was a deeply serious move, for by it he was able to accept overlordship of the Flemish people, and thereby 'conquer' a part of Philip's realm (in a manner of speaking) without having to pay or fight. In shifting his friendships away from the half-hearted German leaders towards Flanders, while keeping Brabant in the alliance, he had forged a much more powerful confederacy, for Flanders and Brabant had a definite interest in English affairs through their dependence on the English wool trade. An alliance with them had the potential to last.

Claiming the throne of France was a complicated business. Not least of the problems was that of which kingdom came first. Was Edward king of 'France and England', or 'England and France'? To the modern reader this might appear a minor point, but to contemporaries it was of grave importance, for it could be construed that it implied precedence and subjection. In October 1337, when Edward had first contemplated adopting the French title, he had played safe, issuing two sets of letters, one styled 'king of France and England' and the other with the order reversed. After 1337 it had been easy to refer to Philip as 'he who calls himself king of France', or 'our cousin, Philip de Valois'. But actually claiming the title was much harder. Philip himself may have contributed to the problem, mocking Edward at first for quartering the arms of England – the three leopards – with the fleur de lys of France. Probably before 1340, Philip pointed out in ridicule that Edward had put the arms of the little country of England in the upper dexter quarter – the most important position – thus relegating the arms of France (the largest and richest kingdom in Christendom) to a lesser position.[2] Edward's decision to reverse this, putting the fleur de lys prominently in the upper dexter quarter, was a direct challenge to Philip, visually demonstrating in vivid blue and gold that he, Edward, was the heir of France.

Philip's response to Edward's claim was surprise and anger. His fury reached a peak on 8 February 1340, when Edward's new seal arrived. That day Edward issued a declaration to the French people, in French, declaring that, as the Flemings had recognised him as king of France, he invited them to do so too. Now Philip could see for himself, engraved on the seal, the French arms quartered with the English. When Philip read the motto – 'Edward, by the grace of God, king of France and England' he was aghast at his audacity. Then he learnt that Edward had issued the same declaration and issued copies of his seal to all the towns in and around Flanders as well as several places in France. Realising he had been challenged and embarrassed, he ordered a search of all church doors and public places for copies of the letter, and decreed that anyone found carrying a copy was to be regarded as a traitor and hanged.

The pope too was surprised and angered by Edward's claim, stating that the 'sight of his letters, with his new title and seal engraved with the arms of France and England, caused surprise'.[3] He insisted that heirs of females could not inherit in France, despite the arguments laid before him by Edward's lawyers. He added that, even if they could, there were others closer to the throne than Edward.[4] Then he went on to castigate Edward for accepting 'evil counsel'. In this way he put forward a vehement protest on behalf of his homeland, with direct accusations that those who had advised Edward were untrustworthy and that the allies of France would do Edward no end of harm.

The pope's surprise at Edward's claim was probably genuine. When Edward had first claimed the title in October 1337, it was probably only the prompt intervention of the cardinals which had prevented him from sustaining the claim. The pope felt that his cardinals had done enough then to dissuade Edward from adopting the title, limiting him to merely disputing Philip's right. This may have been effected through secret threats as well as more open persuasion, and, at that point, this may have included threats to unveil his father, in Italy. Now, thanks to Niccolinus Fieschi, Edward could contain this threat. Perhaps in connection with this matter, it was Niccolinus whom Edward chose to go to explain his actions to the pope. Edward's position was that Philip de Valois had made no attempts to avert war, and although Edward would have been content with a modest attempt at peace, he could see no other option but force.[5] But shortly after Niccolinus's arrival in Avignon, the French, with the help of the pope's marshal, broke into the house in which he was staying and kidnapped him in his nightclothes. Although Benedict was very much in favour of the French at this time, he took the seizure exceptionally seriously, and placed the whole of France under an interdict until Niccolinus Fieschi was set at liberty. To suspend the religious services (including burials, marriages and baptisms), confessions and privileges of an entire kingdom on account of a single offence committed in his own household against a Genoese knight acting for the English king was extreme, to say the least. Philip complained directly about the punishment. Whatever the real purpose of Niccolinus's mission, there was more to his seizure than a violation of diplomatic immunity. He had become as important to the pope as he was to Edward. Pope Benedict hanged all those he suspected of being involved. With regard to his marshal, who committed suicide in gaol before he could be hanged, the benign pontiff had the man's body exposed on a gibbet 'for the birds to eat'.[6]

The English were the most surprised of all by Edward's new title. Although Edward decided on a solution with regard to the order of his kingdoms – 'king of France and England' for international affairs, and 'king of England and France' for matters relating to the British Isles – not even he could justify having more than one coat of arms. For the English to know that their king had adopted the arms of France and set them above those of England was confusing and damaging to English pride. It was threatening too, because his decision to adopt this coat of arms and title was made without any reference or explanation to parliament. Combined with his demands for money and his other high-handed orders since leaving England, it was beginning to seem that he gave little thought to the people of his homeland, and respected their independence even less.

Edward's point of view was very different. Eighteen months on the Continent had broadened his horizons. Here he was, the Vicar of the Holy Roman Empire, the self-proclaimed king of France, and a champion of Christendom: it is easy to see why he did not relish the prospect of returning to a small island to beg for every tenth scraggy sheep off the South Downs. But although Edward's conceit, anger and frustration sometimes blinded him, and made him act rashly, like his self-defeating father, he had not completely lost touch with reality. His claim on France and the vicariate were only made possible by revenues derived from English land and English sheep. If he wanted to reclaim all of Gascony, including the Agenais, and defend England against any counter-attack, then those sheep were important.

Edward had planned to return to England early in December 1339, and had written to the duke of Brabant arranging to leave hostages during his absence, hoping to wriggle out of the terms of his earlier financial agreement. This did not happen, possibly because the Flanders negotiations took longer than expected, possibly because the duke of Brabant refused him permission to leave, or possibly due to Edward deciding that his proclamation to the French throne had to be made while he was still in Flanders, on French sovereign territory. Whichever it was, events were now moving quickly, and even Edward was having difficulty maintaining control. Stuck in Ghent, he probably convinced himself that he could rely on past decisions of parliament to support his adoption of the French title, and that a belated explanation would be acceptable. But his first inclination – to return to England and do his explaining up front – was the better one. In January the commons again refused to grant him a new subsidy. They would confer further and give him a formal answer in February. Such continued resistance from mere commoners had never before been voiced in an English parliament, and it alarmed him. He needed to return to England straightaway.

Edward landed in England on 21 February 1340, having left his heavily pregnant queen in Ghent. Two days earlier the commons had returned their final verdict. They had consulted with those they represented and they would grant no further taxation without concessions. Adapting quickly to the sensibilities of the English, and aware that these men of the shires and towns regarded themselves as representing those who had chosen them – a new development in itself – Edward issued a summons for them to attend another parliament at which he could address their grievances. In order to pre-empt criticism over setting the arms of France above those of England, he explained in the writ of summons that it had not been his intention to prejudice the kingdom of England by assuming the title of France.[7] Indeed, by 29 March, when parliament gathered in his presence for the first time in three years, Edward was in an attentive, concession-ready mode. He was prepared to say what the people wanted to hear, and to grant whatever they demanded.

Parliament had been worried by Edward's repeated high-handedness, and it assembled with a view to listing all of its many demands. Edward had only one requirement: money. If the commons wanted reform, they would have to agree first to finance Edward's war, for that was the bedrock of his policy: to keep the enemies of England on the defensive and in their own lands. To this the commons did agree. In fact they did more than just agree, they encouraged him and supported him in this policy by granting him every ninth sheep, fleece and sheaf for two years.[8] Those who lived in forests and wastes, and foreign merchants, were to be taxed at a fifteenth of their goods, but it was stressed that it was not the wish of the king, nor of the magnates, nor of the commons, that this tax of a fifteenth should be extended to 'poor cottagers or those who lived by their labour' (this was the first time tax relief had been granted for the poor). Parliament also granted a duty of forty shillings on every sack of wool, every three hundred sheepskins and every last of leather exported. This generosity permitted parliament to ask for much in return. Liberties were confirmed, debts to the Crown were pardoned, and delays in the administration of justice were ordered to be dealt with. The use of standard English weights and measures was implemented throughout the kingdom. The method of appointing of sheriffs – widely hated officers of state – was reformed.[9] The Walton Ordinances, which Edward had ordered when leaving England in 1338, were wholly repealed. The outdated custom of Englishry was dispensed with forever.[10] Purveyance was dealt with, as well as rights of presentation to church benefices. A permanent baronial committee, appointed by parliament, was established to oversee all royal taxation and expenditure.[11] Lastly, the question of the subjection of England to the kingdom of France was firmly and unambiguously settled. Edward undertook that 'the realm of England never was or ought to be in the obedience of the kings of France' and 'that our realm of England and the people of the same shall never be made obedient to us, nor our heirs and successors, as kings of France'.[12]

This process of creating legislation – responding to social demands in return for extraordinary taxation – was effectively selling laws. As a result, it has frequently been attacked as a haphazard legislative programme. It certainly suggests that Edward had no domestic legislative agenda of his own. But we have to ask whether a responsive approach to lawgiving was a negative thing. After all, most modern laws are passed in reaction to changing social circumstances. In April 1340 Edward was in no position to know what was required in England; he had been overseas for almost two years. All he knew was that he had to restore his standing in parliament. So the relatively free hand he gave to representatives to set the legislative agenda was not simply due to his need for taxation. It follows that he cannot be credited with the reforms of 1340 except in one important respect: he allowed these statutes to be enrolled. For this

Edward II in Gloucester Cathedral. His overthrow and its implications had the
most profound effect on his son's life. This magnificent alabaster effigy was probably
commissioned by Edward at the same time as that of his brother (*below*).

John of Eltham, Edward's brother, who died at the age of nineteen. Edward subsequently
had bad dreams about his brother's death.

A fifteenth-century image of Edward's mother, Queen Isabella, being welcomed by her brother King Charles of France. Edward was devoted to her.

This image of Edward washing his hands was part of a manuscript presented to Edward around the time of his accession. Personal cleanliness was very important to upper ranks of medieval society.

Another image of the young king, originally from the same presentation manuscript. Edward liked to be depicted with a falcon on his arm: his wedding present from Philippa also showed him with a falcon.

This sculpture of a king on the side of the tomb of John of Eltham has often been assumed to depict his father. But the symbolic empty falconer's glove probably indicates that this is meant to represent Edward himself.

R. Smirke del.

Outline of the king (Edward III, traced from the tracing - the face carefully copied from the Original painting previous to its removal from S. Stephens Chapel.

The paintings which Edward commissioned for St Stephen's Chapel were plastered over when it was remodelled to form a meeting place for the House of Commons in the sixteenth century. Further remodelling by Wren obliterated any vestiges of medieval architecture. The paintings were exposed in the early nineteenth century, and these drawings, by Robert Smirke, are the most accurate copies of the figures of Edward III and Queen Philippa which adorned the east wall. They were lost in the fire of 1837.

Outline of the Queen traced from the tracing with the face carefully concealed from the Original
before it was removed.

Edward, 'The Black Prince', from Edward's tomb in Westminster Abbey. The victor of the battle of Poitiers, he spent the last six years of his life an invalid, and died at the age of forty-six.

Edward's second son, Lionel. Probably the best administrator of Edward's five sons, he spent his most active years in Ireland. He died at the age of thirty.

Edward's daughter, Mary.
She was buried at Abingdon
with her sister Margaret.
They were probably both
victims of the plague of 1361.
Mary was seventeen, Margaret fifteen.

Edward's second daughter, Joan.
One of the first English victims
of the Black Death, she died at
Bordeaux, on her way to marry
Pedro of Castile in the summer of
1348. She was fourteen years of age.

Queen Philippa's tomb effigy. This sculpture was commissioned during her lifetime, and is the earliest royal effigy which we can be sure is an attempt to record the exact features of the deceased.

Edward III's death mask. The plaster mask, showing the drooping mouth (evidence of a stroke), was fixed to a clothed wooden figure and carried in his funeral procession. It provided the basis for the king's eventual tomb effigy.

his contemporaries were prepared to give him some credit. They knew it was something his father would not have done.

*

On 16 April 1340 Edward was jousting at Windsor Castle. Unexpectedly, a messenger arrived from Flanders. Five days earlier, two of Edward's closest companions – the earls of Salisbury and Suffolk – had left the main army and set off to spy out the defences of Lille. They had had with them thirty men-at-arms, and some mounted archers. They were spotted, however, and as they moved around the town, they were gradually surrounded. When the garrison closed in, they were trapped, with their backs to the moat. They had drawn their weapons and fought furiously, even until dark. But when sixty or more men lay dead on the ground, the last seven were overpowered. One – a renegade French knight – was dragged over to a nearby tree and hanged there and then. Both earls and the remaining four men-at-arms were taken captive.[13]

Salisbury and Suffolk – his friends, Montagu and Ufford – to Edward this must have come as a shock. But there was worse news to follow. The earl of Salisbury had been his principal commander in the Low Countries, and his capture flung the whole region into disarray. The French destroyed the towns of Haspres and Escaudœuvres and many villages in Hainault. In May they attacked Valenciennes itself, the capital of Hainault, burning and destroying everything in the vicinity.[14] Sir Walter Manny's brother, Giles, was captured and killed. An allied attack on Tournai failed. Incursions into England from Scotland meant that now, unable to spare troops to defend the border, Edward had to sue for a lasting peace in Scotland, against his wishes. In addition to all this, Philip's fleet was so strong that Edward had to prohibit the export of wool for fear of it being stolen by the French.[15]

To Edward there was only one solution. He had to return to France as quickly as possible and lead an attack on the French army. If he did not, Flanders would be lost to him, and his wife too, still a hostage in Ghent, recovering from giving birth to John, later known as John of 'Gaunt' (Ghent). Edward needed ships, particularly the large Mediterranean galleys which Philip had been able to requisition from the Genoese. He wrote to the pope exhorting him to make sure Niccolinus Fieschi was released from prison so he could arrange for the commissioning of vessels. He also wrote to the Venetians, asking them specifically for forty galleys.

It seems that Edward was just beginning to panic. In his letter to the Venetians he was at pains to point out why they should supply him with galleys and not Philip. He explained the cause of the war – that Philip had occupied his lands in France – and added that:

On this account, King Edward calls upon the said Philip to fight a pitched battle. But for the avoidance of reproach hereafter on account of so much Christian bloodshed, he at the commencement of the war offered, by letter, to settle the dispute either by single combat or with a band of six or eight, or any number he pleased on either side; or that, if he be the true king of France as asserted by him, he should stand the test of braving ravenous lions who would not harm a true king, or perform the miracle of touching for the evil; if unable, to be considered unworthy of the kingdom of France.[16]

It all sounds very self-confident, bragging even. Edward was portraying himself as a leader prepared to risk his life for his political beliefs. But on reflection it is all a little too bombastic; these after all were very distant and very dignified correspondents on the Adriatic. This need to justify himself, personally, in a request for ships to a distant state, was inappropriate. This is especially so when one remembers that Philip was much older than Edward. Edward's need to show that he was a brave and divinely chosen king, brave enough to challenge Philip to single combat, protected by God from the hunger of beasts, hints at a self-conscious need to convince others of his greatness. Such a protest of bravery suggests self-doubt.

The reason for Edward's worry is not hard to find. His whole strategy was collapsing, economically and militarily. On 27 May Edward arranged for his son again to act as regent during his absence overseas. The council of regency was to be headed by the archbishop of Canterbury and the earl of Huntingdon. But they had only been appointed for a few days when the archbishop heard from a messenger of the count of Guelderland that the French were gathering their ships in a great fleet in the Channel to trap Edward when he returned to Flanders. Genoese, Picard, Spanish and French vessels were all drawing together to present an impenetrable wall. Philip had decided that Edward was the cause of, and the solution to, his problems. To capture him now became his highest priority. The archbishop conscientiously told Edward straightaway, but in so doing he made the mistake of telling him what he should and should not do. There were too many ships, he explained, for Edward to consider attacking them. He must remain in England. At this Edward's already-frayed nerves gave way. He exploded in rage at the archbishop, accusing him of being against the war and dictating to him. Faced with this onslaught, the archbishop immediately resigned his office of Chancellor. Edward coldly accepted his resignation, and called two of his most trusted naval advisers to him, Robert Morley, admiral of the northern fleet, and John Crabb. They confirmed what the archbishop had said, saying it was too dangerous to cross the Channel. Edward was furious. 'You and the archbishop are in league, preaching me a sermon to stop me crossing! Let me tell you this: I will cross, and you who are frightened where there is no fear, you may stay at home.'[17] The two naval advisers then said that if the king were to cross, then he and those who crossed with him would be facing almost certain death. But they would follow, even if it cost them their lives.

The chronicler who recorded the above lines was probably trying to accentuate Edward's bravery. However, he did not need to alter the facts to portray Edward as a brave man. Edward was all the braver because he did what he did despite his fear. The inappropriate stresses in the letter to Venice, his lack of money, elements of political misjudgement, his shortage of troops, his giving up of the Scottish war, his admission that the seas were too dangerous to risk the export of wool, the capture of two of his best friends by the French and the risk of losing his wife and son at Ghent, all suggest that now he was under extreme pressure. Given this it is truly impressive that Edward not only gathered a fleet but instilled in his men the belief that they were sailing to Flanders to engage and defeat the enemy. That he was able to inspire them, despite knowing the scale of the task facing them, is astonishing. There were two hundred ships and galleys in the enemy fleet at the mouth of the River Zwin, with nineteen thousand fighting men aboard. Two of the French ships – the *Christopher* and the *Edward* – had once been the pride of his own navy. He himself had only about 120–147 ships and they were mostly much smaller than the large galleys and warships of the French fleet, and fewer than twelve thousand fighting men when he gathered them all at Harwich.[18]

On 20 June, one week late, Edward stepped aboard his largest remaining ship, the *Thomas* and received his new great seal from the archbishop of Canterbury. The archbishop apologised to Edward. Edward accepted the apology and reinstated him as Chancellor, but the prelate, having thought over his position, would not accept. He was too old, he said. He could have added that he was too old to argue politics with a twenty-eight-year-old king who annually made a pilgrimage to see the point of the sword which had killed Thomas Becket, an earlier archbishop of Canterbury. For a second time Edward accepted his resignation. He appointed the archbishop's brother, Robert Stratford, instead. Then, resolved to fight the French, he gave the order for his fleet to sail towards Flanders.

The ships of the fleet all came together over the next two days, keeping close. Small wooden vessels bobbed up and down around Edward's cog: tiny by comparison with some of the vessels they would be facing. Nineteen of the French ships – including a few giant galleys hired from the Genoese – were said to have been larger than anything hitherto seen in the Channel.

Late on the next day, Friday 23 June, as the English approached the Zwin estuary, they all saw for themselves. There was no more arrogant bragging or self-delusion. Every man in the fleet could see what stood between them and their purpose. Masts like a forest rose up before them in the evening light. The ships' prows were all armoured with wooden castles, one after the other, all in a row, totally blocking the mouth of the River Zwin.

Edward gave the order for the fleet to drop anchor, and wait the night. The next few hours cannot have been easy for him or his men, trying to sleep with the movement of the ship, each half-listening for a surprise night attack. No sound but the waves lapping at the side of the boat and the low voices of those talking about strategies for the morning. No refuge from the thoughts of the danger that lay ahead. For the women Edward had brought to attend to his wife and newborn son, it must have been a troubling experience. They knew the horrific consequences if they were captured. Aware of their fears and vulnerability, the king ordered them to be kept well back from the battle.[19]

In the morning Edward saw that the enemy ships had not moved overnight. As the sun came up, he and his men waited for them to leave the estuary, to sail towards him. He probably hoped that they would do what the mounted knights at Dupplin Moor had done: charge into the sights of his archers on the flanks. But the French did not move. Their greatest and largest ships were placed at the front, defensively. If Edward wanted to land in Flanders, he would have to take the fight to them.

Still he waited. It was 24 June, the feast of St John the Baptist. Facing the French, the English archers would have looked into the sun. So Edward continued to wait, close to the coast. He knew that if he sailed north, the French could sail between him and the midday sun. Only in the early afternoon, when he knew that the sun would be behind his ships for the rest of the day, and the wind and the tide were with him, did he give the signal to advance.[20] The first of the three lines of English ships sailed forward, the *Thomas* in their centre, with Edward on board and with the new royal banner of England and France, resplendent in red, blue and gold above him.

Slowly he came within arrowshot of the huge French ships. The French and Genoese crossbowmen waited. The English loosed their arrows. The greater range and the faster speed of the English longbows swept the decks of the French vessels. The crossbowmen were powerless to put up a line of fire. Even with the rising and falling of the boats, the English arrows tore through the lines of men on the French vessels. Realising that the impetus lay with them, the English sailed their ships into the French line and hurled their grappling hooks over the sides, drawing them together. The French responded, sending galleys forward to pick off some of the leading English ships. Four great galleys armed with springalds (giant catapults) sailed towards one English ship, the *Oliver*, and fired large amounts of stone shot into its sails and across the decks of the vessel. Soon many aboard the *Oliver* were killed or wounded. But Edward gave orders to respond to the challenge, and several English ships reached the beleaguered boat, driving off the galleys.

Over the next few hours it became clear that to judge the armies by the numbers of ships and men had been misleading. The first line of the French fleet blocked the second line from attacking, and they blocked the third line. All the English ships massed in an attack on the leading French vessels. The men who now rushed from the English on to the French and Spanish ships were hardened fighters. Foremost among them were the earl of Huntingdon, Sir Walter Manny and John Crabb: men used to warfare at sea as well as on land. The men they commanded had marched with Edward against the Scots. They had marched with Edward against Philip at La Flamengrie. They had thought, talked and dreamed of war for the last ten years. Now, at last, they saw that a momentous victory was within reach. It was as if Edward was a sacred leader who could only lead them to victory, like Alexander. He stood on the deck of the *Thomas*, shouting orders, undaunted, even when a French spear struck him through his thigh. Very soon the *Christopher* had a grappling iron hurled on to its deck, and as the English archers on an adjacent vessel let loose volleys of arrows to pin down the Genoese crossbowmen and to curb the sailors throwing down stones from the mastheads, the English men-at-arms scrambled on board.[21] A great shout went up from the English when they saw the French flag torn down from the *Christopher*. It was all the inspiration they needed.

Late that afternoon, when the foremost English vessels broke through the first French line, the second line was open to attack. Seeing the disaster unfolding, the third line fled that evening. The men of Flanders, who had been watching from the shore, themselves rushed to their boats and put out into the estuary. Attacked from both sides, and with very little chance of sailing around the island of Cadsand and away from the carnage, the majority of the French had no option but to fight to the death. Many threw themselves into the water and struggled to shore, where the Flemings caught and mutilated them. For many more there was no retreat, for their leather or metal armour would have drowned its wearer. And this being warfare at sea, which held special fears for men-at-arms, there were no chivalric courtesies. Probably seventeen thousand Frenchmen were killed or drowned, including both commanders of the French fleet. One of the

French admirals was captured alive, but his skills rendered him too dangerous to ransom. Edward ordered the man to be hanged from the mast of his own ship.[22]

It was the most extraordinary victory, and one for which Edward could take the full credit. Not only had he fought in the front line against heavy odds, the decision to sail had been his, the martial experience and ethos of his men had been down to him, and the strategic use of archers had been his. But even more than these, his leadership was responsible for this victory. He had inspired his men to take on a much larger and better-equipped fleet, knowing that the penalty for failure was death. He may have been half-mad with anger, frustration and worry when he had resolved to set sail; nonetheless he had convinced himself and his men that he could win. In his first great battle against the French – the battle of Sluys, as it came to be known – Edward captured 166 ships. Only twenty-four escaped. He had destroyed French naval supremacy in the Channel.[23]

*

In London they could not believe the news. Only the previous October they had been driving piles and stakes into the Thames, fortifying the city, and arranging for church bells to be rung in warning, fully expecting to see two hundred French ships come sailing up the river to burn the city. Now that enemy fleet no longer existed. They could not believe it until a letter from Edward spelled it out for them.[24] In Ghent too there was great rejoicing. Obviously the men he had led to victory themselves did the most celebrating, 'making much noise and much joy from the instruments they had brought'.[25] Edward himself was deeply affected, and gave thanks to God over and over again. It was a propitious day; he had received victory by divine clemency: it was a great miracle. Thanks were given to God 'who had shown mercy to Edward in his great danger'.[26] The significance of it being the feast of St John the Baptist was not lost on Edward either (although it was probably a coincidence that his newborn son had been christened John shortly before).[27] Thanks to that saint were offered in abundance. Edward could not walk or ride because of his thigh injury, and had to stay on board the *Thomas* for two weeks, but, if he had been able to, he would have no doubt gone on a pilgrimage straightaway. He did not neglect to send a letter to all the archbishops and bishops in England informing them of his victory and desiring their prayers. And he wrote to his son with news of the victory, stressing that the *Christopher* and the previously captured vessels had been retaken together with several other ships as large as the *Christopher*. This was news not just of a victory but of an improved platform for English trade, for it hugely increased the seaborne defences and security of the English wool fleet. As soon as he was well enough, he proceeded to the shrine of the Holy Blood at Bruges and the church of the Virgin Mary at Aardenburg to give thanks for his safe delivery.[28] Only then did he progress to Ghent to see Philippa and his new son.

Edward had spent the time laid up with his injury discussing with van Artevelde how best to prosecute the next stage of the war. The sieges of Tournai and Saint-Omer, which had been planned earlier in the year, remained the top objectives. These were both French-controlled towns on the Flemish border, both of strategic significance to Flanders and of great symbolic value to Edward. Tournai in particular was fanatically loyal to Philip.[29] There was no time to lose. Despite his recent victory, the archbishop of Canterbury had written to say that the council was having difficulty in gathering the wool to fund the expedition. The Peruzzi and Bardi banks were also failing to meet part of a loan agreed for the expenses of the royal household. Edward knew he had to keep the momentum going to avoid a repetition of the 1339 fiasco.[30] He split his army into two parts. One, the smaller, was to attack Saint-Omer under the command of Robert d'Artois. He himself would command the other in an assault on Tournai when he was fit enough.

The expedition began badly. Robert d'Artois was an old man unused to Edward's new strategic thinking and unable to organise and inspire the English archers and men-at-arms. He was not trusted by the Flemish infantry either. He sought to take on the French with traditional methods, and was heavily defeated. Many valuable troops were lost to the alliance, and only remnants of the army made their way back to Edward. The siege did not just fail, it did not begin.

Edward reached Tournai on 23 July, one month after Sluys. As he and his allies were taking up positions around the city, it became clear that it was well-prepared to sustain a siege. Its massive walls had been built for just such a purpose. The River Scheldt ran through the centre of the city, making it impossible to deprive it of water.[31] No attempt to take it by force had ever succeeded. More recently, Philip had stationed a strong French garrison there to galvanise the resistance of the twenty thousand inhabitants. The suburbs had been burnt in advance of the allies' arrival. It looked as though it would be a long siege.

Edward, still high after his victory at Sluys, decided the best way to keep the momentum going would be to challenge Philip to a duel. This was what he claimed to have done already in his letter to the Venetians. Now he actually issued such a challenge. On 26 July he sent a letter to Philip, 'count of Valois'. In it he demanded the throne of France, and complained that Philip had violently withheld from him his rightful inheritance. He went on to say that, since the quarrel was between the two men themselves, 'let the controversy between us be fairly decided by ourselves, body to body, that the great nobility and valour of each other may be seen before all men'.[32] Failing that, he offered a pitched battle between each king and a hundred men. And failing that, a pitched battle between their two armies before the walls of Tournai. The sooner Edward could have a positive and decisive victory on land, the less the cost to him, and the sooner he could advance negotiations into his real object: the return of all the lands he had lost since his coronation.

Philip's reply was to pretend that he knew no one who answered to the name of Philip de Valois. It was a dull response, and it frustrated Edward, who clearly took pride in his being prepared to issue a personal challenge as a king. Everything now pointed to Tournai as where the great land battle would take place. It fell to Edward and his allies to subdue the city as quickly as possible. Against a city whose burghers themselves manned its defences and who volunteered to go out on raiding parties to attack the English, that was not going to be an easy task. It was 26 August – a whole month later – before any determined assault was made on the city walls. Two thousand Flemish sought to break through the northern defences. Despite its weakening state, they failed. They failed again a week later.[33]

As the siege went on, Edward grew more and more disillusioned and angry. His money supplies had again dried up. The German allies who were doing nothing on the east of the city were reprimanded for their slackness. They resorted to the reasonable defence that Edward had not yet paid them. The Hainaulters on the southern fringe of the city were engaging often and having successes in ravaging the countryside. But they too were disillusioned by the inactivity of their allies. The Brabanters fell out with van Artevelde, feeling that he was winning the favouritism of the English king. Matters worsened after a Brabant lord told van Artevelde to 'go back to Ghent and brew beer', prompting van Artevelde to draw his sword and kill him. And still the defences of the city had not been breached. The French army under Philip, with the sixteen-year-old King David of Scotland in tow, was drawing close. Edward knew he would have the greatest difficulty resisting them, but there was no alternative. All the allied armies were drawn together, regardless of their squabbles, to face the French advance on 7 September. The citizens of Tournai took arms and prepared to launch themselves on the rear of the allied troops when the battle was underway. Edward stationed a rearguard to protect his armies, and readied his archers.[34]

In one of the most prescient acts of his pontificate, Pope Benedict had sent secret messengers to both Philip and Edward two weeks earlier. To Philip he had sent the low-ranking William Amici, provost of Lavaur. For once we have a secret messenger's instructions written down, for a copy was kept in Pope Benedict's own register. The reason for sending a low-status messenger was to be explained to Philip; it was so he might move more freely than the cardinals sent in the past. He was to set before Philip the pope's fears for his safety and the safety of his eldest son, John, duke of Normandy. He was to stress how successful the English had been at sea, and how the tide in Gascony was beginning to turn in favour of the English. He was to accentuate the size of the Flemish army with Edward, and to underline the dangers of a revolt in the French nobility against Philip, about which the pope had obviously heard mutterings. Finally, there was a renewed danger of a Moorish invasion. Considering all these things the pope heartily desired there to be peace between the two sides, and suggested that Aquitaine should remain in Philip's overlordship with Edward offering fealty and homage for it, as he had before the war. To Edward he sent his chaplain, William Bateman, a trusted agent of Edward's, explaining that just because he had won one crushing victory did not mean he would always be victorious, 'for one who was conquered seventeen times won the eighteenth battle and another who won two victories was totally defeated in the third engagement'. He also made William write down a series of good reasons why Edward should want peace, namely the problems he was facing through being away from his own kingdom, and the danger of the huge army Philip was bringing against him.[35]

Although the seeds of Pope Benedict's advice had always fallen on stony ground before now, and these low-ranking clerics were not directly successful, both kings listened to these emissaries. Their words prepared the ground for a more personal appeal, on the night of 22 September. At the pope's request, Jeanne de Valois, dowager countess of Hainault and an abbess since her husband's death, came to Edward in his tent. As Edward's mother-in-law and sister of King Philip, and mother to the count of Hainault (whom Philip was threatening to decapitate), she was well-placed to gain access to the leaders and able to beg for peace. She had already wept on her knees before Philip. Now she begged Edward to think of Hainault and the destruction and damage that was being done to her son's dominions. She implored Edward for the love of God to desist from fighting.

Normally Edward would have paid scant attention to such pleas. But he faced a very serious dilemma. A messenger from Tournai to Philip had been caught escaping from the city and had informed the English that the people were close to surrendering. That was certainly the feeling in the French camp; many French nobles were gathering with Philip in fear that their relatives in the city were starving to death. Edward desperately wanted to take Tournai. He saw it as a test of his military capability. But at the same time his army was falling apart. If the city lasted out another two weeks, he would lose altogether, and his army would begin to desert. Money from England had entirely dried up, and he was having to borrow at very high rates of interest just to keep going. Thus Jeanne de Valois' pleas and protestations – made by a holy woman, and a special emissary from the pope – gave Edward an honourable way to begin negotiations with Philip. He could pretend that he was agreeing to parley out of benevolence. He agreed that he would send an embassy to treat with Philip at the chapel of Esplechin, about three miles away.

As Edward admitted frankly in a later letter to the pope, his problem was money. Tournai might have been about to fall, or it might not, but Edward could not afford to go on. In this respect he did exactly the right thing, agreeing to terms, for Tournai was not strategically that important to him, and he stood to gain more from a generous peace than a hard-won victory. Three days after Jeanne de Valois' visit, a truce was agreed, to last until the following midsummer. This would apply to France, the Low Countries, Scotland, Gascony: everywhere that the two kings were at war. All armies and troops, including the Scots, would be required to cease their operations, including sieges, with immediate effect. Those who had made conquests could keep what they had won for the time being. There would be freedom to travel and trade. Prisoners were to be restored. The proclamation was to be read in all the countries affected within twenty-six days. One cannot say that normality was restored – war had become more 'normal' than peace between England and France – but a period of stability and relative safety had been settled.

It has been said that the treaty of Esplechin offered something for everyone except Edward.[36] Philip had succeeded in relieving the siege of Tournai and sending Edward and his army back to England, and in paci-fying the men of the Low Countries. Van Artevelde had protected his leadership of Flanders, had an interdict on his country lifted, and retained the English wool trade. The duke of Brabant and the count of Hainault preserved their frontiers, including several gains in the case of Hainault. They had no obligations to do any more fighting but were still owed a small fortune by Edward. But did Edward really lose by the treaty? If Tournai had fallen, the English would have occupied the city and there would have followed a siege or battle between Philip and Edward. The campaign would have been prolonged, and Edward would have found himself in even more dire financial circumstances, regardless of whether he had been militarily successful or not. If Edward had a clear vision of his situation in September 1340 – and from his letter to the pope it seems that he did – he would have seen that his greatest enemy was not the city of Tournai, nor Philip, but his lack of money. If we consider that it was money which defeated him, as he himself said and as historians unanimously agree, then it may be seen that Edward came out of the siege of Tournai very well, and indeed both the siege and the treaty were something to celebrate. He personally remained undefeated in battle. He had stopped the drain on his finances, stopped the attacks on Gascony and his castles in Scotland without having to spend any more money, retained the services of his allies in the Low Countries, and was free to turn his attention to finance. And for this he had had to make no concessions with regard to his claim on the throne of France, no surrender of lands seized by his allies, and most importantly no lasting peace. It is thus understandable that some contemporary knights regarded it as a victory. A great tournament was held at Ghent in October to celebrate his return from the siege. Some even ranked it alongside the more glorious episodes of Edward's career.[37] Thus, although the siege was not successful, the truce which resulted from it was a success. Through it Edward achieved a stability which he needed more than the city of Tournai itself.[38]

EIGHT

Chivalry and Shame

Despite the Treaty of Esplechin, Edward was not free to go home. The treaty did not erase or even put off his debts, and he remained a virtual prisoner in Ghent. It was an impossible situation: he could not efficiently deal with his financial problems from Flanders, yet he was forced to remain there until he had sorted out his finances. Two months of frustration followed. At the end of October he confronted his creditors, and offered twelve thousand sacks of wool in lieu of his debts; an offer which was not accepted. As his creditors had discovered, too much wool glutted the market and its value dropped. His mood was thus very low when, on 18 November 1340, he wrote to the pope.

Edward's letter is fascinating. In it he states that he had withdrawn from the siege at the pope's request 'even though he had had every chance of success'.[1] This claim to the moral high ground was accompanied by a reiteration of his claim to the throne of France, now reinforced with a detailed legal opinion, and a series of firm demands for permanent peace.[2] The pope dearly wanted to see peace before he died, but, as he said in his reply to Edward, nothing said or presented to him was inclined to make him confident of a permanent settlement.

The letter was important for personal reasons too. Extraordinarily, Edward claimed that the reason why he had received no money at Tournai was that the archbishop of Canterbury was hoping that he would be killed. It seems that the failure to supply Edward with money had amplified his argument with the archbishop in his mind, so that Edward believed that Archbishop Stratford was trying to stop the war by stopping Edward personally. In his frustration, he had twisted this around to believe the archbishop was trying to kill him.

There was something else, even more extraordinary. The three envoys were instructed to tell the pope that the archbishop had (in Edward's words) 'spoken separately to me of my wife, and to my wife of me, in order that, if he were listened to, he might provoke us to such anger as to divide us forever'.[3] Historians have not previously given this intriguing claim much attention. However, we have to wonder what the archbishop might have said to Edward about his cherished wife (and to her about him) that it risked the end of their relationship.

Two possibilities are suggested by the evidence (there may, of course, be others). The first is that it was an accusation of conjugal infidelity. It is very unlikely to have been simply an accusation of adultery on the king's part, for medieval marriages required only the wife to remain faithful, not the husband. Certainly the archbishop may have had other ideas about the sexual mores of kings, and told Philippa of something which Edward had done. But if the archbishop had said the same things about Philippa to Edward – accusing *her* of adultery – this would have been far more serious. It is almost unbelievable, given that Edward and Philippa had a famously strong marriage. However, it has not previously been noted that Edmund of Langley, their seventh child, might have been conceived while Edward was at Tournai and Philippa at Ghent. To be precise: the boy was born on 5 June 1341, which, assuming a thirty-eight-week gestation, implies conception on or around 12 September 1340.[4] As noted above, the siege of Tournai lasted from 23 July until the Treaty of Esplechin, dated 25 September.[5] Edward was back at Ghent on 28 September.[6] If Philippa remained at Ghent throughout, either Edmund was born at least sixteen days before term or he was conceived as the result of an adulterous liaison between Philippa and another man.

These circumstances are very similar to a recent discussion surrounding the conception of Edward IV, which provides a good framework for considering this matter in more depth.[7] The first point is obvious: thirty-five weeks is not particularly premature by modern standards, and occurs in about a tenth of modern confinements. The second – that allegations of bastardy were commonly invented to discredit royal political opponents – does not apply in this case, as whatever the archbishop said to Edward about his wife, it was before he knew that Philippa was pregnant. The archbishop might have invented the story to bring dissent between him and his wife, as Edward supposed, but if so we should wonder why. How could the archbishop have benefited from such claims? No public source mentions the story, not even an enemy one.

The third point of reference for circumstantial evidence of illegitimacy is family relationships. How did Edward behave thereafter towards Philippa? Edward was at the Tower at the time of Edmund's birth. Although it is unclear exactly when in 1341 Philippa returned to England, she probably went straight to Langley to prepare for her seventh confinement. Edward visited Langley frequently in the first half of the year, presumably because she was there, and this would suggest no disruption in their relationship.[8] During one of these visits Philippa asked Edward for permission to export wool to pay her debts overseas. Edward agreed on 11 April, but specifically charged her the full rate of duty on each sack she exported.[9] This might be seen as a sign of ill-will, but, if so, it is an isolated instance. He attended her churching at Langley in early July 1341, and held a series of jousts to celebrate the occasion and the boy's baptism.[10] He took part in the jousting himself in a new breastplate, and gave a large present of twenty marks to the minstrels who played during the feast.[11] If there was any discord, he would appear to have been sufficiently reconciled with Philippa by then to sleep with her, as nine months later their third daughter, Blanche, was born. This suggests that, if there was a rift between husband and wife, it was not a long-lasting one.

The other family relationship which must be considered is that of father and son. Did Edward treat Edmund like his other sons? The answer to this is no. Although he created his eldest three surviving sons earls at very young ages (Edward and John were created earls at the age of two years, and Lionel was married to the heiress of an earldom at the age of three), Edmund was not raised to the peerage as a child, and not created an earl until the age of twenty-one. Similarly, although Lionel was given his own household at a young age, and John of Gaunt was placed in his older brother's household, Edmund remained at his mother's side until 1354.[12] When he was finally elevated to an earldom it was the same day as his three older brothers were raised to dukedoms.[13] Edmund, John and Lionel were all born within three years of each other, and were all placed in Queen Philippa's care in November 1342, but only Edmund was not given a title. In 1347, when Edmund's godfather the earl of Surrey died without an heir, the king allowed him only a minor portion of his godfather's inheritance. Unlike John, Edmund was not mentioned in his elder brother's will, nor in his father's. Lastly, Edmund had fewer leadership qualities than perhaps any other member of the entire Plantagenet dynasty.

The second possible explanation for the archbishop's seeds of discord is similar to the above, but rather than being concerned with the legitimacy of one of the ancestors of the Yorkist claim to the throne, it concerns the legitimacy of the ancestor of the Lancastrian claim, John of Gaunt. It was said that Philippa confessed on her deathbed to William of Wykeham, the bishop of Winchester, that in Ghent in 1340 she had swapped the baby with that of a Flemish woman, who had had a son about the same time. This has always been taken as a mendacious piece of propaganda against John, and, although there are two different sources for this story, one of them – Thomas Walsingham – was definitely pro-Wykeham and anti-John of Gaunt in outlook.[14] It has not previously been linked to the row between Edward and Philippa shortly after the child's birth. However, there are a number of reasons why we should be sceptical of this theory.[15] Most importantly, Edward himself never doubted the legitimacy of John of Gaunt, and promoted him in infanthood, adolescence and adulthood far beyond Edmund, who was only a year younger. John was also the first-named executor of Edward's will. If Edward ever heard of this rumour, he genuinely did not believe it.

In all this debate we must proceed with caution. It would be very rash to assume that there is a serious case to be made for illegitimacy, not least because both John and Edmund were recognised by Edward III as second and fourth in line to the throne in 1376. We do not have any corroborative evidence that what Stratford had said to Edward about Philippa related to her behaviour or the legitimacy of their children. And Edward spent a lot of time at Langley with Philippa, too much to imagine that they had had a serious disagreement. The important fact is that the royal marriage was strong enough to withstand the most damaging personal accusations made by the senior prelate in England. Without doubt this is testimony to the bond which Edward and Philippa had formed over the first thirteen years of their marriage.

*

With deeply unsettling rumours about his wife coming to his attention, and his money pressures weighing on his shoulders, and paranoic fears that the archbishop of Canterbury wanted him to be killed, Edward was keener than ever to escape the Low Countries. Being Edward, he now did so. Early in the morning of 28 November Edward slipped away from the palace at Ghent, pretending he was going riding in the suburbs of the city with a few companions, namely the earl of Northampton, Sir Walter Manny, Sir John and Sir Guy Beauchamp, John Darcy (his steward), William Kilsby (his secretary), and a clerk, Philip Weston.[16] As soon as they could, they galloped to Sluys, and then via Zeeland, they sailed on to England. It was not the way in which Edward had planned to leave Flanders, like a fugitive. Nor was it the best time to try to cross the sea. A winter gale blew up, and caught them in the open, and for three days they laboured against storms. When nearing the mouth of the Thames Edward was very nearly drowned.[17] Thrashing around in the pitch dark, soaking, on a heaving wooden vessel in danger of sinking did nothing to allay his anger. Finally, the ship's navigator brought them into the safety of the river, and slowly in the darkness the ship sailed towards the port of London.

It was nearly midnight, 30 November. The ship came to rest at the wharf adjacent to the Tower. Edward disembarked. Movements across the river at night were against the ordinances of the city, so the guards at the Tower should have been alarmed to see a boat approaching. But there was no reaction. Furious at this lack of defence Edward demanded entry and stormed into the castle, demanding to know what was going on. Where was the Lieutenant of the Tower, Nicholas de la Beche? Out of town, came the nervous reply. That was not what Edward wanted to hear. He could barely control his rage. It was immediate confirmation of everything that his control-fixated mind had come to fear. There and then he wanted to see his ministers, especially the Treasurer and the Chancellor. He wanted to see his justices. He wanted to see the London merchants who could have made loans for his campaigns. And above all else, he wanted to see the archbishop of Canterbury.

Much discussion has taken place about the events which followed, which is usually known as the 'Crisis of 1341'.[18] Most of the conclusions have been constitutional in nature. Taking a broader look at the situation in which Edward found himself in December 1340 – narrowly escaping death by drowning, fleeing on horseback with a handful of knights and two clerks from the demagogue of Flanders, his marriage in jeopardy, and above all else, the frustration of being starved of money so that he had to give up the siege of Tournai almost at the point of victory – one can understand his actions much more easily. He could see for himself the powerlessness his father had experienced, and felt it might overwhelm him too. He was reminded of his own experiences as a youthful king, under Mortimer's sway. However, in trying to counter this fear of powerlessness he exerted power more forcefully, thus emulating his father's tyranny. Those he now accused – especially the archbishop of Canterbury – were old enough and wise enough to remember how to deal with royal tyrants, especially when they were driven by hot-headed fury, as Edward was now.

Robert Stratford, the archbishop's brother, was the first to be accused. He was dismissed from his office as Chancellor and charged with failing to supply Edward with his money, and given until 6 January to prepare his case.[19] The bishop of Lichfield was likewise dismissed as Treasurer. But Edward soon turned his attention to the archbishop himself, whom he saw as his principal enemy in this matter. In February he issued a document containing the charges he wanted to bring against the archbishop. In it he accused him of withholding money, encouraging opposition to the taxes granted by parliament, impoverishing the Crown and abusing his authority to his own advantage.[20] No overt reference was made to Edward's secret fears that the archbishop was trying to arrange for him to be killed.

The archbishop's response to the news of Edward's sudden arrival back in England had been to flee to Canterbury. But having heard the things said about him, he soon angrily counter-attacked. In a particularly vicious letter of 1 January, the archbishop suggested that the king was acting tyrannically. The archbishop made the specific comparison between Edward's behaviour and that of his father, claiming he was

> seizing clerks, peers and other people, and making unseemly process against the law of the land and against Magna Carta, which you are bound to keep and maintain by the oath made at your coronation . . . And since certain [of those] who are near to you do falsely charge us with treason and falsehood, therefore they are excommunicated . . .[21]

He completed his allusions to Edward's tyranny with the thinly veiled threat: 'and what happened to your father, sire, you know well'. Three days later he followed this up with another letter to the king in which he outlined his vision of the constitution. He demanded that he stand trial not before the king but before his peers. Edward's reaction to the implicit threat of excommunication was to summon the archbishop immediately to his presence. The archbishop refused. On 28 January he wrote again to Edward, this time openly threatening him with excommunication. Two days later he forbade the payment of clerical taxation. Edward responded with a famous (or infamous) document known by the name which the archbishop gave to it: *Libellus Famosus* ('notorious libel'). In this letter, Edward heaped scorn and invective upon his ecclesiastical enemy, and accused the archbishop of criminal negligence, of urging clerics not to pay taxes, of failing to support Edward financially as agreed, of impoverishing the Crown and of abusing his position to advance his own career and those of members of his family, implying his recently discredited brother Robert (bishop of Chichester) and his nephew, Ralph (bishop of London). At the end of the document, the archbishop was charged with treason. Edward sent copies of the *Libellus Famosus* all around the country, and had it read widely. He also sent a copy to the pope, amplifying his earlier, secret comments, and claiming that, as the archbishop was preaching sedition, it was dangerous to allow him to remain in the country. He was planning to exile the archbishop.

The two men were locked in an almighty tussle. Both were strong characters, influential and intelligent. Edward was the better propagandist, but the archbishop had religion and intellectual discipline on his side. He also had one huge advantage: Edward's taxation had been so punitive – probably the heaviest there ever was in medieval Europe – that he was bound to attract a large degree of popular support, especially when Edward's agents had been trying to collect the taxation granted by parliament twice over.[22] Thus, at the end of March, when Edward finally caved in and summoned a parliament, the archbishop was in the ascendant. Edward, however, was still angry, and when parliament assembled in the

Painted Chamber at Westminster on St George's Day 1341 (23 April), the archbishop was barred entry. Instead he was directed to go to the Exchequer to answer two minor charges against him. The next day he turned up at the Painted Chamber again, and was directed again to face minor charges in the Exchequer. This time he refused, and forcefully took his place along with the other bishops. Edward, seeing there was a show-down developing in which the archbishop was playing the role of Thomas Becket, refused even to enter the Painted Chamber, thereby disempowering the parliament.[23]

On the third day there was no pretence. The archbishop was told flatly by a sergeant-at-arms that he had orders to bar him entry. This time, he refused to leave until receiving the king's order to do so. John Darcy, his son John, and John Beauchamp proceeded to insult the archbishop where he stood. All this, of course, merely played into the archbishop's hands, especially when he raised his cross above them and cursed them both in the name of God. The earl of Northampton attempted to intervene, but failed to reach an agreement with the archbishop. It was down to an old hand, the aged earl of Surrey, to open the way to a peaceful solution. Regarding Kilsby, the younger Darcy and others of the king's friends, he pointed out that this could hardly be called a parliament when those with no right to be there were in attendance and those who should be leading proceedings were barred. These were brave words, and it soon became clear that they represented the thoughts of many less brave men there. Embarrassed, Kilsby and Darcy left. The earl of Arundel (Surrey's nephew) then proposed that the archbishop's case be heard. After several days of negotiations, an appeal on the archbishop's behalf was presented to the king by a number of prelates and magnates, the Cinque Ports, the mayor of London, and the commons. Edward, having seen his accusations refuted, and his personal invective fail to meet with popular support, was forced to receive the archbishop back into his favour.[24]

The whole episode had been gravely embarrassing for Edward. Parliament had decided that he was in the wrong. But as with his previous clash with parliament in 1340, in one respect he emerges with credit. He could admit that he was wrong, temporarily, at least. What is more, he once more exercised that facility of forgiveness which he had used to his credit so often in the past, with regard to men like Kent's and Mortimer's adherents in 1330, and other prisoners like Crabb who proved so valuable. The archbishop was restored to favour and later served again as head of the council of regency, and was even specifically called upon for his advice. De la Beche was appointed to the household of the heir, Prince Edward, and afterwards became seneschal of Aquitaine. In being able to compromise, and admit fault, Edward was immediately able to command loyalty, and reassert his power as king. And when he had reasserted power, he was able to apply it more freely. There is no better example of his doing this than with respect to the statute which the 1341 parliament forced him to accept. This had some important clauses, such as guaranteeing that peers could only be tried by their peers, and that ministers could only be dismissed in parliament. But on 1 October 1341 Edward simply issued letters stating that he had repealed it.[25] There was no recourse to parliament. It was contrary to the law of the land, he claimed, and had been forced on him against his will. To make sure parliament did not react immediately he broke one of his own statutory promises and failed to summon a parliament the next year. From the parliamentary point of view this was of course reprehensible. But from Edward's point of view it was a necessary step in reasserting his royal prerogative. He learned many things from the events of early 1341, but perhaps the most important was that his ministers had to be ruthlessly efficient and utterly loyal to him. He could not rely on parliament to appoint and dismiss such men.

*

Even though the peace treaty was still in force, Edward was wary of a possible French attack. Before 21 June 1341 news reached him that Philip was secretly planning an invasion. A few days later he received a second blow, in the form of a letter from Ludvig of Bavaria stripping him of his imperial title. In itself this was no great loss – the German alliance had proved militarily worthless and financially crippling – but it was encouraging to his enemies, and coupled with Philip's military preparations it gave cause for concern. When a peace conference was proposed to take place at Antoing, four miles from Tournai, Edward had no hesitation. He sent an embassy consisting of the earl of Huntingdon, the Gascon Bernard le Bret, Sir Bartholomew Burghersh (brother of the late bishop of Lincoln, who had died the previous December), John Offord (archdeacon of Ely) and Niccolinus Fieschi.[26] Edward's representatives were informed that his allies – especially the duke of Brabant – had had enough of war with France, and wanted him to prolong the truce until 24 June 1342.[27] With the Scots once more on the warpath, Edward sensibly agreed.

The truce of Esplechin must have been confusing and frustrating to the Scots. Although they were pleased to draw on French support when it was offered, it was obvious to all that their interests and those of France only partially coincided. The nature of Scottish warfare was different too. It was characterised by very small armies looting, burning and destroying, and then melting back into their communities. It was more of a way of life than a military stand-off. As a result, the treaty did not hold in Scotland.

In April 1341 Sir William Douglas dreamed up a strategy for capturing Edinburgh Castle. Seeing as most Scotsmen did not shave their beards but Englishmen did, he gathered two hundred 'savage highlanders', made twelve of them shave, and then dressed these twelve in rough clothes, like English coal and corn traders. The remainder of his men hid in and around the city. Taking a boat laden with goods, he and his twelve 'traders' disembarked and hauled their wares towards the castle, making sure they arrived very early in the morning. They found only the porter awake, and made a preliminary offer to sell their merchandise cheaply. The porter replied that it was too early to wake the governor or his steward, but gave them entry to the outer ward of the castle. As the great gates swung open, they unloaded their coal sacks in the gateway so that the gates could not be closed and the portcullis could not be dropped. They killed the porter and Douglas blew his horn, the signal for the hidden men to attack. In the ensuing fight they killed all but half a dozen of the English garrison. Edinburgh Castle had fallen.

The following month, delighted at this news, David II left Château Gaillard in France and sailed back to Scotland with his queen and household. He landed on 2 June near Montrose, and very quickly accepted the loyalty of the Scots still fighting for him. With the son of the Bruce in their midst, the Scots felt bold enough again to ride into Northumberland. They pressed all the way to Newcastle, and there set about a siege of the town. David II, however, was an inexperienced commander, and was not confident enough to discipline his captains. As the Scots lay before Newcastle, two hundred Englishmen in the town made an early morning sortie to attack the earl of Moray, who was still asleep in his pavilion. Having captured him and killed many of his men, they returned to the town. When the Scots army realised that one of their leaders had been caught napping, literally, they desperately tried a full-scale attack, which left many of them dead at the foot of the town walls.

On hearing news of the incursion, Edward had appointed the earl of Derby to command the Scottish army. That was on 10 October. Seven days later, the earl was still in London.[28] In fact the earl probably did not take charge at all, for at the end of October Edward travelled so rapidly to Newcastle that Derby would have had difficulty keeping up. News of the attack at Newcastle had been brought to Edward by Sir John Neville, who covered the distance (more than 280 miles) in five days, which was very good going for October. Edward seems to have covered the distance almost as fast, assuming personal control of the forces at Newcastle on 2 November.[29]

The speed of Edward's advance was almost his only achievement on this campaign. The Scots withdrew at the approach of the English, and Edward had a miserable time in Ettrick Forest, trying to bring them to battle.[30] He returned in a despondent mood, and only found a chance to redeem some fragment of glory when he learnt that David planned to hold his Christmas festivities at Melrose Abbey. This gave Edward a strong incentive for remaining in Scotland until then, to make sure that *he* was the one to stay at Melrose. The earl of Derby was directed to hold Christmas at Roxburgh, to safeguard the border and the security of the castle itself.

The notable feature of this campaign were the jousts of war. These were rare events in which knights rode against each other with their lances uncapped and sharpened, as if in battle. Normally jousts were jousts of peace, with lances capped with coronals, although men were often injured or killed from falls or internal injuries in these events too. Sir William Douglas came to Roxburgh, and with eleven of his knights, challenged the earl and his companions to a joust of war. His motive may have been to joust for the prize of the Scottish castles which remained in English hands, for such jousts were recorded as receiving royal licence, and took place at Roxburgh and Berwick.[31] Maybe even the right to hold Christmas at Melrose was decided by a joust of war. If so, Edward's knights won, for there he remained for the latter part of December. Sir William Douglas was so severely hurt in his joust with the earl of Derby that he had to be carried back to Scotland. At Berwick, where twelve knights jousted on either side, two Scots knights were killed and one English knight, Sir John Twyford.[32] The campaign resulted in nothing more than a truce until May. Edward left Melrose on or about 30 December, and came south slowly, through Cornhill, Bamburgh and Alnwick to Newminster, where he remained for two weeks.[33] He then set out on his long journey back to the south-east, to attend the great tournament at Dunstable.

*

This brings us to one of the most famous, or infamous, stories about Edward III: his supposed infatuation for, and rape of, the countess of Salisbury, his best friend's wife.[34] It appears in its fullest version in the chronicle of the Hainaulter, Jean le Bel, who had come to England in 1327. In brief, the story goes as follows. On the Melrose campaign, while Edward was still at Newcastle, a castle belonging to the earl of Salisbury was besieged by the Scots. In the castle was the earl's wife. The governor of the castle was supposedly the earl's nephew, the son of his sister, also called Sir William Montagu (according to le Bel). This Sir William escaped the siege and came to Edward at Newcastle, and begged him to bring assistance to his lady. Edward charged off to the rescue. The besieging Scots army fled, and Edward camped near the castle. He then decided he would take a dozen knights and visit the countess, one of the most beautiful women in England, whom he had not seen since her marriage. On hearing of his approach, the countess threw open the gates of the castle. She knelt in front of him, thanking him for his help, and led him into the castle. The king was utterly smitten by her, and, after brooding over her all evening, confessed his strong feelings. Her response was to beg him neither to tempt nor mock her, for what he was suggesting would bring dishonour to him, to her and to her husband the earl, who was at that time still in prison in France. Nevertheless, Edward continued to gaze at her longingly, his knights quite surprised to see him so besotted. Nothing untoward happened, however, and the next day he departed, and continued on his campaign, returning to England by a different route. However, in mid-August 1342, after her husband's return from captivity, Edward invited them both to a great tournament at London, to which the countess – to whom le Bel now gives the name Alice – came dressed as plainly as possible, suspecting the king's fascination with her was the reason for the invitation. Once again Edward did not pursue her. But, later in the year, when her husband had been despatched to fight in Brittany, Edward returned to her castle under the pretence of inspecting it for security. On this third occasion, in le Bel's words:

The good lady made him as much honour and good cheer as she could, as she knew she ought to for her lord's sake, although she would have preferred him to have gone elsewhere, so much she feared for her honour. And so it was that the king stayed all day and night, but never could get from the lady the answer agreeable to him, no matter how humbly he begged her. Come the night, when he had gone to bed in proper state, and he knew that the fine lady was in her bedchamber and that all her ladies were asleep and his gentlemen also, except his personal valets, he got up and told these valets that nothing must interfere with what he was going to do, on pain of death. So it was that he entered the lady's chamber, then shut the doors of the wardrobe so that her maids could not help her, then he took her and gagged her mouth so firmly that she could not cry out more than two or three times, and then he raped her so savagely that never was a woman so badly treated; and he left her lying there all battered about, bleeding from the nose and the mouth and elsewhere, which was for her great damage and great pity. Then he left the next day without saying a word, and returned to London, very disgusted with what he had done.[35]

According to the story, the countess was never happy again. In a distraught state, she told her husband what had happened on his return from the Continent. The man was overcome with grief and so angry that he decided to leave England. Having settled half his estate on her and his heir, he went to fight the Moors, and died in the siege of Algeçiras.

When Froissart came to this part of le Bel's manuscript he was profoundly shocked. Although le Bel had in several places prefaced his description of events with the words that he had only heard of one evil deed which Edward had ever done (and this was it), Froissart omitted the description of the rape altogether. He left only the fact that Edward had been enamoured of the countess. When he completed the second version of his text, he introduced a charming vignette in its place. In this, Edward played chess with the countess, deliberately not playing well so she would win. When she did win, and he pressed her to accept a valuable ring as her prize, she refused, to which Edward answered that she could be sure he would have taken something of hers if he had won. Instead of the rape scene he wrote

> You have heard me speak of Edward's love for the countess of Salisbury. The chronicle of Jean le Bel speaks of this love less properly than I must, for, please God, it would never enter my head to incriminate the king of England and the countess of Salisbury with such a vile accusation. If respectable men ask why I mention that love, they should know that Jean le Bel relates in his chronicle that the English king raped the countess of Salisbury. Now I declare that I know England well, where I have lived for long periods mainly at the royal court and also with the great lords of the country. And I have never heard tell of this rape although I have asked people about it who must have known if it had ever happened. Moreover I cannot believe [it] and it is incredible that so great and valiant a man as the king of England would have allowed himself to dishonour one of the most notable of ladies of his realm and one of his knights who had served him so loyally all his life.[36]

Clearly the whole episode caused Froissart great worry. When he came to rewrite his chronicle a third and final time, he omitted this careful passage too, so there was no reference at all to the rape.

Later historians have been equally concerned by the story. The great seventeenth-century antiquary William Dugdale would only have known of the 'romance' which Froissart relates (le Bel's version being lost at the time). Dugdale knew that the countess of Salisbury was not called Alice but Catherine. He also was aware that the earl had no nephew called

William Montagu; the only other William Montagu in the family was his young son. So he looked around the family tree and focused on the earl's brother, Sir Edward Montagu. He decided – on what authority is not clear – that the governor of the castle at the time was this Sir Edward, and the 'countess of Salisbury' with whom the king fell head over heels in love was the intended bride of William's son: Joan, 'the Fair Maid of Kent'. Since his source was the third version of Froissart's work, and that had dropped any reference to the rape, the story now became merely that Edward had been touched by the beauty of Joan, his cousin (who was actually about thirteen at the time), and had been in a great study over his feelings for her, but next morning had left, as was decent, gone off to fight the Scots, and returned by a different route.

Modern writers have been no less intrigued by this story. The discovery and publication of le Bel's original chronicle focused attention on the more sordid details, and the discovery of a similar account, including the details of the rape, in a number of continental chronicles further encouraged people to suspect that Edward really was a rapist. However, all the continental stories have a common historiographical root: in other words, they are not all original accounts but copies of one archetypal story.[37] So where did that come from? And does it have a basis in fact?

The first thing to note is that whoever composed the story of the rape knew the movements of the king and Salisbury in 1342 correctly. The English chronicles do not mention many details about the Scottish incursion into Northumberland, but le Bel and Froissart give plenty. David II and his army would very probably have passed by a castle belonging to the earl of Salisbury – Wark Castle – as there was a crossing over the River Tweed nearby. Edward's army also probably stayed near to Wark, for on his return from Melrose in 1341 his wardrobe spent the night of 31 December at the adjacent manor of Cornhill.[38] There was a whole series of tournaments that year over which the king presided, Dunstable in February, Northampton in April, and Eltham in May.[39] Although there is no overt record of a tournament at London in mid-August, there was a great feast, which very probably included jousting, at the Tower on 15 August, when Prince Lionel was married.[40] As already noted elsewhere, the earl of Salisbury himself was indeed abroad in captivity at the time of the supposed infatuation but had been released early in June 1342. Finally, it should be noted that the earl did indeed fight the Moors in the Spanish peninsula, and died not long before the siege of Algeçiras (although in England, not Spain). In this respect there is some accuracy in the story as related by le Bel.

The problem is that, although some of the details are verifiable, most are blatantly incorrect. As Dugdale noted, the countess was called Catherine, not Alice, and it is very unlikely that Edward had not seen her since her marriage for she had been married to his best friend for at least thirteen years. There was no nephew of the earl called 'William Montagu'. There is no evidence of any settlement of the family estates in 1342–44. The version of the story underlying the continental chronicle states that the earl had no heir, which is incorrect. It is very difficult to accept that the countess was at a border fortress during a period of hostility while her husband was overseas. It is even harder to accept that she habitually stayed there. There is no support for the story at all in any English or Scottish chronicle.[41]

Caught between a string of significant errors and some correct facts, one twentieth-century biographer (Michael Packe) tried very hard to make the story fit. He decided that Dugdale was right – that it was Edward Montagu who was the governor of Wark, who escaped to warn Edward that the castle was about to fall – and added that this was how 'William Montagu' was supposed to be the nephew of the 'countess'. Edward Montagu's wife was indeed called Alice. Moreover she was also a cousin of Edward's, being the daughter of the earl of Norfolk, and so may well have been invited to the marriage tournament at London in August 1342. She was about eighteen years of age, and before her marriage to Montagu had been betrothed to his nephew, William Montagu, son of the earl of Salisbury. Packe did not attempt to tackle the question of why Edward Montagu might have left his royal wife and thirteen-year-old nephew in a border fortress during a period of hostility.[42] He considered two details conclusive. First, le Bel mentions at one point that the young William Montagu had to pass a message to his *aunt* the 'countess'. And second, Alice was supposedly killed by her husband and several other men about ten years later. Packe decided that, because Edward did not pursue his cousin's killers with dire vengeance, he was somehow compromised by Edward Montagu.[43]

In all this fact-shuffling and theory-dealing, some fundamental points have been ignored. There are three stories here, rolled into one. They may be connected but they are still separate events: the meeting at Wark, the tournament at London and the rape. One at least – the rape – circulated separately to the others.[44] Therefore we must ask how information about these three events at opposite ends of the country – two of which took place in private – could have reached the person who eventually wrote them down. We might ask why a chronicler of no particularly high status should have known what Edward did or did not do in the countess's bedchamber. Not only that; in order to know what passed between the king and the 'countess' at Wark, the original teller of the tale would have had to be one of the dozen knights picked by Edward to visit the castle with him, or one of the lady's household servants, or a member of the castle garrison. It is exceptionally unlikely that any of these people did not know the woman's name and correct title. It is equally unlikely that they did not know that the governor of the castle was not the earl's nephew, and that William Montagu was the earl's twelve-year-old son. There are too many errors in describing the family to put them all down to 'Chinese whispers' when other facts about the campaign are correctly related. The only way in which the story of the infatuation can be considered credible is if the names and relationships had all been distorted through having been standardised by an unreliable intermediary in the process of making this story fit with the two other events, namely the accounts of the rape and the tournament at London.

Taking this approach of assessing the three elements of the story separately, we may come to some more reliable conclusions. Edward did not rape the countess of Salisbury. The record evidence shows that he had very little time after the earl's departure for France to see the countess.[45] In fact it seems likely that the earl and king sailed together: they were certainly both together on Edward's return journey the following spring.[46] After they returned, the earl's relationship with the king did not break down.[47] Indeed, in August 1343 Salisbury went abroad on Edward's behalf, as a royal plenipotentiary to see King Alfonso of Castile. It is difficult to believe he would have undertaken this if his feelings had been that of an injured husband, nor that Edward would have trusted him with the appointment in such circumstances. Finally, we may be confident that the story is false by closely examining the information underpinning it. The only possible witnesses who could have related the original rape story would have been Edward's valets (due to his instructions to them in his chamber before the rape) and they would have needed further information about the rape itself, presumably from the countess's maidservants. The story could not have spread from the valets to become a common rumour without circulating in the royal household. So it is significant that in later years Froissart, despite having far better access to the key members of the royal household than le Bel, was unable to find anyone who could corroborate the story. Hence we may be confident that the rape story was a piece of propaganda invented by one of Edward's enemies on the Continent.

But who was the 'countess' at Wark – if she was a real person – and who was 'Alice'? Is there any truth in the other parts of the story? As noted above, it is probable that Edward's army camped near Wark, and it is possible that this was due to a request to relieve the castle. It is also possible that Edward was briefly infatuated with a high-status lady staying at the castle, who may have been called Alice. He may or may not have invited her and her husband to the tournament at London in mid-August 1342. If so, it is highly unlikely that she was the wife of the earl of Salisbury. Le Bel wrote his chronicle in and after 1352.[48] By this time there was probably another love story about Edward III circulating: a tale about the foundation of the Order of the Garter (1349). This did relate to a countess of Salisbury, but she was Joan, the 'Fair Maid of Kent' – the same girl whom Dugdale suggested – and she was only thirteen in 1341. As for the elder countess of Salisbury, it is very unlikely she was at a Scottish border castle while her husband was in custody in France. If the woman at Wark really existed, it is much more likely that she was the wife of the castellan of the castle, and this might have been Sir Edward Montagu. But the evidence amounts to just three very tenuous facts: Wark was a castle held by her husband's brother, Edward had not seen her since her wedding (as le Bel claims), as she was married in 1338 and Edward had been abroad, and she did have a young nephew William Montagu, who is quite likely to have served in, or visited, his uncle's household.

So how come a story about an infatuation (whether true or false) became mixed up with one about a rape and another about a tournament, and became twisted into a scandal involving the wife of Edward's best friend? The answer to this is simply that the continental rumour mongers of the 1340s and 1350s wanted to present Edward III in an immoral light. The stories together formed a 'catalogue' of Edward's sins – rape, disloyalty to his friend, adultery – which became widely circulated on the Continent. This in itself is not surprising. What *is* interesting is that le Bel believed the end result, and even Froissart was forced to consider it. Both these men had met Edward. Le Bel had been a footsoldier in his army, and Froissart knew him personally. So it is particularly interesting that le Bel believed this story, and tried partly to excuse it on the grounds that it was 'motivated by love'. This tallies with Froissart's view. He could not believe that Edward had raped the countess but he could believe that Edward was attracted to a noblewoman, and even sufficiently overcome with lust that he attempted a seduction. Edward's liking for women is well-attested. His sexual desire for his wife was evidently compulsive.[49] Furthermore, if we examine the gifts that Edward gave out to members of Philippa's household, we may notice several women benefiting from his largesse. In 1335 he made a grant to Mabel Fitzwarenne, and in 1337 he similarly made grants to Margaret Jorce and Elena Mauley. All these women were 'damsels of Queen Philippa'. Such grants are not suspicious in themselves, but they alert us to the fact that Edward was aware of his wife's female companions, and since none of the grants were ostensibly at Philippa's request we might suspect that Edward himself initiated them. 'Entertaining ladies' (to use Sir Thomas Gray's phrase), in both its sinful and innocent forms, might well have given rise to a single public reputation. Edward acknowledged no illegitimate children in his youth – and so we should not presume he was promiscuous at this time – but he definitely enjoyed and encouraged the multiple flirtations of his sexually-charged court, and he was unashamed about it.

This is probably the most important thing about these stories. It shows Edward's perceived weakness. No one could accuse him of cowardice. No one could accuse him of failing to listen to his people's demands. No contemporary could accuse him of idleness, personal greed, or even foolhardiness. Edward's Achilles' heel was his love of female company, for it was possible to build a moral case against him by representing it as promiscuity. The author of the Vow of the Heron knew this well, and painted a picture of Edward ruling over a lascivious court. The poem underlying the Vow story was probably composed in the Low Countries, in the 1340s.[50] It would thus have been written by a countryman and contemporary of Jean le Bel, at about the same time as the rape story which le Bel heard. Le Bel was particularly biased in favour of Edward, but his informant about the rape scene clearly was not. The count of Hainault himself was somewhat ambivalent, despite being Edward's brother-in-law. It seems there were anti-Edward polemicists in Hainault, and one of these took a story he had heard about Edward's brief infatuation with a woman at Wark and turned it into a tale of rape, centred on the family of the famous earl of Salisbury. A Hainaulter audience in 1352 would not have known any better.

*

The discussions about the alleged rape of the countess have tended to obscure two important events which took place at this time. The first was the news that William Epworth, an officer of the Irish Exchequer, had been thrown into prison. Ireland had long been in a semi-autonomous state, and the Irish Exchequer had grown steadily poorer over the years, so when Edward tried to increase his revenues from the country by revoking all grants made since the death of Edward I, he was bound to cause a dispute. William Epworth was one of the men ordered on 24 July 1341 to reclaim all royal lands which had been granted out to other lords. Three days later Edward showed his lack of understanding of the Irish situation by issuing a writ which stated that he would 'be better served in Ireland by English ministers having incomes and property in England than by Irishmen, or Englishmen who have married and acquired possessions in Ireland and hold nothing in our kingdom of England'.[51] This was an overt attack on the independent culture of the Irish and Anglo-Irish nobility. They responded with determination. They met in a parliament at Dublin in October, and then another at Kilkenny in November, and put forward a series of carefully written and constructed petitions, laying the blame for the policy at the door of Edward's ministers. These petitions gave Edward cause for reflection, and he realised that he was not in a position to lay down the law in Ireland, not without going there. Over the following few months he backtracked, restoring the territories he had tried to take into royal control, giving into almost all the petitions. As with his dispute with Stratford, however much he believed he was in the right, there was a limit to how far he wanted to push an argument.[52]

The second important event of early 1342 was one of the largest tournaments which Edward ever held. It took place at Dunstable, directly after his return from Scotland, on 11–12 February 1342. According to one account, 'all the armed youth of England' were present and no foreigners were invited: the total of knights exceeded two hundred and fifty.[53] In a fuller version of the same chronicle it was noted that the earls of Derby, Warwick, Northampton, Pembroke, Oxford and Suffolk all took part, and the other earls were only excused by reason of old age or illness. The king himself fought as a 'simple knight'.[54] A number of barons from the west of England were present. Even Queen Philippa was there, despite being heavily pregnant again (she gave birth the following month to their eighth child, Blanche). Far in the north, the chroniclers in their monasteries noted it. Stabling alone cost more than £113.[55] A tournament on this scale in February was unusual, for it was almost impossible to set up and complete everything in the short space of daylight.[56] Indeed, it took so long to organise that it was almost dark before the tournament began.

The reason usually given for the tournament at this time is that it was to celebrate the betrothal of the king's three-year-old son, Lionel of Antwerp, to the eight-year-old heiress of the earldom of Ulster, Elizabeth de Burgh. This is supported by the royal wardrobe accounts. But one feature about this tournament stands out. This is the first tournament at which Edward is known to have used a personal motto.[57] Practically everything made for this tournament was embroidered with the words 'it is as it is', in English. Both the king and his son had state beds: Lionel's had love-knots and leaves on it, powdered with silk roses and his coat of arms. The king's bed was covered in green cloth embroidered with silk dragons which encircled the arms of England and France. Its top sheet had 'four circlets in which there are four angels, a final circlet in the middle covered with the helmet and crest of the king, while the field of this sheet is worked with other circlets and scrolls of silk bearing the legend "it is as it is".[58]

Perhaps it was the very mysteriousness of the motto which caused the chronicler who described the tournament, Adam Murimuth, to misunderstand its purpose. Although he was no stranger to heraldic events, he thought it was to celebrate the truce with Scotland. That is hardly likely; truces with Scotland were a common event and never had they been celebrated on this scale by Edward, nor would it have been fitting to have the celebration so far from the border. But more than this, the organisation necessarily rules out the tournament being held at such short notice. Just making the costumes would have taken a considerable amount of time. The accounts reveal that Edward's tailor was paid for making 'various robes, tunics, surcoats and many other garments' for the king and his magnates.[59] Many of these were embroidered with 'it is as it is'. Also, another suit of armour was made for the king bearing the arms of the legendary Sir Lionel, echoing the Dunstable tournament of 1334.

What did it mean, this motto, 'it is as it is'? To date the only historian seriously to have given this any thought assumed that the legend was 'fatalistic' and that its origins were 'probably literary'.[60] A fatalistic message is entirely possible, meaning 'things are as they are and cannot be changed' in a negative, resigned sense. Given his recent Scottish expedition and his possible brief flirtation with a woman at Wark, we might say that the resignation suggested by the phrase reflects his feelings about Scotland, or her, or even the recent chaos in Ireland. But it is very unlikely that all the nobility of England would be gathered for such a purpose. A preferable interpretation is that it relates to the claim on the throne of France: 'it is as it is' being a cold assertion of the immutability of Edward's descent from Philip the Fair. Attractive and sensible as this interpretation would be, it is difficult to see why Edward waited four years after first claiming the title, and two years after properly claiming it, before making this show, and why he made this demonstration in England, not France, and with no foreigners present, and in the depths of winter.

Another interpretation is possible. That 'it is as it is' was not fatalistic at all, but exactly the opposite: a celebration. If one puts the stress on the first 'is', the phrase reads as an achievement – 'it *is* as it is' – meaning 'things have come to be as they should be'. This is supported by Edward's order for twelve red hangings to be made, each one embroidered with 'it is as it is'.[61] These were huge: each one was more than twenty feet long and more than ten feet wide. The cost of these twelve banners was almost £30 (the annual income of nine skilled labourers).[62] Although the statement was certainly mysterious, Edward wanted everyone to see it, and, for those who understood it, we may assume that it was important.

It is likely that 'it is as it is' finally announced the death of the old king, Edward II, to those who knew he had survived Berkeley. We cannot be certain about this, but there are a number of details which support the suggestion. First and foremost, Edward III finally passed on to his son and heir, Edward of Woodstock, the title of 'Prince of Wales' – the only title which his father had never given up – in the next parliament (in May 1343), strongly suggesting the old man had died by then. This was the first parliament for two years, and so it would appear that Edward III had heard about his father's death in the period May 1341–May 1343. Further support for this is that he made a pilgrimage to his father's tomb at Gloucester – his first such pilgrimage – in March 1343, after a near-death experience, indicating that by then his father had very probably been placed in his tomb.[63] An irregularity in a Nottinghamshire chantry ordinance probably arising as a result of Edward II's survival in 1335 was finally sorted out in January 1343, tempting us to push the *terminus ante quem* for Edward's death to 1342 at the latest.[64] Given that Edward II was almost certainly still alive in 1339, and probably died in 1341–42, it seems not unreasonable to connect the 'it is as it is' message in February 1342 with the arrival of the news of the death not long before. It may well be that the appearance of Niccolinus Fieschi in London in November 1341 marks the critical moment.[65]

It seems that at last Edward had the chance to lay his father to rest. It might be said that he had been fortunate to have had the services of the Fieschi and Pope John XXII to guard his father and to keep him secretly. But to reflect that he had lived with the problem of his father's secret survival for the last fourteen years, and had worked his foreign policy, his war and his relations with the pope around this extraordinary situation, and had even managed to meet his father again in Koblenz, is to reflect that Edward had coped successfully with the worst crisis the Plantagenet monarchy had ever faced. He had even managed to initiate and sustain an expansionist foreign policy in spite of it. It also rings a significant change in his life, for Edward from now on could be even more aggressive. From now on, as far as we know, no one had any secrets which could be used to compromise him, or restrain him. From now on, he did not need to tread so carefully. He could be himself like never before.

NINE

The Advent of the Golden Age

Medieval ship captains preferred to sail within sight of land. Having no means of calculating longitude, it was very easy for them to lose direction, and especially so in high winds. When Edward set sail from Sandwich on 5 October 1342 there were gales to contend with, and rough seas, so his captains carefully hugged the coast all the way to Portsmouth. Even then they had to wait for the wind to change direction, so they could proceed across the Channel. Only on 23 October did the coast of England finally disappear from Edward's view, and that of Brittany appear on the horizon.

The choice of Brittany was a profoundly sensible one. Like Flanders, it was a semi-autonomous part of France. If Edward could control it, he would have both a bridgehead in Philip's kingdom and a means of protecting his shipping lanes to Gascony. For years he had toyed with this idea, and had taken care to remain on good terms with John, duke of Brittany. Almost alone among French peers after 1337, John was allowed to keep his English estates and title (the earldom of Richmond). Thus it may be seen that, even when Edward had been trapped in his alliance with the German princes, he had had an alternative strategy in the back of his mind. The opportunity to capitalise on that far-sightedness finally arose in May 1341. As the king was being castigated, denounced and threatened with excommunication by the archbishop of Canterbury, the news arrived that the duke of Brittany had died, without leaving an obvious heir.

As Edward had expected, the duke's death precipitated a bitter inheritance dispute between his half-brother, John de Montfort, and his niece, Jeanne. Normally there was little doubt that a male sibling of the half-blood took precedence over a daughter of a full-blood brother, but the late duke had disliked his synonymous half-brother. So to make sure that John de Montfort did not inherit, the duke arranged the marriage of his niece Jeanne to Charles de Blois, nephew of King Philip. Whatever the law said, John de Montfort would have to fight for his inheritance, and not only with Jeanne and her husband but with the king of France too.

John de Montfort was not unaware of the situation, and he was not unprepared. The moment his brother was laid to rest he took a force and seized Nantes – the administrative centre of Brittany – as well as his half-brother's treasure and most of the other castles of the region. Charles de Blois was left standing, wondering. King Philip proved similarly hesitant. Edward, in contrast, had been waiting years for this opportunity. Having settled the Crisis of 1341 by superficially capitulating to the archbishop's supporters, he sent a knight to John de Montfort to discuss a possible treaty for mutual aid when the truce with France expired.

At this point de Montfort himself hesitated. The problem was not his opposition to Edward but his justifiable anxiety in case his association with the English king should compromise his future standing in France. Philip assured him that he would have a fair hearing with regard to his inheritance in the French parliament. It is possible that John actually believed him, to the extent that he supposed Jeanne's inheritance would be judged unlawful, as the relationship by which she claimed to be the heiress was the same as that by which Edward III claimed to be king of France. But such subtleties were lost on Philip. The French parliament similarly saw the question not in terms of inheritance law but power. On 7 September 1341 they ruled that Philip's nephew, Charles de Blois, should be duke, inheriting through his wife. Before this judgement was given, however, Philip unwisely reprimanded John de Montfort for consorting with the English king, and ordered him to remain in Paris to await the judgement. John de Montfort fled.

Very few people in France in 1341 would have realised what a catastrophic decision their parliament had made. It threw John de Montfort and his legal claim straight into Edward's hands. Perhaps the French parliament thought that Edward, who had just agreed to extend the truce sealed at Esplechin for another year, would be disempowered by the treaty from helping de Montfort. Perhaps they thought de Montfort could be arrested, or paid off, or killed, leaving Charles de Blois free to strengthen the royal hand in Brittany. But if so they reckoned without the determination of John de Montfort's supporters, and in particular his wife, another of those redoubtable fourteenth-century women who did not flinch from the task of leading her troops into battle.

Edward probably understood the situation better than anyone else, and certainly better than the consensus of the French parliament. But having agreed to extend the truce until 24 June 1342, there was little direct action he could take before then. He waited to assess the strength of the support for the de Montfortist faction. All across the region castles and towns fell to the French. At l'Humeau, de Montfort came face to face with de Blois in a surprise encounter, and their armies battled each other for two days before de Montfort retreated to Nantes. After a week the Nantesians forced de Montfort to surrender himself. He went to Paris under the protection of a safe conduct. When he refused to give up his inheritance Philip immediately imprisoned him, disregarding what this said about the value of his own guarantees of safety, and believing too soon that this marked his victory. But Lady de Montfort held out. In fact she did more than just hold out. Having secured Rennes, she led an army to Redon, which she took by force, marching on to establish herself in the walled town of Hennebont, on the southern coast. With a stern realism she proclaimed her two-year-old son as the head of the de Montfortist faction in case her husband was put to death in Paris. And she wrote to Edward imploring him to come to her aid.[1]

Edward was eager to get involved in the battle for Brittany. He did not actually need a lady in distress to heighten his ambitions in that part of France. Nevertheless her example inspired him and many others, and it required him to take action before too late. He ordered a small advance party to set off in April 1342 under the command of Sir Walter Manny. He gave the earl of Northampton and Robert d'Artois command of an expeditionary force to set off later. In the meantime he built up his military reserves at the Tower. Seven thousand longbows were ordered, and three million arrows.[2] As soon as the terms of the truce would allow, he would invade.

Time was running short for all parties. Rennes fell in early May, and Charles de Blois advanced on Hennebont itself, sending his brother to besiege the other de Montfortist stronghold at Vannes. In England, Edward was experiencing delays in sending Northampton and d'Artois. But Manny was underway, and savaging the lands of the Bretons who had failed to support de Montfort. Truce or no truce, he could not afford to wait too long before attempting to help the countess. Manny was a practical and hardbitten man, very experienced and abounding in courage. Although Lady de Montfort worsted Charles de Blois' advance forces in a skirmish at the walls of Hennebont, Manny knew that unless she received assistance quickly, there would be no de Montfortist cause to support, and no bridgehead for Edward in northern France. Thus, despite the truce, Manny set sail for Hennebont.

Within the town the countess was doing her best to inspire her men. She wore armour, and rode around the streets of the town on a destrier, calling on the inhabitants to fight and defend what was theirs and hers. According to Froissart, she ascended a tall tower to observe the attack on the walls, and seeing that the enemy camp was almost unguarded while the assault was on, she took three hundred men-at-arms with her and made a sortie from the town, burning Charles de Blois' supplies and slashing the ropes and walls of his tents and pavilions.[3] There would be no surrender at Hennebont. Charles ordered his commanders to begin a siege, and to starve the inhabitants into submission. Promises were made and rewards offered to all those who would desert the de Montfortist cause. One of the countess's advisers – the bishop of Léon – was won over, and returned to hold a council in which he tried to persuade the countess and her vassals to agree to terms. The discussions went on for two days. The bishop spoke eloquently, and persuaded some of the Breton lords that their cause was lost. With his words ringing around the tower room in which the discussions were taking place, and with the continual thumping of the siege engines ringing in her head, the countess got up from where she was sitting and walked to the window. Looking down, she could hardly believe the sight that greeted her. She gasped: 'I see the help we have been promised for so long has arrived!' Sailing up the estuary were Sir Walter Manny's ships, their sails bearing the cross of St George.

The bishop of Léon might have spoken eloquently but the cross of St George was even more persuasive. Manny's force was small, and its commander had crossed the divide between courage and recklessness so often as not to notice it existed (he later made a sortie just to destroy a single French siege engine at Hennebont because it was disturbing his meal) but it was a significant token of future support. By July the truce had come to an end. The English were on their way.

*

Edward landed in Britanny on 26 October. Already the English had won several significant victories. Lady de Montfort still held Hennebont, her forces now augmented with English troops, and that was a victory in itself. More significantly the port of Brest – where Edward landed – had fallen to the earl of Northampton. The earl had even had the satisfaction of burning a dozen Genoese galleys in the service of the French. Most important of all at Morlaix on 30 September, Northampton had moved to confront a French army under the command of Geoffrey de Charny and had won a decisive victory. Having marched through the night and dug in, and having ordered all his men to fight on foot, he had seized more than one hundred and fifty knights and killed fifty others, besides thousands of men-at-arms and infantry. Back in England the result was wonder, admiration and excitement. Murimuth dutifully recorded incorrectly that 'a few English, namely a force of five hundred men' defeated three thousand French knights in battle. It was more like three thousand Englishmen and Bretons against five thousand Frenchmen, but that was not the way it was reported.[4]

Edward decided that Vannes would be his principal objective. The French had taken it not long before, and thus controlled its harbour, which was of strategic interest to the English. But it was not an easy target. Edward decided on a two-pronged assault by land and sea. He despatched Robert d'Artois with the ships which remained in Brittany while he himself led the overland advance. D'Artois was a brave leader but an unlucky man, and the very last vestige of his little luck was now used up. He was attacked on the way by Spanish and Genoese ships. Leading an attack on Vannes itself with the remains of his navy, he was overpowered and mortally injured. With his death a few weeks later Edward lost a trusted and likeable friend, a man who had never betrayed him but who had never lived up to the confidence he had placed in his military abilities.

Despite the personal loss, it was to Edward's benefit that the positions of command in the field now fell to English lords. There were at least half-a-dozen very able commanders with Edward, including the earls of Derby, Warwick, Huntingdon, Northampton and Salisbury and Sir Walter Manny. Allowing these men to exercise their strengths and to fulfil their ambitions marked a new stage in the development of Edward's success as a king. Thirty years earlier, Robert Bruce in Scotland had run rings around the English by encouraging a cadre of commanders who would seek personal glory and yet be part of a collective struggle. Through encouraging the likes of Black Douglas and Sir Thomas Randolph, Bruce had wrested Scotland from the English. When Edward had begun his French war he had failed to pursue a similar course of action. Instead he had relied on the chivalric ambitions of other heads of state: the indecisive count of Hainault, the wary duke of Brabant, the merchant van Artevelde, and the mercenary Emperor Ludvig. His trust in them was misplaced: they were never going to share his strategic objectives or be part of the confraternity of warriors which would defeat Philip. They would never feel personally bound to Edward's peculiarly English quarrel, and still less to his personal command. But as soon as those responsibilities and expectations passed to his vassals, everything changed. In Brittany Edward began to reassert himself as the King Arthur of a chivalric court of victorious warriors who vied with each other for glory. As Edward destroyed the region around Vannes, the earls of Northampton and Warwick destroyed that around Nantes. The earl of Salisbury devastated the area around Dinan.[5] Throughout Brittany, the army and the supporters of Charles de Blois were on the retreat. The endgame in Brittany was approaching.

Edward had a weakness, however. Being so far from home, he had difficulty raising supplies, and living off the land for any length of time in winter was not easy. He had lost many of his ships. His armies were dispersed across Brittany, and there were not enough of them to face a full French onslaught. In December the main French army approached. It joined up with Charles de Blois' companions who had survived Morlaix, and presented Edward with a force several times the size of his own. It stopped eighteen miles short of the English army. Despite this show of force, as at Esplechin, Edward managed to negotiate a compromise which did not reflect the precariousness of his situation. His treaty negotiators were like his commanders, enthused and personally committed to the struggle which he had started. In this respect it has to be said that Edward's judgement of men to do the job was impeccable. On 19 January 1343 the Treaty of Malestroit was agreed. Edward had to lift the siege of Vannes, but otherwise almost every term was in his favour. The allegiances, gains and losses in Brittany were to be respected, and no further war was to take place in Gascony, Scotland or elsewhere. John de Montfort was to be released. Flanders would remain outside the orbit of French control. The truce was to last for more than three years.[6] Edward had effectively added one more frontier to his war on Philip de Valois. He had conquered a corner of France, and managed to call himself king of it without incurring serious loss.

*

When Edward had opted to lead the land army to attack Vannes he may well have been expressing a personal preference. Although he had commanded at the significant naval victory at Sluys, he was not lucky out on the open sea. Or perhaps we should say that he *was* lucky, for he seems to have survived more near-death experiences at sea than in battle. In 1326 he had been blown off course by a storm when returning to England with Mortimer and his mother. In 1340 he had almost died in a storm at the mouth of the Thames. He had suffered in the gales on his crossing to Brittany. And now, in February 1343, on his return trip he got caught in a catastrophic tempest which seriously threatened his life once more. Several ships in his fleet were lost: swept over and smashed to pieces by the waves. There was, of course, no respite from drowning for anyone on board those unfortunate boats. The whole fleet was dispersed, the sailors doing all they could simply to bring their vessels to port. Murimuth noted how the surviving ships put into ports wherever they could across southern England.[7] The ship carrying Lady de Montfort ended up drifting into a port in Devon. Wreck stories clearly had a wide popular appeal, as most chroniclers note Edward's escape, even the far northern ones. A Franciscan chronicler on the Scottish border noted that Edward incurred many dangers in returning from Brittany, especially from flashes of lightning and unprecedented storms, whereby nearly all his ships were scattered from him and several were sunk in the sea. It is said that not one of his sailors or soldiers was so cheerful amid these storms and dangers as himself, who ever remained fearless and unperturbed through them all; whence he was delivered by God's grace and the Blessed Virgin's intercession, whom he always invoked and chose as his particular patron in all dangers.[8]

On 1 March, he was blown to shore at Melcome Regis, in Dorset.[9] He set off immediately for London, and reached the capital three days later. But this was one storm which had deeply affected him. He seems to have sworn at the height of the gales to go on a whole series of pilgrimages if he was saved. He even seems to have prayed to his recently deceased father to save him. He performed the promised pilgrimages straightaway. In London he gave thanks at the high altar of St Paul's Cathedral. He then took a handful of men and went to his father's tomb at Gloucester, and gave thanks at the high altar there, and at Walsingham Abbey. He went on foot to Canterbury, and gave thanks at the altars dedicated to St Thomas Becket and the Virgin Mary.[10] At each place he promised a costly gift, and a golden incense boat in the shape of a ship was later delivered to each shrine.[11] If Edward stood alone and unafraid on the deck of his storm-beleaguered ship, it was only because he was praying in the fury of the storm, and believed the Virgin Mary, St Thomas Becket and his late father were all looking out for him.[12]

*

On 28 April 1343 Edward opened the first parliament held since the Crisis of 1341. There was much to discuss. One interesting preliminary was to ordain that in future no representatives should come to parliament in armour or with long knives or other weaponry as they had sometimes done in the past.[13] The first main item on the agenda was the Treaty of Malestroit. In the now-accepted fashion, the two houses of parliament deliberated separately, and delivered their verdicts on 1 May. Both houses approved of the treaty, and of the continued search for peace. But if no adequate peace could be obtained, they approved of Edward continuing his quarrel with the French king, and would support him in this. It was a conciliatory statement, made in the light of the military successes in Brittany but also in the wake of Edward's refusal to summon a parliament for two years. Even more conciliatory was parliament's acceptance of Edward's revocation of the statute forced on him on that occasion.

Parliament and Crown had reached an understanding: although the prelates and representatives of the shires and towns might press for reform, the king would not accept extremist measures, or changes which might undermine his ability to run the government efficiently. As a result, the 1343 parliament was a success for Edward. He not only achieved support for his foreign policy, he renewed his royal authority over parliament, so much so that for the next thirty years representatives never questioned Edward's authority over ministerial appointments, nor his right to give royal estates to his chief vassals.[14]

Along with parliamentary acknowledgement of the possibility of renewed hostilities came the agreement to fix wool customs, and a grant of duty to the king on wool for the next three years.[15] Gradually Edward was bringing his finances back under control. He dealt with some of his Continental allies by responding to their demands for payment with letters stating that if he had failed to pay them by a certain date, then their obligations to him would lapse. The debt then was strategically neglected. Not all debts could be treated in this way, of course. Those owing to the Bardi and Peruzzi were a particularly difficult problem. If Edward simply backed out of these, there would inevitably be international repercussions. Indeed, shortly after this, both the Bardi and the Peruzzi banking houses collapsed.

The responsibility for the failure of the Bardi and the Peruzzi has traditionally been ascribed solely to Edward's refusal to honour his debts. This is a serious accusation; it amounts to personal responsibility for the biggest banking crash before modern times. But the view that Edward simply backed out of his financial commitments is mainly based on the opinion of a well-respected Florentine writer, Giovanni Villani, whose brother Filippo was a member of the Peruzzi. Villani said that Edward owed the Bardi 900,000 gold florins (£135,000),* and the Peruzzi 600,000 (£90,000), and that his refusal to pay caused an economic collapse across Florence and much further afield. Such an opinion is neither independent nor justified. Edward never refused to pay his debts. Moreover, recent research has shown that the Peruzzi (whose records survive) did not have the capital to lend Edward this much money, not even a fraction of it.[16] For Edward to have owed them 600,000 florins, they would have needed to have raised further capital in England. They may have done this, but if so they must have received further income or actual repayments, for which Villani does not account. From the English records we may estimate what these repayments were. The total amount borrowed over the period 1337–41 has been calculated at 687,000 florins

---

* After 1340 the conversion rate used for the florin is 3s, rather than 3s 4d. See Author's Note.

(£103,000) from the Bardi, and 474,000 florins (£71,000) from the Peruzzi.[17] Some of this was repaid in cash, and some was repaid through royal grants, especially grants of wool, which allowed the Italians to recoup much of their original investment and to build up their capital. In other words, the total of more than one million florins represents only the borrowings, not the repayments, and thus not the balance owing. It is now thought that the actual amount which Edward defaulted on was nearer the amount he later acknowledged, a mere £13,000.[18] Edward's failure to repay this amount would have dented the companies' profitability, but it would not by itself have proved disastrous. Historians tend to regard the internal disputes in Florence as the cause of the crash, not Edward's failure to repay his debts. It is a telling fact that the third largest Florentine banking house, the Acciaiuoli, also suffered heavily in the 1340s, and many other smaller Florentine banking firms collapsed, despite the fact that they had not lent any money to Edward.[19]

The other important financial measure discussed in the parliament of 1343 was the currency. For the last five hundred years practically the only coins minted in England had been silver pennies. Henry III had tried to introduce a 'gold penny', worth 20d, in 1257, but it had failed. Edward I had issued a new silver coinage in 1279, which resulted in the minting of silver groats (4d), halfpences and farthings, as well as pennies. But most international trade, and much domestic business, was conducted in florins (around 3s) and marks (13s 4d), so silver pennies were of limited use, as they were needed in their hundreds. Edward knew that a successful gold currency would be exported, and English gold coins would be handled and looked at in Avignon, Genoa and Paris as well as more Anglophile cities such as Ghent and Bruges and English dominions such as Gascony. The principle to which he was aspiring was very similar to the modern idea of trademark advertising. Edward would circulate artistically sculpted pieces of gold all around Europe showing him as a truly international monarch. As a result of these discussions, the first important English gold coins appeared in 1344. The largest of these was closely modelled on the French gold currency, showing Edward enthroned, with a leopard on the other side (Edward's own emblem and the heraldic beast on the English coat of arms). These first gold coins proved unsuccessful, being undervalued in relation to the value of the gold, so later in the same year (1344) he ordered the minting of the mighty 'noble', a gold coin worth half-a-mark (6s 8d). This showed the king standing on the deck of a ship. The ship logo drew attention to his victory at Sluys, but even more importantly it showed Edward as a king crossing seas, giving him that international status which he craved. This was a medieval power statement of the first order. It took a few reissues to get the balance of gold and nominal value right, but Edward would not allow his moneyers to fail. The figure of Edward standing on his ship, bearing a shield with the arms of France and England quartered, became one of the most widely known and enduring images of fourteenth-century kingship, being copied in the gold coinage of every subsequent medieval English king.[20]

It was also in 1343 that parliament first pressed Edward to limit the power of the pope. It seemed to parliament that foreigners were increasingly being appointed to the most lucrative benefices in the English church. Edward seized on this. It gave him a weapon with which to attack Pope Clement VI, the newly elected successor to the peace-loving Benedict XII. Clement was, like his predecessor, a Frenchman; in fact he had previously served as Chancellor under King Philip. But his predecessor had been a man with whom Edward could do business, being genuinely concerned to find a peaceful solution to the Anglo-French problem. Clement saw that Benedict's policy had failed. As a Frenchman living at Avignon he naturally decided that the only way forward was to bring such pressure to bear on Edward that the English king would have to back down. During this parliament Edward wrote to Clement stressing how papal appointees often failed to perform their duties. With so many hospitals, monasteries, chantries and other foundations having been endowed by the English for the English, what benefit could arise from their revenues going abroad? Edward argued that God's work was at peril, souls were in danger, and churches were falling into disrepair.[21] By the Ordinance of Provisors, Edward prohibited the receipt in England of papal letters against his interests, and the appointment of any clergy to ecclesiastical positions by such letters.[22] Not only was it enacted with force, with several papal provisions being confiscated, it also resulted in the arrest and banishment of the proctors of the papal peace envoys.[23] Edward realised that he could bring pressure to bear on the pope by representing the nationalist perspective. This was a question of enduring importance to the English. It would not be laid to rest until Henry VIII settled the matter two hundred years later, by removing the Church of England from papal authority altogether.

*

The latter part of 1343 and early 1344 was a time of relative calm and stability for Edward. He was now thirty-one years of age, and stronger than ever. He was approaching solvency once more, and could afford to remedy some of the embarrassing measures he had taken in 1338, such as redeeming his and Philippa's golden crowns from pawn.[24] The pattern of his life reflected the way he had lived ten years earlier: a proud young king going from tournament to tournament and from hunt to hunt, always in the company of knights and women. Among his accounts we find reference to mulberry-coloured Turkish cloth and taffeta for Queen Philippa, Queen Isabella and four countesses to go on a hunting expedition with the king.[25] The same account allows us a glimpse of Edward and the earl of Northampton dressed in white, with eleven earls and knights dressed in green Turkish cloth, and fifteen royal squires waiting on them, all dressed in green. Another reference reveals Edward participating in a tournament at Smithfield on 24 June 1343, jousting for three days against thirteen knights dressed up as the pope and twelve cardinals.[26] No diplomatic niceties here: this was loud and clear political commentary, in which Edward was very clearly setting himself up as England's champion against the pope.

After a summer of tournaments, hunting and sending increasingly uncompromising letters to Avignon, Edward prepared for the next great public event. This was the second of his great winter tournaments at Windsor. On 18 January 1344 he gathered all the armed youth of England, including the earls of Derby, Salisbury, Warwick, Arundel, Pembroke and Suffolk, and many other knights and barons.[27] As usual, he also invited large numbers of women: nine countesses were present, the wives of London merchants and barons, as well as Queen Philippa and their younger children. His mother, Queen Isabella, was also there. With all the other nondescript men, women and servants it amounted to 'an indescribable host of people'. Prince Edward, now thirteen, was given a prominent role, although he probably did not take part in the jousting. Everyone ate and drank liberally and, 'dances were not lacking among the lords and ladies, embraces and kisses alternately intermingling'.[28] Foreign knights came to join in the jousting, and the action – involving Edward, his son and eighteen other knights, who took on all comers – went on for three days. Gifts of money, precious objects and clothes were given, and minstrels played throughout. A great banquet was given on the Monday in which all the women ate in the hall with no men present except two French knights who waited on them. Finally, on the Wednesday evening, at the end of the tournament, Edward spoke to the crowd, and gave instructions that no one was to go home but everyone was to stay the night and hear an announcement he would make the following day.

On Thursday morning Edward was up early. He dressed in his finest new clothes and wore over everything a mantle of exquisite velvet and his crown. The queens likewise were specially dressed, and accompanied him into the castle chapel to hear mass. After the ceremony, led by two earls from the chapel, he stood outside and addressed the crowd. He took a bible, and, turning to the gospels, he swore a vow that he would begin a Round Table in the true spirit of King Arthur, and maintain in it three hundred knights. He added that he would build a great round building within the castle at Windsor where all these men and their ladies could eat together. The building would be two hundred feet in diameter, and surpass any previously seen in Europe. Every year, at Whitsun, he would hold a great tournament at the castle, like this they had just experienced. The earls present joined him in his oath, and afterwards there was more dancing to the minstrels and drums, with a great feast of exotic dishes, before all went home after their five days of merrymaking.

One man had already gone home. In the jousting, William Montagu, earl of Salisbury and for many years Edward's best friend, had been badly injured. On 30 January, eight days after the Round Table tournament ended, he died. The man who had delivered Edward his kingdom, and had dutifully followed him in his expeditions to Scotland, the Low Countries, France and Brittany, was no more. He was taken the short distance to Bisham Priory, which he had founded in the place of Edward's first childhood home, and was buried in the church there.

Edward was back at Westminster when he heard of Salisbury's death. There are no signs of any great outpouring of grief, nor of expensive arrangements for the burial, but nor would we necessarily find these in royal accounts. The official records simply note the bureaucratic process of winding up the earl's affairs. It is perhaps surprising that the chroniclers hardly mention Salisbury's death, and none mention any signs of grief from Edward. If the king attended his funeral then it was in a private capacity, with little fuss. Maybe from this we should wonder whether there was some truth in Froissart's confused story of Edward's lust for the countess. However, there is one sign that the death of his one-time friend caused Edward to stop and think. More than any other man, Salisbury was Edward's partner in chivalric role-playing. He had participated in most of the many tournaments Edward had attended in the seventeen years since he had become king. It was thus no surprise that he was there, jousting alongside Edward, when the Round Table was announced. The loss of Salisbury might therefore be the reason why he only half-heartedly set about the building project.[29] Work began in February as planned, but was soon scaled back due to the expense, and stopped altogether in November. There would be no Round Table. The half-built huge stone circular walls stood empty. It seems the harsh reality of death had stripped the romance away from the tournament at Windsor. Indeed, tournaments altogether lost their appeal for him. Several years were to pass before he lifted a lance in sport again.[30]

*

By the time Edward walked into the Painted Chamber at Westminster to meet parliament again on 7 June 1344, the war of words with the pope had escalated to condemnations as fierce as those Edward had exchanged with the archbishop of Canterbury during the Crisis of 1341. Pope Clement threatened Edward with excommunication, and told him he was in 'rebellion'.[31] This was not likely to result in a comfortable atmosphere for the delegation negotiating peace with France. Things could only get harder for them when Clement openly denounced the English claim to the French throne. In January 1344 Edward responded by directly condemning the papal custom of providing benefices to his companions, and followed this up with an accusation that Philip had broken the truce, as some of Edward's allies had been executed in Paris. Edward's envoys claimed this was a renewal of hostilities, and that English emissaries to the pope were no longer safe in France.[32] The pope expressed his disquiet but did little more. As far as he was concerned Philip was in the right, if only because the politics of restraint demanded that Edward had to be in the wrong.

In parliament Edward put forward the breaking of the truce in the most uncompromising terms. Philip, he declared, had 'falsely and maliciously' put his allies to death with the assent of the French parliament, he had raised armies and attacked Gascony and Brittany, seizing castles, towns, manors and fortlets, and occupying English royal lands.[33] The answer was unanimous. Everyone – lords, prelates and commons alike – all asked Edward to bring this war to a close, 'either by battle, or a suitable peace, if he could get one'. Moreover they asked unanimously that he should confront Philip, and not be delayed by papal intervention, or the peace-making efforts of anyone else. Parliament wanted an end to this war, and the people of England, who by now had borne a heavier tax burden than any other people in history, wanted closure on their own terms.[34] To this end they added an interesting clause to the grant of a new subsidy: the money was conditional on Edward personally crossing over to France with an army to force Philip to submit.

All seemed set now for Edward's next invasion of France. Parliament and king were in accord, over this and many other issues, from opposing papal interference to domestic legal reform.[35] But still Edward did not rush to war. Instead he used parliament's resolutions to bring more pressure to bear on the pope. He made one last attempt to negotiate, repeating his claim to France in a meticulously worded document presented to the pope by an experienced team of negotiators: the bishop of Norwich, John and Andrew Offord, Thomas Fastolf and Niccolinus Fieschi.[36] Clement himself presided over the discussion, perhaps unnerved a little by how strong the arguments were in favour of Edward's claim.[37] Biased he most certainly was, but neither his bias nor his acuity could break the stone wall of

Edward's negotiators. They had powers only to discuss the claim to the French throne, which Edward would not under any circumstances give up. When offered money or a new title, Edward's representatives expressed indignation. In this they did well, for they did exactly what Edward wanted them to do. In December 1344 the conference broke down, with the pope, the cardinals and the French delegation failing to persuade Edward's redoubtable negotiators to admit to any weakness in his position.

*

Edward spent the latter part of 1344 attending to the discussion with the pope, receiving and delaying papal nuncios, and planning his next move in great detail. So concerned was he with this that he seems not to have attended Philippa's churching after the birth of his fourth daughter, Mary, who had been born at Waltham, near Winchester, in October. Instead he remained at Westminster or at the Tower, before moving off to Norwich for Christmas. He had now extricated himself from his financial embarrassment, having redeemed the last of his pawned jewels in October. He was more popular at home than he had been for years. Now he simply needed to put all his assets – armies, inspirational commanders, revenues, diplomatic alliances and technical strategic superiority – simultaneously to good effect.

In January Sir Hugh Neville returned from Avignon to report on the failure of the negotiations under the pope's auspices. Edward met him at Westminster, accompanied by the earls of Derby and Northampton, the archbishop of Canterbury and the archbishop's nephews, the bishops of Chichester and London (the Stratford family having been restored to favour). Edward's thinking until now had been to follow up his intransigent stance by sending Derby to the pope on a secret mission, but he changed his mind.[38] As his advisers told him, diplomacy would achieve nothing unless he could bring real pressure to bear on Philip, and that required action. The longer the truce prevailed, the more Philip could chip away at his authority by pressurising the Gascon nobles and committing minor infringements of the truce in Brittany and Flanders.

Edward's thinking in the spring of 1345 was to divide the command of his army between himself and his two most experienced and successful commanders, the earls of Derby and Northampton. Throughout the first half of the year Derby remained with him, discussing plans and strategies.[39] The earls of Northampton, Huntingdon and Arundel assisted, the latter two being admirals of his fleets. The plan they came up with was to gather a huge fleet of more than four hundred ships at Portsmouth, Sandwich and Southampton to bring a devastating three-pronged attack against the French in Brittany (led by Northampton), Gascony (led by Derby) and Flanders (led by Edward). This would force Philip to break up his army, and, with sufficient archers, the English had a chance to prevail.

The pope, hearing of Edward's preparations, sent a letter in March requiring him to seek peace. He tried to increase the moral pressure on the king by stating that Edward had broken his promise to send further negotiators, and by asking him to join a crusade. These letters came on top of others in which the pope expressed his displeasure at hearing that rumours were circulating in England that he had empowered two cardinals to 'publish processes and fulminate sentences' against the English.[40] Edward had, at the time, refused to give these cardinals safe conducts to come to England, but had eventually received them, in order to say to them personally that he would not countenance any removal or restriction of his rights. The pope was in a weakening position. He only had diplomatic tools and religious threats, and these were ineffective weapons with which to control a man like Edward. No English contemporary doubted Edward's spirituality or his patriotism, whereas practically all the cardinals at the papal court were French, and therefore neither liked nor trusted in England. Even more significantly, the pope underestimated the collective determination of the English camp. He presumed he was dealing with an intemperate and opportunistic leader whose people wanted peace above all else, and would eventually desert their high-taxing king. It was not that Clement was unwise but that he was prejudiced, and thus he believed what he wanted to believe. This did not equip him to understand the situation in England. He also suffered from the unavoidable papal disadvantage of being of advanced years: he could not possibly understand the latest developments in warfare. The very idea that Edward could meet the much larger army of France in battle, and win, was not only outside his experience, it was beyond his imagination.

By the summer of 1345 the three fleets were ready. The earl of Northampton left for Brittany in early June, and, in late July, Derby sailed for Gascony. There he was supported by the recently appointed seneschal, Ralph Stafford, who had mustered the Gascons and laid siege to Blaye after Edward had formally renounced the truce on 14 June. Edward himself was preparing to sail from Sandwich, but at the end of June urgent news arrived from Flanders. There had been an armed rising, and van Artevelde was on the defensive. The count of Flanders stood poised to return. Not knowing what the situation would be in Flanders if he waited any longer, Edward ordered his fleet to set sail on 3 July. He arrived at Sluys two days later, and held a conference with van Artevelde on board his great ship, the *Catherine*.[41]

The events of the next three weeks were momentous for Flanders. To some men of Ghent, van Artevelde was pursuing the alliance with the English for his own personal gain. When van Artevelde returned from Sluys, he was seized and beaten to death by a mob.[42] Edward shrewdly used the murder of his ally as an excuse more directly to intervene. To the count of Flanders he offered the chance of rehabilitation if the count would swear homage to him as the king of France. The count refused, and so Edward was free to neglect his interests and directly to negotiate with the merchant leaders of the three major towns, Bruges, Ypres and Ghent. The burghers of these places found themselves negotiating with a king who controlled the supply of wool to their weavers, and conveniently had an army of two thousand men-at-arms anchored off the coast. Edward made his case, the Flemings all agreed to continue to accept his kingship, and Edward agreed to rid the country of the count of Flanders' supporters. At the end of the month, Edward gave orders for his fleet to sail to a secret destination. Unfortunately his luck with storms once more proved decisive, and his ships found themselves sailing northwards for two days. The secret destination – wherever it was – remained secret. No sailors reached it. Edward realised he needed to regroup and returned to England.

*

Van Artevelde's murder was just one of a series of deaths which cast a shadow over the summer of 1345. Only a few days earlier, while Edward was at Sluys, his trusted confidant John Shorditch was murdered. Shorditch had undertaken much secret business on Edward's behalf, and Edward was furious when told of his death. He had the killers tracked down and summarily executed. In September, at Worms, Edward's brother-in-law and erstwhile ally, the count of Hainault, was killed, leaving no obvious heir. He had betrayed Edward by swearing allegiance to Philip, and his death left Hainault without any leadership except that of his uncle, John of Hainault (the same John who had accompanied Edward to England in 1326). Despite their long association, John now swore allegiance to France, angered that Edward had not paid the money he had previously promised to the count.[43] Edward showed what he thought of this by immediately trying to claim Hainault in right of his wife, even though she was not the eldest of the count's sisters. John retaliated by ensuring that the county passed to Albert, son of his niece Margaret and her husband Ludvig of Bavaria, who was now allied to Philip.

Natural deaths of men close to Edward also occurred at this time. Foremost of these was that of his old ally, Henry, earl of Lancaster, who died on 22 September. One of the now ageing guard who had taken part in the seizure of Mortimer, he was trusted to his dying day. When Edward had gone to Flanders in July, Henry had been appointed one of the advisers of seven-year-old Prince Lionel, keeper of England. Edward and Philippa attended the earl's funeral in person, specially buying black cloth for mourning clothes for themselves and their household.[44]

Less emotional but diplomatically much more important were the deaths of various bishops. When Thomas Charlton, the bishop of Hereford, had died in 1344 the pope had acted quickly to appoint his successor, to enforce his rights.[45] As relations with the pope worsened over the following twelve months it became clear that the next bishop to die would trigger a struggle between the king and the pope. As it happened, the next to go was the bishop of Durham, Richard Bury, who died in April 1345. Perhaps because of the special relationship between this bishop and the king, Edward won this round of episcopal nominations, achieving the election of his clerk Thomas Hatfield to the vacant see. (The pope's words on Hatfield were that he would have appointed a jackass if Edward had nominated one.) But Edward lost the next round of this game of dead bishop's shoes, in June, when the pope's man, Thomas Lisle, was appointed bishop of Ely. Edward decided to make an example of the next church body which dared to oppose him. When Adam of Orleton died the next month, and the monks of Winchester elected John Devenish in his place, against the king's will, Edward took the bold step of fining the monks two thousand pounds.[46] Levying a fine against men who had supposedly given up their worldly wealth only hardened the pope's attitude, which was already hard enough. Clement responded by delaying any appointment to Winchester and maintaining his refusal to permit an arranged marriage between Edward's eldest son and the daughter of the duke of Brabant. Such obduracy was guaranteed not to soften the hearts of the English. Anti-papal propaganda began to circulate: it was rumoured that Clement had declared that the English were 'good asses' who would bear whatever load was thrust upon them.[47] By the autumn of 1345 the English were as eager to fight the pope as they were King Philip. Opposition to the French pope increasingly fused with opposition to the French king. The diatribes written against the French at this point were extreme. 'France, womanish, pharisaic, embodiment of might, lynx-like, viperish, foxy, wolfish, a Medea, cunning, a siren, cruel, bitter, haughty: you are full of bile' was how one contemporary poem began.[48] The English view of the truce was not much better: 'King, beware of truces, lest you perish by them' warned the same writer. Ironically, the only thing holding the English back from launching a full-scale invasion of France at this stage was Edward, and that was only because he already had two armies in the field.

On the death of his father, the earl of Derby had inherited the title Earl of Lancaster. In keeping with his elevation, he had success from the moment he had landed. The siege of Blaye had been an unambitious affair, and he persuaded Stafford to negotiate a local truce. That done, both forces joined together under Lancaster's command and boldly marched to Montcuq, a Gascon castle besieged by the French. After a surprise night march, Lancaster shocked the besiegers into flight, and pursued them north to Bergerac, an important French town on the Dordogne. Barely pausing for breath, Lancaster and his knights (including the ever-present Sir Walter Manny) set about attacking the town. After a number of assaults it surrendered, on 24 August.[49] Thereafter success followed success. Castles fell, valuable prisoners were captured, towns capitulated. Huge amounts of treasure were obtained by Lancaster and Manny. All of this fell to them personally, encouraging them to carry on the fight. And carry on they did, in style. Declining to attack the well-defended city of Périgueux, Lancaster left garrisons at all the surrounding fortified places he could capture. When the French responded by sending a substantial army to recapture one of these, Auberoche, he turned back on himself. Forcing his men on another surprise night march he came upon the French army at dawn on Tuesday 21 October. The result was utter confusion among the French, torn apart by the devastating effect of the English arrows. Despite their superior numbers they could not properly engage the English until the battle was well underway. Just when the French seemed to be stabilising their position and getting the upper hand, Lancaster brought up his mounted knights and men-at-arms, and the garrison of the castle made a sortie to attack the French from the rear. The pendulum of confidence swung in England's favour at the crucial moment of the battle. The rest was devastation. Among the valuable prisoners taken by Lancaster were a count, seven viscounts, three barons, twelve bannerets, many knights, and last, but certainly not least, one of the pope's nephews.[50]

In Brittany the earl of Northampton had success of a much less dramatic kind. He recaptured the Channel Islands but then found himself picking up the pieces of Edward's broken strategy. It was no mistake or defeat which laid his campaign low: it was simply that John de Montfort suddenly fell ill at his castle of Hennebont, and died there on 26 September. It was a devastating blow. As a military leader de Montfort was replaceable but as the heir in whose name the English were fighting, he was not. Worse, back in England, his lion-hearted wife had gone mad, and was unfit to return to Brittany. Not even the six-year-old heir, John's son, was on hand to provide nominal leadership; he too was in England, at Edward's court. The earl of Northampton was forced to maintain his army in the field simply to keep the de Montfortist claim – and Edward's strategy – alive.

The news of de Montfort's death caused Edward to reflect deeply on his situation in October 1345. News of the battle of Auberoche and the subsequent victories of the earl of Lancaster had yet to reach England. The prime strategic factor guiding Edward was the instruction he had received in parliament the previous year: to bring this war to a swift conclusion with no concessions to French interests. It was clear to him now that this meant an English-led attack, entailing huge numbers of English troops, and thus extended supply lines into France, and the assembly of the biggest English military fleet ever assembled. And that was just to get a large enough army across the Channel: the military strategy on the ground was another consideration, the defence of the northern border was another, and the implications of victory yet another. Some necessary preparations could be undertaken straight away. Men could be raised, ships could be acquired and the Scottish border could be secured. But many unknowns remained. Much depended on the progress of the two armies in the field. If Northampton could wrest control of one of the major Breton ports, then Brittany might prove an ideal landing place. If Lancaster continued to enjoy success in Gascony, there might be an argument for taking the army there. In the circumstances Edward did exactly the right thing: he set the date for the navy and army to muster in the spring – 1 March 1346 – and left the details to be decided nearer the date. This left his commanders plenty of time to achieve their respective immediate strategic objectives and allowed him time to gather the huge number of vessels needed for the crossing and to arrange for the defence of the north.

Thus it was that, as Lancaster was wreaking havoc on the French armies in Gascony, and the French king was desperately trying to arrange for the defence of the Agenais and surrounding lands, Edward marched north to the Scottish border. On 8 November Lancaster turned the tide in the Agenais by walking into La Réole, one of the strongest towns in the region, at the invitation of the citizens. Five days later – but long before he heard the news – Edward set off on a high-speed march to the Scottish border. If the October discussions had not specifically recommended that Edward go north, the need became evident on 25 October, when the Scots invaded by Carlisle, and wasted many places in Cumberland.[51] Although Edward himself fell very ill, his purpose in going had been to issue orders, not to lead a campaign.[52] From his sick bed he sent word to the local commanders informing them that a massive invasion of France would take place the following spring, and that they could expect a concerted drive from the Scots at that time. Their task was to resist it.

By Christmas, Edward was back at Westminster and his health

improving. He knew there was another papal nuncio on hand, waiting to introduce two further cardinals to lay Clement's proposals for peace before him. But he had instructions from the 1344 parliament not to delay his conclusion of the war for papal negotiators, and he refused at first to see the nuncio, or even to grant the cardinals safe conduct. Besides, he himself had no wish to see any of them. His grand scheme was now well underway, and he was not for a moment going to entertain sacrificing such an ambitious military expedition for the sake of Clement's pro-French diplomacy. In Brittany, Northampton had won a bitter battle for La Roche-Derrien, and in Gascony the successes which Lancaster was winning were extraordinary. First it had been Bergerac, then Auberoche, then La Réole. Subsequently then almost every citadel and fortress in the Agenais had fallen to the English. Although Edward did not yet know it, Angoulême too had temporarily fallen to John of Norwich. As victory after victory was reported in England, his popularity rose higher and higher. It was, after all, his kingship – his encouragement of a band of worthy knights – which had brought these victories about. In contrast, the pope's popularity had already sunk irretrievably low in the parliament of 1344. Edward had just covered the length of the country and had been left in no doubt that the whole kingdom was behind him. Let Clement put the country under an interdict, and let him excommunicate him! Edward was rediscovering the sort of kingship which England had not seen for fifty years: confident, popular, patriotic and defiant. When he decided eventually to admit the papal nuncio into his presence, it was so he could lecture him on how his cause was just and right, and how it had been Philip who had broken the truce by executing his Breton subjects.

So began 1346, one of the truly momentous years in European history. In the north of England, Edward was preparing for a militia resistance against a Scots incursion. The Scots, aware of the scale of the attack planned on France, were waiting for Edward to leave England. The French were hastily trying to reclaim as much of Gascony as they could, using the army under the command of Duke John of Normandy. They brought thousands of men – Froissart claims no fewer than one hundred thousand – to besiege Aiguillon, where Sir Ralph Stafford and Sir Walter Manny were holed up with about six hundred archers and three hundred men-at-arms.[53] The Genoese were sending galleys – slowly – in support of the French. As for Edward himself, as was made clear at a great council meeting in February, he was set on the path of war. There could be no turning back now. Although a delay set in due to his old enemy the weather, which scattered the ships as they tried to gather in March, nothing was going to deter him from invading France. More than just the French throne was at stake: this was as much about him honouring his promises to the English as his defiance of France and the pope. When the weather turned bad he simply put the muster date back to 1 May. The date had to be set back again, but Edward was not to be deterred. By the end of May approximately fifteen thousand men were gathered in and around Portsmouth, ready to embark on seven hundred and fifty ships.[54] Edward himself was at Porchester Castle from 1 June, waiting. And all of Europe was waiting too. In their towns, parishes and cities across France, Gascony, Flanders, Brittany, Castille and Genoa, they were waiting; in the monasteries and castles, manor houses and street tenements. For no one knew where he would land. Edward had kept his destination a complete secret. Would it be Gascony? Brittany? Flanders? Or somewhere else, somewhere entirely new?

We do not know when Edward made his decision. Neither he nor his closest advisers told anyone. The destination was chosen before he set sail, as the captains of the ships all had sealed instructions where to land in the event of being separated by a storm, but the actual place remained a closely guarded secret. Edward ordered no ships to leave England for a week after the fleet departed, with the exception of a diversionary expedition, due to sail to Flanders under Hugh Hastings. The destination was still a secret on 28 June, when Edward boarded his flagship. Hundreds of vessels followed the great English warships flying their magnificent streamers as they headed westwards, hugging the English coast. The ships had all been equipped with sufficient rations to reach Gascony, and Froissart indicates that that was widely believed to have been the planned destination. A letter written after the landing by Sir Bartholomew Burghersh also states that the king originally intended to go to Gascony.[55] But it was not a Gascony-bound breeze which Edward was waiting for. On 11 July, two weeks after setting out, the strategy was made known. That morning, in the clear sun, the trumpets from Edward's flagship blared out, and the great ships of the English navy unfurled their sails, turned their prows and started sailing south. They were heading towards the Normandy beaches.[56]

TEN

Edward the Conqueror

On 1 July 1346, while Edward was still at sea, Simon Pouillet, a wealthy merchant of Compiègne, was dining with some of his relatives. At the dinner table he happened to remark that, in his opinion, it might be better if Edward were to become king of France, for 'it would be better for France to be ruled well by Edward than badly by Philip'. This remark was noted by some who were present, and mentioned to others, and so on, until it was carried around the town. Eventually it came to the attention of King Philip. His reaction says much about his state of mind. Pouillet was arrested, dragged to the Paris meat market and hanged on a meat hook like a beef carcass. Then he was butchered alive: first his arms being severed, then his legs, then his head. His limbless and headless torso was hung by a chain from the common gallows at Montfaucon, just outside Paris.[1]

About one month before this, an event took place which reveals the morale of the English assailants in France, and perhaps explains Philip's paranoia. His nephew, Charles de Blois, was sweeping across Brittany in an attempt to destroy all Breton support for the English cause. So large was his army that he was successful in persuading many Bretons to switch sides. The English forces were then under the command of Sir Thomas Dagworth (Northampton having returned to England in January). Dagworth's force was too small to face de Blois, and so remained in the fortresses at Brest, Lesneven and La Roche-Derrien. But Dagworth was surprised while making a tour of his outposts. Very early in the morning on 9 June he and eighty men-at-arms and one hundred archers realised they were trapped by the entire French Breton army, numbering several thousand men. Offered no quarter, they dug themselves in, and prepared to fight to the death. They were hugely outnumbered, facing at least twenty if not forty times as many men. They had little chance of even creating an impression on the opposing force. One French knight declared he would himself tie up Dagworth like a parcel and bring him to de Blois. But as the fight raged, something almost unbelievable happened. The English position held. All day they fought, ten, twelve, fourteen hours, right into the evening. They countered attack after attack, and kept going until nightfall. Charles de Blois himself led the last charge and did all he could to break the English line. But Sir Thomas Dagworth and his men, wounded as they were, exhausted as they were, held firm. At the end of the day, having seen de Blois' army fall back, Dagworth realised something close to a military miracle had been accomplished. The French were retreating. Despite fighting for about sixteen hours, and sustaining terrible injuries, he and his troops had come through. It was cause for a letter to the king, and a claim that that day he had led the bravest men that England had to offer.[2]

These two stories are glimpses of a huge contrast in mood in 1346. For twenty years Philip had kept up an awkward war of words and diplomatic squabbling with Edward, at least partly to sustain an image of royal superiority over the upstart grandson of Philip the Fair. And in all that time he had achieved nothing substantial; he had not even lessened the threat to his people. He had not engaged Edward in a full-scale battle, far less defeated him, and he had had to sacrifice territorial rights in order to avoid conflict, which had only resulted in accusations of cowardice. A succession of French popes had proved powerless to help him, and one, Benedict XII, had clearly thought him a fool. Now people openly derided him. But like many unconfident kings before and after, his reaction to dissent was anger and tyranny, and that only exacerbated his difficulties. Edward on the other hand had never stooped to butchering his detractors. His determination to keep the war on French soil meant that he was much more likely to keep the goodwill of his people than Philip. And his policy of continual war coupled with his reluctance to compromise meant that, when he did settle for a truce or a ceasefire, it was always on his own terms. He had every reason to be optimistic.

Optimism was not something to rely on, however, as Edward well knew, and there was still plenty of room for him to miscalculate and lose. Northampton's failure to win a major northern port suitable for an invasion was an indicator of how large Edward's problem was. There could be no failed siege this time, as at Tournai in 1340. Nor could there be a withdrawal, as at La Flamengrie in 1339. This time the armies of France and England had to clash. Philip could not afford to be called a coward again, and Edward had parliamentary expectations to satisfy, that he would bring the war to a successful close. This raised an issue that must have been in the back of Edward's mind: he had never actually defeated Philip on land. Indeed, no one had defeated the French army on French soil for more than a hundred and fifty years.[3] They were reputed to be the best knights in Europe, and certainly constituted by far the largest assembly of trained men who would fight for a single cause. When the two armies did meet, it was probable that Edward would be facing an army two or three times the size of his own. And he could not be sure that the French would not pull some new tactics out to combat his archers. When Dagworth and his men had dug themselves in on top of a hill, it was noted that de Blois had advanced on foot, avoiding the entrapment techniques which Edward's forces had to date relied upon. This was Edward's quandary: he had to bring the French to battle, and defeat them comprehensively on their own soil, knowing he would be outnumbered, and knowing that his tactics were no longer unfamiliar to the enemy. Unless he could choose the place of the battle, and had time properly to arrange his forces, he would be in grave danger of losing everything for which he had fought and negotiated over the past sixteen years.

It is important to remember these dangers, for the character of Edward III has been portrayed as somewhat frivolous compared with such resolute figures from English history as William the Conqueror and Edward I. That would be absolutely the wrong picture to have of him now, on the point of invading France. Edward's ability to enjoy himself has been seen traditionally as reflecting a moral weakness, and his fondness for women has often been cited as a lack of commitment to the business of being a king. But his enjoyment of hunting and male as well as female company should not lull us into forgetting that beneath the lighthearted exterior was a deeply committed and serious core of ambition. He had already shown it dramatically at Halidon Hill and Sluys. It is clearly visible in the very elaborate preparations for this campaign. Although Philippa was about to give birth to another child, Edward did not allow family matters to distract him from his prime purpose.[4] He was now aged thirty-three, Alexander the Great's age at death. Had William the Conqueror or Edward I met their descendant in Normandy in July 1346 they would have recognised a man every bit as resolute as they had been at the height of their powers, and one who was fully aware of the expectations of his peers, his parliament and his people. At times like this Edward was a warrior monk to whom the military guidebook of Vegetius was like a bible and whose reverential prayer all his waking hours was for victory over his adversary.

Propaganda was employed to the full. The very place of landing – Normandy – was partly chosen for its symbolism.[5] The three main reasons for choosing the beaches were probably the proximity to England, the lack of a French army there and the difficulty of preventing a landing. But there was a fourth reason too: England had once been conquered by the duke of Normandy. Now England was returning the compliment. Edward's contemporaries would have understood this as recovering the lands of his ancestors, a powerful symbol of duty in the medieval mind, and in many ways similar to the crusaders' dream of recovering Christ's patrimony in the Holy Land. It was said that Edward tripped on landing, and bloodied his nose, but got up and claimed that it was a welcome embrace from the land of France. William the Conqueror was said to have fallen similarly in 1066, clutching the sands of England as he got up, saying he held England in his hands. Edward certainly came prepared to draw connections between his campaign and that of the Conqueror. In his speech to the invading troops he reminded them of his dynastic right to the duchy of Normandy, which, he told them, inaccurately 'had been taken unjustly in the time of King Richard'.[6] Would not his men fight to right this injustice done by the French to that crusader king? And, like William the Conqueror, he announced that he would send the ships away. There would be no retreat. When he exhorted his men to be valiant, and to conquer the land of France or die, the army responded with shouts and overwhelming enthusiasm that 'they would follow him, their dear lord, even to death'.[7]

Edward's actual landing place – Saint-Vaast-la-Hougue – was on the western side of Normandy, on the Cotentin peninsula. No serious resistance to the landing was encountered; what little there was was quickly swept away by the vanguard, commanded by the earl of Warwick. Many Norman vassals were distrustful of Philip, and whether or not they wanted the old overlordship of England restored, they may have seen a political opportunity to change the king for one less inclined judicially to murder Norman lords such as Olivier de Clisson, who had been hanged during the truce, three years earlier. Godfrey de Harcourt – an important Norman landowner, who had been exiled from France – was with Edward, and may have pointed out that the Norman townsmen were not used to war on this scale, unlike the Flemings and Gascons. They would not be able to form a serious militia to resist Edward. As the English advanced towards Paris, they would be wresting control from Philip all the way.

Soon after landing Edward made his way on to a small hill near the beach. There he knighted his sixteen-year-old son, Prince Edward (the Black Prince), and several other promising young men including the eighteen-year-old William Montagu, second earl of Salisbury, son and heir of his late great friend, and the seventeen-year-old Roger Mortimer, grandson and heir of his late great enemy, the earl of March. He then resorted to Morsalines while his captains oversaw the disembarkation and organisation of all the troops, victuals and equipment, an operation which took a full five days. Edward sent troops to take the ports of Barfleur and Cherbourg which lay nearby. Both towns were looted and burnt. Edward did speak to his men – or as many as could hear him – telling them that he had not come to despoil Normandy but to accept its allegiance; but his exhortation failed to restrain the substantial minority who considered it their prerogative to loot the goods, rape the women, and gorge themselves on the fruits and soft cheeses of Normandy. Even as the troops disembarked the wildest English and Welsh bands – there were about three thousand Welsh spearmen with Edward – roamed between the villages and 'cheerfully' set fire to the countryside 'until the sky itself glowed red'.[8]

On 17 July the English army began the march eastwards, towards Paris. They travelled in three divisions. The first, the vanguard, was under the nominal command of the prince of Wales, assisted by the earls of Warwick and Northampton. The main body of men was under the king's own direct control. The rear was commanded by the recently consecrated bishop of Durham, Thomas Hatfield. With such an enormous force approaching, the first town in their way – Valognes – had no option but to submit, the inhabitants begging only that Edward spare their lives. Edward made a show of granting to all the Normans who accepted his kingship that he would indeed spare their lives and property. But in reality his word alone was not sufficient to control the urges of his men, who looted the town and burnt it as they left. The same happened at the next town they came to, Carentan, which was also subjected to looting and burning despite the king's attempts to save the property of men whom he considered his subjects. After Carentan he knew that, wherever the English army went there would be destruction unless the most strenuous and time-consuming efforts were made to keep the troops in order. In most cases, this was counter-productive. For the French towns in his path, his approaching army was simply a tide of misery.

The inhabitants of the next town on the way to Paris, Saint-Lo, realised in advance what was likely to happen to them, and decided to resist. With a French army in the vicinity, commanded by Robert Bertrand, they prepared to defend their homes. They broke down the bridge and barricaded the streets. But their decision was a naive one. When the size of the English army became clear, Bertrand realised his position was suicidal, and withdrew to Caen, leaving the inhabitants of Saint-Lo to defend their homes as best they could. Had the English been a mere raiding party of a couple of hundred men, perhaps the townsmen could have held them back. But fifteen thousand fresh soldiers was impossible. Edward's carpenters repaired the bridge and the army smashed through the gates and barricades and swarmed over the town, seizing whatever they wanted and killing anyone who got in their way. When the news was spread that the three skulls hanging above the gates belonged to three Norman knights who had been executed against the terms of the truce for supporting Edward in 1343, the inhabitants were doomed.[9] Overt statements that rapes took place are relatively rare in chronicles – killing could be considered chivalrous, rape never – but at Saint-Lo, in le Bel's words, 'several pretty women of the town and their daughters were raped, which was a great pity'.[10] The wealthiest men – cloth merchants – were seized, bound and dragged off, to be shipped back to England and ransomed. As the first town that had actively resisted him, Edward did not say a word to try and prevent the destruction. Instead he gave the order for the whole town to be burnt. He might have lost the power to save those prepared to accept him, but he could still demonstrate what horrors would be inflicted on those towns which resisted.

*

Edward made his men rise early, before dawn. Each morning they were ordered to move out to a certain destination. On the 23rd they were ordered to Torigny, but a change of plan switched them to Cormolain. The next day's march took them to Fontenay le Pesnel, then Cheux. On 26 June, Edward arose, heard mass before sunrise, and ordered the army to advance on Caen.

Edward knew that Caen would be the site of the first important battle of his campaign. Inside the secure walls of the old town and its castle were the forces of the count of Eu, the lord of Tancarville, the bishop of Bayeux and a substantial population, probably in excess of twelve thousand people. There were also about three hundred mercenary Genoese crossbowmen. Outside, waiting for Edward, was a large contingent under the command of Robert Bertrand, including many townsmen of Caen who had insisted on meeting the English in the open, bravely trying to minimise the damage to their town.

The English approached at about three o'clock in the afternoon.[11] Edward drew up his men in battle formation. Seeing the thousands of pennons approaching, the men of Caen realised that they had totally misjudged the scale of the invasion, and fled back within the old town. Fearful though they may have been, their retreat was also a sensible tactical move, strengthening further the town's defences. The French numbered between two and four thousand soldiers and perhaps four thousand adult male citizens; this made it a daunting task to storm the town, as the walls were strong, and seven thousand men (not to mention a few thousand women) could easily defend them for a long period. The king's confessor mentioned in a letter that when he first saw Caen, he thought it was impregnable.[12]

Edward could not afford to think in terms of impregnability for he did not have time for a long siege. He noted that the two great abbeys built by the Conqueror – the Abbaye aux Hommes (where the Conqueror himself lay buried) and the Abbaye aux Dames – lay outside the walls, so that a complete destruction of the town need not destroy his ancestors' burial place or his religious foundations. When the bishop of Bayeux refused even to answer his letter offering to spare the lives of the inhabitants if the town surrendered, and failed also to permit the return of Edward's messenger, the destruction of the town became his determined path.

As it happened, the vanguard had run ahead of his decision-making. As the last of Bertrand's soldiers desperately made for the safety of the old town, the foremost of the troops under the prince and the earl of Warwick had followed them and attacked. A battle ensued in which the archers in the vanguard were confronted by large numbers of men-at-arms. In order to save his valuable archers, Edward sent a message to the earl of Warwick to order them to retreat, but, in the vicious chaos which followed in the streets of the old town, the earl also became drawn into the fighting. Realising there was nothing to do but engage fully, Edward ordered an attack. Everything centred on the bridge between the new and old towns. A contingent of Welsh spearmen, seeing the low tide allowed them to cross the river on foot, jumped in and bravely waded towards the defenders on the far bank, attacking the bridge from the rear. More English piled into the fray until the defenders lost heart and fell back, leaving their compatriots on the bridge to be killed. Some knights took refuge in the upper storeys of the gatehouse. They saw what happened to those caught in the streets. Even the wealthy were killed by the English troops who were (in Froissart's view) 'men of little conscience'. No one was being ransomed. The knights in the gatehouse only survived when one of their number happened to recognise the arms of Sir Thomas Holland amidst the mêlée, and pleaded with him to take them prisoner, so that their lives would be saved.[13]

When the dust settled, more than five thousand Frenchmen lay dead in the streets and in the fields around the town, hacked down as they tried to flee. One hundred and seven knights were taken prisoner along with about one hundred and twenty esquires. Three hundred Genoese archers lay dead, their crossbows all useless after they ran out of bolts. As the town had resisted, a large number of women were systematically raped. Some of the English knights tried to prevent some of the rapes and killings. But Edward did nothing to prevent any of it. He was set on destroying everything, ruthlessly eliminating every obstacle between him and Philip. When he was told that he had lost several hundred soldiers, some killed in the ransacking of the town by citizens throwing stones down from their upper windows, he gave the order to kill everyone within and to burn the town. Only the insistence of Sir Godfrey de Harcourt persuaded him that he had destroyed enough already, that he needed to remain focused on his real ambition, which was to meet Philip in battle, reassuring him with the words 'without more killing we will still be lords and masters of this town'.[14]

Edward accepted Harcourt's advice. It became a pattern for him to insist on the most stringent, horrific punishments for those who had dared oppose him, and only to relent when one of his own men begged him to show mercy. This campaign was not about mercy. It was about him being seen to be 'terrible to his enemies', demonstrating that Philip and the French, and the pope and the College of Cardinals, had to regard him not as the son of Edward II but as the greatest warrior in Christendom, and king of a commensurately great kingdom, capable of re-enacting the most glorious exploits of Arthur or anyone else from history they cared to mention. The self-doubt which he had experienced as a teenager still seems to have been pushing him on, to prove himself, to live up to the prophesies of greatness.

After the battle of Caen Edward spent five days in the town, preparing for the battles that lay ahead. He sent out troops to devastate the countryside around. When he received the capitulation of the citizens of Bayeux, terrified that theirs would be the next city destroyed, Edward told the city's representatives that he would accept their submission only when he could guarantee their safety, with the obvious implications that Philip had failed to do exactly that.[15] He ordered twelve hundred reinforcement archers to be levied in England and despatched to him in Normandy together with their equipment.[16] And he held a council of all his nobles. King Philip had taken possession of the sacred war banner – the Oriflamme – from the Abbot of Saint-Denis on 22 July and was marching to Rouen.

Edward's decision – presumably supported by his nobles – was to go straight for Philip. On 31 July he ordered the army to break camp and head towards Rouen. On either side of the main army rode the marshals, devastating everything, so that a broad trail of incineration and destruction fourteen miles wide was left behind Edward wherever he went. That night he encamped at Troarn, the next at Rumesnil. The following day he marched into the city of Lisieux. On 5 August he was at Le Neubourg, twenty-five miles from Rouen. On that day two cardinals sent by the pope to discuss a new peace initiative were allowed into Edward's presence.[17] Their suggestion was that Edward should accept Philip's offer to restore the counties of Ponthieu and the duchy of Aquitaine to be held on the same terms as Edward II had held them, as feudal tenements of the French king. Edward must have been hard-pressed to retain a diplomatic front. These men were still treating him as if he was a supplicant, the king of a little country, a weak country, unable to question the military and ecclesiastical might of France. Did they not realise he had invaded France and was actively trying to engage the French king in combat? Did they think this was merely to regain his father's territorial possessions? Did they not realise that he did not care whether the pope placed England under an interdict? Where were their letters of authority? They had none, they admitted. He dismissed them from his sight, and gave orders to advance to Rouen.

Edward knew that the French army was growing larger every day. At the beginning of August Philip had crossed the Seine and had briefly headed towards Edward, but then had come news of the landing of the second English army in Flanders, under Hugh Hastings, and intelligence that the Flemings had provided a large force to invade France from the north-east. Philip hastened back to Rouen, uncertain of what to do. As the cardinals wasted Edward's time, Philip ordered the destruction of the bridge over the Seine at Rouen, thereby cutting himself off from Edward. He also sent troops ahead to guard the next bridge upstream, at Pont de l'Arche, and the next at Vernon, and so on, giving him enough time to gather an even bigger army, hoping to sweep around through Paris and crush the English. This posed the question: would Edward attack the capital? His baggage wagons were only able to move slowly, about half the speed of the men, but a large contingent could certainly have reached it sooner than Philip, and could have perhaps burnt the suburbs. But it was a very risky move. To get drawn into street fighting in the largest city in northern Europe, against a massive and hostile population, was to risk being overpowered by numbers.[18] The capital had been defended with barricades, compounding the difficulties. Nor would burning the capital of France have helped him reach the northern bank of the Seine. If Philip moved his army to guard the city, Edward would face an impossible series of obstacles between himself and safety. For good reasons, then, Philip gambled that Edward would not actually attack the capital, though he might threaten it. If Philip could bring another army against Edward from the south, and bring his main force through Paris to attack Edward from the east, he would force Edward back towards Normandy, if not destroy him. In view of this, Philip ordered the huge army under the command of his son, the duke of Normandy, to give up the siege of Aiguillon and begin the long march north.

This decision may have raised a smile in the English camp. It would certainly have raised a fantastic cheer in Aiguillon itself. The town had been besieged for over four months by Duke John, and he had sworn not to rest until he had overrun it. For the three hundred English men-at-arms and six hundred archers within, life had become very difficult. Only the remarkable antics of Sir Walter Manny and his indomitable comrades had prevented the town falling to the huge French army at the gates. Indeed, at times it seems that Manny regarded the enemy's presence as simply a form of entertainment to break the monotony of the siege, making daily sorties to destroy the French bridge being built over the river, and later to forage for supplies. On one of these sorties Manny and his men had found themselves cut off by a French foraging party six times the size of his own. In the ensuing fight, Manny's horse was killed underneath him, and his men were all cut down, but when a rescuing party from Aiguillon reached the skirmish and fought their way through to him, they found him carrying on the fight completely surrounded by Frenchmen, and 'fighting most valiantly'.[19]

Edward destroyed all the manors of the king of France, even those within two miles of Paris, but he did not advance on the city itself. It is likely that he realised the risks were far too great, and the chances of bringing Philip to battle in favourable circumstances were far too small. He was still as determined as ever to fight, but to do so on his own terms required him to cross the Seine. He also knew that, before long, the duke of Normandy's army would trap him if he remained south of the river. So began a desperate chase along the river towards Paris to find a bridge. At Pont de l'Arche the local forces desperately fought off the English vanguard until the main French army arrived. The next bridges were at Vernon, Mantes and Meulan. At these places too the English found either the bridge in ruins, or defended by several thousand Frenchmen. Which left them no option but to press on to Poissy.

By 13 August, the situation must have been beginning to rattle those around Edward, even if he himself remained calm. Yes, they were within twenty miles of Paris. Yes, they were feasting off the king of France's own cattle and drinking his wine. But they were not safe. They had failed to engage the French army. Philip controlled the bridges, and by now his army was much larger than the force at Edward's disposal. Edward was stranded south of the Seine, with no way to go except back to Normandy, and that was unthinkable. There was an army of perhaps twenty-five thousand men between him and safety, and it was still growing in size.[20] If Edward had lost only a thousand men in the campaign so far – and he had probably lost more – then he had about half this number. And a second French army was approaching from the south-east. His freedom was at stake, if not his life. Certainly his leadership was in question unless he made something happen soon. It was of paramount importance that he cross this river.

This was where Edward saw the return on the years and the money he had spent on encouraging chivalric pursuits. By promoting the cult of the knight, Edward had fostered men who saw opportunities for greatness and glory in fighting against odds of six to one. It was said in England that if a French army outnumbered an English one by three-to-one, it would be as fifteen lambs to five wolves. Sir Walter Manny and Sir Thomas Dagworth were not alone among Edward's men in showing outstanding courage and supreme fighting skills. Vignettes of an almost comic nature have come down to us, slipped as they were between the pages of the chronicles of enthralled contemporaries. When Sir Thomas Holland found the bridge at Rouen had been destroyed, dividing him from the French king, he was distraught. Having fought and killed the only two French knights he could find, he stood on the edge of the ruined bridge and repeatedly bellowed 'St George for King Edward!' at the concerned Frenchmen on the other side.[21] Comic as such events may appear to us, Holland's shouting, Manny's extraordinary courage at Hennebont and Aiguillon, and even the wanton destruction of towns and villages by 'men of little conscience' are all indicative of a powerful collective will – one is tempted to say psychosis – to attack the enemy. Edward had encouraged a spirit to fight which was so strong that it was difficult to control. The upside of this was that he commanded a force which was undaunted by any task he set. That promise to follow him 'even to death', which the army had made on landing, was serious.

On 13 August the main army came to Poissy. The bridge itself was broken but, as the English looked at the remains, it seemed that the piles were still in place. Odd beams from the bridge floated here and there on the river's edge. Carpenters were called up. Could the bridge be repaired? It was possible, but if the French attacked in sufficient numbers, those first across would be massacred. Edward ordered the carpenters to begin work at once, and asked Northampton to stand by to defend them. Within a short while a single beam, one foot wide, was laid across the swift-moving river. As the last beam was secured, a French force of one thousand horsemen and two thousand infantry appeared on the far bank.[22] Had Edward's men had any doubt in his leadership, things might have been very different. But Northampton and two dozen knights did not hesitate for a moment. They rushed straight over the narrow crossing, one after the other, swords drawn, and engaged the French in bitter hand-to-hand combat, and held them back, as reinforcements crossed behind them. By the end of the day, between five and twelve hundred Frenchmen lay dead around the north side of the crossing.[23] The English too had lost many men. But Edward had his bridge.

*

The next day Philip learnt that Edward held the bridge at Poissy. His policy of entrapment had failed. He now had no option but to take positive action. He issued a public challenge, declaring that he would meet

Edward's army in the area south of Paris, or north of Poissy (north of the Seine), between 17 and 22 August. Edward told Philip's messenger that he would be delighted to fight Philip, but he would choose the time and place of the meeting himself. When asked where Philip could expect to find him, Edward told him to look for the smoke of burning towns, and promptly gave orders to burn every place between Poissy and Paris, including Montjoye, the French king's favourite residence and the place which gave him his battle-cry ('St Denis et Montjoye').[24]

Philip may have supposed that Edward did mean to fight him south of the capital, in the plains. Perhaps he believed that Edward was so eager to fight that he would rush into poorly defended ground, where his comparatively small army could be surrounded. But Edward was a better military leader than Philip, and a more competent strategist than Philip's advisers were prepared to admit to their king. The day after the feast of the Assumption of the Virgin Mary (15 August) – during which both sides observed an informal truce – the French army marched south, towards Paris. In so doing they opened the door for Edward to cross the Seine at Poissy and march north, escaping their entrapment on the south side of the river.

This move has led many subsequent writers to believe that Edward never really meant to do battle with the French at all, that he was running away. But it is one thing to escape a trap, seeking a more suitable battlefield, and quite another to run away. Edward was doing what the Scots had done to him in 1327, what he had done on the way to La Flamengrie in 1339, and what any skilful strategist would have done in the circumstances. He was searching for a more advantageous place to fight. He even put his plan into a formal letter to Philip on the 15th, stating that his sole intention was 'to put an end to the war by battle', stating 'at whatever hour you approach you will find us ready to meet you in the field' and that 'we do not consider it advisable to be cut off by you, or to let you choose the time and place of battle'.[25]

Having crossed the Seine on the 16th, Edward had the Somme on his north, and he now learnt that Philip had destoyed all the undefended bridges over that river also. If he stopped on the south bank, the massive French army would advance on him there, and surround him. It seemed as though all France was one big spider's web full of rivers on which he could be caught, and the French army a big spider able to crawl towards his army wherever it was trapped. If he came to the Somme, and was cornered, Philip's army could hold back and devour him at its leisure, slowly, without a pitched battle, thereby avoiding the risk of attacking the mass of Edward's archers. The answer therefore was simply not to get trapped. And that meant crossing another big river.

Philip could destroy bridges, but he could not destroy fords. There was only one crossing which would guarantee Edward safety from the French army. This was the ford called Blanchetaque, the 'white spot': a path across the Somme estuary marked with a white stone which was traversable on foot at low tide. At high tide merchants' ships could sail up the river to Abbeville, so there was only a narrow opportunity to cross. This was known to Philip, of course, so he had already despatched Godemar du Fay to oversee its defence, with an élite corps of five hundred men-at-arms and three thousand archers and footsoldiers.[26] This was more than enough to guarantee that it could not be crossed, so Edward sent Warwick to try to force the bridge at Pont-Rémy. There Warwick encountered Sir John of Hainault and King John of Bohemia, who drove him back with heavy losses. Attempts to take the bridges at Longpré and Fontaine-sur-Somme proved equally fruitless. Edward's food supply was now beginning to run down, and Philip was just upstream with his army. Edward was once more vulnerable.

But Edward still had the chivalric fervour of his men on his side. When he needed men who were prepared to risk almost certain death in return for a chance of immortal glory, he had an abundance of volunteers. So, trusting in the valour of his men-at-arms, and the range of his archers, Edward selected the earl of Northampton and Sir Reginald Cobham to lead the perilous attack on Godemar du Fay at the ford.

What happened next was a testimony to how far the English had progressed since that day, nineteen years earlier, when Mortimer had held Edward back from attacking the Scots across the river at Stanhope Park. With incredible courage, Northampton and Cobham proved that it was possible to advance across a river facing large numbers of entrenched, well-armed forces, and drive them from their positions. With one hundred men-at-arms and one hundred archers, they waded into the water, twelve abreast. With the longbows' rapid fire pinning down the front ranks of the enemy, the first group of men-at-arms charged across the river and mounted the bank, despite the returning fire of the Genoese crossbows and the onslaught of the men-at-arms who defied the English longbows. In this way, despite heavy losses, they provided a place for the next hundred men-at-arms to run to, to take the place of the dead, dying and still-fighting first wave. And the archers moved slowly nearer and nearer to the far side, replenished from behind by the next hundred, and then the next hundred. This carried on until they had sufficient numbers to launch a full-scale onslaught on the men of Godemar du Fay. Before long the French men-at-arms realised that their advantage had been shot away by the English archers, and they fled, leaving their infantrymen to be rounded up and killed by the pursuing English knights who now rode freely across the ford. According to a contemporary newsletter, two thousand Frenchmen were killed in the forcing of the passage across the Somme.[27] Soon the English army was across. Not long after that, the tide came in. Philip was cut off from the English. The French were left staring across the river at their elusive quarry. It was not quite comparable to Moses and the parting of the Red Sea, but for the English on the morning of 24 August 1346, it was another of those military miracles for which they were becoming famous. Edward was the first to offer thanks to God.[28]

*

Edward had escaped entrapment. He was still no nearer to victory but at least he could choose when and where he would fight the French king. At first he considered it to his advantage to engage Philip on the river bank at Blanchetaque, and to this end offered Philip an unimpeded crossing. But Philip refused, and returned to Abbeville, where the bridge still stood, held for him by another large force.

Edward was now on home soil, in a manner of speaking. He was in the county of Ponthieu, which was his mother's inheritance, given to him by his father more than twenty years earlier. Froissart specifically attributes the arrival of the army in Ponthieu as the reason Edward stopped near Crécy: to go further would have been to relinquish land he rightly claimed as his own. This is probably correct; keeping the war on French soil was his highest priority. But it needs to be noted that Edward was on familiar ground. He had been here before, on his journey to see Philip in 1329.[29] He had almost certainly been along the road from Abbeville to Saint-Riquier before, and perhaps more than once, for he was in the vicinity in 1325–26 and 1331. How well he could remember the land is another matter. In 1329 he had been a seventeen-year-old on his way to swear fealty to his cousin. Now things were very different. He was twice as old, and had about ten thousand tired men dependent on him; they were hungry, and their shoes were beginning to disintegrate after marching several hundred miles. And they were all about to be attacked by the largest and best-equipped army in Europe.

On Friday 25 August, Edward sent scouts towards Abbeville to find out whether Philip was going to attack that day. They returned to say they could see little sign of action. Sir Hugh Despenser had meanwhile attacked Le Crotoy and returned with plenty of victuals. Edward remained uneasy, concerned that Philip would attack that following night. He gave orders for the army to camp in the open, and to prepare a defensive formation. With still no sign of the French advance, he held a dinner for his nobles and captains. The men remained in their armour. Froissart states that when the lords had retired from the king's pavilion, the king spent several hours in a makeshift oratory, praying for victory, or at least honour. Without honour, he would be nothing, not even self-respecting. At around midnight he went to bed.

Next morning – Saturday 26 August – he was up before dawn. He summoned the prince to him, and together father and son heard mass and received Holy Communion. Then, as the rest of the camp was stirring, they rode out to survey the surrounding area with Edward's principal commanders, including Northampton, Warwick, Cobham and de Harcourt.[30] One can imagine Edward looking over the ground with care, lines from Vegetius echoing in his head. Perhaps he repeated some of them for the benefit of his son, or tested the prince on what he could remember. 'The nature of the ground is often of more consequence than courage.' Or 'if your forces are few in comparison to the enemy, you must cover one of your flanks either with an eminence, a city, the sea, a river or some similar protection'. Edward did not have the sea, and he did not want a river, far less a city. But there was the forest of Crécy. With that to cover one flank he chose to place his standard at the top of a hill. He positioned his men in three battalions in front of it, across the hill. The first would be under the command of the prince of Wales, and would include Warwick, de Harcourt, Cobham, Sir Thomas Holland, Sir Bartholomew Burghersh, Sir Thomas Clifford, Sir John Chandos and many other outstanding knights, with eight hundred men-at-arms and the surviving thousand Welshmen. The second would be under Northampton, with the earl of Arundel in support and a further eight hundred men-at-arms. To himself he reserved the remaining seven hundred men-at-arms, who would hold the rear, and about two thousand archers. It went without saying that the other four thousand or so archers would be on the flanks. Trapping the enemy was the essence of their power.

The baggage wagons were carefully positioned. Some were used to make a corral around the horses, who were placed at the rear of the army, near a windmill at the top of the hill. But some of those carts which had rumbled over the rough roads of France all the way from Saint-Vaast-La-Hougue were placed with the archers. King Philip was about to discover why his army had been able to cover thirty miles in a day and the English could only manage half that. They had been protecting these carts. Strapped beneath them were about one hundred small cannon. Now we can see how meticulous Edward's planning and preparation had been. The powder for these artillery pieces had been made at the Tower of London in March, long before landing in France. It had been hauled across the ford at Blanchetaque still dry. Until now gunpowder had only been used in sieges, with the sole exception of Mortimer's use of 'crakkis of war' on the Stanhope campaign. Those had been dangerous exploding buckets by comparison with Edward's refined guns. As well as small cannon with calibres of roughly four inches (the shot were still stone) he brought his newly developed 'ribalds' – series of bound gun barrels designed to shoot metal bolts, like crossbow bolts. And Edward not only had developed them, he had thought of how to use them too. That was why they were with the archers: to catch the advancing French in the deadly crossfire.[31]

Edward had another surprise, also long in preparation. Beside his usual royal arms he unfurled another banner: a painted dragon clothed in his own arms. It was his answer to the Oriflamme. As the troops marched to their positions, they all saw this new symbol of English power and confidence: 'Drago' they called it, recalling the prophetic symbol of his grandfather, Edward I.[32]

The English captains passed on the orders for pits, one foot deep, to be dug in front of their lines to break the charge of the French men-at-arms. As they worked, four French knights appeared in the distance, surveying the English array. Edward gave orders that they were not to be bothered or interrupted. Let them report to Philip how few they were in number! Let them see Drago! Let them tell the French army to come to them. For Edward was still dependent on being attacked. If his troops were drawn out and down to fight Philip and the French lords on their terms, the battle would be lost. Discipline was everything. He jumped on to a small palfrey and went among the ranks of men, carrying a white wand with which he made his gestures and directives clear to all those who could see him. And they listened. His words were words of honour, he spoke of the glory which they would win, and of the rights they would uphold. Never again would the French king be able to hold the English people in contempt, no, nor the pope. Froissart states that all who heard him, even those who were feeling afraid, were cheered by his presence, so positive and optimistic he seemed. He filled them with self-belief. And he did this as he rode at walking pace through all the ranks. Until ten o'clock he rode among them, exhorting them to do their utmost. He commended them to the protection of God and the Virgin Mary. Then he gave orders for the army to sit down, and rest some more, and have food distributed so that they might be strong when the French came on the scene.

Edward and his leaders met together for one last time in his pavilion. Those who were hungry ate, and they all drank a little. Then the pots and pans were packed up, and sent away to the carts at the rear, and each lord resumed his place with his men, said his prayers, and waited.

Edward might have been unfortunate with the weather at sea, but he surely would have gladly weathered all those storms again for the luck that came upon him now. It began to rain. The English sat or stood and waited in their positions as the summer grass beneath their feet was soaked. And as the grass grew damp so did the crossbow strings of the Genoese who were being force-marched to the front of the French army somewhere beyond their sight. Exhausted, and insulted by their French employers, these Genoese had been chosen to lead the assault on the English, using archers against archers. But these crossbowmen needed time to shoot and reload, and they usually fired from behind their great shields. These shields were still in the wagon trains, somewhere behind them. No time for those, they were told; they would have to fight without them.

It was mid-afternoon when the first ranks of Genoese archers came into view. Behind them, in a long disorderly mass, came the army of France: about thirty thousand men, roughly three times the size of the English force, with more following, yet to arrive. The English ranks were ordered to their feet. The archers restrung their bows. And they waited. The Genoese advanced, and shouting insultingly at the English. Local people had lined the road all the way to the battlefield, and chanting Kill! Kill! Kill! as the French army passed. Now the time to kill had come. Line after line advanced, shouting abuse, their bolts primed for the first volley. They yelled for a third time at the English, hoping to scare them. But the English did not move. Then with the boom of the first cannon, the Genoese loosed their volley of bolts.[33] And with dismay they watched them die up on the air, and fall short. Hurriedly they began to reload in the open, as the next line advanced, taking up the shouting. Still there came nothing from the English but the occasional sighting shot from the cannon. Only when the bulk of the Genoese were in range and about to shoot did the English trumpets ring out for the attack to begin.

If Genoese pride had died in the air with the falling short of those first crossbow bolts, then English pride struck home hard and true with the first English volley. The Genoese were ripped to shreds: 'these arrows pierced their arms, heads and through their armour', said Froissart. Each archer in the English camp could fire between six and ten arrows per minute. If each man fired at the slower rate, to ensure accuracy, and if there were only five thousand archers in the English army, the Genoese – who numbered no more than six thousand – were suddenly struck by thirty thousand arrows per minute, each of which was potentially deadly. We do not know how long they could have kept this up, but if Edward had brought supplies on the same scale as he had ordered them in 1341 (a single order of three million arrows for seven thousand bows) then we may reckon that this rate of fire was sustainable for at least an hour. Chroniclers describe the effect in terms of arrows falling like snow.

Within a few minutes there were very few Genoese who were not dead or dying. Those that survived the attack retreated, shouting, some throwing down their crossbows. But the appalled French commanders refused to allow them to flee. The count of Alençon (King Philip's brother) set spurs to his horse and charged some of them down, slashing at them as an example. Philip himself gave the order to kill anyone who retreated from the battlefield as he saw the Genoese run: 'Kill these scoundrels, kill them all!' were his actual words, reported on good authority.[34] But as his own men realised, killing Genoese crossbowmen would not help them against the English.

Despite this appalling start, the reputation of France as leading all Christendom in arms was much more than mere posturing. Pride ran very deep in the French psyche; military honour was integral to the identity of the French nobility. Even as the French knights saw their mercenaries run, they rallied and readied themselves. These men knew the purpose of their privileges, and recognised the time had come for them to do their utmost duty. They cannot have failed to understand at that moment that they were facing a test as severe as any previously encountered by a French army. Trumpets blared. Wave after wave of knights set their spurs to their horses and charged up the hill in a furious attempt to drive the English from their position, only to suffer humiliating and catastrophic losses on the hillside as their polished armour and surcoats were torn open by the humble arrows of the English archers. Each time they fell back, but, as befitting the flower of European chivalry, they regrouped and charged again. Fifteen charges were thrown against the English. At one point they broke the line, and fought through to reach the first battalion of English men-at-arms. Seeing the standard of the prince of Wales, they made a concerted effort to seize him. The prince, although only sixteen, was strong and brimful of confidence, and as soon as the French knights came to him he rushed at them, slashing at their horses, bringing down their riders, stamping on their helmets and cutting through their lances. As a result, he ran the risk of being surrounded, and briefly it seemed the French had managed to seize him. But they failed to disarm him, and he fought on, while his bodyguard ferociously fought back to save him. At one point he was struck to his knees, and his standard-bearer, Sir Richard Fitzsimon, resorted to the desperate measure of actually laying down the prince's standard in order to draw his sword to defend his master. Another of his men rushed back to Edward to ask for help for the prince. Edward sent it, but by the time it arrived the prince was far from needing it. With

Fitzsimon's help he had regained his feet, and started fighting more furiously than ever, so that by the time the twenty knights from Edward's own bodyguard had reached him, they found him laughing and leaning on his sword beside a long pile of corpses, catching his breath before the next onslaught.

With the chaos of the hand-to-hand combat, and the volleys of arrows still being coordinated by the captains, the trumpets, the whinnying of horses, the cannon booming away, the arrows and the cannon bolts and cannonballs, and the yells, the shrieks and screams, the scene must have been truly terrifying. But one thing was clear to all, no matter where they stood: the English position was holding. Against all the odds, ten thousand were holding back thirty. When he was told of the developments on the battlefield, the fifty-year-old blind King John of Bohemia asked to be led forward. He had demanded to be given command of the French vanguard, for he too had believed they would easily pick off the English. They had even selected in advance who was to have which prisoners. Now he realised that his presumption had contributed to the rout. If he had not demanded the command of the vanguard – if the man in charge of the French advance had at least been sighted – they might have stood a chance. He asked his knights to do him one last service. Would they tie the bridle of his horse to theirs, and lead him to the front line so that he might, for one last time, lift his sword and charge into battle. He was asking them to lead him to his death, and for them to die with him. Solemnly they did what he asked. When the next trumpets blared, and the next great charge against the English rode at full tilt, the closest household knights of the king of Bohemia rode with them, all in one line, stretched out on either side of their king, shouting his war cry for one last time, lances couched and swords aloft. For them there could be no retreat. It was a matter of fighting with the knights and men-at-arms of the first battalion of the English until they were all dead. After the battle their dead horses were found, all still tethered together, with their corpses scattered near the body of their king.

With the last of the French charges failing on the front line, Edward gave the order for the English horses to be led forward. The pages ran to get their masters' steeds and led them out of the enclosure. When the fifteenth charge had fallen back into the mass of men on the slopes of the hill, the trumpets sounded the English attack and the mounted chivalry of England poured around the limits of the front line. When the French infantry saw the standards of Northampton, Warwick, Dagworth, Burghersh and Cobham bearing down towards them, they came to a horrified halt on the slope, and quickly turned and fled. King Philip – a tyrant but certainly not a coward – saw his men desert him in their thousands. And as he watched, on came the English knights. Philip's bodyguard rallied around him, so too some infantry and some of his closest friends and supporters, but the battle they now fought was not for victory, it was for their king's survival. Bitterly they exchanged blows until evening gave way to night. His standard-bearer was killed as he stood beside him. The king's own horse was killed beneath him. An arrow flew into the fray from one of the English archers and struck Philip in the face. The English raised a great shout, and then another as the Oriflamme went down. The sacred war banner of France lay in the mud of the battlefield. John of Hainault realised that nothing now could save the day, and forcing the king on to a spare horse, and keeping hold of the reins, he and a few knights dragged the king from the battlefield. As Edward had previously given strict orders not to pursue the enemy into the night, Philip escaped. Of all the knights and great men who had come with him to Crécy, he had only five barons with him when he departed.

As Philip fled in the darkness towards Amiens, the English regrouped in their positions on the hillside. There was a windmill at the top of the hill; now Edward ordered it to be filled with brushwood and set alight to act as a beacon and a focal point for the English. Still he kept order, wearing his full armour, not even having removed his helmet. Only when he came to the lines of the first battle which had withstood the French attacks, and saw his son Prince Edward with his own eyes, did he remove it. He embraced him and kissed him. 'Fair son, God save you! You are my good son, and you have acquitted yourself nobly. You are worthy to keep a realm.' And the prince bowed to his father, honouring him. He had picked up the crest of the fallen king of Bohemia, an ostrich feather, and repeated his motto as he knelt before his father: '*Ich dien*' (I serve).[35] Edward then began to speak about the battle to all those present. No one was to boast; everyone was to thank God for their good fortune. And they must be on their guard lest there be a counter-attack by a relief force in the night.

There was no other attack that night. The English rested safely with the burning windmill above them and the mounds of corpses and wounded in the darkness below, lying in the cold. There the unfortunate lay in pain, expiring on the killing field, or unable to move, able only to wait for the dawn and the swift cutting of their throats as the English infantry began to pick over the battlefield looking for loot. On the day after the battle there was another fight, between a second contingent of Frenchmen who arrived too late for the battle and who came out of the morning mist to find themselves face to face with the earl of Northampton. Soon they too lay dying. When on the Sunday Edward expressed a desire to know how many had died on either side, he ordered Sir Reginald Cobham, Sir Ralph Stafford and the heralds to establish an accurate figure by collecting all the French surcoats worn by the men-at-arms. Edward ordered that his men now ransacking the battlefield itself could keep all they found as long as they surrendered the surcoats to him. Over the day they covered the whole area of the battle and all the outlying fields and forest, and the site of the battle between Northampton and the reinforcements who had arrived too late for the battle proper. Eleven great princes lay dead, including the king of Bohemia, the count of Flanders, the duke of Lorraine and Philip's brother and nephew, the counts of Alençon and Blois. One archbishop and one bishop lay among the dead, and eight great secular lords. Eighty bannerets – principal knights – were dead, and 1,542 knights and esquires lay just in the area before the English front line, where the prince had been fighting.[36] A great number – thousands – of uncounted infantrymen's bodies were scattered over the battlefield. A further four thousand French men-at-arms and Genoese crossbowmen had been killed by the earl of Northampton in the attack on the following day. In comparison, English losses amounted to about three hundred men.

*

The importance of the battle of Crécy cannot be exaggerated. It demands that we look beyond the limits of Edward's own life to understand his achievement in the broader terms of European history. Leaving aside the political circumstances of the fourteenth century, it was the first major battle between two well-resourced martial kingdoms in which victory was obtained by projectile weaponry rather than hand-to-hand fighting. In that sense it marks the advent of modern warfare. Since his victory at Halidon Hill in 1333 Edward had pioneered the systematic deployment of archers to win a battle. In the mid-1330s he was experimenting with mounted archers. By 1339 he had a projectile-based means of fighting which was exportable, and in 1346 he demonstrated against the best-equipped and proudest military kingdom in Europe that archery could and would defeat the greatest array of chivalry, provided the battlefield was chosen with care. From now on, groups of well-disciplined commoners with longbows could destroy much larger groups of the richest, most-heavily armoured, bravest and well-trained noblemen in Christendom, even when they were backed up with crossbowmen and huge numbers of infantrymen. The banner of aristocratic military splendour which characterises the middle ages had been shredded, not in a single afternoon by a few thousand archers but by thirteen years of careful experimentation and thought as to how projectile-based warfare could be perfected.

The implications of this for European society were profound. It is easy to point to the effects of the approaching plague as a reason for the socio-economic changes by which the medieval peasant was freed from his feudal bonds in the period 1350–1450. Fewer peasants to work the land meant more could sell their labour, and move away from their original manor and its obligations. It is less frequently noted that this socio-economic shift was accompained by a huge change in outlooks and attitudes after the battle of Crécy. Previously medieval society had understood that it was composed of three 'estates' of people: those who fought (the nobility and knightly class), those who prayed (monks and the secular clergy), and those who worked (the peasantry). In reality, 'those who worked' also provided the infantry levies to support their lords; but infantry were raised through a feudal hierarchy, were not well-trained, and they did not generally win battles by themselves. At Crécy all that changed. From now on, 'those who worked' *were* 'those who fought'. A thousand well-trained and well-equipped peasants with longbows were more than a match for a thousand of the best-equipped knights in Christendom. The consequent effect on the pride and military confidence of the English peasantry should not be underestimated.

The effect on the political situation was every bit as profound. Edward had not just won a victory over the French, he had turned many of society's values upside down. He had overturned the common understanding that France was the greatest military power in Christendom, and he had done it in such a way that all could see that this was not a lucky or accidental victory. It was a carefully planned and well-executed systematic destruction of an enemy which could be repeated again and again. This upset the commonly held understanding of God's natural order – the assembled fighting nobility were demonstrably weaker than the peasantry – and paved the way for that combination of political authority and large armies which would eventually see feudalism give way to absolutism. It also threatened papal influence: what help had a French pope been for the French king? If the pope's prayers on behalf of France had so little effect on divine providence, and had not even saved the sacred Oriflamme from being trampled into the mud, how could a papal interdict on England be a sign of divine will? How could it be anything other than a sign of French bitterness?

For Edward, Crécy was a mark of personal glory. He had done what had been prophesied at his birth. He had won a military victory on the Continent and, in so doing, had done something absolutely remarkable. No English army had ever previously won a battle on this scale against the French on French soil. After the long campaigns and the heavy taxation, the news in England that Edward had triumphed was sensational, and the credit went directly to the king. Victory meant that the years of taxation, the strategy, the planning and the very policy of taking the war to France were all seen as a complete success.

For us, looking back on Edward as a man and as a king, it is not just the victory but the Crécy campaign as a whole which is remarkable. If we peel away the concretions of anti-Edwardian polemic written in the nineteenth and twentieth centuries – especially that Edward had been scared into flight by the approach of Philip's army and had been forced to do battle at Crécy against his will, and was lucky – we may see that the entire campaign leading up to the battle had been planned meticulously, managed effectively and led superbly.[37] Today few scholars would deny that in 1346 Edward demonstrated all the qualities for which he was to remain famous for the next four centuries. His courage has to stand high in any list of these. If he had lost his nerve at Crécy or at any time earlier in the campaign – if he had been trapped at Poissy or Blanchetaque, for example – he would have lost not one but every chance of greatness. Great kings do not lose important battles. His reputation at home would have been severely dented, and his ability to raise money to further his firm anti-French policy would have been undermined. Then there is the matter of his leadership. Edward's personal courage would have meant nothing if he had not had men willing to fight for him in extremely difficult situations at Poissy and Blanchetaque. His generalship thus commands respect. But in masterminding the whole policy of an aggressive response to Philip's infringements of his sovereignty, in bringing the English parliament around to support his war, in organising the taxation to pay for it, and in devising the strategy which would ensure victory, Edward proved himself much more than a mere general. The battle of Crécy might have been won by English archers, but the archers by themselves would never have found themselves in France, still less in a position to have won the battle, if it had not been for the king's inspired leadership. All Edward's positive attributes – courage, leadership, strategic thinking, tactical brilliance, discipline, innovation and political astuteness – came together in the Crécy campaign. Together they gave his kingship a touch of greatness.

*

The battle of Crécy undermined Philip's authority but in itself it was a symbolic and strategic demonstration of superiority; it was not a conquest. On the second day after the battle, as the body of King John of Bohemia and the other great men were solemnly buried by the English, and as Philip was issuing orders for all the Genoese archers who had retreated from the battlefield to be hanged, Edward prepared to press home his advantage. Had he seriously wanted to make himself the sole king of France at this time, he should have advanced on Paris. But such an advance would have carried with it many problems, not least the task of trying to persuade more than a hundred thousand Parisians to accept that the Louvre might be occupied by an Englishman. It would have been just as hard in the long term to persuade the English that their royal family might remove itself to Paris and patronise French merchants and craftsmen as much as English ones, and administer French justice, hear French pleas, and attend French parliaments. The idea of a single monarchy might have been militarily viable at this point but it was not a realistic political proposition.[38] Had Edward tried it, no doubt he would have had the same problem as he had in Scotland: a legal monarchy fighting a rival 'nationalist' one, without the means to support an inevitable succession of French campaigns, each of which would probably be organised to coincide with the Scots' harrying of Northern England. It is therefore not surprising that Edward refused to countenance a march on Paris. On 29 August Edward ordered the army to take the road north, towards Calais.

Edward's policy in Scotland had not been to occupy the whole country but to be able to march through the country at will. This was what he now decided to do in France. But to enable himself to bring an English army across the Channel whenever he wished required a permanent bridgehead on the northern coast. For this purpose, Brittany was too distant, too often subject to bad weather, and too hostile to the English. Normandy had been originally intended as a place to build such a bridgehead but victory at Crécy allowed Edward many more options. Calais was the strongest defensive town on the coast – it was practically impregnable – and the nearest port to England, the safest from the weather and the most easily supplied. Edward knew he would never have a better opportunity to set about the long siege which would be necessary to force it to submit.

The siege of Calais is today remembered largely for the story of Queen Philippa begging for the lives of the six burghers who surrendered the town, but this small detail masks a victory as politically important and as strategically significant as that of Crécy itself. It also masks the not-inconsiderable fact that the task of attacking the town was every bit as difficult as engaging a superior French army on French soil and winning. The town was surrounded by water and marshes. It was built on a concentric plan with two strong curtain walls between mighty towers, and ditches also protecting it. It could not be attacked by siege engines or mining, due to the marshes and water. That left Edward only two options: he could try to attack the outer defences using boats and scaling ladders and overwhelming numbers, or he could starve the inhabitants into submission, in conjunction with a slow attempt to break down the walls with stone and iron missiles, and wear down their will. He opted for the latter.

The reasons for this decision continue to be debated by historians. One view is simply that the place was too strongly defended: the walls, for example, being too high.[39] But we have to wonder; given sufficient numbers and a little time, surely every fortified place is vulnerable. And Edward did have sufficient numbers at his disposal. A recently suggested alternative is that Edward was trying to provoke another full-scale battle with Philip.[40] The truth is probably a combination of the two positions, Edward's preferred strategy changing as circumstances around him changed. Yes, he would have relished the chance to fight Philip again on his own terms, and so may have placed himself ostentatiously at Calais to lure him to attack. He certainly stayed there expecting him to do so.[41] But even before Edward arrived at Calais he had sent an order to England to send across all the remaining cannon at the Tower, so he clearly anticipated an assault on the town. However, no full-scale onslaught on the walls took place.[42] Instead Edward built elaborate siege defences around the town, with shops and a marketplace and incorporating stone houses for his leaders and a fine palace for himself. 'Villeneuve-le-hardi', he called it mockingly, 'Brave New Town'. Perhaps he thought that a concerted effort to take Calais would result in the complete destruction of the walls, which he wanted to avoid if he could help it. But with more sombre warning for the besieged, he declared he was prepared to stay there twelve years, if it should take so long to gain the town. And he populated Villeneuve-le-hardi with a very substantial force, up to thirty-two thousand men. If this figure – drawn from army pay records, not the exaggerations of chroniclers – is correct, it would amount to the largest English army raised for an overseas expedition before the eighteenth century.[43]

Calais was commanded by Jean de Vienne, as resolute and committed a man as Philip could have wished to be in command. When the town was first besieged he took a quick and ruthless decision to expel all the poor women and children of the town, so that food could be conserved for the defenders as long as possible. Seventeen hundred women and children thus found themselves trapped between the walls of their home town and the English army, with nothing but the clothes they stood up in. Often in such circumstances such people became used as prey to twist the minds of the defenders, sometimes being killed in front of the walls but more often being left there to starve to death in the sight of their fellow townsmen. On this occasion, Edward was merciful, and not only allowed the women and children to go but gave them a meal as they passed through.

Philip's hope was probably that news of a large Scots attack in England combined with the advance of a French army would drive Edward off from Calais. To this end he summoned his own army to reassemble on 1 October

at Compiègne, and sent to King David asking him for an immediate invasion in the north of England.[44] David, who had been waiting for such a call,
led an army forward at the beginning of October. Edward's northern frontier was not undefended, however. The levies of the north were ready,
commanded by William Zouche (the archbishop of York), Sir Thomas
Rokeby and Sir Henry Percy. On 14 October, as a Scottish foraging party
led by Douglas looted a village near Durham, the archbishop led his men
forward. As they did so, a thick fog came down. The Scots, suddenly realising that they were surrounded by an army which they could not see,
panicked. They fled back to their main army. When told that they were
being attacked, King David responded that they had nothing to be afraid
of, for he had twelve thousand men and there were not that many soldiers
left in all of Northern England. But Archbishop Zouche was one of those
clergymen who not only knew how to pray, he knew how to fight too. Now
he put the two together, preaching to his army that they were defending not
only their homelands but the lands of Durham Cathedral and the shrine of
St Cuthbert. Three days later, at Neville's Cross, the king of Scotland met
an army as large as his own, motivated by fear and pious courage. English
archers devastated two of the Scottish battalions, and forced them to break
ranks. The third, commanded by David, was left exposed. Although he
fought ferociously, even when shot through the nose by an English archer,
he had no hope of escape, still less of victory. He was pursued, overpowered and captured. Sir William Douglas and four Scottish earls were captured
along with him, the earl of Moray being left dead on the battlefield.

The news of the Scottish defeat stupefied the French. It hit them just
two weeks after an English onslaught in the south. Sir Walter Manny, eager
to join in the action at Calais, had obtained a safe conduct letter for himself
and twenty men to go to Edward, but on his journey north he was overpowered and thrown into prison at Saint-Jean-d'Angély. Not a man to
suffer wrongful imprisonment cheerfully, he broke out of his cell and
stormed off. His eighteen fellow-prisoners were unable to escape, but
Lancaster rode to their rescue a little later, as he pressed the boundary of
Gascony further to the northward. And having come this far, Lancaster
decided he would go on to attack Lusignan, where he had some notable
successes. The sack of the rich city of Poitiers in particular, coming on
top of the news of Neville's Cross, paralysed the French. Few men
responded to Philip's summons. No one wanted to march into the hail of
arrows which had massacred so many at Crécy. By the end of October
Philip had given up hope of bringing an army against Edward, and turned
bitterly to accuse his ministers and even members of his own family of
ineptitude and disloyalty. His only hope as far as Calais was concerned

was that Jean de Vienne would hold out for so long that Edward would be forced to give up the siege.

The last thing Edward was going to do was give up. It is in his camp at Calais that we may see him at his most confident and most resolute. The defences he had prepared around Villeneuve-le-hardi were exceptionally strong. He had a huge army with him. Although all his attempts to cross the walls were met with determined resistance, and some French ships did break through to supply the men within, he remained focused on the capture of this important town week-in, week-out. The lack of a relieving army merely persuaded him that he would be spending winter in Villeneuve-le-hardi, so he sent for Queen Philippa to join him for Christmas in his temporary palace. The contrast with the situation of Jean de Vienne could not have been greater. Realising he could not expect a relieving army before the spring, the city's stern commander ousted a further five hundred people into the ditch between the walls and the English army.[45]

So the stand-off continued well into 1347. As each day went by, Edward knew he drew nearer to victory and de Vienne became more desperate. By March it was clear that Edward would not retreat from Calais unless forced to do so. Philip summoned another army in March 1347, and went to the abbey of Saint-Denis to take a newly embroidered Oriflamme. Edward waited, twisting his garrotte around Calais even tighter. Lancaster, who had returned to England from Gascony in January, crossed the Channel to join in the siege. After a French attempt to drive barges towards the town in April was fought off by the earl of Northampton, Edward ordered a timber castle to be built on the sandbank on the seaward side of Calais. He garrisoned it with archers and men-at-arms, preventing any supply ships approaching the town by day or night. He seized every approach road to Calais, and defended them all. He knew that Philip had no option but to attack him. His regnal responsibility demanded it. And this time he was in a far stronger position than he had been at Crécy. In addition to his army of Englishmen he had a force of several thousand Flemings.[46] He was inviting Philip to march to his doom.

The pressure on Philip to meet Edward in battle was growing greater all the time. By the end of June it was extreme. Gascony had been reduced to English control or smouldering ruins, and the flame of English resistance in Brittany was burning more brightly than ever. On 19–20 June the five thousand-strong Breton army of Charles de Blois was defeated in a night attack at La Roche-Derrien by seven hundred men under Sir Thomas Dagworth and a few hundred men of the town, Charles himself being captured in the attack. Philip had lost another nephew to the English. It seemed that whatever Philip did in any corner of his realm, he was powerless to stop the relentless tide of English military success. In the space of two years the English had overrun and looted more than fifty towns and countless villages and monasteries. And there seemed nothing that Philip could do to oust them. He could not even remove Edward from Calais.

The siege had now gone on for nine months. The food had finally run out, and with Edward's comprehensive blockade in force, there was no hope of relief. Jean de Vienne in desperation wrote a letter to Philip and gave it to a Genoese captain to try and smuggle out of the town. He left, in his ship, quietly at dawn on 26 June. The English caught sight of the man, and pursued him in their own vessels. In an attempt to conceal the contents of the letter, in the last moments of freedom the messenger thrust an axe through it and hurled it as far as he could into the sea. Unfortunately for him, all the English had to do was wait for low tide. A few hours later they took the letter to Edward. Now Edward could read for himself of the plight within the walls:

Right dear and dread lord . . . The town is in sore need of corn, wine and meat. For know that there is nothing herein which has not been eaten, both dogs and cats and horses, so that we cannot find any more food within the town unless we eat human flesh. Formerly you wrote that I should hold the town so long as there should be food. And now we are at that point that we have nothing on which to live. So we have resolved amongst us that, if we do not receive help soon, we shall all march out of the town into the open field to fight for life or death. For it is better to die with honour in the field than to eat each other. Wherefore, right dear and dread lord, do what shall seem fitting to you, for if nothing is done soon, you will not hear from me again, and the town will be lost, as well as us. Our Lord grant you a good and long life and give you the will, if we die for you, to acknowledge our sacrifice to our heirs.[47]

Edward, fully realising the power of this letter, copied it, then fixed his own seal to it and sent it to Philip. It was as good as a challenge.

The French army arrived at Sangatte, six miles from Villeneuve-le-hardi, on 27 July. In the town the defenders were overjoyed, and lit bonfires and raised flags in honour of the arrival of the French king. But Edward also watched them as they drew up on the ridge above the marshes, knowing it would be certain catastrophe for them to attack him in his current position. He had his archers, his strong defences and more men-at-arms. He also knew that Philip had no time to spare; the one last attempt to buy time for Calais – sending a fleet of eight barges with food and drink to the besieged – had been captured by the watchful English. Delaying tactics now would prove of no avail. Calais was as good as his.

That evening the two cardinals with responsibility for the peace negotiations between England and France asked for safe conduct to come to the English camp and put proposals before the king. Edward appointed the greatest scourges of French troops to receive them: Lancaster, Northampton, Sir Walter Manny, Sir Reginald Cobham and Sir Bartholomew Burghersh.[48] The following day a French embassy came through the marshes with the cardinals to meet the English negotiators. They recognised that Calais was lost, and that the best which Philip could do was to beg for the lives of those who had held out for so long. But Edward did not need to bother with agreements of this sort, and his negotiators let the cardinals know they had not been empowered to discuss the town, which was already theirs. When the French embassy then tentatively suggested a peace treaty, to include the restoration of all of the duchy of Aquitaine, to be held on the same terms as Edward I had held it, they were told this was a small thing hardly in proportion to the efforts which Edward had made to recoup his rights. For four days the debates continued, everytime the French trying to bring Calais back into the discussions. On 31 July, with nothing else to offer or discuss, they departed.

On the departure of the cardinals, Philip resigned himself to war and the bloody destruction of his kingship. What precisely happened is still obscure, but one thing does seem certain: when the peace negotiations failed on Tuesday 31 July, Philip's negotiators returned from Philip immediately with a challenge to Edward to do battle in an open space between then and Friday evening. This was to be selected by four knights on either side, and safe conducts were to be offered to those who would do the choosing. One chronicle – that of Jean le Bel – states that Edward refused, saying that he (Philip) could see that he was in his realm and despoiling it; if he wished him to leave then he should attack him. However, this is probably incorrect, amounting to no more than le Bel's interpretation a few years later.[49] In his own letter to the archbishop of Canterbury, Edward states that his negotiators received this challenge on the evening of Tuesday 31st. They said they would show the challenge to Edward, and promised a response on the following day. Edward then took advice and 'trusting in God and our right, we answered that we accepted their offer and took up the battle willingly'. This reply was presumably delivered on the Wednesday, together with the safe conducts which Edward ordered to be written. But, as Edward himself states, 'they of the other side, when now they had heard this answer, began to shift in their offers and to speak of the town all anew, as if putting off the battle'. It would appear that Philip's advisers had demanded why they were fighting, if not to save the town? If Edward had agreed to fight in the open, should the town not be the prize? Edward's refusal to talk about the town probably made up Philip's mind for him. He stood to lose not only Calais but a second battle. He could do nothing about the former, but he could at least save his forces a second ignominious defeat. Philip gave orders for his men to burn their own camp and any supplies they could not carry, and to disperse.

A little after dawn on Thursday 2 August 1347, before the walls of Calais, Edward watched as the army of France gave way before him. Anyone of a normal disposition would have been overjoyed, but not Edward. He did not feel victorious. He had promised to make an end to the war, and now he knew his adversary would live to fight another day. He had promised in his letters back home that there would be a second great battle, and a victory, God willing. His mood was therefore blacker than it had been for ages when his attention was dragged back to the plight of the beleaguered town. Sir Walter Manny had been summoned by a messenger to treat with the governor of Calais. After eleven months of bitter siege conditions, and desperate hopes, the crushed garrison realised they had held out in vain. Their king had deserted them.

In the traditional form of chivalric behaviour, the garrison now sought terms. After eleven months of siege, and cheated of his second battle, Edward was in no mind to offer terms at all. When Manny passed this news to Jean de Vienne the governor was at a loss, and pleaded with him to return to Edward to beg for their lives. 'We are just a few knights and squires who have loyally served our master, as you would have done, and have suffered much as a result . . . I therefore once more entreat you, out of compassion, to return to the king of England and beg of him to have pity on us.'[50] Manny relayed this plea to the king who again refused it, insisting that the Frenchmen should submit unconditionally to his will. At this even the hardbitten Sir Walter Manny seems to have been moved, for he answered the king back. 'My lord, you may be to blame in this, for you set a very bad example. If you order us to go to any of your castles we will not obey you so cheerfully if you put these people to death; for they will treat us likewise if we find ourselves in a similar situation.' These words struck home. Manny was alluding to the many small garrisons Edward had left in Normandy, which had been overpowered and massacred after he decided to besiege Calais. After due thought he announced his decision:

> Gentlemen, I am not so obstinate as to hold my opinion alone against you all. Sir Walter, you will inform the governor of Calais that the only grace he must expect from me is that six of the principal citizens of

Calais march out of the town with bare heads and bare feet, with ropes around their necks, and the keys of the town and castle in their hands. These six persons shall be at my absolute disposal, and the remainder of the inhabitants pardoned.

Having heard this offer from Manny, Jean de Vienne ordered the town bell to be rung so the citizens would assemble in the marketplace. In the most famous passage in his chronicle, Froissart repeats how one by one six of the wealthiest men of Calais volunteered to die so that their fellow townsmen would be pardoned. The first to volunteer was Eustace de Saint-Pierre. He was followed by Jean d'Aire, the brothers Jacques and Pierre Wissant, Andrieu d'Andres and finally Jean de Vienne himself.[51]

On 4 August 1347, eleven months to the day since the siege had begun, these six men did as Edward had asked. Carrying the keys of Calais they walked barefoot with ropes around their necks. De Vienne was so weak he could hardly walk, and had to be given a horse. When Manny led them before the king, they prostrated themselves before him, begging for their lives. Edward simply ordered them to be beheaded. Everyone present was shocked, after the courage shown by these men in coming forward. Edward's mind was not inclined to sympathy but to business; his campaign was not yet finished. Even Sir Walter Manny's requests for Edward to show mercy were ignored. According to Froissart, only when Philippa implored him to show mercy did he relent.[52] Aware of the accusations of cruelty which would be brought against him if these men were killed, Edward did what he had always previously done: he relented when begged to do so by someone dear to him.

Forgiveness at the point of death. It was a powerful image, especially for a warrior-king. But it was typical of Edward, right through to his core. He had behaved in exactly the same way when the tournament stand had collapsed at Cheapside in 1331, almost killing Philippa. He had similarly given in to Philippa's plea for him to show mercy when a young girl was brought before him on a heinous charge in 1337.[53] At Caen he had at first ordered a massacre and then relented when begged to do so. In fact, although Edward ordered quite a number of large-scale massacres in France, none was ever carried out. It was as if in each case he was trying to play the dread king 'terrible to his enemies' as well as the compassionate monarch. At Calais, as elsewhere, it was a method which confused and frightened his enemies. But from Edward's point of view, it said everything about him which he wanted to project: magnanimity in victory, mercy, ruthlessness and power.

*

Edward had plans for Calais. Some of the citizens died in the next few days – from eating too much food and drink, when Edward sent abundant food supplies into the town – but most of the remaining townsmen were sent into France. In their place he established a strong English garrison. He destroyed Villeneuve-le-hardi so it could not be reused by Philip in a reprisal attack, and gave rich houses in Calais to each of his leading warriors. His vision for the town was as a landing place for future English armies, and men like Lancaster and Sir Walter Manny would doubtless be on such expeditions. To ensure the financial prosperity of the town he established there a mint and the English tin, lead and cloth staples (the official trading posts). Eventually he would add the valuable wool staple but not until 1363; for the time being that remained at Ghent, to the benefit of his Flemish allies.

Edward never dropped his guard. On 20 August, after the dispersal of the English army, he learned that Philip had summoned the French army to gather again for a surprise attack. Without hesitation he ordered his own forces to return to Calais. He repeated this instruction at the beginning of September, fully determined to meet Philip in battle as agreed before. Edward sounded out his leading magnates and then announced he was going to proceed into France once more 'to do battle with our adversary . . . in order to recover our rights and to take whatever grace and fortune which God shall give us'.[54] But with both sides exhausted, financially as well as militarily, a truce was the preferred option on both sides. In addition, the English army was suffering badly from dysentery.[55] The truce was agreed in mid-September. As before it was to include Scotland as well as France and Flanders. Everywhere Edward's gains were to be respected, and loyalties were not to be broken. The peace, which was planned to last until 8 July 1348, was wholly in favour of the English.

Edward remained for a few more weeks in Calais, and then set sail for England. And as soon as he was out at sea, he got caught in another storm. In England, Edward's voyages had almost become a means of predicting the weather. It was commonly joked that if he was going to France, the weather would be fine, but if he was returning, they could expect storms.[56] After invoking the protection of the Virgin yet again, he landed at Sandwich on 12 October and arrived in London two days later.[57] After two months of seeing to the rewards of those who had fought at Neville's Cross and providing for the administration of Calais, Edward went to Guildford to celebrate Christmas.

Christmas 1347 was a great occasion. He had just completed the longest and most dramatic overseas expedition of any English king since the time of Richard I. Now he could enjoy himself once more. Roll out the tournament banners! For Edward went straight back to enjoying his hunts and his feasts, his celebrations, tournaments and games. Once more we may read in the wardrobe accounts of the extravagant purchases of this proud, happy monarch. For the Christmas games at Guildford Edward ordered:

> forty-two masks bearing the likenesses of women, bearded men, and angels' heads in silver. Twenty-eight crests, fourteen with legs reversed with shoes on, and fourteen with hills and rabbits. Fourteen painted cloaks, fourteen dragons' heads, fourteen white buckram tunics, fourteen pheasant heads with fourteen pairs of wings for these heads, fourteen tunics painted with the eyes of a pheasant, fourteen swans' heads with fourteen pairs of wings for the swans, fourteen painted linen tunics, and fourteen tunics painted with stars.[58]

He himself and all his fellow knights wore long green robes embroidered with peacock feathers.[59] We could almost say that it was business as usual at the English court. Edward's daughter, Joan, was betrothed to be married to the son of the king of Castile. And Philippa was pregnant again.

But in reality, life was never going to be quite the same. On 11 October 1347 Ludvig of Bavaria died while out hunting bears, and the electors chose Edward to be his successor as Holy Roman Emperor. Those prophesies from his youth, of European victories and of receiving the three crowns of the Empire, which once had seemed so daunting, had all come true. But it was not the offer itself that marks the difference, although it was a very rare honour for an Englishman to be offered the triple crown of the Holy Roman Empire. The real difference between Edward before and after Crécy lies in his response. He turned the offer down. He no longer sought to add to his prestige through allusions to prophesies, or the acquisition of great titles. He no longer needed to associate himself with old kings and legends. His own reputation, won through his own efforts, and in new ways, was greatness enough in itself.

At the age of thirty-five he had achieved everything his kingdom had expected of him. The English collectively had a new pride, a new identity, and it was one unparalleled in Europe. Edward's war had begun to galvanise England into a nation, with common interests and, increasingly, a common culture. In the words of the great chronicler Thomas Walsingham 'it seemed that a new sun had arisen for the English because of the abundance of peace, the plenitude of goods and the glory of the victor'.[60]

ELEVEN

An Unassailable Enemy

Edward was probably still encamped before the walls of Calais when he first heard reports that the deadly disease which had swept across Asia had now come to the borders of Europe. To him Asia would have been a semi-legendary place, known only from merchants and distant travellers. He and his contemporaries may well have regarded the disease as divine punishment on the unbelievers in the East for fighting with crusaders of the true faith. But as he sailed into Sandwich in October, the Genoese ships in the Mediterranean a thousand miles to the south docked with a deadly cargo. Cyprus and Sicily experienced the first full onslaught in November 1347. By December it was in Genoa, Marseilles and Avignon. Contemporaries simply called it 'the pestilence'. Today we call it the Black Death.

The Black Death was more than just a disease. Its arrival was arguably the single most important event in European history between the collapse of the Western Roman Empire and the Industrial Revolution. Although the population of Europe, including Britain, had been declining since about 1315, when a spate of poor harvests had been swiftly followed by a cattle murrain, the decline had been small and comparatively slow: no more than a ten per cent reduction over twenty years. A society which was basically confident that God's will protected them was completely unprepared for the shock which followed. As the plague reached a town or village, a number of people very suddenly grew sick and died. What was worse, the plague lingered, so that even if you were not among the twenty per cent to die in the first month or so, there was a good chance you would be caught up in the next month's mortality. And then there were subsequent attacks in subsequent years. Although we tend to think of the Black Death as being the period of the first shock of the disease, between 1347 and 1351 in Western Europe, it came back again and again, with catastrophic consequences every time. Each outbreak disrupted farming, trade and legal systems, so that food production and conveyance collapsed, and violence broke out. The population continued to decline for the next one hundred and fifty years. Society was severely tested, and was forced to develop increasingly flexible systems in order to maintain the political status quo. It was therefore not just the disease which mattered. The economic consequences and the profound psychological shock combined to alter the culture, attitudes, faith, geographical horizons and personal identities of people in fourteenth- and fifteenth-century Europe. To quantify the effect simply in numbers of dead is to miss the point. Europe had been plunged into a horrific and ongoing crisis which cracked the cultural plinth on which society was built.

By spring 1348 the plague was in Normandy. Caen and Rouen experienced particularly heavy death rates. By May it was in Paris. No one could ignore it, nor its unstoppable progress. It was not just the stories of the disease and the dying which gnawed at the conscience of the as-yet unaffected, it was the stories of the houses left empty, whole families dying in rural areas, and their animals dying. The fields sown in springtime lay untended in the summer as the sower and his wife rotted in their house, unburied.

The plague had still not yet arrived in England. While it remained overseas, Edward's reaction was to ignore it. It was not so much a strategy of putting his head in the sand as one of not deserting his royal duties. As a king he was expected to be seen, give audiences, attend parliaments, provide leadership and hear certain law cases. He was expected to be lavish in his hospitality and his spending, the money spent being employment for many. To fail in these duties would be to give in to the plague, and to fail as a monarch. It was not in Edward's nature to give in to anything, least of all a disease which still remained on the Continent.

Edward's priorities in 1348 were the celebration of his military successes of the previous two years and his dealings with parliament. It had been more than a year since Edward had held a parliament, and so he could be said to have broken his promise to summon one every year. The last had met in September 1346, while Edward was at Calais, but this was largely to gather the financial support necessary for the siege. He himself had not actually attended a sitting or heard petitions since the summer of 1344. And some merchants and minor landholders thought that Edward was implementing highly dubious measures. To mark the knighting of the prince of Wales in 1346 Edward had levied a 'feudal aid' of forty shillings on every single manorial unit in the kingdom. This had not been done since the reign of Edward I, and the commons thought it had been pardoned in 1340. Even if it had not, it should have been no more than twenty shillings.[1] A forced loan of twenty thousand sacks of wool in 1347 had not lightened the mood of such men who saw their economic opportunities in a purely personal light. While all England was united in its joy at the string of victories over France, a few of those who spoke for the country had misgivings about how it had been financed.

The first parliament of 1348 was held in January. Its two principal purposes were, as far as Edward was concerned, to discuss the truce recently agreed at Calais, and to address the problem of law and order. Although Edward's earlier efforts to enforce provincial order had mainly been successful, his absence abroad had led to local tax-collectors taking the law into their own hands, and bands of criminals once again being protected by local gentry, through the bribing of local judges.[2] Before he had left England in 1346, he had issued the Ordinance of Justices, to prevent royal judges being bribed, but in his absence this had proved weak.[3] The commons now seized the opportunity to renew their earlier complaint of 'maintenance' by the nobility and gentry. They demanded that the provisions of the Ordinance be extended. They recommended that six persons be appointed in each county – local landowners, not agents of central government – to hear cases of breaking the peace.[4] As for the truce, or rather the need for increased taxation for the resumption of the war, the commons had doubts. They debated the matter for four days and eventually decided that they could not advise the king on this matter, but would support the advice of the magnates.[5] They probably hoped that France would be destroyed cheaply by disease rather than expensively by renewing the war.

Edward was not satisfied with these answers, and a second parliament followed soon afterwards, meeting on 31 March. He was not yet ready to put local justice in the hands of local landowners, probably suspicious that this would simply lead to greater abuse of legal privileges. And he wanted a more constructive answer with regard to the truce. There followed a series of bargains between king and people. Edward accentuated the danger of invasion in order to gain support for the potential renewal of hostilities. Action to control the purveyors for the royal household was taken. Edward agreed not to ransom the Scottish prisoners at the Tower – including Sir William Douglas, the earl of Menteith and King David – so they could not renew hostilities. He made sure of this in the case of Menteith (who had previously sworn homage to him) by having him publicly executed. He agreed to suspend the eyres or tours of his justices in the counties. And he agreed to use his influence to improve the lot of English merchants buying and selling at the wool staple in Ghent.[6] The result was that parliament agreed to a further three years' subsidy: not enough in itself to mount a major campaign, and not too much to bankrupt the kingdom, but enough to satisfy the king for the time being.

*

As the plague hit Paris and killed thousands, in England the king held a series of splendid tournaments. In mid-February he was jousting at

Reading, then later that month at Bury St Edmunds, where he appeared dressed in a huge bird costume, possibly playing an eagle.[7] In early May he held a great tournament at Lichfield.[8] Here he fought in the arms of one of Lord Berkeley's knights, Sir Thomas Bradeston, who had been with him at the arrest of Mortimer in 1330 and had since become one of his most trusted captains. At the same tournament he ordered robes in blue and white to be made for himself and eleven knights of his chamber, as well as the earl of Lancaster and twelve of his knights, and many ladies, including his (Edward's) daughter Isabella.[9] Later that month he held a tournament at Eltham, and a month after that, on 24 June 1348, he held a great tournament at Windsor to celebrate the churching of Queen Philippa after the birth of their eleventh child, William of Windsor. King David, Charles de Blois and many other prisoners of war attended, all decked out in fine new robes at Edward's expense. The younger royal princes were all present too, decked out ostentatiously in velvet: Lionel in azure blue, John and Edmund in purple. After Windsor the next tournament was at Canterbury, probably in mid-August, and another was held at Westminster.[10] Edward travelled, was seen by his people, and dressed himself, his family, his royal prisoners and his entourage splendidly. He was parading his victorious royalty around the country: the champion of England, his conquests made glorious by the honour done to his prisoners.

There are two ways of looking at this huge parade. On the one hand, this is just what Edward did for fun, and after Crécy and Calais he deserved to flaunt his laurels. On the other hand, it would be foolish to forget that the backdrop to this display and ostentation was that the rest of Europe was dying by the million. At the time of the Windsor tournament, England still had not been directly affected. Edward was taking great pride in the ceremonial triumphs he held up and down the country; but he was also displaying a steadying leadership in the face of the dread which now must have permeated the court and country. Many people must have realised that, unless all the ports were closed, England would be the next kingdom afflicted.

The ports did not close. Had they done so, there would have been an outcry in parliament. The merchants would have bitterly complained, they would have been ruined, and they would not have been able to pay their taxes. Edward would have cut himself off from his fellow monarchs, including his daughter, Joan, on her way to Castile to be married to Pedro, heir to King Alfonso. He would have cut himself off from Calais, Ponthieu, Gascony and Brittany. So, as Edward charged down the tournament lists at Windsor, and as his courtiers played romantic games with each other behind their masks, the boats came and went out of the ports all around the country. And because all the ports remained open, there were many potential infection points. Edward had no way of knowing it, but by taking no action to limit the potential places of infection, he was worsening the effects of the disease when it arrived.

*

For Edward, the grief began early. On 5 September his three-month-old son, William of Windsor, was buried at Westminster Abbey. His birth had been greeted by the king with great celebration, Philippa's churching being the cause for the tournament at Windsor at which he paraded his most prestigious prisoners of war. Silver vessels, including several lavish silver bowls befitting a king's son, had been purchased for him in London. A fine cradle had been commissioned (costing five pounds), as well as a daily cradle (costing eight shillings).[11] Edward clearly had expectations of this boy, his only son to be born, like himself, at Windsor. In death, he was treated to a full royal funeral. Gold cloth was purchased, two thousand gold leaves, large quantities of black cloth, and wax candles. The gold cloths were placed over his little body. Sixty pennons stamped with gold lay over and around the bier on which he lay. Around him burned six lamps and one hundred and seventy square candles. Fifty paupers dressed in black circled the shrine, while a chariot covered in black cloth acted as his hearse.[12] Compared to the other infant royal burials, this was striking ostentation, and a sign of a genuine disappointment.

'Disappointment' is a strangely distant word to use, however. For this little boy was not the only member of the royal family to have died. Even before the welter of tournaments had come to an end, Edward had received the tragic news that his beloved fourteen-year-old daughter, Joan, had died of plague on her way to marry Pedro of Castile. Every bit of care had been expended on the arrangements for her journey. Way back on 1 January 1348 Edward had written to the Castilian royal family announcing he was about to send her, and detailing who would accompany her. A month later, somewhat anxious, he had written to make sure that if she should bear Pedro a son, then that boy would be king of Castile. Eleven days later he sent orders to all his admirals and seneschals to assist the bishop of Carlisle who would accompany Joan. After all the precautions Edward could possibly have taken, she arrived at Bordeaux by ship during the height of the outbreak, and died there on 1 July.[13] In the circumstances there was no choice but to bury her at Bordeaux. Edward had lost a daughter who was 'beautiful in body, and abundant in moral virtues and grace'.[14] One can imagine the dread of the messenger returning to England to break the sad news.

If Edward felt he had been unfortunate in September 1348, losing two children, the truth was that he had barely begun to experience the suffering which some had suffered. Agnolo di Tura, a Sienese chronicler, had no illusions about the extent of the calamity:

> I do not know where to begin to tell of the cruelty and the pitiless ways [of the plague]. It seemed that almost everyone became stupefied by seeing the pain. And it is impossible for the human tongue to recount the awful truth. Indeed, one who did not see such horribleness can be called blessed. The victims died almost immediately. They would swell beneath the armpits and in their groins, and collapse while talking. Father abandoned child, wife husband, one brother another; for this illness seemed to strike through breath and sight. And so they died. None could be found to bury the dead for money or friendship. Members of a household brought their dead to a ditch as best they could, without priest, without divine offices. Nor did the death bell sound. And in many places in Siena great pits were dug and piled deep with the multitude of dead. And they died by the hundreds, both day and night, and all were thrown in those ditches and covered with earth. And as soon as those ditches were filled, more were dug. And I, Agnolo di Tura, buried my five children with my own hands.[15]

Although Edward did not know it, plague was already creeping through Dorset. A ship had landed with the disease, probably in early August.[16] Mindful of the threat across the Channel, on 17 August the bishop of Bath and Wells ordered processions to take place every Friday to pray for protection from the disease which had 'come from the East' into France, 'the neighbouring kingdom'. His prayers probably came a few days too late. By October, Dorset was overwhelmed with suffering. Towns which traded with the area ceased to welcome travellers. Those with the wherewithal, aware of the terrible mortality across the Channel, removed themselves to their most isolated estates, and stayed there. All England was plunged into fear.

The first action Edward took to combat the plague was at the end of September, when he ordered prayers and processions throughout England for deliverance from the pestilence.[17] But the second thing he did was far less predictable. He decided to confront the danger head-on, like a soldier. While the rich and powerful throughout England isolated themselves in terrified huddles in their rural manors, Edward decided to go to Calais, and see for himself what the plague held in store. His journey was superficially to take part in the negotiations for continuing the peace treaty: normally a duty for ambassadors. But there was propaganda value in Edward going in person. France was recognised as the source of England's plague: it was in 'the neighbouring kingdom' as the bishop of Bath and Wells had put it. And it was generally understood in England that France was labouring under the mortality. It was said that at Avignon more than thirteen hundred people had died in a single day, and that religious communities of one hundred and forty monks at both Montpelier and Marseilles had been reduced to only seven at the former place and only one at the latter. If mortality as great as this was being experienced in holy, godly communities, what hope did the layman have? Edward's journey to France was a public statement that he and his companions were not afraid, that they could rely on God's protection. In an unprecedented move, he had the news that he was going to France proclaimed in all the towns of England.[18]

Edward departed from Sandwich on 29 October, accompanied by the prince of Wales, the bishop of Winchester and the earl of Warwick. He settled the arrangements for the continuation of the truce near Calais on 13 November, and returned to England on the 17th. By then the first cases of plague had been found in London.[19] Nevertheless Edward returned directly to the capital. As Londoners shut themselves up in their houses, Edward exchanged the Palace of Westminster for the Tower of London.[20] His court had so many people coming and going that no attempt to isolate him would have been of any use. So he decided to carry on, as usual, with his games and celebrations. He held an elaborate games at Otford, for Christmas, at which many guests came. They dressed in the masks of lions' heads, elephants' heads, 'wodewoses' (wildmen of the woods), men wearing bats' wings, and girls.[21] Edward took centre stage in a complete set of armour for himself and his horse in which everything was 'spangled with silver' and his tunic and shield worked with the motto: 'Hay, hay the White Swan by God's Soul I am thy Man'. Nor did he stay at Otford but moved on to Merton for Epiphany (6 January). There his games included the spectacle of thirteen men dressed in masks of dragons' heads parading with thirteen masks of crowned men, or kings. Payments for ten black coats – a very unusual item in Edward's wardrobe accounts at this time – may indicate a mourning tone, but if so one suspects it was so the thirteen kings could be seen to be jousting against those who were in funereal despair.

In the early new year the plague began its huge, deadly sweep through southern England. Modern examinations of the evidence suggest that the mortality in southern England was especially high, around the forty per cent mark, due to the number of ports. In London the numbers of dead crept up, from twenty per day to forty, and then sixty. The chronicler Avesbury noted that from the feast of the Purification (2 February) to after Easter (12 April) more than two hundred bodies were interred every single day in the new cemetery adjacent to Smithfield.[22] This was one of two emergency cemeteries purchased in order for the citizens of London to have a place of burial, and by the end of the plague they had received about sixty thousand corpses.[23] The benefactor who provided this particular cemetery, as well as a chapel dedicated to the Virgin Mary on the site, was none other than Sir Walter Manny, now Lord Manny.[24] There was clearly more to this friend of Edward's than extraordinary courage and indomitable fighting skills.

The plague's relentless progress meant that parliament had to be cancelled. Edward first gave the order on 1 January to delay the assembly until a fortnight after Easter, and then on 10 March he cancelled it until further notice. By then the country and the capital were in chaos. The economy was experiencing chronic deflation, the food supply had collapsed, and law and order was in tatters. To quote the famous description of the chronicler Henry Knighton:

> In the same year there was a great murrain of sheep everywhere in the realm, so that in one place more than five thousand sheep died in a single pasture; and they rotted so much that neither beast nor bird would approach them. And there was a great cheapness of all things for fear of death, for very few took any account of riches or of possessions of any kind. A man could have a horse which was formerly worth forty shillings for half a mark (6s 8d), a big fat ox for four shillings, a cow for twelve pence, a heifer for sixpence, a fat wether for fourpence, a sheep for threepence, a lamb for tuppence, a large pig for fivepence and a stone of wool for ninepence. Sheep and oxen strayed through the fields and among the crops, and there was no one to drive them off or to collect them, but they perished in uncounted numbers throughout all districts for lack of shepherds, because there was such a shortage of servants and labourers. For there was no recollection of such a severe mortality since the time of Vortigern, King of the Romans, in whose day, as Bede testifies, the living did not suffice to bury the dead.[25]

It was at this point that Edward founded – or, to be exact – completed the foundation of the Order of the Garter. On St George's Day 1349, at the very height of the most horrific disease the kingdom had ever seen, Edward held a great tournament at Windsor during which he formally instituted his Order of twenty-six men who would joust and pray together once a year, and conduct themselves everywhere like proud Arthurian knights.[26] How inappropriate, we might say, how insensitive! And yet, the more we examine this foundation, the more we are forced to accept that the plague was one of Edward's key reasons for founding the Order at this particular time.

To understand this, we must review the events described above. As the crisis grew over the course of 1348, Edward held parliaments and a number of tournaments, doing what he did best: pushing himself forward not only as the kingdom's leader but also as its champion. Then his daughter died. In August he established the collegiate chapel of St George at Windsor, and may have meant to found an order along the lines of the Garter soon after, but in September the death of a second child cruelly destroyed any such chivalric dream. Then the country was wholly plunged into despondency with the arrival of the plague. In October, Edward publicly proclaimed he was going to France, where most of the country believed (rightly) that the disease was already raging. It was an act of defiance: a 'publicity stunt'. He then returned to England, and did not attempt to avoid London, where the plague was spreading, but then, perhaps acting on the advice of his physicians, he withdrew and held his games and celebrations at slightly quieter spots, Otford and Merton. And he was probably wise to accept his physicians' advice, for then the true horror of the plague in southern England became apparent. He was forced to cancel parliament. At the same time the most dire rains began to fall, the cattle murrain took hold, and the deflationary cycle started.[27] Against these problems even Edward faltered. But at the very height of the plague, when two hundred men, women and children were being buried in London every single day, and lords and ladies were hiding in their isolated manors up and down the country, when sheep and cattle were dying in their thousands, and the social order seemed to be falling apart, he threw aside the advice of his physicians. His people needed leadership, and he was the king of the English, chosen by God. He could do nothing to halt the plague, but he could demonstrate effective leadership in spite of it. His founding of a chivalric order at this point in time was a second act of defiance against the disease, a second 'publicity stunt'. Edward demonstrated that it was business as usual in England in the only way he knew: a high-profile tournament. It demonstrated to his subjects that their king was not hiding in some out-of-the-way manor, waiting for the all-clear, in contrast to almost every lord and bishop in England.

In this reading of the evidence the key factor influencing the foundation of the Order is the timing of the tournament, at the very height of the plague. This implies that no garters, mottoes or any other objects or phrases associated with the Order were its direct cause. This is not surprising: the idea of founding a chivalric order had probably been in Edward's mind since returning from France in 1347, if not since giving up the Round Table plans in 1344.[28] But it is patently obvious that the emblem of the garter itself has nothing to do with the disease. Likewise, it is highly doubtful that the motto *honi soit qui mal y pense* (evil to him who thinks it evil) was connected with the calamity. So, why this emblem and this motto? What else was going on in Edward's mind at this time?

We could say that, because the garter and motto had been in frequent use at tournaments in the period 1346–48, they were simply adopted because they happened to be there when the Order was formally constituted. But Edward had been planning the Order for at least a year, so it is unlikely that the regalia of the Order were merely incidental.[29] In addition, there is no doubt that a Companionship of the Garter – of twenty-four knights, one of whom was almost certainly the prince – was in existence by the end of 1348.[30] Edward seems to have borrowed this idea, and used it as the basis for his more distinguished and formal Order in April 1349. But this still does not explain where the emblem of the garter comes from. Nor the motto.

A number of modern writers have tried to associate the adoption of the garter and motto with Edward's claim on the throne of France.[31] Although this suggestion is superficially attractive, given the recent conquests in France, it does not stand up to detailed scrutiny. For a start, it is very difficult to see how a garter can be symbolic of Edward's dominance over Philip's kingdom: a man's garter is hardly a fearsome article of clothing. Because of this, it has been suggested that the garter is meant to represent a sword belt.[32] This too is difficult to accept: not least for the common-sense reason that the Order would then have been called the Order of the Sword Belt. We might also object that a sword belt is a far less powerful symbol for an order of chivalry than other knightly accoutrements (a sword, for example). As for the motto, the language in which it was written – French – has often been seen as good evidence that it relates to Edward's claims on the French throne, as Edward's other known mottoes were all in English. Indeed, scholars have repeated this particular argument so many times that it is now said to be a widely accepted 'fact'. But it is a huge assumption, without any evidence to support it. The wording has no political or military overtones at all, and the two contemporary English literary references have nothing to do with the political struggle against France.[33] We should also remember that all Edward's other adopted mottoes were personal, not international statements. 'It is as it is', as we have seen, was probably a tacit announcement of the death of his father, aimed at those in the know. Similarly the apparently love-related motto he used the previous Christmas – 'Hay, Hay the White Swan, by God's Soul I am thy Man' – was anything but international propaganda, requiring either familiarity with the English poem or song from which it came (if literary) or the identity of Edward's 'white swan'.

One fact which has escaped previous writers' attention is that the garter was a chivalric emblem with a history which predated Edward's victories in France. Edward himself purchased pearl garters in the early 1330s, and by his own admission, Lancaster wore garters in his youth.[34] In particular, Lancaster's phenomenal military success in 1345 may have been the reason why now it became an especially prominent chivalric symbol. It had the advantage that it was highly visible, for it could be worn over the plate armour which knights now habitually wore.[35] So when Prince Edward presented garters to the twenty-four 'Companions of the Garter' in 1348, the recipients were probably members of a company – possibly an unofficial jousting fraternity – formed in honour of a victorious war leader, either Edward or the earl of Lancaster.[36] Furthermore, because the *honi soit* motto was integral to the garter badge in the very earliest records (before the foundation of the Order), it follows that it was not necessarily Edward's motto, but either that of the Companionship of 1348 or the originator's own.[37] If the originator was Lancaster, this would explain why the language is different to Edward's other mottoes. French was Lancaster's first language, and, although he also spoke English, French was certainly his language of choice: he wrote a whole book in it, and nothing in English or Latin.[38] Moreover, Edward had good reason *not* to anglicise this motto in 1349, for only a French or Latin tag would have been suitable for an order which marked out with great distinction Hainaulters and Gascons as well as Englishmen. To use an English motto would have alienated all the non-English members of the Order and their companions, and made it an inward-looking, English-only institution, not an outward-looking pan-European one.[39]

There was one other key element to the inaugural Garter tournament in April 1349, and it is most revealing of the atmosphere at court in the tense months while the plague raged around the country. As probably every reader knows, Edward was once thought to have adopted a garter as the symbol of his Order having picked up the countess of Salisbury's garter at a 'ball' after the fall of Calais, saying *honi soit qui mal y pense* to those who suspected that he was holding a lady's undergarment for all the wrong reasons.[40] This story is normally dismissed by modern historians, being too romantic, unsupported by contemporary evidence, and contrary to the received wisdom that the Order was conceived purely as a political or military institution. The story was probably devised in the fifteenth century to explain why the premier chivalric order was denoted by a *garter* (of all things!) and the strange motto.[41] But this level of scepticism has meant that no one has seriously examined it in the light of what we know about the foundation of the Order and its inaugural tournament.

The story of the countess of Salisbury's garter is essentially another love story – like the story of the visit to Wark – in which Edward was depicted as conscious of his own illicit desire for a young and beautiful noblewoman. The high-profile tournaments of 1348–49 were certainly social occasions at which such love-making could – and did – happen. Thomas Burton noted with horror how Edward summoned many ladies to the jousts of 1348, adding 'there was hardly a lady there assigned to her own husband; they were with other men, by whom they were debauched as the lust took them'.[42] Writing about the Lincoln tournament of 1348, Henry Knighton, an Augustinian canon at Leicester, stated that forty or fifty beautiful women attended, and 'inflicted wanton and foolish lusts on their bodies, according to popular rumour. Nor did they fear God or blush at the stories people told, as they threw off the bonds of marriage.'[43] In this light the fifteenth-century story about Edward's flirtation with a married lady who had lost an undergarment seems wholly in keeping.

If we now examine the fifteenth-century story more closely, we note that it does not name the lady concerned in its earliest versions. That is a sixteenth-century addition.[44] So, on the face of it, even though the countess in 1349 was a young and desirable woman – Joan 'the Fair Maid of Kent' – there would appear to be no grounds for connecting her with the tournament. However, surprising though it may be, there is a strong reason for taking Joan seriously as playing a lead romantic role in the inaugural Garter tournament of 23 April 1349.[45] She was about twenty years of age, a member of the royal family, and undoubtedly very beautiful.[46] She was also in the extraordinary situation of publicly having two husbands at the same time. She claimed that she had first married Sir Thomas Holland, one of the founder Garter knights.[47] But she was officially married to the second earl of Salisbury, another of the founder knights. In May 1348 her supposed first husband – who was now the steward of her second husband – stated to the pope that she had been forced into her marriage with Salisbury. He stated that she had previously agreed to marry him and had slept with him, so he now claimed her as his own wife. She supported this story, obviously preferring the steward to his lord. Her marital status was in question for a full eighteen months, and it was not until November 1349 that the pope ordered her to divorce Salisbury and marry Holland, which she did.[48] The crux of the matter is that on 23 April 1349, while the marital rights to this most famous royal beauty were being argued over, her two husbands were on opposing sides at the Windsor tournament: Holland was on the prince's side, Salisbury on the king's. Therefore there is no doubt that the countess of Salisbury was a focus of romantic attention at the inaugural Garter tournament. She was being fought over – literally – by at least two of those present.[49] She did not drop her garter for Edward (women in 1349 did not wear them), and the motto *honi soit* probably has nothing to do with her, but the allure of the countess of Salisbury was indeed connected with the inaugural tournament of the Order of the Garter. Later her wedding dress was given to the collegiate chapel of the Order,[50] and this – coupled with the French story of Edward's infatuation at Wark – is probably why her name finally crept back into the tale after more than two centuries' absence, transformed into the fictitious woman who lost her garter.

This allows us to complete the picture of the foundation tournament of the Order of the Garter. In April 1349, Edward brought together his long-standing ambitions for a chivalric order and realised them in an institution which built on a companionship or jousting fraternity formed to celebrate his victories and those of the earl of Lancaster. The despondency of the plague called for a high-profile publicity stunt, and Edward provided one. It was a lasting statement of his chivalric ideas, just as later his great castle at Queenborough would be a lasting statement of his military genius. But it was also timed as an act of defiance against everything that threatened those ideals. It drew him out of his own personal grief and gave him and the country something positive and glorious on which to focus at the height of the worst epidemic the country had ever seen. Those of his compan-ions who braved the pestilence and journeyed to Windsor to take part in that inaugural tournament were rewarded with founder-member status of the most prestigious and exclusive order of knighthood in Europe. And they took part in a tournament which witnessed some of the most famous knights of the day fight over the most beautiful woman in the land. What better distraction from the plague could there have been than to watch twelve men on each claimant's side battle for his comrade's right to make love to the royal countess? No doubt many contemporaries would have agreed with Henry Knighton in saying that all this was foolish and immoral, but it was in keeping with the chivalric values of the time. Most knights experiencing the horrors of the Black Death would far rather have jousted for the kisses of a beautiful and desirable twenty-year-old princess than sat alongside Henry Knighton in his cold abbey at Leicester, solemnly recording the number of dead recently interred in the local plague pits.

*

Successful though Edward's tournament may have been, people were still dying. After a winter of plenty there followed a season of dearth. Prices went up, and wages doubled. To return to Henry Knighton's chronicle: 'In the following autumn no one could get a reaper for less than eight-pence with food, or a mower for less then twelvepence with food. For this reason many crops perished in the fields for lack of harvesters.'

Knighton's words show us how inflexible medieval society was. When one sector experienced a crisis, the entire community reeled, unable to adapt by assigning tasks to other people. In 1349 many systems simply collapsed. Men who had lost their wives and children could provide a mobile workforce, but only if they broke their feudal bonds and left the manors on which they were bound to work. Faced with starvation, this is what they did in many places. Hence a manorial bailiff, having lost a third or a half of his workforce to plague, now found the remainder threatening to leave unless he paid them double their usual wages. This was threatening the established order. Manorial lords did not normally need to buy food, requisitioning it from their demesne farms. Now, not only had much of their workforce died, and the remainder gone off to work for someone else, their own animals were dying in the fields. They had cows but no one to milk them. They had sheep but no one to shear them. They could not pay their tithes to the church, so the clergy could not function. So many clergymen died that many church benefices remained unfilled. Manors often ceased to exist. No lord, no workforce and no clergy meant no flock in either sense of the word. The unrepaired thatched roofs collapsed in the rains, the cob walls soon were in ruins. One did not need to catch the disease to feel the dire effects of the plague.

Edward's reaction to this is understandable. It was simple logic: all the economic damage would be minimised if those workers who survived remained on their estates and worked for the same wages as before. The danger was that entire manors would return to waste ground as survivors only worked the most economically viable units. Then taxes – such as the sums levied on personal estates (normally a fifteenth in rural manors) – would be greatly reduced in value. Wool taxes too were clearly going to be greatly reduced. Therefore it was with the idea of trying to maintain the status quo as far as possible that Edward issued a royal ordinance. No lords were to offer higher wages to their workers than before the plague, and no labourers were to seek increased payments.

The policy was bound to be unsuccessful. When the labour supply was so short, and the currency supply unchanged, wage inflation was inevitable. Nineteenth-century 'whiggish' commentators, convinced that history is one great march of progress towards modern society, tended to regard Edward's actions as backward-looking, and castigated him for trying to stand in the way of progress towards a free-market economy. But in 1349 it was difficult to understand how society was changing, and impossible to see how high wages or large amounts of derelict property could benefit the nation. Rather we should interpret Edward's action in much the same way as his Windsor tournament of April 1349. It was an attempt to advertise to the country that stability could be maintained. With courage, knights could still travel around the country and joust. Labourers could still be forced to remain on their manors. Edward could – and would – remain in control of his kingdom.

By early September two of the founder knights who had attended the Garter tournament at Windsor in April were dead. Philippa laid gold cloths on the tomb of one of them, Hugh Courtenay, the twenty-two-year-old heir to the earldom of Devon. John Montgomery, governor of Calais, died, and so did his wife. John Offord, the archbishop of Canterbury, died, and so did his successor, Thomas Bradwardine. Sir John Pulteney, four times Lord Mayor of London, died. Most lordly families lost several relations, some noble titles died out. The dowager countess of Salisbury died, so too did Lord Thomas Wake, the bishop of Worcester, the abbot of Westminster, Sir John Fauconberg and the queen of France. Clerks and workmen died in large numbers: the Surveyor of the King's Works, William Ramsey, was one of the most prominent. In Florence, the chronicler Giovanni Villani, hoping to note down the total number of fatalities at the end of the outbreak, became one of them.

It was after all these deaths that the Flagellants arrived. Their presence was yet another shocking jolt to an already-reeling society. Philip de Valois had thrown them out of France, so horrified was he by their self-immolation. Dressed only in loincloths, this unofficial religious order walked from town to town whipping themselves with a heavy whip which had three leather thongs studded with metal spikes. With a few of the brethren leading the others in a dirge, exhorting them to whip themselves to redeem the world of its sins, the group lashed itself until each member was bleeding down his back. Sometimes they whipped themselves until they bled to death. Such extreme physical punishment in the name of God is perhaps not too distant from chivalric ceremonies such as jousts of war, and it may have been because of Edward's martial reputation that the Flagellants came to England in October 1349.[51] But the Flagellants were not welcome. Soon they were driven out of England as they had been driven out of France. Their rules, which held it a sin to converse or have intercourse of any sort with a woman, were not likely to endear them to a king as fond of female company as Edward.

*

In August 1349 Philip decided to break the truce which had prevailed throughout the plague.[52] Perhaps it was thought that English plague losses had been so heavy that Edward could not possibly afford to send an army abroad to protect his French possessions. Perhaps the Gascons, who had carried on their small-scale raids on French property, had committed too many robberies to remain unpunished. Either way, by the end of the month Guy de Nesle was raising an army to attack the English in Gascony.

England was just beginning to emerge from the disease stages of the plague, and to begin to rebuild economically. It was thus with a shock that Edward learnt of the French plans. His reaction was to defend, and for this there was no better leader than Lancaster, whose very name struck fear into his adversaries. But the armies he would lead were another matter. There were no soldiers available. Lancaster took with him about three hundred men and went on a destructive rampage, hoping that through fire, speed and terror he could force the French to renew the truce. But it was not the destruction in the south-west that forced them to the negotiating table: it was Edward himself.

Calais. The town had festered in the minds of the French ever since it had fallen. It was as great a loss to them as Crécy. To regain it, they could try to besiege it, but then they would have to fight a naval engagement with the English, who would break the siege from the sea. So treachery was practically their only option. Aimeric de Pavia was the man they hit upon. He was a Genoese soldier of fortune who had previously fought for France. Indeed, he had been within Calais when Edward had been besieging it. As an experienced and talented sea captain, he had been offered a new position by Edward, anxious to secure his services. Aimeric had accepted, and had been made captain of the king's galleys at Calais. Now Geoffrey de Charny, the famous French commander, approached him with a bribe. The plan was for Aimeric to allow access by night through the postern gate to the town.

Aimeric was a loyal man. He had remained at Calais and starved for the French king's benefit, only to see the French army march away and leave the townspeople of Calais to their fate. That was no way to repay loyalty. So now, at the point of considering betraying the town, Aimeric sent one of his galleys across the Channel with a message for Edward, who was then at Hereford. He told him what de Charny was offering: forty thousand florins (£6,000). Immediately Edward saw the chance of grabbing the money, saving Calais and having an adventure all at the same time. With the prince of Wales, Sir John Beauchamp, Lord Stafford and the young Lord Mortimer – all Knights of the Garter – and Sir John Montagu, Lord Manny, Lord Berkeley, Lord de la Warre and the earl of Suffolk, he rode to Westminster. In order to ensure that no one heard that he was gathering a few hundred archers, he ordered that no one was to leave England, covering his reason by saying it was because of the plague.[53] Then he went down to the coast, and crossed with his knights' retainers and his archers to Calais.

In Calais Edward and the prince went anonymously through the streets, dressed in the clothes of merchants. Few of the townsmen knew they were there. This gave Edward a few days to prepare – the date set for the betrayal of the town was the night of 31 December – and in that time he ordered a false stone wall to be built inside the postern gate. He partially weakened the drawbridge, and stationed a large stone on the battlements of the gatehouse above. Then he and his men settled down to await the betrayal in a room in the castle of the town.

Towards midnight a French advance party under Oudart de Renti rode up to the postern gate. They found the drawbridge down, and the gate open. There was Aimeric de Pavia, waiting for the first instalment of the money. Having received it, Aimeric declared he had no time to count it, but would lead them into the castle to allow them to signal to their fellows that all was well. The room to which he led them was, of course, that in which Edward and his knights were hiding. As the door swung inwards they found themselves confronted with a grim knight in full armour. That first moment of shock was followed by another, for the grim knight then bellowed his war cry: 'Manny! Manny to the rescue!' Sir Walter rushed forward into the group, only to stop short after a moment and declare: 'What! Do they hope to conquer the castle of Calais with so few men?'[54] When the French had surrendered, they were locked in the same castle room. Edward, Manny and the rest of his men then took up their positions behind the false wall which had been built carefully without mortar, resting stones upon each other.

The advance guard had instructions to raise the French flags over the castle if all was safe for the main party to enter the town through the main gate. Edward's men raised the French banners, to lure them forward. When a sufficient number had entered, trumpets sounded, and down went the stone on the drawbridge with a crash, cutting the troops in the town off from their fellow men. And down went the false wall too, to the alternate cries of 'Treachery!' and 'Manny to the rescue!' There the trapped French found themselves facing the banners of Manny, Stafford, Mortimer and the prince. Once more Sir Walter charged forward. This time, unlike any previous encounter, the king of England was beside him, fighting as an unmarked knight beneath the Manny standard. The king tackled Sir Eustace de Ribbemont, one of the principal commanders of the French army, and beat him to his knees. Then, with about thirty knights and a few archers, he ran out of the town to attack the rest of the French.

It was a rash move. Edward and those who had charged with him found themselves facing a large number – perhaps eight hundred – men-at-arms.[55] Edward ordered the few archers who had followed him to take positions on the ridges above the marshes, so that they were free to shoot at any men who approached. And then, pushing back his visor and showing his face to all, he lifted his sword and yelled his war cry 'St Edward and St George!' Any Englishmen there who did not know King Edward personally was with them had no doubt now. The bewildered French men-at-arms suddenly found themselves facing the extraordinary situation of the English king standing before them, outnumbered more than twenty-to-one, and yet preparing to do battle. It would probably have been calamitous had not the prince of Wales heard his father's war cry, and hurried ahead with all the available men, catching up as Edward plunged into the French ranks. The French had not been expecting this – they had thought they would walk into Calais unopposed – and before long the king and his son had fought through their adversaries to seize Geoffrey de Charny and hurl him to the ground while the remainder of the French fled. All the French captains of the attack were captured: de Charny, de Renti and de Ribbemont. Calais had been saved, the money seized, and Edward had gained more valuable prisoners.

Edward was so pleased with himself that he entertained the French leaders to dinner the following evening. A picturesque irony was given to the proceedings by the prince and the other Knights of the Garter waiting on the captured men. Edward wore a chaplet of pearls, and, after the dinner, went among his prisoners talking to them. To Geoffrey de Charny he was stern, saying that he had little reason to love him, since he had sought to obtain cheaply what Edward had earned at a much greater price. But when he came to Eustace de Ribbemont, whom he had beaten in hand-to-hand combat, he took off his chaplet of pearls. 'Sir Eustace', he said,

> I present you with this chaplet, as being the best fighter today, either within or without doors; and I beg of you to wear it this year for love of me. I know that you are lively and amorous, and love the company of ladies and damsels; therefore, say wherever you go, that I gave it to you. I also give you your liberty, free of ransom; and you may set out tomorrow, and go wherever you please.[56]

Edward knew the value of publicity: to give a man he had beaten a permanent reminder of their fight and an incentive to tell people about it was worth far more than mere pearls and a ransom.

*

On 12 January 1350 Edward, now back in England, ordered prayers to be said in thanks for his safe delivery at Calais. The plague was clearly on the wane, and his reputation was higher than ever. The French had once more been forced to the negotiating table, and hard talks had followed. It took until 13 June for an agreement to be reached, during which time both sides remained uneasy. Neither Philip nor Edward was confident that the outcome would be peace; both anticipated renewed conflict, and spent the first half of the year re-arming as best they could.

Edward had one propaganda advantage in his re-armament campaign: the Castilians. After Joan's death on her way to marry Pedro of Castile, King Alfonso had thought better of his alliance with England, perhaps suspecting it would draw him into a conflict with his immediate neighbour, France, and decided instead to further his friendship with Philip. As Philip proceeded to rebuild his maritime forces, he offered a large sum to Alfonso for the use of a Castilian navy. The Castilian ships were huge, famous as towering castles of the sea, and because they were so large they were the ideal means to defeat the English, for lines of crossbowmen could shoot down on the smaller English vessels and clear the decks of long-bowmen. So, as far as the English were concerned, a Castilian navy in the area was a potent invasion threat. Acts of piracy in the North Sea by the Castilians played into Edward's hands. When on 27 March 1350, Alfonso died of plague at the siege of Gibraltar (the only crowned European monarch to die in the Black Death), the threat of piracy worsened. The word on the shipping lanes was that the Castilians aimed to capture the English wine fleet from Gascony.

Even before Alfonso's death Edward had been making plans. On 26 March the orders went out for men to assemble at Sandwich on 6 June. The captains of Edward's flagship, the *Thomas*, were directed to find a hundred sailors in Kent and Sussex. Edward ordered rigging to be purchased 'for the king's ships'. One preparation now considered essential – the secrecy of the mission – was ordered on 23 June, when Edward issued the directive for no one to leave the country. On 10 August he wrote to the archbishop of Canterbury desiring prayers for the forthcoming battle to put an end to the threat of the Spanish invasion. Shortly afterwards he set sail.

The Castilian fleet probably numbered forty or forty-four large ships; Edward had about fifty smaller ones.[57] With the prince of Wales was Edward's third son, the ten-year-old John of Gaunt, whom we might suspect had asked to follow his brother (in whose household he was serving as an esquire). The other vessels were commanded by an array of Knights of the Garter and assorted military heroes: the earls of Lancaster, Northampton, Warwick, Arundel, Salisbury and Huntingdon, Sir Reginald Cobham, Sir John Chandos and the inevitable Lord Manny. Crowds gathered in the harbour at Winchelsea, and the Sussex cliffs were crested with people hoping to see another English victory. Among them were men and women from the queen's household; Philippa remained where she was, six miles from Winchelsea, worried for Edward and her sons.[58]

In order to engage the Castilians, it was necessary either to collide with them or to sail ahead of them and furl the sails, slowing down to meet them. Various captains manoeuvred their ships into position. English archers in the raised wooden forecastles and rearcastles waited until the great Castilian ships were in range, and then loosed their arrows. The new rigging Edward had specially ordered may well have been specifically with the Castilians in mind, allowing archers to be placed high above the English boats and able to attack the Castilians at deck-level. But to fire a longbow is not easy at the best of times, and it would have been far more difficult to shoot accurately from the rigging or crow's nest of the lurching English vessels. Some crossbowmen were picked off by the English, but the choppy waters of the Channel were less conducive to archery than the calm waters of Sluys which had allowed Edward's archers to massacre the French ten years earlier. The only way any Castilian ship was going to be overwhelmed was the old-fashioned way: by catching it, throwing grappling irons on board, climbing up and over the side and attacking those on deck with swords.

Edward led by example. Picking out one of the larger galleys, he ordered his captain to sail straight for it. He presumed that the *Thomas* was sufficiently large to withstand a collision. But when the two vessels crashed into each other, timbers shook, the hull cracked, and immediately the *Thomas* was in danger of sinking. But the forecastle of the *Thomas* tore away that of the Castilian vessel, and left its front mast dangling. Edward was all for drawing alongside and boarding it, but the knights with him urged him to engage another ship, for the one he had rammed was already sufficiently damaged. So Edward disengaged from the first vessel and targeted another, his knights reduced to bailing out water with the sailors. They did not have to bail for long. Another large galley, seeing the royal standard, sailed directly for the *Thomas*, and its captain had every intention of boarding it. As the two ships came alongside and grappled each other, the Castilian crossbows rained bolts down on to the English decks and their experienced archers picked off the longbowmen in the rigging. Rocks piled on the decks of the galleys were hurled down on to the English men-at-arms as they tried to scale the sides of the vessel. The resulting fight was bitterly fierce, with many dead on both sides. But Edward's men once more prevailed. Having gained this new vessel, he hoisted the flag from the *Thomas*, announcing to the other captains that the king had been victorious.

The battle continued until dark. For a while the prince's ship was in danger of sinking, which would have instantly meant the loss of two of Edward's sons, but the earl of Lancaster saw the danger and sailed to his aid, helping him overcome the galley he had grappled. Even after dark one ship carried on fighting against the Castilians. This was the *Salle du Roi*, commanded for Edward by Robert of Namur. The Castilians had grappled the ship, and decided to drag it away from the battle to ransack it, with their sails fully unfurled. In the darkness many men on both sides were killed as they fought across the decks, unable to see, and lost their footing, or were shot by unseen bowmen. Eventually one of Namur's men cut the sails of the ship, deadening their flight, and Namur's men fought off the Castilians.

Contemporaries suggest that, over the course of the battle, between fourteen and twenty-four Castilian ships were captured, and the remainder of the Castilian fleet fled.[59] No English vessels were seized. Some were sunk on both sides, but it was a great victory for the English, hailed in some quarters as a success as bold and as great as Crécy.[60] On landing, a little after dark, Edward went to Philippa and returned to her both Edward and John. It had been a day of courage, destruction and near-disaster, but ultimately it was one more victory for Edward.

When news of the battle of Winchelsea reached France, few would have taken much interest. It was not that the French did not care that their Castilian allies had been defeated in their first engagement with the English, it was because, seven days earlier, King Philip had died. In his career he had chosen to make an enemy of his cousin, Edward, and for that he had been repeatedly outwitted, out-negotiated, betrayed, defeated and humiliated. His insecurity and impatience, leading to his bitter reproaches towards his own people, had only made matters worse. After Crécy he was a broken man. After Calais, his was a broken reign. When his queen had died of plague, he had waited only a month before marrying his seventeen-year-old cousin, Blanche d'Évreux. Philip himself was fifty-six, which raised eyebrows, but what was shocking was that she had been betrothed to his son, John, causing many recriminations from members of the French nobility and the alienation of the heir to the throne. When the truce was announced in June 1350, France was doubly joyful, for it saved them from their own king's ineptitude as well as Edward's ruthless destruction. Philip's death brought an end to a twenty-two-year-long reign which had been as disastrous for France as that of Edward II had been for England. Together they stand as a reminder that, in the middle ages, kings did not have to be good men but they did have to be good kings.

TWELVE

At the Court of the Sun King

In 1350 Edward's confidence could not have been higher. He had been victorious in every battle he had fought. He had survived the plague, had restored the prestige of the royal family, had solved his financial problems, was respected and applauded by his people and held in awe by his knightly contemporaries. He had constantly tried new ideas and techniques, and personally he had inspired and demanded innovations which had resulted in new ways of fighting, governing, raising money and trading. The loyalty and courage of his men had been repeatedly tested to the limit and never found lacking. With such support he had done what no English king – not even his renowned grandfather, Edward I – had done before. He had utterly humiliated the French king, captured the Scottish king, and swept aside the political machinations of the pope, plunging the schemes of all those who opposed him into disarray.

But despite these successes and such high confidence, Edward himself was changing. Even though he had survived the plague, the experience had deeply affected him. It had shown him the limits of his power, and was a horrific reminder to all kings of their weakness against natural disasters. It had affected him as a man too, through the tragic loss of his daughter and the deaths of friends brave enough to join him at Windsor in April 1349, at the height of the epidemic. Above all else it had shown him how transitory his achievements might prove. Had he died in the plague, that would have been the enduring image of him, covered in black pustules and reeking of decay. He had risked his life at the battle of Winchelsea and almost lost his boat and drowned; and all for what? Seventeen galleys? In his own high opinion of himself, it would have been a tragedy if he had died for so little gain. It may have been the plague, or it may have been his age – he was now thirty-seven – or perhaps both, but it is at this point that Edward began to draw back from martial activities and to create more lasting structures. Winchelsea was to be the last time he drew his sword and personally risked his life in the front line of a battle.

Edward had probably begun to think in terms of permanent creations even before Winchelsea. In the Order of the Garter he had created a means to perpetuate a knightly reputation long after an individual was no longer capable of fighting at the highest level. As soon as it was founded, the fame of the Order spread across Europe. In France the newly crowned King John was thinking about founding his own order, the Order of the Star, and other princes and kings were doing likewise. A whole host of orders was in the planning, all based on knightly accoutrements: swords, buckles, collars, even a knot.[1] But there was no doubt which order every knight in Europe aspired to join. When historians write that these orders of chivalry were distinguished by lavish ceremonial and ornate dress regulations they are missing an important point. The distinguishing mark of the Order of the Garter was that it was a select band of just twenty-six knights chosen by the man who was widely recognised to be the greatest warrior-king in Christendom and the epitome of chivalric honour. So great was its reputation that when in 1350 Thomas de la Marche, bastard son of the French king had agreed to fight a duel with a Cypriot knight, John Visconti, they chose to do so not before King Philip but in front of Edward, even though the English king was de la Marche's enemy.[2]

It was with the Order of the Garter in mind that Edward set about his largest and most impressive architectural creation, at Windsor Castle. This was where he had been born; this was where the Garter tournament had taken place, and this, he decided, would be where the heart of the Order would remain. Already he had established the collegiate chapel of St George in the lower bailey. From now on, all Knights of the Garter were to attend the service at Windsor on St George's Day every year. Even if they could not – if, for example, they were overseas – they should celebrate as if they *were* at Windsor, being a travelling advertisement for the glory and dignity of Edward's chivalric order. For his part, Edward would enhance the Order's reputation, building the largest, grandest and most opulent palace in Northern Europe.

Today Windsor Castle has the appearance of a modernised medieval castle, a great symbol easily recognisable from the motorway or on the television as the monarch's home. But in the fourteenth century it was nothing short of a Versailles Palace: the court of the Sun King. Edward's work there amounted to the most expensive building in Britain by a single monarch throughout the whole of the middle ages. To put it in proportion, we often think of Edward I's eight Welsh castles, built between 1277 and 1304, as one of the most significant building programmes undertaken by a medieval king. The entire cost of all eight was £95,000.[3] Edward III spent more than £50,000 on Windsor Castle alone.

And yet few people today connect Windsor Castle with Edward III. People immediately associate the Tower of London with William the Conqueror, and Hampton Court with Henry VIII, just as they do Versailles with Louis XIV of France. But Edward has, once again, slipped through the net of national self-awareness. One reason is the dampening effect of his reputation throughout the nineteenth century, so that his achievements were obscured by writers eager to focus on his failings. But there are two other, simpler reasons as well. One is that Edward's principal works at Windsor are not open to the public; they are very private, as the royal family still lives in them. The other is that they are mostly internal buildings: living and ceremonial quarters, which have been repeatedly adapted to suit the tastes of each monarch since Edward, unlike the stern curtain walls, which retain their militaristic solidity. What the public sees today from outside the castle is largely restored twelfth- and thirteenth-century stonework. It was inside this impressive chivalric shell – the largest residential castle in the world – that Edward created the stone epitome of his vision of kingship and knighthood.[4]

The internal reconstruction of Windsor Castle as the greatest medieval palace in England took about eighteen years. Practically every major artist and craftsman in the country was at some time or other employed on the fabric. A striking mark of the importance which Edward gave to his projected works at Windsor from the outset was his donation of the Neith Cross (a portion of the True Cross and his most precious relic) to the chapel of St George. Actual structural work may be said to have begun with the appointment of the first of a series of clerks of works in April 1350, the first anniversary of the Garter tournament.[5] The earliest works were the buildings for the College of St George in the lower bailey. He removed the huge, unfinished Round Table building he had begun six years earlier and replaced it with a series of half-timbered houses for the canons, clerks and choristers around a series of cloisters. At the same time the chapel was re-roofed and equipped with new choir stalls and windows. A new chapter house was built with a warden's lodge above it. A new treasury was added, a new vestry, and a belfry. The construction and decoration of the collegiate buildings took until 1357 to complete, and cost about £6,000.

It was the king's palatial accommodation in the upper bailey which captured the attention of contemporaries. These works were intended from the outset to be truly impressive. Beginning in 1358 under the direction of a promising royal clerk, William of Wykeham, Edward ordered the rebuilding of the entire upper bailey, beginning at the north-west and proceeding in a clockwise direction. By the early 1360s his expenditure on the castle was running in excess of £5,000 per year. There was a new hall and kitchen, the old hall being converted into a chamber for the personal use of the king. This room alone had twenty windows.[6] He also had a painted chamber, and five other chambers, including one – the Rose

Chamber – coloured with blue, green and vermilion paint and large quantities of gold leaf. Philippa had four chambers, including one hung entirely with mirrors, and another decorated as a dancing chamber. Stone was brought from all over the country, including Somerset, Surrey, Berkshire, Yorkshire and Lincolnshire, to give variety and character to the walls.[7] Although Edward had lost his master mason, William Ramsey, in the plague, he was followed by a whole host of successors, including Henry Yevele, arguably the most important of all medieval English architects. In 1360 alone no fewer than five hundred and sixty-eight masons were employed from thirteen counties. The following year – which saw expenditure on the castle top the £6,000 mark – more than twice this number were employed, drawn from seventeen counties. One chronicler remarked that 'almost all the masons and carpenters throughout England were brought to that building, so that hardly anyone could have any good mason or carpenter'.[8] The chronicler perhaps exaggerated a little, but in one respect he was absolutely correct: all the very *best* craftsmen worked at Windsor. One of the master carpenters at work on the collegiate buildings was William Hurley, the man responsible for Hugh Despenser's great roof in the hall of Caerphilly Castle, built before 1326 (still extant) and many other great buildings of Edward's reign. Edward used all the country had to offer in terms of numbers, skill and experience. At the end of the process he had constructed a palace which was worthy not only of him as the victor of Halidon Hill, Sluys, Crécy, Calais and Winchelsea, but of the English people, who had fought for him at those battles, and won.

*

Edward's huge rebuilding programme at Windsor was by no means his sole cultural contribution. However, the rest have not lasted so well. It is one of the great ironies of Edward's life that the structures and art works which he commissioned from 1350 to be a permanent commemoration of his achievements have not proved as lasting as the memory of those achievements themselves. As mentioned above, few people today associate Windsor Castle with him; but most people have heard of the Order of the Garter. Not a single stone remains from his great vision of military power, Queenborough Castle, on the Isle of Sheppey, but most of us remember the result of the battle of Crécy. Likewise, although most historians today first think of the establishment of parliamentary representation as one of Edward III's major achievements, the great paintings of St Stephen's Chapel, which stood near the current Houses of Parliament at Westminster, have long since vanished.

St Stephen's Chapel, the principal place of royal worship within the

Palace of Westminster, was ordered to be completely rebuilt by Edward I in 1292. Over the next sixty years, progress became a barometer of royal authority. When the king was strong, building rushed ahead; when his policies were challenged, building stopped. Thus it is not surprising that work had progressed very slowly through the last years of the reign of Edward I and through most of Edward II's reign. It was only in the 1320s that the old walls, which had been protected by thatching since 1309 were cleaned off and the slow, scrupulous work of constructing 'the most splendid chapel in England' began again.[9] Little progress had been made by the time Mortimer and Isabella invaded, and brought the work once more to a halt. Building only resumed after Edward III took charge of the country, in 1331. Over the next three years the east end was finished. A lull in construction followed in 1334, while the king was away in Scotland, and facing his first financial crisis in the wage bill from that campaign, but it was not long before work began again, in 1337. This time there was no stopping. William Hurley, the king's master carpenter, and William Ramsey, Surveyor of the King's Works, were put in charge. By 1348 the exquisite chapel – ninety feet long by thirty feet wide – was complete, with a gallery leading directly from the king's chamber into the upper part. At the same time, Edward established a college of canons to celebrate mass there. All that needed to be done now was to glaze, paint and furnish the chapel.

It is, of course, a sad loss for us that the chapel was pulled down after the fire of 1834, which destroyed most of the Palace of Westminster. But what is especially sad is that the decoration was almost entirely lost in that fire. For at St Stephen's Edward commissioned what is generally recognised as the most magnificent English painting programme of the fourteenth century.[10] It is tempting to say that England had not seen painting like this before, for many of the techniques are exclusively connected with painting of the Italian Renaissance: the use of perspective, for example. But, surprisingly, the painters themselves seem to have been English. In March 1350 the master painter Hugh of St Albans was directed to search out the best men of his craft in Kent, Middlesex, Essex, Surrey and Sussex and to bring them to Westminster to work on the painting.[11] Other painters were ordered to do the same in the Midlands and East Anglia. Edward was doing at Westminster with painting what he was doing at Windsor with stonework: conscripting the very best artists his kingdom had to offer. No expense was spared. Paper (still a relatively rare commodity) was purchased for the designs, and peacocks' feathers, swans' feathers, pigs' bristles and squirrels' tails for the brushes, as well as rich paints and gold leaf for the decoration. Every part of the chapel walls was painted. The spaces below the windows were adorned with religious subjects; the corners of the windows were painted or gilded, the walls themselves were covered with angels with extended wings, and doves, eagles, elephants and castles. Beneath the great east window there were painted figures of St George, King Edward, Queen Philippa and ten of their sons and daughters. Only some incomplete sketches made of these images now survive: the originals were destroyed in the fire. A few small fragments of the paintings were rescued, and these are now in the British Museum. Otherwise everything was lost.

Edward did not stop at employing the best painters at St Stephen's: he also employed the best carpenters, glaziers and carvers of stone and wood. Heading up the list of carpenters was, unsurprisingly, William Hurley, the foremost carpenter of his day. They worked on the stalls and the reredos. In 1351–52, twenty to thirty glaziers worked to the orders of the master glazier, John of Chester. The best woodcarver in the kingdom was initially thought to be Robert Burwell, whom Edward had employed at Windsor in 1350; but after a few years it was found that in Nottinghamshire there was an even more skilled man, Master Edmund of St Andrew, a canon of Newstead Abbey. Master Edmund was accordingly brought all the way to Westminster in 1355. He became just the latest of the scores of artists whom Edward drew together from all over the realm. As for stone sculpture, Edward was the first important patron of the fine school of English alabaster carving (his father's effigy at Gloucester being the earliest extant masterpiece), and alabaster sculptures were installed at Windsor and probably also at St Stephen's.[12] The alabaster reredos he commissioned for the high altar of St George's was a particularly large piece: it required ten carts and eighty horses to transport it from Nottingham to Windsor.[13]

By 1355 Edward was the patron of most of the best artists in England. Had all medieval kings acted in a similar way, medieval provincial art may well have been poorer but English royal buildings would have rivalled many of the structural masterpieces of the Italian Renaissance. This may sound like a wild statement, in view of the destruction of the royal chapel and the unique cultural status accorded to the Renaissance, but consider how closely Edward was in touch with the Italians. His extended family links with southern European families (such as the counts of Savoy and Provence, the Fieschi and the Visconti) had, over the years, made him as familiar with Italian culture as his forefathers. For years, through royal gift-giving and gift-receiving, Edward had seen the best that Italian craftsmen had to offer, and had offered back in return priceless works from English goldsmiths' workshops. The banking families of the Peruzzi and the Bardi had practically dwelt at his palaces for several years, and in 1340 the head of the Peruzzi died in London, after spending a year with Edward. His constant embassies to Avignon meant that his high-status ambassadors and low-status messengers were regularly exposed to the culture of the Mediterranean. Some of his doctors were Italian, some of his clerks, and some of his armourers. He purchased paintings and armour from Italy. As a result it would be wrong *not* to regard Edward III as a Renaissance ruler.

No panel paintings belonging to Edward exist now, but documentary evidence shows us that he himself commissioned some and even appointed a royal painter. In 1353 this was 'John, a canon of St Catherine's, the king's picture painter'.[14] Five years later Queen Isabella possessed at least six and perhaps ten Italian paintings, the largest being of seven leaves.[15] This is not a small collection, and her owning such large constructions as six-leaf and seven-leaf paintings suggests that these were being brought to England as a result of a known demand for them, if only in royal circles. Edward similarly used Italian panel paintings in his favourite residences.[16] Most striking of all, Edward was probably the first English king who sat for his portrait, for in 1380 the king of France owned a painted likeness of Edward.[17] We cannot look at this development as being accidental; rather it appears to be another example of Edward's own artistic patronage and links with Italian Renaissance culture.

Much more could be said about St Stephen's chapel, and many books have been written on the subject of the medieval Palace of Westminster, but perhaps one last point is particularly suitable for inclusion in a biography of Edward III. It must be noted that he himself did not begin the chapel, his grandfather did. This may be taken simply as a sign of a continuation of his grandfather's ambitions, but is also indicative of his will to complete his predecessors' foundations. He had already endowed and founded the King's Hall at Cambridge in line with his father's promises. Similarly in 1346 he had founded a convent of nuns at Dartford dependent on the Dominican friars, a unique establishment which was the original idea of his father and grandmother.[18] In these foundations, brought to splendid completion under Edward III, we may detect a sense of triumph, or, more particularly, of a determination to complete what his predecessors had been unable to finish. Edward was keen to tie up the loose ends of the last two generations and eliminate the evidence that the English royal family occasionally failed to live up to its promises. To return to the idea of Edward trying to be 'the perfect king', it is arguable that in 1350 his ambition had gone one stage further, to turn his whole family into a 'perfect dynasty'. If we are right in reading the evidence in this way, then it is surely a remarkable ambition. It was only twenty years since Edward had assented to the execution of his own uncle.

*

Almost nothing now remains of Edward's other great building enterprises. In 1350 he founded the Cistercian Abbey of St Mary Graces beside the Tower, in order to celebrate yet another safe delivery from a storm at sea.[19] This was swept away in the Reformation. So too was the nunnery at Dartford. His palaces at Eltham, Sheen, King's Langley, Queenborough and Moor End (Northamptonshire) and his extensions of Nottingham Castle have disappeared without trace.[20] Of his house at Rotherhithe, only the foundations are visible. Hadleigh Castle is just rubble and jagged ruins.

His work rebuilding Eltham Palace, begun in 1350, lasted for ten years and cost over £2,237. His work there included new lodgings for the royal family, and passages between the king's great chamber and the queen's. He rebuilt the encircling wall, repaired the halls (plural), king's chapel and gatehouses, added a new drawbridge, kitchen, roasting house, saucery, larder and oratory.[21] He restocked and repaired the garden and improved the vineyard. This is an interesting reference to the cultivation of vines in fourteenth-century England which is mirrored in similar payments at the gardens and vineyard at Windsor Castle, from which wine continued to be produced good enough for royal consumption until the end of the reign.

After 1350, Edward began building on a scale which, if not unprecedented, certainly equalled anything previously seen in Britain. In 1351 he acquired Henley from John Molyns and started rebuilding the royal residence there. Having paid £550 for it, he then spent £785 under the watchful eye of William of Wykeham on the principal dwellings.[22] Two years later he commenced work at Rotherhithe, on the south bank of the River Thames. There he spent £1,064 over the next three years on a fine house with a wharf, gardens and vineyards, this to be a convenient stopping-off point on his journeys into Kent. The foundations of this house are still extant, but that is all. The accounts for the garden have survived much better, including the list of seeds, plants and compost purchased.[23] In 1354 he began to rebuild substantial parts of the manor of Woodstock, where his eldest son and daughter had been born. It was particularly with his wife and eldest daughter in mind that he rebuilt a new chamber for the queen and a balcony outside Isabella's suite of rooms so that she might have a view of the park.[24] A few years later he spent more than £500 reconstructing part of Rosamund's Bower, the legendary trysting place of Henry II and his favourite mistress at Woodstock.

The above building programme is remarkable for the fact that it took place alongside the expenditure of more than £5,000 every year at Windsor, and about £1,000 each year at Westminster. In addition there were repairs to all the other royal buildings. In his determination to create a clean, ordered image for his dynasty, Edward spent large amounts of money just maintaining his predecessors' castles and palaces. Quite apart from all the major works he undertook, in the course of his reign he carried out extensive repairs to the castles of Cambridge, Carisbrooke, Carlisle, Corfe, Dover, Gloucester, Guildford, Leeds, the Tower of London (including the construction of the Cradle Tower and the wharf), Ludgershall, Odiham, Porchester, Rochester, Rockingham, Scarborough, Somerton, Wallingford and Winchester.[25] Houses built by his grandfather Edward I, such as Clarendon Palace and Havering, were also extensively repaired.[26] And the most significant and original constructions were yet to come.

At Nottingham Castle in 1358 a major programme of remodelling and repair began, costing more than a thousand pounds. The most obvious result was the construction of Romylow's Tower, the rebuilding and reglazing of the chapels, the rebuilding of the king's kitchen, the queen's hall, the constable's hall and the great kitchen. All of this work was destroyed in the early seventeenth century.[27] In the same year he began work at his great palace of Sheen, near Richmond, at which William of Wykeham administered more than £2,000 on an exquisite new royal house, with fishponds, gardens, tiled courtyards, and chambers with large fireplaces, glazing in the windows, and another one of Edward's favourite additions to any residence: a 'roasting house', somewhere for his meat to be spit-roasted.[28] Edward's work at Sheen was probably entirely destroyed by Richard II after his wife died there in 1394.[29] Anything left standing was destroyed by fire in 1499.

In February 1359, Edward started work on remodelling his father's favourite house at King's Langley. There he spent more than three thousand pounds, including the rebuilding of the bath house. Bathing was a high priority of Edward's, as with other medieval kings. The water supply to the bathroom in the Palace of Westminster had been controlled by bronze taps in the shape of leopards, probably attached to metal cisterns, since at least 1275.[30] Edward II had had the bathroom tiled. But hot water itself in these places had had to be heated in earthenware pots in a furnace, and then poured into a cistern in the bathroom. At Westminster in 1351 Edward made a breakthrough, introducing what was probably the first English bathroom with hot and cold running water, with one bronze tap for hot and another for cold.[31] This was the system he seems to have replicated at King's Langley, where the accounts record a payment for a 'large square lead for heating water'. This hot water would then have been piped – several of his accounts record payments for pipes – into the bathroom, and, having 'turned the water on' (by giving the order for the furnace near the cistern to be lit), he could then control the flow of hot and cold water into his bath as he desired.[32] Sadly Edward's bath house and all the splendid buildings which he, his father and grandfather had built at King's Langley were allowed to fall down by the Tudors. Henry VIII's wives were each granted the manor but spent nothing on it, and what remained was demolished in the seventeenth century.

It was also in 1359 that Edward began work on Hadleigh Castle. Parts of this do survive – a few jagged pieces of tower masonry – but nothing of the great royal apartments which were the focus of Edward's attention. Over the next ten years he spent more than £2,300 on the castle, creating an Essex shoreline residence to balance his planned Kentish shore residence on the Isle of Sheppey.[33] By this stage Edward was beginning to link all his multi-thousand pound residences along the water of the Thames. From Windsor, his chivalric palace, he could travel by royal barge to Isleworth (which he repaired) and Sheen (which he was rebuilding) to Westminster, the Tower of London, and Rotherhithe, a short ride from Eltham.[34] It only required him to add his Isle of Sheppey residence and Gravesend manor for him to have a whole suite of royal palaces and castles which he could reach swiftly. These he began in the early 1360s. In 1362 he acquired the manor of Gravesend from the earl of Suffolk and began yet another lavish building, spending more than £1,350 over the next five years on improving the royal chambers and facilities and decorating the buildings he retained.[35]

If any loss is to be lamented as much as St Stephen's Chapel, it is Queenborough Castle. It was the only new royal castle of the later middle ages and it is remarkable in that it was the last truly military English royal residence. Edward himself took a key role in overseeing the works.[36] This in itself was nothing new: he always had involved himself personally with his acts of patronage, from laying the foundation stone of William Montagu's priory at Bisham (a foundation plaque for which still survives) to overseeing the rebuilding of Roxburgh, Eltham and Windsor.[37] What is interesting about Queenborough is that it seems to have been Edward's own statement in stone about his ideas of defensive building. It was, in some senses, an amusement, almost to show off that he could design a building which was as militarily strong as his grandfather's castles in North Wales or Richard the Lionheart's Château Gaillard (none of which Edward had seen for himself, incidentally).

There is no castle quite like Queenborough. Moreover, there *was* nothing quite like it, for today not a single stone survives.[38] It is known from one seventeenth-century survey and an Elizabethan plan. Work began in spring 1361, Edward himself being present at the start. It was basically an enormously strong encircling wall, three hundred feet in diameter, with no towers except those overlooking the two gates. These gates, which were opposite one another, led into the castle, but not in a usual way. The main gate led to a passage which gave no access to the central part of the great fortress. Instead it acted as a barbican: anyone breaking through the main gate would have found himself trapped in this area, susceptible to arrows and other objects being thrown at him from above, on all sides. If an attacker had escaped from this he would only have been able to reach the outer court. This circular, outward-looking court, which circled the high central part of the castle and its six great circular towers, was built largely to house the trebuchets and the cannon which guarded the sea approach to London. In 1365 Edward installed two great cannon and nine small ones here, making it one of his three permanent artillery fortifications along with Dover (where there were nine cannon by 1371) and Calais (where there were fifteen).[39] The postern gate also was guarded by a barbican, but this one gave way to the inner court of the central stronghold. It was around this inner court that the king's residence was planned. Thus at Queenborough as nowhere else we have the culmination of the royal castle as a palace, fortification and gun emplacement, an architectural master-piece which 'exemplifies the principles of cylindrical and concentric forti-fication carried to their logical conclusion with perfect symmetry'.[40] It cost Edward over twenty-five thousand pounds. He might have thought that such a huge and impressive construction would guarantee its permanence. Alas, its defensive foresight was probably its undoing. Although the mid-seventeenth-century parliamentary commissioners thought its potential as a gun emplacement was small, its concentric self-protection meant that it was too powerful and strategically important to risk letting it fall into enemy hands even at that late date. Parliament ordered it to be pulled down.

*

In the layout of Queenborough and the creation of the naval gun emplace-ment we can see that a technological mind was at work. In the luxury of the hot and cold running water in the bathrooms at Westminster and King's Langley, we can see a similar technological approach. If we knew nothing about Edward and his strategies and patronage of guns and his adapting of longbow crossfire as a fighting method, we might wonder whether these developments were not due to his capable advisers. But the point at which all these technological developments meet is Edward himself. And this brings us to Edward's key area of patronage which has most defi-nitely lasted. The use of the mechanical clock.

The earliest mechanical clock in Europe for which we have clear evidence is often said to be the one put up at Milan in 1335. Earlier attempts to make a mechanical clock, using a weight and ratchet system, were certainly underway in the late thirteenth century, for in 1271 it was recorded that clockmakers were trying to make a wheel which would make exactly one full turn every day.[41] Early in his reign (probably in 1332) Edward saw for himself the realisation of such ideas when he stopped by the monastery of St Albans and found the abbot, Richard Wallingford, building his clock.[42] Wallingford had succeeded in making a machine which both chimed regular hours and showed the movements of the sun and stars. At the time Edward did not recognise the importance of this, especially as it was apparent that the abbot was neglecting his spiritual duties. But by the early 1350s he realised he had been wrong. In 1352 he paid three Italians – one described as 'the master of the clock' – to make him a mechanical timepiece in London. This and a suitable bell on which it would regularly chime the hours were transported from London to Windsor and set up in the great tower there. It had no face but rang the intervals hourly.[43]

Edward's first mechanical clock is a very interesting development in itself, but, when one thinks of the social implications of regulating time in this period, it suddenly becomes apparent that Edward was at the forefront of a profound European revolution. Medieval people divided the day into the twelve hours of the night and the twelve hours of the day. The day started with daylight: so each of the twelve 'hours' of daylight in summer was approximately twice as long as an 'hour' of daylight in winter. Edward, in introducing a regular timepiece, was attempting to standardise time. Moreover he was doing this in his own castle in Berkshire within fifteen years of the introduction of the practice in one of the most advanced cities at the heart of Renaissance Italy. There is something remarkable about this, especially in a war leader. Nor was it just an idle experiment. The clock at Windsor lasted, so that it needed a new bell by 1377 (at which date it was described as being called 'clokke', the earliest recorded use of the English word, derived from the French word *cloche*, meaning 'bell'). Long before then Edward had purchased additional mechanical bell-striking clocks for his palaces at Westminster and Langley (notably the two palaces with hot and cold running water) and his great castle at Queenborough. At Westminster he built a bell tower to contain a great bell inscribed 'Edward'. This weighed four tons, rang the hour at Westminster for more than three hundred years, and has been described as the original 'Big Ben'.[44] The implication of all this is that he was regulating his household and his own life not around the traditional long and short hours of the day but with a standard unit of time measurement.

Although none of Edward's clocks have survived, they nevertheless had an important cultural influence. In the same way, his buildings, paintings and other commissions – even his long-lost plate and costumes – had an influence. Just as Edward's preference for mechanically regulated hours was soon adopted by others, with mechanical clocks being introduced at Salisbury Cathedral in 1386 and Wells Cathedral in about 1390, and soon after that elsewhere around the country, so too his vanished palaces affected architectural development in later generations. Hence it would be foolish to say that his buildings or costumes are somehow less important because they have not survived to this day.

This draws our attention to those other aspects of Edward's cultural patronage which have been obscured by destruction. Literature was never thought to be an area in which Edward scored highly except in regard to his employment of Chaucer. So when one modern scholar discovered that Edward kept a library of one hundred and sixty books at the Tower of London, not counting his books kept in other places, and that these were regularly loaned out to members of the court, the view of Edward as anti-scholarly and unbookish was exposed as a presumption based mainly on a lack of evidence.[45] Also, among the books borrowed by Isabella in 1327 were a history of the Normans and Vegetius's *De Re Militari*, then the best-known and most trusted military guidebook of all. Isabella had no interest in warfare, but her fourteen-year-old son certainly did. Moreover, there is plenty of evidence which suggests that Edward *was* bookish. In 1335 he gave the huge sum of one hundred marks (£66 13s 4d) to Isabella of Lancaster, a nun at Amesbury, for a book which he kept for his own use.[46] He borrowed books too; we know this because he often failed to return them.[47] Some lavishly illuminated texts carry the arms of England and Hainault, and can therefore be said to have been commissioned by him or his wife, or presented to them.[48] Edward's wardrobe accounts also mention romances given as occasional gifts, and list many liturgical books (graduals, missals, antiphons, chorals, martyrologies and gospels).[49] That three or four of these are psalters accords with the idea that Edward himself only normally commissioned books for routine liturgical use or extravagant display. Texts containing historical information which he wanted he either borrowed or purchased from other magnates or ecclesiastical libraries.

This attitude to the latent power of books – which, incidentally, is not dissimilar to that of his intellectual mentor Richard Bury – is amplified by Edward's attitude to learning. The borrowing of a book on the history of Normandy mentioned above quite possibly relates to his own research, as he would have had to know something of the history of Normandy in order to spin the lines he did on the Crécy campaign. In 1332 he paid a clerk to sit down and read through all of Domesday Book to work out which towns had once been royal: not because of any sentiment but so he could think about how to tax them.[50] History was simply a requirement of a king. But his knowledge went further than just kingly necessaries. His interests extended beyond religion, military strategy and good kingship to history and alchemy (an interest he shared with his mother and the earl of Lancaster).[51] His summoning of two alchemists who claimed to have made silver, 'whether they would come willingly or not', should not be taken as a sign of pure covetousness. It should be remembered that a major alchemical text was dedicated to him.[52] Given Edward's propensity to give books away, and considering the destruction of most medieval manuscripts in the sixteenth century, the non-existence today of a magnificent library of beautifully illuminated royal texts owned by Edward cannot be taken as evidence that his court was an anti-intellectual one, or that Edward himself was not interested in the extension of knowledge. We only need to reflect on Edward's foundation of King's Hall at Cambridge, and Philippa's foundation of Queen's Hall at Oxford, to remind ourselves that this was a court which valued learning.

One vivid extension of this interest in the natural world is to be seen in Edward's collection of wild animals. Edward kept a large menagerie of wild beasts, especially large cats, and even paid for them to be taken with him around the country. In 1333 a payment was recorded 'to the keeper of the king's leopards', and the following year the Italian merchant Dino Forzetti was paid for providing Edward with an additional two lions, three leopards and a mountain cat. In 1334 he took these animals north with him when he moved the royal household to York, and kept them there until he turned his attention to France (at which time they returned to the Tower of London). He also owned a bear, given to him several years earlier by King David of Scotland.[53] In later years the royal menagerie was supplemented by gifts of wild leopards and lions, including a gift of live animals from the Black Prince in 1365. Of course, nothing of the royal menagerie remains. But even the idea of Edward III as a collector of rare species has been eclipsed by the knowledge that Henry III had an elephant. That all these beasts were kept at the Tower of London is interesting, as there too was the royal lending library. The Tower of London as a resort of learning is perhaps one of the more unpredictable images to arise from a study of the life and interests of Edward III.

So what does survive of Edward's cultural patronage which we can pick up and see for ourselves today? The answer is precious little. Almost no trace remains of the music of his court, only the payments to his minstrels and the odd motet.[54] Of all the hundreds of gold and silver enamelled cups and goblets which we read about in the royal records, probably only one example of the type from his reign is still in existence. This belongs to King's Lynn, and, ironically, is known as the King John cup, as a result of a confusion with the king who granted King's Lynn its charter.[55] Hardly any cloth survives, except some parts of a horse trapper and some eccle-siastical vestments of the period. All the fantastic gold- and silver-embroi-dered tournament aketons and other chivalric garments have gone. As for jewellery, of all the choice items which are extant, none can be associated personally with Edward. Some texts survive but these do not make light reading. Rather it is in the literary creations encouraged by the successes of his reign that we may find cultural importance, the poetical works of Chaucer, Gower and Langland, the histories of his exploits in the works of le Baker, Froissart, Gray, Murimuth, Avesbury and the author and trans-lator of the longer *Brut*, and the imaginative works, such as the *Travels of Sir John Mandeville* of which various copies are known with supposed dedi-cations to Edward.

Certain artistic works do attest to his patronage. The most glittering and untarnished today are the coins of the realm, in particular the gold coins. From 1344 many attempts were made to establish a successful gold coinage, resulting in a number of highly worked designs: variations on the theme of the king in his boat and a geometrical design on the reverse. In 1351 a new attempt to improve the gold and silver coinage resulted in the renewal of the old silver groat of his grandfather and the introduction of an especially fine series of gold nobles. Of course the skills of the artist who constructs a die for a gold coin are not dissimilar from the skills required to create a seal matrix, and Edward's reign set a new high for that particular art form, not least in his own great seal of the 1360s (the Brétigny seal). To quote the standard work on the subject: 'this remark-ably beautiful seal marks the culminating point of excellence in design and execution in the series of Gothic great seals of England'.[56] In the absence of his architectural achievements, his armour, his clothes, his paintings, his music, his jewellery, his ornaments, his books and his clocks, it is perhaps these small items which give us our most unadulterated glimpse of his artistic and cultural patronage.

There is one further opportunity for us to gaze upon the art of Edward III's kingship. This is his tomb, and the tombs of his wife, brother and eldest son, and to a lesser extent the tombs of his infant children. In some ways it is the most obvious medium to last, and yet in others it is not. Many royal tombs of the period have suffered: those of Queen Isabella and Lionel of Antwerp were lost in the Dissolution of the Monasteries, that of John of Gaunt was lost in the Great Fire of London.[57] But the very highest art of Edward's patronage may be seen in his son's tomb at Canterbury and the two splendid tombs at Westminster. At Canterbury we may look at the prince's armour, and see the sculptured relief of his face. We cannot tell how exact the likeness is but, such is the quality of the work, we can believe that we do see a true representation of the man. We may do the same at Warwick, where the tomb of Thomas Beachamp, earl of Warwick, and his wife Catherine survives intact, replete with a full set of weepers, including portrait images of the Black Prince and probably Edward himself.[58] At Westminster, looking at Edward's and Philippa's faces, we may be sure we look at likenesses. The figure on Edward's tomb monument was sculpted to be realistic, and only tidied slightly. It was based on a death-mask, which is still extant.[59] Philippa's stout figure and friendly face were carved in marble by Jean de Liège during her own lifetime: in other words, carved from life. In this way the idealised faces which sculptors had tradi-tionally placed on dead kings' and queens' tombs came to be supplanted by the likenesses of real people. Edward and Philippa did not need to portray themselves as icons. They themselves had become iconic.

Edward's development as a cultural patron can thus be seen to have acquired many new dimensions after 1349, the year of the plague. Up until that year most of his expenditure had been on war and the culture of war (the completion of St Stephen's Chapel excepted). From 1350, the last time he actually took part in combat, most of his expenditure was on building and artistic projects for the future. With his buildings came his patronage of painters, sculptors and glaziers on a scale not witnessed in England since the reign of Henry III.[60] By 1370 Edward had spent a total of more than £130,000 on building work, and had created palaces which would continue for the rest of the middle ages to be potent emblems of his kingship.

The destruction of all this work is hence all the more surprising, and can only really be explained through the misfortune of fire and the damage of neglect, as tastes changed. That we know these buildings existed is a telling case of documents proving more durable than stones. But it is also an indication of how little we should regard what intervening centuries have thought of a dead king. Edward was the greatest English cultural patron of the later middle ages. Those who argued in the twentieth century that his claim on the throne of France was 'absurd' would have had diffi-culty denying that his preference for a clock-regulated hour and his devel-opment of the use of cannon show every indication of a logical and far-sighted mind. Those who regarded him in the nineteenth century as a brutal warmonger would probably have baulked at the thought that he also founded a Cambridge college, maintained a library, and patronised the art of the Italian Renaissance. And contemporary readers whose image of a medieval warrior-king is that of an unkempt savage might well have difficulty reconciling this image with a man who had hot and cold running water in his bathrooms.

THIRTEEN

Lawmaker

When Edward prepared to face parliament in February 1351, he was a very different man to the eighteen-year-old who had so eagerly awaited his first parliament after taking power, twenty years before. Then he had looked to the forum as a proving ground. Now he had proved everything, and parliament had bowed to his kingship. But although representatives were satisfied with his past performance, one of the developing functions of parliament was to question the king on his policy and, if possible, hold him to account. This was the first parliament he had held for three years, and only the third he had attended since 1344. His promise to hold a meeting with representatives every year was looking frail. It was also the first gathering at Westminster since the Black Death. There were men present who wanted to know what could be done to ameliorate the downturn in the kingdom's fortunes. Some may have wondered what their king had done to incur God's wrath, so that England had not been saved from the horrors of the plague. As for Edward himself, he was well aware that the peace in France would not hold. The new French king, John, was bound to try his luck, hoping to show himself more successful in battle than his father. So Edward faced a difficult task. He needed to buy back public confidence, and to reassure parliament, but at the same time he had to convince a country just emerging from economic collapse to grant him a further subsidy towards the war.

This is, on the surface, how things stood in February 1351. But such an analysis pays no attention to how Edward himself had changed. As Edward's cultural patronage shows, after 1350 he was less anxious to fight and more interested in creating permanent structures. In Shakespeare's famous analogy, Edward was emerging from the fourth age of man, the soldier, 'jealous in honour, sudden and quick in quarrel, seeking the bubble reputation even in the cannon's mouth' and entering the fifth, the justice 'with eyes severe and beard of formal cut'. He said as much in his opening address at that parliament. 'We desire always to do right to our people and to correct wrongs and defaults wherever they may be found in our realm.'[1]

From Tuesday 15 February Edward began to hear petitions. The first asked him to confirm Magna Carta and the statutes of his ancestors and to revoke the subsidy on the country because of the plague.² Predictably enough, Edward agreed to the confirmation of the law but refused to relinquish the tax. The next petition asked him to prevent labourers neglecting their manorial dues in the wake of the plague. Edward responded that a statute would follow. This is interesting: although the remedy to the problem had been devised eighteen months earlier, in the Ordinance of Labourers, it was as a result of a petition in parliament that it became enshrined in law.³ No less significant was the next petition, which begged Edward to prevent papal appointments to English benefices. Parliament objected to overseas clergy taking the income from their English benefices without even visiting the country. This, of course, had been a cornerstone of Edward's policy since 1344. But whereas then he had merely tried to prevent overseas clergy from taking their positions, now in the Statute of Provisors he made the pope's provisions illegal.⁴ A little later another important petition was presented, requesting the return to free trade, a theme from an earlier parliament. Edward assented, and so the Statute of Free Trade was placed firmly on the law books.⁵ Three of the most important statutes of the fourteenth century were thus agreed in principle over a couple of mornings' debate.

Edward's professed desire 'to do right' at that parliament pushed justice high up his list of priorities. This raised some spectres from the past. One was Richard Fitzalan, earl of Arundel, whose father Edmund had been done to death by Roger Mortimer without trial way back in 1326. He now wanted confirmation of his inheritance and assurance it would pass to his heirs.⁶ Similarly, hovering in the background, was Sir John Maltravers. In June his outlawry was annulled. These were old misjudgements which required correction, which Edward was pleased to consider.⁷ Justice of a different sort was needed in the case of Chief Justice William Thorp, who had been arrested and found guilty of corruption the previous year. Edward had declared that corrupt officials would face death, so that was the sentence looming over him when he came to parliament in 1351. Edward, always prepared to order the most extreme punishment, was not always eager to see it carried out. He was therefore looking to remit the death penalty. Thorp was tried before his peers and found guilty, but not sentenced to death. Some years later he was given the chance to redeem himself, and entered Edward's service again.

From all points of view, the parliament of 1351 was a success. Edward managed to secure his wool subsidy for a further two years, despite pleas not to levy it because of the plague. Those deserving justice received it, those requiring the correction of injustices mostly were satisfied, and those putting forward petitions for new laws were mostly rewarded with a positive result. Questions remained in the air about financial burdens and taxation, but the accommodation reached was acceptable to parliament. So it was fitting that, at the end of the parliament, Edward held a second mass creation of higher lords. Harking back to the parliament of 1337, when he had made six earls and a duke, he now created three earls and a duke. Henry of Lancaster now became the duke of Lancaster, in honour of his great achievements in Gascony. Edward's sons Lionel and John were officially granted the titles held for them since infancy: Earl of Ulster and Earl of Richmond. And Ralph Stafford was raised from his barony to become the earl of Stafford. None of these lords were new, in the sense that they were commoners beforehand, but nevertheless, the raising of three men to comital rank, and the raising of Henry to a dukedom, were all in keeping with the style and largesse of a king whose reign was beginning to be viewed in terms of greatness.

*

Not long after King Philip died, Edward had asked the pope to appoint an English cardinal. To put an English voice among the many French ones at Avignon would have been a very sensible move, at least partly correcting the massive pro-French bias there. The pope had responded with a request for Edward to put forward two suitable candidates. Edward suggested William Bateman, the bishop of Norwich, and Ralph Stratford, the bishop of London. The pope, however, saw fit to throw sand in all their faces. On 17 December 1350, in the presence of the newly crowned King John II of France, the twelve cardinals he created included eight more Frenchmen, three Spaniards and one Italian. The English candidates were ignored.[8] In this light it is not surprising that Edward was keen to pass the subsequent petition for a statute prohibiting papal appointments.

French antagonism was extreme in 1351. The feeling in France – and the fear in England – was that King John needed to begin his reign by taking the fight to the English. In March the French won a minor symbolic victory in Brittany in the 'Battle of the Thirty', a joust between thirty French and thirty English and Breton knights. Another blow was struck for French pride when Sir Thomas Dagworth was ambushed and murdered. But it was the English under Sir John Cheverstone who won the more important victory at Saintes on 1 April 1351, capturing the French commander Guy de Nesle. Unfortunately de Nesle was soon ransomed, and the French reversed the English success by capturing the strategic fortress of Saint-Jean-d'Angély, which had been in English hands since its capture by Lancaster in 1346. The English responded with a few raids in Brittany under Dagworth's successor, Sir Walter Bentley, and around Calais under

Lord Manny. It was a situation which could not be called war, yet it was hardly peace.

Then disaster struck. The English garrison of Calais, commanded by John Beauchamp, was ambushed on its way back from a raid. Beauchamp and several other knights were taken prisoner, leaving Calais undefended. The news was immediately taken to England, where Edward was already concerned about an imminent Flemish switch of allegiance to supporting the French king. Emissaries were promptly sent out in all directions. The duke of Lancaster was sent to negotiate with the count of Flanders, heir to the count killed at Crécy, who was more acceptable to his people than his father. Lancaster was told even to offer the hand in marriage of John of Gaunt if it was necessary. The bishop of Norwich and the earl of Huntingdon were despatched to France to seek a permanent peace, hoping thereby to stave off a French advance until Calais could be secured. Edward himself set about raising an army as quickly as he could to secure the town. But the English position was weak. The count of Flanders openly went to King John and threw off his allegiance to England. It was just as well that Bishop Bateman and the earl of Huntingdon were able to secure a truce in September. Edward had suffered two setbacks – Saint-Jean-d'Angély and the Flemish alliance – and King John was able to celebrate in November by establishing a chivalric order of his own, the Order of the Star.

*

Edward was undoubtedly relieved not to be going to war in 1351, and he quickly cancelled his plans to take an army to Calais. The amount he was spending on construction at Windsor, Westminster, Calais, Eltham and Henley could not easily be transferred to fund-raising for war. Nevertheless the encroachments and raids of 1351 had alerted him to the dangers of ploughing all his resources into stone and all his time into hunting and domestic politics. A serious attempt to achieve permanent peace with Scotland was on the point of collapse, even when King David was allowed to leave the Tower of London in February 1352 to return to Scotland to try to persuade his subjects to accept Edward's proposals.[9] A message from France in January reminded Edward very forcibly that there might still be occasions when war would prove advantageous. Edward was thus once more mulling over the prospect of war and its costs as parliament arrived at Westminster.

The parliament of 1352 marks a particularly high point in the relationship between fourteenth-century kings and the country's representatives. A long list of petitions was presented by the representatives in the expectation that Edward would be asking for several years of direct taxation.

In the past, parliament had been asked to agree to taxes in the belief that the king would then, afterwards, listen to their petitions. This time, the order of things was altered. Edward's Chief Justice, Sir William Shareshull, positively encouraged parliament to prepare petitions for Edward to right wrongs or to amend the law. When parliament eventually came back to Edward the deal was that they would agree to the taxation on the condition that he gave a prompt and favourable reply to their petitions.[10]

Edward could not be forced into granting petitions, and it remained up to him whether he accepted the deal or not. In theory, he could have simply imposed taxation and refused any and all terms. But there was an excitement about parliament at this time, and the way it was developing held an attraction for Edward too. The petitions presented to him in 1352 contained a ready-made legislative programme, setting straight a large number of outstanding legal matters going right back to the beginning of the reign. The question of preventing feudal aids being levied without parliamentary consent was raised, so was the problem of purveyors for the royal household abusing their positions, and the enforcement of standard weights and measures throughout the country. Debts owing by Italian merchants, sub-standard coinage, the abuses of forest keepers, and the practice of levying men-at-arms from large non-feudal properties were openly discussed. Edward assented to all of these petitions and many others. In fact, every one of the twenty-three chapters of the great statute of 1352 directly related to the list of petitions handed to Edward by parliament. The laws themselves may have been precisely worded by Edward's civil servants but it cannot be denied that Edward had listened to parliament's demands. Parliament had effectively listed what it considered were Edward's legislative shortcomings to date, and Edward – always eager to be seen in a good light – had done what he could to correct them.

In the midst of this long list of laws were several very important pieces of legislation. There was a new Statute of the Clergy and a law allowing for the payment of fines by those guilty of breaking the Statute of Labourers to go towards reducing the amount of direct taxation necessary. But without any doubt the most important statute made at this parliament was the great Statute of Treasons.[11]

Given the large number of treason trials and executions which took place in the first twenty years of Edward's life, it is surprising that treason had never previously been defined or codified. The word tended to be bandied around very loosely, its references only connected through a sense of a criminal betrayal of trust. But it was clear to all that a servant who murdered his master was not guilty of the same crime as a magnate who went to war with the king. A statute was required to distinguish between general or petty treason and high treason, which was an act against the king and his government. The statute was also required to define exactly what constituted an act against the king. The result was a very interesting list of crimes, in which Edward and his justices referred back to the deeds of Roger Mortimer.[12] Thus we read that High Treason was when a man 'considered or imagined' the death of the king,[13] or of his queen, or their eldest son and heir, or if he violated the queen, the king's eldest unmarried daughter or the wife of his eldest son, or if he went to war with the king in his realm, or adhered to the king's enemies, or if he killed the Chancellor or the Treasurer, or the king's justices, when they were performing their office.[14] These parts of the statute are still in force today. Other parts subsequently repealed state that High Treason included counterfeiting the king's great or privy seal, or coinage of the realm.

Many writers have found it surprising that the Statute of Treasons was passed in 1352, after twenty-five years of Edward's reign, at the very point when the English monarchy was at its most secure. It had been many years since treason had been a feature of the political landscape. But there was an obvious reason, obvious to contemporaries at least. Sir John Maltravers had been found guilty of treason in his absence; now he had been forgiven. Arundel's father had been declared guilty of treason and was found wrongfully adjudged to have been sentenced. The same could be said for Kent in 1330. What crime was it that these men had committed? For if it could be so easily reversed, was treason anything more than going against the king's will? In this new, parliamentary age, it was very dangerous if political representatives could be judged guilty of treason for simply disobeying the king.

It thus appears that the Statute of Treasons was a logical consequence of Edward's determination to rule fairly for all, including the survivors of the dictatorship of Mortimer. This is certainly the way that most modern scholars understand it.[15] Yet we should not presume that there was no more to it than that. It cannot escape a biographer's attention that in these years 1351–54 Edward revisited the events of 1327–30 several times. Maltravers himself returned from Flanders. The Arundel estates were restored and the dead earl pardoned. In 1352 Edward summoned the chronicler Ranulph Higden, one of the most popular chroniclers of the period, to come to a meeting of the great council 'with all your chronicles and those in your charge to speak and treat with the council concerning matters to be explained to you on our behalf'.[16] The same year a special inquiry was ordered to find out whether the archbishop of Cashel (Ireland) had fulfilled his side of a bargain to endow six chaplains in his cathedral to celebrate masses for Edward II.[17] The following year,

1353, Edward himself revisited his father's tomb at Gloucester and remained in the area for about a month.[18] In an unprecedented move he sent his sons to celebrate that year's anniversary of the 'death' of Edward II at Gloucester (he being unable to attend in person due to a council meeting at Westminster on the 23rd). He also paid for offerings to be made on behalf of the dead at Gloucester on the following day, and gave gifts of gold spinet to lay on the tomb on the 24th.[19] Most interesting of all, he seems to have made two visits to Leintwardine in September and November 1353. Leintwardine was a small, out-of-the-way place in north-west Herefordshire, a long way off Edward's usual routes, especially as he usually confined himself these days to the Thames valley. But Leintwardine was where the elder Roger Mortimer had founded a collegiate chantry to sing masses for himself and his family and Edward and the royal family. It was the place in which the souls of Edward II, Edward III and Mortimer were united. In September Edward gave a cloth of gold at the statue of the Virgin there, and in early November he may have made a second visit to Leintwardine to make an offering at the same figure.[20] Finally in 1354, Roger Mortimer the grandson presented a petition in parliament to have all the processes against his grandfather tried. Edward cannot have been surprised by this, and must have discussed it with the heir in advance, for he not only granted the petition, he went so far as to reverse *all* the accusations against the grandfather on the basis that he had not had a fair trial. At the same time he restored to the grandson the title of Earl of March which the grandfather had outrageously demanded in 1328. Had he wished merely to honour the grandson, he could have granted him a new, less contentious title. But with that reversal of his judgement on Mortimer, Edward was finally able to let go of the terrible events of 1330. It seems clear that, from Edward's point of view, the Statute of Treasons was part of a wider revisiting of the past, and was not just a legal formality, as usually thought. We might sum up the personal dimension by saying that, having legally codified what constituted a threat to the Crown, Edward could now wipe the slate clean, and reverse those injustices, semi-injustices and dubious measures which he had been forced to commit in 1330 to enforce his royal authority.

*

While the parliament of 1352 was still assembling, Edward received some extraordinary news, which, problematic though it was, must have made him smile. Despite the truce, an English squire called John Dancaster had led an attack on the castle of Guines. Guines was six miles to the south of Calais, considered impregnable, and the greatest threat to the security of the English town. On the night of the attack, the castle commander was being honoured as a founder member of the new Order of the Star. As the commander of Guines ate off a gold plate in King John's presence, Dancaster and a few other squires in service at Calais, with their faces blackened, climbed over the walls into Guines, killing the sentries and seizing the castle. It was an almost-unbelievable piece of good fortune. But Edward could not ignore that it was a violation of the truce. It had been French emissaries – not an English messenger – who had brought the news to him. Dancaster was refusing to say in whose name he was defending Guines.

It was a serious problem. On the one hand it was so tempting to acknowledge Dancaster's victory as an English success. On the other hand, to resume the war at this juncture was not Edward's highest priority. It threatened to jeopardise his domestic projects. It would also place him very clearly in the wrong, for Edward's justification of the war had arisen in response to Philip's antagonisms, not John's. John was only Edward's enemy because he was his father's son, and thus bound to lead the French in war. On the other hand it could be argued that the French had abused the truce in the same way as Dancaster, when they had attacked and seized Saint-Jean-d'Angély the previous year. As parliament was assembling, Edward took the opportunity to present the question to the representatives. Those who spoke on the matter in his presence were all for war. Edward decided to follow their advice and his own inclination, and to keep Guines. To the dismay of the French, he pardoned Dancaster for any wrongdoing and rewarded him.[21]

The French reaction was immediately to fight. An army assembled at Rennes in Brittany under Guy de Nesle, intended to besiege Ploërmel; another assembled at Saint-Jean-d'Angély and Saintes, and a third assembled near Guines.[22] Edward's response was slow, far slower than it should have been. He underestimated the fury that his decision would unleash. In early March he appointed the newly created earl of Stafford to take command in Gascony. But it was not until 20 April that Sir Walter Bentley was ordered to survey the castles of Brittany and put them in a defensive state. Although the Genoese were already fighting for John in Brittany, only on 6 May did Edward ask them not to assist his enemy. Eventually, on 24 May the writs went out to draw spearmen from Wales and archers from the English counties. Even then Edward was cautious about getting too deeply involved. He waited another three weeks before ordering the coast to be readied for war and equipping fifteen ships for the forthcoming crossing. He seems to have been deeply reluctant to take the necessary steps to fight in France in 1352.[23]

When the English defence did get under way, it proved stunningly effective. A contingent from Calais joined the men at Guines in attacking the French and burning their siege engines, so that the French commander Geoffrey de Charny was eventually forced to retreat. In Gascony, Stafford was successful in striking panic into the hearts of the citizens of Agen, and won a battle at Marmande in August in which he captured seven knights of the new Order of the Star.[24] He then proceeded to relieve the siege of Taillebourg. But the most successful of all was Sir Walter Bentley in Brittany. He relieved the siege of Ploërmel before Guy de Nesle could stop him and then met de Nesle face-to-face on a hill near Mauron, on 14 August 1352. When de Nesle saw how few men Bentley had – the chronicler Avesbury estimated about six hundred – and that they were drawn up in the open, with no protection, no water, no woods, nothing to save them at all, he offered the English the chance to surrender honourably.[25] But Bentley was the successor in office to the famous and fearless Sir Thomas Dagworth, and his reputation was at stake. There was no such thing as an honourable surrender in Brittany. De Nesle ordered his men to advance on foot, hoping to overwhelm the English through force of numbers. The armies clashed 'between the hour of vespers and sunset' and the result was very bloody. Bentley commanded from the front and was himself badly wounded. But the English were victorious. It was yet another extraordinary English success: when his men piled up the surcoats to count the number of dead they reckoned they had killed one hundred and forty knights and five hundred esquires, plus an uncounted number of footsoldiers. A further hundred and sixty men of rank were captured. As the chronicler Geoffrey le Baker noted, the reason why the number of dead knights was so high was because there had been a large number of knights of the Order of the Star present, and at their inaugural feast they had sworn never to retreat. It might have been a noble promise in the hall, but King John's knights paid dearly on the battlefield for giving up one of the most practical of all military manoeuvres.[26]

*

In 1352 Edward held a great ceremony at Windsor to celebrate Christmas. He had just turned forty, which was well into middle-age by medieval standards. For this year's celebrations thirteen devils' costumes were ordered, thirteen Dominican friars' costumes and thirteen merchants' costumes. Edward himself was decked out in a robe embroidered with gold falcons. This would all have no more meaning for us than the most obscure of the games of earlier years if it were not for a single rare manuscript survival. An East Midlands poet seems to have been present at this or a similar games soon afterwards, and was inspired by the occasion to write a poem on the economic state of England.[27]

Poems about economic theory are exceptionally rare, and this one is unique in English medieval history. It is a sophisticated allegory. The poet dreams that he sees two armies come together, and overseeing them is Edward 'worthier in wit than anyone else / to advise, to read and to rule the anger / that both armies had in hatred for the other'. Edward is described as 'the comeliest king crowned with gold' and takes his seat on a silk-covered bench in a pavilion, which is decked out in red with gold bezants and blue garters. High in the canopies are woven the words 'Evil to him who thinks evil of it', the motto of the Order of the Garter. Then the tournament begins. One army is led by 'Winner' and is made up of merchants, lawyers and friars. The other is led by 'Waster' and is composed of men-at-arms and esquires. 'Winner' on behalf of the lawyers, merchants and friars declares his hatred for 'Waster', and accuses the men-at-arms and esquires of spending their money frivolously on drink, good food and having a good time.

This allows us to see the probable format of Edward's regular games and entertainments, so well recorded with regard to clothing but so poorly described as to actual proceedings. Edward was regally on show, presiding, as if he were viewing a tournament. But rather than actually fighting with lances and armour, the armies of protagonists were making declarations in their various costumes. Edward's games in this instance seem to be a form of drama. It is of course possible that the costumes were for specific people to assume other identities for the sake of parody. But the overriding impression is that of political commentary. As we have already seen, satire, especially when it involved the power of the pope, was appealing to Edward.

The poem is also interesting in that it gives us an insight as to how a well-informed and well-connected political commentator viewed the social changes of the first half of Edward's reign. The rising professionals are presented as competing on an equal footing with the landed gentry. This is a novelty in itself; previously the gentry had stood socially head and shoulders above the merchants and all but the most eminent lawyers. It is a recognition of Edward's own policies to date, extending parliamentary power into the gentry and merchant classes, knighting merchants, permitting wealthy men and their families to dress like lords. But if we look at what the poem is really saying, we see there are great tensions arising from this. On one level there is a complaint against the uselessness and selfishness of the old feudal aristocracy, somewhat redundant as a fighting force since Crécy.[28] But the poem is even more subtle than that, for 'Waster' retorts with a devastating attack on 'Winner' and his practice of storing up money and selling goods in times of dearth. Thus this is not just a capitalist's complaint, it is a juxtaposition of the avarice of capitalism contrasted with old-fashioned lordly privilege. The moral of the story is that the rising class of merchants and lawyers are not necessarily more virtuous than those who inherit their wealth, for they will not sustain the poor or anyone else except themselves.

From our point of view, the poem is most interesting for the role the king assumes in all this disputation. Edward was most certainly a champion 'waster', in the sense that he spent more money, was more privileged, and indulged himself more frequently and to a greater extent than anyone else in the kingdom. Yet he is raised above the contest, and placed as a judge. No scandal attaches to his name, nor that of the monarchy; this is not a criticism of his kingship. Rather it is the opposite: it is a vision of society developing and changing under the king's authority. The relatively humble poet selected Edward – and no one else – to preside over this social and moral controversy. Not the pope, not the archbishop of Canterbury, or the prelates *en masse*, nor any duke, prince or combination of earls, nor the Chancellor or justices of the realm, nor the mayors. Not even God, the Devil or the poet himself. In 1352 it was Edward who was seen as the man on whom all the realm depended for its leadership and judgement. At a time of European-wide social unrest, we should not take this for granted. If 'Winner and Waster' had been written in France, we might seriously doubt whether King John would have been presented as the best man to preside over his warring estates of merchants and gentry. And if it had been written in Scotland, the less said about David II (imprisoned at the Tower), the better.

*

On 6 December 1352 Pope Clement VI died. Within days yet another Frenchman had been elected. His successor, Innocent VI, had been one of the cardinals who had approached Edward during the Crécy campaign, and had grossly underestimated the degree of respect which Edward felt he was due as a war leader and heir to the French throne, with the result that the cardinal had been dismissed from Edward's presence. Fortunately for Edward, the change of regime at Avignon also opened up an opportunity for a much younger man, Cardinal Guy of Boulogne, to take a lead in bringing England and France to the negotiating table.

Guy of Boulogne is one of those individuals about whom historians have strong opinions. To some he was quite genuine in his attempts to stop the war, to others he was a 'self-seeking courtier'.[29] There is no doubt that he tried to connect his advantageous birth – he was the son of the count of Boulogne and the uncle of the queen of France – with his peace-making ambitions. Having the ear of King John and being a cardinal made him a doubly dubious agent as far as Edward was concerned, but it did mean that someone, at last, could lay out clearly for King John exactly what was required to make Edward discuss a permanent peace. The problem was clear to him: Edward was never going to pick up the scraps under the king of France's negotiating table, and he was certainly not going to accept French overlordship of any of his hard-won lands. So land had to be given away in sovereignty first in order for the French to achieve the peace and prosperity necessary to make a new start.

Guy's initiative coincided with Edward's own ambitions for a permanent peace. As Edward ordered work to commence on his new house at Rotherhithe, the archbishop of Canterbury, the duke of Lancaster and the bishop of Norwich crossed the Channel to begin negotiations at Guines in March. What they heard – the offer of sovereignty of Gascony being given up in exchange for Edward dropping the title of king of France – was a breath of fresh air, very much in line with what they imagined Edward himself wanted. Discussions came to an end with a promise to follow them up in May 1353, along similar lines. It looked as though a permanent peace might at last be achieved.

Edward was at Eltham that Easter, overseeing the building works of his new palace, giving further directions and having the traditional great feast on Easter Day.[30] His vision of the future in France had so far amounted only to giving up Brittany to Charles de Blois (who was still his prisoner, kept at the Tower) in return for an acknowledgement that Brittany would never fight for either side.[31] A permanent peace was something he had not properly considered. Now, sixteen years after the fight had begun, he found himself pondering the question seriously for the first time. What precisely was it he wanted from the French conflict? His claim had begun as a denial of Philip's insistence on his vassal status and French incursions in Gascony. Edward had originally not meant his claim to the throne of France to be more than a bargaining position, but now that he had been so incredibly successful . . . Was it possible that he could go the whole way and actually claim the throne?

Edward seems to have found it difficult to decide. On 4 April 1353 he appointed John Avenel to take over the lieutenancy of Brittany to implement the terms of the agreement with Charles de Blois. He moved off to Chertsey and Windsor, to inspect the progress of his college there and to hold the tournament and celebrations for the feast of St George. Still he had made no decision about France. At Windsor he and Philippa presided over a gathering of the Knights of the Garter and then took the royal barge back down the river to Thurrock, on the north coast of the Thames. Perhaps he was waiting to hear what the French king thought of what had been proposed at Guines? Still he waited, caught in the indecision of not knowing what he wanted, not wanting to settle for anything less than the maximum, and not knowing what that maximum might be.

Edward's indecision was justifiable in one respect. In May it became apparent that Guy of Boulogne's proposed compromises were too much for King John. He was outraged that his kingship was expected to suffer on account of his father's failings. French refusal, coupled with distrust of Cardinal Guy, was probably why Edward wavered, and delayed sending back his negotiators. John, eager to shrug off thoughts that he might relinquish sovereignty of parts of France, prepared to put his country back on a war footing. But although the attempt to secure a permanent peace had failed for the time being, it had in one sense been successful. It had posed the question which had to be asked in order for there to be a permanent peace. When all the fighting was done, what terms would Edward find acceptable?

*

From Thurrock Edward returned by barge to Westminster. There, on 6 June, he held a feast at which he entertained a number of French lords, as well as the duke of Lancaster and the fourteen-year-old John de Montfort, 'the duke of Brittany', Charles de Blois' rival.[32] Clearly the war was still a talking point. But Edward did not remain at Westminster to discuss the conflict but went down to Wiltshire, where he stayed until August, when he moved to Gloucestershire and the Welsh Marches.[33]

Edward's lack of energy at this time, and the apparent lack of business conducted should make us wonder what he was doing. On 12 July he had ordered the truce to be prolonged until November, but otherwise all the charters and writs emanating from the government were coming from Westminster.[34] Edward had for some years now established his chancery and its subsequent offices permanently at Westminster, so that all charters were written up there and sealed with the great seal. Letters patent and even letters sealed with the privy seal were written up in the king's absence. Edward himself had a third secretariat, the secret seal, which travelled with him.[35] A high level of business must have been delegated. But even if all the letters emanating from the hall at Westminster were written in response to instructions from Edward's secret seal (which they were not), Edward was certainly not overly busy with paperwork in 1353.

Given Edward's preferred recreations, it would be reasonable to suggest that he was hunting or falconing. The chroniclers all mention Edward's love of the chase, and we have proof of it in the huge amounts he spent on hunting and the costly garments he commissioned for hunting parties. At about this time he ordered a perch to be constructed inside his chamber at his new house at Rotherhithe for his favourite falcons to sit on.[36] In August he had to pay compensation to one John Forrester, who had owned three pigs until they were killed by Edward's hunting dogs.[37] The following year he ordered the enclosure of the park at Lyndhurst in the New Forest for hunting.[38] But the likelihood of this explanation does not mean that it is the right one. On 31 July 1353, while Edward was at Clarendon Palace near Salisbury, the king's apothecary John of Lucca, was paid £16 16s 8d for various medicines delivered for the king's use.[39]

Illness is a difficult subject, for the biographer as well as for the sufferer. Had this reference not survived we would not presume Edward was ill at this point in time. Chroniclers – almost always writing in hindsight – tended not to treat illnesses as subjects for comment unless it was a very serious affliction, or coloured the man's personality, or resulted in his death. By comparison, hunting, immorality and tourneying were subjects which they were quite happy to mention in summing up a man's life. As a result we have a picture of medieval knights all heartily and joyfully jousting and hunting together and never once suffering from bad health until they became old or died. This is ironic, given that we also know that these men were charging into each other and seriously wounding each other in peacetime, and brutally maiming each other in war. Many are reported to have been blind in one eye as a result of injuries.[40] Also plague had brought with it a wave of illnesses and morbidity not solely connected with rats. Generally speaking, noblemen born between 1350 and 1450 tended to live shorter lives than their forebears, even if they died peacefully.

Edward was not exempt from the diseases and ailments floating around fourteenth-century England. He had fallen seriously ill in Scotland in 1345. His awareness of his physical vulnerability meant that he maintained a physician and a surgeon as part of his regular household. The employment of these medical men as officers therefore does not mean that he was ill. One reason to have them on hand was the danger of warfare, as shown by the huge discrepancies between the amounts paid to his medical staff for peacetime and wartime service.[41] But another was prophylactic: to maintain the king in good health. The physician advised him about what he should and should not eat at mealtimes, and which astrological periods were the optimum in which to let blood. The surgeon was responsible for his outward appearance, not just his injuries. Even if we knew which medicines were being administered, we would not know how ill he was, or what was wrong with him. All we know for certain is that he required medicines, that his rate of business dropped, and that he left most of his household staff at Salisbury and spent time alone with his closest companions and probably his physician.[42] The other fact we may note is that his illness – whatever it was – did not incapacitate him for long. From Wiltshire he moved into Gloucestershire, and later into Herefordshire. Edward made his trip to the Mortimer shrine at Leintwardine in September. He also went to the shrine of St Thomas Cantilupe at Hereford, then sent his sons to celebrate the obsequies of his late father at Gloucester, and returned to Westminster.

*

Edward's principal purposes in summoning his council in September were to outlaw foreign courts dealing with English affairs (the Statute of Praemunire), to request an extension of the subsidy, and to discuss the Ordinance of the Staple. The wool staple – the place where all English wool had to be sold – was currently situated in Bruges, Flanders. In June 1353, while ill in Wiltshire, Edward had decided to return the wool staple to England, thereby satisfying English merchants' demands at the same time as removing an important overseas privilege from the Flemish. By 1353 the count of Flanders (now fully in command in Bruges) had openly sided with John of France, and had refused to renew his alliance with Edward despite the best efforts of the duke of Lancaster. So there was no further advantage in forcing English merchants to export their wool to Flanders only for cloth buyers to have to re-import it at great expense.

Edward hoped the removal of the staple from Flanders and the establishment of domestic staples for wool, leather, lead and hides would be a sufficient concession to the commons to allow for this business to be dealt with in council. The taxation element meant that the commons had to be involved somehow, but in order to prevent a long list of parliamentary petitions, Edward summoned only a single knight from each shire and a small number of representatives of the towns, and called the meeting a 'great council', not a parliament. The representatives were happy to agree to the removal of the staple from Flanders and the prohibition of courts – especially the courts at Avignon – from dealing with any and all matters touching on English benefices and the rights of the English Crown, and they agreed to the extension of the wool subsidy. What they were not happy with was Edward's attempt to avert the need for holding a full parliament. Petitions were put forward as if Edward *had* summoned a parliament. Edward realised that he could not avoid his newly acknowledged parliamentary reponsibilities simply by calling a small parliamentary assembly a 'great council'. He listened to the petitions. Hence the council of 1353 ended up passing statutes dealing with the granting of pardons, the sale of cloth, the freedom to import Gascon wine at any port and regrating (selling bad or low-quality goods). And to make sure that Edward recognised how parliament saw its position in the legal framework, he was asked to confirm the Statute of the Staple – an important concession to English merchants – in the next full parliament.

The reason for going into the details of these parliaments of 1351–53 at some length is to illustrate the deep engagement which existed between king and parliament at this time. Edward was a man who listened to his representatives, and held dialogue with them, even if he did not or could not agree to their demands. Although it is the mass of legislation passed by his grandfather, Edward I, that caught the attention of early legal historians, prompting them to call that king 'the English Justinian' (referring to the great Byzantine Emperor who codified the Roman Law), Edward III was no less of a legislator. But his methods were different: he was a lawmaker, not a lawgiver. He made laws by responding to parliamentary demands. Sometimes these demands allowed him to promote his own agenda for legislation; at other times the measures were all but forced upon him as a result of his need to maintain a high level of taxation. Sometimes even he had his own wishes presented to him in the form of a petition from a magnate.[43] But the parliaments of Edward III are remarkable for the breadth and depth of the parliamentary dialogue between king and people. So great was Edward's contribution that one modern scholar has assigned him the title of 'Second English Justinian', putting him on a footing equal to that of Edward I, the codifier of English Common Law.[44]

*

Christmas 1353 was spent at Eltham, feasting every day for the traditional twelve days, and then a few days more.[45] In the new year there was an Epiphany tournament, at which Prince Edward (the Black Prince), Sir John Chandos and Sir James Audley took part, dressed in armour covered with red and black velvet.[46] Later in January Edward made his way into East Anglia. His life had become routine. Success and peace had led to building projects and parliaments becoming the events of his reign. Hunting, feasting, falconry, gift-giving and discussions about diplomatic marriages had become the stuff of his private life. Jousts and war were things of the past. Had his life continued in such a manner, one could look at the rest of it as being simply glitteringly rich, dominated by economic and social issues and architecturally splendid. Fortunately for Edward's biographers, there was more to it than that.

The origins of the approaching discontent lay in the political machinations of King Charles of Navarre, one of French history's most duplicitous and least likeable characters. He and his equally unlikeable brother Philip were second cousins of King John, being the sons of Philip d'Evreux and his wife Jeanne, daughter of King Louis X. They were thus royal princes on both their father's and their mother's side, and through their mother it had been claimed that Charles had a prior claim to the throne of France before Edward as well as King John.[47] Charles was also John's son-in-law. In January 1354 the brothers decided they would murder the constable of France, Charles of Spain, a close confidant of King John. Philip entered the inn at which Charles of Spain was staying and had his men stab him eighty times while he tried to escape, naked, from his chamber. He reported the news to his elder brother, who assumed reponsibility for the killing, claiming he himself had ordered it to be done.[48]

Charles of Navarre's behaviour was a deliberate antagonism to the French king, and he rightly expected to be castigated for his crime. He therefore sought the support of the duke of Lancaster, to arrange for an English army to invade France if it should come to war. Lancaster referred the question back to Edward. After a little deliberation, Edward put forward excessive demands for supporting Charles, amounting to a division of the whole of France between them, with Edward being crowned king at Rheims. These were acceptable to Charles of Navarre. In the circumstances, he was likely to agree to anything in return for military aid.

Lancaster was sincere, and himself promised to fight for Charles of Navarre. Edward was also sincere, and promptly gave orders for an army to be raised. Charles himself was anything but sincere. When Cardinal Guy of Boulogne was empowered to make peace with Charles, he used his diplomatic skills to good effect, and managed a cold but clear reconciliation between Charles and John at Mantes, on 22 February. John offered substantial gifts and concessions to Charles, despite his crime, and pardoned him. Then Cardinal Guy left the French royal party to write a sarcastic letter to Lancaster telling him the news. The English had been used and betrayed.[49]

Lancaster was amazed at Charles of Navarre's abuse of his trust. One of Cardinal Guy's comments – that 'the hole by which he (Lancaster) had hoped to slip into France had now been sealed' – infuriated him, and he responded by pointing out that there were many other holes known to him, and the cardinal could not hope to stop them all. The cardinal – who did not approve of the crimes committed – responded by suggesting that Lancaster might find it advantageous sometime to murder one of Edward III's closest friends. It was only half a joke. As the cardinal was well aware, when members of the French royal family murdered royal servants and were rewarded, French politics had reached a new low.

Lancaster was deeply embarrassed and protested his innocence vehemently. He did not need to worry; Edward had no doubts about his friend's integrity. And Edward – or, more probably, one of his far-sighted negotiators – realised the situation was actually to England's advantage. Looking beyond the mere failure of the invasion to the reasons why the intrigue failed, it was obvious that it was due to the weakness of the French monarchy. John was so desperate for support and so devoid of ideas about how to strengthen his realm that he had paid off a hated murderer and rival rather than risk his opposition. The man who had advised him to do this was Cardinal Guy. If Guy was in the ascendant, shadily dealing with all parties secretly, and if he still understood that sovereignty was the key to peace between England and France, might not Guy be the way to bring King John to heel? Moreover, if Edward, with an army in the field, still went ahead and invaded, did Cardinal Guy not stand to lose the most? Edward saw a golden opportunity, and sent the bishop of Norwich and the earl of Huntingdon to reopen negotiations.[50]

It was the right thing to do. Within days of the negotiators' arrival at Guines the basis of a permanent settlement had been agreed. Edward was to renounce the war and his claim on the kingdom of France in return for full sovereignty of the whole of Aquitaine, Poitou, Limousin, parts of the Loire and the town and area around Calais. Both series of delegates agreed, and sealed the provisional treaty, and agreed further that the treaty should be ratified by the pope in October. Edward, it would seem, had finally decided what he wanted. After seventeen years of war, the way to peace was clear at last.

*

On Wednesday 30 April 1354 Edward entered the Painted Chamber at Westminster and met parliament. The discussions at Guines had been secret, and he was obliged not to reveal their content, so the initial address did not mention what had been agreed. Instead it was announced that there were three principal matters to attend to: the Statute of the Staple, to hear petitions of representatives, and the damage to the realm which had been occasioned by the great cost of the war with France. Edward – unable to restrain himself in this moment of victory – promised to reveal the terms of the proposed treaty before the departure of parliament.

So parliament went into session. The petitions of Roger Mortimer and Richard Fitzalan, earl of Arundel for the reversal of the sentences on their forebears were read out and agreed, with the result that Roger Mortimer now became the second earl of March. A spin-off was the important law that henceforth no man of whatever estate should be imprisoned or condemned without him first answering charges against him, a law commendable for its brevity (one single sentence) as well as its fairness.[51] A further fifteen petitions were granted, ranging from a prohibition on exporting iron to confirmation that the Marcher lords should answer for their Welsh estates to the king (as they always had done in the past), not the prince of Wales. But the great event of the parliament was, without doubt, the moment when the ageing chamberlain, Sir Bartholomew Burghersh, announced to the magnates and prelates that there was now a distinct hope that the war could finally and agreeably be brought to a close. As the king had always placed matters of peace or war before parliament, Burghersh asked aloud: 'Would you assent to a treaty of perpetual peace?' And 'unanimously and entirely' the representatives and magnates responded 'Yes! Yes!'

There was huge optimism after this. Edward carried on spending money on his buildings and forest enclosures as if he would need it for nothing else. Philippa was pregnant again, expecting their twelfth child, and England was in a relatively prosperous state. The wool staple was restored to England, and the merchants were satisfied. The prospective end of the French war allowed Edward to renew negotiations for the return of David II to Scotland, and to propose a long period of payment for the king's £60,000 ransom, which would prevent the Scots making incursions into northern England for at least nine years.[52] Edward's only anxiety was that King John would change his mind before the pope ratified the treaty. To this end he instructed Lancaster well in advance. He told him exactly how he wished him to approach the pope at the time they would meet, humbly recognising God's goodness to him and stating that he wished to fight God's enemies. If there was any problem in ratifying the treaty of Guines, Lancaster was to give up Edward's claim to Normandy, Cahors, Quercy and Angoulême, and to renegotiate other combinations of lands. Any boundary disputes could be submitted to the pope for arbitration. He was ordered to entertain all the great men in Avignon, lavishly giving gifts, distributing wine, so that all would see the richness of the English court. The cost of the trip reflects these exorbitant entertainment expenses, amounting to more than £5,000.[53]

Lancaster arrived in Avignon on Christmas Eve and met the pope at a great feast in the papal palace on Christmas Day. The mood was optimistic, and negotiations began in the papal palace there and then. Meanwhile in England, Philippa gave birth to Edward's seventh son, Thomas, at Woodstock, on 5 January 1355. Edward enthusiastically ordered a great tournament to take place in February, on the occasion of Philippa's churching.[54] But not long after this order was given, dire news arrived from Avignon. The French negotiators were not discussing the treaty of Guines.[55] Indeed, it was clear that Cardinal Guy was not fully in touch with the king in Paris, and had fallen out of favour. King John was rather thinking that it was now to his advantage to begin the war again, so he could punish Charles of Navarre and launch a massive attack on Gascony. The French negotiators at Avignon were just going through the motions, playing for time.

In the end the negotiations, the lavish display of wealth and the hopes for peace were all in vain. The entire diplomatic assembly achieved nothing more than a brief renewed alliance with the untrustworthy Charles of Navarre and an agreement to extend the truce until Midsummer's Day 1355. Lancaster left Avignon in a furious mood, loudly declaring that Edward was the rightful king of France. The disappointment in the English camp, and through all of England, was bitter. No one could forgive the French king for this. It might even be said to mark the biggest French diplomatic failure of the war so far. The negotiators between April 1353 and February 1355 had achieved nothing for France but they had focused Edward's mind on the question of what he wanted from the war. Now he had decided, he resolved to do everything within his power to get it.

FOURTEEN

The Pride of England

On 10 February 1355 two students were drinking in the Swindlestock Tavern in Oxford. An argument broke out over the quality of the wine. The students emphasised their dissatisfaction by pouring the unpalatable liquid over the head of the innkeeper. They then broke the jug over his head.[1] Tensions had been simmering for some time between the university and the town, and this proved to be the catalyst for a full-scale riot. More than twenty townsmen and sixty-three scholars died over the next three days. Many others were gravely injured. Even after the fighting had come to an end, the bitterness continued, with the result that many scholars fled and at least twenty students' halls of residence were burnt down. The bishop of Lincoln placed the town under an interdict, and Edward issued a royal commission to investigate. After due process, Edward ruled in favour of the university, granted it a charter so that it controlled the assize of bread, ale and wine in the town, and ordered the mayor of the town and sixty-three citizens to pay a penny each in recompense every year thereafter in perpetuity, to atone for the students' deaths.

Edward had sworn to maintain justice, and in the Oxford 'town v. gown' case he had to show that he would keep that promise. Nor was his favouring the university unexpected: his old mentor Richard Bury was just one of the hundreds of men whose Oxford education had been useful to Edward. What is noticeable about this event is the way in which justice was administered. It was quick, efficient and absolute. In an age when legal disputes could drag on for years, this was dealt with by the king and finalised within a month. It is reminiscent of the argument between two important subjects in 1332 on the eve of the Scottish war. Edward took control of the situation and quickly forced a solution on both parties. There was no time to waste in protracted subtleties and nuances. Edward wanted to remove the issue so he could focus on the forthcoming campaign.

The collapse of the Treaty of Guines had not just frustrated Edward, it had shocked and enraged him. He had been living the life of the potentate, basking in his glory, and perhaps becoming a little complacent. The failure of the treaty had destroyed his ease of mind. It threatened his policy in Scotland as well as France, and he had no choice but to respond. He ordered David II, who was then at Newcastle, to be taken back to his cell in the Tower, and cancelled the negotiations about his ransom. He made preparations for a fleet to go to Gascony. When two papal nuncios reached England in April, desperately trying to patch up some hope of continuing the truce, Edward took the unusual step of responding in person to their requests. Allowing them to enter his council chamber, while he and his magnates were discussing the proceedings at Oxford, he broke off to tell the nuncios flatly that he had no intention of prolonging the truce. He had frequently been asked for truces by 'those of France' (he did not call John a king), and by the cardinals too, and always the French had broken them when it was expedient for them to do so. He would debate the matter with his council, he told them, but that was all. He would let the pope know his decision in his own time, through his own intermediaries. The nuncios were then politely but firmly shown the door.[2]

Nobody attending that council had any intention of trying to dissuade Edward from his set path. Therefore the next act was to consider how to conduct the approaching war. Edward's experience told him that a dual attack through Gascony and Normandy was likely to prove most effective, with a third advance through Calais if necessary. Lancaster had had discussions with the king of Navarre at Avignon, and on the strength of their agreement Edward appointed him commander in Normandy, to join forces with the Navarrese. At the same time the Gascon lords asked for the prince of Wales to lead them against the French. This would mean that Lancaster would be in charge in Normandy, although his experience had been obtained in Gascony, and the prince would lead in Gascony, although he had so far only seen conflict in Normandy. But Edward had confidence in both his son and the duke. Besides, the prince would not be alone with the Gascon armies. He would be supported by the earls of Warwick, Suffolk, Salisbury and Oxford, Sir Reginald Cobham, a thousand men-at-arms, a large number of Welshmen and two thousand archers.[3] And the general plan was that both leaders should advance to a point in central France at which they would meet up. By then it would matter much less where each had landed.

By 24 June – the end of the truce – Edward's plans were nearing completion. But then the weather intervened. The prince found himself becalmed off Plymouth, and Lancaster was stuck off Sandwich. During the delay Edward decided that he too would lead an army, and throughout August he was watching his ships bobbing up and down on the waves outside Portsmouth, held up by the wind. But the prolonged bad weather tossed the English one major piece of good fortune. Lancaster's spies discovered that Charles of Navarre had concocted a secret agreement with King John to betray Lancaster, and to ambush the army after it had landed. Once more the duplicitous Charles had upset Edward's plans. So Edward redirected Lancaster to Brittany. A few days passed, and then he changed his mind again. He would lead both his own force and Lancaster's to Calais. Lord Manny and the earl of Northampton would accompany him. They would leave at Michaelmas, after his seasick men had had time to rest. 'And I want it known throughout France', he declared, 'that soon I will arrive there and do battle with John, and lay waste the land as far forward as I can see.'[4]

More delays followed. Edward and his army disembarked at Calais at the end of October. Despite the count of Flanders siding with John, and the collapse of the alliances with Brabant and Germany many years before, news of his arrival attracted volunteers from those countries. This brought the total number of his troops up to about ten thousand.[5] Edward himself was in an exceedingly confident and aggressive mood. When told that a large French force was gathering at Amiens he declared that he would go there directly 'and show King John the smoke and flames of his country'.[6]

On 2 November Edward set out on the road to Amiens. Three days later, burning the country and villages all around him, he approached Thérouanne. On the way he was met by a French knight, Sir Jean le Maingre, better known by his nickname Boucicaut. Boucicaut had previously been captured in Gascony and was on parole, and so could not take part in the fighting until he had paid his ransom. But that also meant he was safe from further punishment. He was led to Edward, who demanded to know where King John was. Still at Amiens, Boucicaut replied. Edward expressed his surprise. 'Holy Mary! Why is he waiting for me there, when he has so great a force and sees his land burned and devastated by so few men?'

Edward knew that Boucicaut had come mainly to spy on the size of his army, so he showed his confidence in his troops by allowing him to survey them. Boucicaut saw that the English were well-equipped, well-armed, experienced and high in morale, even if the army was smaller than that mustering at Amiens. Some accounts say that he thought the English were too few in number to accomplish Edward's objectives. This is unlikely, given later events, but, whatever Boucicaut actually thought, Edward levelled with him the following day. As the two men watched the English army destroy the countryside around Hesdin, Edward told him that he knew that he was spying, although he was on parole. He added that, given this, he could demand an increased ransom for him. But nevertheless he would let him go, and forgive him his ransom. The condition was that he would go to King John and tell him that Edward expected to see the French arrayed for battle within three days.[7]

Boucicaut did as he was told. But the three days passed, and John did not give battle. He may have been unprepared to do so, awaiting a larger army, or he may simply have been too scared to risk his throne by a head-on confrontation with an English army of ten thousand men. Edward was disappointed. He was also beginning to regret his haste in marching south, for he had left his supply lines prone to attack from the French troops stationed around Calais, and his men had now run out of wine. As soon as the army was reduced to drinking local water from wells and streams, they were prone to illnesses and poisoning. With no sign of a French attack, Edward conferred with his fellow war leaders and decided to try the ploy which had worked at Crécy, to encourage the French to attack them in retreat. He accordingly gave the order to withdraw and encamp outside Calais, destroying everything on the way.

King John rose to the bait. Anxious that he should not be seen in the same light as his father, always shirking battle, he sent his marshal to issue a challenge to Edward. Edward responded with the proposal that he had first made to King Philip in 1340: that the two kings should fight alone, the loser surrendering his claim on the throne of France to the victor. If that was unacceptable, Edward suggested that they each be joined in their struggle by their eldest sons, or perhaps a small number of their chosen knights. Once more, he was pitching his family's divine right against that of the de Valois, a trial by battle in all but name. This was very unattractive to King John, for how could he and the dauphin, Charles, be expected to take on King Edward – the paragon of knighthood – and the Black Prince, who had won his spurs so dramatically at Crécy? He turned him down. He also turned down the next English proposal, and the next. The strategic initiative had to all intents and purposes *become* the battle. Neither side was prepared to fight on terms suggested by the other. Neither side was prepared to attack the other on ground which their enemy had chosen.

Outside the walls of Calais, Edward was more anxious to fight than ever, for he now knew that he had made a second miscalculation in his preparations for the campaign, more serious even than jeopardising his supply lines. On 6 November, while he had been boasting to Boucicaut, a group of Scotsmen led by a French knight had broken into Berwick and destroyed much of the town. Suddenly Edward was aware that he was exposed. And it was his own fault. In 1345 he had been much more careful, arranging the defence of the northern border in anticipation of a Scottish attack timed to coincide with his invasion of France. This time he had rushed things, had changed his mind too often, and had not made adequate arrangements, assuming that David II's custody was a guarantee of peace. He certainly had not foreseen the dangers of small numbers of Frenchmen helping to lead a Scottish attack. Nor did he anticipate that Robert Stewart, the Guardian of Scotland, might want to renew hostilities during King

David's imprisonment, even though that was what the Scots were bound by treaty to do if France was attacked.

Cursing himself, Edward gave the order from Calais for parliament to assemble at Westminster, and issued one last challenge to King John. This too was rejected. The temptation to march forward and attack the French then and there must have been great, but he resisted it. Despite the bravado declarations that he would show John the smoke and flames of his realm, and that he would destroy everything he could see, and despite his showing off to Boucicaut, he was about to leave France hastily, without any reward for his efforts. The thousand volunteers from Germany and the Low Countries were dismayed to see Edward slink away, back to Calais, and back to England, without doing battle. This was not the great warrior-king whose victory they had expected to share.

The 1355 campaign in Normandy was a failure. Edward was not humiliated by the French, but by his own neglect of the necessary strategic precautions. The very fact that he had not covered himself in the glory of another victory was something of a humiliation for the most respected warrior-king in Christendom. Nevertheless, in the circumstances, he did the wise and correct thing. Tactical retreats are rarely glorious but they are often as important as successful battles. If we look at the broader picture, Edward's fundamental approach to the war had not changed since he first went to the Low Countries in 1338. The strategic bedrock of his entire foreign policy (and it is not inappropriate here to use this term) was, in his own words, that 'the best way to avoid the inconvenience of war is to pursue it away from your own country'. The attack on Berwick threatened that policy. It brought war back on to English soil, and that was something Edward could not and would not tolerate. He had to stand by his policy of maintaining the war on foreign territory above all else. Therefore, in considering his campaign of 1355, we have to say that Edward was forced to retreat as a result of his own strategic miscalculations but, having acknowledged his failures, he did the wise thing in withdrawing from France to protect his kingdom's borders.

*

Ten days after challenging King John, Edward was sitting in the Painted Chamber at Westminster, with his magnates and representatives around him. He was in no mood for trifling with merchants or bargaining for a grant. There was a real threat to the kingdom in the north, and he wanted simply to make sure he had the means to attack the Scots and secure the border. He was also still smarting from his enforced withdrawal from France, and determined to ensure financial support for a renewal of his disappointing campaign. The heroic champion Lord Manny was therefore given the task of addressing the assembly and making clear why Edward was demanding a renewed grant of no less than six years' continuation of the wool subsidy.

Sir Walter was an eloquent man. He related the whole history of the struggle for peace, from the treaty discussed at Guines to the failure to ratify the treaty and the duplicity of Charles of Navarre. He told those present about the problems with the weather, and the attempts to do battle, and the French refusal. To his statement Chief Justice Shareshull added the loss of Berwick and the pressing need to respond to the Scots' incursion. After these speeches, the commons withdrew, and shortly afterwards assembled in the White Chamber, and responded with the magnates that they had unanimously decided to grant a subsidy on all wool and leather for the full six years. This was an extraordinarily long period of taxation, never previously known. Edward had been given the purse strings of the kingdom.[8]

Of course there were conditions. The grant was followed by a number of petitions for the redress of injustices and other grievances. To most of these Edward gave a cursory answer. But one in particular caught his attention. It was a petition from his second cousin, Lady Wake, the sister of the duke of Lancaster. She claimed that the bishop of Ely had allowed his men to burn down some of her houses. She had taken legal action against him, and he had been ordered to pay £900 in damages. Edward already knew this, and had rebuked the bishop at the time. But since then the bishop's thugs had murdered one of her servants, William Holm, in a wood near Somersham. Gangs of ruffians were notorious in the early fourteenth century, and Edward had done his best to stamp out organised crime. He had almost entirely eradicated the pattern of magnate-sponsored violence and maintenance (although Sir John Molyns did his best to keep the tradition alive).[9] But it was unheard of for a bishop to be implicated in repeated acts of gang violence. Edward, roused by the threat to law and order, the dignity of the church and the insult to the royal family, ordered that he himself would deal with the case. He further decreed that he would confiscate the bishop's temporal possessions, and demanded that the bishop humble himself before him.[10]

One week later Edward began his long ride north. His mind was set on wresting Berwick from the Scots and then punishing them for their rebellion. He was also angry with the bishop, who had refused to humble himself or even to apologise for his wrongdoing. He was at Newcastle by the end of December, and the army reached Berwick in the second week of January. Even before they arrived, the Frenchmen who had led the attack on the town had abandoned the Scottish cause, leaving the defenders to beg Edward for their lives. Robert Stewart had not anticipated Edward's immediate return and defence of his Scottish possessions. Nor had his men anticipated his wrath. The shame Edward felt in retreating from France only increased his anger. When he heard that his Chancellor and Treasurer had hesitated to confiscate the lands of the defiant bishop of Ely, he was pushed to the point of fury. Now Scotland stood to pay the price.

The campaign which followed became infamous in Scotland as 'Burnt Candlemas'. On 25 January, near Roxburgh Castle, Edward summoned Balliol before him and demanded that he resign the title of King of Scots which he had borne uselessly for the last twenty years.[11] Balliol was given a pension and had his debts paid, and then left Scotland ignominiously, never to return. Edward then set about organising a destructive march across Scotland modelled on those he had used in France. An advancing front – twenty miles wide, in which everything was destroyed and burnt – was now employed to punish the Scots. It began at Roxburgh on 26 January and continued day by day until Edward marched into Edinburgh, the lower parts of which he burnt on Candlemas Day (2 February). Then he moved on to Haddington, which he burnt, allowing the fires to consume the friary there. A bitter winter campaign followed as Edward destroyed everything in his path on the way across the lowlands to Carlisle. His men suffered from hunger and thirst, as the Scots destroyed their own stores to prevent the English having them. The situation was made worse by the loss of his supply fleet in bad storms, but Edward made sure he punished the Scots.[12] A plot to ambush him in Ettrick forest failed when another contingent was sent through the danger zone ahead of his own force. The many Englishmen killed in his place were the only consolation for the desperate Scots whose most ardent supporters were now beginning to see the alliance with France as more of a benefit to the French than to themselves.

There is no doubt that the Burnt Candlemas campaign was hugely destructive. But how successful was it? It did not bring the war in Scotland to an end, and it seems strange at first to suppose it could have done. But to judge Edward's attempt to conclude the Scottish war as a failure on the basis that hostilities were renewed shortly after his death, twenty years later, is nonsensical. So we must ask whether it is possible that Edward believed that Burnt Candlemas would help to bring about a permanent peace. The Scots could not possibly hope to defeat a large English army in the field under Edward's command, so the devastation cannot be regarded as a means of forcing them into a decisive battle. But Edward could have believed that severe reprisals in themselves would bring the Scots to the negotiating table. Certainly he would have hoped that they would think twice before attacking England again at France's request. No doubt he also meant to send a very strong signal to the French, to let them know that he was still capable of inflicting dire suffering on his adversaries. But the most telling sign is that, soon after Burnt Candlemas, Edward agreed peace with the Scots and resumed negotiations to allow David to return to his kingdom.[13] Even more significantly, the negotiations were successful. The conflict with Scotland effectively ended then, not to be resumed during Edward's lifetime, and David returned to his inheritance. Finally, the day on which David's ransom was to be paid, in yearly instalments, was Candlemas. This would be a powerful reminder to the Scots of what Edward had done in 1356 and could do again. It may seem strange that such destruction should be committed in the name of peace but Burnt Candlemas does seem to have been carried out with the intention of ending hostilities, at least while the king of England was a warrior.[14]

*

Historians often stress how expensive Edward's campaigns were, largely because the English records survive in great numbers allowing the figures to be discussed in fine detail. Had the French records survived as well, they would have shown that the defence of France was equally expensive. There was an economic war going on at the same time as the military and diplomatic conflict, and by 1355 England had all but won it. Edward had developed an efficient system of raising enough money to afford the war.[15] Neither John nor his father had ever come close to making ends meet. Frequent attempts had been made to raise money for the French royal treasury by devaluing the currency, but successive devaluations had undermined confidence and could not be continued indefinitely. In 1356 King John was bankrupt. When his government attempted to tackle this matter head-on, raising a sales tax and a salt tax, there were widespread riots.[16]

John's troubles were not just financial. He had been personally damaged by the campaigns of 1355, having again failed to meet the English king in battle. A plot to have him murdered, in which Charles of Navarre was involved, failed in December 1355. In March 1356 a second plot was hatched by the Navarrese king and his Norman supporters. Again the plot was foiled, but this time John reacted violently. He felt he had tolerated Charles far beyond the point of reason. He secretly donned armour and took a large number of men to arrest him and his key supporters as they ate a feast on 5 April. Four men including the count of Harcourt were summarily beheaded in front of the king, sending shockwaves through the Norman aristocracy. Charles himself was incarcerated. Back in Normandy his younger brother Philip of Navarre sent word hurriedly to King Edward that he needed protection and was prepared to acknowledge English overlordship in return.

Important as these setbacks were, John's biggest problem in 1356 was the prince of Wales. Having finally set sail for Gascony on 9 September 1355, the prince had been well-received and successful throughout the duchy. In October he had led a very successful raid through Armagnac, and even reached the walls of Carcassonne before returning to Bordeaux for Christmas, burning everything he could. It was not possible for John to ignore the scale of the devastation: it was even more severe than Burnt Candlemas. Whole towns were destroyed, including Carcassonne itself (although the castle was not attacked) and Limoux, where four thousand houses were burnt. As one newsletter put it, 'since the beginning of the war there has never been such destruction as on this campaign'.[17] The prince's men had looted huge amounts of treasure and added even more to John's financial problems. They even stole financial documents from the towns they burnt in order to calculate how much damage they were doing to the French treasury in lost taxes and unpaid revenue.[18]

Pleased with the success of his son, and satisfied that he had subdued the Scots, Edward turned his attention once more to the solution of the French war. He needed to persuade the French that they stood to gain more from accepting the Treaty of Guines than from refusing it. A sustained war would force John into this position, for he could not be seen to avoid an English army yet again, and he could barely afford to raise an army of his own. Edward meanwhile could be seen to be building lavish manor houses and castles up and down the Thames, and spending thousands every year on his castles and palaces. Everyone in Europe knew that *he* was not facing a financial crisis.

Edward's vision of how to force the French to accept the Treaty of Guines assumed the by-now established form of two simultaneous campaigns: one in the south and one in the north. On 2 May 1356 the pope's formal envoys to Edward requesting a truce were given the same answer as their predecessors. Six weeks later the first small army of eight hundred archers and five hundred men-at-arms arrived in Normandy under the command of the duke of Lancaster, where they met Sir Robert Knolles with five hundred archers from Brittany, and a small army headed by Philip of Navarre and Godfrey de Harcourt. The 2,300 men under Lancaster had specific targets, such as the relief of the king of Navarre's castle at Breteuil, but it is unclear whether this small army was meant to do more than reassure the Navarrese and worry the French. No attempt was made to link up with the prince in the south. Having destroyed the town and castle of Verneuil on 5–6 July, Lancaster put his force in readiness, expecting the French army under John to advance. No attack came. The following day the English retreated, leaving King John to consider whether to take his army south to defend Gascony, to resume the siege of Breteuil, or pursue Lancaster back into Normandy.[19]

It is probably no coincidence that journals were kept for both Lancaster's attack and the prince's.[20] It seems that Edward urged the leaders on both expeditions to have their administrative staff keep a daily record of their feats of arms, in addition to the usual newsletters which he expected. Edward probably also gave some general instructions as to how the leaders were to proceed. In Gascony he stipulated that the lands of the countess of Pembroke were not to be touched, nor those of Gaston Phoebus, count of Foix, a potential ally. But otherwise he was powerless, unable to affect the outcome in any meaningful way. This made him anxious. A sign of his concern is that now he endowed three chaplains to pray for the safe-keeping of the royal family at Durham. Frequently when other men founded chantries and collegiate churches to pray for their families' souls, they included the king, but it was rare for Edward himself to make a grant for prayers for his family. He had been concerned before Crécy, when he had taken his son on a pilgrimage and ensured that he made his will, but now he was doubly concerned, being so distant.[21] His own mistakes of the previous year had reminded him that campaigns could go wrong. And he knew that the prince might be thinking that everything had gone wrong again, for Edward had originally planned that he himself would lead an attack in the north in August to take the pressure off the prince in the south. He had failed to do so. On 1 August he sent a letter giving his son the authority to sue for peace, if it came to the worst.[22]

As he waited in England for news, a drought which had parched the land since mid-March was followed by torrential rains.[23] The usual stream of routine business was presented to him. Orders were given for Balliol's pension to be paid, for the bailiffs of Rochester Bridge to allow building materials for the Palace of Westminster to pass freely beneath it, and for one hundred and twenty archers to be selected for the royal bodyguard. Amid the hundreds of writs, open and sealed letters, and charters, we may read that Sir Thomas Rokeby was appointed Justiciar of Ireland, and that Charles de Blois' ransom was finally settled. Discussions with Philip de Navarre and Geoffrey de Harcourt were concluded. As Edward looked out at the summer downpour, he could only wonder what was happening in Gascony.

It was on or about 10 October that he finally heard the news. It had reached Brittany first, and Lancaster had immediately sent John le Cok of Cherbourg to Edward.[24] There had been a great battle, at Poitiers, on 19 September. The English had been victorious. The prince was safe and well. And, incredibly – astoundingly – King John had been captured.

The king of France had been captured. It was extraordinary. It had never happened before. Edward was exultant, absolutely triumphant! He rewarded the messenger with twenty-five marks, and gave orders for the news to be cried around the country. Archbishops and bishops throughout the realm were asked to offer up thanksgivings for the prince's success. Equally amazed and pleased, they did so, as may be seen in their registers. The whole country was astounded; surely this meant the end – a most glorious end – to the war? Froissart noted that 'great solemnities were made in all churches and great fires and celebrations were held throughout the land'.[25] Two thousand three hundred French knights and men-at-arms had been killed, not including infantry, and two thousand five hundred men of quality had been captured. The figures were so impressive that most writers saw fit to include them in their chronicles.

It was probably Geoffrey Hamelyn – the squire who brought King John's helmet and surcoat to Westminster – who told Edward the detailed outline of the battle. The prince had set out from Bergerac on 4 August and headed north through Périgueux on a long march to Bourges, believing that he would soon hear that King Edward had landed in the north of France. No word came of a second English attack, and the prince had had to reassess his situation on the basis that he would not receive reinforcements. King John was at Orléans with a large army, having destroyed all the bridges over the Loire, and the count of Poitiers' army was at Tours, to the west. The bridge at Tours still stood. To cross there would give the prince a chance of marching north to meet Lancaster, whom the prince wrongly believed was nearby. On 7 September he reached the outskirts of Tours, and looked across the Loire, hoping to see Lancaster's camp fires. There were none. The count of Poitiers refused to be drawn out of Tours. Soon the prince heard that the French royal army was marching south from Orléans. He had no choice but to retreat. The inevitable cardinals, watching like vultures, saw an opportunity, and swooped to offer the prince a chance to sue for peace on terms favourable to the French. He refused, and sent scouts out to search for King John. They found him, at Poitiers, on 18 September. As the prince began to arrange his men on the edge of a wooded hillside, in case of attack, Cardinal Talleyrand returned. He urged the prince to agree with the peace offer he bore. If the prince were to give up his prisoners, and all the land he had captured, and agreed not to make war in France for seven years, he and his men would be spared and allowed to go free. After all, King John had more than fourteen thousand men with him and Prince Edward only six thousand, and only about a thousand archers.[26] The prince acknowledged these facts and told the cardinal that he would agree to the terms suggested on one condition: that they were ratified by his father. That it would take at least a month for Edward to hear the terms, let alone agree to them – which he was very unlikely to do – shows that the prince was not serious, he was just playing for time.

On 19 September the French advanced their crossbowmen and

shield-bearers. King John had unfurled the Oriflamme and issued the order to put all the English and Gascons to death.[27] All prisoners taken were to be killed. The sole exception was to be the prince himself. There was nothing further to be done now in the English camp but to prepare for battle after a night trying to sleep on a hillside in armour. Mass was heard. Prayers were said. Some men took the wagons and carts with their booty down to the river behind their position. The prince went among his men, encouraging them, and dubbing knights.

Two groups of French cavalry had been selected, each five hundred strong, to ride ahead to break up the ranks of archers which, it was suspected, would be arranged on either side of the English position. Their horses had been specially armoured to enable them to do this. But the marshals in charge were unable to see how they could charge into the archers. At first they could not see the English position at all, and so were unsure where it was they were aiming for. They hesitated, and then pride, misinformation and nerves got the better of them, and they charged. As the French crossbowmen came forward, letting fly their deadly bolts at the prince's men in front of them, the English vanguard under the command of the earl of Warwick charged up the hill on the prince's right to attack them on their left flank, driving them back towards the main French army. Warwick's men then found themselves under attack from the first of the two groups of French cavalry. Caught in the open between archers and the charge, they took shelter behind a thick hedge. In the middle of this hedge was a wide gap, through which the French riders now tried to force their way; but the earl of Salisbury anticipated the attack and forced his own men into the breach, fending off both cavalry charges. As the French fell back they impeded the advance of the troops under the dauphin, who nevertheless engaged with the English until his standard-bearer was killed. Then they faltered, and gradually fell back to rejoin the main army.[28]

King John now staked everything on one huge onslaught. His plan was to concentrate his forces on the English position in front of the prince, hoping to overwhelm and crush them through sheer force of numbers. He ordered the entire French army to advance as one massive battalion. When the size of the French army became obvious to the English, and the word went around that the English archers had run out of arrows, they began to panic. Some shouted that they should flee while they had time, for they were beaten. The prince himself rallied the men, responding that the man who said they were beaten was a liar, for how could they be beaten while he was still alive? In the terrifying minutes before the great wave of the French army came upon them, the English ran forward to yank the arrows out of the corpses and the poor wounded and dying, running back to give them to any archer they could find. Across the wide battlefield men realised that they had to stand together now, or they were lost. The prince knew he needed an element of surprise to swing things his way, and ordered a small contingent under the Garter knight, Sir Jean de Grailly – better known as the lord or 'Captal' de Buch – to leave the battlefield and rush to attack the French from behind. But seeing this famous warrior's banners leaving the battlefield, the English thought that he was fleeing, and they began to shout in dismay. At the critical moment, just when the army was about to break up and run, the prince made one of the bravest, most important and unexpected decisions of the entire war. He controlled the urge to flee by ordering his panic-stricken army to advance. The English and Gascons had to steady their nerves or break ranks. Terrified though they were, uncertain as they were, they did not fail. This was true courage. In spite of their fear they marched as ordered, straight towards the Oriflamme, the symbol which meant their deaths. As they advanced, the Captal de Buch was running unseen around the woods towards the French rear. On marched the prince, his trumpeters beside him, his army around him, gathering in resolution. Then at the critical moment the prince signalled to his trumpeters to sound the charge. Men started running. The mounted contingent charged. Archers loosed their last arrows into the faces of the approaching men, then threw away their bows and drew their knives. Infantry, knights and men-at-arms all rushed forwards, waving swords, maces, spears and axes, shouting the war cry 'Guienne, St George!' They crashed into the French infantry, each side furiously intent on one single strategy: to kill every man between them and the enemy leader. In the ensuing struggle, as men wrestled, hit each other with stones, stabbed, slashed and shot each other, it was the English who gradually prevailed. Those who stood by King John were pressed back, without any chance of escape as the Captal de Buch caused confusion in the rear, unfurling the banner of St George in the way of a French retreat. The great men of France fell there, around the billowing Oriflamme, slaughtered as the English and Gascons rushed forward to seize the king. One of the last to die was Geoffrey de Charny, the great knight who had survived Morlaix and Crécy, survived Edward's battle to protect Calais, and had led the attack on Guines. He was cut down as he stood beside his king, holding up the Oriflamme to the last.

It had been a battle totally unlike all the other English victories of the last twenty-three years. It had not been won by archers arranged on the flanks of the army, although the archers had played their part. It had not been won by men-at-arms holding their ground for hours. It had been won by courage, determination and a clear chain of command, keeping the army under control and using its force efficiently in the face of terrifying danger and near-disaster. It was, to use the duke of Wellington's expression, a 'damned near-run thing'. But like that other damned near-run thing, the result was a crushing victory. The news would rock the French pope at Avignon. It would astound all of Europe. And the credit would come to King Edward as well as his son. For he had been the king who had met the challenge of the French and begun the war, he had inspired England to pull together to become a fighting nation, and he had ordered and equipped this campaign and all those which went before against the combined might of France and Scotland. And now he had overcome them both. The kings of both France and Scotland were his prisoners. For the first time in its history, England was more than just the southern part of an island off the northern coast of Europe. It was the dominant military nation in Christendom.

*

There was a sense of euphoria about the English court after the arrival of the news from Poitiers. Edward's feeling that the cardinals never truly gave him the respect he deserved, regarding him merely as the king of a little country, was a thing of the past. Suddenly his letters were full of international business. The Holy Roman Emperor sought a treaty. The Navarrese could now be trusted to keep faith. The Scots could now be trusted to negotiate openly with regard to the restitution of King David. The bishop of Ely fled to Avignon, realising that he could not possibly hope to stand up against a man now becoming widely regarded as the greatest king England had ever had. Even the pope recognised that he needed to take a different approach to Edward. He wrote to him in October begging for there now to be peace between 'our most dear son in Christ, John, the illustrious king of France (whom the event of war has made your prisoner) and yourself'.[29] It no longer mattered how 'dear' or 'illustrious' King John was in the pope's eyes. He was still a prisoner.

King John's capture gave Edward another opportunity to reflect on a permanent peace settlement. The process of the previous years had forced him to decide what precisely he wanted from the war, and under what terms he was prepared to give up his claim to the throne of France. But now the French king was his prisoner what more could he ask for? There would of course have to be a ransom, but beyond that? Which other territories might Edward demand?

As far as the English were concerned, Edward could ask for what he wanted. There was a joke in circulation which went: 'now the pope has become French and Jesus has become English; soon we'll see who will do more: the pope or Jesus'.[30] It was blasphemous, as the chronicler who recorded it admitted, but there did seem to be something of the miraculous about the unending string of victories, and the English were keenly alert to the divine favour shown to their scrupulously religious king. To the medieval mind, as St Peter's successors on Earth for the last half-century had been French, one might have expected the French to be invincible. So for the English to have defeated them in more than a dozen consecutive battles had to be due to more than luck.

Given this, it is perhaps surprising that Edward's territorial demands were only a little more extensive than those agreed at Guines three years earlier. Although we cannot be certain what was agreed on 18 March 1357, it would appear that, as at Guines, he was prepared to renounce both the claim on the throne of France and the war in return for a recognition of his sovereignty to Aquitaine, Saintonge, Angoumois, Poitou, Limousin, Quercy, Périgord, Bigorre, Guare and the Agenais, with the county of Ponthieu (which had been his mother's dowry), and Calais and Guines and the area immediately around them. This decision seems to have meant that some extra territories were retained under the new proposed treaty. But these were not an absolute demand, they were a negotiating position. It was necessary for Edward to demand more territory than he could reasonably hold because, as Trotsky succinctly put it, 'retreat is possible, when there is something to retreat from'. Most twentieth-century historians thought that Edward's reducing his claims marked a strategic failure. But new research has shown that this long-held opinion was based on repeated misreadings of the terms of all the proposed treaties, including the unimplemented agreements.[31] It would appear rather that Edward, believing the war was now over in both Scotland and France, decided he could afford to be merciful and so aimed to achieve little more than the implementation of the Guines agreement and to exchange his French prisoners for a large but negotiable sum.

The new truce with France was agreed by the prince at Bordeaux on 23 March. One slight hitch was that the duke of Lancaster was still besieging Rennes, and was reluctant to end operations. He had been there for nearly six months already, and had sworn an oath not to give up before he placed his banner on the battlements. When the news of the truce reached him, he found himself in a quandary. As the most pious of all Edward's generals (he had personally composed a treatise on religious salvation two years earlier, *The Book of Holy Medicines*) he refused to break his oath. Only in July did he finally agree, achieving a personal compromise between his conscience and the enemy by entering Rennes alone and placing his banner on the battlements for a few minutes before returning to England.

One group who needed no convincing that Edward had the makings of permanent peace was the English parliament. The euphoria following Poitiers had not yet worn off; in fact if anything it was more intense on 17 April, when parliament met, as the prince was expected shortly to arrive back in England with his royal prisoner. The religious tone was still strong, as the case of Cecilia Ridgeway shows. This woman had been condemned to death for murdering her husband, but she proved her innocence by standing mute and going without food and drink for forty days after being condemned. Edward agreed that 'this was a miracle contrary to nature', and pardoned her, presumably to avoid any danger of offending the saintly powers that had conferred such great victories on his people.[32] It was thus in an atmosphere of a divinely favoured England that parliament put forward its petition. Fraudulent sales of wool using false weights were curbed, legal means of gauging quantities of wine were instituted, and the Statute of the Staple was reinforced. Two important measures of long-lasting significance were passed dealing with the laws of probate. Extortionate fees for proving wills were prohibited, and the system whereby the goods of an intestate person were committed to an administrator by the church courts was established. The administrative reform of Ireland was agreed. Edward agreed to protect trades of the fishermen of Great Yarmouth (the Statute of Herrings) and of Blakeney (the Statute of Salt Fish). But the overriding business of April 1357 was peace. Jousts were ordered. Pardons were issued to condemned men in the traditional fashion to celebrate the great victory. And parliament agreed another year's direct taxation (on top of the six years' wool tariff), more out of gratitude than need.

On 5 May 1357 the prince landed at Plymouth with the king of France and rode slowly in procession towards London through Salisbury, Sherborne and Winchester. Everywhere they were fêted. Edward himself sent a secret 'army' of five hundred men dressed in green tunics and armed with bows and arrows, swords and bucklers to prepare a mock ambush of the royal party on the way to the capital. The prince enjoyed the joke, and when the French king saw them, and asked what sort of men these were, the prince told him they were foresters, living in the forests by choice, and that they waylaid people everyday.[33] The reference to the bows and swords – the weapons for which Robin Hood was famed – suggests Edward was alluding to the Robin Hood stories which were becoming popular at the time.[34] Edward also prepared surprises for the prince and the king on their arrival in London. The mayor and aldermen went out to meet the royal party and to escort them into the city. The aldermen were dressed in elaborate costumes of bright colours, the city conduits were filled with wine, the houses were decorated with armour and bows, gold and silver leaves were scattered by beautiful girls sitting in specially made birdcages hung above the road, and crowds thronged the streets. Everyone wanted to see this procession: one of the greatest public events in their lives.[35]

Along with the king of France in the prince's train of prisoners were his young son Philip and three other members of the French royal family.[36] Philip – too young to fight – had stood beside his father at Poitiers shouting out 'Look, father, there!' every time a new assailant had approached the hard-pressed king. Eight other counts had been captured in the battle, and, of course, King David of Scotland was still in custody. The sum of all these captive kings and great lords, plus the visiting lords attracted by the anticipated spectacle, made London the centre of European attention, and it led to a whole season of festivities, beginning with a great tournament at Smithfield. Edward really could be said to wear three crowns now, as the old prophecy had foretold, for a captive king was seated on either side of him at the feast. The seventeen-year-old Geoffrey Chaucer was very probably one of the many thousands who watched the tournament, as the future poet had become a page in the household of Elizabeth de Burgh, wife of the king's son Lionel. In Scotland the effects of the English triumph were felt no less keenly, and the destruction of the kingdom's mighty ally so soon after the Burnt Candlemas campaign helped the Scottish parliament to agree to the terms put forward by Edward, resulting in the Treaty of Berwick on 3 October. Edward and Philippa held a great Christmas feast at Malmesbury and went on to Bristol to watch the first tournament in England to be held at night. This was tournament drama taken to its extreme: knights in plate armour with crested helmets on caparisoned horses jousting in lists illuminated by great fires and thousands of torches, the onlookers' faces red in the glow.

The culmination of all these tournaments and celebrations was the great tournament ordered to take place at Windsor on St George's Day 1358. Edward planned to make this one of the truly great chivalric occasions of his time. The buildings of his new College of St George in the lower ward were now finished, and the stalls of the Knights of the Garter in place. The tournament itself was hosted and proclaimed by the earl of March, one of the leading tournament fighters in the kingdom.[37] Edward issued a proclamation to be taken throughout Christendom that he would offer a safe-conduct to anyone who wished to come to England to watch the tournament. Several Continental dukes came, so too did the king's sister, Queen Joan, and many of the nobility of Gascony, Germany, Hainault and France. Even Edward's ageing mother Isabella stirred herself to attend. The only slight downturn in the glory of the proceedings was an incident involving the duke of Lancaster. While jousting with a knight during a mêlée, another knight charged into him, wounding him severely.[38]

A few days later, at Windsor, King John ratified the peace treaty which had been negotiated at Westminster, known to historians as the First Treaty of London.[39] Its terms were very similar to the Guines agreement. The proposals of March 1357 had been seen by the dauphin in January, and settled. In reality he had very little choice: he was under huge pressure from the French parliament, barely suppressing a revolt over another reformation of the coinage, and was aware that Charles of Navarre had escaped from prison and was putting himself forward as a rival king. In addition an unofficial army of renegade English, German and Navarrese men-at-arms under the command of an Englishman, James Pipe, was pillaging its way up the Seine towards Paris, in total contravention of the truce. So the terms of the treaty were well-received in the city, where the people were sick of paying for the war, sick of being defeated, and sick to think that their own government still could not defend them from free-booters.[40] The only significant problem remained the question of how to raise the money to pay the king's ransom. Edward had demanded the massive sum of one million marks (£666,667). No doubt his own view was that this was not his problem: he could hardly be expected to ransom the king of France cheaply. Moreover he (Edward) had reason to think that he had been more than generous in not exacting further territorial concessions after Poitiers. That he felt he had been reasonable, and that the First Treaty of London was fair, is important to understanding what happened next in the Anglo-French war.

*

Queen Isabella's appearance at the Windsor tournament reminds us that that lady – now sixty-six – was still very much a prominent and active member of the English royal family. One of the most misleading stories of traditional medieval history is that, after the execution of Roger Mortimer in 1330, Edward locked his mother up in Castle Rising, where she went mad and eventually died. This is absolute rot. Although Isabella had been placed under a temporary house arrest at her castle at Berkhamsted in November 1330, she had only remained in that state for a month. Edward was devoted to her, and had her brought to Windsor to join him for that first Christmas after Mortimer's arrest. That this was a genuine closeness, and not just an opportunity for him to gloat over her fall, is shown by his subsequent behaviour towards her, for within a fort-night he had restored her income of £3,000 per year. He spent the next two months with her at Windsor, and often visited her there over the subse-quent two years. After that she often *visited* Castle Rising, which Edward had restored to her along with Hertford, Berkhamsted, Eltham, Leeds,

Cheylesmore and many of her other estates, but she was never imprisoned there or at any of these other places. In 1337, Edward raised her annual income to £4,500. By this time she was a frequent visitor to the court, celebrating his birthday with him, joining in his hunting parties, attending religious ceremonies with him, and watching his tournaments.[41] By 1348 she was again considered sufficiently respectable to represent Edward in diplomatic negotiations with France.[42]

This apparent rehabilitation is made understandable by two facts. First, Edward really had no need to punish her in 1330 as Mortimer had been the one who had posed the threat to his regnal authority, not Isabella. Edward also blamed Mortimer for creating the international dilemma of Edward II's secret survival. If Isabella had participated in not having her husband murdered, Edward could hardly blame her for that. The second underlying fact is that Edward and Isabella had a lot in common, much more than just being mother and son. Edward's interest in alchemy has already been noted; Isabella was also interested in the subject, and made several attempts to obtain the elixir of life which would preserve her once-famous good looks.[43] They both had an interest in spirituality and chivalric literature, as shown by the volumes left by Isabella at her death, which included several religious and Arthurian titles.[44] Like most aristocrats, they were both keen on music: Edward himself kept between five and nine minstrels, and Isabella rewarded liberally the minstrels of all the lords who came to visit her.[45] They were both obsessed even more than their contemporaries with jewels and bejewelled things. In 1357–58 Isabella spent no less than £1,400 on jewellery. The account of her jewels at her death reveals her to have owned many religious pieces – crucifixes, cameos, amulets and rosaries – but also hundreds of non-religious decorative items, such as gold rings with precious stones. One item in particular was described as 'a large brooch containing a thousand pearls'.[46] Edward's and Isabella's similar awareness of the importance of their appearance is highlighted by Isabella maintaining a bathroom, like Edward, and using make-up.[47] Most important of all they knew they were different to other people, for they were royal, and they shared a consciousness of what that royalty meant. It meant divine healing powers, political responsibilities from which one could not run, and (at the extreme) the requirement to put one's life at risk for the kingdom's benefit. To share in such a fundamental and yet minority identity was a powerful bonding force. In any reckoning of the women in Edward's life, Isabella has to loom very large indeed. Thus we may be sure that now Edward was deeply affected by his mother's death.

Edward remained close to his mother to the very end. The pages of her household account book for the last year of her life show that Edward himself came to dinner with her four times between October 1357 and May 1358.[48] He also sent presents regularly: casks of Gascon wine, a falcon, two caged birds and a wild boar. Her grandchildren came to see her: the prince of Wales came with Edward on 26 October 1357, and by himself on 6 April, and with the duke of Lancaster on 19 April. Lionel came to see his grandmother on 2 March 1358, John of Gaunt on 1 February, and Isabella of Woodstock visited with her father and the earl of March on 29 April. All this amounts to more than mere duty: one feels there was a great deal of goodwill towards the old lady.

That Queen Isabella remained sane – contrary to the old myth – is amply demonstrated by her appointment to negotiate with France in 1348, her regular pilgrimages to Canterbury and Walsingham, her involvement in the negotiations regarding Charles of Navarre in 1358, her participation in negotiations regarding the peace with France the same year, repeated visits from important individuals, and her travels to Windsor for the great tournament of 1358.[49] Her social life had greatly benefited from the victory of Poitiers, for the prince brought so many members of the French royal family to England as prisoners that she was able to catch up with many of her cousins. But for the last year of her life she had not been a well woman. On 12 March 1358 she had given her surgeon a gift of forty shillings. Four weeks earlier a messenger had been sent to London on three occasions to fetch medicines for the queen and to hire a horse to bring her physician, Master Lawrence. At the same time medicines were sought in St Albans.[50] Edward probably knew when he visited her on 20 March that she was dying. By then he would also have known that his sister, Queen Joan of Scotland, was on her way south for the great tournament at Windsor. So close was the family that, even though she had not seen her mother for thirty years, Queen Joan nursed her until her death. In these circumstances, it is remarkable that Isabella attended the Windsor tournament. Obviously the occasion was so great, and so important to Edward, that she did not want to miss it. Perhaps having finally seen her son's kingship reach its zenith, she was content. In August, during another bout of ill-health at Hertford Castle, more medicines were sought. On 20 August she summoned Master Lawrence from Canterbury to come with the utmost speed, but before he arrived, she was dead. She had chosen to have a very powerful draft of medicine administered, in a large quantity. So died Edward's pious, aged, once-beautiful and extraordinary mother, Queen Isabella the Fair, on 22 August 1358.

Edward cannot have been wholly surprised by the news of her death but he was nevertheless greatly saddened. Her servants each received a large reward from him.[51] He arranged the watching of her corpse at Hertford, and its transfer to the church of the Franciscans in London. He had the streets cleaned in readiness for the arrival of her corpse at the church. Her wish that she should be buried in 'the tunic and mantle of red silk and lined with grey cindon in which she had been married', fifty years earlier, was respected, and the garment was taken from the wardrobe where it had been lovingly preserved all those years.[52] She was buried on 27 November in the presence of Edward, Philippa and the whole royal family. It was the church where her lover's body had briefly lain twenty-eight years earlier, after his execution. In February 1359 Edward commissioned a fine tomb to be constructed for her, with an alabaster effigy, surrounded by metal railings made by the royal smith at the Tower.[53] In later years, on the anniversary of her death, he went to very great lengths to commemorate her. Every year he paid for three hundred wax torches to burn around her tomb, and for clothes for thirty paupers to bear these torches; for five pounds of spices to be burnt by the men staying at her tomb, and for Parisian towels to wrap around the spices while they were awaiting burning. He ordered three cloths of gold to be placed on the tomb on the eve and on the anniversary of her death every year, and on each occasion alms were given to the Franciscans, Augustinians and Carmelites, and to anchorite recluses in London, and to the prisoners in Newgate gaol, and to 'two poor sisters imploring God' for the benefit of the queen's soul.[54] Finally, the heart of Edward II was placed in Isabella's tomb, on her breast.[55] In terms of ceremony, Isabella's death meant more to Edward than anyone else's to date, even that of his much-loved daughter, Joan.

*

The first £100,000 instalment of King John's ransom was due on 1 November 1359. At the time of sealing the First Treaty of London, Edward had stipulated that every single clause had to be fully accepted and complied with, otherwise he would regard the treaty as being broken.[56] But over the summer the dauphin's government had been brought to the very brink of collapse. First Charles of Navarre had made it clear he was planning to seize the throne. James Pipe's army of marauders had left the villages of the Seine valley in ruins, their men dead, women raped and fields empty of all but the scattered bones of their cattle. Then things had turned utterly horrific. The dauphin himself had faced a revolution in which his ministers were murdered in front of him and he himself was forced to swear allegiance to the mob.[57] The revolution spread into a widespread peasant uprising, the Jacquerie, with terrible destruction and loss of life and property. Even when it was brought under control (by

Charles of Navarre, ironically), the tension remained between the Navarrese supporters and the dauphin. The Parisians refused to accept the dauphin back, and prompted a siege of the city which lasted throughout July. The ransom was thus a relatively minor inconvenience in comparison to the complete breakdown of law and order that summer.

Edward was not inclined to sympathise with the dauphin's plight. What was it to him, if his enemy proved incapable of good government? He had set the ransom; now he wanted it paid, and he refused to reopen negotiations on the matter. His mood was not improved by the funeral of his beloved mother. We will never know exactly how loss or grief may have affected his judgement, but it is reasonable to suppose that his mind was not wholly focused on the French problem in November 1358. The only real pressure for compromise came from King John. Despairing of events back in his kingdom, he now offered Edward whatever he wanted in return for peace.

In January 1359 the anger within Edward, mixed perhaps with frustration and grief began to rise again at a determined French refusal to pay. But King John still implored him to show restraint. John was his prisoner, but he was also Edward's kinsman and his guest. Edward also liked the man. He gave him presents of barrels of fine wine, lodged him in the Savoy Palace – a residence he himself had once used and which he subsequently had given to the duke of Lancaster – and after the ratification of the First Treaty of London he had invited him to go hunting with him at Windsor.[58] Although Edward gave orders on 2 January to gather bows and arrows at the Tower in readiness for a campaign, and ordered an army of archers and Welsh spearmen to be made ready, he still listened to John. John asked him to discuss terms with him, face to face, excluding all the counsellors and diplomats. Edward assented, knowing an army was on the way. But John said the right things, made the right offer, and on 24 March 1359 the Second Treaty of London was agreed between the two kings. John added Normandy, Brittany, Maine, Touraine and Anjou to the territories already ceded to Edward. This amounted to the entire Angevin Empire at its very height – under Henry II – and thus the greatest extent of the English royal family's lordship. In recognition of this generous provision by John, Edward reduced the ransom due to £500,000 and threw in all the other French prisoners, including the other members of the royal family, for free. The first instalment of £100,000 was rescheduled to 1 August 1359.[59] Edward would then release John in return for the security of ten French noblemen and twenty walled towns.

It was an agreement which gave Edward everything he had ever hoped to achieve and more, and he had reason to feel satisfied. He ordered one of the French prisoners, Marshal Audrehem, to take the agreement to Paris for ratification by the dauphin. Then, humoured again by the prospect of a permanent settlement which was very much to his advantage, he turned his attention to family celebrations.

Although now in his forty-eighth year, only one of his children was married, and he had only one legitimate grandchild. This was Philippa, daughter of Lionel and his wife Elizabeth de Burgh, who had been born at Eltham in August 1355. He also had an illegitimate grandson, Roger, who had been born to Edith Willesford, one of the women at Clarendon, after the prince of Wales had taken a fancy to her, but even so, the paucity of descendants was noticeable. The only step he had so far taken to remedy this was the betrothal the previous year of little Philippa to the six-year-old heir of the earl of March, and obviously it would be many years before that match produced offspring.[60] So to make up for lost time he now held a double wedding. On 19 May 1359 (the very day that the Estates General met in Paris to discuss the treaty) Edward's thirteen-year-old daughter Margaret was married at Reading Abbey to the twelve-year-old earl of Pembroke. The following day, in the same church, John of Gaunt (now eighteen) married Blanche, the thirteen-year-old daughter of the duke of Lancaster. All the royal family were there, and many costly gifts of jewellery and goblets were given. Edward himself gave extremely lavish presents to Blanche totalling nearly £400 in value, including 'a large brooch with an eagle and a huge diamond in its breast, garnished with rubies, diamonds and pearls' which alone was valued at £120.[61] Ten days later, at Smithfield, Edward and his four eldest sons dressed up as the mayor and aldermen of London along with nineteen other knights in a great three-day tournament, at which they took on all challengers.[62] Edward was revelling in his victory and the celebration of his family. At times like these, life was one long glorious chivalric parade.

It was probably while awaiting the ratification of the treaty by the French that Edward visited Westminster Abbey to confirm his decision to be buried there.[63] The prophecy said that he would be buried among the Three Kings in Cologne Cathedral. In 1338 he had visited the shrine, but the following year, as relations with the Holy Roman Emperor wore thin, he ruled out any discussion of being buried in Germany, and decided on Westminster.[64] For him, there was clearly no great honour in being buried abroad, even among the Three Kings. He had become the pride of England, for in achieving what was prophesied, he had rendered the prophetic writers' wildest fantasies attainable. Besides, Westminster Abbey was a fine place to be buried. Edward's great-grandparents (Henry III and Eleanor of Provence) and his grandparents (Edward I and Eleanor of

Castile) lay there, as did his brother John and two of his own infant children (William of Windsor and Blanche). St Edward the Confessor, the king who founded the abbey, lay there, behind the high altar. Henry III, who had rebuilt the abbey church, lay just to the north of the saint-king. There was a space directly opposite, just to the south of the saint. That would be where he would be buried, he declared. That was where the great chivalric parade of his life would finally come to an end.

*

What did Edward expect from the Second Treaty of London? No one really knows. Some writers have confidently asserted that Edward never expected the French to accept it, hoping that they would restart the war. Others have been more circumspect, suggesting that Edward was acting reasonably in reducing the ransom for the French king. However, most of these studies have been war-orientated and thus they have ignored Edward's personal ambitions or the changing attitudes of a man approaching old age. There is no doubt that Edward's many attempts after 1350 to bring the war to a successful and permanent end were genuine. Some proposals were extreme, but the reason for their extremeness was to allow Edward to press for the best deal possible, for unless he began negotiating with excessive demands, he would not arrive at the maximum gains. None of the four peace proposals were put forward because he wanted to resume the war: there were easier and more direct ways of starting fighting than protracted peace negotiations. Thus it must have been with regret that he learnt in May 1359 that the Second Treaty of London would not be ratified by the interim French government.

The dauphin was determinedly against the peace his father had negotiated, largely because he saw his inheritance being eroded. The Estates General were inclined to agree. They had not expected an escalated series of territorial concessions, they had expected Edward to lessen his demands. The figures for the ransom were so large that they could not acknowledge that Edward had made any concession. They had forgotten in the course of the debate that he did not need to concede anything at all. The Jacquerie had been none of his doing; rather it had sprung from successive failures of the French government. But such things did not enter the reckoning. What mattered was French public sentiment. When the Estates General and the dauphin refused to accept the Second Treaty of London, they did so mainly out of pride. They had nothing else left with which to fight.

Edward's final campaign was an ambitious affair. The army was reasonably large – in the region of ten thousand men – and the captains were experienced and numerous. The prince of Wales, the duke of Lancaster and the earl of Northampton were present, as were the earls of Stafford, Warwick and March, and, of course, Lord Manny.[65] Edward's younger sons, Lionel, John and Edmund, were also with him, expected to win their spurs as their elder brother had at Crécy. Given the failure of the supply lines in 1355, Edward went well-prepared, with mobile forges, portable cornmills, movable ovens, lightweight boats for crossing rivers, building materials and a huge volume of foodstuffs.[66] Froissart described it as 'the largest army and best-appointed train of baggage wagons that had ever left England'. Edward declared he would stay in France until he had satisfied his objectives or died in the attempt. The permanent solution to the French problem, which had seemed so close in the mid-1350s, was now within his grasp.

Edward sailed from Sandwich on 28 October, arriving at Calais on the same day. One week later the army moved out, in three great columns, to begin the devastation. This time, however, their purpose was not to draw the French army to battle. There was no point: there was no effective army in France. The kingdom was economically broken, its currency was in free-fall and large numbers of renegade and volunteer self-serving armies, like that commanded by James Pipe, were roaming the countryside destroying, plundering and burning. The French administration had difficulty controlling affairs outside Paris, and that city can hardly be said to have been reliable, having so recently tried to rid itself of the dauphin. Edward's purpose in 1359 was a single-minded attempt to demonstrate to the dauphin and the Estates General that they had been foolish to choose war rather than to accept the Guines agreement or the two treaties of London. He went determined to unleash the terrible wrath of a divinely favoured biblical king upon his enemies.

The dauphin had miscalculated. He soon realised that he had no means to resist the invaders. He had no way of raising an army, coordinating resistance or even rebuilding the strategic fortifications of his kingdom. Moreover, his weary father had ransomed his most able advisers in England and sent them back to relieve him of administrative power. They tried to make the best of the situation, ordering everyone threatened by the invaders to abandon their homes and take what they could with them to the nearest walled town or religious sanctuary. Where a town's walls were decayed beyond repair, the town was to be abandoned before the onslaught began. All the French government could do beyond that was to hope, defend Paris, and pray.

Their prayers were answered. Rain began to fall hard, for days on end. Even before 1359 Edward would have ranked as one of the most weather-stricken English kings, but now he was truly soaked. The roads of France became quagmires which prevented his army from moving at more than ten miles a day. The three columns of the army embarked on their ritual desecration of property in a sodden mass of discontent, ransacking the houses in deserted villages as the rain lashed down and saturated their clothes. The commanders too were uncomfortable, themselves soaked, and their prize warhorses' backs blistering under their leather saddles. The three battalions found it difficult to maintain contact with one another. It took them a whole month to reach Edward's principal target, the city of Rheims.

Rheims was the ancient ceremonial place of coronation for the French kings. Edward had brought a crown with him, and there is no doubt he intended to ridicule French objections to the treaty by having himself crowned king in the coronation throne of his ancestors. There could be no greater symbol of his domination over the French monarchy, and no more powerful vindication of his claims to the sovereignty of Gascony and his other French possessions. Thus the English armies closed in on Rheims with a strong will, encircling the city: the duke of Lancaster to the north, the earl of March to the east, the earls of Richmond and Northampton to the north-west and the prince of Wales to the south-west.[67]

The French within Rheims were panic-stricken when they realised that they were to be singled out for attack. They argued among themselves in fear. The proud archbishop was adamant that his palace and ecclesiastical buildings within the city should not be used for military purposes of any kind. But the man whom the citizens appointed to coordinate the defence was a man of higher calibre. Gaucher de Châtillon was as ruthless in his defence of the city as Edward was in his attack. The walls were strong, but he made them higher and stronger. He commandeered the church buildings, fortified church towers, organised the citizens into watches and defensive units, walled up three of the city's gates and dug ditches around the city walls. Streets were blocked with chains, horses requisitioned (including those belonging to the archbishop) and any property which posed a threat to the security of the city was razed to the ground. There was no king in Rheims, nor was the dauphin present. The last-ditch defence of the dignity of the French monarchy was made in their absence.

The English had the experience, skill and means to defeat any army which might conceivably be brought against them, but they did not necessarily have the means to defeat a well-defended city. For two days archers poured a deadly rain of arrows at the defenders as the men-at-arms and infantry filled the ditches with timbers to allow them to approach the walls. The brave citizens did what they had to. Parties of men left the gates and went into the ditches to fight and to try to burn the sodden timbers which allowed the English to approach the walls. Between the rain, the bitter cold, the lack of provisions and the bloody desperation of the men of Rheims, the English were beaten back and forced to consider how long they might have to spend waiting in the mud.

Edward fully understood what made the difference between a successful siege and an unsuccessful one. At Calais he had been able to demonstrate complete superiority through being able to maintain an army for almost a year before the impregnable walls. At Tournai, which also had proved impregnable, he had failed because the city had been well-equipped and his men had grown disillusioned through lack of supplies and money. The question put to him now by Gaucher de Châtillon was whether he was prepared to commit the resources necessary to win Rheims. It would take a long siege, perhaps a whole year, and that would give the French government a chance to reconstitute the French army in sufficient strength to destroy Edward's supply lines, if not directly to attack him. And Edward's supply lines were already proving vulnerable. And at the end of the siege, supposing he was successful, what would he have gained? A city in which he could be crowned like his ancestors but which was strategically worthless. To spend perhaps £200,000 on what would ultimately be a single gesture would be folly, especially when the purpose of that gesture was simply to force the dauphin and Estates General to accept a treaty which King John had already agreed. There had to be another way, and years of devastating France told Edward that there was. A grand march of destruction would bring the French government to its knees.

On 11 January 1360 Edward ordered his army to withdraw from Rheims and march towards Paris. The siege had failed, Edward had been denied the satisfaction of a coronation, but the cost to the French was to prove very high indeed. Everywhere there was looting, killing and burning, accompanied by some of the most hideous massacres. It is difficult to exaggerate the number and range of atrocities recorded, and many more must have been committed which were never written down. There were some incidents which contain an element of chivalric charm: Lord Burghersh invited the resolute captain of Cormicy to survey the mine he had dug under the castle, pointing out that a few wooden pit props were all that held up the walls of the great tower. And there were English losses along the way. The marshal of the army, the earl of March, having taken the towns of Saint-Florentin and Tonnerre, died suddenly while besieging Rouvray, and the poet Geoffrey Chaucer was captured while straying a little too far from the main army, requiring Edward to contribute to his ransom. But on the whole the campaign was a horrifying demonstration of the 'smoke and flames of his country' which Edward had promised John in 1355.

It is very easy, tempting even, to regard the campaign of 1359–60 as a failed siege followed by a trail of wanton destruction. It does not appear an edifying form of conflict. We prefer to read of well-conceived daring exercises being successfully and bravely carried out to achieve specific strategic aims. But warfare is very rarely as neat and tidy as that, and often the most effective methods are the most horrific. And there is no doubt that, after lifting the siege, Edward was able to put far more pressure on the French government by using tactics of shock and horror, similar to those adopted by modern generals with superior firepower at their disposal. Each act in itself was wanton and pitiless, but taken together they constituted a powerful strategy which undermined French resistance. Having no army to bring against Edward, the French administration could only respond with diplomatic entreaties, channelled through the services of the papacy. Five weeks spent besieging Rheims had had little or no effect, but five weeks of widespread destruction left France reeling. After seven weeks it began to yield the desired result. A papal delegation came to Edward requesting a peace conference. Edward's terms were no less than the implementation of the Second Treaty of London, and the French withdrew, professing amazement at his harshness. So the next day the village of Orly was attacked and its population massacred in the parish church. The next day more villages were completely destroyed, their women raped and their men killed. A Benedictine priory where twelve hundred people had taken refuge was burnt by its French garrison after the refugees made an attempt to surrender. Nine hundred died in the fires which the French garrison lit, and the remaining three hundred were killed by the English as they fled. At the gates of Paris a battle between thirty newly dubbed English knights and sixty French knights resulted in the vanquishing of the French. Lord Manny led a contingent to burn the suburbs. All the portents were grim for the French. With the smoke of the burning villages visible to the south, the Parisians started to destroy those last few extra-mural buildings which Manny had left standing.[68]

And then dawned Monday 13 April: Black Monday as it would be known for centuries in England. Even Edward had never seen anything to compare with the weather that day. A storm broke, but it was not just a storm. As the skies darkened and thunder crashed above them, the temperature dropped so suddenly that a wall of ice fell. Huge hailstones rained down, killing men and animals in their thousands. Out in the open, just to the south of Paris, Edward's men had little hope of finding shelter. With the landscape lit by lightning and the thunder above them, and everywhere ice missiles descending, it must have been terrifying. In later years the chroniclers all wrote in awe of the event. Froissart wrote that 'it seemed as if the heavens would crack, and the earth open up and swallow every-thing'.[69] Thomas of Walsingham stated that several thousand men and horses died. The author of the *Eulogium Historiarum* wrote that many men died of snow, hail and rain. Henry Knighton wrote that hail killed six thousand horses and a large number of men. Other sources put the number of dead men at one thousand, including the eldest son of the earl of Warwick, who died of injuries sustained in this storm two weeks later.[70]

There is no doubt that Black Monday was a momentous event, and no doubt that it affected Edward's strategy. But exactly how and to what extent remains a mystery. The view of contemporaries and writers prior to the eighteenth century was that 'Edward, like a good and pious prince, looked upon it as a loud declaration of divine pleasure: wherefore alighting imme-diately from his horse, he kneeled down on the ground, and casting his eyes towards the church of Our Lady of Chartres, made a solemn vow to Almighty God that he would now sincerely and absolutely incline his mind to a final peace with France, if he might obtain good conditions.'[71] Twentieth-century writers, less inclined to understand divine signals as a motivation, were far more cynical, and regarded Black Monday simply as an excuse.[72] But Edward did believe in the connection between God's will and the weather; six thousand dead horses and up to one thousand dead men in a hailstorm was a clear indication that God was not pleased. Therefore we have to ask, was Edward finally brought to the negotiating table by the difficulties of sustaining an army in the field? Or was it down to his belief that on Black Monday he had been spoken to by God?

Edward was forty-seven years of age. Much had happened since Halidon Hill, after which he had given thanks to God for his first great victory. After that he had gone on many pilgrimages, often after surviving a storm or winning a battle. There is no evidence that this was ever a cynical ploy, to make him look religious, let alone that it was cynically motivated on every single occasion. Such was the regularity of his acts of thanksgiving that we must lay aside the postulation that Edward's shows of religion were merely routine. His personal religious zeal might not have been unusual, but we must remember that Edward was living in a deeply religious age. He may have been a great warrior, but so was Lancaster, and Lancaster wrote a book on religious salvation. Also Edward's spirituality had prob-ably increased since the 1330s, not lessened. There had been some signif-icant religious acts over the years, such as donating a figure of St Thomas to Canterbury Cathedral, the pardon to Cecilia Ridgeway, and a commis-sion to search for the body of Joseph of Arimathea at Glastonbury Abbey in 1345. All these do not force us to believe that Edward was a holy man, but neither do they suggest a cynical approach to manifestations of divine will. Edward certainly believed that there was a connection between extreme, life-threatening storms and divine providence. The most obvious example of this is his four pilgrimages, including one to Canterbury from London on foot, and his gift of a valuable golden ship to each shrine after being saved from the storm in March 1343. Therefore Black Monday may well have been pivotal in convincing Edward that the time had come to stop the destruction, settle his military account and accept the best terms that the French were prepared to offer.

The French were of course fully aware of the effects of the storm, and they had been protected in their houses from the worst of it, but they had seen and suffered enough. If Edward was having problems supplying his army in the field, they all knew that he would simply turn in a new direction and savage another place, another string of villages, another few towns. His armies had swerved this way and that between Rheims and Paris, devastating a huge area. The time had come for them to swallow their pride. The question they placed on the table now was whether the territorial concessions of the First Treaty of London, coupled with the reduced ransom demand of £500,000 for all the French prisoners, would be sufficient to appease Edward? In all probability Edward had already decided that this would be the basis for a permanent peace, but, playing the part of a wrathful, Old Testament king, he could not be seen to acquiesce so easily. As with his acts of mercy, he preferred to be asked to temper his fury by others. According to Froissart, it was his greatest friend, the duke of Lancaster, who now assumed this role. 'You can press on with your struggle and pass the rest of your life fighting', the duke is supposed to have said, 'or you can make terms with your enemy and end the war now with honour.' Edward had come to the end of his war. He wisely chose the latter.[73]

The negotiations took place at Brétigny from 1 May 1360 and were finalised on 8 May. Edward agreed in principle to relinquish his claim on the French throne in return for sovereignty of all the territories he had inherited as a vassal and many of those he had subsequently obtained by conquest. Details remained to be sorted out with the captive French king, but Edward was satisfied. He had achieved his aims, and secured everything he had fought for. The claim on the French throne had proved a very powerful negotiating position indeed, but, like the territorial claims of the Second Treaty of London, it had served its purpose, and could now be dispensed with. Edward ordered the English army to march to Honfleur, from which he sailed on 18 May. After landing at Rye, there was feasting in the royal household every day for two weeks.[74]

He had returned in triumph.

FIFTEEN

Outliving Victory

The war was over. After eight years of struggling to capitalise on his dominant military position, Edward had finally achieved a lasting settlement. All that remained was for King John to relinquish sovereignty of the lands agreed and for Edward formally to renounce his claim on the French throne. In October 1360 he crossed the Channel to Calais to see these things done. A few questions remained about the renunciations, and these clauses had to be removed from the final treaty and inserted into a separate document to be discussed further, but otherwise the Brétigny agreement was ratified at Calais on 24 October. Edward returned to England and summoned parliament to meet after Christmas, the ratification by parliament being the very last stage in ending the war.

As every reader knows, the conflict which Edward believed he had brought to an end after twenty-three years fighting is now known as the Hundred Years War. The name is misleading, for it suggests that it was one great, protracted struggle. At several times in the fourteenth century the war came to an end, and peace treaties were entered into – and ratified – in good faith. We tend to forget that different stages of 'the war' broke out for different reasons. Some would say that there was no such thing as the Hundred Years War. What we have so far heard about is just the first phase of the great conflict which was given an ideological unity by presenting the English claim to the throne of France as real. But this first phase was essentially a war of rivalry between Edward III and Philip de Valois, in which Edward's claim was a means to an end, not an end in itself (unlike later stages of the conflict). Almost every aspect of Edward's involvement in the war since hearing of Philip's death had been an attempt to secure a lasting peace on good terms for the English. It is more accurate therefore to think of Edward in 1360 as having achieved a belated but satisfactory end to this war of rivalry.

Edward was now nearing fifty. His original rival was long-since dead. His victories were of such glory and magnitude that he could not have easily repeated them. He was more interested in great building projects than protracted sieges. Besides, his health was not good.[1] His wife's health too was declining. Almost the first thing he did when returning to England in 1360 was to merge his household with Philippa's, with the implication that henceforth they would be together. He was not going to spend the rest of his days fighting a futile war with France which, in his own mind, he had already won. It was time for him to enjoy the fruits of his labours, in peace, and to spend his last days of companionship with his much-loved queen, creating works of lasting beauty.

Edward and Philippa spent Christmas 1360 at Woodstock with their sons and daughters and the king of France.[2] Here Edward wore a coat he had specially commissioned. It was made of black satin embroidered in gold and silk thread with the image of a woodbine – a climbing plant, such as ivy or honeysuckle – and bearing the motto in gold lettering 'Syker as ye Wodebynd' (clinging like the woodbine).[3] This is the fourth and last of Edward's known mottoes, and in many ways it is the most mysterious. If the first ('It is as it is') is to be associated with the death of Edward's father, the second ('Hay, hay the white swan, by God's soul I am thy man') is to be loosely associated with the tournaments of 1348–49, and the third ('*Honi soit . . .*') with Lancaster, then we should be looking for another personal subject as the inspiration.[4] Without further evidence it is impossible to be certain, but it seems that this motto is Edward's own comment on himself and his queen: a reflection on his career and the part she had played in his success. She had been the tree around which he had climbed, twisting like ivy. She was like a pillar to him, a source of courage and self-confidence despite his wanderings and adventures, and had been ever since the day they married. His open appreciation of her loyalty and support after more than thirty years is touching, and inclines us to see the kindness and gratitude of the man. But the motto is also interesting in that Edward clearly compares himself to the searching, questioning woodbine. This is apt; since that frightened, lonely boy-king under Mortimer's dominance, Edward had been feeling his way like the climbing ivy. Even the firm policies on which he relied strategically had been discovered through trial and error: he cannot be said to have inherited them from his father. In looking for the man's own idea of himself we should not ignore this unique case of self-definition. He had always been searching for the way to be a great king, and, now that he was one, he realised that it had only been possible due to the consistent and devoted support of Queen Philippa. She had been the strong emotional foundation for his experiment in kingship. Later events would prove this to be only too true: as her sickness worsened, so did his leadership. She was essential to his continuing to strive to be a great king.

So what does a warrior-king do when he has won his last battle? What does he do when he has sealed the peace treaty on his last war? What does the climbing woodbine seek? Edward, of course, had already given much thought to this question. There were the permanent structures of the Order of the Garter and his religious foundations. There were his many secular building projects, especially Windsor Castle and Queenborough, to which he now could direct more money than ever before. And there was parliament. When he entered the Painted Chamber in 1361 it was to the smiles and delight of the representatives of a grateful people. Even the most ardent anti-war merchants had to be pleased, for now they could expect to be taxed less. Ratification was predictably swift and complete. On 2 February the first ransom instalment was received from the French and, following oaths in the presence of the archbishop of Canterbury, King John was free to return to his devastated homeland.

The parliament of 1361 was more than a mere congratulatory assembly. It was like the great parliaments of the 1350s: it transformed the enthusiasm of the time and the rapid economic development of the country into business decisions and social legislation. The king and representatives locked together in a debate about power over everyday lives. The Statute of Labourers was reinforced, the earlier legislation regarding weights and measures was renewed. Laws were passed restricting the exportation of corn and banning jurors from receiving bribes. Given Edward's interest in hunting, it is interesting to note that a law was passed ensuring that the lord who lost a hawk could legally expect its finder to return it to him. But by far the most important legislation of this parliament was an Act which became the basis of local administration in England for the next half-millennium. Edward agreed, at long last, to the principle that local landholders should have the right to arrest, try and punish minor wrong-doers. In each county there were to be four Justices of the Peace to try offenders. Serious cases were still to be tried by the royal assize courts, but local justice had finally arrived. Two years later Edward expanded the JP's role to include quarterly meetings: the 'Quarter Sessions'. It was only in the nineteenth century that this structure of local government began to be replaced. The basic legislation empowering JPs is still in force today.

Edward and his contemporaries had every reason to believe that the subsequent decade would be an age of great achievements. Parliament could expect legal battles, the king could build and live in splendour. Few at the parliament of 1361, seeing the peace ratified, and realising that English local government had become a reality, could possibly have guessed how the coming year would be marked not by a glorious peace but by tragedy.

*

A number of Edward's close companions had died over the last year. The young earl of March – marshal of the English army, Knight of the Garter and still only thirty-one – had died in France in 1360. Edward had his body brought back to England and gave expensive offerings at his burial at Wigmore and at his obsequies at Windsor.[5] In September 1360 another Knight of the Garter, the earl of Northampton, died. He was Edward's contemporary, one of his bravest generals and one of the few men left who had been there with Edward that night when Mortimer had been arrested, thirty years earlier. Edward gave several expensive cloths of gold for his funeral too.[6] Two more Garter knights were buried at the end of the year: Sir John Beauchamp (standard-bearer at Crécy) and the veteran warrior Sir Thomas Holland, husband of the Fair Maid of Kent and the man who had bellowed across the Seine at the French on the Crécy campaign. Edward's old friends were disappearing fast.

The biggest blow, however, was Lancaster's death, on 23 March 1361.[7] Lancaster had been Edward's most trusted friend for about twenty years. He had won several major battles as sole leader, had fought under Edward's banner, been present at the siege of Calais, and had won countless skirmishes and minor sieges. He had been one of the six earls created in 1337 and the chief negotiator in Edward's search for peace since 1353. It was probably his garters which had resulted in the emblem being adopted by Edward's chivalric order. He had wisdom, strength, courage and luck. Furthermore he had that quality which Edward prized above all others: royalty, as the great-grandson of Henry III, like Edward himself. And he had great piety too. In his *The Book of Holy Medicines* he has left us the most detailed first-hand account of the character of a great magnate at Edward's court. He was not only literate, he prized being able to write, having taught himself. He could speak English as well as French. He was pious, the general theme of *The Book of Holy Medicines* being a description of how his five senses had become infected with the Seven Deadly Sins. And with almost Pepysian self-deprecating honesty he admitted to exactly how this had happened over the course of his life. In his youth he had been tall, slim, good-looking, and vain. He had taken great pleasure in regarding the rings on his fingers and his foot in the stirrup. He had loved dancing and music, and had worn the most exquisite clothes (he thought garters particularly suited him). He had made love to many women, sung songs to them, then 'loved and lost them'. He admitted that he much preferred the embraces of common women to aristocratic ones as they were less censorious of his behaviour. At the time of writing he was in his early fifties, suffering from gout, but still very partial to salmon (his favourite food), spices and strong sauces, and he loved drinking good wine in quantity. Like Edward, in 1360 feasting and hunting were his greatest passions (love-making having fallen by the wayside of middle age), but the song of the nightingale and the scents of

The king.

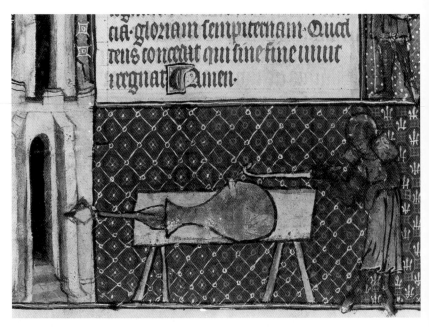

Walter Milemete's treatise on kingship presented to Edward in about 1327 includes many illustrations, including this one, the earliest image of a cannon. It was thought to be a very inaccurate drawing until the discovery of the Loshult gun (*below*).

The Loshult gun, found in Sweden in the nineteenth century, resembles the cannon shown in Milemete's treatise. Edward pushed the development of firearms, but even this primitive weapon had a range of nearly a mile.

Edward overseeing a gun attack on the city of Rheims. Edward did more than any other individual in history to change the nature of combat from hand-to-hand fighting to projectile warfare.

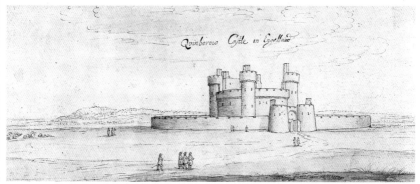

Queenborough Castle, drawn by Wenceslas Hollar. Not a stone survives now of Edward's great castle on the Isle of Sheppey. It was both a royal residence and the world's first purpose-built gun emplacement.

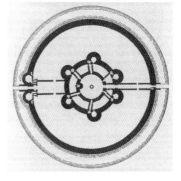

Ground plan of Queenborough Castle.

Edward's sword and shield, at Westminster Abbey. The sword is five feet four inches long.

Edward's signature, 'Pater Sancte' – a cipher on his letter to the pope of about 1329–30 – is the earliest extant handwriting by a member of the English royal family. The original of this letter is in the Vatican.

Windsor Castle, Edward's birthplace. Although the outer walls are largely as they were in the thirteenth century, the inner structures were entirely rebuilt by Edward. At more than £50,000, it was the most expensive single building in medieval England. It was to Edward's realm what the baroque masterpiece of Versailles was to Louis XIV's France.

George III commissioned the American artist Benjamin West to paint a series of scenes representing the noble virtues. This shows Edward leading his army across the Somme, just prior to the battle of Crécy.

By the nineteenth century, the age of chivalry was seen as a time of myth and legend.
This painting, by Edwin Landseer, shows Queen Victoria and Prince Albert dressed as
Queen Philippa and Edward III, at a ball in 1842.

roses, musk, violets and lily of the valley were also dear to him. This was the man whom Edward now lost, an intelligent, sensual, brave cousin, a successful commander, the father-in-law of his son John, and his best friend. At his funeral, in the collegiate church at Leicester, Edward gave four cloths of gold Eastern brocade and four of gold brocade of Lucca in his memory.[8]

Worse was to follow. On 26 February 1361 burning lights had been seen across the sky at midnight.[9] Some said they formed the shape of the cross, and many were afraid. There was an eclipse of the sun, followed by a severe drought. Corn, fruit and hay withered and died in the spring. It was said that not rain but blood fell at Boulogne. Others said that men had seen images of two castles in the sky, from which black and white hosts issued to fight one another. All these strange events were soon explained as forewarnings of a calamitous event. The portents may have been illusory but the calamity itself was not. In May the plague returned.

It is easy for us to take the view that the plague of 1361 was not as bad as that of 1348–49. After all, people knew what to expect, and would have been less shocked. But for exactly that reason the return of the plague – with the widespread expectation that it *would* be as bad as 1348–49 – must have been deeply unsettling. People had thought that the plague had gone forever; so with its return, they became aware that it had not, but might return again and again, as indeed it did. Children were particularly vulnerable. Anyone not born before 1349 had no resistance, and one chronicler speaks of the plague being the Children's Plague as a result of the high infant mortality.

For Edward the return of the plague carried a particular resonance. It challenged him again to show his faith that God would protect him by appearing regularly in public. But would God protect him now that he had won his war? Such reasoning was normal in the spiritual climate of 1361. After the 1360 campaign God had seen fit to summon five Knights of the Garter to his heavenly table, their earthly duties done. Lancaster may even have been killed by the plague, as many chroniclers said.[10] Would God now kill off Edward too?

During the last visitation of the plague, Edward had ostentatiously held the Order of the Garter tournament at Windsor. Since then the Windsor tournament and mass in St George's Chapel had become a fixture of the royal calendar. With plague once more encroaching on the spirit of the nation, the Windsor tournament again became the focal point of Edward's demonstration that royalty did not shrink from mortal diseases. He seized the opportunity to make the 1361 feast of St George every bit as high-profile as its predecessors. As five Knights of the Garter had recently died, he installed other men in their places, including his three sons, Lionel, John and Edmund. Along with the usual blue robes of the Order, black and scarlet lengths of material were ordered in large quantities, possibly for teams of living knights to joust against mourners or the dead. More than two hundred garter emblems were ordered to be sewn, many furs were trimmed as gifts, and more than eight hundred brooches were made to be given out at the king's will.[11]

After the tournament festivities Edward went to Sheppey to oversee the foundation laying of his new town and castle. The plague spread, killing thousands. The cemeteries were reopened. Men of substance began to pack up and head off for their most remote estates. On 10 May Edward suspended the actions of all the law courts as a consequence of the pestilence.[12] Many lesser men, panic-stricken by the approach of the disease, seized what they thought might be their last opportunity to go on a pilgrimage, to atone for their sins. In this way they spread the disease further. By the summer it was rife.

Edward staged two more high-profile events. These took the form of royal marriages. The first, and easiest to arrange, was the wedding at Woodstock of his seventeen-year-old daughter Mary to the young John de Montfort, claimant to the duchy of Brittany, who had grown up at the English court. The second was a much more controversial match: the prince of Wales and Joan, the Fair Maid of Kent. It seems that, not long after Sir Thomas Holland's death, the prince moved in on the widow. This was commonly rumoured to have been a love-match, and it seems almost certain that it was. Joan's marital history was notorious, she had had two husbands already, had given birth to five children and was now about thirty-three years of age. Edward himself had intended his son and heir to marry an heiress from the Low Countries, but the pope had been holding up such a match for years, refusing to grant the necessary dispensation. It was with surprise but no regrets that Edward acquiesced to his son's desire to marry his second cousin. He wrote to the pope that summer to ask permission for the marriage. This was swiftly granted. With great ceremony, the Black Prince and his fair bride were married by the archbishop of Canterbury, at Windsor on 10 October 1361.

Some chroniclers wrote of their shock at this union. Joan – 'the Virgin of Kent' as one writer sarcastically referred to her – was now set to become queen.[13] Froissart (who probably met her on several occasions) described her as both the most beautiful woman in England and also the most given over to love. Not only was she bigamous and believed to be adulterous, she was profligate too. She was quite capable of spending £200 on a set of jewelled buttons: a show of outrageous flamboyance worthy of Edward himself.[14] But Edward, despite the rumours of her unsuitability, seems to have raised no objection to the match. Indeed, he condoned it, sending his own man to ask for the papal dispensation. After the wedding the couple retired to Berkhamsted for the rest of the year, where Edward visited them after Christmas.

No matter how many high-profile events Edward held, no matter how much he tried to show that royal business was proceeding as normal, the plague continued. He could not hold back the tide of death which again swept across the country. After the first suspension of the law courts in May, Edward was forced to suspend them again. Law and order suffered. Women whose husbands had been lost to the disease were forced to marry 'strangers' by their manorial bailiffs, or else lose their homes and lands. Edward was forced to suspend the operations of the Exchequer to try to stop the spread of the disease. Taxation and finance suffered. And among the dying there now were people who mattered to Edward. Although he was probably not in the least upset to hear of the death in June of Thomas Lisle, the embittered bishop of Ely, he would have been concerned by the death in September of the bishop of London, Michael Northburgh, co-founder (with Sir Walter Manny) of the London Charterhouse. Far more distressing were the deaths on 4 and 5 October respectively of Sir John Mowbray and Sir Reginald Cobham. The latter especially had been one of the principal architects of the battle of Crécy. A few days later the earl of Hereford died. Two weeks after that, Sir William Fitzwarin, another Knight of the Garter, became another casualty of the plague. The bishop of Worcester was added to the list a month later.

These deaths were all of little import by comparison with the death of his daughter Mary in September.[15] She was only just married, only seventeen. Shortly afterwards, Edward's youngest daughter Margaret also died. Like her sister, she had not been long married, and, like her sister, she probably died of plague. Sadly the royal family made its way to Abingdon to bury the two royal princesses together in the abbey there. Of Edward's five daughters, he had lost all but one, Isabella.

Blow after blow had rained down on Edward. Death after death. And the questions about his victory in France were beginning to circulate at court. The problems were merely technical, but mere technicalities had undone the peace process before. There were still unresolved doubts about the actual boundary decisions of certain lands which Edward claimed the French had given up, and he demanded that the French king renounce sovereignty of them. John refused, and so Edward refused formally to renounce his claim on the throne of France until the matter was sorted out. This was not a ploy to allow him to begin the war again, as some writers have suggested, for the authority he issued to his son in Gascony clearly anticipated that his claim on the throne *would* be given up.[16] But discussions in plague-stricken London in October 1361 were followed by further discussions in Paris, with no solution. An added complication was that many English soldiers of fortune were trying to make money in France in its crisis years, acting as bands of renegade soldiers, with no political affiliation. In November their antics were brought to Edward's attention, who commissioned John Hound and Richard Imworth to arrest any English men-at-arms or archers found plundering in France. Even though Imworth was an utterly ruthless man, later described as 'a tormentor without pity', it was not easy to stop these self-serving bands of robbers.[17] Twenty-three years of war had led to an attitude of self-interest and violence towards France. It certainly was impossible to reverse that trend overnight.

*

At the beginning of 1362 Edward was in his fiftieth year, heading for that birthday which would bring up his personal jubilee. This was a significant milestone: with it came the unavoidable awareness that he was entering old age. Although fifty might seem barely middle-aged to the majority of modern readers, it was over the hill for most medieval aristocrats. The average age of the five Knights of the Garter who had died in 1360 was forty-three.[18]

The one positive, creative policy which emerges over the two years leading up to his fiftieth birthday is Edward's strategy of giving his sons positions of dignity and responsibility. If he was deeply upset by the loss of his close friends and daughters – and there is no reason to suppose he was not – he seems to have pushed his energies into furthering his sons' careers. By mid-1362 he had settled his ideas for the eldest three. Edward was to be given the title Prince of Aquitaine in addition to that of Prince of Wales, becoming the resident seigneurial lord of that province. Lionel was to start to put his Irish inheritance to good use, bringing that country back into line with royal authority. And John of Gaunt was to be given the lordship of the north. Clearly Edward's idea was to create a series of lesser kings under his sovereignty. Rather than being a king who ruled only a prince and a dozen or so earls, he would be a king who ruled over several dukes and a prince, just as King John ruled over the dukes of Normandy, Burgundy, Brittany and Orléans.

The first filial ship to be launched upon the high seas of international politics was Lionel. In 1360 the Anglo-Irish had been in a desperate situation and had written to Edward urging him to send 'a good sufficient chieftain, stocked and strengthened with men and treasure' to fight the native Irish and restore English rule in central Ireland. As the earl of Ulster, Lionel was the obvious man for the job. Accordingly in March 1361 Edward announced that twenty-two-year-old Lionel would lead an army to Ireland, as King's Lieutenant, and started to make preparations to help him win praise in his first commission. The exportation of corn from Ireland was forbidden in readiness for his imminent arrival. All the sheriffs in England were ordered to proclaim that anyone having lands in Ireland was to sail with Lionel and defend them. All shipping which could threaten the second-in-line to the throne was arrested. A clerk was sent to Ireland to ride around announcing Lionel's arrival. Eventually (after six months) Lionel himself landed, with an army of fifty knights, three hundred men-at-arms and 540 mounted archers.[19] In addition he had with him a thousand bows, three thousand sheaves of the best arrows, a 'copper' (i.e. bronze) gun and sixteen pounds of gunpowder for it, all directed to his wardrobe by his careful father.[20] A further six hundred bows and two thousand sheaves of arrows were despatched in May 1362.

The job which Edward had given Lionel was a tough one. When the Anglo-Irish had written in 1360, their plea was inspired by years of native Irish attacks and English neglect. But neither did they want heavy-handed English intervention. Although Thomas Rokeby had been briefly successful in taming the wilder forces which roamed the borders of the English juris-diction in the early 1350s, the plague had ravaged Ireland to the point where rebuilding was required, not just reformation. Edward's instructions of 1350 to reform the land had proved a dead letter: the land was too poor and the people too hard-pressed to obey new laws which were inad-equately enforced by a king who had never been to Ireland.

Lionel set about his task with gusto, first attacking resistance from the native Irish in Wicklow and then in Leinster. But soon his campaigning ground to a halt. There was no great army he could attack, no national unity which had to be tamed. There were many small, disparate lords and petty kings, whose allegiances to the English varied in strength. The only way to tackle these men was to leave small garrisons in the castles controlling the roads and territories they ruled. The situation was further complicated by the fact that the 'English born in Ireland' were a breed apart from the 'English born in England'. While the latter were loyal to Edward, the former (the great majority) were loyal only when it suited them. They had marriage ties to the native Irish, dressed in Irish clothes and spoke Gaelic. To all intents and purposes they had 'gone native'. Lionel was to spend a total of five years wrestling with the problem, installing many garrisons and returning to England to consult with his father. In 1366, with Edward's approval, he finally enacted the major piece of English legislation in medieval Ireland, the Statute of Kilkenny, which encapsulated Edward's instructions of 1342 and 1350 and enforced an absolute distinction between the English and the Irish, prohibiting inter-marriage and the use of the Irish language, laws and customs by all the English, wherever they were born. In so doing it recognised native Irish independence through cutting off those parts of Ireland that remained outside royal control and more firmly administering those areas in which the English could exercise jurisdiction. This would remain the basis of English rule in Ireland until 1613.[21]

Edward's eldest son, the prince of Wales, had long been marked down for duty in Gascony. Ever since his first campaign there, when the Gascon nobles had actually requested his presence, it had seemed the ideal training ground for his princely qualities. Accordingly, the prince did homage for the duchy of Aquitaine, which his father now elevated into a principality, on 19 July 1362. With his wife he then set out for his new domain, where he arrived the following June, having spent the whole winter on his estates in Cornwall. His administration in the duchy began well, ably led by his constable and fellow Garter knight, Sir John Chandos. Nor did Edward wholly give up decision-making over the principality, unable perhaps to relinquish control of the land which his comrades like Manny and Lancaster had fought so hard to secure. One interesting aspect was a code by which Edward could be sure that letters sent to him purporting to be written by the prince were actually written by him. These were to bear one of the prince's mottoes, '*houmont*' (great courage) or '*ich dien*' (I serve).[22]

The goodwill towards the English in the region remained strong for several years. It was visible in 1364, when the prince needed to raise money. He instituted a hearth tax, and a high one at that, which should have been very difficult to impose on areas which had largely evaded paying taxes altogether for a number of years. There were questions raised in the Agenais, and the county of Rodez, where the count of Armagnac forbade his vassals from paying the tax, but otherwise this controversial measure was accepted throughout the principality. The prince's autocratic manner, however, did not endear him greatly to his subjects, and he personally alienated a number of Gascon lords. Nor did he have the administrative and negotiating capa-bilities of his father. He proved unable to find diplomatic solutions to the boundary disputes occasioned by the Brétigny treaty, and showed himself unwilling or unable to prevent the army of English freebooters from assaulting French possessions on the fringes of the province. In November 1364, when the violence of these freebooting companies had reached desperate levels, the order to put down the violence came not from the prince but from King Edward in England. So it was doubly unwise for the prince to parade himself around in magnificent ostentation: he was undermining his own position by claiming too much credit and undertaking too little responsibility. Thousands turned out to see the christening at Bordeaux of his first-born son, Edward, in 1365, and the occasion should have been used to weld the Gascons more firmly into an English-led unity. But the prince saw the moment as one in which all the glory was for him and his family, not Gascony. Edward of Woodstock had all the courage and martial talent of Edward I and Edward III, but his autocratic attitude and diplomatic skills were reminiscent of Edward II.

Edward's third son, John of Gaunt, was destined for a northern palatinate, secured on the inheritance of his wife, Blanche, one of the two daughters of the late duke of Lancaster. In April 1362 his inheritance doubled, on the unexpected death of his sister-in-law, Maud. This meant that all of the huge palatinate lordship of the duchy of Lancaster – the richest lordship in England – passed to him. Edward had not expected this to happen, and it is possible that he viewed it as unfortunate, as it gave John a greater income and a larger inheritance than his elder brother Lionel could have hoped to enjoy. John was also the sort of man who made enemies for life. Shortly after inheriting the duchy he was accused of poisoning his sister-in-law. Considerable amounts of money and power were hardly likely to teach him to be more circumspect. Nevertheless, from Edward's point of view it was better that such a massive inheritance came to his son rather than to someone outside the royal family. And Edward may have recognised that it might yield some unexpected advantages. He had at various times in the past discussed the possibility of John becoming the heir of David II of Scotland. If that were to become a reality, it would help secure the border, as John of Gaunt would not only be king north of the border but the largest landowner in the area directly south of it. As it happened, when the matter was discussed again in November 1363, it was ruled out by the Scottish parliament, whose members were adamant in their view that they should not have John or any of Edward's sons for their king.

Edward's plans for his fourth surviving son, Edmund, were concentrated on the Low Countries, and in particular Flanders. His idea was that Edmund should marry the daughter and heiress of Count Louis of Flanders, but in order for this to happen, he needed to persuade the pope. In 1362 Pope Innocent VI died, to be replaced by the pious and studious abbot of Marseilles, who became Urban V. Even this most conscientious of religious leaders was unable to overlook the fact that it would be much more in France's interest for the heiress of Flanders to marry a French rather than an English prince, and so Edward's plans were thwarted over and over again.

Edward's fifth son, Thomas, was still young, only seven in 1362, and as yet remained outside Edward's pan-European dynastic ambitions. His last daughter, Isabella, also remained outside his scheme. Her role would of course lie in being a bride to a ruler rather than taking a role in government. Edward had proposed a series of matches for her, but none had succeeded. The count of Flanders had at one point been about to marry her but that had fallen through. Then, in 1351, at the age of nineteen, she had simply refused to go through with a marriage to Bernard, the heir of the Gascon Lord Albret. It was her own decision. Edward had declared his readiness that she – 'our very dear eldest daughter, whom we have loved with special affection' – should marry the heir, but she refused to embark on the boat waiting to take her to Gascony.[23] Extraordinarily, Edward did not hold this against her. Later in the 1350s he gave her annuities and rewards, and she was more constantly with him than any of his other children. It seems that she was set on a love-match, like her elder brother. In 1365, aged thirty-three, she finally chose Enguerrand de Coucy, a lord in England as a hostage for the fulfilment of the Treaty of Brétigny. Edward acquiesced to her desire, and generously endowed de Coucy with a title and made him a Knight of the Garter, but Enguerrand's heart never lay in England, and, once the initial passion with Isabella had worn off, they separated. He went to fight in Italy and she remained with her two daughters at her father's court in England.

On 13 November 1362 Edward finally celebrated his fiftieth birthday. To mark the occasion he summoned a parliament, almost entirely consisting of commoners.[24] He issued a general pardon to wrongdoers throughout the realm in commemoration of his jubilee. More importantly for the petitioners present, Edward granted a new Statute of Purveyance. In it, all requisitioning of goods for the use of the royal household was done away with except that expressly for the king and queen. The title 'purveyor' was removed also, being changed to 'buyer'. This more clearly emphasised that people should be paid for the goods seized at the time they were requisitioned.[25] In addition, restrictions were placed on the buyers for the royal household, rendering them liable to arrest if their behaviour was not deemed to be up to standard. Edward obviously intended this legislation to be a gift to his people. Likewise his confirmation that a parliament should be held every year. The same benevolent intention lay behind his promises that royal officers (escheators) who took wards' estates into royal custody should not charge fees, that fines for breaking the Statute of Labourers should be handed over to parliament, and that the subsidy of wool would not constitute a precedent for indirect taxation in peacetime. Whether or not the representatives at Edward's jubilee parliament were grateful we cannot say, but the legislation flowed, and it flowed in the commons' favour.

The 1362 parliament is today remembered for one piece of legislation above all others: 'pleas shall be pleaded in the English tongue and enrolled in Latin'.[26] This is the first piece of legislation which officially recognised the English language. Since the eleventh century the language of the nobility had been French, and the language of the courts had generally been French, translated into Latin for the permanent record. As this new legislation now recognised, it was not right that men and women should be tried in a tongue they did not understand. But its significance was more than just fairness. The Statute of Pleading, as it was called, gave official recognition to English. It was described as the 'Tongue of the Country', and was thus accorded the status of a national language. In doing this, Edward recognised that a great change was taking place. Whereas in 1300 almost no one of importance in England spoke English – it being very definitely the language of the peasantry – by 1400 almost everyone of importance *did* speak English. Edward himself spoke it and used it in his mottoes. The duke of Lancaster spoke it. Edward's grandson, Edward of York, translated Gaston Phoebus's treatise on hunting into English.[27] In 1362 John Wycliffe – the man who first translated the New Testament into English – was Master of Balliol College. His opponent, the gifted Simon Langham – abbot of Westminster, archbishop of Canterbury from 1366, and in turn both Chancellor and Treasurer – spoke English. Chaucer – the first great poet since Saxon times to write in the English language – was in royal service. Strikingly, from this date on until the end of the reign, parliament was addressed at its opening in English (three times by Langham).[28] By the 1380s English had supplanted French as the language used in grammar schools.[29] English was coming to the fore, and one of the reasons for its speedy rise was its patronage and use by eminent men, including the king's ministers and members of the English royal family.[30]

Just before the end of the parliament, on the actual day of his birthday, Edward promoted his second, third and fourth sons to new, high titles. Lionel became duke of Clarence, in reference to his inheritance of the Clare estates, which, combined with the earldom of Ulster, made him by far the greatest landowner in Ireland. John became duke of Lancaster, acquiring the title of Edward's late general as well as his estates. And Edmund became earl of Cambridge.[31] And of course there was a great feast. On his fiftieth birthday Edward revelled in his great fortune by sharing a little of it out amongst his children, his friends and his people.

*

At Edward's birth, the author of the *Life of Edward the Second* had expressed the hope that Edward would 'follow the industry of King Henry the second, the well-known valour of King Richard, reach the age of King Henry [the third], revive the wisdom of King Edward [the first] and remind us of the physical strength and comeliness of his father'. On his fiftieth birthday Edward could be said to have fulfilled all of the chronicler's hopes for him except reaching the age of Henry III (who lived to sixty-five). But if he looked in the mirror, what did he see? A man at the height of his royal authority, groomed to look the part, admired, famous and feared by his enemies; but also a man who had now achieved his life's ambitions. The eyes were still bright, the face was still handsome and the mind was still strong, but there was nothing left to yearn for.

It would be too soon in an evaluation of Edward's life to say that his regnal authority was weakening. In the mid-1360s that authority was stronger than ever. But the key thread of his kingship – his vision of what kingship could and should be, which had given his life and reign such meaning and dynamism – was now all but extinguished. This has nothing to do with failure, and much to do with success. Edward in 1365 resembled the self-penned character portrait of the late duke of Lancaster. Years before he had danced and tourneyed with the best of them but now he resisted all but the occasional passing fancy. Once he had yearned for victories and accolades; now he preferred to feast himself on salmon and strong sauces, and to drink Gascon wine to join in the merriment of the court feasts. Where were the men with whom he used to drink, laugh and urge on to glory? Where were William Montagu, Reginald Cobham, Thomas Dagworth and the earls of Huntingdon, Northampton and Lancaster? Even the friends who were still alive were not with him now. They were old and retired, gone to their estates to tell tales of their glory days.

The cruelty of kingship gradually became apparent to Edward. His vassals – even the heroes among them – could grow old, withdraw from society, and die in relative peace. But not him; not the king. Too much depended on him. Edward could not grow old without growing weak, and if he grew weak, then England grew weak. Any of his earls could gracefully decline to joust, and claim middle age as an excuse. The king had to be seen still to be prepared for war and to risk his life, if need be. It was incongruous, especially now that he was in his fifties and growing fatter. A favourite red velvet belt with gold and pearls had to be sent back to his tailor in 1363 to be made larger.[32] New war armour was made for him in the same year. Edward wanted little to do with stratagems, war, the pope, or any other challenge. He had earned a little peace, surely? He wanted to complete his great buildings, to spend time with Philippa, to listen to his minstrels, to hear the chiming of his clocks, to look at his paintings, to show off his jewels, to hunt in summer and to loose his falcons in winter, and to be rowed in the royal barge down to Sheppey where his new castle was being built for him.

This sudden decline of ambition may be attributed to Edward's age, or his changing nature, but we should also consider his state of health. As mentioned in a previous chapter, this is a particularly difficult subject area. For instance, we cannot simply rely on occasional payments for medicines to know when he was ill. Edward maintained a permanent medical staff as a part of his household, and so most medical functions would have fallen within the scope of their regular duties, requiring no extra payments. Similarly we cannot assume from the continued activity of government that Edward was physically well. Most work was delegated, and what was not depended only on the king's ability to issue an order, he did not necessarily have to get out of bed. But there is one way we can make a rough estimate of Edward's state of health: we can assess how many medical practitioners Edward was employing from *outside* his household. Often these men were not employed but rewarded, and through tracing these rewards and gifts we do get an idea of how many 'second opinions' were being sought on his medical condition. Apart from the 1349–50 plague year, no practitioner was rewarded as a second 'king's physician' until the years 1364–67, when John Paladyn and John Glaston were both recorded in this capacity.[33] A second physician seems to have been employed regularly in the period 1368–70 and several were employed in the 1370s. As for surgeons, there are various payments to non-household surgeons in 1359, 1362 and from 1368 to his death. It would appear safest to conclude that Edward's health was already suffering, perhaps intermittently, from 1363–64 if not earlier.

If Edward was indeed ill as early as 1363 he was not letting it show. No chronicler records his sickness at this time. Nor could he have played the ailing king if he felt inclined; warrior status does not admit of physical weakness. And as the payment for war armour shows, he was still having to play the part of the warrior-king. When in November 1363 he and Philippa played host to three kings – those of France, Cyprus and Scotland – a great tournament was held in their honour at Smithfield: it was simply what was expected.[34] The regularity of royal tournaments may be considered a second check on the king's health. Jousts continued to take place but whereas in 1348 there had been a royal tournament every month, now it was rare for there to be two in a year. Where was the pleasure in patronising events which only showed how much younger and stronger the new crop of inexperienced youthful strangers were? But such events could not be given up entirely. That would be admitting of weakness, and unkingly behaviour.

Edward's favourite pastimes in the 1360s were hunting and falconry, and he now began to spend more time pursuing these. In the early 1350s he had kept a staff of six huntsmen and seven falconers, but in 1360 he and Philippa maintained thirty-one huntsmen and twenty-three falconers, and it is unlikely that the total number engaged in serving their hunting activities dropped below thirty for the rest of the decade.[35] There were hunting parks attached to most of the royal houses and castles. Edward spent about £80 per year on his hunting dogs alone.[36] He kept fifty or sixty birds of prey – gerfalcons, goshawks, tiercels and lannerets – at his mews, near Charing.[37] When we consider the cost of obtaining the birds in the first place, and then feeding them at a rate of at least a penny a day, and the wages of the many keepers and trainers, and their official robes, Edward's expenditure on hunting can be totalled at around £600 each year, an average baron's annual income. In 1367–68 he spent this sum on his falcons alone. This was much more than other medieval English kings, and much more than he himself spent in earlier and later decades.

It is perhaps in parliament that we can most clearly detect the lessening of political ambition. After the generous and ground-breaking legislation of 1362, that of the 1363 parliament was highly conservative. Edward attempted to set prices for goods, trying to legislate against inflation. He and his officials set down in codified laws exactly what a servant was allowed to wear and eat, and what craftsmen and yeomen were allowed, what lesser gentlemen and their wives and families were allowed, and what merchants, knights, clergymen and ploughmen were allowed. This second sumptuary law was futile, but it shows the conservatism of Edward's mind in the mid-1360s.[38] This was simply how he and his advisers (who drafted the legislation) believed society should be, in a hierarchical ladder from the king down to the servants. At the same time as he was legislating that servants and people of low status could not wear silk or furs, or any embroidered material, he himself was paying hundreds of pounds for the most lavishly embroidered and fur-trimmed clothes. While stipulating that husbandmen should eat no more than two dishes per day, he ordered that eight dishes were to be set before him at every mealtime, and five before the lords with him, three before his gentlemen, and two before his grooms.[39] Even if one takes the view that he was trying to encourage moderation of the ranks of society who felt bound to compete with each other, buying finer clothes than they needed and feasting to excess, his policy of restraint has to be seen as conservative.

Even more telling was the parliament of 1364. It never happened. Although Edward had agreed as recently as his fiftieth birthday that a parliament would take place annually, the meeting due to take place in his thirty-seventh year on the throne did not actually meet until 20 January 1365, four days before the end of the regnal year. Moreover it continued over into the next regnal year, and so Edward managed to avoid having to hold another until May 1366, and that was a brief meeting in which legislation was not discussed. In 1367 he declined to summon a parliament at all, so no more statutes were enrolled until May 1368. This is hardly a sign of eagerness on Edward's part to engage with parliament, or to use the petitions to address the needs and complaints of his people. And some of the legislation that he *did* pass was strategically self-defeating. Over the course of 1363–65 he renewed his attempts to establish monopolies for trade.[40] In 1364 he tried to reverse the legislation of 1361 providing for the judicial powers of JPs.[41] And he renewed his attack upon the pope. Although Urban V was probably the most pious of all the French pontiffs, Edward's frustration over his failure to grant permission for the marriages of his sons made him reissue the Statutes of Praemunire and Provisors in January 1365, ending any chance he had of coaxing Urban V to compromise over the war. Urban finally gave in to Edward's demands that there should be an English cardinal, and awarded Simon Langham a red cap in 1368, but this was due to Urban's judgement, not Edward's pressure. Edward in fact complained about the appointment.

It was not that Edward had suddenly turned into a neglectful king, it was simply that the ambition to be a better king was no longer there. The emphasis had turned from the king seeking success to one whose measure of success was simply to get through each day in a kingly fashion, and to enjoy himself if he had the chance. As a result, he wanted nothing much to change politically. It was in this spirit that he ordained that every man should practise with the longbow. It made perfect sense to encourage the English to continue their domination of projectile-based warfare, but Edward's motive was to ensure that things stayed as they had been in 1346.[42] In 1366, he authorised the Statute of Kilkenny, negotiated by his son Lionel, by which Ireland was divided between those whom Edward wanted to command and those who were beyond English control. Again, in the circumstances this was sensible, but it marked the introduction of a policy of conservatism. The young Edward would have personally tried to bring the whole country under his control. This conservatism did not necessarily lead to bad legislation. In one statute passed at this time, Edward ordered that all goldsmiths had to identify their works with their own specific maker's mark, the origin of the hallmark. We have reason to be grateful; but the motivation was essentially conservative, to keep things as they had been in his heyday.

Edward was not just resting on his laurels, he was preparing to retire on them. He usually confined his movements to the area of the Thames, travelling by the royal barge. One of the reasons for this mode of transport was probably his own declining health. Another was undoubtedly Philippa's medical condition. From 1365 grants made in her name made provision for the eventuality of her dying before the grantee, and her suffering was probably so great in 1365 that she could not travel easily except by barge and litter.[43] It may be that she never properly recovered from the injuries sustained when falling from a horse while hunting with Edward in the summer of 1358; she was making preparations for her tomb as early as 1362.[44] In 1366 the king's own health took a turn for the worse. Payments were made to an apothecary by the king's physician for medicines for him.[45] That summer he left his household for long periods at Windsor Castle and spent considerable lengths of time quietly at his hunting lodges in the New Forest with Philippa, receiving special visitors – such as 'the son of the king of India' – but otherwise laying low, avoiding too much pomp.[46]

*

Philippa's injuries and illnesses go some way to explain one big change in Edward's life. Until now he had never recognised any illegitimate offspring, and may well have had none. Such was the strength of his relationship with his wife that his dalliances with other women – presuming that he had some – had been restrained, even though he had encouraged a culture of intense sexual excitement at his court. But now a girl appeared before him who caught his attention and, having caught it, did her best to keep it. She was one of Philippa's ladies-in-waiting. Edward had of course paid attention to Philippa's female staff in earlier years, giving them grants and presents. The merging of their households in 1360 had brought him into daily contact with them. But to this girl, Alice Perrers, who had – we are told – 'a seductive voice' he gave much more than grants and presents.[47] About 1364 she bore him his first known illegitimate child.

Alice Perrers is the most famous royal mistress between Henry II's 'Fair Rosamund' (Rosamund Clifford) and Edward IV's Elizabeth Lambert (better known as Jane Shore). Arguably she eclipses them both. What she is remembered for is not her captivating beauty or her delightful wit but her avarice and her manipulation. But in considering how her relationship with Edward began we must lay aside this aspect of her behaviour and remember that in 1363 she was just a sexually-desirable servant at court. When it was realised that she was pregnant with Edward's child, she left. She gave birth, perhaps at Southery in Norfolk, to a son who became known as John of Southeray or Surrey.[48] When she returned to court, she received presents and grants, but as yet these were at the king's will. The images of the self-interested, calculating whore and the bewitching she-devil were still a long way from the public mind.

If Edward took a mistress while his wife was slipping into her final illness, we should not be too surprised. He had always had the opportunity to command the sexual availability of women, and adultery on the part of husbands was not considered a great sin. With Edward it is far more surprising that he had not done so more often. He was clearly a potent sire, and therefore if he had had many mistresses, we would expect him to have had a string of illegitimate children, like Henry I (who had more than twenty) and John (who had more than seven). Henry I and John had had these children by a number of women; they were multiple philanderers. Edward III apparently was not. If he was not always loyal to his wife then he was far more circumspect in his romantic interludes than most previous kings. Therefore it is particularly interesting that he now proved loyal also to Alice. She was not paid off but allowed to come and go from court. This is what is strange about this illicit royal union. Edward kept her, and had two more children with her. This was unheard-of in the 1360s. The monastic chronicler Walsingham decided she must have bewitched Edward in order to secure his affections. She may have done, but it was not necessarily in the way that the monk supposed.

*

Throughout the 1360s – not just in the plague years – Edward lost those close to him. His sister Joan died in September 1362, two months before his jubilee. His daughter-in-law Elizabeth de Burgh, Lionel's wife, died the following year. His companion Knights of the Garter died with sad regularity: Miles Stapeldon (a founder member) and Richard de la Vache died in 1364 and 1366. The great soldier Sir Thomas Ughtred, who had been present at Dupplin Moor, had served as an admiral and as a Justice of the Peace, and had fought in all of Edward's wars, died in 1365. The men who came to take their places were all young, nearly thirty years younger than Edward. They were promoted because of their great inheritances or, in the case of Enguerrand de Coucy, because he was betrothed to Edward's daughter. As he walked around his newly completed works at Winsdor and Sheen, Edward must have been saddened that the friends with whom he had laughed and jousted when he had ordered their construction were now gone, replaced by men with whom he had little personal affinity. The castle on the Isle of Sheppey in particular was a testament to his military vision, but who was left alive with whom to share the subtle nuances of military design? He dedicated it instead to Philippa and named the town and castle Queenborough in her honour.

The most significant death of this period was that of King John of France on 8 April 1364. He had dutifully returned to England in January – when his ransom had not materialised – and had fallen mortally ill. Herein lay a problem for Edward. Obviously no more of the ransom would be paid, but, far more importantly, John had not formally renounced sovereignty of the agreed territories before his death. That extra addition to the Treaty of Brétigny had never been ratified. The responsibility for the renunciation fell on the dauphin, who became Charles V. Charles had proved very reluctant to acknowledge any ceding of territory, and now saw an opportunity to capitalise on his father's failure. He could hardly do worse on the field of battle, and, while peace continued, he could rebuild his fortunes and those of France. Any hope of the formal renunciation being made, and a permanent settlement, was thus extinguished.

The problems – although immediately suspected – did not immediately become political reality. In fact the cause of the renewed hostilities came from a quite unexpected direction. In 1362 Edward had agreed an alliance with King Pedro of Castile, known to history by his telling soubriquet 'the Cruel'. At first Pedro had doubted whether it was in his best interests to ally with Edward. His sole purpose was to protect himself against a strong alliance between Aragon and France. But after the death of the French king, he made his mind up, and ratified the Anglo-Castilian treaty. It was just as well for him that he did, for in 1365 the French hit upon a solution to the English unofficial armies, or 'companies', which were ravaging their territories. The great French commander Bertrand du Guesclin offered them the opportunity to attack Castile in the name of Enrique de Trastámara. Back in England Edward realised the danger. English mercenaries were about to fight against his ally. To stop them he issued orders on 6 December 1365 that no Englishmen were to take arms against Pedro. But his orders fell on deaf ears. The English mercenaries commanded by Sir Hugh Calveley, Sir Nicholas Dagworth and Sir William Elmham proceeded with impunity into Castile, under the pretence that they were going on crusade. By the end of March they and du Guesclin had done their work, and Enrique de Trastámara had been crowned at Burgos, the capital. Pedro fled to Bordeaux, a king in name alone.

Although it was the prince who agreed the mission to reinstate Pedro, there is no doubt that it was with Edward's full approval. Edward felt bound to honour his treaty. The matter was discussed at the brief May 1366 parliament, and Edward sent John of Gaunt to the prince with reinforcements and financial support. By this time the English mercenaries, realising that the prince was going to march into Castile, were only too eager to be paid off. On 3 April 1367, at Nájera, the prince and his Gascon army inflicted a crushing defeat on Enrique de Trastámara, who almost alone escaped the carnage and arrest of his army. Du Guesclin himself was captured, as well as Marshal Audrehem, whom the prince had previously captured and ransomed once already, at Poitiers.

It was a stunning military victory, but the prince had terribly miscalculated. Nájera is one of the clearest examples in medieval history of a tactical victory which proved to be a strategic defeat. For when the campaign was over, and the prince's clerks worked how much it had cost, the total was 2.7 million florins (£405,000). There was no hope of regaining such a huge amount of money from impoverished Castile. Worse, Pedro the Cruel saw all the prisoners as traitors, not deserving of ransoms, and murdered as many as he could despite the prince's protestations that these men were valuable to him. Although the prince held a great victory feast when he returned to Bordeaux, in reality he had plunged his principality into chronic debt, having regained about one-eighth of what he had promised in wages of war and supplies.[49]

The crisis in which the prince now found himself was comparable to that which Edward had faced in 1340–41, when he returned from Flanders incognito owing around £300,000. Edward had then weathered the consequent crisis by taking the argument to his political opponents, compromising, and then reversing his compromise after the storm had blown over. The prince could not do this. The crucial difference was that in England there was no alternative to Edward's government in 1341, but in Gascony there was an all-too-eager alternative sovereign in the form of the French king. And King Charles, as every Gascon knew, had yet formally to renounce his sovereignty. When the lords who had fought at Nájera realised that not only would they not be paid for their troubles, they would also be taxed to cover the prince's shortfall, many began to think they would be better served by the weaker, less-assuming French king. It was therefore through the Nájera campaign that the prince precipitated the next stage of the Hundred Years War.

Edward was a relatively passive player in the move to war after Nájera. He was constantly on the back foot, reacting from afar to the plots and strategies emerging in the cauldron of Gascon discontent. But he probably suspected what was happening. In 1333 he himself had been a young king with much to prove and nothing to lose by making war on his enemies. Now King Charles was in a similar position. When the count of Armagnac wrote to Charles in May 1368 appealing against the tax imposed by the prince, the French king saw an opportunity to divide and rule in Gascony. Lord Albret – for many years a die-hard English supporter – felt similarly angry with the prince and openly supported Armagnac. Together with the renewed attacks of the renegade English mercenaries, who had returned from Castile seeking more plunder in France, Charles decided that this was too good an opportunity to miss, and accepted the Gascon invitation to intervene. In so doing, he set himself on the path to war.

Historians have tended to portray Edward's acceptance of the slide into conflict as a sign of his willingness to resume the fight and an ambition to enlarge on his conquest, as if he was some sort of military automaton.[50] But this is a great misrepresentation of his ambitions at this time. He had for years yearned to consolidate his victories in France through a satisfactory peace treaty. He was old, he was ill, and he had lost his companions in arms. More importantly Queen Philippa was dying, and he was determined to stay with her until the end. Already she had commissioned her tomb effigy.[51] For Edward and his wife it was just a matter of waiting, spending what little time they had left together.

Edward attended parliament reluctantly in May 1368. Rather than discuss the deep crisis his son was facing in France, he showered praise on the representatives, charming them. He thanked them for all their support over the years, and they rose to the flattery, calling him their 'highest, most excellent and most redoubted lord'.[52] The statutes enrolled were, however, without a clear strategy. It was as if Edward simply waved them through, or peremptorily dismissed those petitions which were too bothersome. The Statute of Labourers was re-enacted to suit the gentry, sheriffs were prohibited from holding their office for more than a year, and he relinquished his attempts to control JPs. He tried to regulate the wine trade by prohibiting English merchants from buying wine in Gascony, a statute which met with unfortunate results.[53] The only acknowledgement of the impending doom appears in his statute abolishing the wool staple in Calais, which he admitted was threatened by the French breaking of the peace.[54]

It was after parliament that the gravity of the situation became clear. Until now he had maintained a *laissez faire* attitude towards his son's government in Gascony. The prince, after all, was the heir to the throne, and it was necessary for him to learn how to deal with tricky political situations. Edward would not have helped him by stepping in and removing him from authority. But when King Charles accepted Armagnac's request to intervene, Edward had to respond. He wrote to Charles demanding to know what he meant by accepting the appeal. Charles deferred his answer, not wanting to provoke an immediate attack. The prince had no doubts as to the seriousness of the situation and ordered men-at-arms and archers to be raised on his estates in England and Wales, and prepared for war. All became clear in November when Charles assumed his sovereign role and summoned the prince to appear in Paris in May 1369. Edward wrote to his son, clearly of the opinion that he was not fit to govern. The prince wrote back, answering those of his father's 'advisers' (it was not seemly to say that the king himself was wrong) who accused him of maladministration and of bringing dishonour on himself.[55] But the prince was now sick as well as bankrupt. He had caught a debilitating illness in Castile, and was physically too weak to lead an army. Although the prince wrote to Paris saying that he would accept the summons with 'a helmet on his head and sixty thousand men at his back', in truth he was having difficulty even riding a horse.

When news of the prince's illness reached England it was just another blow to the king, who was now psychologically crushed by the events of the year. In addition to his and Philippa's own sicknesses, in September he had heard of the death of his daughter-in-law Blanche, the last surviving child of the late duke of Lancaster and wife of John of Gaunt.[56] Such news, coming on top of the realisation that war was now imminent, and the illness of his glorious son of whom he had been so proud, was dispiriting. But then came worse news: Lionel was dead. Lionel, his second son, named after his Arthurian hero, probably the most intelligent of all his sons. Where would it end? Lionel had been in Italy, had just made a glorious marriage with the daughter of Galeazzo Visconti, lord of Milan. The aged poet Petrarch had himself been there and had lauded the prince. And now he was dead. Messengers came from Italy asking where Edward wanted his son to be buried.[57]

Edward had great difficulty coping with so many disasters. Old and sick, he dismissed many members of the royal household.[58] Expenditure on the royal buildings almost entirely ceased. Any money available would be needed for war. The great palaces of state became silent echoing memorials of his glorious victories and the hope they inspired. At Windsor the winter sun of Christmas 1368 refracted through the glass, and lit up the newly painted walls of the dancing chamber in Philippa's apartments, but there was no dancing. Servants' steps rang out as they crossed the empty room. The clock chimed in the Round Tower. The prophecies of his youth had not prepared Edward for this loss of health, children and friends, this loneliness, this death.

But Edward still had his pride. He still had his throne, and he still had his responsibilities. Slowly his mind turned towards the oncoming war. With him that Christmas were the Chancellor, William of Wykeham (now bishop of Winchester), the Treasurer, John Barnet (bishop of Ely), his sons John and Edmund, and the earls of Salisbury, Warwick and Oxford.[59] These men, together with the earl of Arundel and Guy de Brian, remained with Edward for the next two months as the court moved first to Sheen and then to Westminster. In that time Edward had repeated bouts of illness, his physician John Glaston being sent to fetch more medicines.[60] But despite his personal frailty, Edward was forming the strategy by which he would once again take on his enemies. The earls of Cambridge and Pembroke and Lord Charlton of Powys were among the many lords despatched to the prince of Wales. Richard Imworth and other sergeants-at-arms were ordered to arrest all ships in readiness for an attack on France. On 26 April a ship laden with a cargo of wine – a lavish present from King Charles to Edward – was sent back, the present refused.[61] Archers were selected in their counties, men were arrayed in the towns, stones were ordered to be dug for siege engines, and parliament was summoned to Westminster. On 3 June, Edward asked parliament for its views on the prospect of war. The representatives responded unanimously that they believed Edward should resume the title King of France, and make war on Charles de Valois.

Preparations gathered momentum. Taxation for the forthcoming war was agreed by parliament. Edward wrote to the prince on 19 June that he had reclaimed the title and would invade to reclaim his rights. He seized the revenues of foreign monasteries in England. The peace with Scotland was renewed. He sought also an alliance with Flanders, but Charles got there first, and secured the match by marrying his brother to Count Louis's heiress. In Castile his hopes of an alliance had been dashed by the murder of Pedro the Cruel in March 1369, after which the pro-French Enrique resumed the throne. Aragon, however, was persuaded to remain a neutral partner. But in Gascony itself the prince was already under pressure. Before Pembroke and his reinforcements arrived, the far eastern part of the principality had been overrun. And in late April the French marched into Edward's county of Ponthieu. John of Gaunt was sent to Calais, where he had taken up residence by 16 July. It was expected that the army would follow shortly.

The army did not follow. In mid-July Edward received a message from Philippa. She wanted him near her.

They both knew that she was near death. Her years of suffering were coming to an end. He made his way back up the Thames in the royal barge, towards Windsor. When the boat touched the quay there, the old king was helped out and escorted into the great palace he had built within the walls of his birthplace, and he came to the room where Philippa lay.

When he entered, she saw him, and extended her right hand from beneath the bedclothes, and put it into his right hand. 'We have enjoyed our union in happiness, peace and prosperity', she said. 'I therefore beg of you that when we are separated, you will grant me three requests.' Edward was in tears, but answered 'Lady, whatever you ask, it will be done.' 'My lord', she said, 'I ask you to pay whatever debts I may have outstanding, both in England and overseas. Secondly I beseech you also to fulfil all the bequests or gifts I may have made to churches, both in England and on the Continent, where I have prayed, as well as the legacies I have made to the men and women who have been in my service. And thirdly, when it pleases God to summon you, do not be buried anywhere else but beside my tomb, at Westminster.' Weeping, the king granted his beloved wife her final requests.[62]

Philippa lingered for a few days. Edward suspended the invasion of France while he waited with her. Then on 15 August she died.[63] Edward and their youngest son Thomas of Woodstock were with her at the end. England had lost one of its great treasures, a woman whose spirit was strong and yet never domineering, who managed to keep the peace between her ambitious sons, and who had smoothed Edward's brow as he struggled with his own demons, from the dark figure of the tyrant Mortimer in his early days to the fears and loneliness of his age. She was his oldest and closest companion.

Three months later Edward learnt that another dear friend, Sir Robert Ufford, earl of Suffolk, had died on 4 November. Outside the rain-spattered windows, across the grey cloud-frowned land of England, it had been the worst harvest for half a century.[64] Reports were coming to him that the plague had returned for a third time. On 13 November, the day of his fifty-seventh birthday, plague killed his old friend the earl of Warwick. Edward had outlived almost all his friends and companions in arms. All six of the earls created so joyously and proudly in 1337 were dead. His mother, father, sisters and brother were all dead. His daughters Mary, Margaret and Joan were dead, and his son Lionel. He had buried three other children in infancy. All those who had wished him a long life had unwittingly wished on him this most cruel of fates: to be a man who lived his entire life in the company of friends, children and great men, and watched them die.

Edward prepared for Philippa's funeral with loving care. He could not face leading an army himself, and sent his own retinue across to Calais to join John. But John was more worried about his father than the French, and was back in England by mid-December, intending to spend Christmas with him. John gave precise instructions for a present of thirty fresh rabbits to be presented to his father on Christmas Eve.[65] Edward and John spent Christmas together at King's Langley before being rowed down the river to the Tower of London at the end of the month. Philippa's embalmed body followed from Windsor on 3 January. Edward had ordered that the solemnities were to last six days. But he must have suspected that for him they would never end.

SIXTEEN

A Tattered Coat Upon a Stick

By 1370 many of the joys in Edward's life had died, and all his glories were memories. The nation demanded the same high duty, enterprise and success as he had shown in the 1340s but he was an old, sick man. He appeared a feeble shadow of what he had been in 1346. To Edward, obsessed with his physical appearance, this mattered. And it mattered to him that he was no longer surrounded by his entourage of famous knights. Most of his true friends were dead, and more were shortly to follow them to the grave. As he waited sadly at the Tower for Philippa's body to be rowed down the Thames, Sir John Chandos, one of the founder members of the Order of the Garter, had a sword plunged into his face in a skirmish in Gascony and bled to death. Now only eight of the twenty-five knights who had jousted with him in the Garter tournament of 1349 were still alive, and five of those would die before Edward.[1]

Edward's reaction to the deaths and despondency was to cut himself off further from society. There were no new mass-creations of earls, like those of 1337 and 1351, to replace those who had died. No earls were created at all. Edward withdrew from court, spending time alone with his few intimate companions, issuing instructions through a private secretary. The centre of government was at Westminster, the household was almost permanently settled at Windsor, but Edward remained at Havering, Sheen and Eltham, only attending Westminster when he had to. Much regnal business simply was not done. Whereas in the first ten years of his reign he had granted an average of seventy charters every year, and sometimes more than a hundred, in 1370 he granted just three. In this way he became distant from the court, and unapproachable. He no longer heard what men said, or what rumours were circulating. There was no one left of sufficient stature to speak plainly to him. Only his sons, the prince and John of Gaunt, could talk to him with impunity, but the prince was in Gascony and John was circumspect, mindful of his delicate position as the next eldest son and probable guardian of the realm if his elder brother should die.

It was in this atmosphere of unnaturally silent vast palaces and empty council chambers, that Edward's friendship and devotion came to fix itself on his mistress, Alice Perrers. The sexual satisfaction she gave him was matched by Edward's increasing dependence on her. Devoid of information about public opinion, she became his principal adviser. Of course, she advised him carefully, telling him what she thought he wanted to hear. She also took care to put in a good word for her growing circle of ambitious friends. Men she knew and liked received lucrative commissions and positions. As time went by she grew in Edward's estimation, and he trusted her more. She grew bolder. So their relationship became the subject of gossip at Westminster and Windsor: gossip which Edward feared and avoided.

For the moment, however, Edward's priority was the renewal of the war in France. Exercising his mind on this may well have proved cathartic in the wake of Philippa's death. Three months after her funeral, in April 1370, he ordered John of Gaunt to take an army to Gascony to reinforce the prince's position. At the same time, Sir Robert Knolles was ordered to attack from Calais. It was the classic English strategy which Edward had used with such great effect on so many occasions since 1343: a double attack, from the north and the south. Edward saw no reason why it should not work again, if it could be reinforced with treaties with the Low Countries, Germany and Genoa, whose support he now tried to enlist, with varying degrees of success.

Knolles landed at Calais in July with more than four thousand men and set out on a grand destructive campaign at the end of the month. Once again the fires burnt across France, from Saint-Omer to Arras and Noyon. Sir John Seton, a Scotsman fighting for the English, walked unaccompanied into Noyon with his sword drawn and harangued the garrison until they attacked him. He continued fighting alone until his page shouted to him that the army was passing by the town, and he had better stop fighting now if he wanted to catch up with them. Acknowledging his thanks for the sport, Sir John left the corpse-strewn scene and, taking the reins of his horse from his page, rode off to catch up with Knolles. On went the English, burning, looting and generally doing all they could to encourage attack. But King Charles knew better now than to rise to the bait. The English would have to move on, so he ordered his men not to stand in their way. Instead he would sacrifice the villages and let the villagers look out for themselves. By avoiding conflict he not only avoided defeat, he encouraged the English army to collapse in recriminations and dissent. Other English knights blamed Knolles for failing to bring the French to battle. After all, they complained, what did Knolles know about command? He was just a knight, a brigand, a privateer, a commoner. Most English armies were commanded by earls. Knolles had been promoted above his station, they said. The attack in the north moved into Brittany, away from Paris, and broke up into smaller and smaller forces, each to withdraw or to be attacked separately.

The campaign in the south fared differently. John of Gaunt arrived in Gascony at the end of July and met up with the prince. Although he knew his brother was ill, he did not realise quite how grave his condition was. He was shocked to find him bedridden. But the prince was not dead yet. The French army was in the region of Limoges, and the bishop of Limoges had defected to their cause. This roused the prince to fury. He had liked and trusted the bishop so much that he had made him godfather to his eldest son, and he angrily prepared to make his first journey out of Bordeaux for two years. He was carried in a litter at the head of the army to Limoges, where he set about the attack of the city. On 19 September, having dug tunnels beneath the walls, the pit props were fired and the walls crashed down. The English troops poured into the city. The attack was decisive. The bishop of Limoges and the other leading men of the town were brought to the prince in chains, and the city was looted and burnt to the ground. Taking a leaf from his father's book, the prince sentenced the bishop to death and then waited for the pope to beg for mercy, allowing him to appear magnanimous as well as victorious. But soon everything turned bitter for the prince. Weakened by the journey, his poor health made it impossible for him to carry on. He had to return to Bordeaux, defeated by his own sickness. There he learnt that his son and heir, Edward of Angoulême, had died. Distraught, he made preparations to return to England with his wife and remaining son, Richard of Bordeaux, leaving the chaotic administration of what was left of the principality, including the funeral of his son, in the hands of John of Gaunt.

It is difficult to hold Edward responsible for the lack of achievement in 1370. Perhaps he could have appointed a more able lieutenant in Gascony to take over from the prince. Perhaps he should have foreseen the distrust in Knolles and appointed an earl to lead the northern attack. But there was a limit to how far he could undermine the prince's position in Aquitaine, and earls with both military experience and physical strength were rare in 1370. The real reason for the failures was far deeper, and tackling it went beyond Edward's experience. The English were, for the first time, on the defensive. If Gascony was truly a part of Edward's kingdom then he could only fail with regard to the most important strand of his strategy, which was to keep the war on foreign territory. From now on, unless he continued his war of aggression, pushing further and further into France, the fighting would only be on his lands. The likelihood of his losing was all the greater when he himself was unable to inspire or lead his men, and his principal commanders were all aged and decrepit. So it was that, even though the prince had been successful at Limoges, most of Gascony was overrun and reclaimed for France in the space of a few months. It was no coincidence that Edward failed to achieve the widespread support of European kingdoms in 1370–71, only Juliers and Genoa actively engaging to help him.[2]

*

There were bound to be recriminations when parliament met at Westminster on 24 February 1371. They had not been summoned for twenty months. Edward might have pretended to those around him that by reckoning the new year from Lady Day (25 March), he had just lived up to his promise, but such a contrived explanation was not likely to wash with the representatives. Since they had last met they had hardly seen their king. Moreover, in the last parliament they had voted a substantial tax to be granted to the king for the prosecution of the war, and what had happened? The loss of almost all of Gascony, and the dispersal to no profit of the northern army. What stood between the French king and the shores of Britain? Were there not invasion plans afoot? Where was the English navy?

The news got worse. Shortly after parliament opened, Edward heard that King David II had died. Edward now had few (if any) allies in Scotland. Every representative at that parliament must have considered this a sure sign that a new army would soon be needed in the north. Edward, huddled in his cloak of glorious victories, was not prepared for the angry onslaught which followed. Scapegoats had to be found. Since no one was prepared to accuse the king himself of poor judgement, his ministers bore the brunt. And what did they all have in common? They were all clergymen. The Chancellor, William of Wykeham, was the bishop of Winchester. The Treasurer, Thomas Brantingham, was the newly appointed bishop of Exeter. The keeper of the privy seal, Peter Lacy, was a canon of Lichfield. What did such men know about the prosecution of war? As ecclesiastics, it was not clear whether they could even be held accountable for their maladministration. The dismissal of the clergy became a demand so strong that Edward was forced to give in to the will of parliament. It dumbfounded him. For the first time since the Crisis of 1341, he wavered, lost confidence and immediately lost the political initiative. On 26 March 1371 he sacked all his trusted ecclesiastical officers and replaced them with younger laymen.

Unknown to all concerned, this decision paved the way for further corruption in the royal household. The men whom Edward selected were the sons of men he had once trusted or the suggestions of his only trusted confidante, Alice. Nicholas Carew took over as keeper of the privy seal. Richard le Scrope took over as Treasurer. Robert Thorp became Chancellor. William Latimer, son of the William Latimer who had assisted Edward in 1330, became his chamberlain. These men were generally in their thirties, less well-educated and more unscrupulous than those they replaced. They saw a golden opportunity to make themselves rich and influential. Later that year John Neville, lord of Raby, stepped into Latimer's place as steward of the royal household. With that appointment, all was set for the net of the court clique to close in around Edward, and to stifle him from news of the war, his kingdom and his officers' lining of their own pockets.

It would be wrong to say that all those appointed by Edward at this time were place-seekers and self-interested usurers. Richard le Scrope was the son of a Chief Justice under Edward; he had served as a member of parliament, had fought at Nájera, and knew more than most about financing a war. But his problems were exacerbated by his fellow officers. Latimer stands out as the most corrupt. Although he was experienced in both war and the organisation of manpower, the lure of money was too much for him. He borrowed sums from the Treasury at no interest, then lent it back to Edward for the war effort at high rates, and having pocketed the proceeds, returned the original sum to the Treasury.[3] He had the absolute say in who had access to the king, and had sufficient authority to prevent the earl of Pembroke, commander of one of Edward's armies, from seeing the king in the autumn of 1371. Pembroke had to content himself with an interview with Latimer instead. There were echoes of Hugh Despenser and Roger Mortimer in such behaviour. All it took was for the king to be ill and irresolute and the English government collapsed back into the quagmire of corruption which had characterised it in the years 1322–30.

It was in April 1371, after parliament had broken up, that Edward finally met his son and heir again, after an absence of eight years. It must have been a poignant moment: both knew the other was seriously ill.[4] They had argued over the time apart. Edward had been greatly disappointed by his son's administration in Gascony, and had eventually countermanded his hearth tax in November 1369. The prince likewise had become convinced that his father had lost his diplomatic judgement when Edward sent him yet another treaty with Charles of Navarre, expecting him to seal it, despite the man's countless broken promises. But father and son loved each other deeply, through royalty, family, mutual respect and long-term devotion. They could now also sympathise with one another in their physical frustration, Edward shuffling around in his echoing halls, the prince carried from place to place, unable to walk. For Edward it was as if his last great friend had come home.

It may well have been the prince's presence that gave Edward's self-confidence a boost in the spring of 1371. Maybe the prince pointed out to him how he was being manipulated. Reports of William Windsor's maladministration in Ireland certainly slipped through the courtiers' cordon, for Edward took action in the autumn of 1371 to warn Windsor of his dealings, rebuked him for his taxes and extortions, and eventually recalled him.[5] And in June, at a council meeting in Winchester, Edward found the strength to tackle the petitions of the 1371 parliament in a direct, strong-minded manner. To the demand that he ban ecclesiastics from office, Edward responded only that he would take advice from his council. To almost every other petition, he replied only that 'he would be advised' (meaning nothing would be done in the foreseeable future), or that the existing statutes, customs and laws were sufficient, including his own prerogatives. Even quite reasonable requests, such as the repeal of the statutes prohibiting English merchants from buying wine in Gascony, were dismissed. The demand for the reform of the navy was the one petition to which he was inclined to agree. With his son at his side, Edward recovered his sense of authority, and maintaining it became his chief priority. In his view, parliament needed to be taught a lesson, that they should not presume to thrust policy on him.

There were other reasons for Edward's recovery of his authority in early 1371. The new Chancellor – poorly educated by comparison with his ecclesiastical predecessors – was forced to admit to one of the biggest and most extraordinary mistakes in the history of accounting. The clerical subsidy of 22s 4d per parish would clearly not raise £50,000 because there were only nine thousand parishes in England, not forty-five thousand. How such a gross error was made beggars belief. The request to reform the navy was made in the wake of rumours of a planned French invasion and a French landing at Portsmouth. As soon as there was a threat of war, it seemed parliament panicked, and sought Edward's advice and leadership. This not only flattered him, it gave him a sense of purpose. All these things, combined with Alice's continued attention, helped revitalise him. After attending the solemn commemoration of the anniversary of Philippa's death, he set about planning the next stage of the war.

*

In several of the principal English chronicles there are large gaps at this point in time. Walsingham's *English Chronicle* records nothing between the return of the prince in 1371 and the Good Parliament in 1376. Henry Knighton's chronicle mentions nothing which happened between the death of Lionel in 1368 and Edward's own death. It is as if, with the benefit of hindsight, these writers wanted simply to pass over the last years of the reign. In the comprehensive work of Joshua Barnes the reason is neatly expressed. He describes the year 1372 as 'the first inauspicious year of our great Edward's reign . . .' Inauspicious is the appropriate word. There were only two pieces of good news: John of Gaunt married Constanza, eldest daughter and heiress of the recently murdered Pedro of Castile, and Edmund of Langley married her younger sister, Isabella. Everything else was awful. In January the great warrior Sir Walter Manny – Lord Manny – died, and was buried at the Charterhouse which he had jointly founded in London. Later in the year the earls of Stafford and Hereford died. John of Gaunt – to whom Edward had delegated much routine business – gave rise to hostile gossip about his ambitious nature and his collusion with the self-seekers around the king. John's open and shameless adultery with his children's governess, Katherine Roët, incurred the most vicious criticism, especially when he acknowledged a son by her, John Beaufort. A diplomatic summit near Calais, proposed by the pope, failed to break the deadlock inherent in the combination of French military ascendancy in Aquitaine and Edward's insistence on the recognition of his sovereignty. The English continued to suffer strategic losses: Monmorillon, Chauvigny, Lussac, Montcontour, Poitiers, Saint-Sevère, Soubise, Saint-Jean-d'Angély, Angoulême, Taillebourg and Saintes to mention just the most significant. In defending Soubise, the Captal de Buch – a hero of Poitiers and a Knight of the Garter – was captured. Worst of all, on 22 June, the English fleet – with all its treasure (the payroll for the Gascon army), its archers, men-at-arms and horses – was utterly destroyed by a Castilian fleet off La Rochelle, on the coast of Gascony. The ships were torn to pieces by gunshot and fire, and the terrified horses in the holds stampeded in the smoke-filled darkness, breaking the smaller vessels apart.[6] The commanders, including the earl of Pembroke, were all captured. It was the first major military defeat of Edward's reign.

La Rochelle stunned Edward. The myth of English invincibility had been broken. English domination of the seas had come to an end. But just like that other event which had shocked him – the parliamentary disputes of the previous year – he took energy from the opposition. It was widely presumed that the English would now lose Saintonge and Poitou too. According to Froissart, the king was pensive and silent on hearing the news. At length he declared that he would himself lead a powerful army to France, to fight with the French king, and remain there until he had regained all that had been taken from him, or die in the endeavour.

Edward may well have been reflecting on his grandfather's death, sixty-five years earlier. Then Edward I, faced with the treachery of Robert Bruce in Scotland, had camped on the Scottish border and remained there for the last years of his reign, and actually died while being carried north in a litter at the head of the army. It did not matter then that his army had failed to overwhelm the Scots; what mattered was his personal legacy: he would always be remembered as the king who had died in arms, fighting for his kingdom until the last breath had left his body. That was how Edward III wanted to be remembered too.

Plans had already been in place for an expedition to France in 1372 even before the La Rochelle defeat. John was to take an army to Castile, Edward himself had the idea of joining the prince in leading an army to Northern France, while Pembroke attacked in the south. With the defeat of Pembroke and the loss of the treasure, everything was concentrated on relieving the town and castle of Thouars, where the remaining loyal Poitevin army was concentrated. The French were already besieging the town. All loyal English and Gascon troops were ordered to meet with the king there. He would die before the walls of Thouars, if necessary, away from parliamentary criticism, the household gossips and petty place-seekers.

A treaty was signed with the duke of Brittany. John of Gaunt – already forced to give up his scheme of invading Castile – was now required to give up his earldom of Richmond to allow Edward to offer it to the duke. John of Gaunt's reputation slipped. We do not know whether this was because he had fallen in Edward's estimation, or whether Edward had become aware of the common criticism of his son, but it is interesting that Edward seems to have made a decision that, in the event of Prince Edward's death, his only surviving son, the five-year-old Richard of Bordeaux, should be the heir to the throne, not John of Gaunt. Having settled this, Edward made for Sandwich and the boats which would take him on this last expedition to France.

It would have been interesting to know the outcome if Edward had been able to carry through his plans. He had everyone with him: besides his three eldest sons there were many lords, including the earls of Salisbury, Warwick, Arundel, Suffolk and Stafford. On 30 August he made Richard of Bordeaux guardian of the kingdom, and went on board his flagship, the *Grâce de Dieu*. But three weeks later he was still bobbing about off the coast at Winchelsea. The contrary winds did not let up, his own physical state and that of his eldest son gave him cause for concern, and he learnt that the town of La Rochelle itself had fallen to a besieging French force on 7 September. Edward's world was falling apart around him, and there was nothing in his frailty he could do about it. For another two weeks he tried to sail south. His efforts were in vain. His old adversary the weather was the one thing which had remained dependable all these years. In abject disappointment he called off the campaign.

*

From this moment until the Treaty of Bruges, which was agreed on 27 June 1375, the war in France was a series of unmitigated disasters. There were no big battles, just a huge number of minor losses. The conquest of about one third of France had been easy in comparison to the task of defending it. Each castle and town could be attacked individually by a large army, and so geographically dispersed were the English-held castles, they found it very difficult to defend each other. Under du Guesclin a French army of about ten thousand men simply reduced every defence the English had in the region. By the time of the Bruges negotiations, the area of Gascony which Edward governed was actually smaller than that which his father had ruled.

No one was more aware of the humiliation of the English in France than Edward himself. In his mind the virtues of kingship remained unchanged: a good king should be a strong military leader, able to inspire his men, not an invalid. But Edward could not inspire anyone anymore. When he had been young he had encouraged men to join him in building a new military future for England. At forty he had been hailed a great conqueror, at fifty a great lawmaker, but at sixty he was a great memory. The young nobility of the realm saw him not as an inspiration but as a white-bearded, retired soldier, a man in the sixth age, to return to Shakespeare's theatrical analogy of life: 'the lean and slippered pantaloon, / with spectacles on nose and pouch on side, / his youthful hose, well saved, a world too wide / for his shrunk shank; and his big manly voice / turning again to childish treble'. Edward may or may not have worn spectacles – they are first known in Europe from about 1300 – but no one could look at him as building anything for the future. His day was done.

Edward's eldest two sons were similarly acutely aware of the problems. The prince realised that he was now too sick to return to Gascony and lead the English there to victory, and in the parliament of November 1372, straight after the return from the aborted French mission, he publicly gave up all claim to the principality of Aquitaine. John, who had been styled the king of Castile since January 1373, was not at all resigned to such a melancholy future, and remained optimistic for both the English cause in France and his own pretensions in Castile. But he was insufficiently militarily-skilled to lead an army to victory. His most remarkable attempt to inspire his men – and it was indeed remarkable – was his march across the whole of France in 1373. After landing at Calais in July he led the army all the way to Bordeaux, arriving there in January 1374. It was a brave decision. His army risked attack every step of the way. Passing over the Massif Central in winter was especially hard, made all the harder by John's chivalrous but misguided stipulation that all food had to be paid for, so depriving his army of sustenance. Men were tired and undernourished. Most knights lost their horses, and could not carry their armour on foot, so they discarded it in rivers, or bashed it out of shape with their own hands to prevent the enemy using it. By the end, if they had been attacked they could have done nothing except to fall to their knees and beg for mercy. It was a bloodless disaster.

By September 1374 only Bayonne and Bordeaux remained in English hands, plus two or three castles in Brittany and, of course, the impregnable Calais. In November of that year Edward appointed his son Edmund and the duke of Brittany as his lieutenants throughout France, and there was a campaign in Brittany; but in reality the second French war of Edward's reign was already lost. The fact was that the English military machine needed an active and ambitious warrior-king to lead it. Furthermore, it needed to be aggressive. Without Edward, and confined within the territorial limits of the Treaty of Guines, a defensive war was bound to fail. A measure of how futile the struggle had become by 1375 is the contrasting fortunes of the garrisons of Quimperlé and Saint-Sauveur at the very end of the hostilities. At Quimperlé one of the leading French commanders, Olivier de Clisson, was so harried by the English that he agreed to surrender the town within eight days unless relieved. News of the truce agreed at Bruges came within that period, and, much to the annoyance of the English, the siege had to be given up. At Saint-Sauveur, the same thing happened but du Guesclin insisted that, as the garrison he was besieging had agreed to surrender before they heard of the truce, they should still do so. And they did. The mighty English military machine had been humbled.

*

It has often been said that Edward lost his mind in his final years. This is slightly misleading: he was still sufficiently rational to issue personal instructions in 1374 and retained a degree of lucidity until the last year of his life. But he was not well-informed about the state or government of his kingdom, and his mental health degenerated so that, by 1375, he could not foresee the consequences of his statements. His intellectual capacity declined to the point where we would describe him as feeble-minded. This may have been due to a series of strokes, as sometimes suggested, and there is evidence that it was a stroke which finally killed him. But we should be cautious about making a diagnosis of his condition beyond this without some firm medical evidence. There are many degenerative diseases of the mind known today, as well as others which have not been identified. Also, we do not know which diseases were prevalent in the 1370s which are no longer around. Nor can we tell which diseases are around today which were not then. And we have not even tried to understand the hereditary weaknesses of the family, particularly the descendants of the Navarrese royal family.[7]

The best we can do is to look for evidence for a decline in Edward's mental state. There are indications that in 1374 he was able to issue instructions personally which were enrolled by his secretariat. One example is the reward of a daily pitcher of wine paid on St George's Day 1374 to Geoffrey Chaucer, the great poet. Edward had sent Chaucer to Italy in 1372–73 on a mission to the doge of Genoa (a journey which, incidentally, introduced him to the works of Petrarch, Boccaccio and Dante; he may even have met the aged Petrarch and Boccaccio). Shortly afterwards he made him controller of the customs.[8] But Edward's probable enjoyment of Chaucer's poetry does not imply his judgement was sound in all other areas. In particular, it is well-known that in August 1373, while at Woodstock, Edward gave some jewels and fine treasures which had belonged to Philippa to Alice Perrers. Giving his wife's jewels to his mistress has often been held up as an example of his immorality. This was certainly an error of judgement, but it needs to be put in its proper context. What he actually gave were the jewels and chattels of Philippa's which had previously been given (probably by Philippa herself) to Euphemia, wife of Walter Hasleworth. So Edward was actually giving away Euphemia's property, not treasured items from Philippa's undisturbed wardrobe. Nevertheless, the gift was not managed in some quiet way; it was done openly and tactlessly, with a record being enrolled in the patent rolls.[9] Had the gift been due to Alice's persuasion, she would have quietly pocketed the treasures or had them described in some other fashion, so it seems to have been at Edward's personal order. Thus we may certainly blame Edward for tactlessness in this matter. Two months later there was another royal instruction which also almost certainly came from the king rather than someone operating on his behalf. He ordered all the bridges in Oxfordshire to be repaired because he wished to go hawking there.[10] It seems that in late 1373 instructions were being issued by the king and written up in the usual manner. But already Edward's judgement was weak. He could not foresee the consequences of his actions. Hence it is no surprise that the parliament summoned in Edward's name to assemble in late November 1373 was the last he attended. By the time he listened to Chaucer give an account of his journey to Italy, he was an affable, smiling, white-bearded and forgetful old man, beginning to hum to himself the quiet song of a remembered life.

With Edward incapable of governing, the self-seekers assumed a greater role. Latimer, the chamberlain, not only controlled access to the king, he began increasingly to prevent people from meeting him. Edward still went hunting, and received the occasional visitor, but little or no important business was brought to him. Latimer even developed a system whereby he was allowed to reply in Edward's name to petitions addressed to the king.[11] Latimer also took part in the Bruges negotiations. We have to wonder how much Edward really knew or understood what was agreed in the course of these discussions. He still recognised people, and knew their names and what they did, but important financial and political issues were beyond his comprehension.

This weakness of intellect allowed the self-seekers around the king to catch the gold falling through the wavering royal fingers. Although *we* know how much longer Edward had to live, those in positions of authority at the time did not. All they knew was that he would die soon and that they, in all probability, would be replaced. For men like Latimer, this meant that he could not let too many opportunities to enrich himself pass by. Richard Lyons, a friend of Alice in charge of the royal mint, also suspected that he had only a short while to gather an endowment for his future. And no one fits more completely into this category than Alice herself, whose entire position, status, wealth and safety depended on the term of Edward's remaining life.

No one – contemporarily or historically – has a good word to say about Alice. She may well have been the most self-seeking and corrupt person at Edward's court but that does not mean we should not at least try to understand her situation. And on reflection she certainly deserves more sympathy than she received from the principal writer to describe her, Thomas Walsingham, who detested her. She had met the king when relatively young and perhaps a little naive.[12] Certainly she would have been powerless to prevent his advances towards her when she was serving Philippa. We might even wonder whether the infirm and possibly pain-ridden Philippa suggested to Alice that she might please the king. Edward, after all, could hardly be seen to use the dozen or so regular prostitutes of the royal household, who were common women for the satisfaction of his servants.[13] After Alice gave birth to John of Southeray, she was forever closely linked to Edward, and after Philippa's death, she was apparently his sole bedmate. In short, he needed her, and who was she to deny him, the king? When he began to shower her with presents, and remained faithful to her, what could she do? Here was this great king giving her robes, jewels, status, fame and authority over many servants, and she was not even of a noble family. He had picked her out as a woman, for what she was herself, not because of status or political connections. She must have felt enormously flattered, and privileged to have been raised up as the king's recognised companion, above the wives of knights, barons and earls. Normally a royal mistress was lucky if she had her first bastard child recognised before she was cast aside. For Edward to remain loyal to her was unprecedented. No other medieval king remained as faithful to a single mistress as long as Edward did to Alice.[14]

Alice was intelligent enough to realise that her way to power and wealth was likely to be short-lived. By 1372 she had grown accustomed to royal living, but in the weeks that Edward was away at sea, trying to sail to France, having announced that he would die there, she must have seen all her hopes disappear. She must have been terrified. At that point she would have had seriously to consider what she would do if he never returned. And although he did return, the question remained in her mind. What would she do when he was dead? He was already past sixty: she had only a limited amount of time to safeguard her position and future. Hence her dealing in property and her use of influence to guarantee a future income. Hence her abuse of her position.

Contemporaries could not understand their king's love for this woman. He had delivered them victory after victory. They probably did not know how weak his mind was, how innocent and naive he had become in his dotage. The rumour spread around that a certain Dominican friar, who had attended Alice as a physician, dabbled in magical cures and had given her the secret of a potion by which she could bewitch the king. It seems that it was her physical beauty that had originally 'bewitched' Edward, but that was an insufficient explanation for contemporaries. Edward had been surrounded by beautiful women all his life, so why this one? Especially as she was using her influence with the courts to resurrect maintenance – that odious practice of using political power to protect criminals from trial – which Edward himself had stamped out.

One of Alice's friends was in a similarly tight spot. William Windsor, who had repeatedly been accused by the Irish of extortion, bribery and a host of other crimes, was cleared of any wrongdoing in 1373, perhaps as a result of Alice's intervention in the case. But he remained controversial and unpopular. The Irish pleaded with Edward's government to send the young earl of March to be their governor, and this seems to have been Edward's intention. But in the autumn of that year someone persuaded Edward to send Windsor back to Ireland. The change of appointment was made less than six weeks after Edward's gift to Alice of those controversial jewels which had once belonged to Philippa. It seems likely that Alice persuaded him. This is all the more probable when we consider that Alice and William were making property transactions together at this time. And that was not the half of it. It was probably at this time that Alice and William secretly married.

It seems utterly extraordinary to us – as it did to contemporaries – that this woman could betray the king who had given her so much. To look at the matter from her side, we must realise that she was living in fear. As soon as Edward died she would be nothing, and liable to attack from her political enemies. When the king died she could hardly expect members of the royal family to defend her: they would throw her to the dogs. Hence, to marry William Windsor secretly was to guarantee that she would have a protector after Edward's death. She may have even coerced him: if he did not marry her, she would allow the courts to find him guilty of embezzlement and extortion in Ireland. If this was the case, there would have been very little Windsor could have done. Not even an appeal to the king would have worked, for Edward in his mindlessly smiling state, was besotted with Alice.

The high point of Alice's public position came in 1375, when she attended a tournament at Smithfield with the king. She rode from the Tower through the city dressed as the Lady of the Sun, to the amazement of the Londoners. Ladies led knights on silver chains: a fitting image, in view of Alice ruling Edward in his old age. She planned further tournament displays for the following year, and manipulated her position to be able to acquire whatever she wanted: clothes, jewels, bedhangings, tapestries. Edward was wholly in her power. His world had shrunk to his immediate horizons, his ambitions dissipated. He was conscious only of Alice, his household servants, and his few surviving family members. With them he participated in hunting, hawking and civilised, courtly entertainment. All else had failed.

*

The Good Parliament met at Westminster on 28 April 1376. Edward remained at Havering, and did not attend (except for the opening ceremony). Nor did the prince, physically too weak for business of any sort. So it fell to John of Gaunt to represent the royal family in the Painted Chamber as the magnates, clergy and knights of the shire gathered for the first time in two-and-a-half years. Edward, so obvious by his absence, became the subject of debate.

There are many ironies about the reign of Edward III, but none more obvious than those which arose in this parliament. The leadership fell to the commons, and especially to the first ever Speaker of the house of commons: Sir Peter de la Mare. He was the steward of the earl of March, Edmund Mortimer, great-grandson of the Roger Mortimer whom Edward had ousted in 1330. The steward of the Mortimers was now lecturing Edward on his adultery, half a century after a Mortimer had been committing adultery with Edward's mother. And the word which de la Mare used more often than any other to describe the self-seekers around Edward was 'covyne' (coven); it was a word which Edward himself had used repeatedly in accusing the first Mortimer and his henchmen of their crimes. The judge had become the criminal, the criminal's heir the judge. But the biggest irony lay in the fact that Edmund Mortimer himself was now a member of the royal family, having married Philippa, Lionel's daughter, in 1368. Through his steward, the great-grandson and heir of Roger Mortimer was now speaking up for royal legitimacy and openly decrying an adulterous influence on the Crown.

De la Mare and his associates in the commons had been able to seize the initiative for one very powerful reason. The Bruges treaty only provided for a year-long suspension of hostilities, and without further taxation England would not be able to send an army to France to keep the war on foreign soil. So, when the commons met and flatly refused the subsidy, they were in a very strong position indeed. When John of Gaunt realised that their motive in refusing was a concerted will to move against those who were poorly advising the king, he was furious, and threatened to crush the rebels in the commons. It had to be pointed out to him that, although de la Mare might be a commoner, he had the protection of one of the mightiest men in the land. This was something which John had to consider carefully, for although he was the royal representative at that parliament, the earl of March was now the father of a boy who had a rival claim to the throne. Roger Mortimer, Lionel's grandson, was arguably next in line after the young Richard of Bordeaux. Gaunt had not yet been formally recognised as second-in-line. Thus he was forced to acknowledge that the political will of parliament, including the commons, could not be stifled.

It is impossible not to be impressed by de la Mare's courage. With death threats being muttered around him, and John of Gaunt steaming in his pent-up anger above him, he proceeded to accuse Latimer of a string of crimes, including misrule and extortion in Brittany, theft of Breton revenues from the king, negligence in the defence of Saint-Sauveur and Becherel, seizure of wine and money taken from enemy ships which should have come to the king, embezzlement of four-fifths of the ten thousand marks compensation paid by Sir Robert Knolles for the failure of the 1371 campaign, and embezzlement of four-fifths of the ten thousand pound sum paid by the citizens of Bristol to protect their liberties. He was further charged, along with the London merchant and master of the royal mint, Richard Lyons, of taking interest from the Treasury for money which had been given by foreign merchants to the Crown. Both were also charged with sequestrating imported goods for sale through price-fixing monopolies. The immediate dismissal of Latimer was demanded as an absolute condition, as well as that of Lyons. Some called for them to be executed.

John of Gaunt could not dismiss charges of this magnitude, but nor could he simply acquiesce to the demands. He therefore ordered an adjournment. Lyons, seeing his life at risk, sent a bribe of a barrel of gold worth a thousand pounds to the prince of Wales, who had once been his protector. Prince Edward, now drawing close to death, wanted nothing to do with him, and was suspicious of his brother's motives in adjourning parliament. He refused the bribe. Lyons accordingly sent the gold to the king, whose reputed response was to accept the gift with a smile, saying that he gladly accepted it as Lyons was simply returning what he had stolen from him. 'He has offered us nothing which is not our own', Edward said.[15]

Edward remained largely unaware of the proceedings at Westminster. He would not have known, for example, that Lord Neville, his steward, had tried to make a stand in defending Latimer. Such actions cut no ice with de la Mare. 'You should not be so concerned with other people's actions when you may soon find it very difficult to defend your own,' declared de la Mare. 'We have not yet discussed your case, nor touched upon your conduct.' That shut Lord Neville up. But as Neville and Latimer were still in charge of who had access to the king, Edward heard little or nothing about the total of sixty serious charges brought against them until they were dismissed from their offices, arrested, and had all their possessions confiscated. Richard Sturry, one of Edward's chamber knights, came to tell him of their plight and to plead for his friends. He phrased the news in a way calculated to cause Edward maximum distress. Parliament was seeking his deposition, he told him. They were trying to do to him what they had done to his father.

Deposition. With dishonour. It was what Edward had dreaded all his life. He had strained to do all he could to be a king above criticism in order to avoid that ever happening to him. And yet now, in his feeble-minded state, he saw his worst nightmare coming true. He sought advice from Sturry, who urged him to take immediate action to stop the proceedings in parliament. This would have been very dangerous, and Edward knew it. But what could he do? His distress was exacerbated when it emerged that Alice was being implicated in the accusations levelled against his officers. He saw himself losing those few people whom he trusted, being separated from the one woman he loved, and he himself losing the Crown. He saw himself being left alone, like his father. He implored those with him to take him to Kennington to see his son, the prince, to consult with him. They did so. But on a day which must have torn his heart in two, when he arrived at his son's palace, he found him dying.

The disease which had debilitated the prince for the last seven years was now about to claim his life. The sight of his bedridden son in agony can only have added to Edward's pains. He had already buried seven of his children; it was now clear he would soon bury an eighth, his favourite. Edward ordered the prince to be taken to Westminster where they could spend the final days together.

Edward watched his son die in his chamber at the Palace of Westminster. On 7 June the prince made his will, dictating it in French.[16] He desired to be buried in Canterbury Cathedral, in the undercroft beneath the shrine of St Thomas the Martyr. He chose a French poem to be inscribed on his tomb, and gave details of how he wanted his funeral to be conducted. He asked for his shield, helmet, sword and surcoat to be placed above his grave. He appointed his brother John one of his executors, the others being ecclesiastics and members of his household. After these details were seen to, he turned to his father and begged him to grant him three last requests. He asked him to confirm all the gifts he had made to members of his household, friends and family, including his illegitimate son, Roger of Clarendon. He asked him to make sure all his debts were paid. And lastly he asked him to protect his nine-year-old son, Richard, his heir.

Edward assented to the requests. The scene was reminiscent of Philippa's last days, seven years before, when she charged him with a similar series of final duties. As with Philippa, the prince was a part of Edward's whole life. Roger Mortimer had still ruled England when he had been born. Edward may have recalled the four-year-old boy on his first horse, his little tournament coats made to match those of his father and Lord Montagu. All through the years, his son had made him proud. He may have failed as an administrator in Gascony but he had succeeded in the one field of human endeavour which Edward respected above all others: the battle-field. It had been the prince who had held the English army together that day twenty years earlier, at Poitiers, and brought King John of France as a prisoner to England. And in dying, Prince Edward asked for a simple thing which reminded his father of perhaps the greatest day of his life. He asked that his badge of three ostrich feathers, which he had picked up after the battle of Crécy, would be carved on his tomb, together with the motto he had used that day, '*Ich Dien*'. I serve.

Prince Edward died the following day.

Across the nation the outpouring of grief was genuine and extreme. At St Albans, Thomas Walsingham expressed his pain through literary tears:

> Oh what a death to be mourned by the whole kingdom of England. How untimely you are, death, in robbing us of whatever might be seen to be bringing succour to the English. How sad you make the old king, his father, by robbing him of the desire which not only he had, but which the whole nation had, that his firstborn son might sit upon the throne after him and judge the people righteously. What great grief you cause his country, which believes that now he has gone it is bereft of a protector.[17]

But nowhere was the death of the prince more keenly felt than in Edward's heart. He too had lost his protector, his son and heir, his last hopes for the future.

Edward was in mourning, grief-stricken and hardly able to communicate with the world. So we can only guess at how he greeted the news that parliament had moved against Alice. Sir Peter de la Mare informed parliament that she had relieved the royal purse of between two and three thousand pounds per year. Her use of maintenance was notorious, and, lest there be any doubt about it, parliament stipulated that she and all women were to be prohibited from protecting those accused in the king's courts. Then it was revealed that she had secretly married William Windsor. As a marriage had to be consummated in order to be legal, it was universally assumed – and probably true – that they had slept together.

It was shocking, appalling. Had she not been Edward's mistress, impeachment would surely have followed. But Alice avoided prison and further prosecution on condition that she no longer visited or saw the king. If she did see him, she would lose everything she possessed in England and suffer perpetual exile.[18] Hence we may be certain that there came a day when Edward expected Alice to be with him, and asked for her. And he would have been told that his beloved mistress, his Lady of the Sun, could not be brought to him. He could never see her again. She had married another man. Edward had been committing adultery.

This was too much for Edward. The loss, personal and emotional, hurt him deeply, but the sinfulness too, even though he had loved her in good faith. He was lonely and afraid. In a sorrowful scene he swore an oath by the Virgin Mary that he did not know she was married. In his confused and lamentable state he begged for parliament to show her mercy, not to have her executed, both out of love for him and to preserve some vestige of honour. As for William Windsor, Edward summoned him from Ireland.[19] He wanted him prosecuted. He now knew that he had been used. Anger tore through his grief-stricken soul. On 18 July he purchased a chest in which he locked up the accusations against Windsor whom he regarded as the true culprit.[20] If Edward had any power left him, he would make the man sorry for his betrayal.

*

Among the resolutions of the Good Parliament was a declaration that a council of twelve should advise the king on all matters of weight, thereby reducing the risk of a 'coven' appropriating the royal power again. Edward himself sank into a mood of unfocused remorse and grief. He dwelt on the idea that his son's illness and death were somehow a penance inflicted on him for his treatment of his own father. His loss of Alice seems to have given rise to further grief for his wife. On 6 August he gave instructions to the keeper of the wardrobe to deliver cloths of gold and torchbearers' clothes for commemorating the anniversaries of the deaths of his mother and Philippa.[21] Visitors came and went: some Florentines in exile persuaded him to give them somewhere to stay in London, despite a sentence of excommunication hanging over them. The duke of Brittany left the country without informing him. Edward did not care. He was now waiting for just two things: the burial of his son, which was to take place on 5 October, and his own death.

At the end of September, Edward fell ill at Havering, suffering from an 'enpostyme'.[22] All his physicians despaired of his recovery. Letters were sent out to the clergy on 2 October asking for them to pray for the king.[23] On 5 October, the day of his son's funeral, he appointed trustees to look after his estates. Three days later he gave orders for no fewer than fifty-seven cloths of gold to be offered at churches where his son's obsequies were being celebrated.[24] That same day he made his will.[25] For a man who had achieved so much, it is a very modest list of requests. He asked to be buried in the abbey church at Westminster. He asked that sufficient funds be provided to complete the endowment of the Collegiate Church of St Stephen at Westminster, his Cistercian foundation of St Mary Graces by the Tower of London, and the Dominican priory of King's Langley. He especially gave money to pay for the singing of masses for the souls of himself and Philippa. He confirmed his grandson, Richard of Bordeaux, as his heir and bequeathed him his best bed with all its armorial hangings, as well as four lesser beds and hangings for his hall. To Joan, princess of Wales, he gave a thousand marks, and the free restitution of jewels she had pledged to him. To his 'very dear daughter' Isabella, he gave an income of three hundred marks per year until her daughters were married. Everything else he left to his executors to dispose of as they saw fit. His two youngest sons, Edmund and Thomas, were not mentioned, except for a reference in a supplementary document by which Edward settled the inheritance of the throne. After his death, only males were to inherit: first Richard, then John of Gaunt and his sons, and then, failing them, Edmund and his sons, and finally Thomas and his sons. In this way Edward attempted to destroy any claim his granddaughter, Philippa, might have had on the throne, thereby revoking the royal status of the Mortimer earls of March. It was an act of revenge for the proceedings of the Good Parliament, which he believed had been instigated by the Mortimers. But it was also a sign of how bitter and sad the dying king had become, that he should disinherit his own granddaughter.[26]

In the fourteenth century, wills were normally only made when the sufferer genuinely feared death was close. Thus everyone around him now believed that Edward was about to die. Latimer, whom Edward had appointed one of his executors, was recalled and pardoned. Alice too returned to court at his request. With a council of twelve to guard against maladministration, and Latimer and Neville safely out of office, it was felt that this great king should be allowed some last wishes in his final days. On 16 October a long gown was ordered for him, to guard him against the cold weather.[27] More warm clothes, lined with lambskins and furs, were ordered for him three days later. And three days after that, despite so shamefully betraying him, Alice returned to him, and received his pardon.

The remaining eight months of Edward's life and reign are a sorry tale of his poor health deteriorating further and the country sliding into acrimony and hatred. Had he died shortly after making his will, as he himself expected, no one would have begrudged him having Alice at his bedside. But that she was so easily restored to him, and remained with him for the next eight months, provoked scandal and widespread anxiety. Parliament's will had been flouted. What had changed? Latimer was with the the king, and John of Gaunt was hunting down the key figures from the Good Parliament. Sir Peter de la Mare was arrested and flung into a dungeon in Nottingham Castle, with no prospect of a trial.[28] William of Wykeham lost all his temporal estates. Even the earl of March was forced to surrender his marshal's staff in view of John of Gaunt's threats against him. In November Alice tried to secure Edward's pardon of Richard Lyons. Edward's chamberlain, Roger Beauchamp, would not let her near the king, but she made such a commotion outside Edward's chamber that he heard her, shuffled to the door, and opened it. He accepted the petition, and there was nothing Beauchamp could do to stop him reading it. In his simple state, he pardoned Lyons. In Walsingham's words,

> the whole populace desired Alice's condemnation when they saw that no action was being taken to remedy her wrongdoings, but realised that this evil enchantress, exalted above the cedars of Lebanon, was enjoying extraordinary favour, and all the people of the realm passionately longed for her downfall.[29]

Edward remained at Havering for the rest of the year. On his sixty-fourth and final birthday, he gave presents of lavish robes to his seven serving physicians and surgeons.[30] It was a far cry from his fiftieth, when he had raised his sons to dukedoms and held a great feast. On 25 January 1377 he completed his fiftieth year as king. The jubilee was not widely celebrated. A general pardon was announced. Sermons of the king's new moral purity were preached. But Edward's mortal frame had become little more than the vessel of his sickness. On 3 February 1377, his impostume abated, and eight days after that he was transported by barge to his palace at Sheen, to be nearer to Windsor. Like his mother in her dying, it had become his ambition to attend one last ceremony of the Order of the Garter. As his boat passed Westminster, all the lords who were then attending parliament in the presence of his grandson came out to wave and cheer him.[31] Within the Painted Chamber, clergymen were once again being appointed to the great offices of state, the impeachments of the previous parliament were being overturned, and parliamentary business was beginning to resume the character of bitter in-fighting and political factions it had known under Edward II. The characters were different: it was Edmund Mortimer, not Roger, leading the Marcher lords, and his enemy was now titled the duke – not earl – of Lancaster; but otherwise it was almost as if Edward III had not reigned.

Edward did manage to attend one more St George's Day celebration at Windsor. On 23 April 1377 he lifted a sword to dub the heirs to the great titles of the kingdom. Before him knelt his two ten-year-old grandsons: Richard of Bordeaux, heir of the late prince, and Henry of

Bolingbroke, son and heir of John of Gaunt. Both of these boys were nominated for the Order of the Garter. Edward also knighted his youngest son, the twelve-year-old Thomas of Woodstock, and the young heirs to the earldoms of Oxford, Salisbury and Stafford, and the heirs to the baronies of Mowbray, Beaumont and Percy. Last, he knighted his own illegitimate son John Southeray. Alice's moment of vindication and recognition had arrived.

Edward was taken back to his palace at Sheen to die. Few visited him. An audience with several Londoners who had proved particularly determined to see him revealed him 'placed in his chair like a statue in position, unable to speak'.[32] He seems to have been swaddled like a baby in cloth of gold and muslin and then nailed into his throne for the occasion.[33] The nails might have been gilded but nevertheless it is a striking image. The fate of the victor of Crécy – England's great hero – was to be nailed, half-alive into his throne to sit, vacantly, enduring his last duties. John of Gaunt and a number of bishops were in attendance that day, and the address to the king was delivered by Robert Ashton. But Edward could not comprehend it. Inside that trussed-up statuesque figure of golden senility, his mind plodded on, slowly, its logic awry. When he had recovered his speech a few days later, he summoned the Londoners to him secretly. He urged them to make a great candle bearing the coat of arms of his son John, and to carry it in a solemn procession to St Paul's Cathedral, and to burn it before a figure of the Virgin. What he meant by this we can only guess, but most Londoners clearly thought he had gone mad. In his moments between lucidity and silence, Alice continued to ply her political dealings. One of her undoubtedly positive achievements was to persuade the king to restore the estates of William of Wykeham, which he had lost as a result of John of Gaunt's accusations after the Good Parliament.

The release for which Edward must have yearned finally came at midsummer. On 2 June he made preparations to commemorate the anniversay of the prince's death. On the 4th he granted his last charter. With him that day were his two younger sons and Nicholas Carew, Henry Percy, the archbishop of Canterbury and the Treasurer and Chancellor. Then they left him in his chamber to listen to the silence. Alice alone remained with him, together with a few household staff and chamber knights. In his bed he still talked of hunting and hawking, and the joys he had known. But on the 21st he suddenly lost the power of speech. He had almost certainly suffered a stroke. He lay in his bed, unable to say or do anything. Alice was with him, and a priest also. According to Walsingham, Alice removed the rings from his fingers before she left. Maybe she did.

Maybe Edward had previously urged her to take them when the time came, a final farewell token of his gratitude for her staying by him. To him they no longer mattered. He was drifting into the oblivion which had consumed everything he truly loved. At the last, after Alice had departed, only the priest remained. There were no earls, dukes, princes, or queens: no sons, no wife, not even his mistress. There were no ambassadors, nor dignitaries, nor trumpets. There was just dust floating in the air of the chamber, and one priest praying at his side. The priest urged him to repent of his sins. He alone heard the dying king whisper his final words.

'Jesu, have pity.'

SEVENTEEN

Edward the Gracious

They say that a dying man, at the moment of death, sees his life flash before his eyes. Whether true or not, on hearing of Edward's death, it seems that his subjects saw the reign flash before their eyes in all its glorious achievement. One moment, Thomas Walsingham was writing bitterly 'how distressing for the whole realm of England was the king's fickleness, his infatuation and his shameful behaviour. Oh king, you deserve to be called not master but a slave of the lowest order.' The next, everything was forgiven. Edward was being described as a man of grace.

This sudden turnaround is noticeable even in the arrangements made for his funeral. Absolutely no expense was spared. Everything and everyone was covered in black cloth: the great chamber and chapel at Sheen, Westminster Abbey, St Paul's Cathedral, the royal family, all the hundreds of servants in the royal household, the horse harness and litter to convey Edward's body to London.[1] His body was embalmed 'with balsam and other perfumes and oils to stop it putrefying' by Roger Chandler at a cost of £21. His death-mask was made so that his true likeness, like Philippa's, would be preserved for eternity. This was fixed to a wooden effigy carried at the funeral, dressed in his clothes and shown off, and was later used as the model for his gilt-bronze monumental tomb.[2] His body was wrapped in silk, white 'cloth of Tartar' and red samite, and dressed in cloth of gold. His coffin was lined with red samite.[3] Ceremonial requiem masses were sung at Sheen. When the body was taken to St Paul's via Wandsworth, in a procession which lasted three days (with the cloth specially cut away so his face could be seen), no fewer than one thousand seven hundred torches – amounting to more than three tons of wax – were used at a cost of over £200. Every torch bearer was dressed in black. Bells were rung in every parish. At St Paul's and Westminster, further requiem masses were sung. On the day that his body was finally laid to rest in the church at Westminster, near Philippa's tomb, as he had promised, a great feast was held which cost more than £566: almost twice as much as the great feast at Windsor on St George's Day that year and, with probably the sole exception of the feast at his coronation, more than any other dinner in his whole feast-filled reign.[4] At the time it was probably the most expensive funeral ever held in England.

It marked the beginning of one of the most extraordinary personal exaltations which England has ever known. As a transformation of a military man into godlike hero the most obvious comparison is Nelson, four centuries later. But Nelson's apotheosis pales by comparison with that of Edward. For Edward was not just revered as a great battle hero, he became hailed as the archetypal leader of men, in peace as well as war. By the time his monument in Westminster Abbey was complete, about eight years later, he was deemed worthy of the following epitaph:

Here lies the glory of the English, the flower of kings past, the pattern for kings to come, a merciful king, the bringer of peace to his people, Edward III, who attained his jubilee. The undefeated warrior, a second Maccabeus, who prospered while he lived, revived sound rule, and reigned valiantly; now may he attain his heavenly crown.[5]

Another contemporary, writing at York, described him as

full gracious among all the worthy men of the world, for he passed and shone by virtue and grace given to him from God, above all his predecessors that were noble men and worthy. And he was a well hard-hearted man, for he never dreaded mischance, nor harm, nor the evil fortune that might befall a noble warrior and one so fortunate both on land and at sea. And in all battles and assemblies, with a passing glory and worship, he had ever the victory.[6]

This same writer's view is worth commenting on further, as he was writing a secular chronicle, not a monastic one, and his work proved the most popular of its age. This is therefore as close as we are likely to get to what the proverbial man in the street thought of Edward in the decade or so after his death:

He was meek and benign, homely, sober, and soft to all manner of men, to strangers as well as his own subjects and others that were under his governance. He was devout and holy, both to God and the Holy Church, for he worshipped and maintained the Holy Church and her ministers with all manner of reverences. He was entreatable, and well-advised in temporal and worldly needs, wise in counsel, and discreet, soft, meek and good to speak with. In his deeds and manner full gentle and well-taught, having pity on them that were diseased, generous in giving alms, and busy and curious in building; and full lightly he bore and suffered wrongs and harms. And when he was given to any occupation, he left all other things in the mean time, and held to it. He was seemly of body, and of middling stature, having always to both high- and low-born a good cheer. And there sprang and shone so much grace from him that whatever manner of man beheld his face, or had dreamed of him, he was made hopeful that whatever should happen to him that day should be joyful and to his liking.[7]

The word to note is 'grace'. Many writers use it in describing Edward in retrospect, as they had done in describing his 'gracious' victories in his heyday. A Latin chronicler, drawing from Walsingham's text, broke off to write that Edward 'was glorious, kind, merciful and magnificent above all the kings and princes of the world, and called "The Gracious" on account of that singular grace by which he was exalted'.[8] Such writers were alluding to divine blessing – something beyond mere greatness of action – a greatness and perfection of his nature. Even those who did not refer to him as gracious held him up as a paragon of leadership. A poem written about the time of Edward's death speaks of 'an English ship we had, noble it was and high of tower, it was held in dread throughout Christendom: the rudder was neither oak nor elm but Edward the Third, the noble knight'.[9] Another contemporary piece remembers Edward as 'the flower of earthly warriors . . . against his foes he was as grim as a leopard, towards his subjects as mild as a lamb'.[10]

It did not take long for Edward to become the stuff of legend. With his grandson's reign proving so divisive and lacking in achievements, Edward's name came to represent a golden age. Thus, although the chroniclers of 1377 may well have been moved by genuine admiration for the king they had just lost, those repeating their words in the 1390s were moved by the need for another such hero king. Moreover, what they needed was not a hero who would spend the last fifteen years of his life in physical and political decline but a hero who remained heroic. So they made Edward into one. Although the Edward III of 1372–77 certainly would not count as a hero in any respect, and the Edward III of 1363–71 would not qualify easily either, these periods of his rule were obliterated. How many people writing about Edward in the 1390s could correctly remember the events of 1333–50? Edward's achievements became legendary. He became a sort of Good King Edward, who provided the model for much of the fifteenth century's folk literature and romance. Such an image was not without a basis in fact, but today we would call it caricature. If the 'real King Arthur' were to march forth from the underworld we should expect to see Edward alongside the mysterious Dark Age warrior of that name, for if the king in the fifteenth-century Arthurian poems (including many of the Arthurian stories which we know today) is based on any single identifiable personality, it is that of Edward III. In legends he became what he aspired to be in life.[11]

*

So let us leave aside the legends. The hard fact is that Edward was a hugely successful king, even though he had his share of failures and arguments and died in lonely misery. He was prophesied to be a great conqueror in Europe and he became one. He lived up to every expectation of him recorded at his birth by his father's biographer except one: he died aged sixty-four, one year short of the age attained by Henry III. When he came to the throne the model of great kingship was that of his grandfather, Edward I. He eclipsed that and set a new standard for kings everywhere to admire. If he had died in 1363, having won all his victories and achieved his jubilee, and before his achievements had been overshadowed by later disasters, we would probably know him today as Edward the Great.

To rank Edward's achievements is difficult. One of the greatest was certainly his creation of a new model of kingship. The first stage of this – his recovery of English royal authority from its nadir of 1330 – was in itself a huge achievement. It is astounding that Edward at eighteen not only coped with Roger Mortimer and the débâcle of his father's secret custody in the hands of potential enemies but managed to preserve his mother's dignity afterwards and then pursued an aggressive foreign policy. After that it is hardly surprising that he weathered the political crisis in 1341 as if it were the passing of a few rainclouds. His vision of monarchy, his championing of the *idea* of monarchy – in terms of leadership, spirituality, chivalry, patronage, dress, propaganda, and parliamentary authority – not only aided his own family, it provided an example to all of Europe. By combining chivalric adventuring with military leadership, cultural patronage and political responsibility, he brought together all the real and imagined virtues of a Christian king. It made kingship a very demanding art, and one in which a man past middle age could not realistically hope to succeed, but he demonstrated how successful it could be. For the thirty years between 1333 and 1363 he was the greatest exponent of the art of chivalric kingship there ever was.

An equally impressive achievement was his preservation of peace in England for the duration of his long reign. In 1327 he had been exhorted above all else to work for domestic peace. His policy of keeping the war on foreign soil, clearly articulated in 1339, was novel, successful and hugely to the benefit of England. It was not so much the battles in France which mattered; it was the complete absence of fighting in England. Social historians often point to the prosperity brought by the wool trade as the reason why so many great churches were built in England in the mid-fourteenth century; but the wool trade itself (including the booming cloth trade) would not have flourished as it did if it had not been for fifty years of domestic peace and stability. It is difficult to exaggerate the importance of this. Anyone who assumes that peace was a natural state in the British Isles has only to refer to the preceding and following reigns or the contemporary situations in Ireland and Scotland to see that any weakness in the king's character could easily lead to widespread social, economic and political turmoil.

A third great achievement has to be the status he gave England internationally. In his dealings with the papacy prior to 1346, Edward appears aware of the inferiority of England to France on the international stage, as if he had an international chip on his national shoulder. It was his force of character and his extraordinary determination to play a major role in international politics which changed this. In 1330 France was unquestionably the pre-eminent military kingdom in Europe and the French pope could rely on his links with the French king to dominate Christendom. Edward threatened that spiritual-political alliance more than anyone else. Through his anti-papal legislation and his reinforcement of English royal rights, he helped pave the nation's own religious path, already beginning to diverge from the Catholic Church. Even more importantly for England's national identity, pride and status, he measured up to all his international rivals, be they spiritual, French, Flemish, Brabanter, German, Spanish or Genoese. Even the distant Florentines came to regard England as the military epicentre of Europe.

Edward's fourth major achievement has to be his method of making war. Whether we like it or not, Edward was to warfare what Mozart was to music. He found a new way of doing things, and it proved as good or better than almost everything that had gone before. Until 26 August 1346 international conflicts were not won or lost by firepower alone, they were won by feudal armies of expensively armoured knights. On that day all this changed. Groups of English peasants and yeomen's sons came to be the breakers of the most heavily armoured noblemen. But more than that, Edward's stroke of genius was to take the tactic of projectile warfare – which his commanders had discovered at Dupplin Moor and which he had used at Halidon Hill – and to combine it with the *chevauchée*: the twenty-mile-wide front destroying everything in its path as it progressed through enemy territory. Sufficient destruction forced the enemy to attack, and any enemy advancing on a well-ordered army capable of projectile warfare – whether equipped with longbows or guns – was almost certain to be torn to pieces in the crossfire. Such methods gave Edward the confidence to march across France and win his war of rivalry with Philip de Valois. It was the most effective military strategy of the middle ages, which proved just as decisive when employed by Henry V at Agincourt in 1415. When guns replaced longbows as the weapon of choice, it was not Edward's strategy which was outdated, only the means of putting it into action.

A fifth major achievement is the one which historians have always associated with this reign: the development of parliament. This was, of course, only indirectly an achievement of Edward's. But in view of his cast-iron will on the international political scene, he should be given the credit for proving so malleable on the domestic front. The writer who stated that Edward was 'as grim as a leopard' to his overseas enemies and 'mild as a lamb' to his compatriots was thinking along these same lines. Edward won the affections of his people by refusing to compromise with his overseas enemies and willingly compromising with the representatives of his kingdom. Nor should we give all the credit for reform to those who presented the petitions in parliament. Many statutes were initiated by the representatives, but Edward himself initiated some and the decision to enact all of them lay with the king. Furthermore, the status of the commons in relation to the magnates was allowed to change, and this too can be directly connected with Edward's policy of welcoming the rich merchants into noble society, through knighthoods, social codes and parliamentary authority. When the commons had taken part in the deposition of 1327 they were forced into taking such a bold move by an aristocrat, the earl of March. When the commons took action against the corrupt officials around Edward in the Good Parliament, they did it of their own accord, and it was not the earl of March who led the attack, it was his steward, a commoner. Under Edward III, parliament in general and the commons in particular gained a real voice in the government of the realm. Under his father, such participatory government would not have been allowed to emerge, let alone flourish.

These five great achievements – kingship, domestic peace, England's standing in the international community, modernised warfare and participatory government – are all huge, overarching developments. They are therefore somewhat abstract to us. Their significance is lost when we stand back and see them merely as elements in the development of the nation, even though they were so closely associated with one man. But they each had cultural spin-offs which have proved of lasting significance. The demonstration of kingship in the great palaces Edward built is an obvious one. As pointed out in Chapter Twelve, he was the greatest patron of art and architecture of the fourteenth century, and his cultural influence impressed itself on subsequent centuries, even if only one of his palaces survives today. Similarly, although most nineteenth- and twentieth-century authors completely failed to understand the nature of his claim on the throne of France, that claim was maintained by English kings even after his reputation began to dwindle in the eighteenth century. Not until 1802 was it given up: it was important to the idea of English kingship. Legislative consequences of his parliamentary policy are still to be found in the use of hallmarks, standardised weights and measures, the regular sitting of parliament, the framework of local justice, the crime of high treason and the official recognition of the English language. And perhaps most visible of all the cutural spin-offs is the English flag – the flag of St George – and the very adoption of St George as our patron saint, a consequence of Edward's vision of himself as a warrior-king and England as a fighting nation. When the flag of St George flies today at international football and rugby matches, when it is paraded around on supporters' cars, there is a distant echo of Edward's huge St George banners on his ships as he led England bravely and proudly to war.

As a result of all this, it is very difficult to deny that Edward was a great king. But what of him as a man? Obviously it is very difficult to separate the two, as he *was* a king, by nature, duty and service. Nonetheless, by examining Edward's whole life and remaining focused on him personally, we may go far further than previous writers in summing up his character. In his youth he was ambitious and hopeful but nervous – terrified even – by the dictatorship of Mortimer: a man whom he both feared and admired. He was open to learning, and his enthusiasm for a text could prove unbounded (as shown by his paying a nun one hundred marks for a book which he wanted). But his passion lay in the challenges of kingship, and those inevitably included war. His boyish passion for adventure remained with him right up until his late thirties, and, even after that, stories of far countries and civilisations, whether they be India or Italy, delighted him. He was, quite simply, romantic.

Edward's romance and love of adventuring was not allowed to run away with him, however. Secret business delighted him; dashing off with his companions to see to particular threats and problems was fun. But there was also a straightforwardness about Edward. He wanted to solve his problems himself. He wanted to be in control. The subtle intriguing of a Charles of Navarre was distasteful and alien to him. The shirking of battles by the French and the Scots was frustrating and cowardly. There was nothing glorious or noble about secrecy when it involved deception; but covert missions to capture a ford at low tide, or to arrange a deal with the pope, those were much more his style. This steadfast, dependable straightforwardness is occasionally mentioned by contemporaries. Walsingham goes on at some length about the king's childlike innocence at the end of his life. And his unbeguiling, honest approach may be seen in his political decision-making. Once he had developed a military strategy for attacking France, he stuck to it rigidly. When he had decided what was a reasonable expectation as a result of his French war, he stuck to his decision. When he did try plotting with the great kings of Europe in the 1340s, they all let him down. This is not surprising to us, but he was surprised. He did not understand duplicity.

Edward had the logical mind of a strategician. He did not have the fluid versatility of a schemer – although many of his advisers did – and he did not have the patience of an intellectual. He respected scholarship but did not have the education, patience or desire to get involved in its intricacies. Religious debates left him cold; his religion was laid down for him in his position, and he never questioned it. He knew he was a warrior-king appointed by God, and if he prayed hard and was spiritually dutiful, he would be victorious. That was his faith, and, as far as he was concerned, that was the end of the debate. But that straightforward conviction, unquestioning as it was, allowed him considerable intellectual scope. It did not hamper his logical analysis of a battlefield situation, or his quick-minded appreciation of clocks, parliaments, alchemy, guns and projectile warfare. It even permitted him to reach the heights of genius, as displayed in the strategic brilliance of the design of Queenborough Castle or in the campaign in France in 1346–47. The only time when Edward seems deliberately to have done something to discourage a knowledge-related activity was when, as a young man, he reprimanded the abbot of St Albans for spending too much time and money making his clock and not enough of either on finishing his church. For Edward at the age of ninteen, religious obligations came first, then the exercises of the mind.

Edward's logic and religious conscience go a considerable way to explaining his sense of fairness. This of course is essential to understanding his dealings with parliament; in domestic politics he was often looking for a fair compromise. Distinct signs of his fairness may be seen in such actions as his enactment that men should be tried in their own language, the prohibition of maintenance, and that earls should be expected to live up to their military responsibilities. But it may be seen also in actions less favourable to himself and the nobility, such as his repeated insistence that purveyors should pay for the goods they took. As a man who regarded royal status so highly, we might have expected him to have reinforced the king's purveyor's rights, not limited them. Likewise there is a distinct sense of fairness in his judgement of men, like those accused of his father's murder in 1330. He could simply have seized them and had them executed as scapegoats, but he did not. Nor did he hold the sins of the father against the son and grandson of Roger Mortimer. There was a fine conscience at work in Edward: he did not do things which he suspected he would later regret.

Hence his famous clemency. Edward could be 'terrible to his enemies' – that was expected of a warrior – and his anger sometimes knew no limits, but he could also be merciful and was often magnanimous in victory. The regularity with which he was persuaded to spare condemned men their lives and let them go free was so great that we must treat each such scene as public propaganda. And very successful propaganda it was too: Edward created the image that he was both a wrathful king and a merciful one. Moreover the mercy – with regard to his own subjects at least – seems to have been genuinely instinctive. It is difficult otherwise to understand his forgiveness of Geoffrey Mortimer or Archbishop Stratford. One suspects that in some cases his instincts led him to be too merciful. John Molyns was a criminal through and through, but in 1340 Edward forgave him his crimes, and only in 1357, after repeated offences, locked him up for the rest of his life. Similarly Chief Justice William Thorp deserved worse punishment than he got: according to the law, Edward should have executed him as well as dismissing him. From corrupt ministers and barons to the towns of Caen and Calais, it is the number of men he forgave which deserves notice, not the number he punished.

Edward's mercy to previously loyal servants leads on to another aspect of his character which is repeatedly demonstrated: fidelity. This might seem a strange characteristic to pick, given his reputation as sexually promiscuous, but we cannot escape how grateful Edward remained all his life to those men who helped him overthrow Mortimer in 1330. The reason John Molyns was forgiven for a great number of crimes for almost thirty years was that he was one of those men. Edward remained faithful to those who helped him in his darkest hour. He also remained wholly faithful to his country, as we would expect of a king. And he remained steadfastly loyal to his chosen spiritual protectors, St George, St Thomas the Martyr, and, above all others, the Virgin Mary. Loyalty and fidelity were in his nature. But fidelity of course must include sexual fidelity, and as soon as we mention sex we find him open to accusations of immorality. He encouraged sexual licence at his court: about that there is no doubt. The repeated accusations in English sources of adultery among the women attending his tournaments only gives weight to the immoral character of these events. But these descriptions should not blind us to the complete lack of reference to any bastard children before John Southeray. His eldest son sired two, John of Gaunt had so many that contemporaries described him as a 'great fornicator', but none are attributed to Edward III himself before the age of fifty and the onset of his wife's protracted final illness. The only evidence that he had passing affairs are the French story that he committed adultery while at Calais, and the possibility that there is a kernel of truth concerning his sudden unconsummated infatuation for a young noble-woman at Wark. The first of these was almost certainly propaganda, and the latter is hardly a moral crime. Moreover, to father as many legitimate children as he did required him to stay in close proximity to his queen, and for her to travel with him and to sleep with him often. When Alice Perrers did become his mistress in the early to mid-1360s, Philippa was already gravely ill. Most striking of all, Edward remained faithful to Alice. Therefore his only proven adultery is to have slept with Alice while his wife was preparing to die (and had begun making arrangements for her tomb) and to continue sleeping with Alice after her secret marriage (for which he can hardly be blamed). There may well have been other instances, perhaps many others, but there is no evidence. His inclination was to be loyal. We may in fact go as far as to say he was among the most faithful of all our medieval kings, first to his wife and, after Philippa's physical decline, to his mistress.

So, Edward was loyal, faithful, religious, unintellectual, romantic, adventurous, controlling, encouraging of sexual indulgence, straightforward, logical, fair and merciful. That list includes some surprising contradictions. Romantic and logical? Faithful and yet encouraging of sexual indulgence? But in such contradictions lies the interest of the man. Just as his father is fascinating for his complications of character, so too is Edward. In Edward we have the faithful servant of God who argued with the pope. We have the straightforward man who despised duplicity but who connived at his father's secret custody. We have the fair-minded man who destroyed hundreds of innocent French villages, towns and lives. And we have the merciful man who beheaded a hundred Scotsmen on the morning after Halidon Hill. In each case we may try to explain his actions, but that is not the point. Whatever one says about him, he was a man who contained many conflicting characteristics and motivations. Against his positive attributes we may fairly accuse him of overbearing pride, selfishness, conceit, occasional outbursts of uncontrollable anger, impetuousness, impatience, and probably many more weaknesses, especially in his youth. We may go further and deride him for being merely lucky, if we feel that luck does not count as a virtue, or pity him for being miserable, lonely and unlucky in his later years. But to pretend he was simply a warmonger, a religious cynic and a brutal thug, and that all the cultural achievements of the reign should be interpreted as the side-effects of his passion for women, power and war – as so many historians have done and continue to do – is simply wrong.

One virtue has purposefully been left off the above list and saved for special mention. His courage. It is not a virtue which was particular to Edward – his father and grandfather both had it, and his sons and grandsons displayed varying degrees of bravery – but it deserves special mention nonetheless. For without it none of the above would have happened. In our twenty-first-century comfort, hearing of wars around the world, we do not doubt that the lives of Western political leaders are more or less safe. Those of their generals are probably even safer. But in Edward we see a man who knew that, if anything was to come of his reign, then safety was not an option. He had to risk everything. It was not mere bravado that made him fight as a common knight in his tournaments. Nor was it his sense of adventure that made him stand on foot in the front line at Halidon Hill. It was an awareness that, unless he could show he could conquer his own fears, he had no chance of inspiring his men. At Calais in 1349 he did not need to risk his life as a common knight, fighting de Ribbemont. Nor did he have to stand on deck at Sluys in 1340 or Winchelsea in 1350. On both occasions he went beyond the call of duty. He did put himself at risk, and he repeatedly showed he was prepared to fight, and so he encouraged his men to risk their own lives and go far beyond duty themselves. It was this attitude and this courage that led to the incredible feats of the English armies in the first stage of the Hundred Years War. If there is any one thing for which all people in all times should respect Edward and his contemporaries, it is this: when he had made a political decision which he believed was right, he did not simply give orders for his will to be carried out. He donned armour, drew his sword, and prepared to fight for it himself.

Thus we arrive at the end of Edward's life. But in one respect it is not the end. The great majority of people in England of English ancestry are descended from him, if not the entire population.[12] Although comparatively few people today will be able to prove every generation, the genealogy is less important than the genes. The virtues and the weaknesses of this man have passed into the entire English people, in every walk of life. He may not have been the perfect king he tried to be, but, given the unattainable heights of his ambition, we have to applaud his achievement. For better or for worse, he helped to make the English nation what it is. And for better or for worse, he helped us become what we are.

APPENDIX 1

Philippa of Hainault's Date of Birth

The register of Walter Stapeldon, bishop of Exeter, contains a delightful description of a daughter of the count of Hainault, dated 1319, which has long been thought to refer to Philippa.[1] Stapeldon writes that the girl was, according to her mother, aged 'nine on the next Nativity of St John the Baptist' (24 June). He mentions that her hair was 'between blue [i.e. blue-black] and brown', her eyes were 'brown and deep', her forehead large, and her nose was 'large at the tip' but not snubbed, and 'her neck shoulders and all her body and limbs of good form'.[2] The adjectives used are those of romance literature, with the notable exception that Stapeldon stated she had some off-white teeth.[3] Many historians (including the author of Philippa's article in the *Oxford Dictionary of National Biography*) have accepted that this relates to Philippa, and have assumed as a result that she was slightly older than Edward, being born in 1310. However, this is incorrect.

For a start, the eldest daughter of the count of Hainault was Margaret, who was born in 1311.[4] If Philippa had been born before 1311, she would have been in a much stronger position to inherit the county which passed to her sister on the death of their brother William in 1345. But laying this inconclusive argument aside, there are aspects of the actual entry in Stapeldon's register which should concern us. Although this is in the same hand as the surrounding text, and thus contemporary, the statement that it was Philippa is of later date, in a later hand (probably that of Bishop Grandison), and an insertion in the margin. Therefore the attribution to Philippa is not part of the description. As noted in Chapter One, Stapeldon made two trips to the courts of Flanders and Hainault in 1319: one from January to March, and another in the summer. The reason for the error that Philippa was born in 1310 is a double assumption: that the description relates to Philippa as the insertion suggests, and that the description was made on Stapeldon's return to England after his first trip in March 1319. If correct, this would mean that the girl he described was born on 24 June 1310. However, this overlooks Stapeldon's second trip in the summer of 1319. Edward sent Stapeldon back again to see Count William of Hainault, urging the count to pay special heed to 'certain matters' which

Stapeldon would discuss with him. This second visit was organised before 10 April 1319, the date of Edward II's letter to Count William.[5] However, Stapeldon did not receive his letters of safe-conduct – the equivalent of a passport – until 27 May, and at that point he was in the north, at York.[6] These letters stated he should return from his mission by Michaelmas (29 September). If we then check Stapeldon's register it appears that his reference to the Hainaulter girl appears on folio 142, after entries for May, June and July 1319.[7] The description therefore dates from his second trip to Hainault. This took place between 6 July (when he was at Canterbury) and 7 August (when he was in London). He did not return to see the king at York, but returned to the West Country, and sent his report by letter: hence the appearance of a copy in his register.[8] Therefore his reference to the girl as nine on the 'next' 24 June must refer to the next such date after 6 July, i.e. 1320. So we can be sure that the girl he was describing was born in 1311. This was Count William's eldest daughter, Margaret, who was born in that year, as mentioned above. It would follow that Stapeldon was looking over Margaret of Hainault for the possible marriage to Edward, not Philippa. Other documents confirm that Count William wrote to the pope on 10 December 1318 seeking dispensation for Margaret of Hainault to be married to Edward.[9] Although permission for the marriage was granted by the pope in 1321, as stated in Chapter One, nothing came of the attempt. By the time of Edward's visit to Hainault in 1326, Margaret had been married for eighteen months to Ludvig of Bavaria, the future Holy Roman Emperor; hence she never became Edward's bride.

As a result we may be sure of several things: that Margaret was Edward's first intended bride, and that the description is of her, and that the clerk who inserted the note that Stapeldon's description related to Philippa was doing so on an assumption that only one daughter of the count's was proposed as Edward's marriage partner. We may also be confident that Margaret's birthdate was 24 June 1311. It follows that it is very unlikely that Philippa was born before April 1312. In this context it is worth returning to older narratives, which suggest that she was younger than Edward. Froissart, who knew her in her later years, asserted that she was in her fourteenth year at the time of her marriage in 1328.[10] This implies that she was born between 25 January 1314 and 24 January 1315, and thus about three years younger than her sister Margaret, and about two years younger than Edward.

The Fake Death of Edward II

The definite assertion in my biography of Sir Roger Mortimer, *The Greatest Traitor*, that Edward II was not killed in Berkeley Castle in 1327 startled many readers, academics and laymen alike. The idea that historians could have been wrong for centuries about this matter was greeted with scepticism by most scholars and incredulity by many members of the public. As a result, I devoted a considerable amount of time in 2003–4 to revisiting the subject in much greater detail than it has previously received. After considerable research, rethinking, consultation and discussion, the final result was published by *The English Historical Review*, the leading peer-reviewed journal in the field of English medieval studies. Any reader who wishes to obtain an in-depth perspective on the fake death of Edward II in the period 1327–30 should refer to volume 120 of that journal (November 2005). What follows here is a brief synopsis for those who want a short explanation of why we may have sufficient confidence in this new narrative to begin to interpret Edward III's reign in the light of his father's survival after 1327.

The starting point is an examination of why we as a society have come to retell the popular story of the death. The main answer to this is that it is repeated in various forms in about twenty chronicles from the mid-to-late fourteenth century. In some narratives Edward was smothered, in others he died with a burning piece of copper inserted into his anus, in one he was strangled, and the remainder just state that he 'died'. None say that he did not die. Therefore, when writers of the fifteenth and sixteenth centuries were trying to construct a coherent story of England's past, they looked back to the fourteenth-century chronicles and found them unanimous on the subject of the death. Furthermore, they mostly presumed that the more detailed narratives were more accurate, on the grounds that they provided more information and were thus better-informed. These they assimilated into a popular story which became established and widely accepted before the mid-sixteenth century. The handful of interested antiquaries and textual scholars of the period would have found confirmation of the date of the supposed death in the archives then stored at the Tower. In particular, in the patent rolls they would have found grants to commemorate the anniversary of the death of the king on 21 September, in the royal household accounts they would have found payments for pittances to be given to the poor on the anniversary of Edward II's death, and in the rolls of parliament they would have found direct accusations of murder levelled against Roger Mortimer, Simon Bereford, Thomas Gurney, Thomas Berkeley and William Ockley. This abundance of contemporary record evidence, coupled with the chroniclers' testimony, allowed them and their successors no room to doubt that Edward died on or about 21 September 1327.

What the early scholars did *not* do was to examine the many flaws and irregularities in the evidence. Until the late twentieth century scholars lacked the methodological sophistication to go beyond the face value of the records and chronicles and deconstruct the information structures underlying the various bodies of evidence. Furthermore, by the late twentieth century it had become academically very unfashionable to question whether specific kings were murdered. A general assumption was made that the evidence was insufficient to warrant any major revisiting of the deaths of any of the four secretly 'murdered' kings (Edward II, Richard II, Henry VI and Edward V), and any attempt to research and explain the supposed later lives of the first two and the younger brother of the last in terms of a genuine survival resulted in prompt scholarly dismissal, regardless of the merits of the argument. The result was an example of 'group think', an intellectual stalemate in which the scholarly élite is so hostile to deviation from an accepted orthodoxy that no individual within the élite is in a position to question it, and no individual outside the élite will be taken seriously if he holds such unorthodox views.

If we examine the chronicles of the fourteenth century, we are presented with about twenty texts, one of which – the shorter continuation of the *Brut* chronicle – has many variant versions on the matter of the death. No original contribution to narratives of the death was made after 1356; thereafter all the chronicle accounts are reworkings or direct quotations of earlier statements. The earliest chronicle has Edward dying on 21 September of a grief-induced illness. The 'anal torture' death – probably based on thirteenth-century accounts of the death of Edmund Ironside – first appears in a chronicle written at York by an anti-Mortimer polemicist in the mid-1330s. The first appearance of the red-hot 'poker' (as opposed to a copper rod) is in 1340. But if we examine all the explicit accounts of the imprisonment and death, and reconstruct the information threads repeated in the various stories, the detailed chronicles may be shown to descend from two original accounts, and one of those was very probably no more than an embellishment of the other. The more reliable of these two authors

(Adam Murimuth) actually distances himself from the idea that the king was murdered, saying it was merely 'common rumour', implying that he himself did not know the truth, although he was the only chronicler in the West Country at the time. Furthermore, these two chronicles are demonstrably incorrect in several ways: for instance, they both accuse John Maltravers of being one of the murderers, although he was not at Berkeley Castle at the time of the supposed death and was never accused of murder. The upshot of this is that no chronicle has any reliable information regarding the circumstances of the death, and all the chronicles together contain only one reliable fact: that there was a royal announcement at Lincoln in September 1327 that Edward II had died of a grief-induced illness at Berkeley Castle on St Matthew's Day (21 September).

This turns attention to the record evidence. There is no doubt that the announcement of the death was made between 24 and 29 September (when the court was at Lincoln). In most circumstances, when one knows that a specific royal announcement was made at a certain time and in a certain place, it is not necessary to question the detail any further. However, when a piece of information has a unique, geographically identifiable source, we may be far more rigorous in assessing its reliability. Putting it simply, we may ask the following question: could the person making the official announcement on behalf of the king at Lincoln have known the truth of what he had been led to believe had happened at Berkeley?

The answer to this is 'definitely not'. Edward III heard about his father's supposed death on the night of 23/24 September and began circulating the information with no check on the veracity of the message. This is proved by an original document in the National Archives – DL 10/253 – which is a letter from Edward to his cousin, the earl of Hereford, written on 24 September, in which he states he heard the news about his father's death during the previous night. It could be objected that Edward III checked the identity *after* he started spreading the news, but it needs to be borne in mind that Lincoln is 110 miles from Berkeley. If Edward III – who was only fourteen and under the strict supervision of his mother, one of the instigators of the plot – had been able to order anyone to go directly to Berkeley to check on the identity of the dead corpse, the man could not have got there within five days of the date of the supposed death. Had he done so, and if Lord Berkeley had let him see the corpse, he would have found it already embalmed. This means he would not have been able to identify it, as fourteenth-century royal embalming completely covered the face and features in wax-impregnated cloth. Further examination of the records reveals that there was no credible exhibition of the unem-balmed corpse. As a result of this we may be confident that all the official information about the death of Edward II was based on trust. The 'fact' of the death depends wholly on the assumption that Lord Berkeley's letter to Edward III about his father's death was written in good faith.

The first important fact arising from this is that we can begin to understand the flow of information underlying the extant evidence for the death. Edward III received Lord Berkeley's letter and believed what it said. As a result the death was officially announced, the news spread around the court and the country, chaplains were endowed to pray for the late king's soul, and a royal funeral was arranged to take place at St Peter's Abbey in Gloucester (now Gloucester Cathedral). This is why there is such an abundance of official evidence relating to the death. Lord Berkeley's letter was accepted in good faith.

We can show relatively easily that in one respect the letter was certainly not written in good faith, for it stated that Edward II died of natural causes. In the light of later events, this is not sustainable. The question is rather one of how Lord Berkeley lied: did he lie about the cause of the king's death? Or did he lie about the fact that the king had actually died? In answering this Berkeley himself stated in parliament three years later, in November 1330, that he 'had not heard about the death [of Edward II] until coming into this present parliament'. This seems to be a confession that he had lied in 1327. Various objections – for example, that he really meant he had not previously heard about the accusation of murder – can be shown to be implausible. Nevertheless, even if his statement had been unambiguous, it could still have been untrue. To test its truth, and its implication that Lord Berkeley had lied in announcing the death in 1327, we have to look for any irregularities in the information patterns created as a result of Lord Berkeley's statement that Edward II had died of natural causes.

The first series of irregularities which arise in the wake of the letter state unequivocally that the king was still alive. The plot of the earl of Kent provides the key evidence. Previous commentators have all followed the early twentieth-century scholar Professor Tout in declaring that Kent was 'stupid'. Tout's statement was based partly on the blatantly politicised accusations against Mortimer of November 1330, partly on the anti-Isabella prejudices of the chonicler Geoffrey le Baker, and partly on his own and his contemporaries' anti-revisionist prejudice. As a result of his condemnation, historians have never bothered to investigate the matter from Kent's point of view. Had they done so they would have realised that there is abundant evidence that he was anything but stupid. Certainly he was not executed for his stupidity. He was condemned to death in the parliament of March 1330 explicitly for the crime of trying to rescue the living King

Edward II 'to help him become king again, and to govern his people as he was wont to do beforehand'. There is no good reason to discount this as evidence that the king was alive and that he had been held at Corfe.

The parliamentary view that Edward was still alive in March 1330 has independent support, also previously overlooked. Kent had an informant, Sir John Pecche, who was the keeper of Corfe Castle until September 1329. Pecche cannot be said to have been deluded as to the presence of the king at Corfe prior to this date. His role in Kent's plot was to tell Ingelram Berengar that Edward II was still alive. As Pecche and Kent had the same information, either one must have informed the other or they must have had an independent source. Given his position as constable of the castle, we may be sure that Pecche did not have to accept the news that Edward II was alive – supposedly in his custody – without checking the truth for himself. It is unthinkable that he jeopardised his reputation, estates and life without ascertaining whether the supposedly dead king was in his own castle, given that it was in his power to do so. Pecche's role in Kent's plot is therefore independent corroborative evidence of the parliamentary view that Edward II was at Corfe in 1330. Both of these pieces of evidence in turn support Berkeley's statement that he had not heard about Edward II's death in 1330. And to these we may add two more contemporary documents which state that Edward was alive in 1330: a private letter from the archbishop of York to the mayor of London stating that he had 'certain news' that Edward II was still alive, and of course the Fieschi letter. We thus have a number of good, independent pieces of evidence that Lord Berkeley's letter announcing the death of Edward II was deliberately misleading.

The announcement that Edward II had been murdered was first officially made in the charges against Mortimer and his adherents after his arrest in 1330. These are riddled with inaccuracies, inconsistencies and anomalies. Not least of these are the conscious acceptance of a lie by Edward III of Lord Berkeley's statement as to where he was at the time of the supposed murder, and the failure to order the arrest of the two men condemned to death for the murder until a week after the trial (during which time they were permitted to leave England). Doubts about the accusations were shared by contemporaries: the majority of the manuscripts of the shorter continuation of the French *Brut* (completed in or after 1333) repeat the understanding that Edward II had died of natural causes, revealing a reluctance to follow the new accusations of murder. Similarly, in 1354 all the charges against Mortimer were found to be in error, including that which stated he had procured the murder of Edward II. But perhaps the most interesting aspect connected with the claims that Edward II was murdered is Edward III's treatment of the men responsible for keeping his father safely. He never punished Lord Berkeley in any way at all, letting him keep his lands and lordship and allowing him freely to come to court. And Lord Maltravers was also allowed to keep his lands and lordship. Although he remained in exile in Flanders for several years for his part in betraying Kent, Edward was in correspondence with him as early as 1334. He allowed him to return to England secretly for a meeting in 1335, employed him in Flanders in 1339 and then employed him in Ireland, and rewarded him long before he was officially forgiven for his part in Kent's death. When he finally returned to England in 1351 Edward wrote a letter praising his 'loyalty and goodwill' and specifically stating that he wished 'to do something grandiose for him'. As many people have remarked in the past, Edward's subsequent patronage of the two men responsible for keeping his father safely in 1327 is not consistent with their murdering him.

As a result of these lines of research, it is found that the officially created evidence relating to Edward II's death is based on information arising from a single announcement which was not verified by the king, but which was in line with the political ambitions of Lord Mortimer, and very probably in line with Isabella's emotional attachment to her husband, which remained strong in his captivity and even up until her death. On their instructions Berkeley faked the death, sent Edward II to Corfe Castle to be secretly maintained by Sir John Maltravers while Sir John Pecche was overseas, and embalmed another corpse to be buried in place of the king. Unfortunately for the plotters, Sir John Pecche returned unexpectedly in early 1328 and discovered Edward II at Corfe Castle. Pecche then informed Kent, who subsequently took action to rescue the king. His plot was discovered by Mortimer's agents. Mortimer's threat to the royal authority – which had been great even before 1330 – now became unbearable for Edward III, who saw his uncle condemned to death in parliament for trying to rescue his sadly abused father from Corfe. Having no doubt that his entire dynasty was at risk, Edward III arranged the seizure of Mortimer and eradicated the widespread doubts about his father's fate by finally creating an official, royal version of the 'death': that Edward II had been murdered by Gurney and Ockley on Mortimer's orders in Berkeley Castle. This served both to destroy Mortimer's support and strengthen Edward III's own status as a ruling king, even though he was still under age. The story of the death of Edward II in Berkeley Castle was thus a political fiction invented by Mortimer and twisted by Edward III into a murder story for reasons of political legitimacy. The propaganda fall-out from this has misled scholars and deceived laymen ever since.

A Note on the Later Life of Edward II

Research into the life of Edward II after the collapse of Mortimer's regime in October 1330 is complicated by a number of factors. Unlike the question of his 'death' – which is a finite problem which can be answered logically by examining the information structures underpinning the evidence for the death and scrutinising the evidence for events contingent on his survival – the matters of where he was after 1330 and when he died are potentially limitless. One is caught between the unending possibilities and the shortage of direct evidence. Most important business was conducted orally, through messengers, not in a written format. Therefore there is rarely any written material for us to evaluate. However, despite these problems it is important for readers to have an idea of the nature of the research in progress and some findings, in order to understand how Edward II's survival affected Edward III, as outlined in Chapters Four to Eight of this book.

There is only one piece of written evidence which overtly claims that Edward II was definitely alive after 1330. This is the famous Fieschi letter, written by Manuel Fieschi in about 1336, and known since 1877 from the copy in a cartulary of a mid-fourteenth-century bishop of Maguelonne. (Readers wanting to see the text and a reproduction of the original will find both in *The Greatest Traitor: the Life of Sir Roger Mortimer*.) In brief the letter states that, after the execution of Kent, Edward II was taken from Corfe to Ireland, where he remained for nine months. Up to this point he had the same custodian as had attended him in 1327 at Berkeley, but, after November 1330, he was released (probably partly on account of the danger of being found out by Edward III and partly on account of the fact that the mastermind of the plot, Mortimer, was dead). The ex-king made his way to Sandwich dressed as a pilgrim and then travelled to Avignon, where he saw the pope. If he had walked to Avignon at a rate of about ten miles per day with the other pilgrims travelling south, he would have taken about eight weeks to reach the papal palace, arriving about the end of February or early March 1331. After spending two weeks with the pope, Fieschi's letter states that he went from there to Brabant, and from Brabant to the shrine of the Three Kings at Cologne, then to

Milan, and then to 'a certain hermitage of the castle of *Milasci*', where he stayed for two-and-a-half years, moving on account of a war in the area to another hermitage near 'Cecima, in the diocese of Pavia', where he had been for two years by the time of the letter being written.

There is another well-known document which suggests that Edward II was alive in the 1330s. It has a strikingly reliable provenance. This is the royal wardrobe account written by or under the auspices of William Norwell in 1338–40 which states twice that the William le Galeys who was brought to Edward III at Koblenz in September 1338 claimed to be the king's father. The first of these two references is an undated payment 'to Francisco the Lombard sergeant at arms of the king for the money by him spent on the expenses of William le Galeys who asserts that he is the father of the present king, previously arrested (*arestati*)[1] at Cologne and by the said Francisco led to the king at Koblenz by his own hand, 25s 6d'. Judging from the king's itinerary derived from the same manuscript volume, this delivery of le Galeys must have been while the king was staying at Niederwerde near Koblenz, between 30 August and 7 September 1338. The second entry is specifically dated to 18 October, when the royal party was at Antwerp. Francisco – now fully named as 'Francekino Forcet' – was paid 'for the money received by him for the expenses of William Galeys remaining in his custody, who calls himself king of England, father of the present king, namely for three weeks in December of year twelve (1338) by his own hand 13s 6d'.[2]

In considering these two documents it is important to understand that there are several areas in which they corroborate each other. These are (1) that Edward II was believed by important individuals definitely or possibly to have been alive in the later 1330s, (2) that the person claiming to be Edward II was in the protection or custody of Italians, (3) that his expenses were meagre (fittingly for a man living as a recluse) and (4) that probably both narratives may be connected with the Fieschi family of Genoa and the papal court. As a result of this corroboration it seems it would be wrong to presume that the Fieschi letter is a forgery as no one has managed to find any evidence that it is anything other than what it purports to be. Furthermore, there are reasons to suppose that William le Galeys was not an impostor. Not only was he not punished, he was entertained at royal expense and his keeper was paid in advance for his expenses in December. One logical explanation for the advance payment is that Philippa was expected to give birth to Edward II's grandchild about then (Lionel being born at the end of November).

To carry this debate further requires us firstly to establish what evidence there is to corroborate or deny the Fieschi statement and Norwell's suggestion that Edward II was still alive in the mid-to-late 1330s; and secondly to establish what evidence there is that Edward II had died by a certain date. Contrary to most assumptions, these two questions are not directly connected. If Fieschi's letter was fraudulent, one would still have to answer the question of when Edward II died (given the findings of the research summarised in Appendix Two). And if the letter is correct, it still says nothing about Edward's death.

To begin with the survival of Edward II. In trying to understand the political and social context for the writing of the Fieschi letter an examination of the Fieschi family has been undertaken, as well as the careers of Manuel himself and the two family members of greatest importance in the 1330s: Cardinal Luca Fieschi (d.1336) and Niccolinus Fieschi, also known as 'Cardinal', of Genoa. The author of the letter, Manuel, was resident with Luca (his second cousin once-removed) at Avignon, and served him as a notary, and also served as a papal notary from before 1327 to 1343, when he was made bishop of Vercelli. Luca died at his house in Avignon on 31 January 1336, whereupon Manuel became his executor.[3] On the internal evidence of the letter, unless there is a mistake in the periods spent at the two hermitages in Italy, the letter cannot have been written much before January 1336. Given the fullness with which the letter accounts for Edward's whereabouts up to about January 1336 but not for a period beyond that, it is likely that it was written in the first half of 1336, perhaps triggered by the death of Cardinal Luca.

In *The Greatest Traitor* I suggested that it was Niccolinus Fieschi who brought the Fieschi letter to England in April 1336, a date which would agree with the above analysis.[4] Since writing that, other reasons have emerged to suggest Niccolinus was involved with the delivery of the Fieschi letter. He was a relative, probably an uncle or first cousin once-removed of Manuel's, and a contemporary (probably a second cousin) of Cardinal Luca. He was additionally a lawyer and an ambassador representing not only the pope but also the Genoese state and Edward III, who treated him with exceptionally high regard. If his kinsman Manuel was deliberately trying to mislead Edward III over something as serious as the survival of Edward II in Italy in early 1336, we must ask why Edward III rewarded Niccolinus so enthusiastically on meeting him at the Tower on 15 April 1336. And we must also wonder why he continued to trust him with his secret business, employing him as a high-level diplomat to negotiate peace treaties with the French, Genoese, Sicilians and the pope for the next eight years, undertaking to pay him more than a thousand pounds in fees and expenses for his service between July 1338 and April 1343. When Edward wrote to the pope in 1340 to explain his assumption of the title King of

France, he picked the sexagenarian Niccolinus to be the bearer of his letter, and described him as an 'intimate confidant', and expressly remarked on his 'proven faithfulness and far-sighted circumspection'.[5] Unless Edward never received the Fieschi letter, one cannot believe it was written in bad faith, for if it had been it would be impossible to understand why Edward completely trusted a man closely connected with its author. On the other hand, if the letter was written in good faith, and was received by Edward, it would explain why Niccolinus became so trusted from the moment he arrived at the Tower in April 1336: he was acting as the representative of the custodians of Edward II. It would also explain why Niccolinus was present at Koblenz in September 1338, at the time of the meeting of William le Galeys and Edward III.

Let us return to the letter itself. One important point which has not previously been discussed concerns the two castles. The castle *Milasci* is unlikely to be Melazzo, as identified by Anna Benedetti in the 1920s, as the place has no known reference to the Fieschi family or any other character in this story, and there is no other evidence to sustain this identification. In contemporary documents, Melazzo appears in Latin as *Melagius*, not *Milasci*. There are a number of alternatives, however, of which one demands particular attention. This is Mulazzo, in the Val di Magra, four miles from Pontremoli, a town once belonging to Cardinal Luca Fieschi, given by him in his will to his nephews, and from 1329 to 1336 in the hands of his niece's husband Pietro Rossi. Mulazzo was even closer to the estates of Luca's nephew, Niccolo Malaspina, 'il Marchesotto'.[6] This might be significant as Niccolo Malaspina's other estates (Godiasco, Oramala and Piumesana, among others) were situated very close to Cecima, the place to which Edward II is supposed to have been transferred when war threatened his first sanctuary in about 1334.

Another aspect which has hitherto escaped detailed investigation is the identity of the man who guided William le Galeys to Edward III in 1338. Francisco Forcetti or Forzetti appears in later English accounts dealing with wool exports to Italian companies.[7] He also appears in two other English references: one relating to a Barcelona ship (probably relating to the Barcelona agency of the Peruzzi) which needed to be taken from Haverfordwest to Bristol in December 1342 and the other an appointment in 1344 to guard a Buckinghamshire manor held by an Italian, Tedisio Benedicti.[8] His 'Lombard' (Italian) identity, coupled with his status as a royal sergeant-at-arms, shows that William le Galeys was not 'arrested' at Cologne by a local officer as a law-breaker or local demonstrator, but by an agent of Edward's who was employed (apparently exclusively) on Italian business. That Forzetti was reimbursed for his expenses in bringing William le Galeys from Cologne to Edward at Koblenz (fifty-seven miles) suggests he was specifically charged with this task. Certainly this was not a normal 'arrest' in the sense of it being a response by a local law officer to the antics of a local malefactor. In this context it is very interesting that Forzetti too had a link with the Val di Magra. Tedisio Benedicti (whose Buckinghamshire manor he was guarding in 1344) was a papal sergeant-at-arms and an esquire of Queen Philippa's who came from Falcinello in the Val di Magra, about twelve miles from Mulazzo.[9] Benedicti was probably familiar with at least one international connection of the Fieschi family, Francisco Fosdinovo. The village of Fosdinovo is very close – about three miles – to that of Falcinello in the Val di Magra. This Francisco Fosdinovo came to England in 1337 with Antonio Fieschi (d.1344) and Giffredus de Groppo San Pietro: two men who had very close links with Cardinal Luca and Niccolo Malaspina, 'il Marchesotto'.[10] It is even possible that Francisco [of?] Fosdinovo and Francisco Forzetti were one and the same man. If they were, the implication would be that the man who took William le Galeys to Edward III in 1338 was an agent of Luca Fieschi's nephew and heir.

Given that Edward II was almost certainly still alive in 1330, we should note that the two documents which relate to his whereabouts after that date both suggest that he was in Italian custody. After a very thorough programme of checking and re-checking, I can find no good reason to doubt the outline of the Fieschi letter, and many reasons to believe it genuine. I particularly rate the detail given in the letter on Edward's final days of freedom, the knowledge the letter displays about Welsh, English and Italian topography, the correlations with the Norwell account, the pre-planned 'arrest' and prolonged entertainment of William le Galeys in the Low Countries (as opposed to the death penalty usually meted out to royal pretenders), the extraordinary level of trust placed in the Genoese relative of the letter's author, the fact the letter was written by the notary of Edward II's most important kinsman at Avignon, and the circumstantial links between Edward III, Cardinal Luca Fieschi and his kinsmen and contacts from the Val di Magra. I am also very interested in – and take seriously – the timeliness of certain acts connected to the Fieschi, such as Edward III's ratification of the estate of Manuel Fieschi in August 1342 immediately after his return from a very high-speed visit to Gloucester, the place of his father's tomb. Laying aside the inevitable anti-revisionist prejudices which attend such thinking, there is no sound reason to disregard the outline of the Fieschi letter in postulating where Edward II was after 1330.

On the basis of the foregoing passages, it seems probable that Cardinal Luca Fieschi was the 'godfather' of Edward II's preservation in Italy. First of all we know that, even before he arrived at Avignon, Edward II knew Luca. He was related to him and had met him in his youth, when Luca had come to his father's court.[11] The two men had met several times in 1317 when Luca had been sent by Pope John XXII to negotiate a peace between Edward II and Robert Bruce. They had probably met as recently as May 1325, when Cardinal Luca had obtained royal protection while visiting England.[12] So when Edward II arrived at Avignon in about March 1331, he had a powerful relative in the papal curia whom he knew reasonably well. And Manuel – Luca's notary – was there too. When, after spending time with the pope, Edward II left Avignon, he made his way ultimately to Italy. In so doing he was probably accompanied, and Luca Fieschi is the most likely candidate for arranging his protection from Avignon to Italy. First he went to Brabant and Cologne. Both these places had personal prophetic symbolism for the English royal family (as explained in Chapter One). When he came to Milan he was on territory familiar to the Fieschi, as Luccinus Visconti, brother of the ruler of Milan, was married to Isabella Fieschi, Cardinal Luca's niece. If we are right in supposing that Mulazzo was Edward's next port of call, then, as we have already seen, he was close to the estates of Niccolo Malaspina, Luca's nephew. More than that, the whole district was under the ecclesiastical jurisdiction of the bishop of Luni, and this was practically a pocket appointment of Luca's. The most powerful town in the district, Pontremoli, was a town granted to Luca and controlled in 1331 by Pietro Rossi, the husband of Ginetta Fieschi, Luca's niece. When war threatened the Val di Magra in 1334, prior to the protracted siege of Pontremoli (1335–36), it seems that Edward was moved to a hermitage in the north, near Cecima and the northern estates of Niccolo Malaspina. Here he remained until Luca's death at the end of January 1336. Shortly after this the late Luca's kinsman and notary, Manuel Fieschi, still based in Avignon, wrote the letter to Edward III finally revealing the whereabouts of his father.

One further series of facts involving Luca is worth noticing. On 26 April 1331, approximately six weeks after Edward II is likely to have arrived in Avignon, a clerk called William Aslakeby was licensed to be absent from his church at Sibthorpe for two years while he served in the household of Luca Fieschi.[13] It seems Luca may have requested the assistance of an English priest in his large household at Avignon. Aslakeby was late setting out, still being in England in December 1331, but presumably he went shortly after that, as nothing more is heard of him for the next two years. He was back in England in October 1334, for on the 28th of that month he received licence to be absent for another two years, this time in the service of Manuel Fieschi.[14]

What is particularly interesting about this is that Sibthorpe was a collegiate church, founded by Thomas Sibthorpe in the 1320s to say prayers for the well-being of his friends, his family and Edward II during their lives, and for their souls after death. After Aslakeby returned from Luca Fieschi's household in 1334, the ordinances of the church were rewritten by Archbishop Melton of York. In this revision it was made very unclear whether Edward II was among the living or the dead: his name seems to have been concatenated with that of Edward III.[15] The matter was only sorted out when the ordinances were rewritten again in February 1343; this time Edward II was clearly placed among the dead.

This draws our attention to other collegiate churches and chantries which were founded around this time for the benefit of Edward II's soul. Bablake in Coventry – Queen Isabella's own foundation to pray for the salvation of her husband's soul – was not founded until 1342 and not endowed until May 1344.[16] These expressions of renewed concern for the soul of Edward II in the period 1342–44 tally with the belated creation of Edward of Woodstock as the prince of Wales in parliament on 12 May 1343. This is significant, as prince of Wales was the one title which Edward II never gave up in his lifetime. Therefore, together with other facts directly connected with Edward III (mentioned in Chapter Eight), we have a rough answer to the second of our initial questions, regarding the date of Edward II's death: in the period between the parliaments of 1341 and 1343, probably the autumn of 1341.

In conclusion, there is some evidence which supports the general narrative of the Fieschi letter and suggests that his kinsman and friend Cardinal Luca Fieschi took a central role in protecting Edward II from 1331 to 1336, after which Luca's executor wrote the Fieschi letter to Edward III explaining his situation. In answer to the second of our questions, it would appear that Edward III heard about his father's death in or about late 1341. As this date begs the question where he had been since 1330, and as there is no evidence other than the Fieschi letter and the accounts of William Norwell (1338) to suggest where he had been, and since both of these suggest that Edward II had been in Italy prior to 1338, it seems reasonable to accept the Fieschi letter's explanation of Edward II's whereabouts, in outline at least. It also seems reasonable to suppose he was still in Fieschi custody in 1338, on the grounds that Niccolinus Fieschi was present at the time of his arrival and an Italian (Forzetti) was paid for bringing him to Koblenz. Whether he was returned to Italy after that and died there is another matter, about which we have almost no evidence. All we have to go on is a questionable piece of oral testimony gathered at Sant' Alberto di Butrio in the twentieth century,[17] and the favour shown by Edward III to the Fieschi in the early and mid-1340s, suggesting they remained valuable to Edward after 1340.

All this is of the greatest importance for understanding the life of Edward III. Laying aside the personal ramifications, the political influence it gave the Fieschi and, more importantly, Cardinal Luca's superior, the pro-French pope, would have been considerable. If Edward II was in the custody of Cardinal Luca Fieschi, then both Pope Jean XXII and Pope Benedict XII would have been able to use this as a bargaining lever with Edward. In international negotiations Edward would have been severely compromised. If he was deemed to be complicit in his father's illegal removal from the English throne, he would have been deeply damaged, especially if the pope had authorised Edward II's restoration. If he was found to have acceded to his own uncle's execution for trying to free his father on the pope's orders – as he had – he risked worse trouble. It is therefore very important to know when Edward II died and so when this situation came to an end. That Edward II was probably still alive in 1340 explains why Benedict XII was so strenuous in intervening in the peace process: he knew Edward III was compromised. But a date for his death in late 1341 means that Clement VI would not have been able to exercise this same influence over Edward III. Edward was no doubt rather relieved about that.

Royal Charter Witnesses in Regnal Years 4–5

Name of witness	25 Jan 1330 – 19 Oct 1330	19 Oct 1330 – 24 Jan 1331	25 Jan 1331 – 24 Jan 1332
Henry Burghersh, bishop of Lincoln	72	6	30
John of Eltham, earl of Cornwall	66	13	76
Roger Mortimer, earl of March	56	[arrested 19 Oct 1330]	
Oliver Ingham	54	0	1
William Montagu	31	10	34
John Warenne, earl of Surrey	21	17	11
Henry Percy	18	15	45
Robert Wyville, bishop of Salisbury	18	4	10
Roger Northburgh, bishop of Coventry and Lichfield	16	2	4
John Hothum, bishop of Ely	13	2	4
Gilbert Talbot	13	3	5
Adam of Orleton, bishop of Worcester	12	0	2

Name of witness	25 Jan 1330 – 19 Oct 1330	19 Oct 1330 – 24 Jan 1331	25 Jan 1331 – 24 Jan 1332
William Ayrmin, bishop of Norwich	8	7	31
Simon Meopham, archbishop of Canterbury	5	4	4
Henry, earl of Lancaster	5	24	8
Geoffrey Mortimer	5	[arrested 19 Oct 1330]	
John Stratford, bishop of Winchester	4	30	87
John Bohun, earl of Hereford	3	0	0
Roger Swynnerton	3	0	0
Robert Clifford	2	0	0
Ralph Basset of Drayton	2	0	3
William de Ros	2	0	3
John Cromwell	1	0	1
Hugh Courtenay	1	13	3
Stephen Gravesend, bishop of London	1	0	7
Thomas of Brotherton, earl of Norfolk	1	10	22
William Melton, archbishop of York	0	25	22
Thomas Wake of Liddel	0	2	39

Name of witness	25 Jan 1330 – 19 Oct 1330	19 Oct 1330 – 24 Jan 1331	25 Jan 1331 – 24 Jan 1332
John Beauchamp of Somerset	0	2	1
R Bishop of Chester [sic]	–	1	–
Hugh Audley	0	1	3
Henry Beaumont	0	0	20
William Clinton	0	0	6
Robert Ufford	0	0	4
John Ufford	0	0	2
Thomas Beauchamp, earl of Warwick	0	0	2
William Zouche of Ashby	0	0	1
David Strathbogie, earl of Atholl	0	0	1
Anthony Lucy	0	0	1
Thomas Charlton, bishop of Hereford	0	0	1
John de Ros	0	0	1
William Latimer	0	0	1
Richard Grey of Codnor	0	0	1
Ralph of Shrewsbury, bishop of Bath and Wells	0	0	1

Name of witness	25 Jan 1330 – 19 Oct 1330	19 Oct 1330 – 24 Jan 1331	25 Jan 1331 – 24 Jan 1332
Richard Fitzalan, earl of Arundel	0	0	1
Edward Bohun	0	0	1
Stewards (n.b. stewards of the household nearly always attested charters)			
John Maltravers (steward to 29 July)	56	*[fled 19 Oct 1330]*	
Hugh Turpington (from 29 July 1330)	17	*[killed 19 Oct 1330]*	
Ralph Neville (from 19 October 1330)	0	33	88

The Intended Destination of the 1346 Invasion

The question of Edward III's decision regarding the landing place of his massive expedition to France in 1346 is a difficult one. It is not so much one of *when* he made the decision – although there is doubt about that too – but whether he changed his mind. Did he always intend to land in Normandy? Or were contemporaries correct to believe that he had originally intended to sail to Gascony?

The case that Edward originally intended to sail to Gascony is based on the chronicles of le Bel and Froissart, together with support from a newsletter written five days after the invasion by Sir Bartholomew Burghersh (copied in Murimuth's chronicle). Froissart mentions that the wind was fine for a trip to Gascony when the king embarked but that on the third day it changed, and drove the fleet on to the shores of Cornwall, where it remained at anchor for six days and nights. It was at this time, according to Froissart and le Bel, that Edward changed his mind, persuaded by Sir Godfrey de Harcourt that Normandy was a better destination. Sir Bartholomew Burghersh's letter to the archbishop of Canterbury written on 17 July supports this, stating that Edward made sure all his ships had victuals for a fortnight (the length of a trip to Gascony) and that,

> intending to have passed by the Needles at the end of the Isle of Wight, and so have held his direct course towards the Channel, the wind was so contrary to him that he could not keep to that route by any means, albeit he lay a long while, waiting if God were willing to have given him weather to pass; and since it did not please God that he should go that way, he turned to the land where God should give him grace, and arrived well and in a good state, with all the fleet, in a country which is called Cotentin, in Normandy.[1]

To this one should add the background detail that Burghersh was a well-travelled man, having been sent abroad several times on royal duties, and no stranger to sailing across the Channel. He was also close to the king. So we should perhaps trust his word in a news letter to the archbishop.

There are several reasons to doubt this interpretation. Richard Barber in his *The Black Prince* (1978) stated with confidence that, although the fleet may have been intended for Gascony when originally summoned, its destination had been settled as Normandy by 3 July, when Edward anchored off the Isle of Wight. It was because the wind changed direction after this, when the fleet was at Yarmouth, that Edward ordered the fleet to return to the safety of Portsmouth. Sumption in his *Trial by Battle* (1990) provides a looser interpretation, simply saying that Edward had originally intended to go to Gascony but then changed his mind; he does not say when exactly, but he suggests it was at the meeting on 20 June.

Clifford Rogers in his *War Cruel and Sharp* (2000) provides the most developed argument on this question. He points out that it made more military sense going to Normandy than to Gascony. He suggests that to attack in Gascony would have been a poor strategy, especially if it had entailed raising the siege of Aiguillon, where a few hundred English knights and archers were pinning down several thousand French troops. But to spread rumours that he intended to attack in Gascony and then to launch a surprise attack in Normandy would have been very sensible, and would have directly led to the historical problem with which we are now faced. In support of this interpretation he points out that Edward ordered that no ships at all be allowed to leave England in the eight-day period following his departure, and even concealed his destination to his own chancery officers. If it was widely anticipated in France that Edward would sail to Gascony, he says, 'there would have been little point in taking such precautions in order merely to prevent the French from receiving *confirmation* of what they already expected'.[2] He also claims that 'Edward's own testimony is that he spent ten days on the Isle of Wight waiting, not for favourable winds, but for all his ships to gather', a point noted by Barber too.

The problem is a classic case of where the historian may (if he so wishes) regard the question as a relatively trivial detail, but the biographer does not have this luxury. If Edward was forced to change all his plans and quickly adapt to a radically different situation and series of objectives, then that says different things about Edward than if he always intended to go to Normandy. Similarly if he always intended to go to Normandy and managed to delude everyone, including men like Sir Bartholomew Burghersh, about his intentions, then that says much for his ability to control information and yet retain the confidence of an otherwise misinformed army.

In addition to the various arguments already published, there are at least three further reasons to agree with the Normandy destination. First, as all the above-mentioned writers note, an initial decision – probably the final decision – was made before the fleet set out, as the ships' captains carried sealed orders telling them where they were to assemble in the event of a storm. However, storms were not the only vagaries of the weather which could affect the eventual destination. If the fleet were becalmed for a long period they would not have sufficient supplies to reach Gascony. Thus, if the sealed letters had indicated that ships' captains were to make for a port in Gascony, they would not have been able to do so if lack of wind had delayed them on the way. Similarly, if a storm were to strike in the Channel, the chances of all the waterlogged or damaged ships managing to make the journey with soaked rations and damaged spars all the way to Gascony were small. One could argue that the sealed letters contained a destination which was to be made for *only* in the event of a storm, but if so this would simply reinforce Normandy as the destination, as it was contrary winds, not a storm, which led to the delay.

The second reason is that an eight-day period of secrecy, during which no English vessels left port, would not have been a long enough time to guarantee the secrecy of the journey to Gascony. Travelling that far by ship could take weeks, so an eight-day headstart would not have guaranteed that Edward could have landed in the country around Bordeaux before a spy in England could have informed Philip who could in turn have sent a message to his army in the south-west. A royal messenger with regular changes of horses could transport a message at ninety miles per day in summer. If Edward had been delayed by only a few days, he would have run the risk of disembarking after a long journey only to have to fight sooner rather than later. This causes us to wonder why there was only an eight-days' prohibition if he was heading to Gascony.

The third point – and arguably the strongest evidence for the case that Normandy was the destination all along – is Edward's actions on arrival. He came prepared to speak about Normandy as his patrimony – his ancestors' lands – and he came with a well-worked-out speech. He claimed that it had been illegally taken from the kings of England by France 'in the time of King Richard'. Clifford Rogers touches on this, and considers that the reference to Richard, although it was a mistake, was 'close enough'.[3] However, in appealing to the men of his own generation to right a wrong suffered by Richard the Lionheart, Edward was not making a mistake at all. Any well-informed man (and certainly Edward himself) would have known that it was King John who had lost Normandy, as this formed an important and prominent section of the most popular lay chronicle of the time, the *Brut*, which boldly (albeit incorrectly) talked about 'how King John (Edward's great-great-grandfather) lost Normandy in the first year of his reign'. Moreover either Edward himself or his mother had borrowed (and presumably read) a history of Normandy. So he was not making a mistake but purposefully associating the duchy with England's great crusader king. Of course, Edward could have dreamed up this propaganda during the crossing, but deliberately to misrepresent his own family history seems a well-planned move, and one which had been worked out in advance. Further support to this idea is given in the many and frequent allusions to the conquest of England which are mentioned in Chapter Ten. Finally, if one were to look for a blueprint of how to invade and conquer a country, one would have to consider the events of 1066. Duke William's strategy on that occasion had been a diversionary attack using allies on a different part of the coast, a surprise landing on an unprotected beach, and a confrontation, followed by a march on the capital. Edward's strategy of 1346 follows Duke William's of 1066 in all these aspects, except that he hesitated before attacking Paris.

In conclusion, it is almost certain that Bartholomew Burghersh's belief that he was being sent to Gascony reflects Edward's deliberate spreading of misinformation rather than a change of strategy in 1346. It would appear far more likely that Normandy was his intended destination from the moment he set sail, a decision probably made, as Sumption suggests, on or before 20 June 1346.

The Date of the Foundation of the Order of the Garter

Many aspects of the origin of the Order of the Garter are open to debate, especially the emblem of the garter and the motto associated with it (discussed in Chapter Eleven). However, we cannot properly consider the foundation in the context of Edward's life without coming to some conclusion as to when exactly it took place. Most discussions have removed it from the context of the plague, as if Edward was simply celebrating the merits of his war leaders.[1] This is understandable, given its martial nature and long history, but it is also misleading. It is like discussing the origins of the Victoria Cross medal without reference to the Crimea War: without the latter, the honour might have come into being at some point or other, but not at the time when it did.

The insignia of the Order of the Garter include a blue robe with a silver lining and a blue garter worked in gold with the motto '*Honi soit qui mal y pense*' (evil to him who thinks it evil). The Order was composed of twenty-six knights, including the king and the prince, and it was particularly associated with the chapel of St George at Windsor Castle. The first time the twenty-six knights all met in one tournament and jousted together was at Windsor Castle on St George's Day (23 April 1349). However, as many antiquaries and scholars have discovered over the years, there are a number of garter-related entries in accounts relating to earlier tournaments. For example, twelve garters were manufactured for the Eltham tournament in the summer of 1348.[2] The collegiate chapel of St George at Windsor Castle, which was to be a focal point for future celebrations, was founded on 6 August 1348.[3] Most striking of all, the prince of Wales paid for a plate for a herald of arms 'of the companionship of the Garter' on 18 December 1348, as well as 'twenty-four garters made for the prince for the knights of the companionship of the Garter' about this time.[4] As a result of these payments, which appear in the prince's register, early heralds and antiquaries from the seventeenth century onwards had no doubt that the Order had been founded before December 1348, and the most influential historian of the Order (Beltz) chose the Windsor tournament at Midsummer 1348 as the event at which it was probably founded. The most detailed modern analysis by Juliet Vale, recently described as 'widely accepted', follows this, stating that 'the Order was effectively instituted at the Windsor tournament of 24 June 1348 and that the first formal St George's Day meeting of the Knights of the Garter was that held on 23 April 1349'.[5]

On close examination of the primary source material, some methodological problems appear. For a start, the use of a garter as a symbol does not mean that the Order had previously been constituted in any formal sense. Nor does the use of the '*honi soit*' motto. But there is another much more subtle historical misunderstanding. The membership of the Order was *exclusive*, and so it cannot be said to have been established until its membership was named. This is a crucial point, as can be shown by reference to an earlier tournament, the Lichfield tournament of May 1348. This had two 'battles' of thirteen men – exactly like the arrangement of the eventual Garter knights in their choir stalls at St George's Chapel – and these knights had all worn blue robes with white silk linings at Lichfield. However, although several of them did become founder knights of the Order, most did not.[6] One can say the same for the tournament at Canterbury which took place later in the year, probably in mid-August.[7] If the formal membership had been established by this time, then some of those who took part in these tournaments were appropriating some of the emblems of the Order – or items very similar – with impunity. This is hardly likely, given its exclusive nature. The one element of the Order which does not seem to have been established by the time of Edward's expedition to France in October–November 1348 was a formal membership.[8]

So we must search for the foundation of the Order after Edward's return from France, in November 1348. The tournament at which the two 'battles' took part cannot have been the games at either Christmas or Epiphany (6 January 1349) as many more people took part at both, and neither of these was described as a tournament but as 'games'. The next tournament known is that at Windsor on 23 April 1349. The clearest reference to the foundation of the Order is the chronicle of Geoffrey le Baker, writing in the 1350s, who states that Edward founded it *at* (not before) this tournament on St George's Day 1349.[9] The date is supported by the accounts of John of Cologne who provided the participants with armour, garter-covered robes and garters.[10] The implication of le Baker's description is that the founder members were defined by their being there that day: *they took part*. This explains why so many of Edward's closest friends were not founder members of the Order. Why was the earl of Northampton not a founder member? Why not Sir Walter Manny? Why not Sir Reginald Cobham, Sir Thomas Dagworth, the earl of Huntingdon and the earl of

Suffolk? The reason is simply that they were not there, and did not take part in the tournament. Manny, Northampton and Huntingdon had been sent to France the previous month to negotiate a peace treaty.[11] Dagworth was still in Brittany. Cobham had been made admiral of the Western fleet the previous year, and was not replaced until 1351.[12] That Edward would have wanted these men to be founder members of the Order of the Garter if they had been available is evident from their fame as warriors, from the rewards which Edward heaped upon each of them, and from the fact that all of them were admitted to the Order as soon as there was a vacancy (with the exception of Sir Thomas Dagworth, who died the following year). So eligible were they that Geoffrey le Baker presumed some of these men *had* been admitted. Therefore we can be confident that the founder members of the Order were chosen because they had turned up to fight at a tournament after March 1349 (when Manny, Northampton and Huntingdon went to France), and by far the most likely event is that recorded by le Baker on St George's Day 1349, which implies that that date marks the formal establishment of the Order. This conclusion is stongly supported by the official statute of the Order, which states that it was instituted in the twenty-third year of Edward's reign (i.e. after 25 January 1349).[13] On St George's Day 1349 Edward was certainly drawing from the model of the informal knightly companionships which existed before then, and at least one of these companionships used the emblem of the garter, possibly in reference to Lancaster's self-professed liking for garters;[14] but the existence of these chivalric 'companionships' – garter-wearing or otherwise – should not be confused with the Order itself.

Edward III's Physicians and Surgeons

Edward's household ordinances made provision for one physician and one surgeon. Therefore it would appear that the periods when more practitioners were employed are an approximate indication of when more advice or wider medical services were required, and by implication when the king's state of health was likely to have been poorer. As we cannot rely on payments for 'medicines' always being present when the king was ill – many cures took the form of nutrition or bleeding at certain times of the astrological cycle, or surgical acts requiring no extra purchases – it is instructive to know when Edward was employing more than one practitioner of physic and one of surgery. It is also revealing to note that this body of men who had such influence over the king were drawn from a number of European countries: Italy, England, Ireland, Spain and France.

Edward's first physician, the Italian Pancio de Controne, had been physician to his father before him.[1] He had been present at the coup at Nottingham Castle in 1330 and played a significant money-lending role in funding Edward's planned campaign at the end of the 1330s. He retired before the end of 1339.[2] At the same time, the famous physician, John Gaddesden (author of the *Rosa Anglica Medicina*) was in and around the court, having famously saved one of Edward's uncles from smallpox during the reign of Edward II. However, although Edward personally provided him to a canonry in St Paul's, London, at court Gaddesden seems to have served much the same function in Edward III's reign as he served in his father's, i.e. attending to the children. He seems to have served as physician to the Black Prince and was summoned in April 1341 to attend Joan, Edward's second daughter.[3] No evidence has yet come to light that he ever served as Edward III's 'personal physician'. He died in 1348 or 1349, during the plague.[4]

De Controne's successor as Edward's physician was an Englishman, Master Jordan of Canterbury, who was appointed on probation in 1338 and received confirmation that his appointment was for life in November 1340, after the king attested to his 'expert skill'.[5] Master Jordan was with Edward and his predecessor, de Controne, in the Low Countries in 1338–39,[6] and remained with Edward almost constantly. He was rewarded for his continual service in 1345 and was present at the siege of Calais in 1346–47.[7] He continued to be employed in the 1350s and died about 1360.[8] Master Godfrey de Fromond also appears as the king's physician between January 1349 and July 1350.[9] He does not appear after this date, and it may be that he was employed specifically on account of the plague, not necessarily to cure sufferers but to advise people about precautions they might take to avoid catching it. In the 1360s the title of king's physician seems to have become accorded to several people simultaneously. The Italian John Paladyn was described as such in 1363 and 1367,[10] but before his departure from England shortly after 22 November 1367, the English physician John Glaston was already in royal service. Glaston was first noted as the king's physician in 1364 and he remained in office until Edward's death in 1377.[11] During those years the king also received the ministrations of Master Peter of Florence in 1368–70 and of John Landreyn, John Bray and of Paul Gabrielis of Spain in late 1376.[12] He was also probably attended by William Waddesworth, who sought out and purchased medicines on his behalf in 1376–77.[13] As a result, it would appear that several men were described as 'the king's physician' as he progressively required more medical attention, from around 1363–64.

The king's surgeon similarly seems to have started off as a particular appointment and become diffused as Edward needed more surgical assistance. In the early days his sole surgeon seems to have been Roger Heyton, who died in May 1349, probably of the plague. In June 1341 Edward had reason to use the services of the Irishman William Ouhynnovan.[14] This seems to have been a one-off engagement, however, probably in respect of a particular injury. Heyton may have retired before his death, as the Norman-born William Hamon, prior of Cogges, seems to have been employed on probation as Edward's surgeon from January 1347 (when he was at Calais), officially being appointed a member of the royal household in October 1349.[15] William Hamon was succeeded in the 1350s by Master Adam le Rous, who is possibly to be identified with the Master Adam of 'Pulletria', surgeon.[16] He was in the royal service as a surgeon before May 1357, regularly employed in that capacity, and was still acting as the king's surgeon in February 1374.[17] During the duration of Adam le Rous' service Edward also employed the following surgeons: Richard Wy (who was rewarded for 'long service' in 1359), Peter Gymel in 1362, Richard of Ireland in 1368–70, William Holme in 1371–76 and John Gouche, surgeon to Duke Henry of Lancaster.[18] Finally, at the end of his life, the Irishman John [the] Leech attended him, significantly being described not as 'the king's surgeon' but as 'one of the king's surgeons'. Others in late 1376 included William Wymondham and William Stodeley, as well as

Adam 'the leech' (probably Adam le Rous) and William Holme.[19] Therefore it would appear that Edward's medical needs had prevailed over the household ordinance even before 1360, so that we should probably look to him requiring surgical assistance on and off for much of the last twenty years of his life, and especially from about 1370.

The Descendants of Edward III

Edward is generally credited with twelve legitimate and three illegitimate children. For obvious reasons, there is far greater certainty about the names and vital dates of his legitimate offspring, but even with these there is confusion. If the plethora of Internet sites which deal with royal genealogy can be taken as a good gauge of popular understanding, then there is certainly widespread doubt about whether there was a thirteenth legitimate child, Thomas, or even a fourteenth, Joan. There is also confusion about the dates of birth of the fifteen known children. Finally, and of relevance in considering Edward III's legacy, there is the question about how many descendants he had, and whether he is in fact the last royal common ancestor of the English people.

There is no doubt about the vital dates of Edward of Woodstock, later known as the Black Prince, who was born on 15 June 1330 and died at Westminster on 8 June 1376. He married Joan, the Fair Maid of Kent in 1361 and had by her two legitimate children, Edward (1365–1371) and Richard II (1367–1400). He also had at least two illegitimate sons, Edward (fl.1349; presumed to have died young) and Sir Roger Clarendon (d.1402).[1] Thus it is only from his illegitimate offspring that any line of his descended.

Isabella of Woodstock was probably born on 16 June 1332 (not in March as sometimes claimed).[2] She was promised as a bride to a large number of heirs, including Louis, son of the count of Flanders (1335), a son of the duke of Brabant (1344), the Emperor Charles (1349), and Bernard, eldest son of Lord Albret (1351). She finally married Enguerrand or Ingelram de Coucy, a hostage at Edward's court, in 1365. She had two daughters by him, Mary and Philippa, and died before 4 May 1379.[3]

The next two children are slightly more problematic. Various dates and places are popularly given for the birth of Joan.[4] The nearest we can come to an exact date is to use the record of her mother's 'churching', which took place at Woodstock on 8–10 March 1334.[5] As 9 March 1334 was not a Sunday but a Wednesday, it probably marked an exact forty or eighty days after the birth, which would imply that Joan was born on either 28 January 1334 or 19 December 1333.[6] Edward made allowance for her and his other two children on 6 March of that year.[7] She died of plague in the summer of

1348, on 1 July, on her way to marry the heir of King Alfonso of Castile.[8] Edward's second son, William, was born at Hatfield in January 1337.[9] Philippa's churching feast was held on Sunday 16 February, and so William was probably born in the week ending Sunday 11 January 1337.[10] He died before 3 March 1337 and was buried in York Minster.

The next three children are, after the Black Prince, the most famous. Lionel was born at Antwerp on 29 November 1338. He firstly married Elizabeth de Burgh in 1342 and had one daughter, Philippa, through whom her descendants, the earls of March, claimed the throne. He died at Alba (Italy) on 17 October 1368, shortly after his second marriage to Violante Visconti. John was born at Ghent in early February 1340 and died at Leicester Castle on 3 or 4 February 1399.[11] He was married three times, firstly in 1359 to Blanche, the daughter of Henry, duke of Lancaster, by whom he had three surviving children, including the future King Henry IV, and four who died young; secondly to Constanza of Castile, by whom he had a daughter, Catalina, and a son who died young; and thirdly to his mistress, Catherine de Roët, widow of Sir Hugh Swynford, by whom he had three sons and a daughter. Edmund was born at Langley on 5 June 1341 and died at the same place on 1 August 1402.[12] He married firstly Isabella of Castile, by whom he had three children, and secondly Joan of Holland, by whom he had none.

Edward's next four children all died without offspring. Blanche of the Tower was born and died in March 1342 and was buried at Westminster Abbey. Mary was born at Waltham on 10 October 1344 and married to the duke of Brittany in 1361; Margaret was born on 20 July 1346 and married to the earl of Pembroke in 1359. Both Mary and Margaret died after 1 October 1361 and were buried in Abingdon Abbey. William was born at Windsor in late May 1348. Philippa's churching took place on Tuesday 24 June 1348, and so William was probably born on or after 15 May.[13] He was buried on 5 September at Westminster Abbey.

As mentioned above, one does come across references to another son, Thomas, supposedly born at Windsor in the summer of 1347. This is a mistake. Philippa was not at Windsor in the summer of 1347 but at Calais with Edward. Furthermore, if she had been at Windsor, the child could not have been sired by Edward, who had been in France since July 1346. As Philippa did not join him until shortly before Christmas 1346, no legitimate offspring could have been born before August 1347, which is the probable date of conception of William of Windsor. The reference to Thomas is therefore almost certainly spurious, possibly based on Froissart's reference to Philippa being pregnant at the surrender of Calais. The child is supposed to have been buried at King's Langley. Given the absence of reference to any churching in the records, and no apparent image of another boy on the paintings of the family at St Stephen's Chapel at Westminster, nor a weeper on Edward's tomb (as there were for all the others, including the deceased infants) we can rule out the existence of a son called Thomas before 1355.

Edward's last son by Philippa, Thomas, was born at Woodstock on 7 January 1355. He married Eleanor Bohun, by whom he had five children, and died at Calais in September 1397.

Finally, Edward had three illegitimate children by Alice Perrers – Sir John Southeray, and two daughters, Joan and Jane. It is impossible that the abbot of Westminster, Nicholas Lytlington, was Edward's bastard offspring.[14] John Southeray appears regularly in the records, and there is no doubt that he was an illegitimate son of the king's.[15] In January 1377 he was knighted and married to Maud, a sister of Lord Percy, the future earl of Northumberland.[16] In the arrangements for this wedding a payment is made for his 'sisters'. Much less is known of them. They were still young at the time of Edward's death. Jane married Richard Northland, about whom almost nothing is known. Joan married a lawyer called Robert Skerne from Kingston-upon-Thames. He died in 1437, and the fine brass memorial he ordered to be made, which shows himself and Joan, is still extant.[17]

*

By 1500 many English earls and barons were descendants of Edward III, and so were many Iberian noble families. By 1600 almost the entire English gentry were his descendants. By 1900 hundreds of thousands of people could demonstrate their descent from him. Therefore it is a fair question whether Edward is the last king to be a common ancestor of the English people.

It is of course, impossible to answer this through tracing every single family offshoot. Records do not exist for the vast majority of people born before the mid-sixteenth century, and even some very high-born individuals' families are shrouded in medieval mist. However, it is possible to estimate reasonably accurately whether this statement might be true. By tracing his descendants to a point in time where they constitute a group, with a distinguishable range of social and geographical features as well as predictable nuptial and paternal behaviour, we may then start to make observations about the descendants of Edward III as a subset of the English people as a whole.

Of Edward's twelve legitimate children, only six themselves had children. Together they had at least twenty-four legitimate (or legitimised) children: Prince Edward had two, Isabella two, Lionel one, John eleven, Edmund three, and Thomas five. Prince Edward's legitimate line died out with this generation, but the others carried on. Lionel had four legitimate grandchildren, Isabella one, John at least forty-four, Edmund eight, and Thomas eight. Not all of these survived, of course, and some were born abroad, especially in Portugal (following the marriage of John's daughter Philippa to King John I of Portugal). But twenty-one of them ensured that the bloodlines of four of Edward III's sons continued in England in perpetuity.[18]

If we trace the descendants of these twenty-one great-grandchildren we may establish that Edward III had at least 436 descendants alive in England in the year 1500. This is a minimum, excluding all three of Edward's illegitimate children (whose lines are difficult to trace) and all but four lines of descent from an illegitimate descendant (only including those cases where an illegitimate descendant was recognised and ennobled), and excluding all lines descended from those who married overseas or married into Scottish and Welsh families. It also excludes a number of very young children who might have been born by 1500 but probably were not (dates of birth being difficult to determine in several cases). Many more descendants were alive in Portugal, France, Spain and Scotland and a handful in Ireland and Wales, but these have been excluded in the following calculations. It is important at every step to underestimate the number of descendants flourishing in England to reduce the risk of error or exaggeration, so although the actual number of descendants was certainly much greater than 436, possibly in excess of a thousand, the minimum number has been used.

The population of England in 1500 was about 2.75 million.[19] Therefore, as a proportion of the English population, Edward's descendants amounted to at least this fraction: 436/2,750,000. This does not sound very impressive, but over time the proportion increased steadily. Moreover, we must consider the social privilege and geographical circumstances of the 436. Whereas the descendants of a fourteenth-century Cornish tin miner would be unlikely to have spread very far from Cornwall by 1500, let alone to have reached into the upper classes in other counties, Edward III's descendants were settled in almost every county in England and in all the higher ranks of society. The propensity of the gentry to intermarry their heirs among other gentry families in neighbouring counties meant that the heads of most gentry families would have descended from Edward by 1600.

If all things were equal – if every woman in England was as likely to marry any man as any other, and vice versa – one could say that the maximum proportion of the English who were *not* descended from Edward one generation after 1500 (roughly 1530) would be

$$[1-(436 \ / \ 2.75 \ \text{million})]^2 = 99.9683\%$$

and one generation after that, approximately 1560, the proportion would be $(99.9683\% \times 99.9683\%) = 99.9366\%$. On this basis way we might say that at least 1,879 of the English population in 1560 (estimated at 2,963,505) were descended from Edward III.[20] However, there is a problem in that there were considerable social obstacles which prevented any man from marrying any woman. Although Edward's genes had seeped into the gentry of most counties by 1500 – from Devon to Norfolk and Northumberland – there were significant social barriers which prevented the children of rich fathers from marrying members of the working classes and vice versa. This issue affects the rate of increase of Edward's legitimate descendants in the following way. If the daughter of an earl or a duke was restricted to marrying someone of similar status, then her husband, of course, would have been more likely than not also to be descended from Edward III. Where this happened, two of Edward's decendants would have given rise to one family, not two.

The intermarriage of Edward's descendants as a result of social expectation was at its height in the fifteenth century. As noted above, of the twenty-one great-grandchildren whose descendants perpetuated Edward's lineage, ten (48%) married another descendant, implying five of the sixteen marriages in this generation (31%) were intermarriages. But this proportion seems to decline over the centuries. Of all the marriages noted as taking place in the generation alive in and shortly after 1500, less than 13% were to other descendants of Edward III, so far as can be determined. This is surprising at first, until we reflect that it was only a few great families whose children were all expected to marry peers of the realm. The younger sons and daughters of younger sons and daughters of the gentry increasingly married merchants and local yeomen. Even by 1500 merchants and minor gentry were marrying descendants of Edward III. Thus the proportion of intermarriage which took place as a result of social obligation or bias (as opposed to pure chance) decreased, and this decrease was probably continual. Nevertheless, if the 13% of intermarriage around 1500 is taken as a guide, this would have reduced the number of descendants in the generation centred on 1530 by a factor of 100/113.[21] Rather than doubling to roughly 872 descendants as implied in the previous calculation, the total would have been around 771. Applying the same corrective factor would have led to a further decline in the increment of the next generation, so that the figure for the generation centred on 1560 would be 1,472 of the population of 2,963,505. If we then apply this corrective factor once more to the increment, we arrive at about 3,424 of the population in 1590 (estimated at 3,895,749) and 7,208 of the population in 1620 (estimated at 4,634,570) as being descended from Edward III. A rough check on the acceptability of these figures is possible. If the twenty-two descendants of Edward's alive on 1 January 1380 had increased to at least 436 in 1500 (an increase of 20x over 120 years of slowly increasing population levels), a 16.5x increase over the 120 years from 1500 (a period of rapidly increasing population levels) is reasonable, and almost certainly an underestimate, as intended.[22]

This implies that maybe up to 99.84% of the population of England was *not* descended from Edward in 1620. Nevertheless, continuing to use the correction factor of 13% of all marriages between Edward's descendants being non-accidental status-related intermarriages, we may estimate that the maximum proportions of the population who were *not* descended from Edward were as follows:

1620: 99.84447%	1710: 99.1416%	1800: 95.3596%
1650: 99.7249%	1740: 98.4873%	1830: 91.9774%
1680: 99.5138%	1770: 97.3428%	1860: 86.3703%

Up to this point we have been adjusting for non-accidental intermarriages in every generation at a level of 13%. However, by 1860 the real level was much less than this. Therefore the percentages in the above table are very considerable overestimates of the population *not* descended from Edward. Also, from this point onwards, the emerging capitalist society and the railway network mean that, with the exception of remote areas of the country, the corrective factor applies less and less. If we dispense with this factor from now on, the remaining generations work out as follows:

1890: 74.60%	1950: 30.97%
1920: 55.65%	1980: 9.59%

And, following this patterm, we should expect less than 1% of English children born to English-descended parents after 1995 *not* to be descended from Edward III.

The above working has been exceedingly cautious on several levels. The social bias affecting whom one married did not extend to 13% of all marriages of Edward's descendants in 1860. The population in that year was about 18,682,352, and the above deliberate underestimate suggests that at least 2,546,348 of these were legitimately descended from Edward. Social considerations of ancestry were of importance to the minority: probably fewer than 100,000 members of the aristocracy, gentry and upper-middle classes (less than 4% of Edward's descendants). In addition, the model above allows for a far higher level of intermarriage due to social bias in the seventeenth and eighteenth centuries than was probably the case. The reality is that the upper tiers of society would have become relatively quickly saturated with Edward III's genes, and thus almost every marriage out of class would have resulted in a dispersal of genes down the social hierarchy. Although the contrast in about 1600 is great – most of the nobility and gentry *were* descended and yet 99% of all English people were not – the likelihood of anyone alive today having absolutely no gentry or nobility among his or her eleven, twelve or thirteen great-grandparents (eight thousand or so antecedents) is small. Furthermore, we have been working on minima throughout, and totally ignoring illegitimate conception as a factor to be taken into account. Historians tend to put the proportion of illegitimacy in the sixteenth and seventeenth centuries at around 5% of all births, so the result of neglecting this 5% increase in the number of Edward's descendants in each generation, as we have done above, amounts to an underestimate over a two-hundred-year period of roughly a quarter. To correct this we should increase the numbers of descendants at the end of the sixteenth century by 33%. Obviously if by 1600 there were 33% more descendants than estimated in the above model (including many more among the lower classes, reducing the need for a status-connected corrective factor), the proportion of people of English descent alive today who are not descended from Edward would be negligible.

As a result of this we may regard Edward III as being a common ancestor of well over 80% – probably over 95% – of the living English-descended population of England.[23] It is conceivable that there are exceptional areas in some comparatively geographically isolated corners of the country which welcomed few newcomers before recent times and which have remained largely independent of the mobile middle classes, and have had few or no resident landowners, and never served as a port of any sort, and are isolated from the major highways, but there cannot be many of these. Rural and isolated poor farming communities which themselves practised inbreeding on a regular basis would be the most likely instances, and even then they must be considered exceptional if they have entirely avoided the steady march of Edward III's genes.

Finally, it is worth noting that the above conclusion implies that all the

THE PERFECT KING

post-Conquest kings of England prior to Edward are also common ancestors of the vast majority of the English, with the exceptions of William II, Stephen and Richard I.[24] It also implies that among the common ancestors of the English people are the kings of France before 1314, the kings of Castile before 1252, the counts of Hainault before 1337, the counts of Provence before 1245, the counts of Savoy before 1233, and the dukes of Aquitaine before 1204, not to mention a multitude of earlier French, Italian, Spanish and German noble familes. The same thing may also be said for some of the English magnates who appear in this book. Probably the most notable example is Roger Mortimer, the first earl of March, Edward's erstwhile enemy, whose twelve children yielded more than thirty-five grandchildren, twenty-two of whom had had progeny by 1380. Time has not permitted an accurate estimate of how many descendants of Roger Mortimer were alive in 1500 but it is very likely to have been many more than the total for Edward III, and they would certainly have been equally widely dispersed across all the English counties. The story told at the beginning of this book – of how Edward III survived and surmounted the terror of the first earl of March – is thus a story in which probably everyone of English descent has a stake. The political history of England up to and including the reign of Edward III is the collective family history of the English people.

NOTES

Introduction

1. See Morgan, 'Apotheosis' for an overview of Edward's post-mortem reputation.
2. Brie (ed.), *Brut*, ii, p. 333.
3. Only four medieval English kings lived longer: Henry I (67), Henry II (66), Henry III (65) and Edward I (68). The first English ruler to live to seventy was Richard Cromwell, who died aged eighty-six. Elizabeth lived to sixty-nine. The first English monarch to live to seventy and remain king was George II (1683–1760).
4. This was the first prose biography. There had been an earlier verse sketch of his reign in Thomas May's *The Victorious Reign of King Edward the Third* (1635). Earlier still was the anonymous play *The Reign of King Edward III*, printed in 1596 and 1599, and sometimes ascribed to Shakespeare's authorship.
5. Barnes, *Edward III*, pp. 910–11. The spelling and capitalisation have been modernised.
6. John Kenyon, *The History Men* (2nd ed., 1993), p. 133.
7. *RE3*, p. 182, quoting William Stubbs, *The Constitutional History of England* (4th ed., 3 vols, Oxford, 1906), ii, p. 393.
8. Longman, *Life and Times*, ii, pp. 296–7.
9. Longman, *Life and Times*, ii, pp. 297–8.
10. Warburton, *Edward III*, vii.
11. Warburton, *Edward III*, p. 248.
12. Warburton, *Edward III*, p. 251.
13. MacKinnon, *History of Edward III*, p. 616.
14. MacKinnon, *History of Edward III*, p. 618.
15. MacKinnon, *History of Edward III*, p. 620.
16. Tout, *Chapters*, iv, pp. 287–8, discussing *CPR 1343–45*, p. 371. Another example of Edward trying to remove evidence relating to his father's survival possibly lies in the eradication of details of the visit of the woman who performed the embalming of the corpse buried as that of Edward II in 1327. See Moore, 'Documents', p. 226; *GT*, p. 293.
17. Paul Johnson's *The Life and Times of Edward III* (1973) is the relevant volume in a well-known illustrated series. Michael Packe's *Edward III* is highly entertaining, but he died before it could be completed and it is very slight on the later years and carries many errors. Bryan Bevan's *Edward III: Monarch of Chivalry* (1992) is the third.
18. Perroy, *Hundred Years War*, xxvii.
19. Perroy, *Hundred Years War*, p. 86. Perroy here is presenting this as the judgement of 'the most recent historians' but does not say who they are; and although he presents their view of Philip and applies his own clarification of it, he does not similarly qualify this judgement on Edward, except to add that he was 'an opportunist of genius, who used his adversaries' difficulties to the full, and constantly

modified the detail of his plans in order to adapt them to changing circumstances' (p. 87).

20. Perroy, *Hundred Years War*, p. 69.
21. McKisack, 'Edward III and the Historians', pp. 1–15.
22. Aberth, 'Crime and Justice under Edward III', p. 92.

1: Childhood

1. Johnstone, *Edward of Carnarvon*, p. 64.
2. Denholm-Young (ed.), *Vita*, p. 28.
3. See Hamilton, *Gaveston*; Chaplais, *Gaveston*, pp. 6–22; *GT*, pp. 18–19, 28–30, for the nature of Edward's relationship with Gaveston. An alternative view is Hamilton, 'Ménage à Roi'.
4. A mark of the complexity of the man may be noted in the work of Tout, who, in his *Edward I* (1890), refers to Edward as 'a coward and a trifler' (p. 225). However, the St Albans chronicler states he fought bravely 'like a lioness bereft of her cubs' in trying to save his men at Bannockburn. See Riley (ed.), *Trokelowe*, p. 86. Tout actually quotes this passage in his *Edward II*, p. 10.
5. Denholm-Young (ed.), *Vita*, p. 32.
6. Denholm-Young (ed.), *Vita*, p. 36.
7. Riley (ed.), *Trokelowe*, p. 79. See Gransden, *Historical Writing*, ii, p. 5 for doubts on authorship, which might be more appropriately attributed to William Rishanger.
8. Riley (ed.), *Trokelowe*, p. 79.
9. *CPR 1307–13*, p. 619.
10. It still had not been paid in November 1322. *CPR 1318–23*, p. 611. This was not Edward's fault; the sheriffs had previously ignored an order of 1314 to pay the sum (*CCR 1313–18*, p. 54). Even in 1322 they were trying to get away with paying only half.
11. Smallwood, 'Prophecy of the Six Kings'; Taylor, *Political Prophecy*, pp. 160–4.
12. William Hardy (ed.), *Recueil des Croniques et Anchiennes Istories de la Grant Bretainge . . . par Jehan de Waurin: from Albina to AD 688* (1864), p. 230.
13. My thanks to Susannah Davis for pointing this out to me.
14. The version given in BL Harley 746, transcribed in the appendix to Taylor, *Political Prophecy*, pp. 160–4, does not give the place of birth of Edward of Windsor (as later versions do) but does mention the eagle who will come out of Cornwall, very probably Gaveston. This specifically says that Edward II would die in foreign lands 'il vivera tout son temps en enui et en travaille et en paenie morra'. Previously in this same version 'paenie' is used to describe France, so perhaps should not be read strictly as 'pagan' lands, but overseas in a more general sense.
15. TNA E101/393/4, quoted in *E3&Chiv*, p. 170. Also see *ibid*, p. 51 which notes that a close friend of the Black Prince, Simon Burley, owned a *Brut* and related Arthuriana.
16. The Fieschi letter notes that the dethroned Edward II went to Brabant after seeing the pope in about 1331, after his supposed murder, which may be connected with his faith in the oil's power.
17. Lewis Thorpe (ed.), Gregory of Tours, *History of the Franks* (1974, paperback

reprinted, 1985), pp. 104–6.

18. *GT*, pp. 15–16.

19. Denholm-Young (ed.), *Vita*, p. 36.

20. See Tout, *Chapters*, iv, p. 70. There is no record of the creation itself, and it is possible that the girding of a sword – the usual custom for the creation of an earl – was intended to happen at a later date. Edward was styled earl of Chester before Christmas 1312.

21. *CFR 1307–19*, p. 158.

22. Grant dated 4 August 1313. See *CCW 1244–1326*, p. 392.

23. Grant dated 25 July 1317. *CCR 1307–13*, p. 5; *CCR 1323–27*, p. 7.

24. Grant dated 25 May 1318. *CPR 1317–21*, pp. 141, 162.

25. For examples of writs directed to the earl of Chester before the age of seven, see *CPR 1313–17*, pp. 190, 373, 476; *CPR 1317–21*, p. 200; *CPR 1321–24*, pp. 72, 96; *CCR 1313–18*, pp. 158, 373; *CCR 1318–23*, pp. 23, 254.

26. Riley (ed.), *Trokelowe*, p. 79; Riley (ed.), *Walsingham*, p. 134. This was not in itself such an outrageous suggestion; Edward I's eldest son, Edward II's older brother, who has also been born at Windsor, had been named Alfonso to mark the relationship between the king and the ruling house of Castile which gave him his queen, Eleanor. It was probably vetoed by the king's advisers on account of the hostilities which were so fresh in the minds of the English lords, Edward and Isabella's marriage being part of a peace deal. Ormrod in his *ODNB* article on Edward III states that the name preferred by the French was Philip.

27. Studies of Isabella include Doherty 'Isabella' (D.Phil. thesis); and his somewhat briefer book based on the same study, *Isabella and the Strange Death of Edward II*. See also Menache, 'Isabelle of France', which focuses on the reappraisal of Isabella's character, and John Carmi Parsons' article on her in the *ODNB*.

28. *GT*, pp. 145–7.

29. See Thompson (ed.), *Murimuth*, p. 52. Murimuth was at the time administering the diocese of Exeter after the death of the bishop, James Berkeley of Berkeley, and was comparatively well-informed about the ex-king's incarceration.

30. Menache, 'Isabelle of France', p. 108.

31. Brown, 'Diplomacy, Adultery, and Domestic Politics'.

32. Strickland, *Queens of England*, i, p. 481.

33. See TNA E101/393/4 and E101/333/29. The lists of books in Isabella's possession at her death appear in *E3&Chiv*, p. 170 (where the date of her death is given incorrectly as 1352; she died in 1358).

34. Doherty, 'Isabella' (D.Phil. thesis), p. 39.

35. Margaret, wife of Stephen the Chandler, nurse of Edward, received the manor of Overstone in Northamptonshire in return for her services when Edward was fifteen months old. See *CFR 1307–19*, p. 189. I have found no proof that she was the same woman as 'Margaret of Daventry, nurse of Edward the king's son', but it seems likely in view of the fact that the manor granted to the wife of Stephen the Chandler was only twelve miles from Daventry. In *ODNB*, Ormrod states in his article on Edward III that Margaret of Daventry and Margaret Chandler were two different women who both nursed Edward.

36. The name of Margaret of Daventry appears at the foot of the lists of king's clerks

in the royal household for the years 1328 and 1330. See the appendices to the *CMR 1326–27*, pp. 374, 378. She also appears on the Close Rolls for 10 February 1327 as 'the king's nurse' and was the subject of an order to the sheriff of Lincoln in May 1332, when Edward ordered the sheriff to restore all her goods to her, which had been confiscated because Henry Thorp 'formerly her husband' had been accused of murder. See *CCR 1327–30*, pp. 21, 485.

37. Tout, *Chapters*, iv, pp. 70–1; *CFR 1307–19*, p. 190.

38. The grant is dated 4 August 1313, when the king was at Bisham, which was where the prince had been on 6 July (according to Tout, *Chapters*, iv, p. 70) and probably where he was at the time of the grant. See *CCW 1244–1326*, p. 392.

39. TNA E101/375/3.

40. On 7 April 1314 the sheriff of Oxford was ordered to sell the leftover wine provided for the expenses of the household of the earl of Chester who had been staying there lately. See *CFR 1307–19*, p. 190. On 24 April 1314 the keeper of Ludgershall forest was ordered to provide twenty leafless oaks for Edward's household as it was anticipated that he would be staying at the manor for some time. He was also ordered to provide three oaks for shingles to repair the houses. See *CCR 1313–18*, p. 53.

41. *CCR 1313–18*, p. 57.

42. On 6 June 1314 Hugh Leominster was still at Ludgershall, receiving payments on Edward's behalf. TNA E179/377/7.

43. The king allocated the revenues from Wallingford Castle and Honor to Edward's household on 13 June; one month later the keeper of Henley Forest was ordered to supply Edward of Windsor with thirty leafless oaks for firewood, indicating an anticipated long stay there. See *CCR 1313–18*, pp. 64, 106.

44. Tout, *Chapters*, iv, p. 71. As Tout remarks, on 26 July 1314 John Sapy is to be found acting as steward (*CCR 1313–18*, p. 191). This may have been a temporary appointment. It is worth noticing that Sapy had served in Gaveston's household, amongst others. See *GT*, p. 42.

45. Tout, *Chapters*, iv, p. 71. *CPR 1292–1301*, p. 502. He had been appointed on 10 July 1295. *CCW 1244–1326*, p. 132. He was still Edward's treasurer on 22 July 1316. See Tout, *Chapters*, iv, p. 71 n. 7. He seems to have been favoured by Isabella, who on 16 May 1313 succeeded in persuading her husband to grant the first good benefice that became available to him. See *CCW 1244–1326*, p. 389.

46. He retired to a room within the precincts of the Dominican house at Ely in 1317. *CCR 1313–17*, p. 452.

47. *CCR 1313–17*, p. 430.

48. *CCW 1244–1326*, p. 485. This shows that Damory was appointed 'keeper of the body' etc. before 11 April 1318. Although this is the only explicit reference in the published calendars to his acting in this capacity, in the appointment to enquire into the negligence of the bailiffs of Chester and Flint, dated the same day, he is the first-named (*CPR 1317–21*, p. 134). Similarly he was the first-named when acting on behalf of the prince in conjunction with Robert Mauley (prince's steward) and Nicholas Hugate (keeper of the prince's wardrobe) on 16 January 1319 (*CFR 1307–19*, p. 389), and in conjunction with the same men, described in the same capacities, on 5 June 1320 (*CPR 1317–21*, p. 453).

49. *CPR 1317–21*, p. 134.

50. *CCW 1244–1326*, p. 485.
51. In 1300, when he was appointed one of the keepers of the peace for Oxfordshire, he received special dispensation to follow his lord to Scotland in the king's army. See *CCW 1244–1326*, p. 111.
52. Haines, *Edward II*, p. 408, n. 104, quoting Davies, *Baronial Opposition*, pp. 209–10, who in turn uses the fact that Damory witnessed several charters granted by Despenser, as well as the fact that he remained in office for three years after Despenser assumed authority.
53. *CFR 1307–19*, p. 389. This states that Edward's siblings had already been living with him 'for some time'. The date of the grant is 16 January 1319; Eleanor had been born on 8 June 1318. Initially the king had provided lands in Cheshire and Derbyshire for John and Eleanor's sustenance, but these were transferred to Edward's keeper in January 1319. Later in 1319 Edward also received further grants of lands from his father, including Macclesfield and Overton and the Channel Islands, for their upkeep. See Tout, *Chapters*, iv, p. 72; *CFR 1307–19*, p. 392.
54. We cannot be sure that Edward obeyed the summons, but there is no reason to doubt that he did. His father certainly knew how old he was, and the series of summons sent to him from this date suggest a very clear decision to invite him to witness proceedings.
55. Denholm-Young, *Vita*, p. 109.
56. *CP*, iv, p. 46.
57. In 1321 Lord Tyeys was fined £1000 for his evil practices in the Isle of Wight. See *CPR 1317–21*, p. 546; *CP*, xii/2, pp. 103–4.
58. For summons to him as earl of Chester see *CCR 1318–23*, pp. 413 and 515 (to provide men for the army), p. 527 (to attend parliament), p. 533 and p. 558 (to attend and supply men for the Scottish campaign).
59. Glover (ed.), *Livere de Reis*, p. 345.
60. *GT*, p. 121; TNA E101/379/10.
61. Brie (ed.), *Brut*, i, p. 224.
62. Smallwood, 'Prophecy of the Six Kings', p. 576.
63. Cusance became keeper of the wardrobe on 23 June 1323 and was removed from that position on Christmas Eve 1325. His records were all lost in the disturbances in London following the invasion of 1326. *CPR 1333–37*, p. 41.
64. Tout, *Chapters*, iv, p. 72.
65. Doherty, 'Isabella' (D.Phil. thesis), pp. 93–4.
66. *GT*, p. 161.
67. There is some evidence that Edward II – usually presumed to be a homosexual king – was having a liaison with Eleanor Despenser. See Doherty, 'Isabella' (D.Phil. thesis), p. 139, which mentions frequent visits and gifts, and quotes one Hainault source (Willelmi Capellani) which states they were lovers. See also Doherty, *Isabella and the Strange Death of Edward II*, pp. 101–2 which continues the theme. However, Eleanor Despenser was his own niece, and so one tends to want to reserve judgement on this matter, as to accuse him of adultery with Despenser's wife is one thing; accusing him of incest is quite another. While one cannot rule out the possibility raised by Doherty in *Isabella and the Strange Death* that Despenser sought to impose his sexual will on Isabella – and that this was the 'dishonour' which he

had wrought upon her, we should wish for further details before positively asserting that this was the case. On Edward's homosexuality see Chaplais, *Piers Gaveston*, pp. 7–11; Ormrod, 'Sexualities of Edward II', and Mortimer, 'Sermons of Sodomy'.

68. Doherty, 'Isabella' (D.Phil. thesis), p. 96.

69. Doherty, 'Isabella' (D.Phil. thesis), p. 101.

70. *CCR 1318–23*, pp. 679, 699–700.

71. Trotter, 'Pre-marital inspection'; Buck, *Politics, Finance*, p. 126. Vale (in her *ODNB* article on Philippa) and many others besides Trotter and Buck have incorrectly presumed that the girl was Philippa. See Appendix One for a clarification of this issue.

72. *CCR 1318–23*, pp. 118, 132, 365.

73. Letter of response dated 6 June 1323. *CCR 1318–23*, p. 713. Charles was Edward's great-uncle.

74. Letter of 30 March 1324 to James, *CCR 1323–27*, p. 171. The embassy was despatched 1 October 1324. *CCR 1324–27*, p. 32.

75. *CCR 1323–27*, p. 344. *CPR 1324–27*, pp. 103–4. At this time it was proposed that Edward's sister, Joan of the Tower, should marry Alfonso, heir of Aragon.

76. It has been suggested that Robert Holkot wrote Bury's *Philobiblon*, but he was almost certainly no more than Bury's amanuensis. For the disparaging of the story that Bury was Edward's tutor, see Tout, *Edward II*, p. 336.

77. Crump, 'Arrest of Roger Mortimer and Queen Isabel', pp. 331–2.

78. Tout, *Edward II*, p. 340.

79. On 14 July 1324 the king granted Edward 'La Sauveye' near the stone cross without the bar of New Temple, London, *CPR 1324–27*, p. 4.

80. TNA E101/393/4, E101/333/29. As noted above, she had more than thirty volumes in her possession. She also probably borrowed many more. Borrowing volumes was common among the élite in medieval England.

81. Thompson (ed.), *Murimuth*, p. 171.

82. The age ascribed to Bury here is based on his age as given at the end of the *Philobiblon*, that he was fifty-eight on the day he completed it, 24 January 1344/5.

83. In the *Philobiblon*, Bury mentions Ptolemy, Socrates, Homer, Plato, Pythagoras, Theocritus, Pindar, Euclid, Zeno and Aristotle among the Greeks; Averroës and Avicenna among the Arabs; and dozens of writers from the Roman world, including the historians Aulus Gellius, Suetonius, Sallust and Cassiodorus; the poets Ovid, Virgil, Martial and Lucretius; the grammarians Priscian and Donatus; the orators Cato the Elder and Cicero; the philosopher Macrobius; the natural history writer Pliny the elder; and a number of Church fathers, Tertullian, Boethius, Jerome, Origen, Augustine. Very few English writers were named in Bury's book: John of Salisbury was one; the Venerable Bede was another. In Bury's view, Aristotle reigned supreme. He was 'the arch-poet whom Averroës regards as the law of Nature', by comparison with whom Plato was 'before him in time, but after him in learning'.

84. John Paynel is mentioned as superintending Edward's education in letters. See Ormrod, 'Edward III' in *ODNB*.

85. Nederman (ed.), *Political Thought*, p. 40.

86. For a succinct account of the origins of the War of Saint-Sardos, see Chaplais, *War of St Sardos*, ix–xiii. See also *GT*, pp. 137–9.

87. *CPR 1324–27*, p. 171.

2: A Treasonable Youth

1. *GT*, p. 142; Blackley, 'Isabella and the Bishop of Exeter', p. 230.
2. Denholm-Young (ed.), *Vita*, pp. 142–3.
3. Denholm-Young (ed.), *Vita*, p. 143.
4. There is only one recorded incident which suggests that Edward was sceptical or hostile towards Mortimer at this time. This is an incident reported by Despenser to the bishop of Rochester, who claimed that Isabella would have returned to England straightaway if it had not been for Mortimer, who threatened to murder her if she should try (Doherty, 'Isabella', p. 135; Wharton (ed.), *Anglia Sacra*, i, p. 365). Edward may also have heard this. Three years later Edward III himself accused Mortimer of telling the queen 'that if she went to him (the king) that he would kill her with a knife or in another manner murder her' (*RP*, ii, p. 53). However, we must seriously question who the 'he' was in this statement. Does it mean Mortimer was warning Isabella that the king would kill her? Or was it – as Despenser thought – that Mortimer would kill her? The answer is almost certainly the former. The bishop of Hereford preached a sermon in October 1326 that Edward II kept a knife hidden in a sandal so he would be able to kill the queen if she should come near him, or he would otherwise kill her with his teeth, if he had no other weapon (Hingeston-Randolph (ed.), *Register of John de Grandison*, iii, p. 1542; Mortimer, 'Sermons of Sodomy'). It seems likely that those who have considered this detail have mistakenly presumed that Edward believed that Mortimer threatened to kill the queen if she should leave him, in an act of passion. I am not exempt from this criticism. See *GT*, p. 147.
5. Edward's promise to give this lordship to Mortimer was made while they were in France. As that lordship was in the hands of Despenser at the time (*CChR 1327–41*, p. 55), the implication is that Edward agreed that this would be Mortimer's reward for the removing of Despenser, which suggests that he sympathised with his mother's and Mortimer's hatred of the man. However, it is difficult to be sure that we are not simply witnessing Isabella's promises made in her son's name.
6. Halliwell (ed.), *Letters of the Kings of England*, i, pp. 25–7.
7. *CCR 1323–27*, pp. 579–80; Halliwell (ed.), *Letters of the Kings of England*, i, p. 29.
8. Doherty, 'Isabella' (D.Phil. thesis), p. 142.
9. *GT*, p. 146.
10. Haines, *Edward II*, p. 170.
11. Doherty, 'Isabella' (D.Phil. thesis), pp. 137–8.
12. *GT*, p. 147.
13. Doherty, 'Isabella' (D.Phil. thesis), p. 144.
14. Johnes (ed.), *Froissart*, i, pp. 8–9.
15. Further support for this lies in the appropriateness of the illustrations of the wedding present which Philippa gave to Edward in 1328. See Michael, 'Manuscript Wedding Gift'; Shenton, 'English Court', p. 180. In particular, Shenton points out that in this book Philippa had had Edward depicted with a hawk on his arm. This was an image of himself he liked to project; not only does he appear pictured likewise in Milemete's treatise, he also appears as one of the weepers with a

falconry glove in his hand on the tomb of his brother, John, in Westminster Abbey. Although this figure has been previously associated with Edward II (e.g. Mary Saaler, *Edward II* (1997), plate 3), the use of the falconry glove (with his falcon absent) is far more likely to represent Edward's specific commission.

16. For the size of the invasion force see *GT*, p. 149.
17. Mortimer, 'Sermons of Sodomy'.
18. This was Llywelyn Bren, whom Despenser had had brutally hanged and eviscerated. See *GT*, pp. 87–8.
19. TNA E101/383/8, f.24r, f.24v.
20. TNA E101/383/8 f.5r.
21. TNA E101/383/3, m.1.
22. TNA E101/383/3, m.1.
23. Hingeston-Randolph (ed.), *Register of John de Grandison*, p. 1542; Mortimer, 'Sermons of Sodomy'.
24. Wharton, *Anglia Sacra*, i, p. 367.
25. Riley (ed.). *Walsingham*, i, p. 186.
26. *CCR 1327–30*, p. 1.
27. *GT*, p. 170.
28. Shenton, 'English Court', pp. 135–41. The details of furnishings for the coronation are taken from this source.
29. Shenton, English Court', p. 136.
30. *GT*, p. 170 and p. 288 n. 17.
31. TNA E101/382/8, m.2.
32. TNA E101/383/8, f.25r.
33. This is made on the basis of Lancaster's behaviour towards the king a year later. See *GT*, p. 213.
34. TNA E101/383/8, f.25v.
35. Thompson (ed.), *Murimuth*, p. 52.
36. *WCS*, p. 4 n.13, quoting Sir J.H. Ramsay, *Revenues of the Kings of England, 1066–1399, Volume 2: Edward I – Richard II* (Oxford, 1925), Table I (facing p. 292).

3: The Devil for Wrath

1. Doherty, 'Isabella' (D.Phil. thesis), p. 199.
2. Thompson (ed.), *Galfridi le Baker*, pp. 27, 205.
3. Doherty, 'Isabella' (D.Phil. thesis), p. 204.
4. For example, TNA E101/383/3, mm. 1–3.
5. TNA E101/383/3, m.1.
6. Doherty, 'Isabella', pp. 214–17.
7. Ormrod, 'Edward III' in *ODNB*.
8. The best account of the Weardale campaign is to be found in *E3&S*, chapter three.
9. TNA E101/383/3, m.2.
10. Michael Prestwich, 'Piety of Edward I', in Mark Ormrod (ed.), *England in the Thirteenth Century: Proceedings of the 1984 Harlaxton Symposium* (Woodbridge, 1985), p.

124; Haines, *Edward II*, p. 14.

11. See *GT*, pp. 179–80, where it is suggested that Roger Mortimer was responsible for this decision. However, Maxwell (ed.), *Scalachronica*, p. 80, states it was 'some men of the Marches' who advised this, meaning men of the Scottish Marches.

12. Johnes (ed.), *Froissart*, i, p. 23.

13. Both Froissart, quoting le Bel, and *Brut* agree on the figure of two hundred. See Brie (ed.), *Brut*, p. 251; Johnes (ed.), *Froissart*, i, p. 24. The moonlight is mentioned in *Brut*.

14. Bond (ed.), *Melsa*, ii, pp. 356–7.

15. TNA DL 10/253.

16. The cause of death here is taken from the copies of the earliest lay chronicle, the shorter continuation of the French *Brut*. Most manuscripts state illness, and it seems likely that the original specified grief-induced illness. See Mortimer, 'Sermons of Sodomy'.

17. TNA E101/383/3 m.1.

18. TNA E101/383/3 m.3.

19. TNA E101/383/3 m.3.

20. TNA E101/383/3 m.6.

21. TNA E101/624/14.

22. TNA E101/383/3 m.2. This notes gold thread purchased for decorating purple harnesses for the tournament at Clipstone, and appears between pennons for the Stanhope campaign and commissions for his father's funeral. The tournament probably took place around 15–16 November, when the king was at Clipstone. The following membrane, m.3, includes payments for six harnesses made for the tournament at Worcester between 25–30 November 1327, and harnesses for the tournaments at Clipstone and Rothwell between 24 November–12 December 1327. The king was at Clipstone on 29–30 November 1327 and 9–15 January 1328, and at Rothwell on 18 January 1328.

23. Shenton, 'English Court', p. 35.

24. For the events of September–December 1327, see Mortimer, 'The death of Edward II in Berkeley Castle'. This is outlined in brief in Appendix Two.

25. See Appendix One.

26. Michael, 'Manuscript Wedding Gift', pp. 582–99; *RE3*, p. 47; Ormrod, 'Personal Religion', p. 857; Shenton, 'English Court', pp. 149–50. The music included in the book may have been sung at the ceremony.

27. Most secondary sources give the date as 24 January, following the Bridlington chronicler. Shenton points out that there is doubt, however, noting that the St Paul's chronicler gives the date as 30 January. Shenton suggests 25th or 26th as the household expenditure was highest on those two days, indicating the largest feast which normally would have followed the ceremony. See Shenton, 'English Court', p. 149.

28. TNA E101/383/3 m.3 mentions fifteen shillings 'paid out to those working on manufacturing a harness for the tournament at York and for the twenty-four pennons bearing the arms of St George'.

29. John Wyard was carrying out secret business for the king on 30 March 1327 and 1 January 1328. See TNA E101/383/3 m.6 and E101/383/8 f.25v. On the latter occasion he was given a gold cross bearing a stone and twelve pearls for his secret

dealings at Lichfield.

30. Stones, 'Anglo-Scottish Negotiations of 1327'; Harding, 'Regime of Mortimer and Isabella', pp. 224–8.

31. *Foedera*, ii, 2, p. 731.

32. Doherty, 'Isabella' (D.Phil. thesis), p. 234, stating parliament was ordered to assemble on 26 April. *RE3*, p. 193, states 24 April.

33. Dryburgh, 'Roger Mortimer', Appendix One (Itinerary of Roger Mortimer), quoting BL Harley 1240 ff.43v –44r and Add MS 6041 f.7v, which show Mortimer at Brecon on 20 March 1328; and BL Harley 1240 f.117 and Add MS 6041 f.45r, which show him at Abergavenny on 6 April 1328.

34. TNA C53/115, nos 70, 71, 73, 74, 76.

35. TNA C53/115, nos 72 and 69. Neither man attested charter nos 86, 77, 76, 74, 73, 71 and 70.

36. Letters nominating attorneys granted to Pecche 13 February 1328, he going overseas with his wife Eleanor (*CPR 1327–30*, p. 234). Also complaint dated 18 February 1328 against John Pecche and Thomas de Rous for removing eight horses and £28 in money at Warwick (*CPR 1327–30*, p. 280). He had previously obtained protection for two years, going overseas, 14 February 1327 (*CPR 1327–30*, p. 11). With regard to his position at Corfe, see *CP*, x, p. 343; *CFR 1327–1340*, pp. 168–9; Mortimer, 'The death of Edward II in Berkeley Castle'.

37. Among the terms of this treaty was one promising that the Stone of Destiny (of the Stone of Scone) should be returned to Scotland. A letter from Queen Isabella is extant saying that this was intended (Shenton, 'English Court', p. 144). It did not happen until recent times, however. The Stone was finally returned to Scotland in November 1996.

38. *E3&S*, p. 52.

39. Shenton, 'Edward III and the Coup of 1330', p. 21.

40. Harding, 'Regime of Mortimer and Isabella', p. 243.

41. Lumby (ed.), *Knighton*, p. 451.

42. Brie (ed.), *Brut*, p. 261.

43. For a full analysis of this possibility see *GT*, pp. 221–4.

44. For example, Prestwich, *Three Edwards*, p. 99.

45. Mortimer, 'The death of Edward II in Berkeley Castle'.

46. John Asphale, a friend and accomplice of Kent's, had appointed attorneys to manage his affairs while he was abroad with Kent on 25 April 1329 (*CPR 1327–30*, p. 385). He himself appointed attorneys on 21 May (*CPR 1327–30*, p. 391).

47. Other men planning to travel with Kent still had not left by 1 June 1329. See *CPR 1327–30*, p. 415.

48. For the reason why Kent has been labelled stupid or foolish in the past, and why we may be sure that this is wrong, see Mortimer, 'Death of Edward II in Berkeley Castle'.

49. Crump, 'Arrest of Roger Mortimer and Queen Isabel', pp. 331–2.

50. For example, Maxwell (ed.), *Scalachronica*, p. 85.

51. Crump, 'Arrest of Roger Mortimer and Queen Isabel', p. 332.

52. *Foedera*, ii, 2, p. 775. That the invasion was part of Kent's plot is made clear in Kent's confession and the explanatory letter sent to the pope later. See Thompson (ed.), *Murimuth*, pp. 253–5; *Foedera*, ii, 2, pp. 783–4; *E3&S*, p. 63.

53. On 7 January 1330 Kent witnessed a royal charter. See TNA C53/116, no. 1.
54. The coronation of Queen Philippa had been intended to take place in early 1328, soon after the wedding, but had been delayed. Shenton suggests it was due to the queen's young age; this is a possibility. Another possibility is that it was due to Isabella's will to remain queen, not just queen mother, she being able to wield better influence in that position. The matter remains unclear. For the details of the planned coronation of 1328, see Shenton, 'English Court', pp. 145–6.
55. This and following entries are taken from TNA E101/385/12.
56. Warwickshire County Record Office: CR 136/C/2027. I am indebted to Elizabeth Danbury for drawing my attention to this document. Her publication of the letter is eagerly anticipated.
57. *GT*, p. 217.
58. The fullest account of the proceedings against Kent are to be found in Brie (ed.), *Brut*, i, pp. 263–7, from which this and the other quotations have been taken.
59. *GT*, p. 235.
60. TNA E101/385/4 m.75.
61. Devon (ed.), *Issues of the Exchequer*, pp. 143, 160. The man's name was Thomas Prior.
62. Brie (ed.), *Brut*, i, p. 269.
63. *CChR*, iv, p. 199.
64. Shenton, 'Edward III and the coup of 1330', pp. 25–6; *GT*, pp. 237–8.
65. Maxwell (ed.), *Scalachronica*, p. 86.
66. TNA E372/177/38; TNA E101/469/15.
67. Harding, 'Isabella and Mortimer', p. 317, quoting E403/253.
68. There is a chamber in the south-west tower of the south-west gatehouse at Corfe Castle which apparently has no doors and no windows. The chamber could only have been entered from a trapdoor in the room above. I noted this on a visit to the castle, but it is relevant that in 1331 (note the date) this room was referred to as the prison chamber. See *HKW*, ii. p. 622 n. 6; however also see *ibid*, p. 621 n. 12, in which it is noted that in the sixteenth century the Butavant Tower (now largely demolished) was also known as the Dungeon Tower. Evidence that Edward was actually held at Corfe Castle is outlined in Mortimer, 'The death of Edward II in Berkeley Castle'. In particular the role of Sir John Pecche is pertinent, as is the prosecution of Maltravers for encompassing the earl of Kent's death while he was custodian of Corfe. Also refer to the rumours of Edward's custody there in Brie (ed.), *Brut*, pp. 263–4 and Thompson (ed.), *Murimuth* p. 52, and in the Fieschi letter. See *GT*, pp. 251–2 for the latter.
69. TNA E101/469/15 reads 'pro claustra domini Rogeri de Mortuo Mari, domini Galfridi filii sui et Simoni de Bereford in turello iuxta cameram domini regis de dicto turello usque gardinum xii d'.

4: Absolute Royalty

1. *CPR 1330–34*, p. 97; *GT*, pp. 85–6. The office of King's Lieutenant was viceregal.
2. Haines, *Edward II*, p. 461 n.202 quoting *CCR 1330–33*, p. 67.

3. Doherty, 'Isabella' (D.Phil. thesis), p. 319.
4. *CEPR*, ii, p. 498. The pope wrote that he had heard the news on 3 November, and in a letter dated 7 November gave details of the plot, showing he had unquestionably heard by then. On the same day he wrote stating he had received further news about Isabella's treatment after 19 October at Edward's hands. This is a very telling detail for long-distance communications in 1330. The message had been carried accurately nearly two hundred miles from Nottingham to Dover (presumably: this was the fastest crossing point), across the sea to France, and then more than five hundred miles to Avignon in less than two weeks (20 October to 3 November).
5. *RP*, ii, p. 57. Literally, 'he had not heard about the king's death'.
6. Mortimer, 'The death of Edward II in Berkeley Castle'. This demonstrates how Berkeley was allowed to change his plea from one of not knowing the king was dead to a complete falsehood which Edward knew was a complete falsehood but which he preferred nonetheless.
7. Thompson (ed.), *Murimuth*, p. 62.
8. John de Melburn was the man appointed to look into the estates of the countess of March. See *CPR 1330–34*, p. 13. It was at least six years before a final resolution was reached about Joan's Irish lands.
9. *CEPR*, ii, p. 499.
10. Burghersh was the only man apart from the king to be included with Mortimer's family members in his chantry bequest of 1329–30. See *GT*, p. 222.
11. Maltravers was first given letters of safe conduct to return to England to face a retrial for the earl's death in 1345; he did not return however until 1352. On that occasion he was completely acquitted. For his secret visit in 1335, see *CPR 1334–37*, pp. 88, 89, 111, 112. Those he met included Lord Berkeley, Maurice Berkeley, William Montagu, John Molyns and Edmund Bereford. This was almost certainly in response to Maltravers' letter of March 1334 stating that he had information concerning 'the honour, estate and well-being of the realm', in response to which Montagu was sent to see him in Flanders. See Harding, 'Mortimer and Isabella', p. 332.
12. This was before 1333. *Foedera*, ii, 2, p. 870.
13. Doherty 'Isabella' (D.Phil. thesis), p. 320.
14. Maxwell (ed.), *Scalachronica*, p. 88.
15. TNA E101/385/4 m.79. These games do not appear in the list of tournaments given in *E3&Chiv*, p. 172.
16. *E3&Chiv*, p. 175.
17. The best work on this question is *E3&Chiv*, especially chapter 4: '"Ludi" and "Hastiludia" at the court of Edward III' (pp. 57–75). However, there are many 'games' (as opposed to jousts and tournaments) recorded in the wardrobe accounts which are not noted in *E3&Chiv*.
18. The design of the painting on the table dates from the early sixteenth century but Edward III certainly knew of it, for he had it made into a centrepiece at Winchester, and had it mounted on the wall there (Ormrod, 'For Arthur and St George', p. 22). Given the closeness of the number of knights on the Winchester table to the Order of the Garter, the sixteenth-century painting may reflect an earlier painted or traditional arrangement, perhaps the unofficial Companionship of the

Garter (see Chapter Eleven).

19. See Shenton, 'Edward III and the coup of 1330' for a description of these aketons and their significance.

20. *RE3*, p. 48.

21. Keen, *Chivalry*, p. 179.

22. Keen, *Chivalry*, p. 181.

23. Taylor, *Political Prophecy*, pp. 161–2, quoting BL: Harleian MS 746.

24. See TNA E101/386/14. Although this is dated 11 March 1333, there had been some considerable delay in payment, as the goldsmith, Thomas Walpole, had begun to complain about his £146 17s 8d and had started to seek alternative ways of reimbursement.

25. *CEPR*, ii, p. 500.

26. He asked again about 'crossing the sea' in April 1332 in a letter concerning France. *CEPR*, ii, pp. 503–4.

27. Otway-Ruthven, *History of Medieval Ireland*, pp. 248, 253.

28. Thompson (ed.), *Murimuth*, p. 63. The reason for supposing this was sudden is the itinerary of Edward's wardrobe, which remained at Eltham from 2 April while he himself reached Dover the next day. On this question, there is a payment in a later wardrobe account for '120 ells of russet to be used in the production of twenty tunics and cowls in the monastic style [*ad modum monachorum*] for the king and others of his chamber' (TNA E101/387/14 m.1). If this payment relates to this occasion, then the monastic costumes would have had to be made in advance, and, given the speed of travel, and the lack of preparation otherwise, it is unlikely. These monastic costumes probably relate to another escapade sometime before the date of the document (1334–35). The event is also noted in the Annales Paulini. See Stubbs (ed.), *Chronicles*, i, p. 353.

29. McKisack, *Fourteenth Century*, p. 112.

30. Perroy, *Hundred Years War*, pp. 83–4.

31. Hunter, 'Measures taken for the apprehension of Thomas Gurney', p. 80. Giles of Spain was also instructed to return two other men concerned in the Berkeley Castle plot who had fled to the Continent: Robert Lynel and John Tylli. See *Foedera*, ii, 2, p. 850.

32. *CCR 1330–54*, p. 366. The wording has been slightly paraphrased.

33. The event is described in the Annales Paulini. See Stubbs (ed.), *Chronicles*, i, p. 353.

34. *E3&Chiv*, p. 62.

35. Stubbs (ed.), *Chronicles*, i, p. 353.

36. Stubbs (ed.), *Chronicles*, i, p. 354.

37. This is discussed more fully in *E3&Chiv*, p. 62.

38. The collapse of the stand is described in the Annales Paulini (see Stubbs (ed.), *Chronicles*, i, p. 354). The forgiveness of the workmen is noted in Hamilton (ed.), *Hemingburgh*, ii, p. 303, n.2.

39. Ormrod, 'Personal Religion', p. 872.

40. *RE3*, p. 94, using *RP*, ii, pp. 62, 446.

41. Musson, 'Second "English Justinian"', p. 73.

42. When England and Scotland bound themselves to mutual defence in 1328, France was specifically excepted, due to Scotland's prior treaty with the French. See Perroy,

Hundred Years War, p. 89.

43. *E3&S*, pp. 76, 97.

44. TNA E101/386/3 f.4r. Although the New Year technically began on 25 March, 1 January (the feast of the Circumcision) was when presents were exchanged at court.

45. *Foedera*, ii, 2, p. 831. The following list is based on the same source.

46. See Appendix Eight.

47. *E3&Chiv*, p. 63.

48. TNA E101/386/2 m.7.

49. *E3&S*, pp. 81–3. They had set sail on 31 July.

50. Maxwell (ed.), *Lanercost*, pp. 270–1.

51. *Foedera*, ii, 2, p. 842.

52. The distinction is more than just a historical nicety. David II was the king of Scotland, as his father Robert Bruce had been. Balliol's father – a client king – is usually referred to by the term King of Scots, and this term is usually used to designate client kings unrecognised by many of their Scottish contemporaries.

53. *E3&S*, p. 120. See also Maxwell (ed.), *Lanercost*, ii, p. 274.

54. *E3&S*, p. 96.

55. *RE3*, p. 95.

56. *E3&S*, p. 107.

57. *E3&S*, pp. 121–2.

58. *E3&S*, pp. 121–2.

59. This is now in the Statens Historika Museum, Stockholm.

60. This was using variant forms of modern gunpowder. See Medieval Gunpowder Research Group, Report no. 2 (Middelaldercentret, Denmark, August 2003). This is available online at http://www.middelaldercentret.dk/gunpowder2003.pdf at the time of writing (May 2005).

61. *GT*, p. 181, quoting Barbour, *The Bruce*, ii, p. 479.

62. Tout, *Chapters*, iv, pp. 470–5.

63. *E3&S*, p. 121. Edward requested only one old siege engine to be assembled for use at Berwick; the other two were to be newly made.

64. *Foedera*, ii, 2, p. 856. Most of the following list of events are drawn from the same source.

65. TNA E101/386/3 f.2r.

66. Bond (ed.), *Melsa*, ii, p. 368.

67. Brie (ed.), *Brut*, i, p. 281.

68. TNA E101/386/10 m.1.

69. *CCR 1333–37*, p. 152.

70. *E3&S*, p. 124.

71. Wyntoun, quoted in Maxwell (ed.), *Scalachronica*, p. 95, states that there were more Seton boys, but this is not borne out by the daughter of Sir Alexander Seton inheriting his lands.

72. *E3&S*, p. 129.

73. Ormrod, 'Personal Religion', p. 859, n.57.

74. Childs and Taylor (eds), *Anonimalle*, p. 167.

75. Thompson (ed.), *Galfridi le Baker*, p. 51.

76. *E3&S*, p. 138.

77. Childs and Taylor (eds), *Anonimalle*, p. 167. The Anonimalle chronicler does not mention the previous wave of the attack led by Balliol. See Maxwell (ed.), *Lanercost*, p. 279.
78. Brie (ed.), *Brut*, i, p. 285.
79. *E3&S*, p. 138.

5: *Warrior of God*

1. Brie (ed.), *Brut*, ii, p. 291.
2. James and Simons (eds), *Laurence Minot*, p. 26.
3. TNA E101/386/8 m.9.
4. TNA E101/386/10, m.2.
5. For example: Thompson (ed.), *Murimuth*, p. 69.
6. TNA E101/386/10, m.2.
7. By far the best work on Edward's religion is Ormrod, 'Personal Religion'. A subsequent short article by Bryce Lyon, 'What were Edward III's Priorities: the pleasures of sports or charity?' used this and added some conclusions based on his edition of William Norwell's wardrobe account book (TNA E36/203). However, Lyon's methodology is highly reductive and his conclusions should be discounted. He argues that, because Edward's special alms-giving in the period 1338–40 amounted to £439, plus daily alms-giving of £137, and yet hunting cost him £873 (total household expenditure being £23,746), this amounts to alms-giving having a lower 'priority' than hunting. One cannot sensibly compare financial payments for purchases which are completely different in nature and infer that such payments are quantifications of will, inclination or some ill-defined 'priority'. The laws of demand and supply affected prices for commodities then as now, and Edward's payments reflect externally determined prices as much as personal taste. Also Lyon's work disregards some basic facts: that Edward was in an unusual situation (in a foreign land, having to entertain foreign potentates); that many religious gifts were in kind and occasional (such as his foundations of religious institutions); and that the total of alms-giving noted by Lyon – in excess of £300 per year – would have been more than that of any other individual in England.
8. Ormrod states that 'there is very little to suggest that Edward was aware of the great theological debates raging in Oxford, even though William of Ockham, Thomas Bradwardine, Richard FitzRalph and John Wyclif were all at some stage employed in the service of the crown' (Ormrod, 'Personal Religion', p. 854). This is almost certainly true. However, he was aware of the men who were conducting the debates, even if he did not understand what they were saying. The employment of Ockham at any stage of his career is notable. Similarly the employment of the Aristotelian Walter Burley on a mission to Avignon to request the canonisation of Thomas of Lancaster is a good sign that Edward was familiar with how others are likely to have viewed him. Burley was also probably entrusted with educating Edward's son and heir, Edward of Woodstock. Also we must note Edward's appointment of the future archbishop Thomas Bradwardine as his own chaplain and confessor in 1338. Bradwardine was the well-respected scholar who

wrote denouncing the error of Pelagius regarding free will; he remained in
Edward's service for several years, until appointed archbishop of Canterbury just
before he died in 1349.

9. Ormrod, 'Personal Religion', pp. 862–5.

10. Ormrod, 'Personal Religion', p. 874.

11. TNA E101/386/3 ff.1–3.

12. Ormrod, 'Personal Religion', p. 857.

13. TNA E101/388/5 m.15. This is described in context in Chapter Six.

14. TNA E36/204 f.75r, relating to the early 1340s, records a second visit to this statue.
Another cult he patronised was that of St Thomas of Canterbury, especially visiting
the point of the sword which killed the saint, which was still at Canterbury, venerated as a relic in its own right.

15. *Foedera*, ii, 2, p. 895.

16. Edward was fourteen at Stanhope Park, when 1800 pennons of Saint George were
carried with him.

17. TNA E101/386/18 m.23.

18. On 22 February 1333, before the Berwick campaign, Edward sent Richard Bury
and John Shorditch to Avignon to see Pope John XXII. Their mission was 'to negotiate secret business of the king and business relating to his kingdom' (TNA
E101/386/11). No expense was spared in trying to assist the passage of Bury's affairs.
The king and council wrote to three of the pope's kinsmen who had been engaged
as royal councillors in the previous reign – Arnold de Unsa, Peter de Via and
Arnold de Trie – asking them to support Bury and Shorditch. Funds were made
available for much gift-giving to soften them up. These three councillors were all
given silver-gilt goblets from the king. The pope was given 'a silver-gilt goblet worth
£66.13s.4d. purchased at Avignon with a stand and lid and decorated with various
gemstones' (TNA E101/386/11, m.1). Several cardinals were given pensions of fifty
marks per year, including Napoleone Orsini Frangipani, cardinal deacon of Saint
Adrian; Gaucelin d'Euse, cardinal bishop of Albano; Annibale Gaetani di Ceccano,
cardinal bishop of Naples; Cardinal Bertrand du Pouget, the pope's nephew; and
Peter Montemart, cardinal priest of St Stephen in Celiomonte. Whatever Bury's
and John Shorditch's business was, it was clearly of the highest importance to
Edward III. Part of their secret business was to discuss Scotland, but there was
more to it than that. On 5 July Bury agreed to pay four thousand florins 'each
florin worth 3s 4d' (£666 13s 4d) per year to the pope, supposedly in lieu of papal
taxation in England and Ireland (*Foedera*, ii, 2, p. 864; E101/386/11 m.1). Having
made over all this money they waited until October 1333 for the pope to answer
whatever was the last part of their secret business. When he finally answered he
declined to address the matter of Scotland, but with regard to the other matter he
was inclined to give 'a favourable response' (*CEPR*, ii, p. 512). What that was we
do not know. Bury and Shorditch returned to England in November. The pensions
of fifty marks for the cardinals were paid once and never again. If taxation was
really the purpose of Bury's mission, it is difficult to see why it was described as
'secret business' in the royal accounts, and why he did not return more swiftly. One
possible explanation lies in the instigation of the 'secret business' coinciding with
the arrival at court of Niccolinus Fieschi (TNA E101/386/9, where he appears
under his alias 'Cardinal'). Niccolinus was later to become closely involved with

much of Edward's secret foreign business, and was a relation of the author of the Fieschi letter (see Appendix Three). Hence his appearance at court in February 1333, and the robes he was given as a reward, might suggest that Edward finally had some information as to his father's protector at that time.

19. Edward restored to her her dower lands of Ponthieu and Montreuil on 24 September 1334. *Foedera*, ii, 2, p. 893.

20. *CEPR*, ii, p. 512.

21. *CEPR*, ii, p. 501.

22. Philippa's churching was at Woodstock on 8–10 March 1334, with by far the greatest expenses due on the 9th; so it seems reasonable to suppose that Joan was born about thirty-three days earlier, on 9 February 1334. See TNA E101/386/16 m.7. However, if the biblical sixty-six-day 'uncleanness' applied (as this was a female child), then this would indicate a January birth. See Appendix Eight. See also Shenton, 'English Court', p. 160.

23. This was set in motion in June 1335. See *Foedera*, ii, 2, p. 910.

24. Set in motion in July 1334. See *Foedera*, ii, 2, p. 890.

25. I have been unable to determine what the 'M' might have stood for.

26. TNA E101/386/18 m.58.

27. For the list of armourers in 1330 see *CMR 1326–27*, p. 381. The names given in the text for 1333–34 are drawn from TNA E101/385/7 (esp. m.2, where John of Cologne is specifically paid for providing tunics 'in the German style'), E101/386/18 and E101/387/15. Late in November 1333 the king had received a delivery of Italian and French plate armour (TNA E101/386/11 m.2).

28. TNA E101/388/13 m.3.

29. Laking, *Arms and Armour*, i, p. 145.

30. TNA E101/386/18 m.59.

31. For example, the 'hood of brown scarlet circled with pearls made for the king which he gave to Robert Ufford'. See TNA E101/386/18 m.59.

32. For example, 'the seven hoods of brown scarlet fringed with feathers, gold and pearls; the fringe of each hood having 408 pearls: one hood for the king, one for the earl of Cornwall, one for William Montagu, one for Edward Bohun, one for William Bohun, one for Robert Ufford, and one for Ralph Neville. The fringe of the king's hood is lined with large pearls.' See TNA E101/386/18 m.59.

33. TNA E101/386/18 m.59.

34. TNA E101/387/14 m.70. This includes a payment for 'a palfrey saddle given to the earl of Chester' at some point between 20 March and 20 August 1334. The prince would have been four years and two months old on the latter date. The reference to his armour is from Barber, 'Edward of Woodstock', *ODNB*.

35. TNA E101/386/15 m.1. Payments included saltpetre and sulphur.

36. *E3&Chiv*, p. 172.

37. *E3&S*, p. 170.

38. Indirect taxation was brought to bear upon dioceses which had recently lost their bishops. See Bryant, 'Financial Dealings of Edward III', pp. 761–3.

39. The subsidy allowed by parliament was assessed in a new way, with the emphasis on the sum required from a community, not individuals' ability to pay. See Willard, 'Taxes upon moveables', pp. 69–74.

40. TNA E101/387/15 m.23; *E3&S*, pp. 175, 178.
41. *E3&S*, p. 176.
42. *E3&S*, p. 177.
43. Stubbs (ed.), *Chronicles*, ii, p. 120.
44. Wages were reduced when an army crossed the border, on the basis that the men were free to steal when on enemy territory.
45. *E3&S*, p. 193.
46. Waugh, *England in the Reign of Edward III*, p. 80.
47. *E3&S*, p. 198.
48. It had previously been ordered to assemble on 11 June. See *E3&S*, p. 198.
49. *E3&S*, p. 200.
50. *CChR*, iv, p. 348.
51. Maxwell (ed.), *Lanercost*, p. 291; *E3&S*, p. 205. Given the low levels of compensation paid – £10 and £20 – it is unlikely that the damages amounted to the destruction of either monastic house, as Nicholson suggests. See also Barnes, *Edward III*, p. 96.
52. Maxwell (ed.), *Lanercost*, p. 291.
53. Sumption, *Trial by Battle*, p. 145.
54. Maxwell (ed.), *Lanercost*, p. 293.
55. *E3&S*, p. 217, n.5.
56. *E3&S*, p. 224.
57. *E3&S*, p. 226.
58. Brie (ed.), *Brut*, ii, pp. 291–2.
59. 15 March 1336, at Westminster, the king dined with the papal nuncios and the envoys of the king of France, the archbishop of Canterbury, the bishop of Lincoln, the earls of Warwick and Buchan and other magnates of England. See TNA E101/387/19.
60. TNA E101/387/19 m.3.
61. *CPR 1334–38*, pp. 246, 252.
62. *CPR 1334–38*, p. 247; *Foedera*, ii, 2, p. 937.
63. TNA E101/386/9. This states that 'Cardinal' and his companion received a robe each on 23 February. Protection was granted for Bury on 26 February (*CPR 1330–34*, pp. 408–9). The secret nature of Bury's business is stated in TNA E101/386/11 m.2: 'for secret negotiations touching the the king and his kingdom'.
64. See Appendix Three.
65. On 14 July 1341 Niccolinus Fieschi was commissioned by Edward to treat with Philip de Valois (*Foedera*, ii, 2, p. 1168). Six days later he was summoned to the king in Flanders for the making of a treaty at Antoing (*CCR 1341–43*, p. 268; *Foedera*, ii, 2, p. 1169). See also the safe-conduct for Niccolinus Fieschi going to the pope as an envoy from the king to treat of peace with France, 1 September 1344 (*CPR 1343–45*, p. 341).
66. That Luca and his family were kinsmen of Edward I, II and III is stated several times in the English records, but precisely how they were related is unclear. See Appendix Three, n.11, for contemporary references to consanguinity and suggestions regarding a blood connection.
67. Royal Commission on Historical Monuments, *An Inventory of the Historical Monuments in the City of Cambridge* (1959), ii, pp. 209–10.
68. Welander *Gloucester Cathedral*, notes five visits before 1330 and then one in 1334 and none until a flying visit in 1349. I cannot find the source of his reference to a visit

in 1334. No letters patent or closed were issued from Gloucester in the period from July 1330–September 1337. To his list I can add the 1337 visit (TNA E101/388/5 m.4); 1342 (CCR 1341–43, p. 578); 1343, (Thompson (ed.), *Murimuth*, p. 135; TNA E36/204 f.75v); and 1353 (TNA E101/392/12 f.18v)).

69. Welander, *Gloucester Cathedral*, pp. 155, 160. Abbot Wygmore died 28 January 1337, having been abbot for seven years.

70. In 1337 the choir of the church around the tomb of the supposed Edward II was begun to be rebuilt. It was reconstructed in the new London style of architecture (later known as Perpendicular), previously employed only at two royal chapels, both of which had been overseen by the Surveyor of the King's Works, William Ramsey, Edward's chief mason. Ramsey only oversaw £4 of building work at St Stephen's, Westminster, in 1337, and in 1338 there seems to have been no work carried out. Not until 1340 did serious works resume there. It is therefore probable that in 1337–39 he concentrated on the work at Gloucester, directing works carried out at the expense of the Gloucester monks. See *HKW*, i, pp. 177, 182, 207–8, 279, 515–17. If he oversaw the placing of the body of Edward II into the tomb it would not be surprising, as many years after his death, it was his daughter who placed Edward II's heart in Isabella's tomb.

71. TNA E101/387/19 mm.4–6.

72. Sumption claims John of Eltham presided; the wardrobe account of Ferriby suggests it was the queen. See Sumption, *Trial by Battle*, p. 162; TNA E101/387/19 m.6.

73. Barnes, *Edward the Third*, p. 103.

74. Bothwell, 'Edward III, the English Peerage and the 1337 Earls', pp. 36–7.

75. See the entries for John in *DNB* and *CP* (under 'Cornwall'). The last wedding had been agreed on, and papal approval had been obtained.

76. Ormrod, 'Personal Religion', p. 855.

77. TNA E101/388/5 m.14 for the bad dream about John.

78. Balfour-Melville in his *Edward III and David II* (p. 11) states that Edward had already left Perth. This might be true: his wardrobe accounts suggest as much (TNA E101/387/19 mm.8–9). But Edward was not with his wardrode. He stayed at Perth. See note 82 below.

79. 'Morrust de bele mort' in Maxwell (ed.), *Scalachronica*, p. 101.

80. For example, a Leicester writer states he was ill; a canon of St Paul's emphasises that his death was not due to war. See respectively Lumby (ed.) *Knighton*, i, p. 477; Thompson (ed.), *Murimuth*, p. 78. Also see James, 'John of Eltham', esp. pp. 67, 73–4.

81. Barnes, *Edward III*, p. 107.

82. Although his wardrobe was at Berwick on 13 September, Edward himself seems to have remained at Perth until the 16th. See TNA E101/387/19 mm.8–9; *CCR 1333–37*, p. 703. *CPR 1334–38*, p. 362. See also James, 'John of Eltham', p. 76, showing that a letter from Edward was written at Perth on 7 September, after the household had left the town (it left on the 3rd, and was at Kinkell Bridge on the 4th, contrary to James's assertion). This is supported by the Close Roll entries for 7–8 September (*CCR 1333–37*, p. 701). See also James, 'John of Eltham', p. 77, quoting an entry in Edward's name entered on the *Rotuli Scotiae* for his presence at Perth on the 13th. Contrary to James's assertion that 'there is no doubt that

Edward was at Berwick on 12 September' the Close Rolls specify that a writ issued at Perth on 12 September was 'by the king' (*CCR 1333–37*, p. 705). Although James's suggestion on p. 77 – that the chancery was split up in transit at this time – is probably correct, it is unlikely that the part which issued the letter 'by the king' was not the one with him at the time.

83. Edward's route probably followed that of his wardrobe, from Perth to Kinkell Bridge, then Cambuskenneth, Stirling, Berwick, Belford, Newcastle, Bishop Auckland, Darlington, Knaresborough, Blyth and finally Nottingham. If he reached Nottingham on 22 September (see next note), and presuming the reference to his presence at Perth on 16 September relates to a morning activity, this equates to about 380 miles or more in a maximum of seven days, which is very fast progress indeed. An alternative explanation is that Edward moved with his wardrobe, and the references to his letters of 4–16 September at Perth relate to clerks' carrying out his business in response to his verbal instructions after he had actually left the town. The only evidence that this was the case, however, is the large amount spent on household expenses at Newcastle on 14 September, the Feast of the Exaltation of the Cross, and this by itself seems inconclusive. If Philippa had been there, for example, she might have hosted a major feast in Edward's absence.

84. TNA E101/387/19 m.9 states that 22 September was the first day of the council at Nottingham (*HBC* has 23rd). The chancery (part of it at least) would appear also to have made it to Nottingham by then, as shown by a charter (10 Edward III, no. 15) dated then, and *CPR 1334–38*, p. 363; *CCR*, p. 706. Sumption dates Edward's arrival to 24 September (Sumption, *Trial by Battle*, p. 165).

85. Sumption, *Trial by Battle*, p. 169.

86. The king's progress south meant that his wardrobe reached the capital on 8 January; a local chronicler states the body entered the capital on 10 January. See TNA E101/387/19 m.13; Stubbs (ed.), *Chronicles*, i. p. 365.

87. The date of the Gloucester tomb has usually been assumed as early to mid-1330s. This is based largely on the assumption that Edward II died in 1327. Such a date is possibly correct nonetheless, as Edward III certainly wanted the public to believe that his father was buried there, and an ostentatious tomb, with regular masses in its vicinity to the man's memory, was a good way to persuade people. The use of the French royal arms as a border to the English leopards on John of Eltham's tomb suggests the tomb was crafted before 1340, when Edward quartered his mother's arms with his own, giving prominence to France. If one craftsman made both exceptional and pioneering alabaster effigies, as is probable, it is unlikely that the Gloucester one was made as much as ten years before the Westminster one. Similarly, both canopies to the two tombs have been attributed to William Ramsey, who also provided the alabaster effigy of Edward's daughter Blanche in 1343. One is inclined to believe that Ramsey was responsible in whole or in part for all the royal tombs at this time, and his appointment as Surveyor of the King's Works in 1336 is a crucial date. No records survive to allow certainty, but at present a date of 1336–39 for the completion of both Edward II's and John of Eltham's tomb monuments seems probable.

88. TNA E101/387/19 m.13.

89. Barnes, *Edward III*, p. 108.

6: The Vow of the Heron

1. This is a greatly shortened account of the Vow of the Heron. A full version appears in an English translation, with notes, in James and Simons, *Laurence Minot*, pp. 69–83. This was the edition I used in writing this book. A more recent edition, with an introduction which redates the poem to about 1346, is J.L. Grigsby and N.J. Lacy, *The Vows of the Heron (Les Voeux de héron): a Middle French Vowing Poem* (New York, 1992).

2. The description of Edward's claim on France being 'absurd' is taken from the *Encyclopaedia Britannica* (14th ed., 1939), vol. 11, p. 888.

3. For the linkage between Edward's claim on the throne of France and his rights in Aquitaine see Craig Taylor, 'Edward III and the Plantagenet Claim to the French Throne', pp. 155–69; Templeman, 'Edward III and the beginnings of the Hundred Years War', pp. 71–3.

4. *CEPR*, ii, p. 561.

5. See Perroy, *Hundred Years War*, p. 91. The invasion threat of September 1336 is when Perroy suggests Edward decided war was inevitable.

6. Taylor, 'Edward III and the Plantagenet Claim to the French Throne', p. 157.

7. See Bothwell, 'Edward III and the "New Nobility"', which questions whether this should be seen as a new nobility, as Edward failed permanently to ennoble more than a handful of his followers. This argument presupposes a definition of nobility itself which did not change; it seems that Edward pushed men into quasi-noble positions, and elevated men to less permanent positions of nobility, somewhat akin to his avoidance of employing feudal armies in favour of paid trained men and mercenaries. Indeed, the two might be regarded as similar means of military resourcing.

8. The skilled labourer here is a thatcher. The daily rate for a master thatcher at this time – 3d – has been taken from Dyer, *Standards of Living*, p. 215. Presuming 250 working days per year, this equates to an annual income of about £3 2s 6d. Comparisons with other artisans are available in this same work.

9. TNA E101/388/2 m.2.

10. See Sumption, *Trial by Battle*, pp. 185–95 for a full description of the background to this. In fact Edward gave d'Artois a pension of £800 per annum (on 3 May) and the rights to dwell in three royal castles (23 April); it is therefore very unlikely that he ever seriously contemplated surrendering him; and thus Sumption is very probably correct in saying these were 'final' demands. Everything points to these being diplomatic niceties continued for the sake of form.

11. Montagu's doubts are expressed in Maxwell (ed.), *Scalachronica*, p. 104.

12. Maxwell (ed.), *Lanercost*, p. 303.

13. Fryde, 'Parliament and the French War 1336–40', p. 245.

14. See Sumption, *Trial by Battle*, pp. 212–13 for a neat description of this economic strategy proposed by William de la Pole and Reginald Conduit.

15. *Foedera*, ii, 2, p. 976.

16. Sumption, *Trial by Battle*, pp. 207–10.

17. *RE3*, p. 193; Fryde, 'Parliament and the French war 1336–40', p. 252; Thompson (ed.), *Murimuth*, p. 80. Sumption, *Trial by Battle*, p. 211, refers to a council between

18 and 26 August. It was on 21 August that Edward appointed the archbishop of
Canterbury and the earl of Northampton to explain to the people of Kent about
the decision of the council at Westminster, but that was probably the July council
(*Foedera*, ii, 2, p. 990). Sumption's referenced sources (*Foedera* and *Scalachronica*) do
not mention the dates of the council. *HBC* (2nd ed., p. 520) mentions the councils noted in the text for May, July and 26 September, summoned on 18 August.
18. Templeman, 'Edward III and the beginnings of the Hundred Years War', p. 77.
The example of the archbishop of Canterbury and the earl of Northampton
speaking to the people of Kent comes from *Foedera*, ii, 2, p. 990.
19. Each year would have amounted to some £38,000, thus three years amounted to
about a third of his total borrowing. See Fryde, 'Parliament and the French War
1336–40', p. 248.
20. *Foedera*, ii, 2, p. 1001. The matter of precedence is discussed in Ormrod, 'Problem
of Precedence', pp. 133–53.
21. *CEPR*, ii, p. 565.
22. *CEPR*, ii, p. 566.
23. Thompson (ed.), *Murimuth*, pp. 80–1.
24. See Sumption, *Trial by Battle*, pp. 218–20 for some excellently written passages on
Burghersh. Sumption is wrong in one respect, however. On p. 217 he states that
Edward declined to give the cardinals safe passage until November: letters of safe
conduct were sent on 13 October. See *Foedera*, ii, 2, p. 1002. See also Fryde, 'Dismissal
of Robert de Wodehouse'.
25. Hunt, 'Dealings of the Bardi and the Peruzzi', p. 155. In 1339 his debts were put
at £300,000 (Fryde, 'Dismissal of Robert de Wodehouse', p. 75), but this does not
take into consideration the repayments which must have been made before then,
as implied by Hunt. Stratford, in arriving at the figure of three hundred thousand, was probably presenting the worst case scenario he could justify documen-
tarily in 1339. In late 1337 his borrowing was probably no more than a third of
this total.
26. TNA E101/388/8 m.4.
27. TNA E101/388/8 mm.4, 6. These included 'fifty-six surcoats of red stiffened
cindon decorated with oak leaves lined with white cameline cloth . . . thirty-seven
hoods of blue cloth . . . and a further sixty surcoats of red cloth lined with white
cloth and blue hoods' for the knights taking part.
28. TNA E101/388/8 m.6.
29. At these games, Edward, William Montagu and the earl of Derby were resplendent in tunics of white cloth, trimmed with fur and green cloth, 'decorated with
the image of a castle made of silk and trimmed with gold, displaying towers, halls,
chambers, walls and other such things, and within the walls divers trees of gold,
and on the breast of each tunic an embroidered figure in gold standing under a
canopy on the battlements; the hems of these tunics being designed in such a way
as to resemble the moats and ditches of this castle surrounded by a green field'.
30. Fryde, 'Parliament and the French War 1336–40', p. 246.
31. Harris, 'War and the emergence of the English Parliament'; Richardson and Sayles,
The English Parliament in the Middle Ages, chapter xxi, parts i and ii.
32. Fryde, 'Parliament and the French War 1336–40', pp. 244, 249–50.
33. Specific instructions to pillage were included in the ordinances for the Norman-

French invasion of March 1338. See Thompson (ed.), *Murimuth*, pp. 257–63.

34. This is based on Sumption, *Trial by Battle*, p. 232, and p. 606, n.92. But note that Sumption dates the letter being carried to France to May 1338, and then on p. 295 dates it to November 1337, a much more likely date, a month after it was written. Also note that Edward again made provision for an embassy on 21 June 1338 to treat with 'our cousin of France', which also carried letters addressed to 'King Philip' as a diplomatic stand-by. See *Foedera*, ii, 2, p. 1043.

35. For William of Pagula and purveyance see Given-Wilson, *Royal Household*, p. 44; Nederman (ed.), *Political Thought*, pp. 63–139. Purveyance is a central theme to his work; the old woman's hen quotation in Given-Wilson repeated here appears on p. 86 of this edition.

36. *Foedera*, ii, 2, p. 1027

37. *Foedera*, ii, 2, pp. 1024–5. On 16 March he was at the Tower; on the 23rd at Newcastle, on the 28th at Berwick, and back at Langley on the 6th. According to an *inspeximus* of a charter, he was back at Langley by the 5th.

38. TNA E101/388/5 m.15.

39. Maxwell (ed.), *Lanercost*, p. 314.

40. Lyon *et al.* (eds), *Wardrobe Book of William Norwell*, L. The editors are rather slipshod in supposing that Edward, duke of Cornwall disembarked with them. The heir to the throne remained in England as regent, appointed on 11 July. See *Foedera*, ii, 2, p. 1042. The reference to John Chaucer comes from *DNB*, presumably using *Foedera*, ii, 2, p. 1042. Sumption states that Philippa only followed at a later date; it is not clear what his source is for this. The Norwell accounts include a payment for maintenance of her household from 22 July, without specifying that she was then in England. See Lyon *et al.* (eds), *Wardrobe Book of William Norwell*, p. 226. The wardrobe account TNA E101/388/13 m.2 mentions her being transported from Westminster by boat on 19 October, but the same account notes Edward being transported by boat from Westminster at the same time, and it is exceptionally unlikely that he returned to England at this juncture. The date may relate instead to the date of satisfaction of the debt.

41. TNA E101/388/9 f.23v. The basins given to Isabella were given at Bury St Edmunds on 11 July; those to Joan were given on 30 June at Walton.

42. Wyon and Wyon, *The Great Seals of England*, pp. 30–1; *Foedera*, ii, 2, p. 1050.

43. TNA E101/388/8 m.4. See *E3&Chiv*, p. 79 for other references to streamers and ships. It is likely that streamers bearing St George's arms were also used, made not for this but for a previous occasion.

44. *Foedera*, ii, 2, p. 1053.

45. Lyon *et al.* (eds), *Wardrobe Book of William Norwell*, LXXIX. On the strength of the persuasive arguments advanced by Edwin Hunt regarding the business of the Bardi and the Peruzzi, it seems very unlikely indeed that such high levels of lending as £70,000 were obtained in this period as a single outstanding balance of debt from the Italian banking companies. Norwell's account book states less than £8,700 came from them at this point; and the level of borrowing by Edward over the period 1336–39 is perhaps best viewed as sustained by constant, if erratic and irregularly documented, repayments, including the donation of wool to their southern Mediterranean monopoly. See Hunt, 'Dealings of the Bardi and the Peruzzi', and its later summing

up in his book, *Medieval Super-Companies*, which deals with the Peruzzi.

46. Lyon *et al.* (eds) *Wardrobe Book of William Norwell*, p. 212.
47. Lyon *et al.* (eds) *Wardrobe Book of William Norwell*, p. 206. It appears as £65 10s in Ormrod, 'Personal Religion', p. 860. It could be that Ormrod has silently corrected Lyon *et al.*; I have not checked the original.
48. The interpretation of events in this and the following passages is drawn from Sumption, *Trial by Battle*, pp. 241–3.
49. Thompson (ed.), *Murimuth*, pp. 84–5, n.10.
50. TNA E101/388/8 m.1.
51. Johnes (ed.), *Froissart*, i, p. 47.
52. *Foedera*, ii, 2, p. 1058.
53. Dino Forzetti or Forcetti was the English agent of the Bardi in the 1320s and the 1330s; Francesco Forcetti was the Sicilian agent of the Peruzzi from 1299 to 1341.
54. Lyon *et al.* (eds), *Wardrobe Book of William Norwell*, p. 212.
55. *Foedera*, ii, 2, p. 1067.
56. *CPR 1340–43*, p. 45. This, like all but two of the later references to Forzetti concerned shipping wool to the Bardi and Peruzzi. The two exceptions are for a cargo on board a Barcelona ship, which Forzetti was ordered to take intact to Bristol, with its crew, in December 1342 (*CPR 1340–43*, p. 569) and for him to guard a manor of Tedisio Benedicti de Falcinello, one of Philippa's esquires and a papal sergeant-at-arms, in November, 1344 (*CPR 1343–45*, p. 565).
57. Sumption, *Trial by Battle*, p. 240.
58. Barnes, *Edward the Third*, p. 136.
59. *CEPR*, ii, p. 569.
60. *CEPR*, ii, p. 570.
61. Fryde, 'Dismissal of Robert de Wodehouse'.
62. *Foedera*, ii, 2, p. 1065.
63. Fryde, *Parliament and the French War 1336–40*, pp. 2153–4
64. Bothwell, 'Edward III and the "New Nobility"', p. 1127.
65. *CEPR*, ii, pp. 574–5.
66. The letter appears in Thompson (ed.), *Murimuth*, pp. 91–100; Riley (ed.), *Walsingham*, i, pp. 201–8. A translation is in Barnes. *Edward the Third*, pp. 126–30.
67. Taylor, 'Edward III and the Plantagenet Claim to the French Throne', p. 156.
68. Riley (ed.), *Walsingham*, i, pp. 206–7; Barnes, *Edward the Third*, p. 129.
69. McKisack, *Fourteenth Century*, p. 149. Perroy does much the same thing in his *Hundred Years War*, p. 106.
70. The letter from Benedict which appears in Riley (ed.), *Walsingham*, i, pp. 208–13 is wrongly placed by Walsingham, correctly being 1 November 1338. The mistake has been followed by Barnes in his *Edward the Third*, pp. 130–3.
71. *EHD 1327–1485*, p. 65; Thompson (ed.), *Galfridi le Baker*, p. 64. Sumption dates this event to 10 October. See Sumption, *Trial by Battle*, p. 284.
72. Johnes (ed.), *Froissart*, i, p. 54.
73. Fryde, 'Parliament and the French War 1336–40', p. 257.
74. Fryde, 'Parliament and the French War 1336–40', p. 259. Although Fryde states that there was no exaggeration in the amount of three hundred thousand pounds, it is likely – given more recent findings – that the amounts owed to the Italian bankers at least had been reduced by repayments which have not been recorded

as systematically as the debts. The same points raised by Edwin Hunt regarding the Peruzzi should also be considered with regard to William de la Pole. See Hunt, 'Dealings of the Bardi and the Peruzzi'.

75. See Appendix Three. If Edward II was being held by the Fieschi on papal instructions, then this might explain the reluctance to claim the throne of France between October 1337 and January 1340, despite the frequent assertion that Philip had intruded illegally.

76. *WCS*, p. 1.

77. Obviously neither Magna Carta (1215) nor the first invitation to the commons to send representatives to a parliament (1264) was a royal initiative (both were baronial). The Norman Conquest was, of course, the initiative of William as duke of Normandy, not as a king of England.

7: Sluys and Tournai

1. Maxwell (ed.), *Lanercost*, p. 248.
2. Thompson (ed.), *Galfridi le Baker*, p. 66.
3. *CEPR*, ii, p. 579.
4. This was stretching the facts, as Charles of Navarre, to whom the pope had been referring, had not been born in 1328, when Edward claimed he should have inherited from his uncle, King Charles.
5. *Foedera*, ii, 2, pp. 1107–8, 1126.
6. Bond (ed.), *Melsa*, ii, p. 386; Barnes, *Edward the Third*, pp. 157–8.
7. Ormrod, 'Problem of Precedence', p. 147.
8. *RE3*, pp. 20, 22, 83 etc; Waugh, *England in the Reign of Edward III*, p. 215. Natalie Fryde suggests that this was another tenth merely called the 'Ninth' as it required the ninth sheep of every ten to be given to the Crown as opposed to the 'Tenth' or tithe, which was given to the clergy. See Fryde, 'Edward III's Removal of his Ministers', p. 152.
9. Originally sheriffs had been Exchequer appointees. On Edward's departure from England in 1338 he had ordered in the Walton Ordinances that each county's sheriff should be elected by the coroner and four knights of the shire. This was now done away with, and the right of appointment was once more given back to the Exchequer. See Jewell, *English Local Administration in the Middle Ages*, p. 193.
10. This was the old law dating back to the Conquest which stated that if a man was found slain, he was presumed to be Norman unless proved to be English. If it could not be proved that he was English, those living in the hundred in which he was found were fined.
11. *RE3*, p. 51.
12. *EHD 1327–1485*, p. 70.
13. Sumption, *Trial by Battle*, p. 312.
14. Sumption, *Trial by Battle*, pp. 312–17.
15. *Foedera*, ii, 2, p. 1120.
16. *Calender of State Papers and Manuscripts Relating to English Affairs Existing in the Archives and Collections of Venice and Other Libraries of Northern Italy 1202–1509* (1864), i, pp. 8–9.
17. Thompson (ed.), *Murimuth*, p. 311.

18. Sumption, *Trial by Battle*, p. 323. Differing figures with a full discussion appear in *WCS*, pp. 192–3. Rogers agrees that there were many fewer ships in the English navy, either 120 or 147. Records suggest about 3,700 men-at-arms, knights and infantry and just under 8,000 archers, plus sailors.

19. Barnes, *Edward the Third*, p. 182.

20. Thompson (ed.), *Murimuth*, p. 106. Nicolas in his *Royal Navy* states that he waited for the tide, and that no writer mentions the wind, apparently not noticing Murimuth's words on the subject.

21. Small boats full of stones had been hoisted up the masts for the purpose of preventing the English boarding the larger vessels. See Nicolas, *Royal Navy*, ii, p. 52.

22. Sumption, *Trial by Battle*, p. 327; Nicolas, *Royal Navy*, ii, p. 57.

23. Sumption, *Trial by Battle*, p. 327 has 190 ships; Rogers corrects this misreading in *WCS*, p. 193.

24. Nicolas, *Royal Navy*, ii, pp. 39, 60.

25. De Vries, 'Siege of Tournai', p. 70.

26. Thompson (ed.), *Murimuth*, p. 313.

27. Goodman, *John of Gaunt*, pp. 28–9. It is thought that John was named after his godfather, John of Brabant.

28. Ormrod, 'Personal Religion', p. 861. Nicolas, *Royal Navy*, ii, p. 60, quoting Froissart.

29. De Vries, 'Siege of Tournai', p. 72.

30. Hunt, *Medieval Super-Companies*, pp. 208–9.

31. De Vries, 'Siege of Tournai', p. 72, states that Edward cut off the water supplies. This is presumably on the evidence of chronicles which state that he damned the river (see ibid, pp. 87–8). However, damming the Scheldt would have been a difficult task. Also it would not have affected the water table height, and a city like Tournai would have had many wells. It seems more reasonable to agree with Sumption on this point; Edward created bridges over the running river, not dams. See Sumption, *Trial by Battle*, pp. 349–54.

32. Barnes, *Edward the Third*, p. 188.

33. Sumption, *Trial by Battle*, p. 352; de Vries, 'Siege of Tournai', p. 73.

34. Sumption, *Trial by Battle*, pp. 355–7; de Vries, 'Siege of Tournai', pp. 73–4.

35. *CEPR*, pp. 581–2.

36. De Vries, 'Siege of Tournai', p. 75, quoting Alfred Burne and May McKisack. See also ibid, p. 77.

37. *E3&Chiv*, p. 66.

38. See de Vries, 'Siege of Tournai', pp. 73–4. Although E.B. Fryde is quoted as saying that the failure of the siege of Tournai cannot be blamed entirely on money, which is true, the alternative perspective is not considered: what if the siege had been successful? Since this consideration would also have affected Edward's judgement in calling off the siege, the money problem needs to be seen as the real battle, not the siege itself.

8: Chivalry and Shame

1. *CEPR*, ii, pp. 583–4.

2. Taylor, in his 'Edward III and the Plantagenet Claim to the French Throne', p. 164,

thinks that the November 1340 document simply served as a 'positioning paper' to set before the pope and cardinals, with the more detailed dossier to follow in 1344. Even so, the synopsis of the argument put forward at this time is hardly lightweight. See *CEPR*, ii, pp. 584–8. To these three negotiators the pope added the now-freed Niccolinus Fieschi, on Edward's behalf, his argument apparently being distinct from that of the other three.

3. *CEPR*, ii, p. 585.

4. The date of birth is recorded in Riley (ed.), *Walsingham*, i, p. 253. The *terminus ante quem* for the churching appears to be before 8 July, according to Ormrod, 'Royal Nursery', n.34, so certainly the birth cannot have been any later than 5 June. Ormrod suggests the birth might actually have been earlier than 5 June, not later, thus increasing the likelihood of Edmund being illegitimate.

5. *Foedera*, ii, 2, p. 1135.

6. Sumption, *Trial by Battle*, p. 360.

7. Michael K. Jones, *Bosworth 1485: Psychology of a Battle* (2002). For the continued debate see Michael K. Jones, 'The Debate: was Edward IV illegitimate?' in *Ricardian Bulletin* (Summer 2004), pp. 18–24, including the response by Joanna Laynesmith.

8. Edward was at Langley from 30 January to 7 February, on 12 and 15 February, 5–19 March, 2–20 April and 5–10 June, and from 20 June–6 July (information supplied by Professor Ormrod from his unpublished notes on the itinerary of Edward III). Subsequently Edward remained at London or Westminster. Philippa was said by the old *DNB* to have returned with Edward in November 1340, but this seems unlikely in view of Murimuth's detailed list of the men who fled from Ghent with the king and the manner of their escape: high-speed flight on horseback would not have been appropriate for a pregnant and possibly sick queen with none of her ladies. She may have stayed in London with Edward prior to moving to Langley.

9. *CCR 1341–43*, pp. 59–60 (11 April); p. 180 (15 April). The full rate was forty shillings. Edward had not long before given permission for one of the cardinals to export sixty sacks of wool every year, entirely free of duty; and in 1342 he gave permission for Robert d'Artois to export wool at the old rate of 6s 8d per sack. See *Foedera*, ii, 2, pp. 1141, 1215.

10. TNA E101/390/2. The earls of Salisbury and Surrey joined him in the lists. A total of thirteen shields made for the king and covered in gold and silver leaf, decorated in the arms of each of the two earls, suggest a small but intimate party. Interestingly, the godfathers chosen for the baby were the abbot of St Albans (who baptised him) and the old earl of Surrey and his nephew, the earl of Arundel: the same two men who had persuaded Edward to relent and hear the archbishop's case in parliament the previous month. See *CP*, xii, pp. 895–6.

11. TNA E101/388/11; E101/389/8 m.19.

12. Ormrod 'Royal Nursery'; *CP*, xii (2), pp. 895–6.

13. Thomas of Woodstock was also not created an earl until his early twenties, but Thomas was very much younger, nearly fourteen years younger, than Edmund, and to make him an earl in infancy would have drawn attention to Edmund's comparatively low status.

14. Thompson (ed.), *Chronicon Angliae*, pp. 107, 398; Taylor, Childs and Watkiss (eds),

St Albans Chronicle, p. 61. In Walsingham's (St Albans) account Philippa gave birth to a girl, not a son, and so swapped the children. A more credible reason is given by the author of the *Anonimalle Chronicle*, who explains that a nurse accidentally suffocated the baby – presumably laying on it in bed – and swapped it for John. See Galbraith (ed.), *Anonimalle*, pp. 104–5.

15. It is very unlikely that it was the subject about which the archbishop of Canterbury spoke to Edward and Philippa 'apart' (unless he spoke through messengers) because Philippa had not returned to England since giving birth to John. In addition, Philippa had not felt the need to conceal her daughter Isabella of Woodstock. Also, Wykeham never claimed this himself in any extant source; chroniclers claimed it on his behalf, possibly as a result of rumours. Lastly, but importantly, this story was not original. In 1318 John of Powderham had claimed that he was the genuine heir of Edward I, having been 'taken from the cradle', and that Edward II was an impostor, the child of a carter 'subtly brought into the Queen'. For this see Denholm-Young (ed.), *Vita Edwardi Secundi*, p. 86; Stubbs (ed.), *Chronicles of the Reigns of Edward I and Edward II*, i, pp. 282–3; Hingeston (ed.), *Capgrave*, pp. 185–6; Bond (ed.), *Melsa*, ii, pp. 335–6.

16. Thompson (ed.), *Murimuth*, pp. 116–17.

17. Maxwell (ed.), *Scalachronica*, p. 112.

18. See for example Fryde, 'Edward III's Removal of his Ministers'; Lapsley, 'Archbishop Stratford and the Parliamentary Crisis of 1341'; Jones, 'Rex et Ministri: English Local Government and the Crisis of 1341'.

19. *RE3*, p. 83.

20. *RE3*, p. 83.

21. *EHD 1327–1485*, p. 72.

22. Lapsley, 'Archbishop Stratford and the Parliamentary Crisis', p. 15. For Edward's taxation being the worst in medieval Europe, see *WCS*, p. 21.

23. Lapsley, 'Archbishop Stratford and the Parliamentary Crisis', p. 194. For the parliament to be properly so, the king or his designated representative had to be present.

24. How far he was received into favour is debatable. Ormrod in *RE3* (p. 84) claims that the power of the Stratford family was permanently eclipsed by this episode. But Murimuth relates several occasions when Edward specifically sought advice from Stratford after this. See Thompson (ed.), *Murimuth*, pp. 157, 159, 160. Also it should be noted that in 1350, when Edward was asked to put forward two candidates to become English cardinals (a very rare distinction), one of the two men Edward proposed was Ralph Stratford, bishop of London (Thompson (ed.), *Galfridi le Baker*, p. 112).

25. *RE3*, pp. 25, 52.

26. *Foedera* ii, 2, pp. 1168, 1169.

27. Sumption, *Trial by Battle*, pp. 383, 385.

28. Hardy, *Syllabus of Rymer's Foedera*, i, p. 324. Fowler, *King's Lieutenant*, p. 37, states 7 October.

29. *Foedera*, ii, 2, p. 1181; Fowler, *King's Lieutenant*, p. 37.

30. Maxwell (ed.), *Scalachronica*, p. 112.

31. See Maxwell (ed.), *Scalachronica*, p. 112; Thompson (ed.), *Murimuth*, p. 123; *E3&Chiv*, p. 66.

32. Lumby (ed.), *Knighton*, ii, p. 23.

33. TNA E36/204/f.20v.
34. The best discussion of the event is Gransden, 'Alleged Rape'. The details of le Bel and Froissart are given considerable attention by Packe, *Edward III*, pp. 103–23.
35. Packe, *Edward III*, p. 120.
36. Gransden, 'Alleged Rape', p. 334.
37. Gransden, 'Alleged Rape', p. 335.
38. TNA E36/204 f.20v.
39. *E3&Chiv*, p. 173.
40. TNA E34/204 f.28v.
41. Edward made an arrangement on 22 October 1341 to pay Edward Montagu wages of war. This might mean he had received word from him at Wark, or he might have been with him in England. See *CPR 134–44*, p. 269.
42. Packe, *Edward III*, p. 117.
43. Packe, *Edward III*, p. 122. Despite Packe's theory, the circumstances of the death of Alice, wife of Edward Montagu, do not constitute evidence that she was the rape victim. Any number of other reasons could have arisen for her husband to have killed her, and the death was many years after the supposed rape. Also it would have been difficult to hold a man guilty in law for murdering his wife when she was his chattel, even if she was the king's cousin german. This does not mean she was not the woman of the narrative, but the fact is incidental to the story under consideration.
44. The version in the French chronicles only deals with the rape. See Gransden, 'Alleged Rape', pp. 333–4.
45. The crime is supposed to have been committed between Salisbury's departure overseas and Edward's own sailing. The navy assembled at the port of Sandwich on 29 September, and then waited for favourable winds, skirting around the coast to Portsmouth, from which Edward finally sailed on 23 October (TNA E36/204 ff.32r–33r; Thompson (ed.), *Murimuth*, p. 128). Although Salisbury was preparing to sail on 3 September, he was still in England on 26 September, when he was present at a dinner with the royal family and various other magnates (TNA E136/204 f.31v).
46. *CCR 1341–43*, p. 9.
47. The countess supposedly confessed all to her husband on his return from the Continent. As mentioned above, the earl and king returned together. Soon afterwards Edward wrote to an emissary of the Grand Master of the Knights of St John requesting that a cousin of the earl's be allowed admittance to that order of knights: a small favour to the earl, not a sign of any great upheaval. There is no sign of any settlement of the earl's estates in the period 1342–44. Finally, when Montagu died, it was not fighting the Moors but two weeks after a great tournament held by Edward at Windsor, in which Montagu had taken part (Thompson (ed.), *Murimuth*, p. 232).
48. Gransden, *Historical Writing*, ii, p. 84. This was when he was back in Hainault.
49. In the first twenty years of their marriage, Philippa was pregnant for nine of them. This is remarkable for the period, considering Edward was away from her for much of the time.
50. Gransden, 'Alleged Rape', p. 341.

51. Quoted in Frame, 'Crisis of 1341–1342', p. 91.

52. This passage is largely drawn from Frame, 'Crisis of 1341–1342'; Otway-Ruthven, *History of Medieval Ireland*, pp. 259–60.

53. Thompson (ed.), *Murimuth*, p. 223.

54. Thompson (ed.), *Murimuth*, pp. 123, 124.

55. *E3&Chiv*, p. 140, n. 107, quoting E36/204 f.21v.

56. Edward had held January tournaments in the past, including one large-scale one at Dunstable in 1334, but they were rare. See *E3&Chiv*, pp. 172–3.

57. TNA E101/390/1 m.2: 'cum sermonibus Regis it is as it is'. It is worth noting that Lionel's bed of state did not carry this motto, suggesting the double purpose of the event. Shenton, 'English Court', p. 152 associates all of this account with the marriage of Lionel in London on 15 August 1342. TNA E101/389/14 m.2 does not suggest this. However, if Shenton is right, then the points made here would apply to the marriage/announcement later in the year. It is quite possible, given the way these accounts were written up, that some confusion of items purchased for two distinct events has occurred, or that confusion has arisen from them being reused.

58. TNA E101/389/14 m.2.

59. Among these were 'a long robe with a short, flouncy, buttoned surcoat made in advance from cloth given to the king by the duke of Cornwall', 'three flounced, buttoned tunics of green Brussels cloth for the king and two knights' and 'thirty-two tunics of striped cloth with individual white hoods to be trimmed for the king's squires'. See TNA E101/389/14 m.1.

60. *E3&Chiv*, p. 65.

61. TNA E101/390/1 m.2.

62. The skilled labourer here is a thatcher. The daily rate for a master thatcher at this time – 3d – has been taken from Dyer, *Standards of Living*, p. 215. Presuming 250 working days per year, this equates to an annual income of about £3 2s 6d. Comparisons with other artisans are available in this same work.

63. Thompson (ed.), *Murimuth*, p. 135. See Doherty, *Isabella and the Strange Death*, p. 140 for a description of the unusual lead coffin.

64. The final rewriting of the ordinances for the chantry at Sibthorp to reflect the fact that Edward II was definitely dead was in January–February 1343. The rewriting to reflect an ambiguity – that he may have been alive – was written in 1335. See Appendix Three.

65. Niccolinus probably returned before 3 December when an order to pay him the arrears of his wages was made. See *Foedera*, ii, 2, p. 1183. He was still in London on 22 December 1341 when he dated a receipt for £50 at London (TNA E40/508 i). He remained in London while the knights were all at Dunstable. Another receipt of his is dated 11 February 1342 at London (TNA E40/508 ii).

9: *The Advent of the Golden Age*

1. For the progress of the war in Brittany see Sumption, *Trial by Battle*, pp. 370–410. This part has been drawn from pp. 387–91. See also Perroy, *Hundred Years War*, pp. 114–17.

2. Bradbury, *Medieval Archer*, pp. 93–4. He quotes 130,000 sheaves; I presume these were regular sheaves of two dozen arrows each.

3. Johnes, (ed.), *Froissart*, i, pp. 106–7.

4. Sumption, *Trial by Battle*, p. 400; Thompson (ed.), *Murimuth*, pp. 128–9.

5. Sumption, *Trial by Battle*, p. 405.

6. Sumption, *Trial by Battle*, p. 407.

7. Thompson (ed.), *Murimuth*, p. 135.

8. Maxwell (ed.), *Lanercost*, pp. 324–5. The Lanercost chronicle was at this time being composed in Carlisle by a Franciscan friar. Only later was it edited at Lanercost.

9. TNA E36/204, f.42v.

10. Thompson (ed.), *Murimuth*, p. 135; Ormrod, 'Personal Religion', p. 80.

11. TNA E36/204, f.75v.

12. On this note, it is worth remembering that these saintly figures were the closest not only to Edward but the royal family. Edward I and Edward II had also strongly supported the Virgin and St Thomas of Canterbury. The offerings to them at Canterbury after this storm are in particular reminiscent of Queen Margaret, Edward I's first wife, who believed St Thomas had saved her life during a storm and had named her first-born son Thomas in recognition of the fact in 1300.

13. *RP*, ii, p. 135. This was despite a law of 1313 forbidding the presence of armed men in parliament.

14. For the parliament of 1343 see *RE3*, pp. 25, 60, 61, 102, 120, 155–7, 174.

15. *RE3*, pp. 67, 174.

16. Hunt, 'Dealings of the Bardi and Peruzzi', pp. 155–6. The records are published in Sapori, *I Libri dei Comercio dei Peruzzi*. See also Hunt, *Medieval Super-Companies* (especially chapter eight: 'The Collapse').

17. Hunt, 'Dealings of the Bardi and Peruzzi', p. 150, quoting E.B. Fryde, 'Public Credit, with Special Reference to North Western Europe', in *Cambridge Economic History of Europe* (Cambridge, 1965), iii, p. 460.

18. Hunt, 'Dealings of the Bardi and Peruzzi', pp. 162.

19. Hunt, 'Dealings of the Bardi and Peruzzi', p. 150; Villani, *Nuova Cronica*, book 13, chapter 55. It is of course possible that the Acciaiuoli and other firms suffered due to the defaulting of creditors ruined by the Peruzzi crash, a point which Hunt does not explore; but it would be an assumption simply to presume that this was the reason, especially given the figures which Hunt and Fryde have determined.

20. The notes on coins have been drawn from Seaby's *Standard Catalogue of British Coins* (24th ed., 1989) and *AC*, pp. 490–2.

21. Thompson (ed.), *Murimuth*, pp. 141–2.

22. A.D.M. Barrell, 'The Ordinance of Provisors of 1343', *Historical Research*, 64 (1991), pp. 264–77. In this article the Ordinance is shown to have been supported by direct action to confiscate provisions and prohibit clerics from acting on such provisions. Letters to the sheriffs to carry out its threats are also extant.

23. Mollat, *Popes at Avignon*, p. 263.

24. The great crown was redeemed in 1344. Measures to redeem Queen Philippa's crowns had been taken in September 1342. See *Foedera*, ii, 2, p. 1210.

25. TNA E101/390/2, m.1.

26. Thompson (ed.), *Murimuth*, pp. 146, 230–1; *E3&Chiv*, p. 173.

27. The date here is not straightforward. Thompson (ed.), *Murimuth*, p. 231 states 8 February, a Sunday, which was the usual day for a major tournament to start. However, this same account states that the earl of Salisbury was present, and was wounded, and died eight days later. Salisbury died on or before 31 January, as proved by *CFR 1337–1347*, p. 358, when the escheator was sent to make an inquisition into his lands. The inquisition itself suggests he died the previous day, 30 January. An alternative date (19 January) appears on p. 155, but this was a Monday. However, it might relate to the day that the jousting started, as no fighting at a tournament took place on the first day, a Sunday, only prayers and eating. If the meeting began on Sunday 18 January, and the jousting started on the 19th, then the last day would indeed be eight days before the 30th, when Salisbury died.

28. Thompson (ed.), *Murimuth*, p. 231 quoted in translation in *EHD 1327–1485*, p. 74.

29. *HKW*, ii, p. 870; Thompson (ed.), *Murimuth*, p. 156; Riley (ed.), *Walsingham*, i, p. 263.

30. *E3&Chiv*, p. 173 suggests four years. However, Barber, *Black Prince*, pp. 45–6 states that Edward took part in the Lichfield tournament on 9 April 1346. Unfortunately he does not reference his source for this detail.

31. Mollat, *Popes at Avignon*, p. 263.

32. *CEPR*, iii, p. 7.

33. *RP*, ii, p. 147.

34. *WCS*, p. 221.

35. For example, statutes passed at the 1344 parliament included reforms such as ceasing commissions of enquiry, the appointment of Justices of the Peace, the right to purchase wool, the freedom of the seas, the law of trespass and when soldiers' wages were to be paid. Also there was a Statute of the Clergy, making a distinction between rights for secular and temporal judges, among other things. See Ruffhead (ed.), *Statutes at Large*, i, pp. 240–5.

36. *Foedera*, iii, 1, p. 19.

37. For the strength of the English claim, see Taylor, 'Edward III and the Plantagenet Claim to the French Throne', pp. 161–2, 168.

38. Fowler, *King's Lieutenant*, p. 49.

39. Derby witnessed almost every charter granted from January to June 1345. See TNA C53/131 nos 2, 3, 4 and 8; C53/132 nos 13, 15–21.

40. *CEPR*, iii, pp. 15–16.

41. Johnes (ed.), *Froissart*, i, p. 142.

42. Sumption, *Trial by Battle*, pp. 461–2.

43. Johnes (ed.), *Froissart*, i, p. 145.

44. TNA E101/391/1; Riley (ed.), *Walsingham*, ii, p. 266.

45. Thompson (ed.), *Murimuth*, p. 158.

46. Thompson (ed.), *Murimuth*, p. 173.

47. Thompson (ed.), *Murimuth*, p. 175.

48. James and Simons (eds), *Laurence Minot*, p. 86.

49. Fowler, *King's Lieutenant*, p. 56; Sumption, *Trial by Battle*, p. 465; Johnes (ed.), *Froissart*, i, p. 130.

50. Sumption, *Trial by Battle*, pp. 468–9.

51. Maxwell (ed.), *Lanercost*, p. 325.

52. Matthews, *Royal Apothecaries*, p. 29.

53. Sumption, *Trial by Battle*, p. 486; Johnes (ed.), *Froissart*, i, p. 149.
54. Sumption, *Trial by Battle*, p. 497, who gives this number of ships and suggests 7,000 to 10,000. The matter of the size of the army – and the figure of fifteen thousand men – is discussed in greater depth in *WCS*, pp. 423–6.
55. Thompson (ed.), *Murimuth*, pp. 200–1.
56. A discussion about whether this was the intended destination appears in Appendix Five.

10: Edward the Conqueror

1. *WCS*, p. 229; Sumption, *Trial by Battle*, p. 500; Barber, *Black Prince*, p. 49; Barnes, *Edward III*, p. 342.
2. Sumption, *Trial by Battle*, p. 496.
3. This of course does not include the defeat at Mons in 1304, Mons being then part of Hainault.
4. His daughter Margaret was born at Windsor on 20 July.
5. See also Appendix Five for further discussion on the choice of Normandy as the landing place in 1346.
6. *WCS*, p. 218, quoting Villani, *Cronica*.
7. *WCS*, p. 218, quoting Villani, *Cronica*.
8. *WCS*, p. 241.
9. Sumption, *Trial by Battle*, p. 506.
10. Barber, *Black Prince*, p. 53; *WCS*, p. 245.
11. They came to Caen 'at the hour of nones' according to Avesbury in Thompson (ed.), *Murimuth*, p. 361. Sumption (*Trial by Battle*, p. 508) assumes this is nine o'clock in the morning. However, the medieval clock counts from the first hour, approximately 6 a.m. See *OED* under 'nones'.
12. Thompson (ed.), *Murimuth*, pp. 213–14.
13. The details of the attack on Caen are very muddled, both in original sources and in various writers' interpretations. I have broadly followed Rogers, using Froissart, Avesbury and Murimuth as a supplement. Sumption's account differs from Rogers in several respects.
14. *WCS*, p. 248; Sumption, *Trial by Battle*, p. 510; Johnes (ed.), *Froissart*, i, p. 156.
15. *WCS*, p. 252; Barber, *Black Prince*, p. 55.
16. Sumption, *Trial by Battle*, p. 510.
17. This date is taken from *WCS*, pp. 252–3. Sumption, *Trial by Battle*, p. 513, has the date of 3 August and states that Edward received them at Lisieux. Barber, *Black Prince*, p. 56, also states that Edward received the cardinals at Lisieux; Rogers however points out that Edward had kept them waiting for several days.
18. Both Sumption and Rogers in their considerations of Edward's strategy at this time presume that Edward could have attacked Paris and that it would have been in his interest to do so. Given the points raised in the text here, this seems very unlikely. Paris was a walled city, with an adult male population of at least fifty thousand, and many women would have fought for the city too, dropping heavy objects from upper storeys if nothing else. The city could be divided along the lines of the river, if necessary, and thus leave it as four separate parts (north bank,

south bank, Île de la Cité and Île Saint-Louis). Edward would have been unable to use his archers as an organised force in the narrow streets. With the French army combined, Edward would have lost the advantage of his archers' trapping the enemy in its crossfire, would have faced several thousand Genoese crossbowmen, and the hand-to-hand fighting would have been between about twelve thousand Englishmen and eighty thousand Frenchmen, the Parisians fighting on familiar ground and protecting their homes and families. To my mind Edward would not have put his forces in this situation under any circumstances, and thus would not have attacked Paris except to burn it. Even then the geography of the city astride an island in the river would have prevented much more than the southern third from being burnt. In mid-August 1346, the prospect of engaging Philip's army in battle was considerably more attractive.

19. Johnes (ed.), *Froissart*, i, pp. 149–50.
20. Sumption, *Trial by Battle*, p. 517 estimates eight thousand men-at-arms, six thousand Genoese besides a large number of infantry.
21. Sumption, *Trial by Battle*, p. 514.
22. *WCS*, p. 255.
23. Barber, *Black Prince*, p. 58; Avesbury in Thompson (ed.), *Murimuth*, p. 370; *WCS*, p. 256, where the variations in the numbers of dead are mentioned.
24. James and Simons, *Laurence Minot*, p. 74.
25. *WCS*, p. 260, quoting TNA C66/219 m.21v and *CPR 1345–48*, pp. 516–17. Rogers adds a useful discussion on the variant forms of this letter.
26. *WCS*, p. 262; Sumption, *Trial by Battle*, pp. 521–4.
27. Avesbury, in Thompson (ed.), *Murimuth*, p. 370.
28. Johnes (ed.), *Froissart*, i, p. 162; Thompson (ed.), *Murimuth*, p. 216.
29. The king's household stopped twice at Crécy in May/June 1329 (I am grateful to Dr Paul Dryburgh for this information). Although this does not prove that the king himself passed this way, it makes it very likely. The TS itinerary of Edward III in the Map Room at TNA does not mention Crécy, but if Edward himself did not stay at Crécy or date any documents there, one would not expect it to do so.
30. Northampton is not usually named among those who decided on the battlefield, but given his experience and his pioneering use of the archers' strategy at Morlaix, it is inconceivable that Edward did not consult him on this matter. Sir Richard Stafford was included in Froissart's first redaction as one who chose the battlefield. See *WCS*, p. 264, n. 149.
31. Tout, *Chapters*, iv, pp. 470–1; Tout, 'Firearms', p. 670. The latter mentions that there were about one hundred ribalds, as well as some heavier pieces expressly made for the passage to Normandy in 1345. In his earlier (1905) volume of Longman's *Political History of England*, p. 364, Tout had expressed his belief that there were only three cannon present, a view which his own researches in the administrative records revised. See also Sumption, *Trial by Battle*, p. 528, who follows Tout. Although Tout ('Firearms', p. 671) notes that no payments for shipping them abroad were recorded until after the battle of Crécy, this is consistent with Edward's usual practice of payment in arrears, often long in arrears, and so should not be taken as evidence that these cannon were not the ones at the battle. Burne in his *Crécy War* mentions the cannonballs found later on the battlefield.
32. Thompson (ed.), *Galfridi le Baker*, p. 83.

NOTES

33. That the cannon were fired in conjunction against the Genoese in this first wave of attack is mentioned by Villani. See also Burne, *Crécy War*, pp. 193–203.

34. Froissart expressly states his source was John of Hainault, who was with Philip in the latter stages of the battle, and who was almost certainly with him at this point. Hence this exclamation, which normally would have been suspect, is probably genuine.

35. Barber, *Black Prince*, pp. 68–9, noting that a chaplet of pearls engraved with his motto had been paid for before the Crécy expedition set out. The motto appears in his own hand on a writ and on his tomb in Canterbury Cathedral, and the ostrich feathers appear on his crest, so there is no doubt that he personally adopted them both, the only question is exactly when. Arderne (possibly his own physician) stated he adopted the ostrich feather from the king of Bohemia; although there is no sign that the feather was the king's crest, this does not invalidate the story, as Edward may have picked it up believing it belonged to the late king.

36. *WCS*, p. 270.

37. For a full discussion of the historiographical developments concerning the 1346 campaign, see *WCS*, pp. 217–37, and the same author's Alexander Prize-winning essay 'Edward III and the Dialects of Strategy'.

38. See Burne *Crécy War*, pp. 204–7 for the view that 'the Hundred Years War might have been concluded in a single campaign' if Edward had marched on Paris at this time. Burne, as a soldier himself, did not consider the political consequences of success, only the ways of achieving it.

39. See for example Barber, *Black Prince*, p. 73; Sumption, *Trial by Battle*, p. 537.

40. *WCS*, pp. 273–85.

41. This is shown by a letter dated 4 September 1346. See de Vries, 'Hunger, Flemish Participation and the Flight of Philip VI', p. 146.

42. Some small-scale attacks took place, according to some chroniclers. See de Vries, 'Hunger, Flemish Participation and the Flight of Philip VI', p. 140; Sumption, *Trial by Battle*, p. 558.

43. *WCS*, p. 273, making use of the pay records, and Sumption, *Trial by Battle*, p. 537, using the same sources, state that thirty thousand troops came and went at various times. Ormrod, 'Edward III', *ODNB* states thirty-two thousand were present. Sumption, *Trial by Battle*, p. 578, reasonably suggests that the numbers steadily grew, so that they started at ten to twelve thousand and reached thirty-two thousand by July 1347, when the French were about to attack. Alternatively we may consider that many might have gone home, in which case we should disregard the figure of thirty thousand and expect there to have been between twelve and thirty thousand.

44. De Vries, 'Hunger, Flemish Participation and the Flight of Philip VI', p. 141.

45. Chroniclers vary on whether Edward allowed these men to pass or let them starve in the ditch. Henry Knighton, writing about fifty years later, states that they were forced to starve in the ditch, a view followed by Sumption, *Trial by Battle*, p. 577. Le Bel, writing earlier, is of the contrary view. See de Vries, 'Hunger, Flemish Participation and the Flight of Philip VI', p. 142.

46. *WCS*, pp. 278–9.

47. Thompson (ed.), *Murimuth*, pp. 386–8.

48. Thompson (ed.), *Murimuth*, pp. 391–5.
49. For the debate about the challenge, see Barber, *Black Prince*, p. 77; Sumption, *Trial by Battle*, p. 580; de Vries, 'Hunger, Flemish Participation and the Flight of Philip VI', pp. 149–52; *WCS*, pp. 278–81.
50. Johnes (ed.), *Froissart*, i, p. 186.
51. Froissart only mentions four of the six, and states that de Vienne was not one. A manuscript found in the Vatican Library in 1863 is the source for the other two, according to descriptions of the famous Rodin sculpture, but I am unaware of the precise reference of this. Rodin-centred writing tends to differentiate between Jean de Vienne and Jean de Fiennes, as Rodin made de Fiennes the youngest of the burghers and altogether a different man to the keeper of the town. But it would have been hard for the captain not to put himself forward as one of the men if he accepted the terms of the surrender. De Fiennes is simply the spelling of de Vienne found in the Vatican manuscript. This assertion is supported by Baker, who also states that Vienne came to the king, mounted, and offering his sword. See Thompson (ed.), *Galfridi le Baker*, p. 91. A similar story is related by the Meaux chronicler. See Bond (ed.), *Melsa*, iii, p. 67.
52. According to Froissart, Philippa was heavily pregnant at the time. However, William of Windsor was probably born about 24 May 1348 as Philippa's churching was held on 24 June (TNA E101/391/14 m.3). This would suggest he was conceived exactly two weeks after the surrender of the city, on 18 August. See Appendix Eight. Paul Strohm has used this accentuation of the queen's royal child-bearing status to emphasise her female, intercessory role. Although there probably is much dramatic exaggeration in Froissart's account (and that of le Bel underlying it), Strohm's argument ignores the fact that as much interceding was done by men as women in fourteenth-century chronicles, including Froissart's. Walter Manny had just successfully pleaded with the king in this instance; later the king would withdraw from France after the intercession of the duke of Lancaster, according to Froissart (see Chapter Fourteen). The key thing is that the intercession was made in each case by the closest person to Edward present, which is what one would expect. The gender reading here says much more about the modern reader's quest for novel interpretation than the historical events of 1347. See Paul Strohm, *Hochon's Arrow* (Princeton, NJ, 1992), pp. 99–105.
53. *CPR 1334–38*, p. 486.
54. Quoted in *WCS*, p. 282.
55. Bond (ed.), *Melsa*, iii, p. 65. Brie (ed.), *Brut*, ii, p. 544 mentions deaths due to the flux.
56. Bond (ed.), *Melsa*, iii, p. 74.
57. *Foedera*, iii, 1, p. 138. Baker has 14 October: see Thompson (ed.), *Galfridi le Baker*, p. 96. Barber gives no source for his assertion that Edward landed in early November (which must be a mistake as the official letters in *Foedera* do not support a November date). It was probably the Meaux chronicler, who states 1 November: see Barber, *Black Prince*, p. 78; Bond (ed.), *Melsa*, iii, p. 67. For the storm see Riley (ed.), *Walsingham*, i. p. 271.
58. TNA E101/391/15 mm.9–10. A translation appears in *E3&Chiv*, p. 175.
59. TNA E101/391/15 m.9.
60. Riley (ed.), *Walsingham*, i, p. 272.

11: An Unassailable Enemy

1. Barnes, *Edward III*, p. 417. This actually relates to the second parliament in 1348. See *RP*, ii, p. 201.
2. Bellamy, *Law of Treason*, p. 78; *RE3*, p. 107.
3. *RE3*, pp. 106–7; Musson, 'Second "English Justinian"', p. 81.
4. *RP*, ii, p. 174.
5. *RP*, ii, p. 165; *RE3*, pp. 176, 179.
6. *RP*, ii, pp. 201–4.
7. *E3&Chiv*, p. 71; the dating is revised in Ormrod, 'For Arthur and St George', p. 19.
8. TNA E101/391/15 m.6.
9. TNA E101/391/15 mm.6–7. This states that coats with hoods were made 'for the person of the king and those of eleven knights of his chamber – Walter Manny, John de Lisle, Hugh Courtenay, John Grey, Robert de Ferrers, Richard de la Vache, Phillip de Spenser, Roger Beauchamp, Miles Stapelton, Ralph Ferrers and Robert Mauley – so that each receives two ells of blue cloth for their coats and three-quarters of half an ell of white for their hoods'. Here we have the livery of the later Order of the Garter being purchased for non-Garter knights, indicating the Order had not been established as an exclusive body of knights by this time. The like costumes were purchased for Giles Beauchamp and his son John, John Beauchamp of Warwick, Peter Brewes, Thomas Lancaster, Joanna Brocas, the earl of Lancaster and twelve of his knights, Isabella, the king's daughter and her ladies, the ladies Juliers, Wake, Segrave and Darcy, and several of their damsels, Eleanor Merkyngfeld, Phillippa Bohun, Alice Belet, Joanna de la Mote and Burga Vaux.
10. Ormrod, 'For Arthur and St George', p. 19, elaborating on dates in *E3&Chiv*, pp. 172–4. The Westminster tournament (if it took place) very probably predates 5 September as thereafter there were no tournaments during the period of mourning for two of the royal children.
11. TNA E101/391/14 m.3.
12. TNA E101/391/15 m.13.
13. Ormrod, 'Royal Nursery', n. 83, quoting E101/391/17, which states that John Badby returned to England after the princess's death on 1 July.
14. Thompson (ed.), *Galfridi le Baker*, p. 97.
15. Agnolo di Tura, *Cronaca Senese*, quoted in William Bowsky (ed.), *The Black Death* (New York, 1971), pp. 13–14, in turn quoted in Gottfried, *The Black Death*, p. 45.
16. Zeigler, *Black Death*, pp. 119–21. Avesbury's date, quoted on p. 120, does not relate to 29 June, which is the feast of Saints Peter and Paul, but the feast of St Peter ad Vincula (clearly stated in the text) and thus 1 August. See Avesbury in Thompson (ed.), *Murimuth*, p. 406.
17. Hingeston-Randolph, *Register of John de Grandison*, ii, pp. 1069–70.
18. *Foedera*, iii, 1, p. 175. Prior to this, on 8 October, Edward had ordered that men-at-arms who wished to travel with the king were to assemble at Sandwich on 26 October.
19. Avesbury in Thompson (ed.), *Murimuth*, p. 407.

20. See Ormrod, 'English Government and the Black Death of 1348–49', p. 175. Edward seems to have been at Westminster on 1 December and at the Tower on the 10th. The latter reference especially seems to indicate his actual presence in London, as it was a ratification of a treaty by the king himself sealed at the Tower. See *Foedera*, iii, 1, p. 178.

21. *E3&Chiv*, p. 175, quoting TNA E372/207, m.50; E101/391/15.

22. Avesbury in Thompson (ed.), *Murimuth*, p. 407.

23. Thompson (ed.), *Galfridi le Baker*, p. 99.

24. Manny was ennobled at the fall of Calais or soon after. See *CP*, viii, p. 573.

25. *EHD 1327–1485*, p. 90.

26. For the precise date of the foundation of the Order see Appendix Six.

27. For the rains, see Brie (ed.), *Brut*, ii, p. 301. Here the author states that the rain fell from Christmas to Midsummer (24 June). In Riley (ed.), *Walsingham*, i, p. 272 Walsingham states that the rains fell every day from Midsummer to Christmas.

28. Eight months before the foundation of the Order, in August 1348, he founded the college of priests at Windsor which was to serve it. See Appendix Six.

29. Ormrod, in 'For Arthur and St George', shows how frequently Edward was at Windsor in the first half of 1348, and argues that the idea for the development of the Order should be dated to this time.

30. *E3&Chiv*, p. 84, quoting *Register of Edward the Black Prince*, iv, pp. 72–3. The companionship of twenty-four knights plus the king is incidentally the same number as there are spaces for on the round table which hangs at Winchester (see Chapter Four). This was probably mounted on the wall of the hall in 1348/9 (Ormrod, 'For Arthur and St George', p. 22).

31. The most recent attempt is Ormrod, 'For Arthur and St George', esp. p. 24. See also *E3&Chiv*, pp. 80–2; Sumption, *Trial by Fire*, p. 3; Ormrod, 'Edward III' in *ODNB*. Barber in his article on Edward of Woodstock in *ODNB* also states that the foundation was political, 'reflected in the choice of heraldry and motto: the gold and blue of France is combined with words that refer to Edward's claim to France: "Shame on him who thinks evil of it."' This is a succinct summing-up of an academic consensus for which there is no actual evidence. In addition, Barber's statement is slightly misleading: the robes of the Order were not blue and gold but blue with a silver lining. The garter itself (a less visible item) was blue and gold, but this colour scheme might just as readily relate to the colours of the mythical coat of arms of King Arthur – whose Round Table was inspiration for the earlier company established at Windsor in 1344 – as those of the kingdom of France.

32. Ormrod, 'Edward III' in *ODNB*.

33. For example, in *Winner and Waster*, the context is Edward's chivalric situation judging the classes of society. In *Gawain and the Green Knight*, the words appear at the end of the manuscript, without a specific setting, but the theme of the poem is moral (like the motto) not political. The possible appearance of a similar phrase in the *Vow of the Heron* is possibly no more than a common turn of phrase of the time, but, even if not, it is of foreign authorship; therefore one would be surprised if it did *not* have a political context. See Ormrod, 'For Arthur and St George, pp. 24–7.

34. Edward ordered payments for 'a pair of pearl garters' along with other jousting equipment for his own use in February 1333 (TNA E101/386/9 m.12) and 'a pair

of pearl garters encrusted with gold' for himself in March 1334 (TNA E101/386/18 m.58). These are characterised by their pearls, however, not their motto like later garters. With regard to Lancaster's garters, see Fowler, *King's Lieutenant*, p. 194. Although there is no proof that Lancaster wore garters before 1348, several observations have led the present writer to conclude that it is very likely that he did, and that it was originally a personal badge. Firstly, the garter bearing a motto (as opposed to pearls) does not appear before 1346–47, and so may be connected temporally with the conquests of 1345–46, of which Lancaster's was the most impressive campaign before Crécy. Secondly, writing about his misspent youth in 1354, he mentions his vanity in wearing rings, shoes, armour and garters. The passage reads '*Et par surquiderie est orgoil tant entree en moi par mes pieez come autrement, quant jeo me siu meismes mal avisee, il me semble, ceo qe nul autre ne sembloit: ceo estoit qe le piee me seoit bien en l'estru, ou autrement de chausure ou de armure, ou de daunser ou legier piee, et les garters qe bien me seoient a mon avys – qe gaires ne vaut; et si jeo en oïse poynt parler, ma fole joie en estoit greignure de tant et passoit mesure tout outre*' (version taken from web edition of the *Livre de Seyntz Medicines* provided by the Anglo-Norman Online Hub, http://www.anglo-norman.net/texts/). His statement that his garters 'suited me well in my opinion – that were worth but little' (*qe bien me seoient a mon avys – qe gaires ne vaut*) suggests a personal vanity, not something thrust upon him through the ceremony of an institution. If it meant the latter, he would be saying that wearing garters *as a Knight of the Garter* was something which puffed him up with sinful pride, bringing the Order itself into disrepute. It would also mean that in his opinion the badge for the Order of the Garter was worth 'but little'. It was clearly not his intention in this work to cast any doubt on the merits of the Order or its badge. Also, as he was writing in 1354, it is unlikely he was referring to the recent past, or the period after 1345 (when he was in his mid-thirties, hardly a youth any more). As Fowler says, 'these were the reflections on youth of a middle-age man suffering from gout' (*King's Lieutenant*, p. 194).

35. This point is made by Barber in his article on Edward of Woodstock in *ODNB*.
36. Although the prince had not fought in Gascony, he had certainly been with Lancaster and the king at Calais, and this companionship may well have formed as a jousting fraternity around the earl during the siege. As to whether the record of this payment was an advance order for garters to be handed out at the inaugural tournament of the Order (and only described as a companionship informally), it should be noted that the early references to garters as gifts (including those mentioned in Nicolas, 'Observations on the Order of the Garter') do not add up to twenty-six. There is little room for doubt that an informal, smaller companionship existed before the Order.
37. Nicolas, 'Observations on the Order of the Garter', pp. 34, 40–1, 119–21.
38. *Le Livre de Seyntz Medicines* is extant in two manuscripts, at Stonyhurst College and Cambridge University (Corpus Christi College). Although he claimed to be ill at ease with French (see the *ODNB* article on him), this was clearly nothing more than a self-effacing statement of a man who was conscious of the fact his writing in French was not up to literary standards. See Fowler, *King's Lieutenant*, p. 196. Had he been more conversant with English (an exceptionally unlikely situation for an aristocrat born in about 1310), he would have written in that language.

39. The same principle applies to the inscriptions on Edward's coins: they were not in English because they were struck in the knowledge that they would have an international audience.

40. This story is related in some late fifteenth-century chronicles and was mentioned by the antiquary John Selden, writing in 1614. But Froissart – who did not shy away from such romantic interludes, and who elaborated on the previous story of the 'countess of Salisbury' – does not mention her or any other lady in this respect. Barber in his article on Edward of Woodstock in *ODNB* states the story 'seems to have no basis in reality'. See also Ormrod, 'For Arthur and St George', p. 28, where a fuller description of the identifiable origins of the story is to be found.

41. 'No one now believes in the authenticity of this story', according to Ormrod, 'For Arthur and St George', p. 28.

42. As quoted in Barber, *Black Prince*, p. 94.

43. Lumby (ed.), *Knighton*, ii, p. 58.

44. Ormrod, 'For Arthur and St George', p. 28.

45. For the old identification and its lack of credibility today see Ormrod, 'For Arthur and St George', p. 29 n. 71, citing Galway and Barber.

46. With regard to her age, her parents married in about 1326. She cannot have been born after 1329, due to her father's execution in March of 1330 and the birth of her brother John in April of that year. She was Edward's first cousin on his father's side and his second cousin through his mother.

47. See Wentersdorf, 'Clandestine Marriages of the Fair Maid of Kent'; Barber, 'Joan suo jure countess of Kent' in *ODNB*. Whether she had really married him (or just claimed she had) is not clear.

48. Chamberlayne, 'Joan of Kent's Tale', p. 8.

49. In addition it is worth noting that she later married another participant in the tournament, the Black Prince.

50. *E3&Chiv*, p. 53.

51. Avesbury in Thompson (ed.), *Murimuth*, p. 407.

52. Sumption, *Trial by Fire*, p. 51.

53. *Foedera*, iii, 1, p. 191. This was dated 1 December.

54. Johnes (ed.), *Froissart*, i, p. 193.

55. Barber, *Black Prince*, p. 96.

56. Johnes (ed.), *Froissart*, i, p. 195.

57. Froissart states forty Castilian vessels. Forty-four is the figure given by Barber, *Black Prince*, pp. 99–100, and Burne, *Crécy War*, p. 228. Sumption, *Trial by Fire*, pp. 66–7 follows Avesbury in saying that there were twenty-four great Spanish ships. See Avesbury in Thompson (ed.), *Murimuth*, p. 412.

58. Johnes (ed.), *Froissart*, i, p. 199.

59. See Barnes, *Edward III*, p. 452. Fourteen is the number in Johnes (ed.), *Froissart*, i, p. 199; seventeen in Thompson (ed.), *Galfridi le Baker*, p. 111; twenty-four in Brie (ed.), *Brut*, ii, p. 304.

60. Sumption, *Trial by Fire*, p. 67, states that the victory was inconclusive, perhaps following Barnes, *Edward III*, p. 452, who claims that night prevented the English from obtaining an 'absolute victory'. However, a battle in which about half of the enemy ships were captured and none of one's own, and in which the enemy is put to flight is a victory by any reckoning. Barnes' notion that this did not constitute

an absolute success – meaning the destruction of every enemy ship – would be out of proportion with the idea of a success in a land battle, in which to kill half the enemy and put the rest to flight would be an overwhelming success.

12: At the Court of the Sun King

1. The French Order of the Star was founded in 1351; the Neapolitan Order of the Knot in 1352, the Holy Roman Emperor's Order of the Golden Buckle in 1355, and the Savoyard Order of the Collar in 1363. See Keen, *Chivalry*, p. 179. The sole predecessor to the Garter which Keen notes is the Order of the Band, founded by Alfonso of Castile in 'about 1330'.
2. Thompson (ed.), *Galfridi le Baker*, p. 112; Barnes, *Edward III*, p. 453; Riley (ed.), *Walsingham*, i, p. 275.
3. Edward I actually only spent eighty thousand pounds; Edward II spent a further fifteen thousand pounds on the eight Welsh castles, bringing the total construction costs to ninety-five thousand pounds (an average of about twelve thousand pounds each). *HKW*, i, p. 161.
4. The 'largest residential castle in the world' comes from the *Guinness Book of Records* (21st ed., 1974), p. 118, which incidentally also claims that the major part of the castle is of twelfth-century date, underlining how Edward III is generally not associated with the building today.
5. *HKW*, ii, p. 872.
6. Brown, *English Castles*, p. 209.
7. *HKW*, ii, p. 881.
8. *HKW*, ii, pp. 881–2.
9. *HKW*, i, p. 514.
10. *AC*, p. 498.
11. *HKW*, i, p. 518.
12. Stone, *Sculpture in Medieval England*, pp. 160–2, 190. The employment of a carver from Nottinghamshire at St Stephen's suggests alabaster would have been used there, as well as at Windsor, which is documented.
13. *E3&Chiv*, p. 53.
14. Devon (ed.), *Issues of the Exchequer*, p. 160. He was employed on the chapel of Windsor Castle that year.
15. *E3&Chiv*, p. 52.
16. *AC*, p. 21.
17. Harvey and Mortimer, *Funeral Effigies*, p. 34.
18. Ormrod, *Personal Religion*, p. 873.
19. Ormrod, *Personal Religion*, p. 858.
20. The remains of the medieval palace of Eltham include nothing of Edward III's work. The extant hall was built by Edward IV and the fragments of masonry in the retaining wall were commissioned by Queen Isabella. See *HKW*, ii, p. 932.
21. *HKW*, ii, pp. 931–2.
22. *HKW*, ii, p. 961.
23. *HKW*, ii, p. 992.
24. *HKW*, ii, p. 1017.

25. *HKW*, ii, pp. 587, 593, 599, 623, 639, 655, 659, 699–701, 725, 731, 768, 788, 811, 818, 831, 838–9, 850–1, 863. There are some exceptions to Edward keeping royal castles in good condition. Most interesting is his almost total neglect of Canterbury Castle, which although being seriously in need of repair in 1335 was completely ignored by Edward. He spent less than two pounds on the upkeep of the castle in his reign.

26. *HKW*, ii, pp. 917, 959.

27. *HKW*, ii, pp. 762–3.

28. *HKW*, ii, pp. 995–7.

29. Given-Wilson, *Royal Household*, p. 31; Harvey and Mortimer, *Funeral Effigies*, p. 37.

30. Salzman, *Building in England*, p. 276.

31. Salzman, *Building in England*, p. 276.

32. For example copper pipe was purchased for the wardrobe in 1347–49. See TNA E101/391/14 mm.8–9.

33. *HKW*, ii, p. 663.

34. Brown, *English Castles*, p. 136.

35. *HKW*, ii, pp. 946–7.

36. He was there in early 1361, when work began. See Given-Wilson, *Royal Household*, p. 33.

37. For the foundation stone, see *AC*, p. 498. Edward visited both Eltham and Windsor in 1353. See TNA E101/392/12.

38. The only parallel which Brown draws is with the Castel del Monte in Apulia, Italy, which Edward would never have seen. See Brown, *English Castles*, p. 135.

39. Tout, 'Firearms', p. 675.

40. *HKW*, ii, p. 793.

41. Gimpel, *Medieval Machine*, p. 153, indirectly quoting Robert the Englishman.

42. Gimpel, *Medieval Machine*, p. 156. The meeting (recorded by Walsingham) is most likely to have taken place in February 1332, as from 1334 Abbot Wallingford was physically disabled and the only date Edward seems to have visited St Albans between 1330 and 1334 was on or about 21 February 1332, according to the itinerary in TNA Map Room.

43. Brown, 'King Edward's Clocks', p. 285.

44. Morgan, 'Apotheosis', p. 861. For comparison, the modern bell, 'Big Ben' weighs thirteen tons, and was cast in 1858.

45. *E3&Chiv*, pp. 49–51.

46. Devon (ed.), *Issues of the Exchequer*, p. 143. The question of what this book was is interesting. It was purchased from Isabella of Lancaster, a sister of the earl of Lancaster. It is possible that it was an early copy of the pro-Lancastrian longer continuation of the French *Brut*, which would certainly have been described as a 'romance' and which had been written up at York around 1333. It is unlikely therefore that Edward already had a copy. Also it contains an update of the Prophecy of the Six Kings, in which Edward III is amplified as the conqueror of Europe. This might explain the unprecedented price and Edward's personal association with the book. See Brie (ed.), *Brut*, pp. 74–5.

47. Ormrod, 'Personal Religion', p. 857.

48. Alexander, 'Painting and Manuscript Illumination', pp. 141–3. These manuscripts are Walter Milemete's *De Nobilitatis Sapientiis et Prudentiis Regum* (Christ Church, Oxford, E.11), the *Secreta Secrorum* presented by Milemete to Edward at the same

NOTES

time (BL Add. 47680), a small psalter (Dr Williams Library, London, Ancient 6), a lavishly illuminated larger psalter (Bodleian Library, Oxford, Douce 131), another psalter (BL Harleian MS 2899). Another item might be the psalter confiscated in the sixteenth century and given to Queen Mary (BL Royal 2 B vii). To these should be added Philippa's wedding present to Edward.

49. For examples of liturgical books see E101/386/3 ff.2–3; for presents of romances see for example E101/390/7, which mentions a romance delivered to the queen. Isabella owned many such books at her death.

50. Devon (ed.), *Issues of the Exchequer*, p. 142.

51. French *et al.*, *Medicine*, p. 34, mentions his alchemical interests and gives further references. His historical interests are shown by his borrowing of the history of the Normans (*E3&Chiv*, p. 52) and his borrowing of William Newburgh's *Historia Rerum Anglicarum* (Ormrod, 'Personal Religion', p. 857). Perhaps one could add to these his summoning of the chronicler to bring all the chronicles in his keeping to him in 1352 (Gransden, *Historical Writing*, p. 43). These are just lucky survivals of references: there were very probably many more borrowings of historical works.

52. French *et al.*, *Medicine*, p. 49, n. 73.

53. Shenton, 'English Court', pp. 168–9.

54. For example the music in the wedding present manuscript.

55. *AC*, p. 435.

56. Wyon and Wyon, *Great Seals of England*, p. 38.

57. Isabella was buried in the church of the Greyfriars, London; Lionel was initially buried at Pavia but was later reburied in Clare Priory, Suffolk; John of Gaunt was buried in old St Paul's Cathedral.

58. Although the painted coats of arms have long-since gone from beneath these weepers, the central east-facing weeper on the tomb (in the choir of St Mary's, Warwick) is similar to the image of the Black Prince on Edward's own tomb at Westminster and the figure of the prince on his Gascon coins. It is counterbalanced on the western side, in the centre, by an elderly king in a long robe which is highly reminiscent of images of Edward himself. Thomas died in 1369.

59. Harvey and Mortimer, *Funeral Effigies*, pp. 30–5.

60. Henry III's total accounted expenditure on his buildings was in the region of £160,000. Edward's total was well over £130,000. See *HKW*, i, pp. 109, 162. In comparing the artistic expenditure of Edward and Henry the authors of *HKW* state that Edward rivalled Henry and that Windsor, St Stephen's and Queenborough 'need fear no comparison even with the royal buildings of the thirteenth century'. Edward I's expenditure was of a much more military character; his Welsh castles (which accounted for about two-thirds of his total expenditure) were not intended to be royal residences like Henry III's and Edward III's works.

13: Lawmaker

1. *RP*, ii, p. 225.

2. *RP*, ii, p. 227.

3. Although in the long run, the provisions of the statute were unsuccessful, this was

THE PERFECT KING

because it took time for the benefits to landowners of a flexible market to become apparent. Not least of these was the local administration of breakers of the law, an important step in contributing to the legal authority of the gentry. See *RE3*, p. 32; McKisack, *Fourteenth Century*, p. 335.

4. See G. G. Coulton, *Medieval Panorama* (Cambridge, 1949), p. 126 for an old and rather extreme interpretation of this as representing a break from Rome.

5. *RE3*, p. 162.

6. *RP*, ii, pp. 226–7.

7. That Edward was positively pleased to be able to reverse the judgement on Maltravers is shown by his letter of October 1351 to the steward of his chamber praising Maltravers, specifically mentioning his 'goodwill and loyalty', and stating that 'he wished to do something grandiose for him'. See TNA E101/391/8, m.2.

8. In England it was reported that eleven Frenchmen had been appointed. See Thompson (ed.), *Galfridi le Baker*, pp. 111–12.

9. See Sumption, *Trial by Fire*, pp. 143–50 for a résumé of the situation 1350–55 in Scotland.

10. Unwin (ed.), *Finance and Trade*, p. 226.

11. Bellamy, *Law of Treason*, pp. 59–101; *RE3*, p. 52; McKisack, *Fourteenth Century*, p. 257; Musson 'Second "English Justinian"', p. 82.

12. Mortimer's crimes are repeated or touched upon in many of those specified in the great Statute of Treasons. He had conceived of the death of the king (Edward II) in that he had pretended the man was actually dead. He had violated the king's wife (Isabella) in the sense that he had become her lover. He may well have 'conceived of the death' of the king's son and heir – Edward III – in the plot against him at Nottingham in 1330. Mortimer had also taken an army against the king in 1321–22 and 1326, although he had not actually fought with him on either occasion. Pro-Mortimer supporters had killed the Chancellor (Robert Baldock) in 1326, although he was not conducting his office at the time.

13. The wording of this is '*quant home fait compasser ou ymaginer la mort nostre Seigneur le Roi*'.

14. Ruffhead (ed.), *Statutes at Large*, i, p. 261.

15. For example, McKisack, *Fourteenth Century*, p. 257, states that 'the primary object of the statute was probably legal, rather than political'. Bellamy only considers the law of treason in its legal and historical context. Even though he states that 'the dominant theme in the history of treason under the first two Edwards was then the development of conviction on the king's record' (p. 55) he does not consider a biographical aspect to the statute apart from Edward's apparent immunity from plots. Instead he takes the view (quoting Sir William Holdsworth) that 'the king's intent was primarily to extend treason for political purposes'. See Bellamy, *Law of Treason*, p. 60.

16. Gransden, *Historical Writing*, ii, p. 43. In this context it needs to be noted that Higden was more responsible for the spread of the story about the death of Edward II being due to a red-hot poker than anyone else. The story of the 'anal rape' murder first appears in the longer continuation of the *Brut* chronicle, written in the mid-1330s, but it achieved its widest publicity through Higden's *Polychronicon* which survives in more than 160 Latin manuscripts, and (like the *Brut*) informed most of the chronicle-writers of the later middle ages.

17. Ormrod, *Personal Religion*, p. 855.
18. TNA E101/392/12 f.18v. He left the region to attend a council at Westminster on 23 September.
19. TNA E101/392/12 ff.33r; 34v; 35r.
20. TNA E101/392/12 f.34v. Both visits were personal, in that the household did not attend. In September the wardrobe was at Gloucester; in November at Northampton.
21. Sumption, *Trial by Fire*, pp. 89–90. Thompson (ed.), *Galfridi le Baker*, pp. 116–17.
22. Sumption, *Trial by Fire*, p. 91.
23. *Foedera*, iii, 1, pp. 239–45.
24. Sumption, *Trial by Fire*, p. 96.
25. Sumption, *Trial by Fire*, p. 94 notes that French chroniclers put Bentley's army at 1,500, but suggests that the actual figure was about half this.
26. See Avesbury in Thompson (ed.), *Murimuth*, pp. 415–17; Thompson (ed.), *Galfridi le Baker*, p. 120; Sumption, *Trial by Fire*, p. 94.
27. *E3&Chiv*, pp. 73–4, drawing on the work of Sir Isaac Gollancz, points out the similarities between the king's dress in the poem and the dress known to have been worn at this time by Edward.
28. Dyer, *Standards of Living*, p. 87.
29. Perroy accuses him of being a self-seeking courtier in *Hundred Years War*, p. 129. Sumption is more generous in *Trial by Fire*, p. 112.
30. TNA E101/392/12 f.8r.
31. Sumption, *Trial by Fire*, pp. 100–1.
32. TNA E101/392/12 f.13r.
33. TNA E101/392/12 ff.13r–18v.
34. For example, all letters close dated to this year – 27 Edward III – were issued from Westminster with only six exceptions (out of about five hundred). The exceptions were issued from the Tower (4 March, 20 January and 23 February); Windsor (23 April, 29 May) and Eltham (30 March). See *CCR 1349–54*, pp. 525–626 (pp. 532, 537, 543, 576, 589, 590 for the exceptions). Much the same can be said for the years 1351, 1352 and subsequent years, and for some earlier years.
35. *RE3*, p. 70.
36. Woolgar, *Great Household*, p. 195.
37. TNA E101/392/12 f.43v. Damages were often paid by the royal household, especially for the large numbers of houses they burnt down. In this year (1353) £6 6s was paid on 18 May 1353 to Alice Mande and £5 to John Benefield as compensation for their houses having been burnt down during the king's stay at Mortlake. Nor were priories exempt: on 5 December 1353 the prior of St Andrew's, Northampton, was paid £1 for damage caused during the king's stay.
38. *HKW*, ii, p. 984.
39. TNA E101/392/12 f.17r. This was probably John Adam, born in Lucca but raised in London. For some of Edward's apothecaries, including John Adam of Lucca, William Stanes, John Donat, and Bartholomew the Spicer, see Matthews, *Royal Apothecaries*, pp. 26–9. For further references to John of Lucca, William Waddesworth and John Donat see TNA E101/392/12 f.17r; E101/398/9 f.25r; and E101/396/2 f.40v respectively. See also Appendix Seven.

40. For example Henry, earl of Lancaster (d.1345), William Montagu, earl of Salisbury (d.1344) and Thomas Holland, Knight of the Garter (d.1360) all were supposed to be blind in one eye.
41. Matthews, *Royal Apothecaries*, p. 26.
42. Master Jordan of Canterbury was in receipt of several grants around this time. For example: *CPR 1350–54*, pp. 321, 357, 501. The last relates to his daughter.
43. For example, the case of Mortimer's claim on the earldom of March mentioned earlier in this chapter. Historians in the past have too readily divided petitions and royal assent, but it seems Edward himself suggested that some petitions should be put forward. This probably also applies to the Statute of Treasons as a whole, for this seems to have had a strong support from the community and been part of Edward's revisiting of the past at this time. If Edward himself was behind more of the petitions presented to him in parliament (for example: requesting that views put to him unofficially by courtiers and visitors should be put to him formally in parliament), current thinking on the king's role in the formation of Statute Law needs to be reconsidered. It was not a straightforward contest between king and parliament.
44. Musson, 'Second "English Justinian"', p. 88.
45. Royal household expenses increased from about £36 per day to £49 on 22 December, £61 on the 23rd, £102 on the 24th, £223 on Christmas Day itself, £126 on the 26th (St Stephen's Day), and remained at a level between £50 and £100 for the next fortnight. See TNA E101/392/12 f.27v.
46. Barber, *Black Prince*, p. 105.
47. This was easy to argue against however, as at the time of the death of King Charles the Fair (1328) Charles of Navarre had not been born, and his mother – as a woman – could not have inherited the French throne. See Fowler, *King's Lieutenant*, p. 122; Taylor, 'Edward III and the Plantagenet Claim to the French Throne', pp. 159–62.
48. Sumption, *Trial by Fire*, pp. 124–5; Fowler, *King's Lieutenant*, p. 122.
49. Sumption, *Trial by Fire*, pp. 128–30; Fowler, *King's Lieutenant*, p. 126.
50. For the alternative view that Edward was on the back foot at this time, see Fowler, *King's Lieutenant*, p. 130. See also Rogers, 'Anglo-French Peace Negotiations', pp. 195–7. For the cardinal's shady dealings see Fowler, *King's Lieutenant*, p. 131.
51. Ruffhead (ed.), *Statutes at Large*, i, p. 285.
52. During the nine-year period the king would be on parole, his behaviour guaranteed by the presence in England of the heirs of twenty of the leading magnates. See Sumption, *Trial by Fire*, p. 152.
53. Fowler, *King's Lieutenant*, pp. 135–8.
54. *E3&Chiv*, pp. 63, 174. The tournament took place on 22 Februuary.
55. Although the English often have been blamed for the failure of this treaty, this stems largely from a misreading of a late chronicle by the influential historian le Patourel. The matter was convincingly settled by Rogers, 'Anglo-French Peace Negotiations', pp. 196–200. Although published slightly earlier, Sumption, *Trial by Fire*, pp. 140–2 arrives at the same conclusion.

14: The Pride of England

1. Usually it is said to be beer that they were drinking; the account in Avesbury states wine. See Thompson (ed.), *Murimuth*, pp. 422–3. Pouring drink over the head of a regrator or bad seller of drink was the practice usually adopted in towns for the punishment of unscrupulous merchants.

2. Avesbury in Thompson (ed.), *Murimuth*, p. 424. For the safe conducts for the nuncios, see *Foedera*, iii, 1, p. 297.

3. Avesbury in Thompson (ed.), *Murimuth*, p. 424; *WCS*, p. 294. Hewitt, *Black Prince's Expedition*, pp. 20–1, discusses the strength of the army and concludes that the actual figures were slightly lower.

4. *WCS*, p. 296, quoting Jean le Bel.

5. *WCS*, p. 297.

6. *WCS*, p. 297, quoting Jean le Bel.

7. *WCS*, pp. 299–300, quoting Jean le Bel.

8. *RP*, iii, pp. 264–5. A grant of indirect taxation for this length of time was not made again until the reign of Henry V, after the battle of Agincourt.

9. Molyns was at times uncontrollably violent. Although of great service in the early part of Edward's reign, taking part in Mortimer's arrest, for example, and acting as the king's agent in arresting all the Italians in 1337, he was arrested in 1340 and locked in the Tower of London. He escaped from the Tower and then refused to answer the justices. He lost his lands, committed murder, and was only gradually restored to royal favour. War saw him flourish again, but in the peaceful years of the 1350s he found himself the subject of attack in parliament for his excessive fines and his use of violence. Despite his charitable donations, he spent the last years of his life in prison, at Nottingham and later at Cambridge. His tomb is said to be in the church at Stoke Poges.

10. Aberth, 'Crime and Justice under Edward III'; Wilkinson, 'A Letter from Edward III to his Chancellor and Treasurer'.

11. Avesbury transcribed the charter, giving the date. See Thompson (ed.), *Murimuth*, p. 453.

12. Avesbury in Thompson (ed.), *Murimuth*, pp. 450–6; Lumby (ed.), *Knighton*, ii, pp. 84–6; Balfour-Melville, *Edward III and David II*, p. 17; Sumption, *Trial by Fire*, pp. 188–90.

13. As Rogers points out, the peace was specifically between Northampton and Douglas but this was tantamount to a peace between the two countries, as Northampton was Edward's appointed lieutenant on the border. Given the speed with which the negotiations resumed, and the failure of the Scots to accept the earlier suggestions of 1350–51 (when it was proposed that one of Edward's sons should be David's heir), it seems that the reason Edward took away Balliol's title in advance of the Burnt Candlemas campaign was to remove him from the equation when talks resumed afterwards.

14. See *WCS*, pp. 336–40, for a similar argument. For the payment at Candlemas, see Balfour-Melville, *Edward III and David II*, pp. 17–18. The Candlemas association means we should not assume that the eventual Scottish peace negotiations were due to the victory at Poitiers.

15. See *RE3*, p. 87 for an exposition of the English situation. He shows that the campaigns of 1355–56 cost a total of just £110,000, at a time when the customs revenues alone could provide £87,500 per annum.
16. Sumption, *Trial by Fire*, pp. 195–205.
17. See the newsletters sent to the bishop of Winchester about this campaign transcribed by Avesbury in Thompson (ed.), *Murimuth*, pp. 434–49. The campaign is discussed in Barber, *Black Prince*, pp. 110–30; Sumption, *Trial by Fire*, pp. 174–87; *WCS*, pp. 304–24; Hewitt, *Black Prince's Expedition*, pp. 43–77.
18. *WCS*, p. 314, quoting Avesbury in Thompson (ed.), *Murimuth*, p. 442.
19. Avesbury in Thompson (ed.), *Murimuth*, pp. 458–68; *WCS*, pp. 344–7.
20. The journal of Lancaster's raid, covering 22 June–16 July, is in Avesbury's chronicle, in Thompson (ed.), *Murimuth*, pp. 462–8. The journal of the Black Prince's expedition, covering the period 4 August–2 October 1356, is in Haydon (ed.), *Eulogium Historiarum*, iii, pp. 215–26.
21. For the Durham endowment see Ormrod, 'Personal Religion', p. 855. For the pilgrimage in 1346 and will-making, see Barber, *Black Prince*, p. 46.
22. Barber, *Black Prince*, p. 132.
23. Avesbury in Thompson (ed.), *Murimuth*, p. 468.
24. Hewitt, *Black Prince's Expedition*, pp. 138, 194.
25. Quoted in Hewitt, *Black Prince's Expedition*, p. 139.
26. *WCS*, p. 377, gives the most detailed breakdown of the figures.
27. Quoted in Hewitt, *Black Prince's Expedition*, p. 132.
28. The early stages of the battle are very confused. Most primary accounts vary considerably, and most secondary accounts differ even more. In trying to put a brief description together I have only used *WCS*, pp. 373–84; Barber, *Black Prince*, pp. 138–44; Sumption, *Trial by Fire*, pp. 238–42; and last (and surprisingly least) Hewitt, *Black Prince's Expedition*, pp. 118–21.
29. Barnes, *Edward III*, p. 518.
30. Lumby (ed.), *Knighton*, ii, p. 94.
31. Rogers, 'Anglo-French Peace Negotiations'.
32. *Foedera*, iii, 1, p. 353.
33. Barber, *Black Prince*, p. 152.
34. The Robin Hood stories were famous by the time of the earliest extant literary reference to him in *Piers Plowman*, written about 1377. See Holt, *Robin Hood*, pp. 16, 158.
35. Barber, *Black Prince*, p. 152.
36. Numbers of captured members of the French royal family are drawn from Lumby (ed.), *Knighton*, ii, p. 90.
37. Barber, *Black Prince*, p. 155. See n.8 where it is noted that March borrowed £1,000 from the prince probably to pay for the jousting.
38. Maxwell (ed.), *Scalachronica*, i, p. 128. As Barber notes, Fowler in *King's Lieutenant*, p. 197 doubts whether Lancaster was there; that he was is shown by the household account book of Isabella, who was certainly there. She had dinner with Lancaster and the prince on 19 April, when she was on the way to Windsor. See Barber, *Black Prince*, pp. 155, 260 n.8; Bond, 'Last days of Queen Isabella', p. 459.
39. Sumption refers to this treaty as the Treaty of Windsor, due to its ratification there, thus distinguishing it from the Second Treaty of London. This is pragmatic

but inconsistent, as he describes the Treaty of Brétigny as such (referring to the place of negotiation) rather than as the Treaty of Calais (where it was ratified). Most historians since Roland Delachenal, who worked out the sequence of peace treaties in his *Histoire de Charles V* (1909), have used First and Second Treaties of London (8 May 1358 and 24 March 1359 respectively).

40. Rogers, 'Anglo-French Peace Negotiations', p. 202; Sumption, *Trial by Fire*, pp. 298–304.

41. Doherty, 'Isabella' (D.Phil. thesis), p. 325. See Chapter Nine for references to tournaments and hunting.

42. *Foedera*, iii, 1, p. 170. The plan, however, came to nothing, and she did not leave England.

43. French *et al.*, *Medicine*, pp. 34, 49 n.73.

44. Isabella's books are listed in *E3&Chiv*, p. 170. The original is TNA E101/393/4, supplemented with E101/333/29. In 1357 she also loaned two Arthurian books to the king of France in his captivity. See Bennet, 'Isabelle of France', p. 219.

45. For Edward's nine minstrels see Given-Wilson, *Royal Household*, p. 298 n.126. Isabella's rewards to the minstrels of visitors, including the minstrels of the earls of March and Salisbury, appear in Bond, 'Last Days of Queen Isabella'.

46. TNA E101/393/4, f.9r.

47. For the bath see Bond, 'Last Days of Queen Isabella', p. 465. For the make-up see French *et al*, *Medicine*, p. 84.

48. See Bond, 'Last Days of Queen Isabella'. The days Edward ate with her were 26 October 1357; and 20 March, 29 April and 2 May 1358.

49. Bond, 'Last Days of Queen Isabella', p. 467; Bennet, 'Isabelle of France', p. 222.

50. Bond, 'Last Days of Queen Isabella', pp. 462–3, 469.

51. Bond, 'Last Days of Queen Isabella' on all points. The frequent visits by men such as the count of Tancarville, Marshal Audrehem and the sire d'Aubigny show that the French were very welcome in her household, whether she was staying at Hertford Castle or at her house in London.

52. TNA E101/393/4 f.4v.

53. For Isabella's alabaster effigy, see *HKW*, i, p. 468; Duffy, *Royal Tombs*, pp. 131–2. For the iron railings see TNA E101/393/7 m.14 and Duffy, ibid. Although no accounts survive for either Edward II's or Isabella's effigy, the appearance of early alabaster sculptures on both tombs, as well as John of Eltham's tomb, suggests that all three were royal commissions. The earlier ones were probably all made by William of Ramsey. The first effigy of Blanche of the Tower was provided by William Ramsey (see Duffy, *Royal Tombs*, p. 131), and the now-vanished canopy over the tomb of John of Eltham has been attributed to him, as has the tomb of Edward II at Gloucester (on the strength of similarities between the canopies of this and that of John of Eltham).

54. TNA E101/394/10 m.2.

55. According to Stow, writing in the sixteenth century, the heart of Edward of Carnarvon was buried beneath Isabella (Haines, 'Afterlife', pp. 73–4, 84 n.76). Agnes Ramsey, the daughter of William Ramsey – the royal master mason who had probably overseen the works at Gloucester at the time when Edward II was most probably interred there – was paid £10 and £96 18s 11d in connection with

the construction of the tomb 'as a result of an agreement made with the queen's council made during her life' (TNA E101/393/7 m.13). It appears likely that the Ramsey family had not only taken care of the body of Edward II but his heart also, and had probably been guarding the latter for the best part of the last seventeen years.

56. *WCS*, p. 389.
57. This was in February 1358. See Sumption, *Trial by Fire*, p. 312.
58. Bennet, 'Isabelle of France', p. 218. For the presents of barrels of wine, see *Foedera*, iii, 1, p. 411. Later he lodged him in Hertford Castle (Isabella's residence at the time of her death) and Somerton Castle. See *Foedera*, iii, 1, p. 442.
59. Rogers, 'Anglo-French Peace Negotiations', pp. 205–8.
60. Holmes, 'Edmund Mortimer, third Earl of March and Earl of Ulster' in *ODNB*, gives 1358. An allowance from the Mortimer estates was made in 1360 for the maintenance of Philippa. See *CP*, viii, p. 447.
61. TNA E101/393/10 m.1.
62. Barber, *Black Prince*, p. 155.
63. Ormrod, 'Personal Religion', p. 872.
64. He issued instructions for his brother's body to be moved to the Confessor's chapel and asked that the best places in that chapel be reserved for him and his family. See Duffy, *Royal Tombs*, p. 125.
65. Sir Walter Manny was ennobled in 1347, being first summoned to parliament as Lord Manny on Edward's thirty-fifth birthday (*CP*, viii, p. 574).
66. Sumption, *Trial by Fire*, p. 425.
67. Sumption, *Trial by Fire*, p. 428.
68. Sumption, *Trial by Fire*, pp. 440–2.
69. Froissart quoted in Rogers, 'Anglo-French Peace Negotiations', p. 212.
70. Riley (ed.), *Walsingham*, i, p. 289; Haydon (ed.), *Eulogium Historiarum*, iii, pp. 228–9; Lumby (ed.), *Knighton*, ii, p. 112. Further references to the extreme cold are given in Sumption, *Trial by Fire*, p. 623 n.73 and Barnes, *Edward III*, p. 583.
71. Barnes, *Edward III*, p. 583.
72. Edouard Perroy regarded the whole campaign as a 'lamentable escapade', and had no doubt that it constituted a 'failure' (Perroy, *Hundred Years War*, p. 138). Writing in 1959, with little understanding of Edward's complicated negotiating strategy and no sympathy for his religious outlook, Professor le Patourel regarded the subsequent peace as a French 'victory' because Edward was unable to impose the terms of the Second Treaty of London (le Patourel, 'Treaty of Brétigny', p. 33). Others are discussed in *WCS*, p. 417.
73. Froissart's account has the duke ending his speech with the warning that 'we might lose in a single day all that we have gained in twenty years', but this is doubtful. It is difficult to see how Edward could have lost anything in a single day, unless Black Monday was to be repeated. There was no French army in the field.
74. Prior to May 1360, household expenditure was low, around £16–£22 per day. After landing at Rye it climbs to nearly £109 on 1 June and £135 on the day after (TNA E393/11 f.50r). Then the daily amount drops back to about £15 or less until about the end of August.

15: Outliving Victory

1. Master Adam of Pulletria, the king's surgeon, was in attendance on him in late 1360. See TNA E101/393/15 m.2.
2. Thompson (ed.), *Chronicon Angliae*, p. 49.
3. TNA E101/393/15 m.5. See *OED* for the earlier meaning of 'woodbine'.
4. Similarly the Black Prince's motto *'Ich Dien'* (I serve) has a personal source rather than a literary one. The origin of his other motto, *'houmont'* is unknown, but no literary source has been found. It seems rather unlikely therefore that literary sources were the origins of the fourteenth-century royal mottoes, as Vale suggests in *E3&Chiv*, p. 65.
5. TNA E101/393/11m. f.61v.
6. TNA E101/393/15 m.10.
7. Ormrod, 'Henry of Grosmont, Duke of Lancaster', in *ODNB*. *CP* has 24 March.
8. TNA E101/393/15 m.14.
9. The following portents are taken from Brie (ed.), *Brut*, ii, pp. 313–14; Haydon (ed.), *Eulogium Historiarum*, p. 229; Riley (ed.), *Walsingham*, p. 290.
10. Most chroniclers claim this, but in the form that places his name in the roll-call of the dead for the whole year. However, his making his will ten days before he died, in early March, suggests a death not from plague but a slower decline. This was before the plague spread, an event usually associated with May 1361 and later.
11. TNA E101/393/15 mm.1, 7, 14.
12. *Foedera*, iii, 2, p. 616.
13. For a description of the marriage arrangements see Barber, *Black Prince*, pp. 172–5.
14. Barber, *Black Prince*, p. 174.
15. Goodman, *John of Gaunt*, p. 42, states that Mary died before 13 September 1361. She died thirty weeks after her marriage, according to the entry (under Richmond) in *CP*, vol x, p. 823.
16. For example, Ormrod in his article on Edward in *ODNB* suggests the possibility that Edward forced the compromise at Calais because he still had dreams of conquering more of France. Barber in *Black Prince*, p. 178, points out that the letters of authority issued to the prince in Gascony assumed the renunciations had already been made, a fact which can hardly have been unknown to John Freton, the author of the grant of Aquitaine. While Edward himself may not have authorised this anachronism, an irregularity such as this in a chancery as experienced and sophisticated as Edward's can only have been authorised by a very senior figure, almost certainly the Chancellor himself, William Edington, who would have known Edward's mind on the matter.
17. Given-Wilson, *Royal Household*, p. 53. Imworth had his house burnt down and was dragged from sanctuary and beheaded during the Peasants Revolt (1381).
18. March was 31, Northampton 48, Lancaster about 50 (according to Ormrod in *ODNB*), Beauchamp about 44 and Holland about 40.
19. Lionel landed on 15 September 1361. McKisack, *Fourteenth Century*, pp. 231–2; the complement of men is from Ormrod, 'Lionel of Antwerp' in *ODNB*.
20. TNA E101/394 m.3. The small amount of powder suggests that this was a handgun, perhaps one for Lionel himself to use on the unsuspecting Irish.
21. McKisack, *Fourteenth Century*, p. 233.

22. Barber, *Black Prince*, p. 178. The practice is reminiscent of Edward's own code-words 'Pater Sancte' in his own hand when writing to Pope John XXII in 1329.

23. Ormrod, 'Edward III and his family', p. 409; Gillespie, 'Isabella, Countess of Bedford', in *ODNB*.

24. Only thirty-eight magnates were summoned compared to 174 commoners representing 86 cities, towns, etc. See *RE3*, pp. 92, 180.

25. The prompt payment clause was consistently ignored. See Given-Wilson, *Royal Household*, pp. 45–6.

26. Ruffhead (ed.), *Statutes at Large*, i, p. 311. For a full discussion of this legislation, and the wording on the parliament roll and the statute roll, see Ormrod, 'Use of English'.

27. Barber, *Black Prince*, p. 187.

28. McKisack, *Fourteenth Century*, p. 524.

29. Ormrod, 'Use of English', p. 751, quoting Trevisa.

30. A somewhat contrary view is put forward in Ormrod, 'Use of English'. Ormrod suggests that the Statute of Pleadings performed one of three purposes: 1. as part of a package of concessions offered by Edward in return for renewed taxation; 2. to affirm the authority of the Justices of the Peace; and 3. a statement of English independence from France. None of these are particularly convincing. With regard to the last of these, while independence may have informed a decision underlining English authority, one has to ask why this did not happen at an earlier date, say 1340? The answer surely lies in the limited uses of English among the nobility and their households. As for the local justices, this may have been a pragmatic gesture on their behalf, certainly, but if so it amounts to little more than a recognition that for effective local government there needed to be an effective mode of communication, and so this again reflects developments in language beyond the king's control. The most likely of these three explanations is the first, but it surely is too cynical to link the recognition of the language purely with taxation. The recognition of English served many purposes – nationalist, pragmatic, etc. – but it also and probably most importantly linked the king and his government with the people. In this reading, the Statute of Pleadings was more about Edward's view of kingship as much as any cynical bartering with parliament.

31. It is not known why Edmund was only created an earl when his two brothers (who were not much older) were created dukes. As discussed above it might be because Edward wondered about his legitimacy (see Chapter Eight). It might be, however, that Edward simply did not like or trust him as much, or that Edmund was just not interested in a responsibility-laden political position. But Edward had installed him as a member of the Order of the Garter, and clearly had plans for him in the marriage with Flanders.

32. TNA E101/394/16 m.6.

33. See Appendix Seven for a detailed list, with references.

34. TNA E101/392/15 m.13.

35. Given-Wilson, *Royal Household*, p. 278.

36. Given-Wilson, *Royal Household*, p. 61.

37. Given-Wilson, *Royal Household*, pp. 61–2.

38. For the legislation see Ruffhead (ed.), *Statutes at Large*, i, pp. 315–16; for the comments of Thomas Walsingham see Riley (ed.), *Walsingham*, i, p. 299.

39. Henisch, *Fast and Feast*, p. 176.

40. Unwin (ed.), *Finance and Trade under Edward III*, p. 246.

41. He was prevented from doing so by parliament in 1368. See Ormrod, 'Edward III', *ODNB*.

42. Bradbury, *Medieval Archer*, p. 93.

43. Juliet Vale, 'Philippa of Hainault' in *ODNB*.

44. Haydon (ed.), *Eulogium Historiarum*, p. 227 (fall); Duffy, *Royal Tombs*, p. 133.

45. TNA E101/396/2 f.40v. The physician in question (John Glaston) also left court for twenty-two days in order to obtain further medicines. These were 'for the king's person' so there is no doubt that it was Edward who was ill, not Philippa.

46. TNA E101/396/2 f.38v (king of India); *HKW*, ii, p. 985 (times spent in New Forest). The wardrobe was based at Windsor from 12 April–24 July 1366, then shifted to Havering until 10 September, then came back to Windsor for the period 12 September–31 January 1367. See TNA E101/396/2 ff.3r–29r. I have been unable to find out who this 'king of India' might have been.

47. Taylor, Childs and Watkiss (eds), *St Albans Chronicle*, p. 43.

48. Galway, 'Alice Perrers's son John', p. 243; Given-Wilson and Curteis, *Royal Bastards*, p. 138.

49. Barber, *Black Prince*, pp. 208–9.

50. For example, Sumption, *Trial by Fire*, p. 572, whose view is that Edward did not want to renew the peace precisely so he could enlarge his claim on France, and Ormrod, 'Edward III' in *ODNB*, whose view is similar, although more cautiously expressed than Sumption's.

51. Work on her tomb began in 1362. In 1367 she commissioned the tomb effigy. See Duffy, *Royal Tombs*, p. 133.

52. *RE3*, p. 68.

53. One result of this was that the 1368 vintage remained in the warehouses at Bordeaux, unbought, unshipped and undrunk, with the consequent loss of the wine tax to the prince. See Barber, *Black Prince*, p. 213.

54. Ruffhead (ed.), *Statutes at Large*, i, p. 327.

55. Barber, *Black Prince*, pp. 217–18.

56. Goodman, *John of Gaunt*, p. 46.

57. Duffy, *Royal Tombs*, p. 133.

58. Given-Wilson, *Royal Household*, pp. 78, 82.

59. TNA C53/151 no.1. This appears in the *Calendar of Charter Rolls* as Westminster but the MS states Windsor. The date of this charter is 23 December 1368.

60. Ormrod, 'Edward III', in *ODNB*, quoting TNA E101/396/11.

61. *Foedera*, iii, 2, p. 864.

62. Johnes (ed.), *Froissart*, i, p. 428. The wording has been modernised.

63. Goodman, *John of Gaunt*, p. 47 gives 15 August. Duffy, *Royal Tombs*, p. 133 gives 10 August. Ormrod in his *OBNB* article on Edward gives 15 August; Vale in her article on Philippa gives 'shortly before 14 August'. The 15th appears to be correct; see TNA E101/401/2 f.38r.

64. McKisack, *Fourteenth Century*, p. 336.

65. Goodman, *John of Gaunt*, p. 47.

16: A Tattered Coat Upon a Stick

1. Those alive in 1370 were the prince, the Captal de Buch, the earls of Stafford and Salisbury, Lord Mohun, Sir Hugh Wrottesley, Sir Neil Loring and Sir Walter Paveley. The three knights who survived him were Wrottesley, Loring and the earl of Salisbury.

2. Other countries remained neutral: Flanders and Navarre, for example, which each signed a treaty. Scotland also remained neutral, despite pressure from the French. David II, falling behind with the payment of his ransom, came to London to visit Edward and to explain the failure to raise the money. Edward allowed him to defer payment on the condition that he did not fail a second time. See Balfour-Melville, *Edward III and David II*, p. 21.

3. Given-Wilson, *Royal Household*, p. 72.

4. In his *ODNB* article on Edward, Ormrod states that the speed of his medical decline should not be exaggerated: 'at least until the mid-1370s there is evidence that he continued to take an active, if sporadic, part in the business of govern-ment'. But this is a limited view. Government – as in the issuing of instructions – did not need Edward to be physically able, just sane and coherent. Most of Edward's other activities *did* require him to be physically able, and so it is misleading to use the issuing of orders as a measure of his health. The very long period of medical assistance detailed both in the records of medicines and medical practi-tioners inclines the present writer to take the opposite view, that we should not exaggerate his healthiness. This view is further supported by the decline in the volume of his business, his isolation, and the lack of travelling. Even the level of his hunting reduced.

5. Lydon, 'William of Windsor', pp. 253–4; *Foedera*, iii, 2, pp. 924, 928.

6. Rogers (ed.), *Wars of Edward III*, p. 194.

7. It is noticeable that Isabella's three brothers died between the ages of 27 and 33, and Edward's own brother died at twenty, and the sons of his sister Eleanor also died in their thirties. Of course it is perfectly possible that this was a coincidence – that they all just happened to die relatively young – but another explanation would be a hereditary illness, such as an X-chromosome-related weakness which affects only men (although carried by women). If it was carried to John of Eltham by Isabella, and also affected her brothers, the X-chromosome in question would have to have been inherited from her mother, Joan of Navarre, and in this context it is interesting to note that her father Enriques died at about 30. However, so many royal people died young in the fourteenth century that we should not rush to any conclusions. Also it is obvious that Edward did *not* die young, so if his uncles, brother and nephew were all carried off by an X-chromosome problem, it would be unlikely also to explain his decline, for it would appear that the 50% chance of inheriting the relevant chromosome from his mother would have gone in his favour.

8. We might say that Chaucer had fallen in with Alice Perrers and her circle, and that the reward was really her doing. This idea is explored in Braddy, 'Chaucer and Dame Alice Perrers' and revisited in the same author's 'Chaucer, Alice Perrers and Cecily Chaumpaigne'. The date of the gift being the feast of St George and

the gift being so akin to the annual present of wine accorded to later poets laureate might incline us to suspect that this was a reward for a reading of his poetry. Certainly Chaucer had already composed *The Book of the Duchess* on the late wife of John of Gaunt by this time. Also it should be noted that Chaucer was receiving his pitcher of wine while Alice was banished from court in 1376. She did not return until 22 October, but Chaucer was being given a gallon of wine every day on 14 October. See TNA E101/398/9 f.28v.

9. *Foedera*, iii, 2, p. 989.
10. *Foedera*, iii, 2, p. 990.
11. Given-Wilson, *Royal Household*, p. 148; Ormrod, 'Edward III' in *ODNB*.
12. As she wrote her will in 1400, it is unlikely that she was born much before 1340, and quite likely that she was born after that date. It is therefore unlikely that she was older than her early twenties, and may have been a teenager when she met Edward.
13. See Given-Wilson, *Royal Household*, p. 60 for the regulation of these women.
14. Alice was Edward's mistress from at least 1364, and possibly from the union of Edward's and Philippa's households in 1360, until Edward's death. It is not known how long Elizabeth Lambert or Shore, otherwise known as Jane Shore, was Edward IV's mistress, but it was unlikely to have been anything like as long as thirteen years. In any case, Edward IV had several other concubines throughout his period of enjoyment with Elizabeth.
15. Taylor, Childs and Watkiss (eds), *St Albans Chronicle*, p. 21.
16. Nichols (ed.), *A Collection of All the Wills*, pp. 66–77.
17. Taylor, Childs and Watkiss (eds), *St Albans Chronicle*, pp. 38–9.
18. Taylor, Childs and Watkiss (eds), *St Albans Chronicle*, p. 51.
19. Taylor, Childs and Watkiss (eds), *St Albans Chronicle*, p. 46, n.56.
20. Devon (ed.), *Issues of the Exchequer*, p. 200. Alice was banished from court at this time, so this is very probably Edward's action, not her buying a chest to lock away the accusations against her husband.
21. TNA E101/397/20 m.29.
22. Galbraith (ed.), *Anonimalle*, p. 95; Ormrod, 'Edward III' in *ODNB* states that the problem at this time was a large abscess. An impostume was the word used for various ailments. The definition in the earliest English dictionary composed by a doctor of physic, Dr Bullokar's *English Expositor* (1616), is 'a quantity of evil humours gathered into one part of the body. There are two kinds hereof. One when inflamed: blood, being turned to corrupt matter, filleth some place. The other when without any inflamation: nature thrusteth those humours into some part apt to receive them'.
23. Raine (ed.), *Letters from Northern Registers*, pp. 410–11.
24. TNA E101/397/20 m.29.
25. Nichols (ed.), *A Collection of All the Wills*, pp. 59–65.
26. His executors were John of Gaunt, the bishop of Lincoln, the bishop of Worcester, the bishop of Hereford, William Latimer, the Chancellor John Knyvett, the Treasurer Robert Ashton, the Chamberlain Roger Beauchamp, the Steward John de Ypres, and Nicholas Carrew, Keeper of the Privy Seal. For the disinheritance of the earls of March, see Bennet, 'Edward III's Entail', especially p. 592.
27. TNA E101/397/20 m.7.

28. Taylor, Childs and Watkiss (eds), *St Albans Chronicle*, p. 59.
29. Taylor, Childs and Watkiss (eds), *St Albans Chronicle*, p. 57.
30. TNA E101/397/20 m.8.
31. Ormrod, 'Edward III' in *ODNB*.
32. Taylor, Childs and Watkiss (eds), *St Albans Chronicle*, p. 103.
33. On 5 May 1377 various exotic cloths and one thousand golden nails, a peck of muslin and three woollen scarlet carpets were brought to Sheen for making of a throne for the king so that he might sit up in his chamber. TNA E101/397/20 m.10.

17: Edward the Gracious

1. TNA E101/397/20 mm.11–12, 20, 30–32; E101/398/9 f.31v.
2. Stephen Hadley, a member of the household, was reimbursed £22 4s 11d for an effigy in the likeness of the late king, a sceptre, an orb, and a cross with a silver gilded crucifix, as well as for divers other costs incurred in preparing the body for burial (TNA E101/398/9 f.23v). For the most recent work on the wooden effigy, which is still extant, see Harvey and Mortimer, *Funeral Effigies*, pp. 31–5.
3. TNA E101/397/20 m.12.
4. TNA E101/398/9. Cooking expenses at the coronation were just in excess of this, at £585 (Shenton, 'English Court', p. 135).
5. This translation has been taken from Morgan, 'Apotheosis', p. 861.
6. Brie (ed.), *Brut*, ii, p. 333.
7. This has been slightly modernised for ease of reading.
8. Riley (ed.), *Walsingham*, i, p. 327.
9. Morgan, 'Apotheosis', p. 863, quoting Bodleian Eng. Poet. MS a.1.
10. Morgan, 'Apotheosis', p. 866, quoting BL Harley MS 1808.
11. Keiser, 'Edward III and the Alliterative "Morte Arthure"'.
12. See Appendix Eight for the reasoning underlying this statement.

Appendix 1

1. The original is now in Devon Record Office, Exeter, ref: Chanter 2.
2. Hingeston-Randolph (ed.), *Register of Walter de Stapeldon* (1892), p. 169.
3. Trotter, 'Pre-marital inspection', p. 3.
4. Nederlandse Genealogische Vereniging, 'Karel de Grote (I)', *Gens Nostra*, nos. 10/11, Oct/Nov 1990, 382.
5. *CCR 1318–23*, p. 132.
6. *CPR 1317–21*, p. 336.
7. Devon Record Office: Chanter 2, f.142r.
8. See Hingeston-Randolph, *Register of Walter Stapeldon*, p. 555 for his itinerary.
9. A. Wauters, *Table chronologique des Chartes et Diplômes imprimés concernant l'Histoire de la Belgique*, viii, 1301–20 (Brussels, c. 1907).
10. *DNB*, quoting Luce (ed.), *Froissart*, i, p. 285.

Appendix 3

1. In contemporary English sources *arestati* can mean 'conscripted' or 'commanded', as well as 'arrested'. One finds the word used to describe the enlisting of craftsmen and painters for Edward's works at Westminster, for example.
2. Norwell's account book has been published. For these references see Lyon *et al.* (eds), *Wardrobe Book of William Norwell*, pp. 212, 214. The entries are also published in Cuttino and Lyman, 'Where is Edward II?', p. 530.
3. Alessandra Sisto, *Genova nel duecento: il Capitolo di San Lorenzo*, Collana Storica di Fonti e Studi 28 (Genoa, 1979), p. 167.
4. *GT*, pp. 259–60.
5. *Foedera*, ii, 2, pp. 1107, 1126.
6. Niccolo was the son of Luca's sister Flisca and Alberto Malaspina, Marchese di Oramala (*Dizionario biografico degli Italiani*, vol 48 (Rome, 1997), p. 502; Fayen (ed.), *Lettres de Jean XXII*, no. 203).
7. In October 1340, January 1341, March 1341 and June 1342 he was appointed in connection with the collection and shipping of wool on behalf of the Societies of the Bardi and Peruzzi. See *CPR 1340–43*, pp. 45, 75, 145, 174. On the strength of this we might speculate that he was related either to Dinas Forcetti or Forzetti, a Florentine agent of the Bardi in England. There is no evidence in Sapori's edition of the records of the Peruzzi that he was related to Francesco Forcetti/Forzetti, the Sicilian agent of the Peruzzi.
8. *CPR 1340–43*, p. 569; *CPR 1343–45*, p. 565.
9. *CEPR*, iii, pp. 3, 11, 23.
10. *CPR 1334–38*, p. 467. Antonio was Luca's nephew. Giffredus was the attorney of Bernarbo Malaspina, the bishop of Luni, another nephew of Luca and brother of Niccolo Malaspina. Bernarbo had accompanied Luca to England in 1317 and witnessed his will at Avignon in 1336.
11. As stated in Chapter Five, there is no doubt that Luca Fieschi and Edward II acknowledged each other as kinsmen, as many records describe Luca as 'the king's kinsman'. For examples, see Hilda Johnstone, *Letters of Edward. Prince of Wales 1304–5* (1931), p. 54; *CCW*, pp. 388, 511; *CPR 1292–1301*, p. 608 (relating to Luca); *CPR 1317–21*, p. 14; Timmins (ed.) *Melton Register*, v, no. 423 (relating to Luca's nephews Adrian and Innocent respectively) and *Foedera*, ii, 1, p. 274 and *CPR 1313–17*, p. 340 (relating to Carlo, Luca's brother). How the Fieschi were related to the Plantagenets is harder to establish. In approaching this question we may first examine which members of the Fieschi were – and which were not – acknowledged as royal kinsmen. Those specified above as being connected were all descended from Tedisio Fieschi (d. abt 1248). All the Fieschi descended from Tedisio's brothers, Opizzo (d. abt 1268) and Alberto (d. before 1226) – including Manuel Fieschi and his cousins and uncles – were never described as relatives of the royal family. So the connection must lie in Tedisio's marriage or later. Next we may observe that no Fieschi claimed kinship with the English royal family prior to 1278. This includes all of Tedisio's children, namely: Alberto (d. 1278), Ugolino (d. abt 1274), Niccolo (d. abt 1304), Cardinal Ottobono (Pope Adrian V, d.1276), Rolando (fl.1267), Percevalle (d.1290), Vernazio, Federico (d.1303), Agnese, Caracosa

and Beatrice (d.1283). This is significant, as at least three of these sons visited England in the later thirteenth century. The first reference to a blood connection is a petition written in July 1278 by Brumisan, widow of the aforementioned Ugolino, son of Tedisio, on behalf of her son Raimondo, who had been given an English income of fifteen marks per annum by the aforesaid Cardinal Ottobono which had not been paid for some years (*Foedera*, ii, 1, p. 559). This cannot relate to a Fieschi relationship, as Brumisan specifically claimed that she was a kinswoman of Edward I's through her father, whom she says was descended from the counts of Savoy. This checks out: she names her father as 'Jacobo de Cateto' (Giacomo del Caretto), who was the son of Enrico del Caretto (d.1231) and Agate (d.1247), daughter of Guillaume II (d.1252), count of Geneva, whose mother was of the Savoy family and whose sister, Beatrice of Geneva, married Tomasso I (d.1233), count of Savoy and was thus the grandmother of Eleanor of Provence, Edward I's mother. This makes Brumisan a third cousin of Edward I, not her husband. As a result, we may be certain that the earliest reference to a kinship tie between a male member of the Fieschi and the English royal family is that of 1301, when Luca first visited England (*CPR 1292–1301*, p. 608). This implies that the kinship probably has nothing to do with the marriage of Beatrice Fieschi (d.1283) and Tomasso II (d.1259), count of Savoy, which took place in about 1250, as this marriage never led to claims of royal kinship by Beatrice's brothers when they came to England in the later thirteenth century, and would not have entailed a blood connection anyway. The only remaining possibility is that Luca and Carlo were connected with the Plantagenets through their mother, Leonora or Lionetta (wife of Niccolo Fieschi), whose maiden name is unknown. As Luca claimed to be also connected to Jaime II of Aragon when he was appointed a cardinal, this indicates that his mother was almost certainly descended from the house of Savoy, as Jaime II's mother, Constanza (d. 1302), was the daughter (by her second husband) of Beatrice of Savoy (d.1257), daughter of the above-mentioned Tomasso I (d.1233), count of Savoy. As Leonora was probably born in the 1230s (Luca was born about 1275), it is just possible that she was a daughter of Beatrice of Savoy by her first husband, Manfred III (d.1244), count of Saluzzo. This would in turn connect her to the earls of Lincoln, and it is perhaps significant that several ecclesiastical incomes granted to the Fieschi were in the diocese of Lincoln. So, although we may be sure the connection was through her, and that she was descended from the counts of Savoy, we cannot be certain of the exact link until we know the name of her father.

12. *CPR 1324–27*, p. 119.

13. Brocklesby (ed.), *Melton Register*, iv, no. 638.

14. Brocklesby (ed.), *Melton Register*, iv, no. 757.

15. In 1326 Edward II was definitely alive. But in 1335 the passage relating to him and Edward III (as king) was phrased very strangely: 'et nostra ac inclite memorie domini Edwardi filii regis Edwardi secundi' (Hamilton Thompson, *English Clergy*, p. 258). This has to relate to Edward II somehow (as Edward III's charter of July 1338 states that it does) but the only way it can do that is to read 'domini Edwardi secundi, filii regis Edwardi', which it does not. Also this would exclude Edward III, whose name should also appear. It certainly appears very prominently among those benefiting from prayers in the 1343 version, which unambiguously separates the dead Edward II from Edward III. It is possible that the wording is deliberately

ambiguous. However, it is also possible that a mistake has been made in copying the ordinances into the register.

16. Knowles and Hadcock, *Medieval Religious Houses*, p. 328 (1342 foundation); TNA C143/274/14 (endowment).
17. Cuttino and Lyman, 'Where is Edward II?', p. 531.

Appendix 5

1. Thompson (ed.), *Murimuth*, pp. 200–1.
2. *WCS*, p. 232.
3. *WCS*, p. 218.

Appendix 6

1. See for example, Ormrod in *RE3*, p. 27, whose view is that honour was the only criterion for 'election' to the order.
2. *E3&Chiv*, p. 82.
3. *E3&Chiv*, pp. 53, 82, 83.
4. *E3&Chiv*, p. 84, quoting *Register of Edward the Black Prince*, iv, pp. 72–3.
5. Ormrod, 'For Arthur and St George', p. 20, referring to *E3&Chiv*, p. 83, and mentioning that it was accepted by two other recent writers on the subject: D'A.J.D. Boulton, *Knights of the Crown* (Woodbridge, 2000), pp. 115–16; Hugh Collins, *Order of the Garter* (Oxford, 2000), p. 13.
6. TNA E101/391/15, m.6. The account itself dates the Lichfield tournament to 9 April 1348 but Professor Ormrod disagrees, suggesting May, in line with Edward's itinerary. Among those knights who would be founder knights are John Lisle, Hugh Courtenay, John Grey, Miles Stapeldon, John Beauchamp and the earl of Lancaster. Among those who were not founder members are Walter Manny, Richard de la Vache, Philip Despenser, Roger Beauchamp, Ralph Ferrers and Robert Mauley.
7. According to Barnes, *Edward III*, p. 419, the prince of Wales, Sir John Grey, Sir Robert Mauley, Sir John Chandos, Sir Roger Beauchamp, the earls of Lancaster and Suffolk and Sir John Beauchamp were at the Canterbury tournament. Most of these men were founder members of the Order, but Mauley and Suffolk were not. See Ormrod, 'For Arthur and St George', p. 19 for the dating of the Canterbury tournament. After 5 September, there were no tournaments (due to the death of the royal prince and his sister) until April 1349.
8. This statement is based on the assumption that there was no formal constitution of the exclusive membership between the Canterbury tournament and Edward's journey to France, on 29 October 1348. No tournament is known to have taken place during this period.
9. Thompson (ed.), *Galfridi le Baker*, p. 109.
10. *E3&Chiv*, p. 83.
11. *Foedera*, iii, 1, p. 182.
12. *HBC*, p. 129.

13. *E3&Chiv*, p. 84; Barber, *Black Prince*, p. 84.
14. Fowler, *King's Lieutenant*, p. 194, quoting the earl's own *Livre de Seyntz Medicines*. See Chapter Eleven.

Appendix 7

1. *CPR 1334–38*, pp. 43, 50, 117, 172, 507. The last is the final reference to him as the king's physician, being dated 30 August 1337.
2. Lyon *et al.* (eds), *Wardrobe Book of William Norwell*, pp. 303, 348, 389, 439. De Controne received a gift from Edward on the last day of August 1339 of £1,000. He crossed to the Low Countries with Edward in 1338 with six esquires and twenty-two horses. He was reimbursed at the rate of 4s per day for his services and 4d per day for each of his six esquires.
3. Ormrod, 'Royal Nursery'.
4. Martha Carlin, 'John Gaddesden (d. 1348/9)', *ODNB*.
5. He is first described as the king's physician on 20 November 1338, when he was granted twenty marks annually at the Exchequer until a stable income could be arranged for him. See *CPR 1334–38*, p. 194.
6. Lyon *et al.* (eds), *Wardrobe Book of William Norwell*, p. 303.
7. *CPR 1343–45*, p. 380; *CPR 1345–48*, p. 509.
8. He was still in office on 16 September 1359. See *CPR 1358–61*, p. 274. See also Gask, 'Medical Staff of Edward the Third', pp. 50–3.
9. *CPR 1345–48*, pp. 229, 330, 552.
10. Rawcliffe, *Medicine and Society*, p. 111; *Foedera*, iii, 2, p. 703 (1 June 1363); *CPR 1367–70*, p. 58.
11. £20 annuity for life 23 March 1364 *CPR 1361–64*, p. 477; TNA E101/396/2 f.40v (1366); E101/396/11 (1369, quoted in *ODNB*); E101/397/5 f.36r (1371–72); f.79r (1372); E101/398/9 f.25r (1376–77).
12. *CPR 1367–70*, pp. 103, 412; *CPR 1374–77*, pp. 352, 354, 368; TNA E101/397/20 m.8.
13. TNA E101/398/9 f.25r.
14. *CPR 1340–43*, p. 84.
15. *CPR 1345–48*, pp. 394, 447.
16. TNA E101/393/15 m.2. This is dated 1360.
17. *CPR 1354–57*, p. 542; *CPR 1358–61*, p. 105; *CPR 1361–64*, p. 138; *CPR 1370–74*, pp. 202, 401.
18. TNA E101/397/20 m.8; *CPR 1358–61*, p. 231; *CPR 1361–64*, p. 270; *CPR 1367–70*, pp. 46, 402; *CCR 1369–74*, p. 153; *CPR 1370–74*, pp. 135. 140; Gask, 'Medical Staff of Edward the Third', pp. 53–5; Fowler, *King's Lieutenant*, p. 217.
19. TNA E101/397/20 m.8.

Appendix 8

1. For Roger of Clarendon see Given-Wilson and Curteis, *Royal Bastards*, pp. 143–6. It is almost certain that John de Galeis was not a son of the Black Prince, as he is not mentioned in the will, nor was he brought up at court.

2. The date of 16 June comes from *CP*, ii, p. 69 which does not cite its source. The date of March 1332 is in Alison Weir, *Britain's Royal Families* (Pimlico, 2002), p. 95, based on the understanding that Philippa was churched on 30 April. This is incorrect. Philippa's churching in 1332 was held on Sunday 19 July (see *E3&Chiv*, p. 173; TNA E101/386/2 m.7). Shenton states that Isabella was born in May as her churching took place in June, but this reasoning seems to be based on the presumption that Philippa had to be with the royal household, which left Woodstock as mentioned in Chapter Five before the end of June. Edward returned to Woodstock (where Philippa had probably remained) in July. However, we do not know exactly what the royal custom was – in the case of female children – between birth and churching. If the biblical period for a female child was observed (Leviticus xii, 2–5), this would entail a wait of eighty days between the birth and the churching. This means that it is possible that Isabella was born in May, but not for the reasons which Shenton gives. See Shenton, 'English Court', pp. 157, 159.

3. *DNB*; *CP*, ii, p. 70 (date of death).

4. For example, Alison Weir, *Britain's Royal Families* (Pimlico, 2002), p. 95, has 'before May 1335'. The confusion probably stems from some late payments for the baptism of the king's daughter which date from April 1335. For example TNA E101/387/9 m.5 (17 April 1335). Some contemporary documents refer to her as 'Joan of the Tower', confusing her birthplace with that of her aunt.

5. TNA E101/386/16 m.7.

6. Normally churchings were held on a Sunday, forty days after the birth of a male child, and possibly eighty after a female (although we cannot be certain that biblical practice was adhered to). However, in 1355 Philippa was not churched after Edmund of Langley's birth until 22 February, Edmund having been born on 7 January (see *E3&Chiv*, p. 174). It might have been a difficult birth. Either way, the period of forty days should not be too rigidly adhered to.

7. *Foedera* ii, 2, p. 880.

8. Ormrod, 'Royal Nursery', n.83.

9. Shenton claims that William was born 'just before Christmas 1336', but this is on the strength of the wardrobe being at Hatfield on 20–21 December. This is more probably the time when the king accompanied Philippa there, and then departed. The king returned to Hatfield for the churching, which certainly took place on 16 February 1337.

10. TNA E101/388/2 m.1.

11. Murimuth states that Gaunt was born 'in principio mensis Februarii', which Shenton translates as 1 February. If this was the case, it has to be wondered why the more usual 'primo die Februarii' was not used. It is thus more likely that this should be translated as 'at the beginning of February'. See Thompson (ed.), *Murimuth*, p. 104; Shenton, 'English Court', p. 162.

12. With regard to his birth, *HBC* (pp. 36, 419) has his birth in June 1342, which on the face of it would explain how come he may have been conceived despite his father's absence from his mother in September 1340 (see Chapter Eight). However, TNA E101/388/11 clearly has Philippa's churching at Langley in 1341, so the widely accepted date of 1341 is correct, not 1342. As to the specific date, Shenton has argued that the churching took place on 7 or 8 July, on the strength of a

payment to a minstrel. This is probably too late, as shown by Ormrod in his 'Royal Nursery', n.34.

13. TNA E101/391/14 m.3.
14. See *ODNB*; Given-Wilson and Curteis, *Royal Bastards*, pp. 136–7.
15. Galway, 'Alice Perrers's son John'.
16. TNA E101/397/20 m.9; Given-Wilson and Curteis, *Royal Bastards*, p. 138.
17. Given-Wilson and Curteis, *Royal Bastards*, pp. 136–7.
18. These were (1) Elizabeth Mortimer (1371–1417) who married Henry 'Hotspur' Percy (1361–1403); (2) Constance Holland (1387–1437) who married (2ndly) Sir John Grey (d. 1439); (3) John Holland (1395–1447), duke of Exeter; (4) Edmund Beaufort (1406?–1455), duke of Somerset; (5) Elizabeth Ferrers (d. 1434), who married John Greystoke (d. 1436); (6) Mary Ferrers (d. 1458), who married Sir Ralph Neville (d. 1458); (7) Richard Neville (d. 1460), earl of Salisbury; (8) William Neville (d.1463), earl of Kent; (9) George Neville (d. 1469), Lord Latimer; (10) Edward Neville (d. 1476), Lord Abergavenny; (11) Eleanor – the illegitimate daughter of Thomas Holland and Constance (daughter of Edmund of Langley) who married James Touchet (d. 1459), Lord Audley; (12) Richard Plantagenet (1411–1460), duke of York; (13) Humphrey Stafford (1402–1460), duke of Buckingham; (14) Henry Bourchier (*c.* 1408–1483), earl of Essex; (15) William Bourchier (1412?–1469?), Lord Fitzwarin; (16) John Bourchier (1415?–1474?), Lord Berners. In addition, the following five great-grandchildren of Edward III inter-married with the above or their children and had offspring by them: Anne Stafford (d.1411), who married John Holland (1395?–1447), duke of Exeter; Isabella (1409–1484) who married Henry Bourchier (*c.* 1408–1483), earl of Essex; Anne Neville (d.1480) who married Humphrey (1402–1460), duke of Buckingham; Cecily Neville, who married Richard Plantagenet (1411–1460), duke of York; Eleanor Neville (d.1472) who married (2ndly) Henry Percy (1392–1455), earl of Northumberland. In the above reckoning lines which died out before 1500 have been ignored. Joan Beaufort (d.1445), who married James I of Scotland and later Sir James Stewart, has also been ignored in order to eliminate overestimating the number of descendants in England (as opposed to Scotland) and the descendants of Humphrey (1390–1447), duke of Gloucester (through his illegitimate daughter, Antigone) have also been ignored to eliminate overestimating the number of descendants in England (as opposed to Wales).
19. It was almost certainly no higher than the 2.77 million which has been widely accepted as the population in 1541. E.A. Wrigley and R.S. Schofield, *The Population History of England 1541–1871* (1981), pp. 531, 566.
20. E.A. Wrigley and R.S. Schofield, *The Population History of England 1541–1871* (1981), p. 531.
21. This factor is because 113 descendants would have been required to make every hundred marriages which included a descendant.
22. This includes the children of Gaunt who were later legitimised but not the illegitimate children of Edward himself or Edward the Black Prince (whose lines have not been included in the determination of 436 descendants by 1500). The twenty-two descendants here mentioned being: King Richard II; Mary and Philippa (daughters of Isabella of Woodstock); Philippa, countess of March (d.1380) and her four children (Elizabeth, Roger, Philippa and Edmund Mortimer); John

of Gaunt and his four legitimate children (Philippa, Elizabeth, Henry IV and Katherine), plus his four Beaufort offspring (John, Henry, Thomas and Joan); Edmund of Langley and his three children (Edward, Constance and Richard), and finally Thomas of Woodstock (1355–1397).

23. Somewhat strangely, this analysis is independently supported by the work of a group of American, French and Argentinian research physicists who concluded in 1999 that 'by going about thirty generations into your past, you and all your contemporaries will be related to everyone who lived then, at least to those who had offspring and who lived within that particular geographical or cultural realm'. This was based on a statistical analysis of the properties of the genealogy of Edward III back to Charlemagne. Although fewer generations than this separate Edward III from us – twenty to twenty-four being the average – the level of genetic saturation the physicists were looking for was nothing less than 100%. However, it is not clear to what extent the vagaries of class and geography were taken into account in this study. See 'Physics News Update', No. 428 (American Institute of Physics, 1999).

24. These three left no children, except Richard I, who did have one illegitimate son, Philip, to whom he gave the lordship of Cognac.

FULL TITLES OF WORKS APPEARING IN THE NOTES

A large number of articles and books were consulted in the course of writing this biography. Many were used just for background, and many others were checked only to confirm a lack of relevant information. It would be misleading and page-consuming to include all these works as sources. Similarly it would be pointless to repeat the entire bibliography of my book, *The Greatest Traitor*, which inevitably underpins the second and third chapters of this study. The following is therefore not a bibliography as such but merely a list of the full titles of works which appear in shortened form in the notes. Some items frequently cited are referred to only by abbreviations (e.g. *RE3* for Ormrod's *Reign of Edward III*). These are included in this list under both the abbreviation and the name of editor or author. Works which appear only once in the notes have usually been fully identified there, and do not appear in this list.

With regard to manuscript sources, these appear fully referenced in the notes. Approximately three hundred items in the National Archives (TNA) were looked at in the preparation of this work by Dr Paul Dryburgh and myself. The classes most frequently used were E101/382–400 (wardrobe accounts and associated documents) and C53 (charter rolls). The charter witnesses' names were drawn in part from the transcript in the Map Room at TNA, and in part from the originals (Appendix Four was based on the original rolls). The reference to the original roll has been given in all cases for ease of checking and consistency of style. In addition a few dozen manuscripts from other classes were consulted. These were not systematically searched; in most cases the items were identified through the online catalogue.

In the following list, place of publication has been given in all cases other than London. Record societies' and series' names have been omitted wherever possible.

John Aberth, 'Crime and Justice under Edward III: the case of Thomas de Lisle', *EHR*, 107 (1992), pp. 281–301

AC: *Age of Chivalry* (see next entry)

Jonathan Alexander and Paul Binski (eds), *The Age of Chivalry: Art in Plantagenet England 1200–1400* (1987)

J.J.G. Alexander, 'Painting and Manuscript Illumination for Royal Patrons in the Later Middle Ages', in V.J. Scattergood and J.W. Sherborne (eds), *English Court Culture in the Later Middle Ages* (1983)

E.W.M. Balfour-Melville, *Edward III and David II* (1954)

Richard Barber, *The Black Prince* (1978)

Joshua Barnes, *The History of that Most Victorious Monarch Edward III* (Cambridge, 1688)

J.G. Bellamy, *The Law of Treason in England in the Later Middle Ages* (Cambridge, 1970)

Michael Bennet, 'Isabelle of France, Anglo-French Diplomacy and Cultural Exchange in the Late 1350s', in J.S. Bothwell (ed.), *The Age of Edward III* (Woodbridge, 2001), pp. 215–26

Michael Bennet, 'Edward III's Entail and the Succession to the Crown, 1376–1471', *EHR*, 113, 452 (1998), pp. 580–609

F.D. Blackley, 'Isabella and the Bishop of Exeter', in T.A. Sandquist and M.R. Powicke (eds), *Essays in Medieval History Presented to Bertie Wilkinson* (Toronto, 1969), pp. 220–35

F.D. Blackley, 'Isabella of France, Queen of England (1308–1358), and the late medieval cult of the dead', *Canadian Journal of History*, 15, 1 (1980), pp. 23–47

W.H. Bliss and C. Johnson (eds), *Calendar of Entries in the Papal Registers Relating to Great Britain and Ireland*, ii–iii (1895–97)

Edward A. Bond (ed.), *Chronicon Monasterii de Melsa* (3 vols, 1867)

Edward A. Bond, 'Notices of the Last Days of Isabella, Queen of Edward the Second, drawn from an Account of the Expenses of her Household', *Archaeologia*, 38 (1854), pp. 453–69

J.S. Bothwell, 'Edward III, the English Peerage and the 1337 Earls: estate redistribution in fourteenth-century England', in J.S. Bothwell, *The Age of Edward III* (Woodbridge, 2001), pp. 35–52

James Bothwell, 'Edward III and the "new nobility": largesse and limitation in fourteenth-century England', *EHR*, 112 (1997), pp. 1111–40

Jim Bradbury, *Medieval Archer* (Woodbridge, 1985; rep. 1998)

Haldeen Braddy, 'Chaucer and Dame Alice Perrers', *Speculum*, 21, 2 (1946), pp. 222–8

Haldeen Braddy, 'Chaucer, Alice Perrers and Cecily Chaumpaigne', *Speculum*, 52, 4 (1977), pp. 906–11

F.W.D. Brie (ed.), *The Brut* (2 vols, Oxford, 1906–8)

Reginald Brocklesby (ed.), *The Register of William Melton, Archbishop of York 1317–1340*, iv (Woodbridge, 1997)

R.A. Brown, H.M. Colvin and A.J. Taylor, *History of the King's Works: the Middle Ages* (2 vols, 1963)

R.A. Brown, 'King Edward's clocks', *Antiquaries Journal*, 39 (1959), pp. 283–6

R. Allen Brown, *English Castles* (1954, rep. 1970)

Elizabeth A.R. Brown, 'Diplomacy, Adultery, and Domestic Politics at the Court of Philip the Fair: Queen Isabelle's Mission to France in 1314', in J.S. Hamilton (ed.), *Documenting the Past: Essays in Medieval History Presented to George Peddy Cuttino* (Woodbridge, 1989), pp. 53–83

Kathryn Brush, 'The *Recepta jocalium* in the wardrobe book of William de Norwell, 12 July 1338 to 27 May 1340', *Journal of Medieval History*, 10 (1984), pp. 249–70

W.N. Bryant, 'Financial Dealings of Edward III with the County Communities, 1330–1360', *EHR*, 83 (1968), pp. 760–71

Mark Buck, *Politics, Finance and the Church in the Age of Edward II: Walter Stapeldon, Treasurer of England* (Cambridge, 1983)

Alfred H. Burne, *The Crécy War: a Military History of the Hundred Years' War from 1337 to the Peace of Brétigny, 1360* (1955)

CCR: Calendar of the Close Rolls Preserved in the Public Record Office, Edward I, Edward II & Edward III (21 vols, 1892–1913)

CChR: Calendar of the Charter Rolls Preserved in the Public Record Office, 1226–1516 (6 vols, 1903–27)

CCW: Calendar of Chancery Warrants Preserved in the Public Record Office, 1244–1326 (1927)

CEPR: W.H. Bliss and C. Johnson (eds), *Calendar of Entries in the Papal Registers Relating to Great Britain and Ireland,* ii–iii (1895–97)

CFR: Calendar of the Fine Rolls Preserved in the Public Record Office, Edward I, Edward II & Edward III 1327–1347 (5 vols, 1911–15)

Joanna Chamberlayne, 'Joan of Kent's tale: adultery and rape in the age of chivalry' *Medieval Life*, 5 (1996), pp. 7–9

Pierre Chaplais, *Piers Gaveston: Edward II's Adoptive Brother* (Oxford, 1994)

Pierre Chaplais (ed.), *The War of Saint-Sardos* (1954)

W.R. Childs and John Taylor (eds), *The Anonimalle Chronicle, 1307–1334, from Brotherton Collection MS 29* (York, 1991)

W.R. Childs and John Taylor (eds), *Politics and crisis in fourteenth-century England* (Gloucester, 1990)

Adam Clarke, J. Caley, J. Bayley, F. Holbrooke and J.W. Clarke (eds), *Foedera, conventiones, litterae, etc. , or Rymer's Foedera 1066–1383* (6 vols in 4, 1816–30)

CMR: Calendar of Memoranda Rolls (Exchequer) Preserved in the Public Record Office, Michaelmas 1326 – Michaelmas 1327 (1968)

CP: G.E. Cokayne, revised by V. Gibbs, H.A. Doubleday, Geoffrey H. White, Lord Howard de Walden and Peter Hammond (eds), *The Complete*

Peerage of England, Scotland, Ireland, Great Britain and the United Kingdom Extant, Extinct or Dormant (14 vols in 15, 1910–98)

CPR: Calendar of the Patent Rolls Preserved in the Public Record Office, Edward I, Edward II & Edward III (25 vols, 1891–1916)

Charles George Crump, 'The arrest of Roger Mortimer and Queen Isabel', *EHR*, 26 (1911), pp. 331–2

G.P. Cuttino and T.W. Lyman, 'Where is Edward II?', *Speculum*, 53, 3 (1978), pp. 522–43

James Conway Davies, *Baronial Opposition to Edward II* (Cambridge, 1918)

Kelly R. De Vries, 'Hunger, Flemish Participation and the Flight of Philip VI: Contemporary Accounts of the Siege of Calais 1346–47', *Studies in Medieval and Renaissance History*, n.s. 12 (1991), pp. 131–81

Kelly R. De Vries, 'Contemporary views of Edward III's failure at the siege of Tournai, 1340', *Nottingham Mediaeval Studies*, 39 (1995), pp. 70–105

N. Denholm-Young (ed.), *Vita Edwardi Secundi* (1957)

Frederick Devon (ed.), *Issues of the Exchequer* (1837)

Dizionario biografico degli Italiani (Rome, 1960–)

DNB: Leslie Stephen, Sir Sidney Lee (eds) *Dictionary of National Biography* (63 vols, 1885–1912); see also *ODNB*

Paul Doherty, 'Isabella, Queen of England, 1296–1330' (University of Oxford D.Phil. thesis, 1978)

Paul Doherty, *Isabella and the Strange Death of Edward II* (2003)

Paul Dryburgh, 'The Career of Roger Mortimer, 1st Earl of March (c. 1287–1330)' (University of Bristol Ph.D. thesis, 2002)

Mark Duffy, *Royal Tombs of Medieval England* (Stroud, 2003)

Christopher Dyer, *Standards of Living in the Later Middle Ages* (revised ed., Cambridge, 1998)

E3&Chiv: Juliet Vale, *Edward III and Chivalry* (1982)

E3&S: Ranald Nicholson, *Edward III and the Scots: the Formative Years of a Military Career 1327–1335* (Oxford, 1965)

EHD: A.R. Myers (ed.), *English Historical Documents 1327–1485* (1969)

EHR: English Historical Review

Arnold Fayen (ed.), *Lettres de Jean XXII* (2 vols, Rome, 1908–12)

Foedera: Adam Clarke, J. Caley, J. Bayley, F. Holbrooke and J.W. Clarke (eds), *Foedera, conventiones, litterae, etc. , or Rymer's Foedera 1066–1383* (6 vols in 4, 1816–30), ii–iii

Kenneth Fowler, *The King's Lieutenant: Henry of Grosmont, First Duke of Lancaster, 1310–61* (1969)

Robin Frame, 'English Policies and Anglo-Irish Attitudes in the Crisis of 1341–1342', in James Lydon (ed.), *England and Ireland in the Later Middle Ages: Essays in Honour of Jocelyn Otway-Ruthven* (Blackrock, 1981)

Roger French *et al.* (eds), *Medicine from the Black Death to the French Disease* (Aldershot, 1998)

E.B. Fryde, 'Dismissal of Robert de Wodehouse from the office of treasurer, December 1338', *EHR*, 67 (1952), pp. 74–8

E.B. Fryde, 'Parliament and the French war, 1336–40', in E.B. Fryde and E. Miller (eds), *Historical Studies of the English Parliament* (Cambridge, 1970), pp. 242–61

Natalie Fryde, 'Edward III's Removal of his Ministers and Judges, 1340–1', *Bulletin of the Institute of Historical Research*, 44 (1971), pp. 153–61

V.H. Galbraith (ed.), *The Anonimalle Chronicle 1333 to 1381* (Manchester, 1970)

Margaret Galway, 'Alice Perrers' son John', *EHR*, 65 (1951), pp. 242–6

G.E. Gask, 'The Medical Staff of King Edward the Third', in Sir Zachary Cope (ed.), *Sidelights on the History of Medicine* (1957), pp. 47–56

Jean Gimpel, *The Medieval Machine* (2nd ed., 1992)

Chris Given-Wilson and Alice Curteis, *Royal Bastards* (1984)

C.J. Given-Wilson, *The Royal Household and the King's Affinity: Service, Politics and Finance in England 1360–1413* (1986)

John Glover (ed.), *Le Livere de Reis de Brittanie e Le Livere de Reis de Angletere* (1865)

Anthony Goodman, *John of Gaunt: the Exercise of Princely Power in Fourteenth-Century Europe* (1992)

Robert S. Gottfried, *The Black Death* (1983)

Antonia Gransden, 'The alleged rape by Edward III of the Countess of Salisbury', *EHR*, 85 (1972), pp. 333–44

Antonia Gransden, *Historical Writing in England II: 1307 to the Early Sixteenth Century* (1982)

GT: Ian Mortimer, *The Greatest Traitor: the Life of Sir Roger Mortimer, 1st Earl of March, Ruler of England 1327–1330* (2003)

R.M. Haines, *The Church and Politics in Fourteenth-Century England: the Career of Adam Orleton, c. 1275–1345* (1978)

R.M. Haines, 'Edwardus Redivivus: Afterlife of Edward of Carnarvon', *Transactions of the Bristol and Gloucester Archaeological Society*, 114 (1996), pp. 65–86

R.M. Haines, *King Edward II: his Life, his Reign and its Aftermath, 1284–1330* (Montreal, 2003)

J.O. Halliwell (ed.), *Letters of the Kings of England* (2 vols, 1846)

H.C. Hamilton (ed.), *Chronicon domini Walteri de Hemingburgh* (2 vols, 1848–49)

J.S. Hamilton, *Piers Gaveston, Earl of Cornwall 1307–1312: Politics and Patronage in the Reign of Edward II* (1988)

J.S. Hamilton, 'Ménage à Roi', *History Today*, 49, 6 (June 1999), pp. 26–31

D.A. Harding, 'The regime of Isabella and Mortimer, 1326–1330' (University of Durham M.Phil. thesis, 1985)

T.D. Hardy, *Syllabus . . . of Rymer's Foedera* (3 vols, 1869–85)

G.L. Harriss, 'War and the Emergence of the English Parliament, 1297–1360', *Journal of Medieval History*, 2 (1976), pp. 35–56

Anthony Harvey and Richard Mortimer, *The Funeral Effigies of Westminster Abbey* (Woodbridge, 1994)

F.S. Haydon (ed.), *Eulogium Historiarum sive Temporis: Chronicon ab Orbe Condito usque ad Annum Domini MCCCLXVI* (3 vols, 1858–63)

HBC: Sir Maurice Powicke and E.B. Fryde (eds), *Handbook of British Chronology* (2nd ed., 1961)

Bridget A. Henisch, *Fast and Feast: Food in Medieval Society* (1976)

H.J. Hewitt, *The Black Prince's Expedition of 1355–1357* (Manchester, 1958)

H.J. Hewitt, *The Organization of War Under Edward III 1338–62* (Manchester, 1966)

F.C. Hingeston (ed.), *The Chronicle of England by John Capgrave* (1858)

F.C. Hingeston-Randolph (ed.), *The Register of John de Grandison: Part Three, 1360–1369* (1899)

HKW: R.A. Brown, H.M. Colvin and A.J. Taylor, *History of the King's Works: the Middle Ages* (2 vols, 1963)

G.A. Holmes, *The Estates of the Higher Nobility in Fourteenth Century England* (Cambridge, 1957)

G.A. Holmes, 'The rebellion of the Earl of Lancaster, 1328–91', *Bulletin of the Institute of Historical Research*, 28 (1955), pp. 84–9

J.C. Holt, *Robin Hood* (revised ed., 1989)

W.H. St John Hope, 'On the Funeral Effigies of the Kings and Queens of England', *Archaeologia*, 60 (1887), pp. 517–70

Edwin S. Hunt, 'A new look at the dealings of the Bardi and the Peruzzi with Edward III', *Journal of Economic History*, 50, 1 (1990), pp. 149–62

Edwin S. Hunt, *The Medieval Super-Companies: a Study of the Peruzzi Company of Florence* (Cambridge, 1994)

Joseph Hunter, 'Measures taken for the apprehension of Sir Thomas de Gurney, one of the murderers of Edward II', *Archaeologia*, 27 (1838), pp. 274–97

T.B. James and J. Simons (eds), *The Poems of Laurence Minot, 1333–1352* (Exeter, 1989)

Tom Beaumount James, 'John of Eltham, History and Story: Abusive International Discourse in Late Medieval England, France and Scotland', in Chris Given-Wilson (ed.), *Fourteenth Century England* (Woodbridge, 2002), pp. 63–80

Helen M. Jewell, *English Local Administration in the Middle Ages* (Newton Abbot, 1972)

W.R. Jones, 'Rex et ministri: English local government and the crisis of 1341', *Journal of British Studies*, 13, 1 (1973), pp. 1–20

Thomas Johnes (ed.), *Chronicles ... by Sir John Froissart* (2 vols, 1848)

Hilda Johnstone, *Edward of Carnarvon* (Manchester, 1946)

Maurice Keen, *Chivalry* (1984)

George R. Keiser, 'Edward III and the Alliterative '"Morte Arthure"', *Speculum* 48, 1 (1973), pp. 37–51

David Knowles and R. Neville Hadcock, *Medieval Religious Houses, England and Wales* (1953)

Sir Guy Francis Laking, *A Record of European Arms and Armour Through Seven Centuries* (5 vols, 1920–22)

Gaillard Lapsley, 'Archbishop Stratford and the Parliamentary Crisis of 1341', *EHR*, 30 (1915), pp. 6–18, 193–215

J.H. le Patourel, 'The treaty of Brétigny, 1360', *Transactions of the Royal Historical Society*, 5th series, 10 (1960), pp. 19–39

William Longman, *The History of the Life and Times of Edward III* (2 vols, 1869)

J.R. Lumby (ed.), *Chronicon Henrici Knighton, vel Cnitthon, monachi Leycestrensis* (2 vols, 1889–95)

J.R. Lumby (ed.), *Polychronicon Ranulphi Higden*, viii (1882)

J.F. Lydon, 'William of Windsor and the Irish Parliament', *EHR*, 80 (1965), pp. 252–67

Bryce Lyon, 'What were Edward III's priorities: the pleasures of sports or charity?', *Revue d'histoire ecclésiastique*, 92 (1997), pp. 126–34

Mary Lyon, Bryce Lyon and Henry S. Lucas (eds), *The Wardrobe Book of William Norwell, 1338–1340* (Brussels, 1983)

James MacKinnon, *The History of Edward the Third* (1900)

Leslie G. Matthews, *The Royal Apothecaries* (1967)

Sir Herbert Maxwell (ed.), *The Chronicle of Lanercost* (Glasgow, 1913; rep. 2001)

Sir Herbert Maxwell (ed.), *Scalachronica: the Reigns of Edward I, Edward II and Edward III as Recorded by Sir Thomas Gray ...* (Glasgow, 1907, rep. 2000)

K.B. McFarlane, *The Nobility of Later Medieval England* (Oxford, 1973)

A.K. McHardy, 'Some Reflections on Edward III's Use of Propaganda', in J.S. Bothwell, *The Age of Edward III* (Woodbridge, 2001), pp. 171–92

May McKisack, 'Edward III and the historians', *History*, 45 (1960), pp. 1–15

May McKisack, *The Fourteenth Century, 1307–99* (Oxford, 1959)

Sophia Menache, 'Isabelle of France, queen of England – a reconsideration', *Journal of Medieval History*, 10 (1984), pp. 107–24

M.A. Michael, 'A Manuscript Wedding Gift from Philippa of Hainault to Edward III', *Burlington Magazine*, 127 (1985), pp. 582–600

Michael Michael, 'The little land of England is preferred before the great kingdom of France: the quartering of the royal arms by Edward III', in David Buckton and T.A. Heslop (eds), *Studies in Medieval Art and Architecture Presented to Peter Lasko* (Stroud, 1994), pp. 113–26

G. Mollat, *The Popes at Avignon 1305–1378* (trans. from 9th French ed., 1963)

S.A. Moore (ed.), 'Documents relating to the death and burial of King Edward II', *Archaeologia*, 50 (1887), pp. 215–26

D.A.L. Morgan, 'The political after-life of Edward III: the apotheosis of a warmonger', *EHR*, 112 (1997), pp. 856–81

Ian Mortimer, *The Greatest Traitor: the Life of Sir Roger Mortimer, 1st Earl of March, Ruler of England 1327–30* (2003)

Ian Mortimer, 'The death of Edward II in Berkeley Castle', *EHR*, 120 (2005) pp. 1175–1214

Ian Mortimer, 'Sermons of Sodomy: a reconsideration of Edward II's sodomitical reputation', in Gwilym Dodd and Anthony Musson (eds), *The Reign of Edward II: New Perspectives* (Woodbridge, 2006), pp. 48–60

Anthony Musson, 'Second "English Justinian" or Pragmatic Opportunist? A Re-examination of the Legal Legislation of Edward III's Reign', in J.S. Bothwell (ed.), *The Age of Edward III* (Woodbridge, 2001), pp. 69–88

Cary J. Nederman (ed.), *Political Thought in Early Fourteenth Century England* (Tempe, Arizona, 2002)

Sir Nicholas Harris Nicolas, 'Observations on the Institution of the Most Noble Order of the Garter', *Archaeologia*, 31 (1846), pp. 1–163

Sir Nicholas Harris Nicolas, *A History of the Royal Navy from the Earliest Times to the Wars of the French Revolution* (2 vols, 1847)

J. Nichols (ed.), *A Collection of All the Wills Now Known to be Extant of the Kings and Queens of England . . .* (1780, reprinted New York, 1969)

Ranald Nicholson, *Edward III and the Scots: the Formative Years of a Military Career 1327–1335* (Oxford, 1965)

ODNB: Oxford Dictionary of National Biography from the earliest times to the year 2000 (60 vols, Oxford, 2004). [No volume numbers or page numbers have been given as the online corrected version is expected to remain the most up-to-date. References were drawn from this immediately on publication, so checking the printed version will reflect the source used.]

W.M. Ormrod, *The Reign of Edward III* (updated ed., Stroud, 2000)

W.M. Ormrod, 'Agenda for Legislation, 1322–c1340', *EHR*, 105 (1990), 1–33

W.M. Ormrod, 'Edward III and his family', *Journal of British Studies*, 26 (1987), pp. 398–442

W.M. Ormrod, 'The English Government and the Black Death of 1348–49', in W.M. Ormrod (ed.), *England in the Fourteenth Century* (Woodbridge, 1985), pp. 175–88

W.M. Ormrod, 'For Arthur and St George', in Nigel Saul (ed.), *St George's Chapel, Windsor, in the Fourteenth Century* (Woodbridge, 2005), pp. 13–34

W.M. Ormrod, 'The Personal Religion of Edward III', *Speculum*, 64 (1989), pp. 849–911

W.M. Ormrod, 'A Problem of Precedence: Edward III, the Double Monarchy, and the Royal Style', in J.S. Bothwell, *The Age of Edward III* (Woodbridge, 2001), pp. 133–54

W.M. Ormrod, 'The Royal Nursery: a Household for the Younger Children of Edward III', *EHR*, 120 (2005), pp. 398–415

W.M. Ormrod, 'Sexualities of Edward II', in Gwilym Dodd and Anthony Musson (eds), *The Reign of Edward II: New Perspectives* (Woodbridge, 2006)

W.M. Ormrod, 'The Use of English: Language, Law and Political Culture in Fourteenth Century England', *Speculum*, 78 (2003), pp. 750–87

A.J. Otway Ruthven, *A History of Medieval Ireland* (1968; reprint, New York, 1993)

Michael Packe (ed. L.C.B. Seaman), *King Edward III* (1983)

J.J.N. Palmer (ed.), *Froissart: historian* (Woodbridge, 1981)

Patourel (see le Patourel)

Edouard Perroy (trans. W.B. Wells), *The Hundred Years War* (1951)

Michael Prestwich, *The Three Edwards: War and State in England, 1272–1377* (1980)

James Raine (ed.), *Historical Papers and Letters from Northern Registers* (1873)

Carole Rawcliffe, *Medicine and Society in Later Medieval England* (1999)

RE3: W.M. Ormrod, *The Reign of Edward III* (updated ed., Stroud, 2000)

H.G. Richardson and G.O. Sayles, *The English Parliament in the Middle Ages* (1981)

H.T. Riley (ed.), *Chronica Monasterii S. Albani, part 1: Thomae Walsingham Historia Anglicana* (1865)

H.T. Riley (ed.), *Chronica Monasterii S. Albani, part 2: Willelmi Rishanger quondam monachi S. Albani et quorundam anonymorum Chronica et Annales regnantibus Henrico Tertio et Edwardo Primo . . . 1259–1307* (1865)

H.T. Riley (ed.), *Chronica Monasterii S. Albani, part 3: Johannis de Trokelowe et Henrici de Blaneforde* (1866)

Clifford J. Rogers (ed.), *The Wars of Edward III: Sources and Interpretations* (Woodbridge, 1999)

Clifford J. Rogers, 'The Anglo-French Peace Negotiations of 1354–1360 Reconsidered', in J.S. Bothwell (ed.), *The Age of Edward III* (Woodbridge, 2001), pp. 193–214

Clifford J. Rogers, 'Edward III and the dialects of strategy, 1327–1360', *Transactions of the Royal Historical Society*, 6th series, 4 (1994), pp. 83–102

Clifford J. Rogers, *War Cruel and Sharp: English Strategy Under Edward III 1327–1360* (Woodbridge, 2000)

RP: J. Strachey, John Pridden and Edward Upham (eds), *Rotuli parliamentorum: ut et petitiones, et placita in Parliamento (1278–1503): together with an index to the Rolls of Parliament, comprising the petitions, pleas and proceedings of Parliament ... A.D. 1278–A.D. 1503* (8 vols, 1767–1832)

Owen Ruffhead (ed.), *Statutes at Large, from Magna Charta to the end of the Last Parliament, 1761* (8 vols, 1763)

L.F. Salzman, *Building in England Down to 1540* (Oxford, 1952, rep. 1997)

Armando Sapori, *I Libri dei Comercio dei Peruzzi* (Milan, 1934)

Caroline Shenton, 'The English Court and the Restoration of English Royal Prestige 1327–1345' (University of Oxford D.Phil. thesis, 1995)

Caroline Shenton, 'Edward III and the coup of 1330', in J.S. Bothwell (ed.), *The Age of Edward III* (2001), pp. 13–34

Walter Skeat (ed.), John Barbour, *The Bruce*, Early English Text Society (3 vols, 1870–77)

T.M. Smallwood, 'Prophecy of the Six Kings', *Speculum*, 60 (1985), pp. 571–92

Peter Spufford, *Handbook of Medieval Exchange* (1986) [The sterling/florin exchange rates are quoted on pp. 198–201]

Lawrence Stone, *Sculpture in Britain in the Middle Ages* (2nd ed., 1972)

E.L.G. Stones, 'The Anglo-Scottish negotiations of 1327', *Scottish Historical Review*, 30 (1951), pp. 49–54

J. Strachey, John Pridden and Edward Upham (eds), *Rotuli parliamentorum: ut et petitiones, et placita in Parliamento (1278–1503): together with an index to the Rolls of Parliament, comprising the petitions, pleas and proceedings of Parliament ... A.D. 1278–A.D. 1503* (8 vols, 1767–1832)

Agnes Strickland, *Lives of the Queens of England* (8 vols, 1882)

William Stubbs (ed.), *Chronicles of the Reigns of Edward I and Edward II* (2 vols, 1882–83)

Jonathan Sumption, *The Hundred Years War: Trial by Battle* (1990)

Jonathan Sumption, *The Hundred Years War: Trial by Fire* (1992)

James Tait (ed.), *Chronica Johannis de Reading and Anonymi Cantuarensis* (Manchester, 1914)

Craig Taylor, 'Edward III and the Plantagenet Claim to the French Throne', in J.S. Bothwell (ed.), *The Age of Edward III* (Woodbridge, 2001), pp. 155–70

John Taylor, Wendy R. Childs and Leslie Watkiss (eds), *The St Albans Chronicle: the Chronica Maiora of Thomas Walsingham, 1376–1394* (Oxford, 2003)

Rupert Taylor, *The Political Prophecy in England* (New York, 1911; rep. 1967)

G. Templeman, 'Edward III and the beginnings of the Hundred Years War', *Transactions of the Royal Historical Society*, 5th series, 2 (1952), pp. 69–88

A. Hamilton Thompson, *The English Clergy and their Organisation in the Later Middle Ages* (Oxford, 1947)

E.M. Thompson (ed.), *Chronicon Angliae ab anno domini 1328 usque ad annum 1388* (1874)

E.M. Thompson (ed.), *Chronicon Galfridi le Baker de Swynebroke* (Oxford, 1889)

E.M. Thompson (ed.), *Adae Murimuth, Continuatio Chronicarum* (1889)

T.C.B. Timmins (ed.), *The Register of William Melton, Archbishop of York 1317–1340*, v (2002)

Thomas Frederick Tout, 'Firearms in England in the Fourteenth Century', *EHR*, 26 (1911), pp. 666–702

Thomas Frederick Tout, *Chapters in English Administrative History* (Manchester, 6 vols, 1923)

Thomas Frederick Tout, *The Place of Edward II in English History* (2nd ed., Manchester, 1936)

David Trotter, 'Walter of Stapeldon and the pre-marital inspection of Philippa of Hainault', *French Studies Bulletin*, 49 (1993), pp. 1–4

George Unwin (ed.), *Finance and Trade under Edward III* (1962)

Juliet Vale, *Edward III and Chivalry* (1982)

Vries (see de Vries)

W. Warburton, *Edward III* (2nd ed., 1876)

Scott L. Waugh, *England in the Reign of Edward III* (Cambridge, 1991)

WCS: Clifford J. Rogers, *War Cruel and Sharp: English Strategy Under Edward III 1327–1360* (Woodbridge, 2000)

David Welander, *The History, Art and Architecture of Gloucester Cathedral* (Stroud, 1990)

K.P. Wentersdorf, 'The Clandestine Marriages of the Fair Maid of Kent', *Journal of Medieval History*, 5 (1979), pp. 203–31

Henry Wharton (ed.), *Anglia sacra; sive, Collectio historiarum . . . de archiepiscopis & episcopis Angliae* (1691)

B. Wilkinson (ed.), 'A Letter from Edward III to his Chancellor and Treasurer', *EHR*, 42 (1927), pp. 248–51

B. Wilkinson, 'The Protest of the Earls of Arundel and Surrey in the Crisis of 1341', *EHR*, 46 (1931), pp. 177–93

James F. Willard, 'Edward III's Negotiations for a Grant in 1337', *EHR*, 21 (1906), pp. 727–31

James F. Willard, 'Taxes upon moveables', *EHR*, 30 (1915), pp. 69–74

C.M. Woolgar, *The Great Household in Late Medieval England* (1999)

Alfred Benjamin Wyon and Allan Wyon, *The Great Seals of England* (1887)

Philip Ziegler, *The Black Death* (1969)

Henry III, d. 1272, king of England,
m. Eleanor of Provence, d. 1290

Edward I, d. 1307, king of England
m. 1stly Eleanor of Castile, d. 1290 — m. 2ndly Margaret of France, d. 1318 (see Table 3)

Edmund, d. 1296, earl of Lancaster, m. Blanche of Artois, d. 1302

Children of Edward I (1stly Eleanor of Castile):

Joan of Acre, d. 1307, m. Gilbert Clare, d. 1295, earl of Gloucester
[one son, three daughters]

Elizabeth, d. 1316, m. 2ndly Humphrey Bohun, d. 1322, earl of Hereford

Edward II, d. 1327, king of England until 1327, m. Isabella of France, d. 1358 (see Table 3)

Children of Edward I (2ndly Margaret of France):

Thomas of Brotherton, d. 1338, earl of Norfolk, m. Alice Hayles

Edmund of Woodstock, d. 1330, earl of Kent, m. Margaret Wake, d. 1349

Children of Edmund, earl of Lancaster:

Thomas, d. 1322, earl of Lancaster

Henry, d. 1345, earl of Lancaster, m. Matilda de Chaworth

Elizabeth's children (Humphrey Bohun, earl of Hereford):

Humphrey Bohun, d. 1361, earl of Hereford

William Bohun, d. 1360, earl of Northampton, m. Elizabeth Badlesmere, d. 1356

Children of Edward II:

EDWARD III, d. 1377, king of England, m. Philippa of Hainault, d. 1369 (see Table 2)

John of Eltham, d. 1336

Eleanor of Woodstock, d. 1355, m. Reginald, count of Guelderland, d. 1343

Joan of the Tower, d. 1362, m. David II, king of Scotland, d. 1371

Children of Thomas of Brotherton:

Margaret, d. 1400, m. 1stly John Segrave, d. 1353; m. 2ndly Sir Walter Manny, d. 1372

Alice, d. pre 1351, m. Edward Montagu, d. 1361

Children of Edmund of Woodstock:

Joan, d. 1385, countess of Kent, m. 1stly Thomas Holland, d. 1360; m. 2ndly Edward, d. 1376, prince of Wales (see Table 2)

Children of Henry, earl of Lancaster:

Henry, d. 1361, earl of Derby (to 1345), earl (later duke) of Lancaster, m. Isabella Beaumont, d. 1361

[six daughters]

Children of William Bohun:

Humphrey Bohun, d. 1373, earl of Hereford
[two daughters]

Children of Eleanor of Woodstock / Reginald:

Reginald, d. 1371, duke of Guelderland, m. Mary of Brabant (see left)

Children of Joan of the Tower / David II:

Edward, d. 1372

Children of Margaret (Brotherton):

Anne Manny, d. 1384, m. John Hastings, d. 1375, earl of Pembroke

Children of Henry, earl of Derby/Lancaster:

Matilda, d. 1362

Blanche, d. 1368, m. John of Gaunt (see Table 2)

Lower branch (Brabant):

John, d. 1355, duke of Brabant

Mary, d. 1399, m. Reginald, count of Guelderland, d. 1371

Jeanne, d. 1406, duchess of Brabant, m. William d. 1345, count of Hainault

Table 1: THE ENGLISH ROYAL FAMILY BEFORE 1330

EDWARD III, d. 1377, king of England, m. Philippa of Hainault, d. 1369

Edward ('the Black Prince'), d. 1376, m. Joan, d. 1385, countess of Kent (see Table 1)

Isabella, d. 1379, m. Enguerrand de Coucy, d. 1397, earl of Bedford

Joan, d. 1348

William of Hatfield, d. 1337

Lionel, d. 1368, duke of Clarence, m. Elizabeth de Burgh, d. 1363

John of Gaunt, d. 1399, duke of Lancaster

m. 1stly Blanche of Lancaster, d. 1368 (see Table 1)

m. 2ndly Constanza of Castile, d. 1394

m. 3rdly Katherine Roët, d. 1403

Edward, d. 1371

Richard II, d. 1400

Mary, d. 1404, m. Henry of Bar, d. 1401

Philippa, d. 1411, m. Robert de Vere, d. 1392

Philippa, d. 1380, m. Edmund Mortimer, d. 1381, earl of March

Philippa, d. 1415, m. John, d. 1433, king of Portugal

Elizabeth, d. 1425, m. 2ndly John Holland, d. 1400, duke of Exeter

Henry IV, d. 1413, king of England, m. 1stly Mary Bohun, d. 1394

Catalina, d. 1418, m. Henry d. 1406, king of Castile

John Beaufort, d. 1410, marquess of Dorset

Henry, d. 1446, bishop of Winchester

Thomas, d. 1426, duke of Exeter

Joan Beaufort, m. 1stly Robert Ferrers, d. 1396; m. 2ndly Ralph Neville, d. 1425, earl of Westmorland

Robert of Bar, d. 1415, m. Jeanne de Bethune

Elizabeth Mortimer, d. 1417

Roger Mortimer, d. 1398, earl of March

Philippa Mortimer, d. 1400

Edmund Mortimer, d. 1409

[six sons, two daughters]

[three sons, two daughters]

[four sons, two daughters]

[one son, one daughter]

[four sons, two daughters]

[one son]

[nine sons, seven daughters]

EDWARD III, d. 1377, king of England, m. Philippa of Hainault, d. 1369 (continued)

Edmund, d. 1402, duke of York, m. Isabella of Castile, d. 1392	Blanche, d. 1342	Mary, d. 1361, m. John de Montfort, d. 1399, duke of Brittany	Margaret, d. 1361, m. John Hastings, d. 1375, earl of Pembroke	William of Windsor, d. 1348		Thomas, d. 1397, earl of Buckingham, later duke of Gloucester, m. Eleanor Bohun, d. 1399

Under Edmund, d. 1402, duke of York:

- Edward, d. 1415, earl of Rutland, later duke of York, m. Philippa Mohun, d. 1431
- Constance, d. 1415, m. Thomas le Despenser, d. 1400, earl of Gloucester
  - [three sons, two daughters]
- Richard, d. 1415, earl of Cambridge, m. Anne Mortimer, d. 1411
  - [one son, one daughter]

Under Thomas, d. 1397, duke of Gloucester:

- Humphrey, d. 1399, earl of Buckingham
- Anne, d. 1438, m. 2ndly Edmund, d. 1403, earl of Stafford; m. 3rdly William Bourchier, d. 1420, count of Eu
  - [five sons, three daughters]
- Joan, d. 1400
- Isabella, d. 1402
- Philippa, d. 1399

Table 2: THE ENGLISH ROYAL FAMILY AFTER 1330

Philip III (the Bold), d. 1285, king of France
m. 1stly Isabella of Aragon, d. 1271
m. 2ndly Mary of Brabant

Philip IV (the Fair), d. 1314, king of France, m. Joan, d. 1305, Queen of Navarre

Charles, d. 1325, count de Valois, m. 1stly Margaret of Anjou, d. 1299

Margaret, d. 1318, m. Edward I of England (see Table 1)

Louis, d. 1319, count of Evreux, m. Margaret d'Artois, d. 1311

Louis X, d. 1316, king of France, m. Margaret of Burgundy, d. 1315

Philip V, d. 1322, king of France

Isabella, d. 1358, m. Edward II of England

Charles IV, d. 1328, king of France

Charles, d. 1346, count of Alençon

Margaret de Valois, d. 1342, m. Guy, d. 1344, count of Blois

Jeanne de Valois, d. 1342, m. William, d. 1337, count of Hainault

Philip VI (de Valois), d. 1350, king of France, m. Jeanne of Burgundy, d. 1348

Charles d'Evreux, d. 1336, count of Étampes

Philip d'Evreux, d. 1343, king of Navarre (see far left)

Jeanne, d. 1349, Queen of Navarre, m. Philip d'Evreux, d. 1343 (see far right)

John I, d. 1316, king of France

EDWARD III, d. 1377 (see right and Tables 1 & 2)

Louis, d. 1346, count of Blois

Charles de Blois, d. 1364, m. Jeanne, d. 1384, duchess of Britanny

John II (the Good), d. 1364, king of France, m. Bonne of Luxembourg, d. 1349

Philip, d. 1375, duke of Orleans

William, d. 1345, count of Hainault, m. Jeanne of Brabant (see Table 1)

Margaret, d. 1356, countess of Hainault, m. Ludwig of Bavaria, d. 1347

Philippa, d. 1369, m. EDWARD III (see left and Tables 1 & 2)

Jeanne, d. 1374, m. William, d. 1362, count of Juliers

Isabella, d. 1361, m. Robert of Namur, d. 1391

Charles the Bad, d. 1387, king of Navarre, m. Jeanne of France (see right)

Philip of Navarre, d. 1363, count of Longueville

Charles V (the Wise), d. 1380, king of France, m. Jeanne de Bourbon, d. 1378

Louis, d. 1384, duke of Anjou

John, d. 1416, duke of Berry

Philip, d. 1404, duke of Burgundy

Jeanne, d. 1373, m. Charles the Bad, d. 1387, king of Navarre (see left)

Table 3: THE FRENCH ROYAL FAMILY

INDEX

INDEX

1, 80, 123, 130, 188, 212, 215, 237, 274, 294, 310, 366, 376, 422

Fitzsimon, Richard: 240, 241

Fitzwarenne, Mabel: 197

Fitwarin, Fulk (d. 1336), Lord Fitzwarin (1315): 77

Fitzwarin, William (d. 1361): 349

flagellants: 270

Flanders: 87, 95, 97, 135, 145, 162–164, 166, 169, 171–173, 175, 177, 178, 180, 182, 185, 186, 202, 207, 215–218, 222, 226, 231, 249, 254, 296, 298, 307, 353, 363, 366, 403, 410

Flintshire: 23

Florence: 102, 152, 210, 270, 387

Florence, Peter of: 431

Foix, count of: *see Gaston*

Fontaine-sur-Somme: 235

Fontenay le Pesnel: 228

Fordun, John: 131

Forrester, John: 306

Forzetti, Dino: 290

Forzetti or Forcetti, Francisco: 152, 154, 412, 414, 415, 417

Fosdinovo: 415

Fosdinovo, Francisco: 415

France: 33–34, 40–46, 59, 69–70, 76, 91, 92, 112, 117, 118, 130, 180, 329, 362, 430, 436; ambassadors of 97, 121, 127, 146, 215, 251, 300, 310, 312; kings of 440, *see also* Philip IV, Charles IV, Philip VI, John II, Charles V; queens of *see* Evreux, Jeanne of Burgundy; parliament of 124, 129, 203, 214, 330, 335, 336, 339; war with 95, 96, 118, 124, 125, 132–136, 140–147, 150, 151, 154–166, 172–181, 189, 202–207, 215, 216, 218–255, 270–276, 299–305, 310–317, 320–343 365, 366, 370–372, 374–378

Franciscan Friars: 110, 207, 333

French language: 5, 35, 265, 266, 355, 385

French Revolution: 165

Friesland: 24

Froissart, John (c. 1337–1404): 5, 13, 46, 47, 88, 161, 193, 194, 196, 197, 204, 213, 221, 222, 236–239, 253, 291, 323, 337, 340, 342, 348, 375, 404, 423, 434

Fromond, Godfrey de: 431

Gabrielis, Paul: 431

Gaddesden, John (d. c. 1349): 430

Gaelic language: 351, 352

Galeys, le: *see* Edward II

gambling: 97, 103

games: 87, 88, 114, 255, 262, 301, 302

Gascony: 8, 18, 38–40, 45, 59, 97, 108, 132, 136, 137, 139, 141, 147, 157, 169, 179–181, 202, 207, 210, 214–216, 218–222, 226, 249, 259, 266, 270, 271, 274, 295, 300, 301, 304, 308, 312, 314, 321–325, 329, 338, 350, 352–354, 363–366, 369–372, 374, 375, 377, 385, 423–426; *see also* Aquitaine

Gaston Phoebus (1331–1391), count of Foix (1343): 322, 355

Gaunt: *see* John of Gaunt

Gaveston, Piers (c. 1281–1312), earl of Cornwall (1307):

18, 19, 26, 27, 29, 39, 40

Gawain (Arthurian knight): 97

Geneva: 141

Geneville, Joan (1286–1356), Lady Mortimer (1304), countess of March (1328): 85

Genoa and the Genoese: 128, 171–173, 205, 206, 210, 221, 222, 229, 235, 239, 240, 245, 250, 256, 271, 300, 370, 372, 379, 412, 413

George III (1738–1820), king of England (1760): 13, 165

Germany: 41, 116, 140, 143, 144, 150, 151, 155, 157, 159, 160, 178, 315, 317, 329, 330, 370

Gibraltar, siege of: 274

Ghent: 139, 163, 166, 169, 171, 173, 176–178, 181–185, 210, 217, 258, 434

Giffard, John (1287–1322), Lord Giffard of Brimpsfield (1299): 31

Glasgow: 123

Glaston, John: 357, 366, 431

Glastonbury Abbey: 89, 341

Gloucester: 31, 48, 66, 71; abbey of St. Peter (now Gloucester Cathedral) 65, 129, 133, 201, 208, 282, 299, 307, 408, 415; abbot of *see* Staunton; Castle 285; earldom of 30, 138; earls of *see* Clare, Audley

Gloucestershire: 305, 307

Gneth Cross: *see* Neith Cross

Godiasco: 414

Gouche, John: 431

Gower, lordship of: 30

Gower, John (d. 1408): 291

Grâce de Dieu: 376

Graham, John (d. 1348), earl of Menteith: 258

Grailly, Jean de (d. 1377), Captal de Buch: 325, 375

Grandison, John (d. 1369), bishop of Exeter (1327): 403

Gravesend: 286

Gravesend, Stephen (d. 1338), bishop of London (1318): 52–53, 78, 420

Gray, Thomas (d. 1369): 82, 87, 131, 198, 291

Grey, Richard (d. 1335), Lord Grey of Codnor (1308): 421

Gregory XI (1331–1378), pope (1370), prev. known as Pierre Roger de Beaufort: 375

Groppo San Pietro, Giffredus de: 415

Guare: 327

Guelderland, count of: *see* Reginald

Guernsey: *see* Channel Islands

Guesclin, Bertrand du (d. 1380): 362, 363, 377, 378

Guildford: 87, 254, 255, 285

Guines: 299–301, 304, 305, 310–313, 318, 321, 325–327, 330, 337, 378

Guise: 160

guns and gunpowder: 42, 101–103, 107, 118, 237–239, 241, 247, 287, 292, 399

Gurney, Thomas (d. 1333): 64, 85, 92, 97, 406, 410

Gymel, Peter: 431

Gynwell, John (d. 1362), bishop of Lincoln (1347): 313

Haddington: 319

THE PERFECT KING

Langham, Simon (d. 1376), abbot of Westminster (1349–62), bishop of Ely (1362–66), archbishop of Canterbury (1366–68), Treasurer (1360–63), Chancellor (1363–67), cardinal (1368): 355, 359
Langland, William (c. 1325–c. 1390): 13, 291
Langley (King's Langley): 183–185, 284–288, 368, 434
Latimer, William (c. 1301–1335), Lord Latimer (1327): 2, 373, 421
Latimer, William (1330–1381), Lord Latimer (1335): 373, 380, 384, 388
Latin language: 5, 35, 54, 266, 355, 394
Launge, John and Joan: 20, 33
Lavagna, counts of: see Fieschi
Lavaur: 179
Le Crotoy: 236
Le Neubourg: 230
Leech, John [the]: 431
Leeds Castle (Kent): 25, 285, 330
Leinster: 351
Léon, bishop of: 205
Leicester: 83, 129, 267, 268, 347, 434
Leintwardine: 299, 307
Lengleis, William: 115
Lennox, Malcolm of (d. 1333), earl of Lennox (1291?): 107
Leominster, Hugh of: 27, 29
Lescout, Arnaud de (d. 1320), bishop of Poitiers: 20
Lesneven: 223
Lewes: 130
Libellus Famosas: 187
Libourne: 142
Lichfield: 259, 428; bishop of see Northburgh
Liège, James of: 116
Liège, Jean de: 292
Lille: 163, 171
Limburg: 140
Limoges: 371, 372
Limousin: 310, 327
Limoux: 321
Lincoln: 64, 71, 267, 407, see also parliament; bishops of see Burghersh, Gynwell
Lincolnshire: 280
Lindisfarne: 103
Lionel (Arthurian knight): 115, 131, 200, 365
Lionel of Antwerp (1338–1368), earl of Ulster (1351), duke of Clarence (1362): 153, 184, 194, 199, 218, 259, 291, 295, 329, 332, 335, 337, 348, 350–353, 355, 359, 361, 365, 367, 375, 383, 412, 434, 436
Lisieux: 230
Lisle, Gerard: 55
Lisle, Thomas (d. 1361), bishop of Ely (1345): 218, 318, 319, 326, 349
literacy of the nobility: 35; 41, 75, 355; see also books
Llantrissant: 50
Llywelyn Bren: 23
Lochindorp: 130
Loire, River: 310, 323
London: 18–20, 26, 31, 33–35, 48–49, 52, 79, 87, 108, 122, 124, 134, 137, 142, 148, 176, 185, 190, 192,

194–196, 201, 208, 212, 254, 262–264, 287, 288, 328, 329, 333, 342, 387, 390, 392, 404, see also Westminster; bishops of see Gravesend, Stratford, Northburgh; Charing 358; Charterhouse 349, 375; Cheapside 93–94, 111, 253; Franciscan church 333; mayors of 188, 328, 409, see also Bettoyne, Pulteney; Newgate Gaol 333; St Mary Graces 284, 388; St Paul's Cathedral 49, 56, 76, 108, 133, 208, 390, 392, 430; Savoy Palace 34–35, 334; Smithfield 212, 262, 329, 335, 357, 382; Tower of 33, 48, 51, 76, 83, 86, 102, 110, 127, 128, 133, 136, 183, 185, 186, 194, 204, 237, 247, 258, 262, 278, 284–286, 289, 290, 296, 303, 304, 314, 333, 334, 368, 388, 405, 413, 414; Treaties of 330, 333, 334, 336, 337, 340, 342
Longman, William: 7–8
Longpré: 235
Loos: 151
Lorraine, Raoul of (1320–1346), duke of Lorraine (1329): 243
Loshult, Sweden: 102
Louis IX, Saint (1215–1270), king of France (1226): 40
Louis X (1289–1316), king of France (1314): 309
Louis XIV, 'the Sun King' (1638–1715), king of France (1642): 279
Louis I (1304–1346), count of Flanders (1322): 139, 142, 145, 162, 163, 216, 217, 243
Louis II (1330–1384), count of Flanders (1346): 296, 307, 315, 353, 354, 366, 433
Lucca: 347
Lucca, John of: 306
Lucy, Anthony (d. 1343), Lord Lucy (1321): 421
Ludgershall: 26, 285
Ludlow: 70
Ludvig (1282–1347), duke of Bavaria (1294), Holy Roman Emperor (1314): 47, 141, 143, 144, 150, 151, 154, 155, 159, 166, 189, 206, 217, 255
Lusignan: 248
Lussac: 375
Luxemburg, count of: see John
Lyndhurst: 306
Lyons, Richard (d. 1381): 380, 384, 389
Lytlington, Nicholas (d. 1386), abbot of Westminster (1362): 435

Maccabeus, Judas (d. 160 BC): 97, 111, 393
Macclesfield: 27
MacKinnon, James: 9–10, 18
Magna Carta: 58, 77, 187, 293
Magnus Ericson (1316–1377), king of Norway and Sweden (1320): 132
Maguelonne: 411
Maine: 334
Maingre, Jean le, called 'Boucicaut': 315–317
maintenance: 95
Malaspina, Niccolo, 'Il Marchesotto': 414–416
Malestroit, Treaty of (1342): 207, 208
Malmesbury: 329
Maltravers, John (c. 1290–1364), Lord Maltravers

528

INDEX

Valois, Philip de: *see* Philip VI

Vannes: 204, 206, 207

Vegetius Renatus, Flavius: 225, 237, 289

Venice: 171–173, 177

Vere, John (1312–1360), earl of Oxford (1331): 123, 199, 314

Vere, Robert (1362–1392), earl of Oxford (1371): 390

Vere, Thomas (c. 1337–1371), earl of Oxford (1360): 366

Vere, Thomas (d. 1329): 55

Vernon: 231, 232

Verneuil: 321

Versailles Palace: 278

Vesci, Lady (d. 1343): 78

Victoria (1819–1901), queen of England (1837): 13

Victoria Cross: 427

Vienne, Jean de: 247–250, 252, 253

Villani, Giovanni (d. 1348): 209, 210, 270

Villani, Filippo: 209

Villeneuve-le-hardi: 247–250, 254

Vincennes: 40

Vineyards: 284

Virgin: *see* Mary

Visconti, family of: 282

Visconti, Galeazzo (d. 1378), lord of Milan (1349): 365

Visconti, John: 278

Visconti, Luccinus (d. 1349), lord of Milan (1339): 416

Visconti, Violante (d. 1386), duchess of Clarence (1368–68): 434

Vita Edwardi Secundi: 19, 22, 356

Vow of the Heron: 134, 164, 198

Waddesworth, William: 431

Wake, Blanche (d. 1380), Lady Wake (1316): 318

Wake, Margaret (d. 1349), countess of Kent (1325?): 45, 69, 77

Wake, Thomas (1298–1349), Lord Wake of Liddel (1317): 55, 68, 78, 270, 420

Wakefield, Henry (c. 1335–1395), bishop of Worcester (1375), Treasurer (Jan.–July 1377): 390

Wales and the Welsh: 23, 27, 48, 50, 63, 68, 79, 102, 108, 123, 124, 227, 229, 237, 286, 300, 311, 314, 365, 436; prince of *see* Edward II, Edward of Woodstock

Walkefare, Robert: 2, 83

Wallingford: 26, 48–50, 113, 285

Wallingford, Richard (c. 1292–1336), abbot of St Albans (1327): 288, 399

Wallingford, William: 162

Walsingham Abbey: 108, 208, 332

Walsingham, Thomas (c. 1340–c. 1422): 255, 341, 361, 375, 380, 386, 389, 390, 392, 394, 399

Waltham Abbey: 128

Waltham (Bishops Waltham): 215, 434

Walton: 47; *see also* Ordinances

Walwayn, John (d. 1326): 34

Warburton, William: 8, 9,

Ware: 18

Warre, Roger de la (1326–1370, Lord de la Warre

(1347): 271

Wark Castle: 113, 194–196, 198, 200, 266, 268, 401

Warenne, John (1286–1347), earl of Surrey (1304): 18, 130, 184, 188, 419

Warwick: 292; earls of *see* Beauchamp

Wear, River: 60–61

weather, bad: 60, 61, 120, 121, 155, 185, 202, 207, 208, 217, 222, 239, 254, 264, 322, 337–342, 367, 376, 377, 425

Wells: 96, 289

Werde: *see* Niederwerde

West, Thomas: 2, 73

Westminster: 43, 53, 128, 140, 213, 215, 220, 259, 271, 296, 299, 305, 307, 366, 369, 370, 384, 433; *see also* parliament; Abbey 21, 54, 65, 76, 94, 133, 153, 260, 292, 335, 367, 387, 392, 393, 434; abbot of 270, *see also* Langham, Lytlington; Palace of 188, 213, 262, 280–286, 288, 310, 318, 322, 385; St Stephen's Chapel 280–283, 286, 292, 388, 435

Weston, Philip: 185

Whitby Church: 120

Wicklow: 351

Wight: *see* Isle of Wight

Wigmore: 75, 99, 346

Willesford, Edith: 335

William I, 'The Conqueror' (c. 1027–1087), duke of Normandy, king of England (1066): 8, 11, 225, 226, 228, 278, 426

William II, 'William Rufus' (d. 1100), king of England (1087): 440

William (1286–1337), count of Hainault and Holland (1304): 24, 34, 41, 43, 46, 67, 132, 139, 140, 403, 404

William (1307–1345), count of Hainault and Holland (1337): 139, 140, 144, 159, 161, 180, 198, 206, 217, 403

William (d. 1362), count (later duke) of Juliers (1328): 122, 139, 140, 144

William of Hatfield (1337–1337): 133, 136, 433

William of Windsor (1348–1348): 259, 260, 336, 434

William of Windsor (d. 1384): *see* Windsor

Willington, Henry (d. 1322): 31

Willington, Ralph (d. 1348), Lord Willington (1338): 55

Wiltshire: 305, 307

Winchelsea: 376; battle of (1350): 274–277, 280, 402

Winchester: 51, 72, 77, 79, 88, 215, 218, 328, *see also* parliament; bishops of *see* Stratford, Orleton, Edington; Castle 285; earl of *see* Despenser

Windsor: 19–21, 26, 32, 171, 212, 213, 259, 263, 264, 267–270, 277–280, 284, 286, 288, 296, 301, 304, 329, 330, 332, 334, 345–348, 360, 361, 365–370, 389, 392, 427–429, 434

Windsor, William (d. 1384), Lord Windsor (1381), King's Lieutenant of Ireland (1369–72), Governor of Ireland (1373–76): 374, 381, 382, 386, 387

Winner and Waster: 302, 303

Wissant: 73

Wissant, Jacques and Pierre: 253

Wodehouse, Robert (d. 1346), Treasurer (1329–30,

535